HWLC 6TH FLOOR   VISION

BANKRUPT

D0863418

BANKRUPT

Global Lawmaking and
Systemic Financial Crisis

Terence C. Halliday
and Bruce G. Carruthers

Stanford University Press
Stanford, California

Stanford University Press
Stanford, California

© 2009 by the Board of Trustees of the Leland Stanford Junior University.
All rights reserved.

No part of this book may be reproduced or transmitted in any form or by any means, electronic or mechanical, including photocopying and recording, or in any information storage or retrieval system without the prior written permission of Stanford University Press.

Printed in the United States of America on acid-free, archival-quality paper

Library of Congress Cataloging-in-Publication Data

Halliday, Terence C. (Terence Charles)
 Bankrupt : global lawmaking and systemic financial crisis / Terence C. Halliday and Bruce G. Carruthers.
    p. cm.
 Includes bibliographical references and index.
 ISBN 978-0-8047-6074-4 (cloth : alk. paper) -- ISBN 978-0-8047-6075-1 (pbk. : alk. paper)
 1. Bankruptcy. 2. Bankruptcy--International cooperation. 3. Financial crises. I. Carruthers, Bruce G. II. Title. K1375.H35 2009
 346.07'8--dc22
                              2009001215

Typeset by Bruce Lundquist in 10/14 Minion

R0424403737

CHICAGO PUBLIC LIBRARY

To Aidan, Alexander, Arlen, Jackson, Lucas, Nathaniel, and Titus

To Esther and Sam

Table of Contents

Figures and Tables

Preface

Plus ça change, plus c'est la même chose.
[The more things change, the more they stay the same.]

FOR VETERANS of the Asian Financial Crisis, the unraveling of the world economy in late 2008 has a familiar but chilling resonance. In late 1997 and early 1998 a quick succession of national financial crises in East Asia portended a regional crisis that might have plunged the world economy into systemic breakdown. It was this fear that galvanized the G-7 and G-22 to urge emergency action. Led by the U.S., leaders of advanced economies pressed international financial institutions (IFIs) in the short term to halt the downward slide of national economies teetering on the edge of bankruptcy. In the intermediate term, states and international organizations in the global center set about forging national and international institutions that would forestall future crises of similar or greater scope. The creation of robust bankruptcy systems featured prominently in this institutional architecture.

Despite these efforts, a potentially greater crisis now threatens the global economy. It is a threat that began not in smaller developing or transitional economies but in the American financial system at the heart of global finance. Yet again we see the International Monetary Fund (IMF) rushing to the aid of nations that need an immediate infusion of capital (so far, Iceland, Ukraine, Hungary, and Pakistan). Again the world's leading economies (now the G-20) meet in a quickly convened conclave to coordinate a concerted action plan. And again, it is likely international organizations will intensify efforts to build legal apparatuses and frameworks—new global norms, new global regulatory regimes, new national regulatory bodies with globally authorized features—to prevent recurrence of the present threat to markets of debtor and creditor nations alike.

How does the *legal* response to financial crisis work in practice? Do the states that lead the world's economy also produce institutional change? How do international organizations craft global norms for laws and institutions to make markets more resilient? Can global actors effectively press their standards on nation-states and insist on institution building to protect the integrity of national financial systems? How responsive are faltering nation-states to the demands of their international last-resort creditors?

One obvious way to find some answers is to examine previous crises. The Great Depression surely is one, but it occurred in a radically different global economy. The aftermath of World War II, with the establishment of the Bretton Woods system, provides another, but it, too, unfolded in such a different set of circumstances as to be not quite comparable. Most proximate and salient is the Asian Financial Crisis, now ten years old. Although there are many differences, it is plausible to apply some of the lessons of the last ten years in the present crisis.

This book shows in detail how the international community responded in the last major financial crisis to a perceived deficit in national and international regulatory institutions. It identifies the key global actors, shows how they competed and cooperated with each other, analyzes the types of norms they crafted, and reviews the actions they took. This book also shows how systemic financial crisis unfolded on the other side of the global/local divide. It reveals how three countries experienced financial crisis, how they reacted to foreign emergency interventions, and how deep and enduringly the institutional reforms penetrated everyday activity.

Above all, our book explores how and when institutions change, even in the most extreme of circumstances. It describes remarkable advances on some fronts (e.g., obtaining global consensus on norms) but halting progress on others (e.g., implementing effective institutional change in nation-states). Institutional change, we shall show, comes hard. Indeed, effective institution building to forestall financial crisis is so difficult that it calls into question just how deeply globalization has penetrated beyond financial markets and into the legal institutions that undergird them.

Globalization and Its Limits

The aphorism "the more things change, the more they stay the same" insinuates that change and continuity coexist. However much change catches our eye and absorbs our attention, much remains unchanged. Contemporary discussions of globalization and economic change could do well to heed its message, for many scholars, journalists, and popular commentators talk about globalization as if it were unprecedented and as if it were causing dramatic and simultaneous change around the world. To be sure, our world is more interconnected and interdependent than it has been in the past. One person can sneeze in Guangdong province in southern China, and two days (and a plane ride) later someone else contracts SARS in Toronto, Canada. Cost-cutting at Wal-Mart headquarters in Arkansas leads to layoffs and redundancies in Malaysia and Cambodia as clothing suppliers lose their contracts. The subprime mortgage crisis, originating in the U.S., causes banks around the world to lose billions of dollars and national financial systems in every region to falter.

Such interconnections expose people's employers, jobs, and general economic well-being to far-off events and forces. If these constraints and influences are proximate, then individuals have the chance to shape, modify, or ameliorate them, or at the very least to anticipate their impact. Being in the same political jurisdiction gives citizens the opportunity to pressure their governments for action to help solve such problems (of course, they need not be successful) or to exhort local firms to be good corporate citizens. But in a global world, the events and forces that shape people's lives increasingly lie outside their national political jurisdiction. Malaysia can pass a law regulating layoffs, but that law won't stop Wal-Mart from cost-cutting. Municipal governments in South Carolina may offer tax incentives to keep textile mills, but those incentives won't prevent the textile industry from migrating to Mexico or China. This mismatch between polity and economy is one of the central challenges of globalization: How can we live in a world of global connections and worldwide interdependencies extending beyond the reach of local or national government? How can we manage global market forces that exceed the political grasp of individual national governments?

Of course, by many measures of globalization, the current era is *not* unprecedented or extraordinary. In 1913 on the eve of World War I and under a British-led, gold-standard financial system, the world economy was characterized by substantial international flows of capital, goods, and even people (Obstfeld 1998). International economic integration collapsed during the war, fell apart further during the Depression, and did not return to levels comparable to those of 1913 until the 1980s. Even today, international flows of people remain more restricted than they were in the early twentieth century.

But some things have changed. Globalization not only affects trade in goods and services, and flows of capital into and out of countries, but increasingly is shaping the fundamental legal, political, and social institutions that undergird market economies. Globalization now encompasses the flow of ideas around the world, ideas about how best to organize an economy, how best to manage corporate governance and restructuring, and how best to encourage investment and economic growth in effective ways. Trade in models, paradigms, ideas, and policies now rivals that of goods and services.

The collapse of the Eastern European socialist bloc and China's decision to pursue market reform effectively made capitalism the only game in town. But what kind of capitalism? Neoliberal doctrines were embraced by international financial institutions like the IMF and World Bank in the 1980s and 1990s (the so-called Washington Consensus; see Stiglitz 2002: 16), and this doctrine stipulated privatization, liberalization, fiscal austerity, retrenchment of the welfare state, deregulation, and "hard currencies" as the path to economic success. The Reagan and Thatcherite "Revolutions" in the U.S. and U.K. gave credence to these policies (Prasad 2006). Such ideas also embraced the so-called rule of law as the best way to provide a stable framework of predictable contract law and enforceable property rights. It seemed that only one version of capitalism was to hold sway.

Despite the application of neoliberal doctrine to Latin American economies during the 1980s, to transitional economies in the early 1990s, and then to East Asia in the late 1990s, some scholars detect a strong and enduring difference between Anglo-Saxon liberal market economies (typified by those of the U.S., U.K., Australia, Canada, etc.), on the one hand, and Continental coordinated market economies (including those of Germany, France, Scandinavia, Japan, etc.), on the other. These two groups of countries differ over the structure of their labor markets, social welfare protections, financial markets, and patterns of corporate governance. This line of scholarship argues that such varieties of capitalism are durable and will continue to exist (Hall and Soskice 2001). It also implies that one-size-fits-all policy recommendations are mistaken (Stiglitz 2002). Furthermore, scholars have noted that the regulation of global business is increasingly occurring between states rather than within them, at the level of international organizations like the World Trade Organization (WTO), regional meta-governments like the European Union (EU), or multilateral trade agreements like the North American Free Trade Agreement (NAFTA) (Braithwaite and Drahos 2000). Such arguments offer a cautionary corrective to those who expect global pressures unproblematically to produce rapid institutional convergence to a single national model of capitalism.

But if rapid convergence isn't happening, institutional change certainly is. Sometimes countries make changes in the wake of an economic or political crisis, and sometimes they do so under external pressure from organizations like the IMF. Typically, however, change occurs as the result of a confluence of factors and a configuration of causes, both domestic and foreign. Institutional change is seldom unicausal. Moreover, institutional change initiated wholly from the outside is unlikely to be effective. To avoid "window dressing" concessions or purely symbolic change, proponents almost always need to have internal political partners with an autonomous interest in reform.

In this book, we study change in a legal institution that plays a central role in governing corporate failure, economic restructuring, firm rehabilitation, and firm liquidation: namely, corporate bankruptcy law. This kind of law sits at the nexus between the legal system and the market economy. It defines corporate "failure" and sets the rules that govern what happens to insolvent firms. It dissolves one set of ownership claims and creates a new set as it transfers assets out of the control of the insolvent debtor and into the hands of creditors. And it overturns corporate governance arrangements by empowering new sets of stakeholders. Bankruptcy law constitutes the hard budget constraints that distinguish capitalist from command economies (Kornai 1992), and it structures the flow of credit that fuels all modern market economies. Given its importance for debtor-creditor relationships, it seems likely that bankruptcy law will vary depending on the kind of financial system a country possesses (Allen and Gale 2000; Zysman 1983).

A number of countries reformed their bankruptcy laws independently and sporadically during the 1970s and 1980s. Two notable cases were the U.S. in 1978 and the U.K. in 1986 (Carruthers and Halliday 1998). But starting at the end of the 1980s, and throughout the 1990s, bankruptcy law became a topic of concern to major international financial institutions, global lawmaking bodies, and international professional associations. Each organization participated in a loose, expert-led, ongoing set of international conversations and deliberations about the centrality of bankruptcy law, and what constituted good law. Their interest was sparked by a combination of real-world events and growing recognition of the role that institutions play in economic development.

Bankruptcy reform began to occur in waves as first the transitional economies of Eastern and Central Europe passed new laws when they created market economies, and then East Asian economies reformed their laws in the wake of the Asian Financial Crisis. In some cases, countries reformed their laws more than once. Countries began to borrow ideas and models from each other, and some international organizations began to design and promulgate the underlying principles or basic rules of "good" bankruptcy law and "best practices." Furthermore, some actors learned to appreciate that simply to pass good laws and put them on the books are not enough: effective implementation of law is critical if the benefits of "good" commercial law are to be achieved. To be effective, formal rules needed to be enforced by institutions with sufficient capacity and adequate resources.

To understand this accelerating process of legal reform, and to explain why and how so many different organizations became interested in bankruptcy law, we engage a number of different ideas about the causes of institutional change, patterns of legal change, the importance of predictable law in capitalist economies, processes of legal rationalization, the relationship between standardization and predictability, varieties of capitalism, and the connection between law, finance, and economic growth. Furthermore, we recognize that legal reform is often an ongoing process in which law-on-the-books is implemented as law-in-action, which itself may engender new law-on-the-books. This cyclical process we name the *recursivity of law*, in recognition that the process of implementation is often problematic, or complicated, and can result in a substantial difference between law-on-the-books and law-in-action (Halliday and Carruthers 2007b). This gap is a staple of sociolegal research. Here, we place it into a larger context of legal reform, which acknowledges that the groups who most influence enactment are frequently not those who most shape implementation. Indeed, sometimes those who can exert the greatest control over enactment of formal law have very little influence over implementation. Legal practice can lead to new law-on-the-books, just as new formal law can lead to new practices.

Our book reports the results of a two-pronged research strategy. On the one side, we have undertaken intensive research of global norm-making organizations through participation, observation, interviewing, and documentary analysis. From 1999 until 2007 we tracked closely the emergence of an international legal field of norm-making organizations as they struggled toward convergence on a single set of global standards.[1] We have asked: When did they become interested in this kind of legal reform? Are their relationships with each other antagonistic or cooperative? What kinds of approaches have they taken? What has led them to embrace particular models, paradigms, principles, or "best practices"? How are they able to press their recommendations onto audiences that range from welcoming to hostile?

While the power and importance of such well-known organizations cannot be denied, the world is not a blank page upon which the IMF or World Bank can write what it pleases. The impact of IFI recommendations, for example, is very much dependent on the interaction between the IFI and the particular countries it advises, influences, or lends money to. The same is true for the World Bank and similar organizations. Furthermore, even countries that embrace these recommendations and pass new laws still face the formidable problem of implementation.

In recognition of these complexities, the second prong of our research examines episodes of legal reform from the domestic viewpoint of three countries: Indonesia, South Korea, and China. These three countries give us useful variation in that China is a transition economy, but the other two are not. South Korea enjoyed a much higher level of economic development than the other two and in many respects has a fully "modernized" economy (e.g., it joined the Organisation for Economic Co-operation and Development [OECD] in 1996). And because they felt the brunt of the Asian Financial Crisis so severely, the IMF and World Bank had considerable financial leverage over Indonesia and South Korea but not over China.[2]

Four Questions

We weave our analysis around a series of key issues. The first and most important concerns the *relationship between states and global markets.* Scholars have long recognized that markets do not emerge "automatically" or out of "thin air." Rather, they exist because their institutional preconditions have been satisfied. Usually, these foundations are provided by the state (Fligstein 2001; Moss 2002; North 1981; Polanyi 1944). States constitute markets by providing property rights, enforcing contracts, and promulgating other basic rules of the game. In turn, however, markets affect states by providing the economic base out of which states extract the resources necessary to fund their activities. In capitalist democracies, markets also determine the general well-being of citizen-voters, who in turn choose their political leaders on the basis of how well the economy is performing. Markets and states coexist and coevolve.

Were market boundaries and political boundaries perfectly aligned, this reciprocal relationship between states and markets would remain relatively simple. States would encourage economic activity within their boundaries by devising rules that supported markets. But they are not coterminus, and in fact some markets have become very much larger than any political jurisdictions. Many market transactions occur between polities, as opposed to within them. This situation leads to a kind of "mismatch" problem between nation-states and global markets. At the same time that the world has become economically integrated, it has remained politically fragmented (Gilpin and Gilpin 2000). Economic markets exceed the political grasp of any single nation, even one as large as the United States. As a result, for a given political jurisdiction or state actor, global markets are hard to regulate and difficult to control, and such markets have the power to frustrate or constrain public policy. Countries are vulnerable to economic interdependencies that they cannot govern.

In addition, neoliberal waves of privatization and deregulation in the 1980s and 1990s mean that in many countries, states have loosened their grip over the markets they formerly regulated or administered (Levi-Faur 2005). Instead of direct public command and control, markets are governed through a combination of networks of professionals (e.g., accountants, lawyers, managers) and organizations (various private groups, industry associations, and other nongovernmental organizations [NGOs] and international nongovernmental organizations [INGOs]) whose accountability to national publics is relatively limited even though they have been delegated regulatory responsibility (Braithwaite and Drahos 2000; Picciotto 1997).

For the private economic actors who operate within such markets, the mismatch creates a different set of challenges. It means that those engaging in global transactions or relationships necessarily face the problem of legal pluralism: their business goes through multiple legal jurisdictions, so they may have to deal with different and even conflicting sets of rules. This pluralist legal order frequently adds unwelcome uncertainty to global transactions and makes them riskier for all but the most sophisticated players. Suppose a lender has extended a substantial sum to a firm that operates in twenty countries and that has gone bankrupt. These twenty countries have twenty different bankruptcy laws, and it is not clear how or where a creditor should best proceed if it wants to recover its money. Advocates of legal harmonization among countries propose that it beneficially reduces transaction costs and legal uncertainties faced by private actors.

Mismatches that lead to legal variability are not always bad for private economic actors, however, in part because such differences enable them to play a game of "institutional arbitrage" (akin to regulatory arbitrage), exploiting differences to put pressure on jurisdictions with less desirable features. A typical scenario would be one in which investors shift their money from high-tax jurisdictions to low-tax jurisdictions, putting pressure on the former to lower their taxes or suffer continued disinvestment. Such arbitrage situations can set off races to the bottom, or to the top, but either case over time is conducive to *convergence.*

In sum, the mismatch appears to give considerable leverage to private economic actors in relation to public authorities. So long as state powers are bounded by the political limits of the nation, private economic actors navigating international markets can, *when it suits them*, evade, elude, and circumvent the rules and restrictions that states try to impose. But nation-states have not remained passive, outmaneuvered by more nimble and mobile private actors. Nations can respond by cooperating with each other to build international economic institutions and establish a legal connective tissue that spans the gap between nation-states. Indeed, the export of legal codes from colonial powers (like Britain) to their colonies during the nineteenth century exemplified a global diffusion of law. More recently, however, this connective tissue consists of bilateral or multilateral treaties, and membership in transnational governmental bodies (like the EU or WTO), in efforts to harmonize their discrepant rules, and sometimes in more informal (memoranda of understanding) or implicit understandings. Even as state regulation has receded at the national level (as governments deregulated and liberalized various markets during the 1980s and 1990s), re-regulation was occurring in the space between countries.

A second major issue concerns whether the recent period of globalization has led to *institutional or legal change.* Various arguments can be adduced (e.g., that globalization produces convergence, that globalization leads to greater international flows of ideas, policy paradigms, models, etc.) suggesting that the combination of integrated markets and fragmented polities will bring about institutional change. At the very least, greater global economic integration has created enormous demand for institutional arrangements to help govern transactions, provide credible information to market participants, enhance the security of ownership interests and allow for reliable transfer of such interests, and so on. The scale and complexity of global markets have in some respects simply outrun supporting institutional structures, and key political and economic shocks (e.g., the first OPEC oil crisis, the Latin American debt crisis, the collapse of socialism in Eastern and Central Europe, and the Asian Financial Crisis) have propelled institutional elaboration, extension, and modification.

Institutional change can occur from a number of different directions (Clemens and Cook 1999). Institutional rules can be more or less mutable, they may possess internal contradictions, and there may be multiple or competing alternative rules. Any of these situations produces institutional variation that, if it is to lead to significant change across an entire field, must somehow spread. The means of diffusion include networks, coercion, learning, and emulation. Some of these factors suggest that change is more likely to occur among marginal or peripheral organizations or actors (Clemens and Cook 1999: 452, 458). Clemens and Cook's discussion resonates with our analysis given how much corporate bankruptcy law, as a set of institutionalized rules, differs from country to country and possesses variable mutability. Furthermore, professional and expert networks span the globe, knit together this area, and provide ample opportunity for diffusion, learning, and emulation. And organizations like the IMF and World Bank have the financial leverage to coerce (or at least strongly encourage) countries to change their laws.

Theories of institutional change can inform our analysis, but given our interest in law, we also draw upon theories of *legal change*. Among other things, we can engage ideas about the rationalization of law, first posed by Max Weber but also by others more recently (see, e.g., Carruthers and Halliday 2007). Some scholars have focused on the importance of structural contradictions for lawmaking (Chambliss and Zatz 1993), while others have viewed law in a more functionalist perspective, perceiving it to adapt to the changing needs of society, elites, capitalists, business, or some other group. Some view legal change as primarily having to do with the creation of new formal law; others, with changes in how given formal law (law-on-the-books) is interpreted or implemented. Here we treat these possibilities in combination.

From political science, arguments about public policy feedbacks (Thelen 1999) suggest that one of the most important factors shaping the change of law is law itself. Extant policies, including law, can themselves engender supportive and opposing political constituencies and can expand or contract bureaucratic capacities. This argument about feedbacks implies that regardless of the particular political, bureaucratic, and social forces that put a policy in place at one point in time, that policy in turn changes those forces and how they affect subsequent policy. To give one example, the beneficiaries of a new law may not have been involved in the passage of the law (indeed, they may not even have existed as an organized political group), but once the law is in place, they crystallize as a supportive constituency who would oppose repeal or substantial modification of that law. Thus, interest groups shape law, but law shapes interest groups, so a feedback process occurs.

The fact of institutional change does not say anything about the direction of change. This leads us to our third major issue: *institutional convergence*. In particular, we consider whether there is global convergence in insolvency rules and if so, what is producing it. The issue of convergence has become something of a set piece in discussions of globalization, with early arguments stating that globalization was going to lead to rapid convergence among prices, products, business forms, and public policies. The next round of scholarship noted that in fact, rapid convergence was not occurring (see, e.g., Boyer 1996; Garrett 1998). Simplistic convergence arguments became something of a dead horse to be ritually flogged while noting the limits of globalization and criticizing exaggerated claims about its effects.

Yet, in the arena of corporate bankruptcy law, convergence is not such an implausible outcome. The 1990s have witnessed widespread revision of such laws in many different parts of the world. Furthermore, numbers of powerful organizations have become active in trying to devise and promulgate models, principles, normative standards, and paradigms for good bankruptcy law. Some of these organizations possess considerable financial leverage (e.g., IMF and World Bank) and can press their favored alternatives on loan recipients. Other organizations (e.g., United Nations Commission on International Trade Law [UNCITRAL], OECD, International Federation of Insolvency Practitioners [INSOL]) possess additional political, technocratic, or rhetorical resources to promote their alternatives.[3] Since many of these organizations have been trying to coordinate their negotiations, it is plausible that one or two alternative models might emerge and then be diffused globally, resulting in considerable convergence. But convergence could also occur if creditor or investor groups, which possess considerable international mobility, push hard for laws that favor their interests. Through a process of investment and disinvestment, countries that offered such laws would benefit while those that didn't would suffer, and over time laws would converge around a pattern that was good for investors.

If the emergence of global standards increases the likelihood and degree of convergence of legal institutions and helps to motivate institutional change, we have still to consider a fourth issue: *construction and propagation of global normative standards.* We do not consider such standards to be necessarily and strictly legal, although they have some lawlike features. To address this question, we must consider the activities of international organizations during the late 1990s. We also examine how the mobilization and deployment of technocratic and professionally based expertise shaped the diagnosis of "problems" and the prescription of "solutions." Because of differences in their training and in the knowledge they draw upon, different professions (e.g., lawyers vs. accountants vs. economists) have distinct and often conflicting perspectives on the same situation, and when these experts are based in different organizations (e.g., a Ministry of Justice vs. a Ministry of Finance), professional disagreements can turn into bureaucratic conflicts. Despite such differences, all the groups that mobilized in the late 1990s shared a belief that bankruptcy law, appropriately enacted and implemented, played an important role in supporting a market economy. They also agreed that such law was highly technical, and its revision required input from experts.

Beyond this basic consensus, however, competing visions were proposed, negotiated, and revised in various venues and organizations around the world. For instance, even if all agreed that a proper and effective corporate bankruptcy law helped with the reorganization of insolvent firms, it wasn't clear whose proper and effective law was best: British? U.S.? German? French law? National disagreements often emerged as experts embraced standards that happened coincidently to be rather close to the way things were done in their own home country. Experts also disagreed about whether it was better to frame standards at the level of general guiding principles (which would allow for more local variation) or to specify definite rules that ensured some measure of standardization across countries. Complicating still further these professional and organizational differences is the fact that the various forums in which proposals were made and negotiated varied considerably in their internal structure. Some were basically informal conferences in which the usual experts were rounded up and set the task of discussing an issue, but others (e.g., UNCITRAL) had formal deliberative proceedings in which delegates participated and then voted on a particular proposal. Since many of the same interested parties participate in multiple forums multiple times, it is clear to them (as well as to us) that such parties are differentially empowered across forums. To give an example, the U.S. government possesses a powerful influence over the IMF by virtue of the size of its financial contribution to the IMF. By contrast, in a setting like UNCITRAL, the U.S. can send a delegation, but so can all other member countries. Operating through the IMF privileges the U.S. much more than via UNCITRAL. Clearly, such internal structural differences affect what kinds of understandings, agreements, and endorsements emerge.

The creation of new standards is heavily influenced by real-world events. During the late 1990s, the major international financial institutions were simultaneously devising standards, norms, and principles for bankruptcy law, and at the same time advising particular countries (especially in East Asia) about how to revise their bankruptcy laws. Revision of national law and promulgation of international standards went on at the same time. Contrast this with the early 1990s, when many transition economies passed new bankruptcy laws, again with the advice of the IFIs. At that point, however, the IFIs did not use their advisory activity as an occasion to codify underlying principles of good bankruptcy law. The dramatic failure of East Asian economies motivated a more systemic and less ad hoc consideration of bankruptcy law than did the even more dramatic failure of socialism and subsequent transition to capitalism.

Propagation of global norms, standards, and models occurs through the kinds of channels identified by DiMaggio and Powell (1983), and it is easy to think of examples of each of the mechanisms they discuss: mimetic isomorphism (e.g., when Australia follows the lead of Britain), coercive isomorphism (e.g., when the IMF forces a country to change its laws as a condition of bailout loans), and normative isomorphism (when professionals and policy specialists use their authority as experts to define certain laws as appropriate or best). It is obvious that all three operate in the field of corporate bankruptcy law, albeit at different times and in different ways. But it is not obvious that they will lead here to the kind of outcome emphasized by DiMaggio and Powell, namely, *isomorphism* (their term for *convergence*).

We address these questions throughout the following sections of the book. After we introduce our theoretical framework, Part I examines in detail the activities of diverse global institutions as they struggled during the 1990s to apprehend the importance of bankruptcy law, as they came to an internal and external consensus about what "good" law is, and as they began to promulgate models and standards of "good" law so that various countries would change their own laws. In Part II the three country case studies indicate how the balance between global and local forces played out in particular situations. Part III elaborates how much the effects of global pressures are mediated by and filtered through local national situations, even when countries are heavily dependent on global institutions (as during a financial crisis). Such mediations hold true for both the enactment of formal law and its implementation, and for recursive patterns between law-on-the-books and law-in-action. In conclusion, we reflect on the theoretical and pragmatic implications of our research for understandings of globalization, law, and markets.

Acknowledgments

THE PLEASURES of researching and writing this book derive substantially from the great number of extraordinarily engaging, expert, and cooperative people who have willingly spent countless hours and effort supporting our enterprise. In the course of our research on international organizations and field work in China, Indonesia, and Korea, we have interviewed hundreds of informants. To all we express our deepest gratitude for carving out time from packed schedules and for bearing with endless questions, provocations, and half-baked theories with good humor and insight.

We thank especially principals at international organizations (IOs) who went the second and third extra mile and met with us repeatedly at diverse sites across the world, gave us access to private and public meetings, and trusted us with frank and forthright characterizations of their situation and those of other IOs. We express particular appreciation to Sean Hagan, General Counsel, International Monetary Fund; Clare Wee, formerly Assistant General Counsel, Asian Development Bank; and more recently to Vijay Tata, Legal Vice-Presidency, World Bank. We are most grateful to Jernej Sekolec, Secretary, United Nations Commission on International Trade Law, and Jenny Clift, Secretary of the Working Group on Insolvency, for giving the American Bar Foundation observer status in the Working Group on Insolvency so we might participate in all its meetings. Elena Miteva at the Organisation for Economic Co-operation and Development has integrated us into the Forum on Asian Insolvency Reforms (FAIR) for several years. UNCITRAL delegates from INSOL (Neil Cooper), the American Bar Association (Chris Redmond, Susan Block-Lieb), and many other state and nonstate delegations have been open and available for extensive discussions at our biannual cycles of meetings in New York and Vienna. The IMF, World Bank, and OECD FAIR provided seminar forums and constructive critiques of our developing analyses of insolvency reforms.

Our research has been enabled by superb research assistance from Teri Caraway, Lijun Chen, Khurram Husain, Hayun Kang, Ryon Lancaster, Faiza Mushtaq, Pavel Osinsky, and Gibb Pritchard. This work could not have been completed without the efforts of these fine scholars.

We have benefited greatly from careful readings of various chapters by Susan Block-Lieb, Rhoda Weeks-Browne, Jenny Clift, Sean Hagan, Zou Hailin, Michel Nussbaumer, Ceda Ogada, Soogeun Oh, Sebaastian Pompe, Mardjono Reksodiputro, Gerard Sanders, Fred Tumbuan, Clare Wee, and Wang Weiguo. Two excellent readers from Stanford University Press offered outstanding comments on the entire initial manuscript. And we have profited enormously from the very many reactions we received from readers of previously published articles and chapters as well as from participants in conferences, seminars, and meetings where we have presented our work. We absolve them of all responsibility for any factual errors and for interpretations we present despite all their best efforts to enlighten us.

We acknowledge gratefully permissions to reprint parts of articles and chapters previously published by Blackwells (Bruce G. Carruthers and Terence C. Halliday. 2006. "Negotiating Globalization: Global Templates and the Construction of Insolvency Regimes in East Asia." *Law and Social Inquiry* 31 (3): 521–584); the University of Chicago Press (Terence C. Halliday and Bruce G. Carruthers. 2007. "The Recursivity of Law: Global Norm-Making and National Law-Making in the Globalization of Corporate Insolvency Regimes." *American Journal of Sociology* 112: 1135–1202); and Hart Publishing (Terence C. Halliday and Bruce G. Carruthers. 2007. "Foiling the Hegemons: Limits to the Globalization of Corporate Insolvency Regimes in Indonesia, Korea and China." Pp. 255–301 in *Law and Globalization in Asia: From the Asian Financial Crisis to September 11*, edited by Christoph Anton and Volkmar Gessner (Oxford: Hart Publishing).

Our research has received extensive financial support from the American Bar Foundation and National Science Foundation (Grant SES-0214301). To both institutions we express deep thanks and especially to the indefatigable support of Bryant Garth and Robert Nelson, Directors of the American Bar Foundation. Kate Wahl at Stanford University Press has patiently encouraged us to bring this book to completion for longer than we care to remember.

Not least we happily say thanks to our families, who have never failed to show enthusiasm for our arcane research nor to grow weary of the frequent flyer miles that inevitably accompany global research projects. Our wonderfully encouraging and tolerant wives, we are relieved to say, have endured with mostly good humor another ten years of bankruptcy law. Terry Halliday dedicates the book to seven grandsons who have never known life without T-shirts winging their way from exotic research sites. Bruce Carruthers' dedication is to Sam and Esther, always dear to his heart.

BANKRUPT

1   The Legal Constitution of Markets

T HE 1997 ASIAN FINANCIAL CRISIS alarmed many besides the Asian Tigers.[1] Rapidly accumulating national financial meltdowns not only threatened the economic stability of East Asia but sent tremors across the global economy. So great was the alarm that the G-7 pressed for a restructuring of the international financial architecture.[2] Powerful global actors strenuously advocated worldwide projects of institution building and lawmaking, all directed to produce more robust markets. Within these was the law that governs corporate restructuring or failure—corporate bankruptcy law.

For the G-7, and the international organizations (IOs) subject to its influence, the Asian Financial Crisis spread so quickly and dangerously in part because orderly processes for dealing with failed firms simply did not function in any of the previously acclaimed Asian Tigers. This analysis led to an obvious prescription: robust markets required predictable mechanisms for weeding out inefficient firms or for giving them temporary protection while they reorganized themselves to compete effectively. In practice, however, this part of the reform package would involve much more than a change of laws. International organizations sought to implant entire corporate restructuring systems—substantive and procedural law, courts, out-of-court restructuring organizations, restructuring professions—and to integrate those with reformed banking systems.

Awareness of the integral role of bankruptcy systems in national and global markets did not emerge de novo in 1997. The dramatic transition from command to market economies in Central and Eastern Europe in the early 1990s focused the minds of consultants, bankers, investors, institution builders, and lawmakers on precisely what laws and institutions were needed in countries developing a market economy. The reform package included laws and organizations to handle something hitherto unknown under communism—corporate failure.

Even before the events of the 1990s, bankruptcy law was on the agendas of national lawmakers and bankruptcy practitioners. Along the road to European integration, finance ministers and Brussels civil servants alike recognized that cross-border trade would bring cross-border bankruptcies and that they needed a framework to handle the collapse of a multinational firm with assets and creditors in Spain, Ireland, Germany, or Britain. For precedent they needed only to look across the English Channel or across the Atlantic. In the 1980s several massive corporate collapses, most notably the Maxwell communications empire, sent creditors, insolvency practitioners, judges, and government officials scrambling to deal with a multinational whose affairs were organized in hundreds of subsidiaries spread across many national jurisdictions.

The effort to retrieve value from failing companies stemmed substantially from two earlier national initiatives (Carruthers and Halliday 1998). In 1986 the British Parliament enacted the English Insolvency Act, which Mrs. Thatcher's government had intended as a way to help save companies before they were beyond hope. She also intended to alter how company directors did business—to "clean up" the market, as her ministers proclaimed, and make it safe for the British investing public. Even more influential was the passage in 1978 of the U.S. Bankruptcy Code. In this far-reaching reform, Congress enacted the most ambitious effort yet to shift the concept of bankruptcy law from a legal mechanism for liquidating a company to an enabling mechanism for company rescue. This emphasis on corporate rehabilitation would eventually propagate across the world.

In short, starting from scattered law reforms in the 1970s and 1980s, a quickening pattern of legal change came to characterize one of the hallmarks of capitalist markets. The chief legal instrument for weeding out failing firms found its way into the formulas of global organizations and sovereign states as they tried to build a new national and transnational market architecture. This book shows how it happened. Previously we analyzed the landmark legislation in the United States and Britain that marked the beginnings of this worldwide movement (Carruthers and Halliday 1998). Here we attend to the more recent years that brought this global movement toward fruition. It is a process that allows us to engage various arguments about the causes, consequences, and pattern of globalization and also about the role of law in supporting a market economy. Furthermore, we can consider the role of experts and their ideas in policy reform and institutional design.

This global enterprise brought law and markets into a paradoxical conjunction. On the one hand, the world's dominant capitalist nations and many powerful IOs sought coherent global standards to rectify the absence or inadequacy of laws that rendered markets so fragile. On the other, IOs offered so many competing standards that the fate of any one was placed into the hands of nation-states who were their ultimate "consumers." This "market" for standards shaped the standards for markets. Law's global markets, therefore, made law the arbiter of markets and markets the arbiter of laws.

Pragmatism and Theory

The reform of bankruptcy law and institutions resulted from a conjunction of pragmatic concerns, which concentrated the minds of practitioners and policymakers, and theoretical questions, which opened up explanations of legal change, markets, and globalization. Reform participants included people who were simply concerned to assist troubled economies and others who pondered social science theories about the relationship between law and markets and how globalization affected economic development. The ideas that shaped reform ranged from the narrowly practical to the sweepingly grandiose.

For decades, bankruptcy law belonged to the arcane margins of legal practice and interested only those unfortunate companies that failed, or the professionals who ushered them out of business. Although the repercussions of multinational collapses and the reconstruction of Eastern European economies brought bankruptcy law closer to center stage, it was the Asian Financial Crisis that finally made global actors realize that a concerted campaign was necessary to protect financial sectors, countries, and the world economy from financial shocks (Stiglitz 2001, 2002). But how to do this? One big issue concerned the role of law itself. Many possibilities for corporation liquidation or reorganization exist outside law, including private restructurings by creditors, reorganizations on the advice of major consulting firms, and use of formal mechanisms set up by the state. In other words, procedures to deal with corporate failure can be provided without law. Yet law offers particular benefits: arguably it is more orderly, less arbitrary and ad hoc, more transparent, more concerned with equity, more mindful of the public interest, and, most important, binding on all actors involved.

To champion a legal core to corporate insolvency regimes raises many practical and theoretical questions. The world is divided into legal families that derive from centuries of culturally embedded political and economic development. To construct an international financial architecture that rests on national legal systems poses an enormous challenge. Which global actors would have the capacity or the legitimacy to craft global standards and then persuade nations to enact them? How much flexibility would those standards offer to nations pursuing reform in widely variable circumstances? What kind of relationship would be crafted between legal, in-court mechanisms and nonlegal, out-of-court methods? Would nation-states conform to these standards, and how effectively could they frustrate global legal change? If laws were enacted and institutions erected, would they be implemented? And even if all went the way of global actors, and laws were enacted and implemented, could they deliver the results promised?

The interdependency of law and capitalism is a central issue for the sociology of law. For Max Weber, the possibility of market exchanges that went beyond local and personalistic relationships depended upon law that was formal, unambiguous, and enforceable by authorities with jurisdiction over market actors (Swedberg 1998; Weber 1978). Markets, like law, require legitimation. Economic sociology also posits that national and global markets depend on rules and considers the sources and bases for those rules (Fligstein 2001). Is predictable law necessary for modern capitalism, as Weber argued? And does the global spread of markets produce convergence among varieties of capitalism (Halliday and Carruthers 2007b)? The success of global legal norms, moreover, precisely turns on the capacity to legitimate particular conceptions of law's regulatory functions vis-à-vis markets. What kinds of global norms emanating from which institutions are sufficiently legitimate? What global scripts, templates, or standards are available to cope with the vast diversity of laws, nations, and firms worldwide? And how are these adaptable to local circumstances and legal cultures?

Research on markets and law takes on a different hue from the perspective of the globalism and antiglobalism conflict (Santos 2002; Silbey 1997). Who formulates the norms and rules to govern global markets? The most powerful countries? Global capital? International professionals? Is a global consensus possible, and if achieved, how are global norms propagated? And if propagated, how are they received by national policymakers? Their local reception can range from welcome adoption to hostile resistance, with ambivalent adaptation in between. To understand the globalization of law and markets, we must be able to identify its agents, the scripts they craft, the mechanisms they deploy, the powers they exercise, and the structuration of global/local relationships (Halliday and Osinsky 2006). Ultimately, such an account must address convergence at the center and periphery around global norms and the actors that articulate them.

Globalization

Globalization set the stage for reform at the end of the twentieth century. As an idea, "globalization" proceeds from a premise of universality (Boyle and Meyer 1998). Whether global flows consist of goods, services, ideas, beliefs, capital, or cultural artifacts, the idea connotes that nations and peoples, organizations and individuals, will be connected and progressively integrated across the world. Furthermore, in many arenas it is presumed that particular goods, services, or ideas will prevail—that universal ideals, norms, or standards will originate in a global center and be diffused throughout global peripheries. In many conceptions, globalization means convergence or homogenization: a fully globalized world is one in which there is greater global uniformity and less local variety than before. The tension between global forces and local structures, and the domination of the former over the latter, means that power inequalities accompany globalization (Arrighi 2003; Santos 2002; Silbey 1997).

To understand how law features in globalization, we need to identify global norms, structures, standards, and ideals and understand where they originate. We must also explain their propagation and whether it produces convergence. There are four distinct approaches that address this conjunction of law and markets (Halliday and Osinsky 2006). World polity theory holds a strong view of global norms (Berkovitch 1999; Boyle and Meyer 1998; Schollmeyer 1997; Supit 1998). Its proponents maintain that global norms of rationalism, universality, and human rights represent the cultural triumph of Western civilization. A strong global consensus within "world society" originates from Western Europe and North America and is progressively diffused throughout the world. These norms are more self-validating than imposed by dominant actors. By contrast, world systems theorists recognize global economic integration but attribute little importance to global norms (Boswell and Chase-Dunn 2000; Wallerstein 2002). Dominant economic actors at the global center are resistant to normative constraints on their power. To the extent there is legal regulation of markets, it is contested between, for instance, capital and labor. Scholars of postcolonial globalism also point to a global hegemony, albeit more broadly construed, whereby nations and institutions at the global center exercise economic and intellectual dominance over weak peripheries (Darian-Smith 2004; Santos 2002; Silbey 1997). Global norms privilege those of a particular "local" and are better understood as globalized localisms (Santos 2000). Scholarship on law and development similarly proceeds on the assumption that global actors have forged a consensus around an ideology of law and markets that they subsequently have propagated in two successive waves (1960s–1970s, 1990s–2000s) to poor and weak countries the world over (Salacuse 2000; Trubek 1996).

With the partial exception of world systems theory, these approaches all embrace a similar concept of universal global norms, standards, structures, or rules. They also posit that such norms are formulated asymmetrically because of the exclusion of weak nations and marginal actors. Mostly, however, these theories advance on the basis of a reified and unitary concept of the "global." As an explanatory concept it is rarely more than a monolithic black box. There is little recognition of the internal contests and conflicts among global actors striving for ascendancy in the formulation of norms. To be sure, these theories recognize the conflict between central powers and peripheral players, although the battle is invariably won by the center. The battle within the global center, over whose law regulates global markets, gets overlooked. Furthermore, there is scarce attention to those who play a key role in the creation of global norms, most notably professionals. With some notable exceptions (Braithwaite and Drahos 2000; Canan and Reichman 2001; Merry 2005), too little theory specifies the conditions under which global consensus on norms will be possible.

In some measure, these theoretical lacunae follow from a methodological shortcoming. Social scientists mostly lack access to the councils of global norm making. Forced to rely either on the public documents that global actors release, which themselves are forms of opinion shaping, or on a potpourri of journalism, autobiographies, and official histories, social scientists face two problems. They either place undue reliance on official self-representations, and thus are caught by projected self-images, or they rely on reified concepts that owe more to theoretical deduction than empirical induction. One consequence of the latter is a tendency to overestimate global consensus and global capacities, a lapse that can misrepresent the force and impact of globalization. What is required, therefore, is access to the crafters of global norms, observation of norm making as it occurs, and access to the internal documents, successive drafts of competing proposals, and intermediate formulations that trace out the creative process.

In this book we open up the black box in which global norms are debated and decided. In the course of our fieldwork, we established long-standing relationships with the key individual and institutional actors who have competed over the formulation of global norms on bankruptcy law. Over seven years, we conducted hundreds of interviews with these actors, as they have advanced alternative sets of norms. We have had access to drafts of standards under deliberation, not just the finished products, and we participated in many meetings of international organizations as they negotiated over global norms. And, most important, we had former "observer" status inside the United Nations Commission that brought the global consensus to fruition.

This unusual access to global policymaking led us to appreciate globalization as both a concept and a process. Globalization comprises both structural changes and discursive representations of those changes (Fiss and Hirsch 2005). The *structural* dimension concerns changes in global flows of people, ideas, money, and material objects. The *discursive* dimension concerns the meanings that motivate, rationalize, and interpret structural changes, including diagnoses, policy frameworks, political framings, epistemologies, and the like. A global normative consensus therefore signifies the combination of a dominant discourse and congruent structural capacities that undergird its development and propagation. We consider norms to be more fully globalized when their structural and discursive aspects are extensive (broadly include nation-states worldwide), intensive (penetrate deeply inside localities), spread rapidly, and implemented in practice (i.e., they are effective) (Held et al. 1999).

Explicating these processes requires careful analysis of global and local arenas. An adequate theory of globalization must attend closely to four elements (Braithwaite and Drahos 2000; Halliday and Osinsky 2006). First, to get beyond reification and vacuous overgeneralization, it is necessary to identify *actors* at the global center, local actors who encounter global forces, and the actors that intermediate between the global and the local.

Second, an adequate theory requires analysis of *technologies* and *scripts*. Global norms can be institutionalized in a wide variety of forms—best practices, UN resolutions, international conventions, treaties, model laws, cases from the WTO and international courts, standards and principles. Every form represents a particular method for solving a coordination problem, resolving a conflict, or achieving convergence. Formal attributes of technologies vary their authority, flexibility, and effectiveness.

Third, institutionalized global scripts are propagated by agents exercising *power* through an array of *resources* or *mechanisms*. International legal actors rely principally upon economic coercion, the propagation of models for nations to adapt and adopt, persuasion, systems of reward, and various kinds of reciprocity and coordination. In short, the globalization of law and markets is an expression of power. Differentials of power must be explicated between global actors and peripheral states, within the global center, and with the global periphery. Fourth, as a *process*, globalization is structured through international organizations, epistemic communities and professional networks, aid programs and intergovernmental networks, trading relationships, and migration.

Much of the complexity that surrounds globalization arises from the interconnections among these elements. For instance, we know that certain actors are predisposed to particular scripts, mechanisms, and forms of power. We expect that, where possible, powerful global actors will try to avoid heavy reliance on raw power and utilize soft power exercised through collaboratively developed norms. In its extreme form, when a dominant power prevails, the latter is the path to hegemony—universal acceptance of the rightness and "normality" of one course of action. In less extreme forms, it takes the paths of classification, labeling, and framing to develop universals that may be considered "modern," "efficient," and "advanced."

The contours of globalization vary by the arena in which it unfolds: there is no single world stage. The conjunction of markets and law presents a particularly intriguing research site because the propensity for convergence varies so sharply between them. On the one hand, global integration is far advanced in capital markets and in trade and commerce. Until recently, the dominant trend had been toward free capital movements, free trade, and market liberalization generally, and structures were well developed to facilitate many aspects of global business—even if the Asian Financial Crisis showed these were far from complete. But the globalization of markets contrasts with the strong local connections of law. Insofar as law is institutionalized by national sovereign authorities, its development is embedded in local cultural, social, and political relations and therefore is less responsive to extraterritorial trends. Insofar as markets are structured and supported by legal systems, one accelerator of globalization appears to be joined to a brake of localism. Part of our task, therefore, is to show how the actors in the field of bankruptcy law negotiated their way between global market pressures and the local embeddedness of commercial law.

The conjunction of law and markets not only brings together two distinct social organizations but also poses a tension between them: globalization of markets has far outpaced globalization of commercial law. The misalignment between these two institutions (Westbrook 2000) is precisely what sparked global economic actors after the Asian Financial Crisis. Beneath their call for an international financial architecture, built on robust national institutions, lay a tacit notion of market-law symmetry. Markets too poorly regulated and disciplined by law, stated the G-7 and G-22, are dangerously unstable (G-22 1998b, 1998c). Law must be brought into symmetry with the market. But insofar as reform activates another asymmetry—the power differences between global and local actors—the reform process will be fraught with contingency.

Configuring the Global

The concept of globalization, as a process, typically begs the question of what is the global. How does what we term *global* come to be? Which actors are drawn into domains of global activity, and what are their social, economic, and political locations? How do global alternatives converge onto global norms? In short, how is the global institutionalized in a given arena or domain?

Extending Djelic and Quack's (2003) discussion, we propose three vantage points from which to approach these questions. The global may be constituted from *above*, via the imperial or quasi-imperial acts of global powers (Berle and Means 1968; Goldman 2005; Merry 2003). The global may be constituted from *below*, at the insistence of nations, subnational groups, or other interest groups that view global norms and mechanisms as a suitable way to resolve their problems (Sassen 2006). And the global may be constituted from *across* domains, when solutions to problems in one arena appear suitable for problems in another, and so move laterally.

In the globalization of bankruptcy law, we examine each of these directions. From above, colonial or neocolonial legacies might produce significant convergence on a small cluster of solutions emerging out of the legal families of common law, French and German civil law, and Dutch and Scandinavian civil law (Pistor et al. 2002). This convergence could be selectively reinforced by U.S. domination in the post-WWII era, by ideologies of legal regulation and rule of law that reflect the American market economy, and by U.S. power over international organizations.

From below, demand for transnational legal mechanisms could come from nation-states, multinational corporations, and professionals and judges seeking an orderly way to manage corporate failures. Demand could stem from efforts at transnational regulation of international commerce (e.g., between Canada and the U.S., Britain and the U.S.) or regional regulation that accompanied economic integration (e.g., European Union). Professionals are only one of many groups for whom economic restructuring presents valuable opportunities.

From across, any effort to articulate between the market and law in the insolvency field can potentially borrow from similar regulatory efforts elsewhere. The IMF and World Bank developed protocols for macroeconomic restructuring and institution building that long predated concern with bankruptcy. The UN Commission on International Trade Law could point to decades of success at drafting model laws and conventions to govern sales, contracts, and other aspects of business practice. And the regional development banks were already building legal systems in Central Europe and Asia in domains other than bankruptcy law (Pistor and Wellons 1999). In other words, globalization can proceed through something like a lateral contagion effect, where lessons learned in one arena spill over into others.

These explanations are not necessarily contradictory, but they pose quite different trajectories for change. The movement toward a single global standard in the insolvency area can be seen as a series of trial-and-error steps toward models that combined legitimacy, adaptable technology, and leverage. Nevertheless, since actors placed different weights on these attributes, and because competition among actors complicated the process, the path was by no means predetermined. The complexity and contingency of this process can be better appreciated by a brief consideration of each element.

Legitimacy

If global actors wish nation-states to adopt global norms, and if governments are to adopt norms that suit their aspirations, then the norms must be seen as legitimate (Boyle and Meyer 1998; Hurd 2002, 2005; Smismans 2004). Legitimacy matters on both sides of the global/local encounter. With respect to the global center, the issue of legitimacy for IOs has again attracted the attention of political scientists (Hurd 2007). It is clear that most international organizations either do not wish to rely on coercion or do not have the capacity to do so. In fact, it is usual in recent years that powerful sovereign states prefer to proceed without the fact or appearance of naked coercion. In contradistinction to classic realpolitik, therefore, IOs and globally dominant countries seek to establish their authority through legitimation mandates. If the objects of action by IOs can be persuaded of the rightness of prescribed action, then compliance is more likely and implementation less problematic.

Three such mandates have been identified (Cronin and Hurd 2008; Hurd 2008a). First, IOs are more legitimate when their membership and decision making include representatives of the entities that are the objects of norm making. This *representative* basis for legitimacy depends on the activation of criteria, which are quite diverse, for persuading prospective audiences that an organization's products have been formulated by actors who share their interests. Second, IOs seem more legitimate when their internal decision making proceeds by standards of *procedural fairness*. All actors incorporated into the deliberative process should be aware of the rules of deliberation and be treated equitably in their application. Third, in a kind of circular reasoning, IOs are more legitimate when they are seen to be *effective*. If an IO has previously been successful in achieving its goals, in producing standards that were adopted, then it will be considered more legitimate in prospective endeavors.

At the global level, efforts to obtain legitimacy mean that organizational actors weigh their legitimation warrants against legitimation deficits. Each global actor has, or may be able to construct, elements of legitimacy that audiences find credible. But legitimation warrants may be offset by legitimation deficits. Whether by virtue of their goals, reputations, ties to illegitimate allies, disreputable past practices, offensive ideologies, or incapacity, among others, international organizations carry delegitimating attributes that diminish their capacity to influence. As a result, one dynamic in global norm making turns on efforts by international organizations to balance their own legitimation warrants and deficits, but also to seek compensatory alliances with partners whose legitimacy bolsters and complements that of the IO.

Legitimacy is also an issue for the global periphery. In global/local encounters, much depends on the willingness of national actors to grant legitimacy to global agents. Legitimacy always requires an accepting subject, an actor willing to obey or comply in acknowledgment of legitimate authority. In this sense, the power of global actors depends not just on their inherent organizational attributes but on how they are perceived. The perceptual side of legitimacy reflects its relational aspect. Effective global norm making is integrally interactive—and this grants some power to the subjects of legitimation initiatives. In short, processes of legitimation take place within international organizations, among international organizations, and between those organizations and their national/local intended subjects.

We take issue with the world polity approach to legitimacy. While applauding its emphasis on cultural factors, we find the portrait of "world culture" overly monochromatic, unitary, and consensual. By this account, a world culture emerged over the last centuries, embracing a core set of principles whose legitimacy is now unquestioned. Its principles are universalism, individualism, rational authority, rationalizing progress, and world citizenship (Boli and Thomas 1997: 172–173, 180). This culture then becomes the driving force behind many changes similar to the ones we study: "Many features of the contemporary nation-state derive from worldwide models constructed and propagated through global cultural and associational processes" (Meyer et al. 1997: 144–145). For example, the global spread of higher education in the twentieth century reflects the institutionalization of a new model of society, characterized by democratization, human rights, scientization, and development planning (Schofer and Meyer 2005: 900). Thus, there is global isomorphism in higher education (p. 909). But for our purposes, this radically oversimplifies the legitimation process: a reform or policy is legitimate only to the extent that it reflects world culture. It overlooks the work that IOs must perform to legitimate their activities, and it provides no guidance when sharply competing reform alternatives come to embrace world culture.

Technologies

For our purposes, a social technology is a social arrangement or set of rules aimed at achieving a particular outcome or solving a particular problem in a regularized manner. IOs are production centers of such technologies. Some they borrow and others they invent (although rarely de novo). All technologies encapsulate a set of understandings or agreements about the nature of a problem and how to solve it. The goal is to package them in a form that will be persuasive to potential audiences or constituencies.

The process of innovation at the global level parallels that within nation-states. Rarely are technologies imposed on IOs, but limitations may be placed on which technologies they may employ or the breadth of their scope. More often technologies are borrowed, either from national exemplars or from other IOs, and frequently with some alterations. Nevertheless, we will show that in the attempt to align markets with law in the arena of corporate insolvency, technologies are mostly invented to suit the specific challenges that confront them. IOs' capacity for invention depends substantially on their ability to attract the world's leading professionals and scholars to their organizations (and not just as employees). And if the participants themselves are not the inventors, they can act as conduits through their connections to professional associations, scholarly societies, epistemic communities, practice settings, and international networks where innovations also originate. To integrate professional expertise within IOs is a fundamental challenge that determines their ability to manage global complexities appropriately.

Technologies in the legal field vary by how binding they are. In the terminology of legal scholarship, they may be "hard" law or "soft" law (Abbott and Snidal 2000). Hard law has the force of legal authority, complete with sanctions. Soft law has persuasive force, with ample room for maneuver by national policymakers. Legal technologies are affected by the process of their formulation. Devising a precise and binding global convention is vastly more difficult than formulating a set of advisory principles. IOs face trade-offs between the arduous attempt to negotiate a legitimate, binding, and universally applicable hard law, as against producing an equivocally binding soft law more quickly and at less cost.

The legitimacy of legal technologies depends also on their particular attributes. This is especially important in soft law, where promulgation is not accompanied by binding sanctions. IOs can increase the persuasiveness of their instruments, templates, and scripts by building into the technology attributes that convey either a positive valence (e.g., that "the majority of advanced nations have adopted") or a negative valence (e.g., shaming language against a particular country) (Block-Lieb and Halliday 2006; Halliday, Carruthers, and Block-Lieb 2008).

Technologies vary also by their relative weighting of diagnosis and prescription (Chapter 3) (Halliday and Carruthers 2007). All formulations of norms for national legal systems proceed on some kind of diagnosis. Sometimes that diagnosis is implicit (e.g., that a country lacks an independent judiciary), but in other cases it is systematically conducted (e.g., formal measurement and evaluation) and may be publicized in full or in part. Altogether these variations in diagnosis and prescription provide even more degrees of freedom for IOs to create technologies.

Leverage

In addition to the attributes of IO decision making and their products, the influence of IOs over local actors depends on IO leverage. Building on the most comprehensive research on global business regulation (Braithwaite and Drahos 2000), we find that global actors exercise leverage through very particular means. The most visible is *economic coercion*, notably through the use of conditionalities by international financial institutions that demand legal and institutional changes as a condition of financial assistance. More common is *modeling*, when IOs offer nation-states model laws or model bankruptcy systems to which they may adapt their own institutions. Leverage also proceeds through *persuasion*, when IOs and professionals in their circle host conferences, write articles, and give speeches in regional meetings about the merits of particular scripts or national models that adhere to those scripts. Persuasion can be coupled with *incentives*, sometimes financial, as in foreign aid or technical assistance loans, and sometimes moral, when IOs suggest that a country's reputation will be enhanced by its conformity to global standards.

The leverage exercised by global actors is unevenly distributed and situation specific. Part of the explanatory task is to find which mechanisms are applied in what situations. For example, economic coercion will be available only to international financial institutions (IFIs) with a capacity to make financing contingent on reforms. The availability of instruments for leverage depends also on the attributes of nations, whether they are willing to accept donors' conditions, or whether they need financial resources or approbation. We will show that the balance of power between nation-states and global actors and the "proximity" of national actors to global processes affect which forms of leverage come into play (Chapter 8). In short, leverage depends on complicated relationships between capacities of global actors, the situation of the nation-state, and the relations between them.

Legitimacy, technology, and leverage have complex interactions with each other. An economically powerful actor, such as the IMF or World Bank, may be able to use economic coercion, and indeed its use may appear advantageous in the short term, but in the intermediate and longer term blatant pressure can delegitimate these organizations and engender domestic resistance to their policies. The United States may believe it has the best corporate bankruptcy system, and it may seek to export it to the rest of the world, but for some nations, overt conformity to U.S. models will be unacceptable to domestic constituencies (e.g., China). IOs may develop superb technologies through legitimate processes, but inadequate leverage will leave polished scripts languishing on shelves.

Our formulation reveals the complexity inherent in developing global norms. Legitimacy stems from all three sources of globalization—from above, below, and across. Technologies, too, stem from multiple sources. And the availability and efficacy of forms of leverage are variously dependent on whether they originate from above, below, or across. These interactions reinforce the complex role of IOs and also the likely indeterminacy of their absorption into a coherent international field of law. Nevertheless, we shall show that over a period of twenty years competitive actors in the international field managed to produce a highly legitimate bankruptcy product that was conducive to convergence and open to adaptation, with attendant forms of leverage that might be deployed in diverse situations. How this occurred is our empirical puzzle. How it is to be explained turns on the interplay of dynamics around legitimacy, technology, and leverage.

Recursivity of Law

The institutionalization of legal regimes for global markets presents a massive challenge for legal change, especially within nation-states. The most critical moment comes when global and local factors combine to produce domestic legal change. What are the dynamics at this critical juncture?

Domestic Legal Change

The problem of explaining legal change within countries is difficult enough. Sociolegal scholarship has centered its activities on a classic distinction—between law-on-the-books and law-in-action (Cotterrell 1995; Lempert and Sanders 1986; Sutton 2001). Its primary focus for decades was on the gap that inevitably opens up between formal law (i.e., statutes, court cases, and regulations) and everyday practice (i.e., how the subjects of law comply, obey, and deviate from it). But sociolegal scholarship itself has effectively abandoned inquiry into the origins of law-on-the-books itself.[3] Instead, this task was appropriated by political science. But political scientists, in turn, have shown little interest in what happens after enactment of new statutes, implicitly assuming what sociologists of law know to be false, namely, that law-on-the-books smoothly becomes effective law-in-action.

We offer an alternative framework that centers around the recursivity of law and that includes both lawmaking and law implementation (Chapter 10) (Halliday and Carruthers 2007b). These produce mutual tensions that produce cycles of reform oscillating between law-on-the-books and law-in-action (see Figure 1.1).

In this framework, lawmaking cycles are anchored by two poles. At one end is lawmaking itself, narrowly construed. For heuristic purposes, we designate law as the formal products of legislatures (statutes, statutory amendments), courts (cases, regulations, interpretations), and executive agencies (regulations).[4] At the other end is practice, where law is perceived, applied, implemented, and acted upon, whether in conformity or not with the intentions of the lawmakers or the letter of the law.

Legal change that involves state law of any kind proceeds through cycles between formal law and law-in-practice. Law-in-practice is an outcome to be explained (traditional sociology of law) as well as a further stimulus for lawmaking, just as law-on-the-books must be explained and followed into action. The premise is that neither formal law nor practice can be explained adequately without attention to the other. A theory of legal change requires that we situate any particular moment of lawmaking or implementation into a context of prior sequences, for the form and substance of prior cycles variously enable and constrain prospective lawmaking.

Episodes and Cycles   In many areas of legal change, reforms are not constant. Years and decades may pass without any significant alteration in either formal law or practice. Reforms frequently proceed in distinct episodes, with perceptible beginnings and ends. They begin when underlying problems in social practice or mobilization of interests or contradictions and tensions build up pressure for change of law, combined with the political opportunity to do so. Often a triggering event—a tragedy, scandal, or crisis—is necessary to precipitate lawmaking at a given moment.

Cycles also have endings: when contradictions are resolved, or consensus is reached, or legal meanings settle, or an underlying cause fades away. Cycles also end when exogenous pressure is removed, an oppositional party runs out of resources, political attention shifts to other issues, or all parties are exhausted.

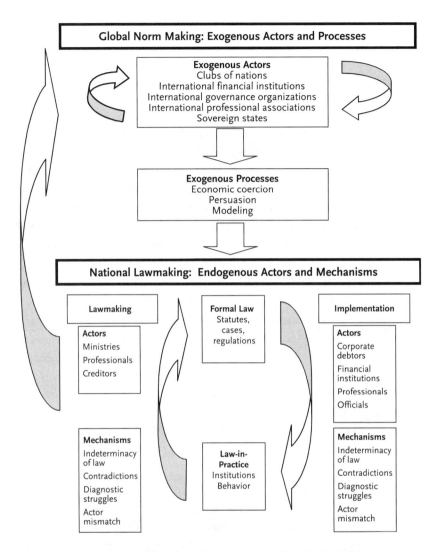

FIGURE 1.1 Recursive Cycles of Bankruptcy Lawmaking in Global Contexts
SOURCE: Adapted from Halliday and Carruthers (2007b).

Cycles of rapid and regular adjustments of formal law and practice will slow and reach some point of equilibrium.[5] Practice continues, and a de facto law may consolidate, shift, and change, but formal law can remain static, often for decades. As historical institutionalists increasingly point out, much legal change can occur while statutes remain static (Streeck and Thelen 2005).

Mechanisms   Cycles of reform are driven by internal tensions between formal law and practice. We identify four such dynamic tensions.

1.   It is a fundamental insight of sociolegal and critical legal scholarship that all lawmaking involves *indeterminacy* and *ambiguity* (Pistor and Xu 2003). New concepts or doctrine allows for multiple interpretations and requires clarification. Creative professionals can use the law in unanticipated ways, such as creative compliance—a form of sophisticated noncompliance (McBarnet and Whelan 1997). One piece of the law may be inconsistent with another part. The law itself may be inconsistent with other laws or with constitutional principles. Indeterminacies and ambiguity open up gaps in practice. To reduce ambiguity, inconsistency, and uncertainty, practitioners, interest groups, and lawmakers will often press for another round of reforms.

2.   Laws also internalize *contradictions* (Chambliss and Zatz 1993). Ideological contradictions occur when the balancing of interests in lawmaking builds counterposing ideals into the law. Contradictions endow the formal law with an inherent instability that can be exploited and translated into competing applications in practice. Since states themselves are variously differentiated into branches of government, and branches incorporate competing agencies, structural contradictions often accompany lawmaking. But ideological and structural contradictions are recipes for further rounds of regulatory promulgation or judicial rulings until the contradictions are resolved.

3.   Any legal change proceeds on the basis of social diagnosis, the imputation of a state of affairs, the identification of a problem, or the definition of a situation that requires a policy-led remedy. The power to impose a diagnosis is the first step toward prescribing a particular solution. As a result, in politics and law *diagnostic struggles* occur between parties competing to persuade the public and lawmakers that their particular definition of the problem is accurate. The linking of diagnosis and prescription in professional work (Abbott 1988) has its metaphorical equivalent in politics. Collective actors strive to define the problem in terms that will be conducive to their preferred solution. If a tendentious diagnosis hardens into law, then implementation provides an arena for the losers in the definitional contest to resist in practice and push for another round of reform.

4. Cycles of reform are also driven forward by pathologies of *actor mismatch*. There are five parties to practice and reform: (a) *practitioners* who implement the law; (b) *diagnostic actors* who individually or collectively interpret problems that require solution; (c) *stakeholders* who will be influenced by the law (or its absence); (d) *lawmakers* who are the proximate actors in lawmaking; and (e) *veto players* who overlap with lawmakers and have the capacity to stop any prospective formal law. If key actors in practice are excluded from lawmaking and have no "voice," then they are likely to use the arena of practice to resist law they do not support. Here again an effort to effect changed practice will increase the probability of another round of reform.

Global Contexts

The recursivity of law within countries increasingly responds to global circumstances. By the same token, global forces are themselves partially constituted out of local factors and frequently reflect the imprint of a particular nation or coalition of states, so-called globalized localisms (Santos 2002; Sassen 2006). The shape of the "global" varies from one to another domain of law, and its contours have to be discerned inductively. It is especially useful to make comparisons across domains in order to examine which actors are present (and absent) in which areas of law.

In the bankruptcy field we identify five sets of global actors who helped design the global bankruptcy standards that shape bankruptcy lawmaking within nation-states (Part I):

1. Clubs of nations (e.g., G-7, G-22, Organisation for Economic Cooperation and Development [OECD]) set political agendas, release or prioritize resources, concentrate expertise, and create collegial and collaborative environments.

2. International financial institutions (e.g., IMF, World Bank, and regional development banks) execute in part the directives of the G-7 or G-22, develop global norms, diagnose and prescribe treatments for nation-states, and channel resources to developing countries.

3. International governance organizations (e.g., United Nations) provide inclusive global forums for national representatives and technical experts to produce global norms.

4. Peak or confederations of associations of professionals (e.g., International Bar Association, International Federation of Insolvency Practitioners) and networks of specialists offer technical expertise, provide professional authority, and seek to advance professional interests in the formulation of standards and their enactment and implementation.

5. Core nations (e.g., U.S., Germany, France) push collective efforts from behind the scenes, seek indirect influence through international bodies, and provide resources to multilateral and bilateral aid programs to developing nations.

We will show that relations among these are complicated by their interpenetration. The U.S. was a leading player in the G-7, IMF and World Bank policies, and UN norm making; U.S. professionals exerted technical and policy influence not only through their associations but via participation in OECD and UN activities. What appear as discrete categories of international bodies in practice devolve into a community of discourse and influence with a very small core of key individuals. Paradoxically, in contrast to the massive scope of programs aimed at almost two hundred countries, the actual designers, agents, and organizers of global norm making form an intimate, if not always concordant, community. So small was this community that interorganizational conflicts and contests were influenced by the social skills and even the personalities of key figures (Canan and Reichman 2001).

In the context of recursive lawmaking we identify two movements that integrate the "global" and "local." We have already pointed to a dynamic that will be explicated in detail in Part I: global norms themselves emerged from cycles of trial and error, formulation and reformulation, innovation and adaptation among the global actors. Before and during recursive cycles of lawmaking at the national level there were iterations of norm making at the global level. It must be emphasized that these did not proceed independently of each other. The experiences drawn from transitions and crises in nation-states were drawn into global norm making; the norms developed by global actors were propagated across developing nations. In short, global institutions and local experiences were partially co-constitutive. Yet it would naïve to suppose this interchange was symmetrical. Powerful nations in the global financial center put their stamp on global norms much more than did peripheral nations.

In sum, lawmaking in a global context can be framed as an intersection of three sets of cycles: (1) iterations of *norm making and lawmaking* by global actors, (2) recursive cycles of *lawmaking* by nation-states, and (3) recurrent exchanges between global iterations and national cycles. And running through the cycles are bilateral and multilateral flows of information and resources, modeling and imitation, between and among countries bound by region, legal family, or a close trading relationship.

Asymmetries of Power

These cycles unfold in a field of power. To capture this important aspect, we locate global/local interactions within a two-dimensional context (see Figure 8.1). Interactions vary depending on where they occur in this space.[6]

One dimension concerns the balance of power between the national and global. This balance varies over time, across contexts, and between countries. For example, in some issue areas national autonomy takes precedence: national norms and institutions are stronger within one issue area (e.g., security) than another (e.g., finance and investment). The balance varies over time, so with respect to global institutions like the IMF a country like Thailand was in a stronger bargaining position in 1995 than in 1998 (at the height of the Asian Financial Crisis). And, of course, the balance varies between different countries. Economic and military powers like the United States or China cannot be treated like small countries (e.g., Luxembourg or Madagascar). In general, we expect that nations in a strong position will be less receptive to global scripts. But the balance can sometimes shift dramatically and quickly reset the terms of the interaction.

The second dimension concerns the cultural and social "distance" between the local and global. There is significant variation in how congruent extant local institutions and practices are with their global counterparts. Greater congruence means a shorter distance between local and global, and therefore less of a tension or incompatibility between them. It makes for a less conflictual global/local interaction. Some global institutions are already more or less "localized." For example, both the World Bank and the IMF are global institutions. Yet, as an organization, the IMF remains highly centralized in terms of both personnel and organizational capacity. By contrast, the World Bank is more decentralized and maintains long-term personnel and offices in various recipient countries. As a result, the World Bank has more local knowledge, expertise, and capacity than the IMF. Or it may be that a global institution represents a regional or selective perspective (e.g., the EU, the OECD, or the Asian Development Bank [ADB]).

Localization of the global works in other ways as well. Sometimes, particular countries are able to make global institutions conform to their own local institutions (Braithwaite and Drahos 2000). For example, international airline safety standards and protocols have essentially adopted U.S. safety standards and protocols, so a country that conforms to those has in effect (and often without knowing it) imported U.S. standards. In this situation, the distance between U.S. and global standards is zero. Furthermore, global institutions can be co-opted to serve local interests or used to pursue a local agenda. Such "two-level games" occur, for example, when a government obtains an IMF loan because the conditions attached to the loan give the government extra leverage over domestic political opponents (Vreeland 2003, 52–53). In this way, the IMF is used by a national government to "force" a government to do what it wants to do but otherwise cannot. Or, not infrequently, a domestic interest group enlists a global actor as an ally to increase its domestic influence, as we shall show with the IMF's involvement in Indonesia. Finally, global institutions can be "localized" informally, through selective or creative implementation. In such cases, the global rules appear to have been directly imposed on a nation and incorporated into its laws, but the adoption may be only formal.

On the other side of the dichotomy, local institutions can be more or less globalized. Some countries already possess "world-class" capacities, expertise, and institutions, so for them to deal with global institutions is not such a challenge. For example, when the Mexican Central Bank deals with global financial institutions like the IMF or the Bank for International Settlements (BIS), it possesses staff economists who were trained at the same U.S. graduate schools (e.g., Harvard, Chicago, MIT) as their foreign counterparts (Babb 2001). Consequently, Mexican Central Bank economists speak the same language, possess the same professional credentials, and may even be part of the same graduate school networks, as individuals from global institutions. The *ex ante* "distance" between the local and global affects how the interaction between them unfolds, and this distance varies depending on how localized is the global and how globalized is the local.

Taken together, these two dimensions help to explain how particular global/local interactions unfold. Distance indicates how far apart the two sides of the interaction are at the outset. The greater this distance, the greater the potential tension between the two, the greater the need for mediation, and the more formidable the challenge to satisfy the demands coming from the global and local sides. The balance of power helps to determine which side is more likely to be moving toward the other. To take one extreme, an interaction between equally powerful local and global institutions that have little distance between them is likely to be uneventful and will not lead to dramatic change on either side or pose substantial translation or framing difficulties.

Our emphasis on power differences among competing actors again distinguishes our approach from the world polity perspective (Meyer et al. 1997). Rather than suppose that global technologies derive from a long-term consensus built around core values of world culture, we observe technologies emerging from one unequal struggle and their implementation unfolding in another unequal struggle. Following Beckfield (2003) and Bartley (2007), we recognize that there is considerable inequality of involvement and influence within the international governmental organizations (IGOs) and the international nongovernmental organizations (INGOs) that provide much of the "connective tissue" within the world polity.

Since globalization cannot be understood by focus on the global alone (Sassen 2006), we approach it from two directions. Not only must we examine flows from the global to the local but we must also investigate the global/local encounter from the vantage point of the local. Because we expect that these encounters will vary across the dimensions in Figure 8.1, we varied our choice of cases to study—the nation-states of Indonesia, South Korea, and China—in terms of their different power relations with the global and their proximity to the global.

The imbalance of power going into the Asian Financial Crisis was greatest in Indonesia. Although it had recorded remarkable economic development during the preceding decades, its vulnerability at the point of the Crisis in 1997 was extreme. Moreover, Indonesia had limited geopolitical significance for the global powers, and its institutions were far from conforming to global standards. After September 11, 2001, however, the Bush administration's policies toward terrorism, money laundering, and political Islam raised Indonesia's significance for U.S. foreign policy, a shift that ultimately relaxed U.S. pressure for commercial legal reform.

South Korea also had experienced rapid economic growth long before the Crisis. By the mid-1990s its admission into the OECD, the club of the world's wealthiest nations, signified it had successfully made the rare transition from third to first world. It had geopolitical significance for the U.S. stemming from the aftermath of the Korean War, in which it stood as a front line against communism. Thereafter it anchored U.S. interests in Northeast Asia.

Nevertheless, an asymmetry of power was reflected both in its dependence on the U.S., in particular for security, and even more, in its stunning financial vulnerability at the moment of the 1997 Crisis. Compared to Indonesia, however, Korea's relative size and geopolitical significance reduced the imbalance of power with the U.S. insofar as its demands for financial assistance in 1997 and 1998 had both economic and geopolitical significance. Its growing wealth, successful development, and heavy investment in higher education brought Korea into closer cultural proximity with global institutions. Korean scholars and officials were intimately familiar with the same Western elite universities and as well integrated into international organizations as their counterparts from global centers.

China's situation differed from those of Indonesia and South Korea in important ways. Given its size, rapid economic development, and emerging geopolitical power, China could not be treated imperatively by global actors. Moreover, its quite different degree of integration into global capital markets made it much less vulnerable to the financial forces that hurt other Asian countries in 1997. It rode out the Crisis relatively unscathed, thereby giving global institutions little opportunity to intervene. Yet China could not boast Korea's proximity to the global. Its involvement in global institutions and the engagement by experts and officials with leading Western universities and global organizations were not as limited as for Indonesia but fell far short of where Korea stood. In this sense, China was a case with a relatively even balance of power with global institutions but greater cultural and social distance. These differences among the three countries influence many aspects of the global/local encounter and help explain why globalization does not unfold as a uniform process.

Processes

In studies of convergence between global and national regimes it is easy to show correspondences and affinities but hard to explain how they occurred. Why were certain features of a global standard adopted and others rejected, modified, or adapted? Why did some elements of new legal regimes deviate from global standards? It is too easy to commit the fallacy against which sociolegal scholarship has been traditionally arrayed—assuming that formal concurrence of a national institution with a global standard means that local behavior has changed in any way whatsoever. Arguably the now well-established findings on symbolic compliance of regulatory subjects within states can be replicated on the global stage (Boyle and Meyer 1998). We must acknowledge that putatively weak actors—nation-states in a disadvantageous position within the global balance of power—are nevertheless able to resist and adapt to global forces, and we must explain the conditions under which such resistance is possible.

Studying recursive processes of lawmaking in the global/local context, we face contentious issues in scholarship on globalization. Some theorists predict an inexorable march toward global integration, whether of markets, law, or both. These "globalizers," as they are styled by Held et al. (1999), represent the most optimistic school of globalization scholarship, advancing a teleology of inevitability that belies either the prospect of resistance from the global periphery or the powerful inertia of indigenous institutions. Often, this prediction of irresistibility is accompanied by expectations that nation-states will progressively lose their power and that sovereign authority will slowly erode. It portrays weak actors helpless in the face of overwhelming flows of global capital, goods and services, cultural phenomena, and people.

We uncover three processes (intermediation, foiling, and recursivity) that help to make global/local encounters both contingent and contested. It should be emphasized that these contingencies occur *not* in a realm of law where theory would predict most local resistance, such as inheritance or religious law, but in an area that is closely tied to the leading edge of globalization, namely, commercial law. To the extent that bankruptcy law influences the flow of capital and facilitates investment and trade, as its global champions avow, its implementation should be relatively unproblematic. In short, the capacities and proclivities of nation-states to resist what is alleged to be good for them will be low.

Intermediation

We investigate the hypothesis of easy isomorphism between local structure and global norms, first, through the process of *intermediation* (Chapter 8). The global and local can be conceived in different ways,[7] but whatever the conception, each side adjusts, albeit asymmetrically, to the presence and possibilities of the other (Slaughter 2004). And all such conceptions possess a common feature: there are actors who stand between one structure and the other, who can turn both ways, who sit at nodes in networks through which communications back and forth will pass. These actors possess the status of intermediaries (Merry 2006).

Two powerful metaphors recur in explanations of globalization and law, and each invokes the process of intermediation. The organic metaphor of *transplants* connotes healthy plants being uprooted from their native ecosystem and replanted in new soil, perhaps even by grafting onto a host plant. Scholars have divided sharply over how easy it is to transplant law, especially since law inevitably involves grafting or layering the imported law over the law already in place (Harding 2002; Nelken 2002; Watson 1974). However, the general consensus is that intermediaries significantly influence the probability of success (Berkowitz, Pistor, and Richard 2003; Nelken 2002; Pistor and Xu 2003). In law the most critical intermediaries are legally trained personnel—lawyers, judges, legal academics, and often legally trained civil servants. However, their impact varies significantly from country to country.

The probability of successful transplants also depends on previous relationships between adopting and origin countries (Berkowitz, Pistor, and Richard 2003; Pistor 2000). Transplanting can occur imperatively, in the colonial context, through the hierarchy that runs from the colonial office in the colonizing society to the local officials in the colonies. There, local encounters between the colonial official and the indigenous populations are integral to the effects of this "planned planting." Transplanting also occurs diffusely, through contact and informal adaptation, such as the regularized relationships that grow up between trading partners, a process more akin to floating seeds or spores that haphazardly happen to land and take root (Harding 2002). In the former case, contemporary intermediation may be structured through institutionalized patterns of professional education. In the latter case, strong geopolitical and trading relationships between countries can lead to institutionalization of similar ties. In a world economic system, stronger economic ties are likely to be accompanied by denser networks of potential legal mediators.

Scholarship on transplants implies that intermediation operates at multiple levels. Global/local intermediation occurs when agents of either global or local principals directly interact with each other. The density and dynamics of those interactions depend on the institutionalized patterns we have already discussed. But an even more important form of intermediation is local and indirect when lawyers, judges, and other professionals mediate legal change that has been principally initiated from outside a country (Djelic and Quack 2003). Successful reception and implementation depend critically on local actors, so much so that law and finance scholars propose that a "transplant effect" will occur when laws that originate from outside are not adopted, in significant part because of the reluctance of local legal intermediaries to implement new law (Berkowitz, Pistor, and Richard 2003).

Despite considerable agreement that intermediation significantly influences the impact of globalization, that fact is asserted far more emphatically than the process is actually described. Current scholarship rarely penetrates the black box of intermediation. Who are these actors, and what are their attributes? Where do international organizations find intermediaries, and how do they ensure their competency and loyalty? How do the agents of global and local actors deal with each other? And can local actors strengthen their position by mobilizing their own intermediaries? Answering these questions will enable us to refine the elements of a theory of globalization that attends to actors, mechanisms, and structures in varying fields of power.

A second metaphor of intermediation, used by contemporary anthropologists of law and economic sociologists, is that of *translation* (Campbell 2004; Merry 2004, 2005). If we conceive of global norms as scripts, then local actors mediate the rendition of the global script into local languages and idioms. Like transplanting, the positioning of intermediaries as translators or brokers grants them considerable power (Burt 1992). They are constrained by their own primary discourses, but they operate between two systems of meaning, and their capacity to translate depends on their relative fluency in either discourse. Problems in translation arise from more than inadvertence. Since the process of translation is an exercise of power—construing meaning in one realm in relation to meaning in another—principal-agent problems recur for both global and national institutions. Hence either side can be expected to seek intermediaries capable of translation and capable of checking each other. Translation is potentially conflictual as various legalities "clash, mingle, hybridize, and interact with one another" (Merry 2004: 574).

Our investigation of intermediation, using the concepts of transplants and translation, is directed toward "mapping of the middle," as Merry (2006: 38) aptly puts it. This cartography of a terra incognita for social scientists attends to the role of intermediaries as brokers who translate "down" from the global center or "up" from the global periphery. Framings of meaning, and contests of framings, between global scripts and local usages are integral to this exploration because intermediaries have some flexibility in how they negotiate their way among alternative translations—whether to transliterate an alien global script into a local lingua franca, to create a hybrid of the global and the local, or to vernacularize the global so it conforms (or not) to the principles but not the rules of global agents.

But intermediaries are more active agents than translators, who are bound to the discourse of their respective interlocutors. Campbell (2004) evocatively styles agents of institution building in global contexts as *bricoleurs*. Through their interstitial positions they relate the global to the local by mixing and matching varieties of indigenous and foreign elements in an activity known as "bricolage," creating new solutions out of an admixture of preexisting elements. Bricolage can be either substantive, recombining existing options for instrumental outcomes, or symbolic, combining elements that are culturally acceptable and legitimate in the local context. Yet, like the production of global scripts, bricolage is a process of trial and error. Contradictions get internalized into interim solutions whose instability generates further efforts to resolve the global/local encounter. In short, translation and bricolage are embedded within recursive cycles of reform. The settling of recursive reforms partly depends on the creativity of intermediaries to constitute an outcome that satisfies all parties, domestic or international, which have the power to drive successive cycles of reform.

Finally, the significance of intermediaries is played out differently in *enactment* and *implementation*, the two sides of recursive lawmaking. In the former, intermediaries situated between the global and local will dominate. In the latter, local intermediaries, exercising a pragmatic, everyday power, will determine whether the law-on-the-books is anything more than a symbolic gesture to foreign interests.

Foiling

We have argued that intermediation occurs in a field of power. All intermediaries are not equal. Their availability and capabilities for translation and bricolage vary by the cultural and social proximity of the global to the local, and the balance of power between them. We have thus far emphasized the agency of the global rather than the autonomy, power, and creativity of the national or local. But the arguments of James Scott (1985, 1990) alert us to local actors who wield "weapons of the weak." The examples of Malaysia and Argentina intimate a broader truth: countries extremely vulnerable to the vagaries of international capital flows and the interventions of the IMF can resist, with some impunity, the enormous pressures of IFIs and the world's more powerful economies (Stiglitz 2002). In global financial markets, where globalization purportedly is most advanced, what possibility do nation-states have to go their own way? Are their laws and markets compelled to conform to global standards, *or* can they carve out sufficient room for an indigenous design?

We approach these questions in Chapter 9 by arraying our case studies along a continuum of vulnerability during the Asian Financial Crisis (Carruthers and Halliday 2006). At one end lies Indonesia. Highly vulnerable to global financial markets at the moment of the Crisis, and exposed thereafter to the full force of international intervention, Indonesia exemplifies the biggest difference between weak and strong. This tremendous asymmetry of power suggests that Indonesia would conform most exactly to global standards, with limited capacity to resist.

In the middle of the continuum lies Korea, a country quite vulnerable at the moment of the Crisis and critical to U.S. geopolitical interests. Yet Korea's fundamentals were basically strong. Because Korea was a newly minted firstworld economy, socially proximate to global centers of education and finance, its economic stumble proved temporary. The country rebounded smartly, and its financial obligations were paid off with dispatch. In these circumstances, we expect that at the depth of the Crisis Korea had little capacity to resist the powerful. Its rapid rebound, however, should have produced more degrees of freedom and more opportunities to push back against the IFIs.

At the other end of the continuum, China escaped the worst of the Crisis. Its growing foreign reserves and its close control of capital flows shielded it from the harms suffered by its smaller neighbors. In these circumstances China seemed least vulnerable to external pressures and most able to devise its own path. But the Crisis was more than an isolated economic disaster. It signified the rocky integration of East Asian countries into the global financial system. Insofar as China depended on massive foreign investment to fuel its expanding economy, a necessity driven partly by domestic politics, it must placate the expectations of world capital markets in the development of its domestic financial architecture. This architecture is increasingly legally constituted, as the massive wave of commercial law reforms signifies over the past fifteen years. We expect, on the one hand, that China was not immune from pressures emanating from the Crisis nor those building from its investment needs; and, on the other hand, that its singular status as a huge, rising economy gave it most capacity to resist narrow conformity to global scripts. China might have to do something, but exactly what remained an open question.

Our investigations indicate that ostensibly weak countries can foil hegemonic power (Halliday and Carruthers 2007a). Countries develop repertoires of resistance, weapons of the weak, through which they manage to carve out zones of independence from external pressure. In these openings they deviate and design, reject and adapt, conform and contest as their situations permit. These repertoires are artfully matched to the historical moment, sensitive to changes in geopolitical circumstances, calibrated to asymmetries of power. They are not available to all countries, and they are not equally mobilized by every country. But they do reinforce our argument that globalization is contested and negotiated, not simply imposed or imprinted, even when the power differentials are pronounced (Santos 2002).

We therefore part company with scholars and journalists who foresee an inevitability to globalization, even in an arena most amenable to global influence. No global institution has the unilateral capacity to impose on a nation-state. While there is no question that formal convergence occurs, implementation gaps open up between formal law and practice. In fact, it is a brilliant strategy of weak actors to retreat from a battlefield where they most often lose (i.e., enactment) to that terrain where they have a good chance to win (i.e., implementation). Resistance occurs at both points—enactment and implementation. But the war may be won, not in the theater of conventional legal "warfare" but in the theater of local guerrilla resistance.

Recursivity

The capacities for foiling and resistance by national and local actors help to make global legal change recursive (Chapter 10). The purpose of local dissidents is often to frustrate the grand architectural design of externally imposed enactments. The greater their ability to frustrate global agents of change, the more likely that reform cycles will continue. The greater skill exercised by local actors to write their own scripts, the more likely that global agents will be compelled to negotiate variations on their own themes. Indeed, recursivity itself may be an index of resistance. Reform cycles continuing over a protracted period could signify that local/local and global/local struggles compel successive efforts to obtain a stable political settlement.

In principle, recursivity can occur on a purely local level. Cycles of enactment and implementation are driven by local actors through the processes we have identified, and legal change will be explained in terms of local factors. But for law that governs national markets integrated into a world economy, domestic recursive lawmaking exists in dynamic tension with iterations of global norm making.

Recursivity in a global context depends on global processes and global/local interactions. If a global consensus has not been reached among the world community, then variable and unstable responses from national lawmakers can arise in two ways. In one circumstance, global norms themselves are unformed, inchoate, or incoherent. This was precisely the situation for global corporate bankruptcy norms until 1999. In another circumstance, diverse IOs produce competing norms that differ in substance, form, or both. In 2001 an Asian country reforming its bankruptcy system was faced with an à la carte offering of the Asian Development Bank's evaluative standards, the International Monetary Fund's "key issues," the World Bank's *Principles*, and intimations that the United Nations was developing yet another set of norms. As IOs wrestled with their own legitimation issues, national policymakers were confronted with a range of options, each with its own merits. In such a context, recursivity in domestic lawmaking can result from changing adherence from one to another set of norms. Multiple norms, in other words, set the stage for bricolage.

Recursivity is affected by how global/local negotiations unfold. Translation between the two levels gets constrained by the fit between imported elements and national regimes. It is influenced by local politics, by which organizations sponsor externally driven innovations, and by the institutional capacities of domestic institutions to effect change. Given this, we should expect substantial national variation even if external models were identical (Campbell 2004). The negotiation of both the fit and the transition to practice may proceed through successive cycles of lawmaking.

Transplants depend heavily on the receptivity and competence of local professionals. Their incorporation into the negotiations will affect their inclination to implement formal law in practice. Strong resistance can produce further rounds of formal lawmaking. Transplants often involve "layering" a new source and type of law over that already in place (Harding 2002). Inconsistencies and conflicts will arise through the addition of yet another layer of law, leading to further rounds of clarification, amendment, and adjustment. Bricolage has similar effects to layering. It requires the selective recombination of elements already institutionalized within a country. The experimentation required to settle upon a combination that works will be reflected in repeated efforts at lawmaking. Foiling can be both a cause and consequence of recursive lawmaking. By opposing what global actors or national lawmakers have institutionalized in statutes, regulations, and cases, local actors and factions provoke lawmakers to try again, this time addressing their objections.

Externally engaged legal change is likely eventually to settle (Grattet and Jenness 2001). *Settling*, we argue, is a theoretical challenge for legal change in a global context because it is seldom addressed. Although it is either assumed (i.e., legal change will automatically follow from exogenously induced reforms) or ignored, ending an episode of legal change inevitably involves some kind of resolution of global/local negotiations and domestic power struggles inside nation-states. Settling is often deceptive. IFIs may settle for formal legal changes because these publicly signal to IFI boards and members that interventions have succeeded. National policymakers may in one situation be content with symbolic compliance, one form of settling, but in another situation expect reformed practice, a much more difficult endeavor. We examine, where possible, what it takes for a legal reform to settle. However, by definition settling takes time. We have tracked recursive legal change in Indonesia, Korea, and China for almost ten years. In the wake of the Crisis, major formal and institutional changes have taken place. We observe evidence of settling in formal law, but evidence of settling in practice remains less certain.

Settling partly relates to changes in the political and economic contexts of a country. A shift in political agendas from economic crisis to international terrorism can affect the terms on which domestic settling occurs. When the U.S. suddenly discovered that it needed Indonesia as an ally in the war against terrorism, it diverted resources and lightened the pressure it indirectly applied through IFIs to prioritize market reform (Halliday and Carruthers 2007b). Arguably, Indonesia can now settle for less thoroughgoing bankruptcy reform than would have been the case had 9/11 not occurred. Domestic concerns also induce settling. China's comprehensive corporate bankruptcy law reform went through countless drafts between 1994 and 2006, even grinding to a halt between 1996 and 2000. What explains enactment in August 2006? One view has it that China's top leaders were nervous that any faltering in their breakneck economic expansion would intensify the social unrest that is occurring in those parts of China where workers have been left behind. Economic growth requires capital from abroad, and the European Union pressed strongly for law reforms as a condition of its continued investment

Law and Markets: Variations on a Theme

Many pundits of globalization have pointed to a world of economic homogenization. As national markets were progressively integrated into the global economy, core institutions would inevitably look more like each other. An international financial architecture surely heralded a world where capitalist edifices bore close resemblance to each other. Insofar as law was an integral part of the framework, it followed that national laws would also become perceptibly isomorphic.

Among scholarly observers of legal convergence, however, dissent over the homogenization thesis could not be more vigorous. At one extreme, legal scholars asserted that legal transplants were unproblematic. Sociologists of the world polity perspective construe macrolegal change as part of the global convergence upon the universalistic values of Western rationality, efficiency, individualism, and rights. At the other extreme, anthropologists of law and postcolonial globalists pronounced the homogenization thesis passé. They see rejection and resistance, hybridization and translation, everywhere in the Global South. In between, law and finance writings counterpose trends toward the proliferation of converging creditor rights with obvious national divergences and indeterminacies. Law is inherently incomplete.

Our particular domain—corporate bankruptcy law—in principle could go either way. As commercial law, and part of the new international financial architecture, it should exemplify high convergence on a global standard. However, since bankruptcy is also deeply embedded in local legal culture and institutions, and in divergent attitudes to debts and debtors, it should exhibit low convergence.

Our evidence and interpretations provide some comfort to each of these perspectives, but ultimately we align with none. We present evidence that law's global competitors quickly settled for cooperation, and significant convergence has occurred at the global center. Over twenty years, from fragmented, uncoordinated, and even conflicting initiatives by regional and global actors, there emerged a fairly coherent global script and an institutional division of labor among the IOs. The convergence is *substantive*, insofar as it centers on the reorganization of failing companies and not simply their liquidation; it favors debtors, who get a second chance to compete in the market; it protects creditors, who always fear for the value of their assets; and it shifts public policy concerns, such as protecting workers, to other domains of law and policy. The convergence is *formal*, insofar as it has been articulated by the United Nations Commission on International Trade Law (UNCITRAL) in a technology that approximates the legislative statutory form, complete with overarching objectives, statutelike chapters, and recommendations. The convergence is *systemic*, insofar as it advocates a system of institutions, not only including substantive and formal law but state institutions, most notably courts and regulatory agencies, and quasi-public, quasi-private, out-of-court agencies and expert professions. The convergence is *pragmatic*, inasmuch as it is also expressed in diagnostic instruments used by international financial institutions to grade conformity with the global standards, a pragmatism linked in the private capital markets with optimal conditions for investment, and in public finance with threshold conditions for IFI lending.

Global convergence has been enabled by institutional trade-offs and a coalescing division of labor among global actors. Through successive rounds of trial and error, potentially rival IOs and governments sought a solution that combined legitimacy with a practicable technology wed to forms of leverage ensuring its probable implementation. As the actors each discovered their own limitations, they progressively converged on a global standard negotiated within and promulgated by UNCITRAL. Nevertheless, we do not assume that this moment of global convergence is either complete or settled. UNCITRAL left several difficult areas, such as corporate groups in bankruptcy, untouched. Moreover, alternatives left within the global script, institutional rivalries, differences in mission and resources, changes in personnel, and alterations in leverage guarantee that negotiation among global actors will continue.

Enactment is the primary sphere of action for global actors and national policymakers, the place where the concordance of global norms and national laws gets negotiated. In the process of enacting or reforming formal law, national institutions differentially align themselves with global standards. But this is precisely where global standards have the greatest chance of making an impact. Often this alignment involves symbolic politics, where either negotiating party signifies results to its respective constituencies. It is the politics most easily observed and measured by cross-national surveys and commensurating social science techniques. Uncritical attention to this level of politics artificially magnifies the degree of convergence.

Implementation is another political arena altogether. It is the primary arena for local intermediaries, agents of continuity or change, sponsors of globalism or its foes. It is to implementation that ostensibly weak national and subnational actors can retreat, disappearing by degrees from the surveillance instruments of global overseers. On the stages of local implementation now appear the corporations and managers, lawyers and accountants, trade creditors and workers, who had little or nothing to say either to global standards or their national correspondences. They have the quiet capacity to kill entirely what was announced with a flourish in the national press and IO annual reports. And if they do not destroy it, they may bend it out of recognizable shape.

We highlight global norm making and the operations of global actors, their scripts, mechanisms, and exercise of power. Ultimately, however, all global politics become local. Global institutions are substantially created out of local ones, and they are instantiated locally. There they meet national heritages that constrain the range of possibilities as they descend into a welter of economic interests, ideological crosscurrents, and institutional incapacities. The local recipients of global influence do not remain inert. A single international crisis can alter a recipient's geopolitical significance and hence its priorities and resource allocations. Transnational reference groups in one decade can be displaced in another. The pool of intermediaries may expand and contract and change loyalties. Thus, the balance of power between the global and local is also constantly shifting with the result that the pressure for convergence itself rises and falls.

In sum, the recursivity of law is manifest everywhere in the conjunction of law and markets. It manifests itself in iterations of global norm making that in our case reach a negotiated settlement, albeit its ultimate impact is unpredictable. It manifests itself in successive cycles between formal lawmaking and everyday practice, as enactment and implementation engage each other en route to a possible settlement. It manifests itself in the extent to which the global and local take account of each other—whether global norms are responsive to local experiences and sensibilities, and whether local lawmakers and practitioners will comply with global standards.

Our case studies challenge the assumption made by IFIs and many scholars that law will be the principal market-ordering mechanism. In the three countries of East Asia we follow closely, none reached their economic takeoff by giving law much countenance at all. Indeed, their startling rates of economic growth occurred despite the substantial marginalization of law. Policy decisions, arbitrary executive power, relational capitalism, and at most, regulatory rule making, substituted for the formal legal rationality Weber identified with the growth of capitalism. Many IOs and scholars now presume that a crucial tipping point has been reached past which national economic development and global market integration require more law. But this presumption is more an ideological commitment or theoretical postulate than a concept grounded empirically.

If law cannot be assumed to be the dominant structuring institution for the social organization of markets, and if it can be shown that national laws conform variably to a unified standard for bankruptcy regimes, then it seems that convergence has its limits. Some of those limits can already be observed at the point of enactment, but they will only be amplified once reform gets to the point of implementation. Many variations are already evident around the central themes composed by global standard setters.

This result should not be surprising. Political economists have discovered two principal variations on the basic capitalist themes. If there are varieties of capitalism in Europe and North America (Hall and Soskice 2000), might there be more in Latin America, Asia, Africa, or Oceania (Crouch 2005)? And if there are varieties of capitalism, then we might expect variety among capitalist laws. Even within legal families, two common law countries with liberal market economies, Britain and the United States, manifest pronounced variations in their bankruptcy systems. When Australia and Canada are added to the pool of former British colonies, the variation widens further. Comparable variations occur across Continental Europe, and they widen in those former colonies or modernizing nations that looked to France or Germany for models to adopt. A new and unprecedented convergence on global themes may go some distance to create an international financial architecture that constrains the range of national variation. Convergence at the center may even be echoed by formal convergence at the periphery (after all, Eritrea was the first country to adopt UNCITRAL's Model Law on Cross-Border Insolvency). Nonetheless, this is a long way from homogenization. And it is an even greater distance from implementation. The politics of enactment and implementation that constitute the recursivity of law will eventually articulate the relationship between law and markets. We will show that the processes of legal change we identify not only reveal the contingency of globalization but suggest its limits.

The recursivity model is also a model of institutional change. We stress that formal enactment and implementation are two quite different, albeit connected, stages of institutional change, and that to focus on one at the expense of the other can be quite misleading. It appears, for instance, that in the global context of formal enactment convergence proceeds apace and that, as world polity scholars would have it, increasing isomorphism among national institutions is driven by a dominant, almost monolithic, world culture. Instead, we find global institutions to differ among themselves with competing global models and differentially empowered stakeholders. Furthermore, change is supported (and opposed) by complex alliances that cut across political, professional, and organizational lines and that link local and global actors. With Streeck and Thelen (2005: 14–15), and following sociolegal scholarship, we emphasize not only that formal rules are incomplete and ambiguous but also that their implementation never follows in a mechanical or determinant fashion. Political conflicts that produce formal institutional change will subsequently set the stage for a politics of implementation in which those who are politically weak during enactment often emerge with surprising strength. Implementation gaps (sometimes also called "decoupling") then set the stage for subsequent episodes of formal enactment. And so the recursive loop cycles on.

2 Managing Corporate Breakdowns Across National Frontiers

A S O F 1988, no trade bloc of advanced nations had reached any agreement on the harmonization of insolvency laws, no instruments had emerged for coordination of cross-border insolvencies, no universal models existed for national insolvency systems, and comparatively few national governments or global governance bodies understood the full import of insolvency law for market stability and economic development. By 2004, major trade blocs could draw on an array of voluntary and binding instruments for harmonizing their insolvency proceedings, a global model law existed for handling multinational corporate failures, a global legislative guide for national insolvency systems had been adopted by the United Nations, and global multilateral institutions as well as national governments viewed robust insolvency regimes as a necessary element of domestic and international financial architecture. How did this remarkable shift come about?

Construction of a Global Normative Architecture

In the following three chapters we examine closely the construction of a global normative architecture. Professionals, together with other national, regional, and global actors, drove forward an international search for cross-national, then global, solutions to problems of corporate rehabilitation and failure. The twenty-year journey toward a rationalized normative order proceeded by trial and error, a series of successive experiments, the mixed results of each informing the next. At its best, this was a cumulative process. At its worst, experiments died, never to be revived. It began with ad hoc solutions and rather localized private initiatives. It concluded with systematic and public deliberations on a global scale. In short, this was an iterative process fueled as much by failure as success. Iterations of experimentation continued until the most powerful actors in the global arena reached consensus upon a technology they considered legitimate and operational.

From the mid-1980s to the mid-2000s metacycles of insolvency lawmaking advanced through three phases (Table 2.1). In the first phase (this chapter) advanced economies in close trading relationships endeavored to find orderly ways of liquidating or reorganizing companies whose operations and assets were spread across several national jurisdictions. This came partially to fruition in the Model Law on Cross-Border Insolvency. A second and more ambitious phase of lawmaking (Chapter 3) was precipitated by the fall of communism and punctuated by the Asian Financial Crisis. Multilateral institutions, such as the Asian Development Bank (ADB), European Bank for Reconstruction and Development (EBRD), IMF, World Bank, and OECD, advanced from ad hoc, episodic interventions to substantive and procedural models of entire insolvency systems. The third phase (Chapter 4) brought all these efforts, both cross-border and national lawmaking, to a climax with the completion of the UNCITRAL Legislative Guide on Insolvency in 2004 (hereafter Legislative Guide).

In less than a generation, therefore, the international field of insolvency law obtained at least a formal "symmetry" with the global markets it purported to regulate (Westbrook 2000, 2002b). The regional impulse to greater market integration among advanced economies by close trading partners in the 1980s broadened to a globalizing impulse that now potentially encompasses all trading nations.

Cross-Border Initiatives

Seldom has corporate failure been personified more tragically than the mysterious drowning of English magnate Robert Maxwell, who fell off the back of his oceangoing yacht, by accident or intent, and lost his life even as his global corporate group stumbled toward financial collapse. Behind the worldwide headlines that announced Maxwell's death lay the Maxwell Communication Corporation (Maxwell Corp.). With some four hundred subsidiaries worldwide in

TABLE 2.1 Global Expansion of Insolvency Norms, 1986–2004

Initiative	Economies	Formal Instrument and Purpose
Cross-Border, Advanced Economies (late 1980s–later 1990s)		
MIICA, 1986–1989	Advanced, adjacent	Model law—harmonization of procedures
Concordat, 1993–1996	Advanced, adjacent	Protocol—harmonization of procedures
Maxwell Protocol	Advanced	Protocol—coordination of procedures
Council of Europe Istanbul Convention, 1990	Advanced, adjacent	Convention—harmonization of procedures
European Union Convention, 1990–1996	Advanced, adjacent	Convention—harmonization of procedures
Model Law on Cross-Border Insolvency, 1990–1997	All economies	Model law—harmonization of procedures
American Law Institute Transnational Insolvency Project	NAFTA: Canada, U.S., Mexico	Principles—coordination, harmonization of procedures
European Union Regulation on Insolvency Proceedings, 2001	Advanced, adjacent	Regulation—harmonization of procedures
National Insolvency Regimes, Emerging Economies (late 1990s–2003)		
Model Bankruptcy Code	Emerging markets	Model law—harmonization of substantive law
Workout Principles	Emerging markets	Principles—harmonization of private procedures
Asian Development Bank Report	Emerging markets	Standards—convergence of substantive law and procedures
International Monetary Insolvency Procedures	Emerging markets	Statutory options—convergence of substantive law and procedures
World Bank Principles	Emerging markets	Principles—convergence of substantive law and procedures; convergence of courts and professional regulation
National and Cross-Border, Advanced and Emerging Economies (1999–2004)		
United Nations Commission on International Trade Law Legislative Guide, 1999–2004	Emerging markets Advanced	Legislative Guide—convergence of substantive law and procedures

industries ranging from information services and electronic publishing to general publishing, the company's default on a loan of $2 billion in late 1991 placed the multinational corporation in imminent threat of attacks and dismemberment by creditors across the world.[1] A specter of fights between creditors in one country or another, the liquidation of viable enterprises, and the loss of jobs presented one of the greatest challenges yet to the capacities of professionals and legal systems, creditors and managers, to disentangle an extraordinarily complex corporate empire and to save what value remained in it.

Although the publicity was unprecedented, the Maxwell Corp. was not the first multinational corporate group to confront the jurisdictional limits of market regulation. In North America large companies like Bramalea and Olympia and York challenged practitioners and courts in Canada and the U.S. to find ways forward in the absence of adequate formal law or regularized institutional responses.[2] More generally the expansion of multinational corporations and international trade through the 1980s created an increasing need for mechanisms to handle the failures of corporations with operations and assets across national frontiers. Yet the diplomatic failures of the European and North American negotiators to produce continental frameworks for cross-border cooperation signaled that harmonization of substantive law or treaties were not promising solutions. Harmonization within Europe required such immense steps to overcome deeply entrenched differences among several varieties of capitalism and law that it faltered repeatedly as a viable option. Even a treaty between two such close trading partners as Canada and the U.S., both advanced capitalist societies and both common law jurisdictions, could not be brought to satisfactory completion (Table 2.2).

In these negotiations, insolvency lagged other areas of market regulation. Compared to trade regulations, tax treaties, and various mechanisms of judicial cooperation that were already harmonized among countries (Braithwaite and Drahos 2000),

[t]he contrast in international insolvencies is dramatic. A multinational business that fails, or that tries to reorganize in response to impending insolvency, must face a maze of often conflicting insolvency laws in the several countries where its assets and creditors are located. Furthermore, it finds no international means to discipline and integrate domestic insolvency so that it may marshal all of its assets and satisfy all creditors in one proceeding, in one place. The multinational debtor's estate is often inequitably dismantled, as in one jurisdiction

after another creditors find favor in local courts and take local assets to satisfy
their claims with regard to other creditors or jurisdictions. Thus, the fairness to
debtor and creditors alike that is sought with such diligence in domestic insolvency proceedings becomes an idle dream in most cross-border insolvencies.
(Powers, Mears, and Barrett 1994: 233–234)

TABLE 2.2 Cross-Border Initiatives, Advanced Economies, 1986–2004

Initiative	Agent	Entities Regulated	Formal Instrument: Enabling Institution	Key Audiences: Veto Player(s)
MIICA, 1986–1989	Professional association (IBA)	States: Cross-border	Model law— harmonization of procedures: Legislature	Executive, legislative branches: Governments
Concordat, 1993–1996	Professional association (IBA)	States: Cross-border	Protocol— harmonization of procedures: Courts	Practitioners, judges: Courts
Maxwell Protocol	Courts	Courts	Protocol— coordination of procedures: Courts	Professional counsel: Courts
Council of Europe Istanbul Convention, 1990	Regional suprastate body	States: Cross-border	Convention— National legislatures	States
European Union Convention, 1990–1996	Regional suprastate body	States: Cross-border	Convention— National legislatures	States: European Government
Model Law on Cross-Border Insolvency, 1990–1997	World governance body	States: Cross-border	Model law— harmonization of procedures: Legislature	Executive, legislative branches: Governments
ALI Transnational Insolvency Project	Professional association (ALI)	States	Principles— Courts Legislative recommenda-tions— Legislature	Practitioners, judges: Courts Legislatures
EU Regulation on Insolvency Proceedings, 2001	Regional supra-state body	States: Cross-border	Regulation	States

A Private Professional Proposal:
The Model International Insolvency Code (MIICA)

Into this vacuum stepped the global peak association of lawyers, the International Bar Association (IBA), which by 1994 could boast "representation from over 150 bar associations" of some 2.5 million lawyers and an individual membership of sixteen thousand lawyers from 160 countries (Leonard and Besant 1994: vii). The IBA Committee on Insolvency and Creditors' Rights broached in 1986 an instrument for advanced countries that would require harmonization not of substantive law but of procedures on a very narrow front. Driven by U.S. lawyers, the IBA project embraced a principle of universality over territoriality. Whereas countries historically practiced a kind of "grab rule," in which the imperatives of territoriality unleashed a local scramble for assets where "everybody fights for what they can get, everyone is like a vulture" (Riesenfeld quoted in Panuska 1993: 382; Westbrook 1991), the principle of universality held out a vision of one, unitary insolvency administration that would draw all parties in all jurisdictions across several countries into a harmonious, coordinated proceeding. Coordination would replace chaos (Powers, Mears, and Barrett 1994).[3]

Capable of application in all jurisdictions everywhere, this globalizing vision rested on core premises of lawyers' epistemology—"a basic threshold of fairness and equity" (MIICA, Third Draft, 1988, Section 1, and Statement of Principles, in Leonard and Besant 1994: 263). The lawyer-drafters considered that both principles served concomitantly to dispel "uncertainty and lack of predictability" in international commercial transactions by producing "assurance and predictability" in insolvency proceedings (MIICA, in Leonard and Besant 1994; Powers, Mears, and Barrett 1994).

To produce legal certainty in service of both economic and legal principles, the IBA Committee advocated creation of a model law rather than a convention. A convention was a thoroughly institutionalized form of multilateral relationships among countries. As a legal technology, however, it required that negotiators obtain complete consensus on precise wording that would be adopted without alteration by all countries that acceded to it and would accept it as binding in their own law. However, although a convention was a form of strict harmonization that was self-executing (i.e., binding in domestic law), the difficulties of reaching agreement were formidable, and the domestic politics involved in take-it-or-leave-it accession not to be underestimated.

In contrast to a convention, which required nations to accede to a single, identical instrument, the IBA's proposal sought to design a technology that would produce sufficient harmonization without creating a legal straitjacket. Its concept offered what might be termed an *elective harmonization*, that is, a choice by nations to adopt in toto a model statute offered by the IBA, or to accept it in general with limited modifications in principled ways. While universality should remain the prevailing principle, the IBA drafters envisaged adoption with "considerable modification in order to be effectively integrated with existing domestic legislation" (MIICA, in Leonard and Besant 1994: App. 1, 259). The drafters signal a flexibility in their instrument that combines adherence to the master principle with variation on details, thus offering a trade-off between complete harmonization, with all its benefits for certainty and the likelihood of implementation. As Clift (2002) puts it, a model law is a permissive standard. Nations can deviate from the model although they are encouraged not to do so.

The elements of MIICA covered three main topics: (1) the duties of a court to recognize proceedings of courts in other countries; (2) the procedures for recognizing proceedings in other jurisdictions; and (3) a provision added in the later stages of discussions to allay fears that adoption of MIICA would preclude a nation from subsequently signing a bilateral or multilateral treaty (Panuska 1993). In seven brief sections covering less than two pages, MIICA treated the recognition of foreign representatives (e.g., lawyers, insolvency practitioners) in courts; the setting up of ancillary proceedings and the powers given representatives in other countries; some guidance on which law to apply; and some definitions of "foreign representatives" and "foreign proceedings." The full text of MIICA included several additional pages of commentary that elaborated, for each section, the purposes of the section, the sources of the recommended statutory language, and an explanation (MIICA, in Leonard and Besant 1994: App. 1, 259–268).

For professionals, the Model Code had significant jurisdictional and practical consequences. A South African insolvency practitioner dealing with a liquidation or reorganization in South Africa would also obtain the right to pursue assets of the company in Germany or the United States, once the foreign proceeding was recognized in those courts (Lechner 2002: 1008). This global reach for lawyers and insolvency practitioners would enable them to follow assets and creditors wherever they were located to obtain standing in foreign courts. For many practitioners, this provision was the most critical for the successful unitary treatment of a multinational reorganization—and among the most critical for an international professional association.[4]

MIICA's drafters not only sidestepped the impossible standard of a universalism that required all or nothing but adroitly maneuvered around controversial decision rules that might equally have subverted the Model Code. For instance, the Model Code provides clear guidance neither about the choice of forum (which court in what country will have primary jurisdiction?) or choice of law (what country's law will govern proceedings?), two key aspects of an international insolvency proceeding. No provisions are included about how courts or practitioners should decide where the principal proceeding will be located or what law it should apply (its own or that of another jurisdiction?). Westbrook (1991: 484) views this tactic of silence as a way of permitting the assumption to be made that which jurisdiction was the home country and would be the center of a cross-national insolvency proceeding would be obvious. Applying an explicit test might derail drafters and legislators and sink the Model Code's chances of adoption. But these pragmatic choices came at a price, for they also would reduce predictability of parties about gains and losses if they proceeded under a MIICA-type regime (Westbrook 1991: 484–485).

The pragmatism of the Model Code reflects its designers—experienced insolvency practitioners from advanced economies. Pragmatism could not disguise the fact, and the drafters had no hesitation in revealing, that the inspiration for most of the Code came from Articles 304–306 of the U.S. Bankruptcy Code. Other laws from several countries (primarily England and Canada) are mentioned as sources. Although the three drafts of MIICA were widely circulated and debated by country teams and international meetings of the IBA Committee, a strong American influence nevertheless pervaded MIICA, even if the American drafters felt compelled to drop some provisions of Sections 304–306 that were objectionable to civil law practitioners.

This lawyers' product seemed to solve many of the implementation problems inherent in conventions and treaties. Moreover, the auspices of the IBA gave the initiative a patina of international legitimacy, despite its strong American provenance. The IBA Committee could properly claim that the early and repeated involvement of professionals from several continents, which span several legal families, indicated that practitioners, at least, could find some common ground that might then provide a foundation for legislative initiatives.[5]

Yet even this relatively simple and flexible instrument faced formidable challenges. Unquestionably its legitimacy was founded less on representation than expertise. There was little doubt that its drafters had technical authority and deep reservoirs of experience. Yet that very fact underlined MIICA's status as a purely professional product—and only one profession, that of law. Even on technical terms it was not clear quite which countries with what degrees of sophistication in their insolvency systems could participate in a MIICA "system" (Panuska 1993: 399; Westbrook 1991).

To legitimate its prospective efficacy, the Code needed a strong early adoption by a leading nation to precipitate a wave of subsequent adoptions across advanced countries. However, the U.S. found it difficult to be the first mover since MIICA eliminated some critical details in U.S. bankruptcy law. Some Europeans were lukewarm about MIICA because they suspected it was a "Trojan horse" for the introduction of the American practice of allowing management to stay in control of reorganizing companies ("debtor-in-possession"), which all European jurisdictions rejected (Lechner 2002: 1006).[6] So the European Community adopted a "wait-and-see" approach as to what would happen elsewhere. Not surprisingly, smaller countries waited for a move by a major trading nation.

Five years after the Code's final endorsement by the IBA in 1989, no countries had adopted MIICA, although leading IBA proponents asserted in 1994 that many countries were still "considering" adoption.[7] Apart from inherent problems in the instrument itself, the very strength of MIICA's expert auspices proved to be a weakness. By focusing the attention of leading lawyers in many countries on the problem, a solution emerged quite quickly. A professional association, however, had no capacity to exercise leverage over the legislators in nation-states who would be the critical gatekeepers for enactment of the Code. Expert suasion counted for not enough. Indeed, only once the Model Code had been finally endorsed by the IBA Committee did lawyers fan out across the world to enlist the support of legislators.

From this experience, UNCITRAL later drew the conclusion that a model law process requires that national government officials and representatives must work alongside experts at the formative stage and their approval should be obtained at every stage thereafter (Clift 2002). A temporal separation of designers of legal instruments from their implementers undermines the political viability of instruments, since they do not spring from established power bases. Although the institutional target of the MIICA proposal was the courts, statutory enactment was required to institutionalize a cooperation regime. Excluding states from the deliberative process meant that legislators had little investment in the Code, however expert its developers.[8]

Yet even with its failure to be implemented, MIICA's experiment was not a total loss. In fact, it became a progenitor of several subsequent initiatives.[9] The Code designers accomplished setting a new agenda for international co-operation and showed what might be possible. MIICA valorized decisively the principle of universality, itself no little distinction (Westbrook 1991: 484). And the choice of instrument—a Model Code—signaled that this technology, developed and executed with more sensitivity to political contingencies and legitimation auspices, might be the best-adapted instrument to forge international cooperation, a challenge UNCITRAL would take up just a few years later (Clift 2002).

Court-Based Protocols for Cross-Border Insolvencies

The impending collapse of the Maxwell group precipitated a quite different response by professionals. Because some 70 percent of the book value of the company was vested in U.S. subsidiaries, and Maxwell management did not want to lose control of the company, Maxwell's lawyers filed for protection from creditors under Chapter 11 of the U.S. Bankruptcy Code in the Southern District of New York on December 16, 1991. The filing would permit management to stay in place and propose a reorganization plan. The following day in London, Maxwell's English counsel placed the company into administration under the Insolvency Act 1986. Effectively, Maxwell put its fate in the hands of two separate jurisdictions with very different provisions on management control, the powers of creditors, and the prospects of reorganization (Flaschen and Silverman 1994).

Since "the opportunities for confusion, chaos and paralysis were self-evident," the two distinguished judges on either side of the Atlantic entered into intensive discussions with Maxwell Corp.'s English Administrators (accountants/insolvency practitioners from Price Waterhouse) and Maxwell's U.S. Examiner over a strategy for coordinating proceedings. Only twelve days later, on December 31, 1991, the English High Court approved and adopted an Order and Protocol to govern a coordinated response. The U.S. Bankruptcy Court followed suit on January 15, 1992 (Flaschen and Silverman 1994).

The Protocol stated its objective was to "harmonise" the proceedings of the two courts in order to "facilitate a rehabilitation and reorganisation" of Maxwell Corp. (Flaschen and Silverman 1994: Order, Annex 1). The agreement hammered out by the professionals and the courts essentially gave the English court primacy so long as certain concerns of due process and fairness in the U.S. were heeded by the English court (Nielsen, Sigal, and Wagner 1996). The Protocol gave the U.S. Examiner rights to appear in the English High Court, rights to investigate the financial situation of the company and to harmonize his plan for company reorganization with the English Administrators, and rights to appoint other professionals and investment bankers as needed.[10] Further, for transactions of certain kinds and above a certain monetary level, the English Administrators would require the approval of the U.S. Examiner, and for other transactions make a good-faith effort to obtain his agreement. The Chairmen of Macmillan, Inc., and Official Airline Guides, Maxwell Corp.'s largest American subsidiaries, would remain in place (effectively as "debtor-in-possession"), and the English Administrators and U.S. Examiner would work together to create a new Board (Flaschen and Silverman 1994: Protocol, Annex 1). In all instances, the Order and Protocol intended to promote harmony in order to maximize the value of the estate for all creditors.

In addition, the English High Court and U.S. Bankruptcy Court were required to resolve many legal issues about choice of forum, choice of law, and scope of rulings by either court, among others. The Protocol and subsequent court opinions relied heavily on mutual respect and reliance on comity, a governing principle in private international law.[11] Said Judge Brozman of the U.S. Bankruptcy Court, "Lurking in all transnational bankruptcies is the potential for chaos if the courts involved ignore the importance of comity."[12] As a result of the absence of an international convention on cross-border insolvencies, said Mr. Justice Hoffman of the English High Court, "the only way forward is by the discretionary exercise of jurisdictional self-restraint" (Flaschen and Silverman 1994: 47). That the courts displayed comity and self-restraint seems plain, since the Maxwell Corp. reorganization proceeded more smoothly than Olympia and York.

The very success of the Maxwell reorganization, however, turned on the serendipity of an ad hoc solution when a case involved two advanced countries, two experienced and flexible judges, and several veteran professionals. Compared to MIICA, the Protocol had very modest goals: resolving the potential conflicts of a single case between two leading common law courts. Although the Protocol served a temporary purpose, it nevertheless intimated a more permanent need—an instrument that would be accessible for any court in an advanced jurisdiction that might readily be appropriated by courts and practitioners in cross-border insolvencies. Maxwell indicated that such an instrument could be more easily developed and implemented within the legal system than the array of more demanding instruments—conventions, treaties, model laws—that required legislative mandate. In this, presumably, a lawyer- or judge-led initiative would have a distinct advantage. A lawyers' association should be able to mobilize more readily through legal institutions than the polity.

Constructing a Model for Court Protocols: The IBA's Concordat

Slow adoption of MIICA and the promise of the Maxwell Protocol left an opening for an instrument that might be generalizable to many jurisdictions but neither reliant on political will nor at a level of detail that made agreement improbable. Such an instrument must be precise enough that it facilitated predictability but at high enough a level of abstraction to subsume variation across jurisdictions—in short, a master Protocol.[13]

In the course of their writing on international insolvency law, two New York corporate insolvency lawyers, Mike Sigal (Simpson Thacher & Bartlett) and Karen Wagner (Davis Polk), concluded that the whole area "was a real mess" with "very few unifying principles and very few ways to run insolvencies in more than one country." In order to bring some rationality into this chaotic domain, they began to draft a Concordat—a set of principles that might govern relations among courts in cross-border insolvencies.[14] Rather than proceed alone or through their firms, Sigal and Wagner enlisted the IBA's Committee on Insolvency and Creditors' Rights to take on an international project to complete and propagate a consensually refined instrument through the collaboration of the IBA's membership. IBA's Committee J began work in 1993 with a core of six people, including Sigal as Cochair with a Swiss lawyer, John Barrett from Houston, and Bruce Leonard from Toronto. Both Barrett and Leonard were Chairs of Committee J during the 1990s and leaders in IBA initiatives.

Drafting proceeded through several iterations, alternating between international forums and national reactions. Conferences in London and Australia discussed the first draft in 1994. Thereafter the IBA consulted with lawyers in twenty civil and common law countries with advanced and developing economies.[15] The Concordat was approved by the IBA Council in 1996 (Nielsen, Sigal, and Wagner 1996).

Sigal and the IBA drafting team construed the problem they confronted in terms of the increasing number and complexity of cross-border insolvencies without any workable mechanism for resolving them (Concordat 1995: 1). On the one side, countries do not like giving up their sovereignty, or courts their powers. Countries also jealously protect the privileges and priorities for claims they have built into insolvency law. On the other side, it was clear that previous political solutions had not worked: "in the past, treaties which have attempted to follow only the universality theory have met with failure." The insistence on universality, for instance, doomed the European Commission proposal released in 1980, which envisaged only one proceeding to cover all jurisdictions within the European Union (EU), with no possibility of secondary or ancillary proceedings (Nielsen, Sigal, and Wagner 1996: 562, 539). Thus, a "nonpolitical solution" must assure countries that their political values institutionalized in insolvency law would remain unthreatened within a cooperative transnational framework.

For Sigal, predictability was the value most demanded by the market.

> [T]he issue is predictability. The markets can price anything. Take a country that had a high priority for employees. You can price that. How many employees you have? What's the budget? How long is the priority for? You can price that. I think the issue of predictability is more important than a uniform law. . . . By predictability, it's clear what the statute is. And regularity, that you will get this result. . . . [T]he thing that really scares people off is you don't know what will happen.[16]

If predictability could not be delivered through legislatures, it was necessary to rely on courts. A Concordat-type instrument, which relied on higher-order principles, "would never work for a legislature, because one of the premises here is that these are just some general concepts. They need to be tailored as circumstances require by the courts and the judges."[17]

In an important sense, therefore, the Concordat responds to a double failure: that of politicians following the diplomatic and treaty route; and that of lawyers following the legislative route. The Concordat was a quintessentially *professional* solution where lawyers created a refined technology and relied on their own institution, the courts, and their professional counterparts, the judges, to implement the technology. In sum, it is a case of "practitioners allying with courts to produce practical solutions."[18]

For one leader of the IBA, the practitioner-led initiative through the Concordat reflected the essence and creativity of the common law: "the genius of the common law is that it invents things as the commercial needs arise. In 1995, it dealt with the way to meet cross border situations. And I think the [common law] genius is that we can invent solutions. MIICA is in that tradition and so is the Concordat."[19] The designers of the Concordat aimed to harmonize proceedings across national boundaries by producing an insolvency system that is "reasonably predictable, fair and convenient." A rationalized, harmonious insolvency system would encourage international commerce for its own sake.[20] Said Sigal, "[S]o it was kind of a vehicle for . . . the courts to try to rationalize insolvencies that were beyond the borders of one country."[21]

The drafters of the Concordat invoked a threefold basis of authority for their instrument. First, it relied on practice and experience, including from those courts that had already experimented with coordination protocols. In that sense it sought to invoke the legitimation mandate of effectiveness. Second, it derived "primarily from principles of private international law." The drafters insisted that they proceed according to well-established precedents in other areas of commercial international law. Third, the Concordat Principles themselves frequently relied on principles drawn from the EU and Council of Europe (Istanbul) conventions (Nielsen, Sigal, and Wagner 1996: 542).

The Concordat was founded on ten Principles.[22] Many of these represent breakthroughs in concept and form. First, while the Concordat unabashedly expresses a commitment to universalism, it goes beyond the simple duality of universalism versus territoriality by recognizing that a relaxed or "modified universalism" may be necessary in many circumstances (Nielsen, Sigal, and Wagner 1996). Second, the Concordat claims it can operate in every combination of plenary and secondary court relations, including combinations of courts that differ sharply in their commitments to universal or territorial ideals.[23] Third, the Concordat does not expect that all Principles must be adopted for coordination to be effective. Fourth, as an advance over MIICA, even where a Principle may be applicable, the Concordat in some instances provides alternative expression of a given Principle to foster further flexibility where severe differences occur among regimes. Fifth, since the Concordat is not a legislative but a judicial instrument, it can be adapted far more readily than a statutory or diplomatic product as experience dictates.

Thus, the putative appeal of this new technology inhered substantially in the skillful manipulation by the designers of formal features of the instrument itself. When the Concordat is compared to earlier instruments, we find that the designers (1) raised the level of abstraction, (2) narrowed the scope of application, (3) increased alternatives, (4) focused on procedure rather than substance, and (5) avoided high barriers to implementation. They acknowledged sovereignty and territoriality where necessary but permitted sufficient discretion and flexibility to courts without hindering coordination or fore-stalling predictability.

Moreover, anticipating difficulties that had impaired previous efforts, the drafters engaged in tactical maneuvers. They expressly sought to *lower* expectations by stating precisely what the Concordat was not intended to do, that is, to substitute for a treaty or statute or be treated as "a rigid set of rules." Instead, they presented the first release of the Concordat as an interim step on the way to treaties and statutes. And they stressed the Concordat was intended to be adaptable rather than rigid, "a living document" (RevDraft 2, in Nielsen, Sigal, and Wagner 1996: 537–538).

Despite its procedural emphasis, the American-led design opens up the possibility of a substantive emphasis on reorganizations rather than liquidation. The Concordat even allows for situations that would draw countries without reorganization law into a cross-border reorganization plan (RevDraft, Principle 9, p. 26).

In contrast to MIICA, the Concordat obtained recognition very quickly in a case presided over by Judge Lifland in New York and Judge Farley in Ontario, both judicial advisors to the drafting team. Evergreen Beverages, a large multinational firm with operations in the U.S. and Canada, filed simultaneously for reorganization in the courts of Ontario and New York in December 1995. Counsel for both sides presented a Protocol based explicitly on the Concordat to the courts as a basis for coordinating proceedings. The Protocol drew directly from the Concordat.[24] This first start did not augur rapid and extensive adoption among advanced countries. By one measure, as of 2002 the Concordat has been used relatively rarely: some eight cases between the United States and Canada; and several other cases between the U.S. and Israel, the Bahamas, the Cayman Islands and England, Bermuda and Switzerland (Clift 2002).[25] By another measure (Leonard 2001), as of 2001 protocols "continued to develop and expand." Leonard noted that some twenty to thirty protocols had been used since 1995 after the completion of the Concordat "and the trend towards the use of protocols shows no sign of abating." In 2000–2001 alone protocols were being used between several courts in the U.S. and Canada (Leonard 2001).

European Strivings: Harmonization Among States
While Canadian and U.S. jurisdictions sought instruments of cooperation between themselves and with U.K. courts, the Europeans were continuing on

a decades-long quest for harmonization that seemed always to elude them, even at the penultimate moment when success seemed assured.

The succession of failures stemmed from a combination of factors, many related to the instruments themselves, and others to the politics of the European Community (EC), and subsequently, European Union.[26] In its first attempt to find a European Community–wide basis for resolving cross-border disputes, Commission experts worked on a Convention from 1963 to 1980, producing first one draft and then another, but without success. Their efforts served as precisely the kind of object lesson that had led the IBA to propose its Model Code: to obtain the universal assent required by a convention certainly solved a legitimation problem, but the process itself proved impossible to bring to a successful conclusion. After three years of study by the European Commission Council, in 1985 the Council was forced to drop further work in the face of continuing disagreements.

In hindsight the reasons for its failure seem obvious, for it strove for an impossible ideal—a unity of proceedings in which one court would handle all the affairs of a corporate insolvency that crossed any or all national frontiers within the European Community. Given the extraordinary diversity of common and civil law countries, of large and small economies, and of radically different financial structures and policy preferences, this high road to legal rationalization through complete harmonization was a bridge too far. Member-states were not ready for the strict principle of universality it embodied. And U.S. critics maintained that it did not adhere to the principle of equality among all creditors. It discriminated between parties within and outside the European Community (Nielsen, Sigal, and Wagner 1996; Woodland 1994). Furthermore, the instrument of a Convention also raised a high bar for enactment.

In the wake of this failure, the Council of Europe, a supranational organization of twenty-five states, tried again, also by striving for agreement upon a Convention. Learning from the failed European Community experiment, however, it relaxed the demanding standard for a unity of proceedings Europe-wide and instead made two breakthroughs that reflected MIICA's innovations and would anticipate later advances. On the one hand, it allowed liquidators to operate in more than one country, effectively allowing them to pursue assets wherever a multinational company held them. On the other hand, and even more important, it opened up the possibility that the main proceeding could occur in one country, but subsidiary, complementary, or ancillary proceedings could take place in others. In other words, it also re-laxed a strict version of the principle of universality. This more promising instrument was produced in 1990 (Istanbul Convention), and by 1993 seven states had indicated their support of it, though none had ratified the Conven-tion (Fletcher 1999; Nielsen, Sigal, and Wagner 1996; Woodland 1994).

Meanwhile, in 1989 Ministers of Justice of the European Community agreed to try again for yet another cross-border convention. They set up a Working Group under the chairmanship of Manfred Balz, who would sub-sequently emerge as one of the key figures in global insolvency reform move-ments. Experts appointed by European Community countries contributed information via questionnaires to the Working Group, which produced a draft Convention.

Unlike the abortive European Commission proposal, this version lowered the bar by deliberately *not* seeking to unify or harmonize laws, but rather to coordinate proceedings among European Union jurisdictions. Following the precedent of the Istanbul Convention, the tension between the principles of universality and territoriality was resolved by the principle of "controlled uni-versality." Alongside a main proceeding that is opened in one country might be secondary proceedings in others. In addition, liquidators could exercise their powers throughout the EC, subject to various protections. And within countries, secured creditors and priority claims (preferential creditors) might be settled in their country with any surplus funds being sent to the main forum. Moreover, an attempt was made to maintain a rule of equality among creditors.[27]

Foreign critics acknowledged the advance toward modified universalism but indicated that several issues remained unresolved. For choice of law in a given jurisdiction, no rule was proposed. For choice of forum, most particu-larly where the main proceeding should be situated, the presumption that it should be in the country where a company was incorporated was not very sat-isfying, given that many companies carry on their principal business activi-ties away from their state of incorporation. And while the Convention left an opening for the possibility of company rescue, the Convention did not apply well to reorganizations (Westbrook 1991: 487; Woodland 1994: 4–5).

These relaxed, less intrusive provisions, which were more respectful of territorial interests, were persuasive to member-states, and by 1995 twelve of fifteen states had signed. Shortly thereafter so did the Netherlands and Ire-land. The United Kingdom's decision again demonstrated the fundamental implementation hurdle of conventions—they require all states to accede before they have value for any. Reportedly, the U.K. refused to sign because of its anger at the way other EU countries had treated it during the "mad cow" disaster in British agriculture. Privately, however, the thinking was that the U.K. believed that in some manner signing the Convention would threaten its sovereignty over Gibraltar, and that the U.K. could not tolerate. In either case, the Convention died for a political reason quite unrelated to the merits of the Convention itself—yet another impediment of seeking coordination via the route of international conventions.

A Global Ambition: The UNCITRAL Model Law

Together, the legal technologies developed by the IBA and the courts established several bridgeheads for the advance toward a global, rationalized solution for multinational corporate insolvencies. MIICA demonstrated simultaneously that a Model Law might be achieved, but the auspices for a Model Law must transcend a particular professional association for it to be taken seriously by governments. The Concordat indicated that principled cooperation between relatively similar courts could significantly improve the efficient management of large and complex corporate failures. Yet, for all its promise, the Concordat would probably apply only in a small fraction of common law cases, and whether it could operate in civil law systems was not at all clear. Perhaps as significant, each of these instruments adhered to a doctrine of universality, but tempered by pragmatism. Their designers sought what might be possible, not simply what would be ideal, a necessary trade-off emphasized yet again by the faltering efforts of the EU to produce an insolvency convention.

Despite their advances, MIICA, the court protocols, and the Concordat are all partial solutions for advanced economies in close trading relationships. The EU Convention, which appeared likely to be signed by all EU nations in the mid-1990s, and the comity of some pioneering North American courts offered regional solutions among rich countries of the Global North. So, too, the effective protocols on a few major cases between Canada and the U.K. and the U.S. and the U.K. show that advances made in legal technologies for coordination of insolvencies across borders apply only to a limited number of countries in particular regions of the world.

By the mid-1990s, therefore, rationalizing technologies with global scope remained far out of reach, if not out of mind. Into this vacuum entered a new collective actor that could claim legitimation warrants missing from prior efforts, an actor, moreover, aspiring to a legal instrument that would embrace not only advanced economies across the world but the transitional and emerging economies being increasingly drawn into global trading relationships.

Already well versed in the production of model laws, in 1992 UNCITRAL hosted a conference on uniform commercial law in the twenty-first century where practitioners proposed that UNCITRAL consider work on a cross-border insolvency law.[28] Heavily encouraged by the International Federation of Insolvency Practitioners (INSOL), UNCITRAL tested the support for and feasibility of this proposal by staging a joint conference with INSOL in Vienna in April 1994. The practitioners, judges, academics, lenders, and government officials at the conference agreed that a model law might be possible if it narrowed its focus to enable judicial cooperation and the access of foreign insolvency representatives to courts in different jurisdictions. This would permit an insolvency proceeding to advance harmoniously across multiple jurisdictions.[29] A further UNCITRAL-INSOL conference held a year later in Toronto, and restricted principally to judges and government officials, concurred and recommended that UNCITRAL develop a legislative instrument, preferably a model law, to achieve these aims.[30]

UNCITRAL's Working Group on Insolvency met only four times in two-week sessions to reach agreement on a draft text that it presented to a March 1997 meeting of practitioners, judges, and academics. With their support, the UNCITRAL Commission approved the Model Law in May 1997, thus reaching consensus for a global law in less than four years, a remarkable feat given the repeated failures of the EU to achieve its more ambitious goals over several decades.[31]

The UNCITRAL Commission and later UN General Assembly approved a double-barreled instrument.[32] One part, the Model Law itself, was written as a statute, comprising thirty-two Articles subsumed under five chapters. The other part consisted of a Guide to Enactment aimed at legislators and executive branches of government. The Guide acts simultaneously as a commentary on the reasoning behind each Article, a justification of UNCITRAL's initiative, a legitimation of its particular multilateral deliberative process, and a careful positioning for prospective legislators of what the Law does or does not intend to accomplish.[33]

The Model Law (Arts. 1–8) allows ample flexibility for adaptation to variation among countries over the institutions through which they administer liquidations or reorganizations (e.g., courts or administrative agencies). It clearly states that countries may include or exclude any kind of collective proceeding and any kind of financial actor. The Model Law (Arts. 9–14) treats the legal standing of foreign representatives in domestic insolvency proceedings and establishes that foreign creditors should be treated "no worse" than local creditors (Art. 13).

Subsequent provisions (Arts. 15–24) deal with recognition of foreign proceedings and various forms of relief that courts can grant in cross-border situations and ways courts can speed up the process (Art. 16), together with issues of cooperation among courts across jurisdictions and insolvency representatives in different jurisdictions (Arts. 25–27).

UNCITRAL staked its singular claim for recognition of its instrument on three grounds. It explicitly acknowledged its debt to what it had learned from prior efforts, not least from MIICA and the Concordat produced by the IBA, and the EU Convention on Insolvency Proceedings, which at that time it expected (wrongly, as it happens) to be implemented shortly. Further, UNCITRAL boasted a breadth of participation unparalleled by any prior initiative—the contributions of thirty-six member-states, forty observer-states, and thirteen international organizations.[34] Here, UNCITRAL accomplished an inclusiveness of interested parties that had escaped previous initiatives. More important, however, UNCITRAL combined its claim to legitimacy with the prospect of pragmatic efficacy. The UNCITRAL process enabled a rapprochement among practitioners (lawyers, judges, insolvency practitioners), who were thoroughly familiar with the practice of international insolvency, and states, whose officials could facilitate adoption by legislatures and thus make a model law binding for all cross-border insolvencies affecting a given country. This fusion of expert and political authority placed the UNCITRAL negotiations on a new plane of practicality with a high promise of implementation. At once UNCITRAL was able to combine expert and representative authority with the prospect that many of the representatives in its Working Group on Insolvency would have a personal stake in national implementation.

UNCITRAL also situated its technical product within the theory of modified universalism (Westbrook 1991), aiming for the universal while showing itself reasonable and ready for concessions to nations where territoriality still prevailed. The experience of previous failures and the participation of state officials added to a new political realism about what might be possible.

In part, these advances in the auspices of the new instrument and its stress on realistic expectations born of experience resulted from a different professional strategy. Whereas the IBA, an international organization of lawyers only, had adopted a strategy of "going it alone," INSOL mobilized its diverse membership in alliance with a multilateral institution (UNCITRAL) that had a record of producing legal products familiar to governments around the world. Unlike the IBA's, INSOL's membership included not only lawyers but insolvency practitioners, many of whom were qualified primarily as accountants. Later, INSOL expanded its membership to judges and even bankers. Although INSOL's President at the time was an American lawyer, Richard Gitlin, the association's worldwide membership included representatives from jurisdictions where lawyers play a relatively minor role in corporate insolvencies and accountant/insolvency practitioners dominate. Moreover, a strong influence within INSOL emanated from British and Commonwealth countries where insolvency practitioners (whether originally qualified as lawyers or accountants) traditionally had extensive powers, often as agents of banks, to liquidate (and occasionally restructure) companies, so far as possible without the interference of lawyers or courts. In this they followed the lead of Britain, whose insolvency practitioners traditionally sought to keep law, lawyers, and courts at arm's length (Carruthers and Halliday 1998).

An epistemological divide therefore separated the orientation of the IBA from that of INSOL. We can overdraw the contrast by observing that the instruments developed by the IBA were premised on the lawyers' values of equity and fairness—it is true, in the service of efficiency, but nevertheless an efficiency constrained by legal procedure and controlled by courts. INSOL's orientation reflected the sentiments of an organization with a perceptible affinity for English and much British Commonwealth insolvency practice, in which accountants and insolvency practitioners championed swift, decisive action in order to preserve lenders' assets. Although the UNCITRAL process compels professionals with different epistemological orientations to find common ground, it is not surprising to find that the Model Law places a premium on "speed, speed, and more speed," to "act first, think later" (Berends 1998).

The Model Law construes the problem it seeks to solve as a situation where law lags behind the market. While there exists a "continuing global expansion of trade and investment," national insolvencies are "ill-equipped" to deal with bankruptcies across national borders. As a result, "inadequate and inharmonious legal approaches" impede "the rescue of financial troubled businesses." The administration of cross-border insolvencies is neither fair nor efficient. Assets of the debtor are not protected and are readily dissipated; value certainly is not maximized. The lack of law encourages lawlessness, most notably in fraud committed by companies that conceal assets or shift them around so they cannot be drawn into an insolvency proceeding. Market consequences are severe: "the absence of predictability . . . impedes capital flow and is a disincentive to cross-border investment."[35]

UNCITRAL itself, therefore, advances implicitly the alignment of market and legal logics that undergird the more self-reflective early reform efforts. Predictability and certainty stimulate investment, economic growth, and global trade. Harmonizing and coordinating legal frameworks permit predictability and certainty. Indirectly, therefore, global legal instruments facilitate global economic development and expansion. Indeed, according to Jay Westbrook, one of the drafters of the Model Law and a leading theorist of cross-border law reform, the UNCITRAL Model Law reflects a functional necessity for markets and law to be in symmetry, for "a globalizing market requires a globalizing insolvency law" (Westbrook 2000).

The Guide and the provisions of the Law reveal a tailored strategy to evade prior traps and to position the Law for acceptance by practitioners and politicians in every legal system, an aspiration of extraordinary proportions. Following the example of the Concordat, the Guide immediately seeks to adjust expectations. It states repeatedly that it does *not* attempt to unify substantive law across jurisdictions and it *does* respect variations across legal systems. In addition, says the Guide, the Model Law does *not* create new substantive rights, nor does it demand reciprocity between nations participating in coordinated proceedings.[36] In short, compared to the regional efforts of the American Law Institute for the NAFTA countries and the European Union, the Model Law offers itself as "more modest in its goals but more global in its application" (Westbrook 2002: 3).[37]

Much of UNCITRAL's strategy turns on the form of the instrument itself. In order to lower the barrier for legislative drafters, the Law is written in the form of a legislative text that could be enacted into any country's national law with few changes, such as filling in some blanks. The Guide emphasizes repeatedly how much flexibility the instrument permits: provisions can be left out, and provisions can be modified. On occasions legislators may choose among alternatives, either of which is acceptable.

Even the terminology of the Model Law was invented to be sufficiently general that it would not conflict with terms-of-art in particular legal systems. Such key terms as "foreign proceeding," "foreign main proceeding," "foreign non-main proceeding," "foreign representative," "foreign court," and "establishment" were created so that they do *not* coincide with terms used in any extant legal system, nor will they conflict with any technical meanings in various legal systems. In fact, they are defined by their purposes or functions to encompass all the rich diversity of professionals, proceedings, and firms found in any market, legal system, or cross-border insolvency.[38]

In addition, the Guide further advocates its flexibility over what kinds of collective proceedings could be included within the terms of the Model Law. It raises the level of generality to encompass the vast majority of legal systems that variously employ compulsory or voluntary approaches, apply to corporate or individual subjects, and allow liquidations or reorganizations.[39] It also remains flexible about what kinds of debtors can be included. Countries can choose to be entirely inclusive of all debtors, individual and corporate, industrial, service, or financial; or they may exclude some, such as financial debtors like banks and insurance companies.[40]

Because the perpetual stumbling block of prior efforts relates to national sovereignty and the jealousy of nations and courts over control of their own affairs, the globalizing instrument remains deferential to territoriality in several ways. It accepts that priorities among creditors will differ across countries. It indicates that local creditors' rights should be protected. And it acknowledges that secured transactions in local situations should be respected ahead of transactions of foreign creditors.[41]

Given sensitivities that a Model Law might interfere with policy preferences of a country, the Guide states clearly that a public policy exception is possible. If an aspect of the Model Law contradicts a constitutional principle of a nation, for instance, then an action governed by the Model Law could be resisted (Art. 6., §§ 86–89, p. 46).[42]

The Law and Guide appeal to the interests of all parties to cross-border insolvencies. For practitioners, in addition to opening up work on a global scale, the Model Law sells itself as broad enough to encompass a multiplicity of situations where there is a foreign ("in-bound") request for a practitioner to be recognized in a national proceeding; an "out-bound" request by a court or representative that its proceedings be recognized in other countries; a situation in which coordination is needed between proceedings going on concurrently in two or more states; or a situation in which foreign creditors wish to participate in proceedings in a given country.[43] For courts it offers clear procedures without the need for reciprocity. It also enables courts that in the past might have been reluctant to directly contact courts in other jurisdictions without formal authority to now "pick up the phone." For lenders it argues for economic benefits, since the law would forestall situations where creditors will not be paid or investment will be impaired. For governments it offers an alternative to the prevailing situation where viable businesses are not rescued and jobs are lost. It offers, therefore, an escape from hard budget constraints (Carruthers, Babb, and Halliday 2001).

If the price of all these potential payoffs is to make a choice for political expediency in the trade-off between the certainty that might have been delivered by an almost impossible-to-achieve convention versus less predictability that would be delivered by a more-likely-to-be-achieved model law, then it is a price UNCITRAL willingly pays in order to get a global technology suited for an increasingly pressing problem of international trade.

The Model Law draws upon the doctrine of "modified universalism" that had been articulated by Jay Westbrook and also lies behind the initiatives of the European Union in the 1990s. The wording of the Model Law and Guide repeatedly asserts the cardinal principle of speed. Courts, say the Guide, need to act "at the earliest possible time," sometimes providing a "rapid freeze," at others "'urgently needed' relief."[44]

In addition, cross-border insolvencies should take the form of global, collective proceedings. All parties and assets should be drawn into a coordinated set of proceedings where cooperation is the dominant value. The Model Law authorizes courts to coordinate with each other "to the maximum extent possible."[45] Both legal and financial transparency should be maintained.

Further, the Model Law proceeds on a principle of "procedural legitimation" for foreign representatives in an enacting country (i.e., that representatives authorized in another country can obtain recognition and standing in a foreign country); and a principle of nondiscrimination among creditors, namely, that creditors should not be treated worse than local creditors in a foreign country.

Together these principles intend to serve the virtues of predictability and certainty in law insofar as they are intended to produce predictability and certainty in the market, but with the pragmatic reasoning that they must be effected with a politically feasible technology. Thus, UNCITRAL seeks to effect a tight synergy in the implicit theory of politics, markets, and law that pervades the model statute and its commentary: markets require law, and law requires politics. Crafted almost entirely by lawyers, the Model Law presumes that markets are legally constructed and institutionalized through politics.

In pursuit of a pragmatic strategy, the UNCITRAL Working Group insisted on its narrow procedural focus, introducing new substantive principles neither into private international law nor into local law. Yet the blurred distinction between procedural and substantive law effects here what it does frequently produces in domestic legislation—through procedure some substantive openings occur. The Model Law makes clear in its Preamble that a primary purpose is the "facilitation of the rescue of financially troubled businesses." The valorization of reorganization recurs through the Guide. More important, however, the procedural terms of the law itself increase the likelihood of reorganizations across jurisdictions; simultaneously, they champion reorganization as a substantive policy value and permit countries without reorganization provisions in their laws to participate in cross-border reorganizations. Just as Europeans might have feared MIICA as a Trojan horse to introduce the U.S. pattern of management control in business turnarounds, countries committed to liquidation regimes might recognize the Model Law as a Trojan horse for the advancement of a shift toward reorganization in their domestic law.

Given UNCITRAL's strenuous efforts to remedy the faults of its predecessor initiatives, how effectively has it produced a winning formula? Since 1997 UNCITRAL reports that it has been the basis for cross-border laws enacted in Eritrea (1998), Japan (2000), Mexico (2000), South Africa (2000), Montenegro (2002), Poland (2003), Romania (2003), Serbia (2004), British Virgin Islands (2005), the United States (2005), Colombia (2006), Great Britain (2006), and New Zealand (2006). Both the IMF and the World Bank build it into their recommendations for bankruptcy regimes in developing nations. We shall see in Chapter 4 that it was later assimilated into the UNCITRAL Legislative Guide on Insolvency (2004). After more than a decade of trial and error, the Model Law proved it had become "an idea whose time has come" (Westbrook 2002a: 4).

Practice and Theory, Technology, and Power

In just ten years, professionals and multilateral governance organizations produced a new international legal order for cross-border insolvencies. Actors entered this nascent field with diverse interests and capacities. Professionals diagnosed problems and invented solutions for their own sakes and those of their clients, solutions that arose out of their distinctive knowledge sets of skills and theory and that were best suited for their preferred modes of mobilization. Courts sought practical solutions for a class of problems in commercial disputes where private international law proved inadequate and where public international efforts had failed. Multilateral institutions such as UNCITRAL sought areas of law where a good probability of success existed for a politically viable technology. Advanced nations sought technologies that would recognize their territorial distinctiveness but would facilitate their engagement in international trade.

The prospect of reconciling diverse interests around a particular technology turned significantly on a little-examined global assumption on which all parties could agree. Both the national and global actors converged on a single, unifying, functional theory of law and markets. The market component of their theory had two elements. First, markets require certainty and predictability in order to grow in both scope and scale. Since regulatory boundaries threatened certainty, mechanisms must be found to transcend such boundaries. Second, entrepreneurial risk produces failure. However, value might be preserved in corporate failures and companies reorganized and made newly competitive if markets were optimally regulated. The legal component of the theory argued that a certain kind of law and certain types of practice would deliver the certainty and predictability it was assumed that markets require. Construction of this legal field progressively demonstrated that neither harmonized substantive law nor procedural unification was necessary. If the right kind of law and practice could be discovered, it would produce the "symmetry" of markets and law that proponents believed would deliver economic growth in a globalizing market. In short, global markets needed global law.

Hence, the success of creating the new insolvency field represents much more than "an idea whose time has come." The designers of this legal field were challenged to discover or invent precisely what combination of technologies and enabling powers would deliver legal and market certainty and predictability.

The problem posed by localized practices in a globalizing world sparked experimentation, doctrinal development, and technological advances. Professionals advance their private practices through invention of new techniques, forms, and instruments (Carruthers and Halliday 1998; Powell 1993). Braithwaite and Drahos (2000) rightly state that capitalist legal systems in general are highly inventive, creating new forms of property, such as intellectual property, and then developing norms and models to bring regions and then the entire world into a seamless regulatory system. Cross-border solutions advanced along similar lines. At the outset legal and accounting practitioners put their inventive skills to work by seeking particular solutions to immediate difficulties faced by their clients. At the other end of the knowledge spectrum, however, academic jurists were beginning to develop a theory to stimulate and justify the technologies being invented by professional designers. Scholars recognized that the great divide between universalist and territorial theories of insolvency must be bridged, for universalism by itself led to political stalemate, and territoriality led to fragmentation and disharmony. By creating a new theory, modified universalism, the jurists signaled that the ends of legal and market certainty might be served in doctrinally justifiable ways. The theory further served the critical purpose of rebutting prior assumptions that complete harmony across legal systems must be the condition of unified insolvency proceedings.

This alignment of skill and doctrine, practice and theory, led to a series of experiments as first one, then another, invention was tried, modified, and tried again, until a robust technology emerged. Each technology comprised as many as four elements—the process by which the technology was created, the form it took, the substance of the instrument, and the means by which it was implemented. Designers successively varied each of these in order to discover a winning combination (Table 2.3).

1. The *process* of drafting might be undertaken by government officials, private practitioners, judges, professional societies, states, or multilateral organizations. The process was critical for three reasons: the sophistication and diversity of skills that could be built upon, the degree of difficulty in reaching agreement, and the legitimacy of the process as it influenced implementation of a new technology. It took several efforts to find a workable result that, it turned out, required all categories of stakeholders, experts as well as governments, to deliberate in a carefully controlled, neutral "legislative" environment.

2. Global norm makers had available several *forms* of legal technology, some thoroughly familiar from private and public international law, and others in the process of elaboration and adaptation. Even within these, however, reforms shaped the scripts with a variety of expedients: leaving undefined key concepts that might be controversial; defining concepts in ways that did not conflict with any indigenous usages; raising or lowering levels of specificity of the instrument (e.g., from pro-

TABLE 2.3 Dimensions of Legal Technologies for Cross-Border Insolvencies

	Convention	Protocol	Concordat	Model Law (UNCITRAL)
Process	Drafting by state officials Negotiation among states	Agreement among courts and insolvency representatives	Consultation and drafting among experts	Narrow: Consultation among experts Broad: Consultation among stakeholders
Form	Statutory No options No selective adoption	Court order Detailed, case-specific rules	Principles General rules of cooperation Rights of representation Commentary	Statutory language Alternative options Selective adoption Judicial discretion No reciprocity Guide to Legislators
Substance	Philosophy: universalism Substantive unification Liquidations only	Philosophy: comity Liquidation and reorganization	Philosophy: comity Liquidation and reorganization	Philosophy: modified universalism All countries Liquidation and reorganization
Feasibility of Implementation	Officials to agree States to accede in toto Binding upon accession	Courts, professionals agree Binding by court order	Courts, professionals agree Advisory to court	Vote of UN Commission Enactment by sovereign legislatures Advisory to lawmakers

tocols designed for two countries to the Concordat designed for any number of countries); not confronting vexing issues that might later be left to courts (e.g., choice of law, choice of forum); offering higher-order principles instead of more precise rules; providing opt-out options for potentially contentious rules; providing alternatives for rules that might achieve the same end; and offering explanatory commentary to justify and educate, among others.

3. Similarly, designers also varied the *substantive* provisions of each instrument. Philosophical foundations varied along a continuum from a juridical theory of universalism to a modified universalism to territorialism.

The jurisprudential breakthrough provided by the scholars occurred when a middle ground was found between what appeared as two unpalatable or impractical options. The scope of some was broadened to encompass more issues, whereas the scope of others was narrowed to embrace more nations. Some focused on liquidations while others encouraged reorganization. Some demanded reciprocity; others did not.

4. Finally, each technology was chosen with awareness of the trade-off between ambition in the instrument itself and the feasibility of *implementation*. Designers experimented with combinations of voluntary implementation for more exhaustive instruments and binding implementation for less ambitious instruments.

Much of the debate over technologies and their embedded scripts turned on the legitimacy of forums, processes, and outcomes. Unlike the foundations of legitimacy in the Security Council (Hurd 2002, 2007) and some other international organizations, the springboard for a legitimate process and product originated from expertise. Initial efforts were initiated by professionals. Their authority stemmed from their technical skills, their experience, and their sponsorship by major professional associations. This basis of legitimation was amplified to a degree by a far-reaching consultative process among professionals from diverse legal families. But the expert authority of legal specialists and scholars had two obvious limits: other professionals—accountants and insolvency practitioners among them—had their own expertise, and they could not be assumed to be in accord with the lawyers; and specialist expertise, while valuable and even necessary, falls far short of the representativeness conventionally expected of lawmaking—or even norm-making—forums. This manifest deficit of undue reliance on expert authority was overcome only when official forums, such as the European Union and UNCITRAL, brought insolvency into established deliberative processes. Both the latter could add to their legitimation warrants by pointing to prior successes in cognate arenas of law and regulation.

The creation of legal technologies must also be understood as an effort to meld two forms of rationalization: rationalization of markets and rationalization of law. For markets, designers—mostly professionals—assumed that expansion of trade, investment, and economic growth required the removal of barriers that are irrational from a market standpoint, such as differing laws, national barriers, and arbitrary decision making. Thus, the value of harmonization, and the certainty and predictability it would yield, mattered to merchants of commerce as much as merchants of law. For law, designers strived for a satisfying solution that would deliver sufficient rationality in the legal regime to produce the rationality supposedly needed for globalizing markets. We will pursue later the forms of rationalization that designers manipulated in order to produce harmony, predictability, and cooperation. We can say here, however, that the technologies include both substantive and procedural provisions, where procedure comes ultimately to prevail, albeit procedure with a distinct substantive tint.

The creation of the insolvency legal field demanded that technology be harnessed to power. Just as technological progress required that several segments of professions bring their distinctive expertise into a common cause, a final settlement on an instrument demanded that political feasibility and leverage be sufficient to ensure deployment of a technology. Alongside technological experimentation, therefore, the creation of the field emerged through political learning and political experimentation, as first one then another design idea was matched with one or another means of political implementation. For instance, the IBA early discovered that a model law without a partner for implementation would yield much less than a concordat developed in consultation with judges who could promulgate it in their own courts. Further, European Community drafters learned that setting the political requirement too high by aspiring to a strictly binding process would consign an innovation to oblivion.

This process in the insolvency field exemplifies the logic identified by Braithwaite and Drahos (2000) for business regulation more generally. Political learning occurred because the designers formed loose professional circles that allowed continuity across experiments. Many of the same reformers recurred in several of the initiatives. Judge Lifland, for instance, one of the most experienced U.S. bankruptcy judges, was involved in the Protocol used in the Maxwell case, in design of the Concordat, and as a member of the American delegation to UNCITRAL's Working Group on Insolvency. Mike Sigal, a drafter of the IBA Concordat, was a delegate to UNCITRAL's Working Group on Insolvency. Richard Gitlin, a leading counsel in the Maxwell reorganization, was integrally involved with INSOL's initiatives to work with UNCITRAL. Bruce Leonard, a Canadian practitioner who led the bankruptcy section of the International Bar Association, also became a participant in UNCITRAL's Working Group. Moreover, professionals wrote, and a succession of articles by designers and academic critics enabled, a body of cumulative commentary, with an eye to lessons learned, which provided a more informed basis for each new experiment (Fletcher 1990, 1996, 1997, 1999; Wade 1990; West-brook 1991, 1994, 1996, 2000, 2001a, 2001b, 2002a, 2002b).

These webs of knowledge, constituted by practitioners, academics, and judges, became webs of influence through the process of enrollment (Braith-waite and Drahos 2000). "Weak" academics and individual practitioners suffered not only from legitimation deficits but from an inability to compel implementation. Indeed, there was much doubt that they could even achieve the enactment of global norms. Enrollment occurs when a weaker actor is able to persuade a stronger actor to take on its cause. In the case of cross-border insolvency, enrollment started modestly and ended ambitiously. For instance, in order to get better coordination among courts, Sigal and Field enrolled the International Bar Association. While this broadened the base of expertise and consensus to a prestigious professional association, that orga-nization did not have either the legitimacy or leverage to make a major im-pact. More leverage came when Gitlin and his British counterparts persuaded the English and New York courts to adopt a protocol binding on the parties. This began with agreements and ended with binding court orders. The most notable instance of enrollment can be found in INSOL's successful effort to enlist a UN norm-making body into the global search for a cross-border solu-tion. Through this move INSOL radically widened the bases of legitimation for cross-border norms. UN-mandated norms might not convey the force of bilateral reciprocity or IFI economic coercion, but they offered an often more effective lever—the persuasion that a global standard now existed on which all progressive countries might model themselves.

The successive experiments to create a definitive solution exemplify the re-cursivity of law. This had two elements. On the one side, reformers drove *iter-ations* of norm making that were not binding but prescriptive and persuasive. Efforts to formulate different types of technologies and scripts, independent of any binding authority, cycled not between enactment and implementation, but rather between proposed adoption and nonimplementation. On the other side were *recursive* cycles of lawmaking where a new technology and script became binding in a particular instance, such as the Maxwell case, and were elaborated in subsequent cases. The EU regulations combined these—several unsuccessful iterations to obtain consensus on "enactment" eventually were realized in a binding adoption by EU member countries. Complicating fur-ther these cycles of reform were the sites from which they originated. *Private* individuals and organizations propose one technology, observe its failures, and then offer another to compensate for those failures. *Public* lawmaking occurs when a body with sovereign authority, or a supranational legislature, makes multiple attempts to develop and implement a solution. The EU's several failed attempts to develop conventions that culminated in the EU Insolvency Regulation of 2000 exemplify precisely such cycles of multiple products that fail to be implemented until a product appropriately matches the political exigencies for implementation.

In the development of the insolvency field these cycles complemented and intertwined with each other in a temporal sequence. The first cycle began unsuccessfully with the failed public lawmaking of the EU. A second private lawmaking cycle followed with the IBA's unsuccessful MIICA and then by a more successful iteration. The recursive process reverted to the public domain and ultimately succeeded with the cycle of invention represented by UNCITRAL's Model Law.

It is the interplay of these private and public cycles that answers the question raised in the Part I Preface. Private and public actors confronted and construed a problem of cross-border economic and legal coordination. Through one cycle after another they experimented with solutions that would combine an adequate technology with legitimacy and leverage. The inventiveness of professionals coupled with the institutional capacities of the UN ultimately brought this reform process to completion and, in so doing, created a new international legal field where global law and global markets might exist in symmetrical relations with each other. Admittedly, this was a narrow front and limited ambition. It is true that we observe only law-on-the-books—globally and nationally—not implementation in everyday commercial practice. But ten years later the adoption of the UNCITRAL Model Law by major states signifies that a modest ambition was a shrewd choice by the nascent community of international insolvency actors. It established that a global consensus could be forged by cooperation among private and public actors. It showed that what began as bilateral could become multilateral, what was regional might become global, what started as local experiments could be translated into global templates. In establishing a precedent, it also raised aspirations for bolder and more far-reaching challenges. Until they confronted bolder challenges, global actors took pride in a modest achievement that nevertheless putatively brought a new kind of legal regulation to every kind of capitalism—advanced, transitional, and emerging.

3 Constructing Global Norms for National Insolvency Systems

THE INSOLVENCY of a handful of huge multinational corporations precipitated cross-border frameworks for handling corporate bankruptcies in advanced economies. The collapse of the Soviet Union triggered a global movement of much greater proportions. The fall of Communist regimes in the late 1980s and the demise of their command economies produced an avalanche of lawmaking and institution building to create nascent markets. Bankruptcy regimes featured prominently in the bundle of commercial laws that creditor nations and multilateral institutions believed to be necessary to solidify viable market economies (G-22 1998b). Leading trading nations and international financial institutions, professionals, and international governance organizations provided funding, expertise, and technical assistance to transitional economies from the Baltic to Central Asia, all with the intent of erecting the institutions that regulate exit of failing firms from the market.

But the scramble of institution building in transitional countries was not the only site for widening and widespread law reforms. The Mexican debt crisis in 1994–1995 signaled that many countries were financially vulnerable. Their institutions showed limited capacity to handle either the volatile flows of capital across their borders or the buildup of domestic economic pressures. But, surprisingly, it was not the laggards in the world economy but the Asian Tigers that urgently impelled commercial law reform and institution building. The Asian Financial Crisis in 1997–1998 motivated dominant economic powers and international institutions toward a new realm of activity—to codify experience, aggregate best practices, enunciate core principles, and articulate standards. Modest steps in this direction had already been taken by the International Bar Association (IBA) and INSOL in the mid-1990s. After 1997, efforts amplified to an unprecedented scale. Between 1999 and 2004, regional and global institutions, aided by professionals and advanced countries, produced an array of new legal scripts for the design of bankruptcy regimes in developing and transitional economies. By setting in motion these rationalizing endeavors, national and global actors pushed the insolvency field of law toward its ultimate phase—a single global standard for bankruptcy systems worldwide.

The enterprise of creating norms for national insolvency systems contrasted markedly with those of formulating mechanisms for cross-border restructurings. The magnitude of the new challenge vastly exceeded that of cross-border insolvency. Compared to solutions designed for a few relatively homogeneous economies in the Global North, reformist institutions now aspired to global scripts that could embrace the Global North and Global South, advanced and developing nations, countries with common and civil law heritages, national economies integral to the global trading system, and those barely integrated into it. Global scripts would be pressed upon countries whose legal systems might be outdated, moribund, undeveloped, or built on the premises of entirely different legal or political ideologies.

Added to this vast heterogeneity across the world's nations, the ambition to design a global standard for complete bankruptcy systems ran directly into the face of the distributional conflicts inherent in substantive bankruptcy law. Classic struggles between creditors and debtors, management and labor, secured versus unsecured creditors, the state versus market actors, all would now need to be confronted on a global scale with the potential for worldwide commercial consequences.

The entry of major lending nations and multilaterals into national insolvency lawmaking demonstrates that they perceived the stakes were substantial. The fall of the Soviet Union gave Western nations a moment for geopolitical realignment through national reconstruction. Since bankruptcy is a defining characteristic of market economies, and the rule of law is a defining characteristic of liberal politics, leading creditor nations had a brief window of opportunity to help institutionalize markets and to forestall any economic or political relapse. Whereas the former Soviet nations also opened up new credit markets, the Asian Crisis underlined the need for institutional safeguards to forestall market volatility and systemic fragility. Again, insolvency regimes became part of the packet of institutional reforms considered necessary to short-circuit the domino effect of financial failure that spread from corporate to global financial crisis. At once, therefore, leading creditor nations sought to stabilize financial systems and position themselves competitively vis-à-vis each other for entry into emerging credit markets.

The tension between a common interest in stability and a sectional interest in competitive advantage also marked the engagement of IFIs and professions. A unified global standard for insolvency regimes would reinforce a coherent, international financial architecture. Yet IFIs themselves competed over norms, practices, and the prestige of setting global and regional standards, not least, which international organization would take the ultimate prize of setting the global standard. Similarly, burgeoning trade relations expand markets for professional services in corporate liquidation and reorganization. However, the shape of insolvency regimes differentially benefits lawyers or accountants and restructuring specialists. For all the major actors in the insolvency field, therefore, the phase of national insolvency lawmaking nests competition within cooperation, thus producing uneasy relations of mutual support alongside incipient rivalry.

Given the scope of this new enterprise, the diversity of settings to which it would be applied, the rivalries among actors trying to forge a global standard, and not least, the deep embeddedness of substantive bankruptcy law in the traditions of nation-states, the prospects for agreement on global norms would seem to be low. Skepticism could as readily be found in professional circles as in scholarly expectations. Our task, therefore, is to explain why the dire prognostications of skeptics were unwarranted. Who were the actors that stepped into the legal and regulatory vacuum? How did they position themselves in relation to each other? And by what means did actors advance their respective technologies and scripts as candidates for a global standard? We shall refine and elaborate the interplay of technologies, legitimacy, and leverage we have already seen activated in the cross-border negotiations. We shall show how, as the stakes of a successful outcome rose, global actors invested heavily in scripts they thought best adapted to their own capacities and the prospect of acceptance.

The Logic of Action by International Actors

Through the early 1990s, regional and international organizations built institutions in transitional countries on an ad hoc basis. This is not to say that there were no continuities in their country-by-country initiatives, but these remained tacit, not explicit. The Asian Crisis signaled that an apparently regional phenomenon had global implications. Transitional and developing countries the world over presented the same problem—the need for a systematic approach. To take on the entire world required a shift from case-by-case remedies to the construction of global templates. In so doing, actors faced a conundrum.

On the one hand, actors encounter varieties of markets, varieties of capitalism. In the West varieties of capitalism produce different types of insolvency regimes. If the frame is widened to include nations as diverse as Japan, India, China, and Indonesia in Asia, as well as nations in Latin America, then the variety of markets multiplies. By the same logic so, too, should diversity increase among insolvency systems. Hence the combination of heterogeneous markets and heterogeneous modes of regulating those markets compounds the difficulties already confronted by regional institutions in Europe and Asia. On the other hand, international organizations confront their own institutional imperatives. Some relate to the evolving missions of the organizations themselves and, more particularly, of their legal departments. Others relate to the constantly shifting division of labor among potentially competitive organizations in the same legal field.

Actors

Five classes of actors mobilized to place their stamp on global scripts (Table 3.1). First, *clubs of nations* undertook global norm making after the Asian Financial Crisis. The G-7 charged the World Bank and other IFIs to begin building institutions that would forestall recurrences of the Asian Crisis elsewhere. The G-22, a club of "systemically important" nations, adopted a policy statement on the critical need for debtor-creditor regimes that might reduce the scope of crises and facilitate swift workouts of indebtedness. Second, *international financial institutions* were given frontline responsibility by the G-7 for developing global norms and facilitating their implementation. While this was a primary charge for the World Bank and International Monetary Fund, the call was also heard by the European Bank for Reconstruction and Development (EBRD) and the Asian Development Bank (ADB), whose members had been hardest hit by the financial shocks. Third, the two *international professional associations* already engaged in cross-border initiatives transferred their energies to the global project. In some respects they worked

TABLE 3.1 Global Norm-Making Initiatives and Technologies by Transnational Actors

Initiative/ Product	Legitimation Warrants	Diagnostic Instrument/ Approach	Formal Instrument/ Technology	Leverage
Clubs of Nations				
G-22	Economically significant states	World financial system	Principles	Persuasion
Organisation for Economic Co-operation and Development (OECD)	Quasi-representation Neutrality Expert warrants of participating organizations and nations	None	None	Persuasion Peer pressure
International Financial Institutions				
European Bank for Reconstruction and Development (EBRD)	Experience Expertise (narrow) Technical assistance Investment	National surveys	Surveys	Technical assistance Ratings for public and private lenders Implicit shaming
Asian Development Bank (ADB)	Experience Expertise (narrow) Technical assistance	National reports (national experts, consultants, ADB staff)	Standards	Technical assistance Public shaming
International Monetary Fund (IMF) *Insolvency Procedures*	Experience Expertise (narrow)	Internal reports; consultants	Normative model: Objectives Approved alternatives	Conditionalities for loans Technical assistance Evaluations

World Bank *Principles* and Assessment Templates	Experience Expertise (broad)	Assessment Templates/ Reports on the Observance of Standards and Codes (ROSCs)	Principles	Conditionalities for loans Technical assistance Evaluations
International Professional Associations				
INSOL Workout Principles	Technical expertise	None	Principles for multicreditor workouts	Technical authority
International Bar Association (IBA) Model Bankruptcy Code	Technical expertise	None	Model Law on Liquidations—harmonization of substantive law	Technical authority
IBA expedited procedures	Technical expertise	None		Technical authority
International Governance Organizations				
UN Commission on International Trade Law (UNCITRAL)	Representation Expertise	None	Legislative Guide	Persuasion Technical Authority Representative authority
Sovereign States				
United States	Expertise	None		Economic power Symbolic ascendancy Technical experience

SOURCE: Adapted from Halliday and Carruthers (2007b).

alone, promulgating their own standards. But, where possible, they sought partners—who also sought them. It is no accident that the G-22 Working Group on International Financial Crises relied heavily upon a draft of bankruptcy standards prepared by INSOL. Fourth, later on, *international governance organizations* joined the movement. In the case of the Organisation for Economic Co-operation and Development (OECD), this was primarily regional, in the OECD's regional Asian forums co-hosted with the ADB, World Bank, and national aid agencies. The ambition of UNCITRAL, last to join the movement, was to coordinate and ultimately integrate all the previous efforts into a global consensus. Fifth, and not least, *sovereign states*, most notably the United States, mobilized directly and indirectly, sometimes working bilaterally with developing countries but more often working multilaterally on the crafting of global norms.

In principle, such a phalanx of organizations and states could mobilize huge resources on behalf of this global project. In practice, the very organizations impelled to take a leadership role confronted numerous incapacities and organizational impediments.

Internally, the organizations confronted their own incapacity to cope with the range of variation in types of markets. They faced incapacities of knowledge. To "go global" requires a kind of intellectual work and fundamental analysis that most international organizations are not able to provide. Norm making about the implantation of new institutions is enormously complex. And harnessing that knowledge from outside organizations presents additional challenges, although the OECD, World Bank, and UNCITRAL showed some adeptness in doing so. The professional associations mustered contributors principally from advanced economies, and disproportionately in Europe and North America, to their private enterprises. However, even the largest IFIs have limited resources. The legal departments of IFIs, which had primary responsibility for bankruptcy lawmaking, did not have sufficient staffing capacity. To these incapacities can be added incapacities of time: the more time constrained an institutional mandate, where multilaterals must operate in financial emergencies, the less nuanced can be global institutional responses to local particularities.

Moreover, every global institution, and particularly multilateral development banks, operates in an external environment where it is subject to the shifting fortunes of the world economy, regional crises, and the financial vigor of the leading national economies. They respond to pressures from principal donors, shifting development agendas, and criticism from clients and borrowers (Mallaby 2004). At any moment these external pressures confront an institution's own inertia. The international organizations are constrained by their own history, mandates, and structure. On one side the challenge recurs for organizational elites to adapt their mandates, for instance, in response to exhaustion of an original function (IMF), or to criticism (World Bank) of current functions, or to new opportunities (Babb 2003; Mallaby 2004). On another side the staffing of international organizations poses the problem of how to maximize the value of skills, expertise, and creativity as mandates change. A critical turning point occurs in the development of the insolvency legal field, for instance, when Legal Departments in IFIs shift from their traditional service roles as in-house lawyers to service, surveillance, and law-making activities, which required quite different skills.

Technologies

The attributes of actors influence their choice of legal technologies. As an organizational imperative, to manage with the enormous pressure of potential collapsing economies, huge sums of money, and tiny windows of opportunity, IFIs are compelled toward technologies that permit efficient intervention. For instance, the more time pressured and shallow an institution's technical resources, the more likely it will need to develop standardized, or "one-size-fits-all" technologies that can be readily deployed in any new crisis, no matter where it occurs or in what circumstances. The less time pressured an institution, the less an excuse there is for not developing a differentiated intervention that reflects the reality of variations in economic and legal systems.

Private institutions have more flexibility in the invention and creation of technologies and, in so doing, can be a proving ground for public institutions (Halliday 1987). Moreover, private professional associations are composed of the specialists who have the advantage of presiding over implementation, the point where the practicality of norms gets proved in practice. This advantage is counterbalanced by the remoteness of private officials from power, by the non-self-executing character of their technologies.[1] Public international institutions have the advantage that nation-states comprise their primary constituencies, thus setting up a shorter distance from formulation to enactment of norms, on occasion through self-executing and binding technologies.

In the cross-border legal technologies we observed varieties of soft and hard law, mostly procedural in content. As such they sidestepped most of the difficult substantive and policy issues at the heart of insolvency regimes. In the more ambitious goal of formulating substantive global norms, two refinements occur. On the one hand we shall observe that normative standards are articulated not only by *prescriptive* principles and rules but also by *diagnostic* techniques (Table 3.1). The former promulgates positive standards, always based on a diagnosis, whether explicitly or not. The latter evaluates the state of play in a nation's laws or practice against criteria that may or may not be made explicit. Diagnosis and prescription can be given different weights. It is crucial to recognize, however, that implicit prescription can advance through explicit diagnosis—that diagnosis itself is a normative enterprise. The interplay of diagnosis and prescription can be seen across all types of technologies—principles, best practices, model laws, standards, and surveys, among others.

A further refinement in the development of technologies can be found in the formal properties of scripts themselves. This will be particularly evident in UNCITRAL's Legislative Guide on Insolvency, treated in the following chapter. But it can also be seen in each of the alternatives advanced by IFIs. International institutions have a repertoire of possibilities for the crafting of scripts. One critical decision rests on how to balance themselves between higher-order formulations and more specific recommendations. Some scholars argue that this decision is partly forced upon institutions in virtue of their composition and decision-making processes (Patchel 1993; Schwartz 2002; Schwartz and Scott 1995; Scott 1994). If captured by powerful interest groups, private legislatures, or their functional equivalents, can write precise rules. If locked in a stalemate among competing powerful actors, then rule-making bodies will opt for vague formulations. Other scholars observe that a decision on how to balance principles versus rules turns on choices made by organizations about how best to adapt to legal arenas (Braithwaite 2002). Those with simple regulatory demands in slow-changing environments without powerful interests can issue precise rules with good effect. Those complex arenas with fast-changing circumstances and powerful economic interests will obtain more legal certainty when they rely on general principles. But the choice is never zero-sum. Scripts may combine abstract and precise formulations in numbers of ways, as we shall see.

The significance of higher versus lower orders of abstraction becomes even more complicated when brought into juxtaposition with diagnosis versus prescription. For diagnosis, a broader and abstract standard has the benefit of accommodating much practical variability across diverse nation-states. But in so doing, it also allows more discretion for the evaluator and less precise guidance for implementers. For prescription, precise rules offer the illusion of precision for local enactors and implementers of rules, but they lose flexibility and adaptability in the process of implantation, a rigidity that almost ensures a transplant effect (Pistor et al. 2002). However, more abstract principles becoming the core of a global script permits not only adaptive flexibility by local implementers but also a formula for avoidance.

Legitimation

The formal properties of global technologies and scripts also include forms of self-validation. Global scripts may vindicate themselves by a rhetoric that impels acceptance by its readers. In this sense IFIs employ the scripts to legitimate rhetorically their claim for approval and adoption. This adds yet another element to the amalgam of bases for legitimation that have been identified for international organizations (Cronin and Hurd 2008; Hurd 2002, 2005, 2007, 2008a).

Each of the organizations that stakes a claim to the primacy of its global script already, before putting pen to paper, has tacitly or openly advanced its right to lead global norm making in terms of legitimation standards. Where possible, organizations emphasize their representative inclusion of constituencies to which norms are directed. Additionally, they frequently adopt procedures that provide at least the appearance of fairness in decision making. Their influence will be magnified if they can also show that they are likely to have an impact because they have a resume of effective prior initiatives.

We argued in Chapter 2 that a basis of legitimation based on representation must be extended in some international organizations beyond mere representativeness. In fact, representation itself is far more contestable than appears at first blush (Hurd 2005). It means quite different things to competing actors. But in international organizations where technical knowledge is critical, reliance on delegates who represent nation-states or interest groups is often not sufficient. Global norms will not be considered legitimate if the primary specialists in complex fields of knowledge are excluded. Thus, representation as a basis for legitimacy of international organizations that deal with complex fields must include both political and technical representation.

The legitimation struggles of international organizations play themselves out within the organizations themselves as well as in relation to external constituencies. Within IFIs the charge for leadership of norm creation lay within the legal departments of each IFI. But historically those departments were assigned a rather marginal service role where their technical expertise facilitated the real work of the economists and finance specialists at the heart of the institution. Lawyers in each institution needed to redefine their roles internally and to reconstitute their own departments. Moreover, they needed to convince the bankers, economists, and development specialists that they shared the economic ideology of the institution while offering their own distinctive value to the IFI's mandate.

Global organizations, especially multilateral quasi-public institutions, have multiple and often conflicting stakeholders (Barnett and Finnemore 2005; Mallaby 2004). Insofar as legitimacy also implies a subject that is oriented to the organization (Suchman 1995), the multiple stakeholders represent multiple potential sources of legitimacy. Organizational theory proposes that successful innovation depends in part on showing some isomorphism of the new with the old, of the innovation with the already accepted, in short, of the yet-to-be legitimate with the already legitimate (DiMaggio and Powell 1983). But in a division of labor this presents a complication. Each IFI and its legal department found itself in a tension between showing its similarities to others while carving out its distinct niche in the international "market" for normative technologies.

Persuading multiple stakeholders of the "rightness" of a deliberative process and technology suggests that various elements of the legitimation package will be directed to different constituencies. Representation of all nations in a deliberative chamber will be more persuasive to national lawmakers than to legal experts, just as the latter is likely to have more impact on professionals who implement law than the former. For the same reason, this multiplicity of stakeholders complicates the task of script writing, because they must appeal simultaneously to diverse constituencies. Thus, drafters of global scripts bear a heavy load. For acceptance by often conflicting stakeholders—internal IFI management, donor nations, private international bankers, recipient nations, experts—the script internalizes both substantive tensions in the norm-making field and varied rhetorical gestures.

Leverage

Legitimation conveys its own leverage in the form of persuasion. How international organizations choose to craft their scripts represents a judgment about what will produce a desirable outcome. But part of the legitimation problem for international organizations is posed precisely by the forms of leverage they have available. The challenge for the most powerful of the IFIs, the World

Bank and IMF, is that their immense leverage through financial conditionality is delegitimating for many national leaders, who resent the muscular intrusion of IFIs into domestic policymaking. To compensate for this loss of legitimacy, they may need to depend on other mechanisms to carry their own warrants of expertise and authority. The intrinsic merits of a particular model represent one possibility. The crafting of a global script to vindicate an IFI's orientation is another. Professional associations like INSOL and the IBA, as well as the OECD, cannot depend upon economic power or financial incentives to have their scripts adopted. They have neither. All the more they must rely upon the inherent value of their models, or the guarantees of expertise that are implicit in their formulation.

In brief, all international organizations have shortcomings that impede the adoption of their norms worldwide. They exist in a field of power where they may choose to cooperate or compete. One alternative is to go it alone and try to triumph through unilateral action. Another is to seek alliances—to wed expertise with hard power, or one kind of legitimation with another. Yet another is to constitute a division of labor where actors demarcate a particular territory in which they have mutually agreeable primary responsibility. The division of labor might be defined in terms of audiences, technologies, or types of scripts. Part of the empirical puzzle, therefore, is to discover how individual organizations negotiate their relationships with others in the same field and whether they define those relationships primarily in cooperative or competitive terms. What alliances emerge and why? Is a general consensus possible around an agreed division of labor? Or will the global norm-making enterprise result in multiple standards from competitive players in the global arena?

The scale of the challenge to create global norms for bankruptcy systems compelled IFIs and other global actors to experiment with rationalizing products that could produce convergence from a starting point of extreme diversity. More than this, however, they were compelled to come to terms with each other.

First Steps

International organizations quickened their pace of norm making and broadened their aspirations in the years following the collapse of the Soviet empire, a decade punctuated by national and regional debt crises, all of which portended the danger of a global financial crisis.

After the Fall of the Berlin Wall

In the years framed by the fall of the Berlin Wall in 1989 and the onset of the Asian Crisis in 1997, scattered initiatives appeared from professional groups and international governance organizations. The International Bar Association's Committee J on creditor-debtor law decided to move on from MIICA and the Concordat to the heart of substantive bankruptcy law itself. In the early 1990s several British and Continental lawyers spearheaded a project to create a Model Bankruptcy Code that restricted itself entirely to liquidation.[2] Cross-border measures would go so far as to permit coordination across frontiers, they reasoned. But ultimately convergence on a common regime would produce a preferable solution. Since liquidation is the bedrock of bankruptcy law, and the ideal of corporate rehabilitation at that time was still somewhat controversial, they narrowed the agenda to liquidation law alone.

The organizers from Denmark, Britain, and the Netherlands initially surveyed liquidation law in some twenty-five countries. From this information, they identified eight or nine topics and set up a task force, chaired jointly by a common law lawyer and civil law lawyer, on each topic. Compilations of subcommittee drafts were discussed at IBA meetings in New Delhi in 1997, Copenhagen in 1998, Barcelona in 1999, and Milan in 2000. But the effort never caught fire. Subcommittee drafts differed in quality and thoroughness. Some chose to postulate principles; others sought the specificity of model laws. Often disagreements between legal traditions were so deep that the divide could not be bridged. Not least, the enterprise failed to attract much support within the IBA, most notably from American lawyers who were largely absent. To them it also seemed regressive, since it did not treat rehabilitation of companies, which is at the heart of U.S. bankruptcy law. By the late 1990s, the project came to an end, overcome by other initiatives that were more expansive, better resourced, and more broadly supported.

INSOL, in the meantime, took a different course altogether. Centered in London, INSOL, in its earlier years, reflected the imprint of its origins—an affinity with the style of insolvency practice in Britain and many Commonwealth countries. Here it was not lawyers but accountants and insolvency practitioners who dominated bankruptcy practice. Accountancy-qualified and specialist insolvency practitioners were long accustomed to working with bankers to restructure companies short of bankruptcy or to liquidate them within bankruptcy (Carruthers and Halliday 1998). English insolvency practitioners were vocal in their aversion to lawyers and courts, partly because the practice was dominated by nonlawyers but also because lawyers and courts were thought to increase costs and delay resolution, both of which could be deadly to troubled companies. In addition, England had little history of rehabilitation of companies within the bankruptcy law. Its system was weighted toward creditors and their rights to seize assets of failing companies outside bankruptcy proceedings, again a recipe for corporate dismemberment.

In 1994 INSOL created within it a Lenders' Group—bankers experienced at corporate financial restructuring outside insolvency law.[3] Encouraged by the Bank of England, the leading workout banks in Britain met to form the core of this specialty forum within INSOL. Since England's 1986 insolvency legislation had not been very successful as a framework for restructuring companies, England's banks evolved a practice, coordinated by the Bank of England, to restructure troubled companies before they were forced into bankruptcy. Styled as "the London Approach," this informal out-of-court practice was quite simple in its basics (Armour and Deakin 2001; Flood 1995).[4] When a major company was headed toward collapse, the Bank of England wielded its extraordinary authority and called the company's principal creditor banks into a conference. Together they would hammer out a gentleman's agreement for restructuring the company's debt. This had all the merits that insolvency practitioners championed: the absence of lawyers and law, swift action before the company was too wounded to recover, coordinated action among potentially competitive creditors, and a morally binding solution.

Since corporate collapses were scarcely confined to England, and collapses in one country now more frequently spilled over into others, the Lenders' Group decided to globalize its local practice. It persuaded major accounting and law firms to write summary papers on informal practices in "major countries." Armed with these materials, the Group set out to discover if there were continuities across countries that might form the basis for a transnational protocol. They found considerable variation in specifics, but underlying these were several principles that accorded fairly well with the London Approach. Since too much specificity in rules would doom the enterprise to failure, they created a technology whose script was organized at two levels.

At the highest level of abstraction the INSOL Lenders' Group offered a "Statement of Principles for a Global Approach to Multi-Creditor Workouts," which presented eight, and later nine, Principles.[5] Principle One, for instance, read:

> Where a debtor is found to be in financial difficulties, all relevant creditors should be prepared to co-operate with each other to give sufficient time (a "standstill period") to the debtor for information about the debtor to be obtained and evaluated and for proposals for resolving the debtor's financial difficulties to be formulated and assessed, unless such a course is inappropriate in a particular case.

The Principles, asserted its sponsors, were binding among those who subscribed to them. At the second level, however, there were "nonbinding comments" and "a lot of commentary on best practice."[6]

Leaders of the INSOL initiative, including London bankers Terry Bond (HSBC) and Adrian Marriette (Barclays Bank), took the Principles on the road, touring Asia, the U.S., and elsewhere, seeking to persuade bankers, insolvency practitioners, and bankruptcy lawyers of the merits of adoption.[7] To these audiences they acknowledged that most countries already had some informal out-of-court procedures. The advantages of adopting Principles in common, they averred, were numerous: they would "reduce the learning curve, reduce cost and uncertainty, bring local and foreign parties closer together, add value to the process," and ultimately achieve "better returns to creditors than through insolvency," and, more fundamentally, "avoid more widespread economic damage." But this could only be accomplished if there were enforceable local insolvency laws.[8]

In the final analysis, however useful the Principles—and it remains an open question how applicable they are in markets and legal systems quite different from those in England (Meyerman 2000)—they emerged from a professional association that could be construed as having a vested interest in their adoption. Whatever the intrinsic merits of the Principles, their legitimacy relied upon the technical expertise of INSOL professionals, the Bank of England's international prestige, and INSOL's own modeling and persuasion. It seemed politically expedient, therefore, for INSOL to seek alliances with international organizations that wielded greater economic power and moral authority. INSOL turned to the IMF and World Bank, successfully urging both organizations to include or at least endorse its Principles in their own nascent global norm making. Later it would urge similar adoption by UNCITRAL.

In the meantime there were also reformist stirrings at the OECD. An umbrella organization of the world's strongest economies, the OECD has a Corporate Affairs Unit (Directorate for Financial, Fiscal and Enterprise Affairs) based in Paris, which is charged with improving the quality of corporate governance and corporate restructuring in nations around the world. In the early 1990s, the Unit, staffed principally by lawyers, initiated an effort to make the activities and financial transactions of corporate managers and owners much more transparent to creditors and investors. In the course of the 1990s, the crisis in the Russian economy drew the Corporate Affairs Unit into a revision of Russian insolvency law, which the OECD helped coordinate with the EBRD, and that in turn led to a broader global interest in insolvency, especially following the Asian Crisis.

The Global Mandate

When Thailand, Malaysia, Indonesia, and South Korea, the much-vaunted Asian Tigers, suffered severe economic reversals in 1997 and early 1998, the shock waves registered across the world, most notably in the financial capitals whose private and public lenders suddenly were also at risk. East Asia might be manageable, but if the collapse also brought down other midsized developing countries, such as Brazil and Mexico, a regional crisis could spread and produce a new world depression. This worst-case scenario kept the lights burning late at the IMF and World Bank and at the regional development banks.

While the U.S. and other major financial powers worked with private and public banks to meet the immediate threat from East Asia, the clubs of countries that set global economic agendas pushed for a longer-term response. For the Clinton administration, the crisis reinforced the need for a "global financial architecture," resting not only on transnational institutions but on robust national financial institutions. In their tighter interdependency, global financial markets and a global trading system become as vulnerable as their weakest links.

The G-7 in 1998 charged global regulatory institutions, notably the World Bank and IMF, to begin designing preventive mechanisms. Most precise for the bankruptcy field was the reaction of the G-22. Self-described as a group of the world's "economically significant" nations, the finance ministers and central bank governors of the G-22 formed three working groups on international financial architecture: (1) Transparency and Accountability, (2) Strengthening Financial Systems, and (3) International Financial

Crises.[9] Reporting in April 1998, the Working Group on International Financial Crises emphasized insolvency systems: "effective insolvency and debtor-creditor regimes were identified as important means of limiting financial crises and facilitating rapid and orderly workouts from excessive indebtedness" (G-22 1998a, 1998b).[10] Indeed, of the four main sets of recommendations made by the lengthy Report, two focused extensively on bankruptcy law. Said the Report:

> Recent events in Asia have highlighted the critical importance of strong insolvency and debtor-creditor regimes to crisis prevention, crisis mitigation and crisis resolution. Effective national insolvency regimes contribute to crisis prevention by providing the predictable legal framework needed to address the financial difficulties of troubled firms before the accumulated financial difficulties of the corporate sector spill over into an economy-wide payments crisis. Such a predictable framework is also essential to the orderly resolution of corporate financial difficulties, and thus is an essential element of any regime for orderly and cooperative crisis management.[11]

In addition to strong "laws," strong "insolvency regimes," and "necessary frameworks," the G-22 called for effective enforcement apparatuses, such as courts and tribunals, staffed by competent professionals, as well as incentives and appropriate frameworks for restructuring corporate indebtedness outside courts or government agencies.

However great its authority as a club of nations, the G-22 had limited technical resources. For these it turned to INSOL. The G-22 drew upon INSOL's expertise, and explicitly acknowledged its reliance, in the promulgation of a set of principles and key features of effective debtor-creditor regimes. It pronounced:

> Effective insolvency regimes maximise the ex post value of the firm, whether it is liquidated or reorganised; provide a fair and predictable regime for the distribution of assets recovered from debtors; and facilitate the provision of credit for commercial transactions by providing an orderly regime for the distribution of the proceeds of debtors' assets. (Chap. 2.5.1)

These Principles form the core of later scripts written by the IMF, World Bank, and UNCITRAL.

Altogether, proposed the Working Group, implementation of the G-22

Principles will improve the management of risk, send advance warnings of impending financial crises, solve debt problems in private financial markets, reduce spillover of financial crisis from one country to another, strengthen national financial institutions, stimulate sound credit decision making, improve creditor coordination, and reduce the frequency and severity of international financial crises. These Principles also recognize a fundamental shift in credit that occurred during the 1980s, from a small number of large international banks to large numbers of new debt instruments traded on markets, a shift that official institutions could no longer effectively regulate.

International Financial Institutions

The regional and global financial institutions each responded to the Crisis in its particular way, selecting its technology and crafting its scripts with varying balances of diagnosis and prescription, legitimation and leverage. These vary along two dimensions (Table 3.2). The first dimension concerned the form of the norms. Some IOs emphasized diagnostic instruments, whereas others moved directly to prescriptions. A "complete" repertoire of normative instruments combined both. The second dimension had to do with the explicitness of the norms. In some cases, IFIs made their diagnoses manifest. Countries could view their standings in relation to others in both Asia and Central and Eastern Europe (e.g., ADB, EBRD). But in other cases diagnosis was tacit (e.g., IMF, World Bank).[12] Similarly some IFIs, such as the EBRD, left their prescriptive norms implicit, whereas most others expressed them explicitly.

TABLE 3.2 Variations in Normative Scripts Created by
International Organizations

	Form of Norms	
Explicitness of Norms	*Diagnostic*	*Prescriptive*
Tacit	International Monetary Fund World Bank	European Bank for Reconstruction and Development
Manifest	European Bank for Reconstruction and Development Asian Development Bank World Bank	Asian Development Bank International Monetary Fund World Bank

Manifest Diagnosis, Tacit Prescription:
The European Bank for Reconstruction and Development

The youngest of the IFIs pioneered formal technologies for insolvency regimes. Founded in 1991, the EBRD was the first new European multilateral institution to be formed in the wake of the fall of the Berlin Wall and the demise of the Cold War (Weber 1994). The EBRD differentiated itself from existing regional and global IFIs in that it would lend only to countries that adopted liberal market economies and democratic political regimes. Lending focused on private sector development and especially on small and midsized businesses that were thought to drive liberal markets and politics (Weber 1994: 19–20).

The EBRD placed a strong emphasis on institutions. The EBRD's Transition Report in 1999 stated explicitly that the move from command to capitalist economies "concerns institutional change." The "central lesson of transition is that markets will not function well without supporting institutions, a state that carries through its basic responsibilities and a healthy civil society" (EBRD 1999: 4–5). The EBRD clearly understood that "establishing the appropriate laws and regulations is not sufficient. They must be embodied in the social norms, practices and behaviours of both government and the private sector—institutions need social capital and social foundations" (EBRD 1999: 9–11).

Although the Legal Department began its existence with a stronger emphasis on transactional than transitional lawyering, involvement of bank lawyers with local practitioners in the lending activities of the EBRD reinforced a Bank culture that not only acknowledged the "fundamental role of a sound and effective legal system" but implicitly understood that law-in-action, the behavior of law, mattered as much as law-on-the-books (Newburg 2001: 1). From 1991 to 1995 the Legal Department's core activity centered on servicing the investment relationships of the Bank. Yet in its 1991 colloquium on law reform, the Legal Department signaled that it would pursue programmatic initiatives (Newburg 2001: 1). Although EBRD lawyers undertook consultations on many reform initiatives in its first four years, the Legal Department institutionalized and expanded its reform effort by the establishment in 1995 of a team dedicated to law reform, which was subsequently expanded in 1997 to a Legal Transition Programme (Bernstein 2002: 3–4).[13] In pursuit of its ambition "to improve the investment climate in the Bank's countries of operations by helping to create an investor-friendly, transparent and predictable legal environment," the Legal Department created a group of lawyers who would coordinate reform efforts in six substantive areas—secured transactions, concessions, financial markets, telecommunications, corporate governance and company law, and insolvency law (Averch et al. 2002).[14]

Although the Programme undertook many specific initiatives across the region, the Legal Transition Survey had most significance for insolvency reforms in which the Bank had done relatively little (Bernstein 2002: 4–5).[15] The Survey covered all twenty-six EBRD countries of operation and several areas of law,[16] and it remained distinct from later IFI initiatives on insolvency in several respects.

Influenced by the Chief Economist within the Bank, by law and development ideas, and by the Bank's own investment experience, the EBRD, in classic sociolegal fashion, argued that pristine substantive law mattered little if it did not inform actual practice. The Survey therefore measured both *extensiveness* (whether a country covered a breadth of areas sufficient for bankruptcy law in a developed country and whether its coverage of each area conformed with the EBRD standards) and *effectiveness* (a judgment that "legal rules are clear and accessible and adequately implemented administratively and judicially").[17]

The conformity of countries to this regional standard was assessed on a five-point scale: laws and practice were comprehensive, adequate, barely adequate, inadequate, or detrimental. For instance, in 1999 a country would be ranked as "comprehensive," at the top of the scale, in these circumstances:

> Insolvency law [was] perceived as comprehensive and highly effective as [an] exit mechanism. Countries have insolvency legislation that is perceived as comprehensive and clear with respect to issues such as legal definition of insolvency, the role of the courts and trustees during the liquidation, the priorities of creditors and reorganization proceedings. Insolvency law is also perceived as being effectively implemented in almost all instances.[18]

The EBRD rated entire countries *numerically* on both implementation and effectiveness for a particular law such as insolvency.[19] Comparisons of all countries were then published in annual scorecards contained within a handsome publication, *Law in Transition*, which continues to be widely circulated within Central and Eastern European (CEE) and Commonwealth of Independent States (CIS) countries.

By taking repeated surveys, the EBRD purported to measure progress from year to year. This enabled the Legal Department to laud countries for moving forward or to chide them when they were in retreat. The commentary uses report-card language to flag a rise or fall in performance: "Kyrgyzstan's score has improved" or the "Czech Republic received a slightly lower rating" or "Bulgaria has had problems."[20]

The EBRD's instrument in the 1990s was predominantly diagnostic. It undertook the Survey without publicizing a detailed set of standards or the precise evaluation criteria, which in effect it drew from prevailing standards in advanced legal regimes.[21] Its publications include two very general sets of norms. One comprises the paragraph-long summary of a country. Another, in 1999, can be found in a more detailed three-page overview of main topics in a bankruptcy law. The EBRD acknowledged that these norms followed those being developed by the World Bank.[22] The overview briefly sketches with broad brush strokes some general parameters of both substantive law and institutions.[23]

At the outset, it advises countries to situate themselves somewhere along the continuum of debtor- versus creditor-oriented regimes.[24] The EBRD is not neutral about the direction of lawmaking on those five criteria. It advocates a balance of debtor and creditor interests. It argues for a combination of cash versus balance sheet tests for commencement, "given the relatively low standard of accounting practices in many transition economies." It insists that every liquidation law be accompanied by reorganization alternatives, anticipates the need for professionalized insolvency professions, and recommends the formation of specialized commercial courts where competent judges are given adequate discretion.

The EBRD's predominantly diagnostic technology employs a rhetorical structure that legitimates its standards in several ways.[25] The instrument appeals to a preponderance of practice in advanced countries or to what is "normal" in "industrialized economies' insolvency systems." Positive and negative exemplars of compliant nations are offered. For example, whereas the "1994 Bulgaria Law provides this clear priority for secured creditors," Ukraine has "extensive and time-consuming impediments" to filing a petition.

In 2002 the EBRD intensified and narrowed its evaluative approaches with the commissioning of a Legal Assessment Survey. Rather than rely on a survey of perceptions among multiple actors in a country, the EBRD commissioned two international leaders of insolvency reforms to appraise the formal law of bankruptcy in twenty-seven EBRD countries of operation.[26] The Legal Assessment Survey created norms based on "acceptable international standards and practice," said its authors, explicitly invoking other international organizations that, by 2002, had published their own standards and norms.[27] It assesses each country's laws against the standard, and then rates them on a scale.[28] As with the Legal Transition Survey, the EBRD intends to provide annual updates, which simultaneously track change and prod countries to close the gap between the standards and their rating.[29]

The EBRD therefore stood apart from later norm-producing IFIs. Compared to the IMF and World Bank, it placed its initial emphasis on evaluative instruments rather than the formulation of explicit norms and standards. Since it reported compliance *without* specifying publicly the standards against which compliance was measured, countries needed either to consult directly with the EBRD to discover the norms from which they deviated or they later were encouraged to consult the norms articulated by other IFIs.

Indeed, through its three phases of diagnostic activity (Legal Indicator Survey, 1997–2002; Insolvency Sector Assessment, 2002–present; Legal Indicator Survey, 2004–present),[30] the EBRD has forged what it characterizes as a "virtuous circle of legal reform." It begins with standards, it proceeds through diagnostic national assessments, it communicates results privately to governments and publicly in its dissemination vehicles, and these optimally lead to technical assistance by the EBRD.[31]

Throughout the publications and documents of the EBRD recurs a theoretical model that echoes the underlying ideology of all the IFIs. That model holds that certain attributes of legal environments contribute to financial behaviors that produce economic growth. The EBRD specifies the attributes of legal environments comprehensively. The kind of legal system needed to stimulate growth will consist of "sound" legal rules, based on internationally accepted principles, that are transparent and fair (Bernstein 2002: 2). Law will be predictable. Complementing law must be effective institutions to implement and enforce law; these institutions should be developed or upgraded either before or during reform of substantive law (Bernstein 2002: 7n20). Laws and institutions rely on a conducive legal culture (Corell 2002: 1). Together these attributes of the legal system will contribute to investment, sustainable economic development, and a "vibrant market economy." A secondary theme, occasionally sounded, is that what is good for the economy (independent judiciaries, respect for contracts and property rights) is also good for free societies (Corell 2002: 1). If this underlying philosophy is true for commercial law in general, it also applies to insolvency law, for, the argument goes, strong insolvency systems attract credit, and credit is a necessary building block for sustainable economic development.

Of all the IFIs, the EBRD during the development of the Legal Transition Programme has been most strongly influenced by interdisciplinary scholarship, most notably, sociolegal studies, development economics, law and development, and institutional economics. The result is an unusually nuanced approach to the fundamental tension between global uniformity and national particularities that stalks all IFI initiatives.

Manifest Diagnosis and Manifest Norms:
Asian Development Bank

The ADB was first into the arena with a systematic normative template, producing two reports on insolvency between 1998 and 2000. Founded in 1966, the Bank is owned by sixty-seven member countries, developing and donor, regional and nonregional,[32] with the goals of reducing poverty, promoting economic growth, supporting human development, and protecting the environment (Wee 2000). Although the Bank's two largest shareholders, Japan and the United States, account for some 30 percent of its subscribed capital, the culture and leadership of the Bank are strongly influenced by Japan.[33] The Bank extends mainly public sector but also some private sector loans for infrastructure development, totaling in 1999 almost $5 billion.[34] For many projects it obtains cofinancing from other private and development banks.[35] The Bank also makes a small number of direct equity investments.[36] In addition, it provides technical assistance grants for agricultural development, energy, finance, industry, social infrastructure, transportation, and communications, among others.[37] Through these grants the Bank most influences lawmaking.

While the Bank had offered minor technical assistance grants for law reform over decades, its law and development program took a leap forward in 1995 with the appointment of Barry Metzger as General Counsel. A partner of private investment bank Coudert Brothers, Metzger had long experience in Asia. As important, he was also part of a network of law and development intellectuals that revolved around the longtime China expert Jerry Cohen, at Harvard University.[38] After his appointment, Metzger nudged the Legal Department away from its primary focus on traditional lawyers' work and toward advisory, assistance, and development roles (Metzger 1996). Activities in lawmaking became more intensive, comparative, programmatic, and prescriptive. The groundwork was laid when the ADB became the first multilateral institution to adopt a policy on "good governance" and, more precisely, on "the important contribution which the institutional framework in a country makes to such a country's ability to achieve sustainable economic development." To attain the standards of good governance, namely, transparency, predictability, accountability, and participation, the ADB insisted on the importance of legal rules, legal institutions, and legal personnel (Metzger 1996).

Metzger also confronted the most fundamental question of law and development by funding a project to evaluate whether law, in fact, does matter for development. Scholars at Harvard University analyzed six Asian countries during the period 1960–1995[39] and concluded that law reforms can indeed make a positive contribution to economic development when they are consistent with economic policy (Metzger 1996; Pistor and Wellons 1999). As late as 1995 insolvency law was not considered sufficiently important to be included in the ADB's law and development study. Yet in 1995 and again in 1996 the ADB funded two projects to support China's efforts to restructure insolvent state enterprises.[40]

The ADB's turn from a case-by-case to an evaluative and normative instrument came with a project initiated in 1997 to evaluate systematically the state of bankruptcy regimes across Asia.[41] Turning again to Ron Harmer, together with John Lees, an experienced Hong Kong insolvency practitioner,[42] the ADB surveyed eleven economies whose bankruptcy laws reflect quite different traditions (Pistor and Wellons 1999).[43]

To ensure systematic comparisons, the ADB created an extensive checklist of questions to put to country specialists. In its 1999 preliminary Report, the ADB forthrightly criticized countries for "the lack of frameworks for the systematic restructuring of debt" or of efficient mechanisms for liquidation of companies. It predicted that in the aftermath of the Asian Crisis this would "pose impediments to economic recovery, complicate the rehabilitation of financial sector institutions, stifle foreign investment, and inhibit the growth of the region's domestic debt markets."[44] Moreover, said the Report, the Asian Crisis reinforced the inadequacies of court systems and professions and the weakness of enforcement apparatuses.

Nevertheless, the Report drove a careful path between universalist and particularistic extremes. On the one hand, it fully acknowledged that considerable variation existed among insolvency regimes in advanced countries and that some problems manifest in developing countries, such as the successful prosecution of corporate fraud, are also present in advanced countries.[45] On the other hand, it argued both for commonality in the commercial environment of most insolvency regimes and for recognition that basic principles of all insolvency regimes might be similar, though implementation might vary considerably.[46]

The Report explicitly acknowledged that cultural influences might engender resistance in Asia to law as the arena in which to handle either liquidation or reorganization. "The majority of the local studies clearly evidence that the financial difficulty of a corporation is, more often than not, accompanied by an attitude of concealment and denial on the part of the owners and managers." Owners feel a "stigma" is attached to financial failure that brings "business and social disgrace."[47] These limitations, proposed the Report, might be overcome "by recourse to modern forms of both formal and informal rescue processes."[48] The Report provided summary accounts of how the insolvency systems of each country, formal and informal, dealt with liquidation and reorganization and showed particular interest in the recent development of informal processes, a concession to a distinctively Asian way of conducting business.

The structure of financing and corporate organization also led to Asian deviations from the structures of Western countries. The Report observes that banks in several countries are able to establish significant equity holdings in corporations, many corporations and corporate groups are controlled by families, and the conglomerate form is widespread. In addition, political factors might be directly implicated in business, whether through partisan ownership of major companies or through government-directed lending to financial sectors or even specific firms.

While the 1999 Report began to lay out the "essential elements of rescue" and the basic elements of informal workout processes,[49] the final Report (ADB 2000) takes the bold step of establishing "good practice standards." The ADB admits to the difficulties of "universal concepts," an admission reinforced by its grouping of countries by legal heritages.[50] Yet it affirms its earlier belief that there are "common basic policies" and "principles" across all countries irrespective of legal tradition or stage of economic development. Its logic is that these common features can be identified and from them can be crafted "well established, widely accepted and respected standards" that will be relevant, suitable and practical.[51]

The ADB consultants approached standard setting from two angles. One involved the inductive development of standards through empirical comparisons of successful and unsuccessful systems in Asia with extrapolations from successful systems in other parts of the world. From another angle, however, the principles might be tested by a pragmatic standard: will they deliver the economic and commercial goals of good insolvency law, whether to serve microeconomic processes (e.g., removing uncompetitive firms from the market, maximizing value of assets); satisfy broader commercial needs of creditors for certainty, predictability, stability, efficiency, and equitable treatment; and lessen unemployment or encourage commercial morality?[52] In short, will an insolvency regime deliver the functional results of a vibrant, growing economy?

On this dual foundation, the ADB erected a set of thirty-three "good practice standards" that cover core topics of bankruptcy law.[53] These are at a fairly high level of abstraction, but they are certainly more specific than either INSOL's Principles or the G-22's governing debtor-creditor Principles. Each standard is expressed as a "should" statement, such as Good Practice Standard 1, "An insolvency law regime should clearly distinguish between, on the one hand, personal or individual bankruptcy and, on the other, corporate bankruptcy." Given the formulation and justification of the standard, the ADB then rated every country on a three-point scale. Does it *apply* the standard? Does it *apply in part* the standard? Or does it *not apply* the standard? The evaluations were presented in a clear table and summarized for every country at the end of the Report. Following the categorical ratings of each country for each standard, the Report provided summary observations, commented on the experiences of particular countries, and sometimes made recommendations.

The Legal Department of the ADB does not have heavy financial leverage to exercise over countries in its region. As a result, it must rely more heavily on the intrinsic form of its methodology and rhetorical expression in its script. The ADB obtains some symbolic leverage by appropriating a cultural process indigenous to the region—the power of losing or gaining "face." Because standards are publicized and each country is publicly ranked on each standard, all countries can see whether they perform comparatively well or poorly. For countries that perform poorly, their officials and legislators are shamed before their regional peers. Thus, simultaneously, the ADB subjects every country to expert review (what the ADB wants) and peer pressure (how other countries perform).

It is clear that the ADB Report also shares the wider consensus of a shift toward reorganization, but it champions this less than the other IFIs do. There are traces of an Asian exceptionalism to the Report, a sense that out-of-court mechanisms may be preferable to in-court processes, that courts and lawyers are not the optimal institutional locus in countries where law historically has been marginal to social and economic ordering, that key institutions (e.g., courts, professions) are underdeveloped, and that the threat of liquidation must be severe enough to induce debtors to restructure their companies. Of all the IFI reports, the ADB Report stands farthest from the influence of American law and practice.

Tacit Diagnosis, Manifest Norms:
The International Monetary Fund
Like the EBRD, the IMF had been providing country-by-country advice on insolvency reforms for transitional nations through the 1990s. The Asian Crisis and the urging of the G-22 compelled the Legal Department toward creation of a broader policy product. In a shift of emphasis from a reactive to a preventive orientation, the IMF moved from its iterations of country initiatives, which were diagnostic and prescriptive on an ad hoc basis, to a higher level of rationalization, in which experiences were codified in a normative code.[54]

The IMF has a global mandate since it is a lending institution of last resort for countries with critical balance-of-payment problems. As a result, any set of norms must be able to encompass the full range of cross-national variability. Yet, ironically, although it is the world's leading multilateral lending institution, its internal resources are limited. The Legal Department's staff was small in 1997, rarely are country resident staff available as resources, and in the typical situation the IMF has little time, since it characteristically functions in emergency conditions. Each staff lawyer must cover many countries. At the same time, its external constraints are substantial, for the IMF is linked closely to the U.S. Treasury Department, its largest donor, and its headquarters are located in Washington, D.C., a stone's throw from Treasury and the White House. Further, many of the IMF's largest donors vary in their type of capitalism and correlative type of insolvency regime. Altogether these place the IMF in a field of countervailing forces. Most important for our purposes, however, the IMF has enormous direct leverage over countries in emergency circumstances, for it can set conditions of compliance in order to secure release of moneys to a country. All this would suggest that the IMF will be pushed toward a homogeneous standard and needs to invest less heavily in persuasive rhetorical stratagems.[55]

While IMF interventions in emergency situations are its most visible activities, in no small part because they attract criticism for its economic prescriptions and use of conditionality as a weapon (cf. Stiglitz 2002), it can also exercise influence through several other mechanisms. One is the so-called Article IV review that the IMF is mandated to carry out regularly on all its member countries. This report of a country's macroeconomic status can also include an appraisal of those legal institutions that affect the economy.[56] Here its principal leverage is persuasion with a measure of shaming, since edited versions of Article IV reports are now made public. In addition to, and sometimes informing, the Article IV reports, the IMF has teamed up with the World Bank to provide Reports on the Observance of Standards and Codes (ROSCs) in twelve areas of commercial activity.[57] These are detailed analyses of a country's regulatory codes. Both the evaluative instrument and the subsequent reports are kept confidential. Finally, the IMF can offer technical assistance, although on a tiny scale compared to most other IFIs. Given this bundle of potential interventions in a nation's economic and legal affairs, therefore, economic coercion can be brought into play only at the extreme. Otherwise, the IMF must rely on modeling, persuasion, and shaming. All this, notwithstanding its function as a lender of last resort, may cast a long shadow over a country. It can behoove prudent national leaders to bring their laws and institutions into conformity with IMF standards as insurance in the event of some future call upon IMF funds.

In 1999 the IMF Legal Department published a booklet entitled *Orderly and Effective Insolvency Procedures* (colloquially labeled the "Blue Book" in virtue of the color of its cover; hereafter *Insolvency Procedures*) (IMF 1999). *Insolvency Procedures* was created in the first instance as a coherent statement for IMF lawyers who were fanning out across the world seeking to upgrade insolvency systems. Implicitly, however, it had an audience inside the Fund— the economists who dominated the Fund's professional staff. *Insolvency Procedures* effectively makes the claim that lawyers and law matter. Insolvency regimes, it shows, affect macro- and microeconomic processes and affect the vulnerability of nations to crises.[58] By educating economist institution builders, the Legal Department legitimated its own distinctive contribution to IMF interventions.

Although *Insolvency Procedures* was designed principally as an internal document, the Legal Department well recognized its value as an aid to policymakers in developing institutions. The distillation of IMF interventions in developing countries might accomplish three goals: it would show why insolvency reform is relevant to a policymaker, not only for resolving a crisis but for promoting growth; it would identify issues that every insolvency system must address; and it would articulate key policy choices, with their negative and positive consequences.[59]

The opening lines of *Insolvency Procedures* immediately pose the economic benefits of good insolvency law. The first words of the Foreword rest the claims on "experience" of the Fund in the ways "an effective insolvency system" will be a "pillar" of the domestic banking system, the "critical role" it plays in dealing with problems of insolvent state-owned enterprises, the mechanisms by which it enables "adequate private sector contribution" to the resolution of financial crises, and the incentives and framework it provides to effect negotiation among debtors and creditors "in the shadow" of the law.[60] That is, the most intractable and dangerous problems confronted by IMF economists—systemic instability in banking systems, privatization, recapitalization, and orderly debt servicing—can all be ameliorated by good law.

This argument is reinforced in the initial paragraphs of the Introduction: "Recent experience has demonstrated the extent to which the absence of orderly and effective insolvency procedures can exacerbate economic and financial crises." If creditors cannot be paid, future credit will be "adversely affected." Without "orderly procedures," debtors' rights will be at risk. Good insolvency law will foster growth and competitiveness and may even prevent economic crises. Hence the claim for insolvency law rests firmly on fundamental issues for economists and policymakers: prevention of economic crisis, stimulation of markets, economic growth, and recovery from economic crisis.[61]

This lawyers' brief for integral involvement in market building through lawmaking then turns didactic. Insolvency law accomplishes this, argue the IMF lawyers, in two main ways "that are generally shared by most systems." "Most systems" of insolvency law pursue the objective of "allocation of risk among participants in a market economy in a predictable, equitable, and transparent manner."[62] In addition, an insolvency system is designed "to protect and maximize value for the benefit of all interested parties and the economy in general." Rehabilitation or reorganization of companies offers a significant alternative for countries to pursue this goal.[63] Effectively, therefore, the lawyers weave tight links between a highly instrumental conception of the law and what it can do for economies in normal and extreme circumstances.

Insolvency Procedures does not rest its auspices on IMF experience alone. It legitimates its normative prescriptions on two grounds. On the one hand, the IMF assures its audience that prescriptions in *Insolvency Procedures* are consistent with the wave of institutional initiatives by multilateral organizations. It "builds upon" and is "consistent with" the G-22 Principles. By acknowledging in its Preface the comments it has received from other international organizations—the World Bank, OECD, EBRD, and International Finance Corporation (IFC)—it does more than extend a courtesy. The Legal Department informs internal and external audiences that *Insolvency Procedures* stands in solidarity with its institutional peers and implies that it expresses a convergence of experience and opinion.

On the other hand, the IMF's external validation rests on expert legitimation. For reasons of efficiency and economy, the Legal Department relied on seven distinguished international leaders for commentary. Careful choice allowed the IMF to cover differences among regimes in advanced countries and to draw upon the combined experience of key participants in many national and international initiatives. Manfred Balz, for instance, was a drafter of the new German insolvency law, the former Chairman of the Group on Bankruptcy of the EU Council, and General Counsel of Deutsche Telekom. He is a frequent consultant to the IMF on insolvency reforms in developing countries. Richard Gitlin, an American, is styled a specialist in transnational insolvency law, but Gitlin and his firm had participated in some of the most notable early cross-border cases and had been counsel to the Indonesian government during the Crisis. Professor Junichi Matsushita is a leading insolvency expert from Japan and a delegate from Japan to UNCITRAL. Professor Jean-Pierre Sortais from France specializes in insolvency law. Professor Jay Westbrook, University of Texas at Austin, was co-head of the U.S. delegation to UNCITRAL on Cross-Border Insolvency, and the Reporter on the North American American Law Institute (ALI) project to harmonize insolvency law. One of Britain's most distinguished insolvency lawyers, Philip Wood, has written widely on insolvency developments in many countries. And Professor Christoph Paulus from Humboldt University is a distinguished comparative lawyer who specializes in insolvency. This selective consultation of experts from all the leading economies further ensured that the IMF's dominant stockholders were represented. Alongside these selected practitioners and scholars, *Insolvency Procedures* acknowledges the involvement of the world's main peak association, or association of associations, of insolvency practitioners, INSOL.

The Legal Department makes no pretense to be democratic, representative, or broadly consultative. Those values are beyond its organizational
modus operandi and its internal resources. As a result, the IMF involved no
representatives of countries to whom this product would be directed. The
legitimating cluster of values rests entirely on professional expertise and the
implication of multilateral cooperation.[64] Ultimately, it is a lender's product
for a borrower audience.

Insolvency Procedures begins with general objectives and a list of common
issues that it asserts all insolvency regimes, of whatever legal and historical
provenance, must confront: a substantive legal framework and an institutional framework.

The institutional framework includes courts, insolvency professionals,
and supporting professionals. *Insolvency Procedures* deals relatively little with
institutions, despite the institution-building efforts of the IMF in Asia and
elsewhere. But it warns that the substantive law must be tailored to the institutional competency of a system. The more discretion the law allows, the
better its infrastructure needs to be.[65] This suggests the concession to the level
of legal development that is not expressly articulated but nevertheless recognizes the extreme variability of markets and legal systems to which insolvency
reforms are being urged.

The legal framework incorporates policy choices around nine substantive
issues and related procedural matters. The substantive issues are construed
with universal application and broad-brush alternatives. Thus, every system
must "identify the debtors that may be subject to insolvency proceedings,"
and the two main alternatives are either to include all debtors of any type or
to exclude some debtors, such as financial institutions or state-owned enterprises. Similarly, a country must decide who will manage a company when it
is being reorganized: the management in place, a court-appointed administrator, or some combination of these.

Within the chapters on the legal framework, *Insolvency Procedures* follows
a similar pattern: (1) an opening statement of broad objectives that policymakers should strive to attain, followed by (2) detailed discussions of specific
elements of an effective system, followed in turn by (3) a "principal conclusion" that summarizes the preference of the Legal Department. A principal
conclusion is expressed as a principle, for example: "The law should enable
creditors to play an active role in the insolvency proceedings. To that end, it
should allow for the formation of a creditors' committee, with the cost of such

a committee being an administrative expense."[66] The principal conclusions approximate in form the standards expressed by the ADB Report. Altogether *Insolvency Procedures* offers eleven conclusions on liquidation, eleven on rehabilitation, three on institutions, and one on cross-border procedures.

The principal conclusions posit certain irreducible, minimal core features of insolvency systems that are justified by their economic effects and their usage in model legal systems. In this respect *Insolvency Procedures* pushes countries toward convergence. Yet the conclusions equally clearly signal that alternative variants will be acceptable beyond the threshold criteria. This two-level structure is formally expressed in consistent distinctions between categorical recommendations ("should" or "must") and optional recommendations ("may," "consider," or "advisable," etc.). Such a format protects the Legal Department from the epithet of a "one-size-fits-all" solution and implicitly indicates to the economists that they might expect more variation in the substance of law than might be usual in economic prescription.

To cope with enormous cross-national variation, however, the Legal Department does simplify its task by expressly excluding many topics from its purview. It makes its problem manageable and limits the variance it confronts by excluding consumer bankruptcy, governmental actors, and financial institutions. It does not treat the relationship of insolvency to corporate governance or to secured transactions. It deals little with problems of institutions, especially judiciaries. And it treats much less extensively than the ADB with "out-of-court" or informal procedures. Above all, it seeks to sidestep "social or political" considerations—those difficult issues of public policy and party ideology that might have destined any insolvency initiative to early defeat.[67]

What are the theoretical premises and propositions that infuse this script? The language clearly signifies that the IMF conceives of bankruptcy law not as a substantive or procedural matter only but as a "system" embedded within state institutions (such as courts), within economic negotiations in the shadow of the law, and in markets for professional services. The IMF's orientation is distinctly instrumental: systems are "designed" to serve economic goals and not merely inherited, so it is implied, as an institutional given. Although *Insolvency Procedures* periodically refers to "efficiency," arguably the dominant criterion of the economists, it differentiates itself from economic theory by offering two standards for lawyers—orderliness and effectiveness, as noted in the book's title.[68] Moreover, it signals from time to time the problem of insolvency's distributive implications. The beneficiaries of an "effective and orderly" regime are not simply creditors but also potentially shareholders and management, as well as employees. In this respect, the Legal Department clearly prefers those insolvency regimes that seek to balance the rights of all parties in the credit network over those that champion the secured creditors—usually large banks—at the expense of others.

The IMF therefore advances a strong substantive theory of insolvency that advocates a pro-rehabilitation philosophy, although the Fund is quick to add that reorganization must be anchored in solid liquidation law. Based on pitfalls in the Fund's own institution-building experience, *Insolvency Procedures* states there must be a way to get debtors to negotiate in a reorganization and this can best be achieved by threatening something worse—the breakup of their entire company. The institutional turn of the Fund is reflected in the Legal Department's insistence that formal institutions matter. A strong institutional infrastructure is even more important than whether a regime falls on either side of the old pro-debtor versus pro-creditor divide among legal systems.[69] This includes officials—"judges and administrators that are efficient, ethical, and adequately trained."[70] Formal systems matter not only in their own right but because "our painful experience is that unless you have a formal system with a minimal leverage you will not get an effective out-of-court settlement."[71]

Ultimately, however, the Legal Department aligns itself with pragmatic sociolegal theory and the EBRD in its belief that "law-in-action," not drafting elegance, must be the crucial test. "A pro-debtor law that is applied effectively and consistently will engender greater confidence in financial markets than an unpredictable pro-creditor law."[72] The notion recurs that markets require predictability; and if creditors must choose between good substantive law with unpredictable administration and less appealing substantive law with highly predictable results, the latter will be preferred.

The Legal Department's institution-building experience leads it to a rather sophisticated notion of behavior in the shadow of the law. In part this is a matter of expediency. In crisis situations, formal institutions, especially those that are underdeveloped, cannot handle the volume of cases. And if institutional structures are not well developed, or there is a preference in the commercial culture to proceed informally, then out-of-court procedures make sense. Thus, the Fund strongly advocates out-of-court frameworks so long as they are anchored to an effective and predictable in-court procedure. As befits experienced lawyers, they perceive that law casts a long shadow over the economy, well beyond the small fraction of cases that ever turn up on its dockets. This realist view of formal legal versus informal near-legal processes echoes the ADB's emphasis on out-of-court agreements, especially in countries where formal institutions have neither the competence nor the trust required by financial markets.

The underlying theory of law and economic development in the Blue Book echoes the underlying consensus among IFIs that good law broadly understood increases credit, which stimulates economic activity, which in turn produces economic growth (and, by implication, reduces poverty). This chain of reasoning applies to insolvency law since an "effective law" imposes discipline on debtors; it provides an alternative to state intervention and financial support (thus supporting privatization and market self-correction); it enables financial institutions to protect their assets (and thus reduce their vulnerability and prospective reliance on state bailouts); and it enables private creditors to contribute to resolution of a crisis (and thus removes part of a burden from the Central Bank or multilateral lenders of last resort).[73] The normative framework, therefore, enables the penetration of law deep into the fabric of the economy.

If *Insolvency Procedures* shares a theory of law and economy with the EBRD and ADB, it also indicates the cumulative impact of an emerging division of labor among international organizations. Not only does the IMF acknowledge the input of other international organizations and INSOL but it explicitly incorporates UNCITRAL's Model Law on Cross-Border Insolvency into its final recommendation. This is a mutually beneficial move. For UNCITRAL it links a model law without any kind of financial leverage to an institution that is renowned for applying such leverage. For the IMF it legitimates its position by adopting a global model that was formulated by the most representative process available in global decision making—the forums of the United Nations.

Finally, it is clear that the IMF had been engaged in case-by-case diagnosis of countries before *Insolvency Procedures* was written. *Insolvency Procedures* provides an implicit standard for a diagnostic instrument that the IMF did not at that time formalize, at least for public consumption. The IMF Legal Department did commit itself, however, to the joint development of a ROSC on national insolvency systems in collaboration with the World Bank, which would have primary responsibility for its design. Thus, *Insolvency Procedures* set up a manifest set of norms against which informal and, later, formal diagnostic instruments would operationalize.

Manifest and Tacit Diagnosis, Manifest Norms: The World Bank

Last into the field of insolvency norm production came the World Bank. The Bank began to draft its norms at the time that the IMF and ADB had already published theirs, which enabled the Bank to benefit from work already done and to differentiate itself from other institutions. Indeed, the Bank's lead lawyer on this project used its later arrival in the field as a potential springboard for the Bank to bring prior efforts to fruition in a global synthesis. But this opportunity confronted a challenge: precisely when the Bank began to draft its offering of a global script, a vigorous movement was under way from international professional associations and other IFIs to shift the locus of norm making away from IFIs to the United Nations Commission on International Trade Law. The Bank thus faced the choice between differentiating its product from that of UNCITRAL, proceeding in parallel and competitively with UNCITRAL, or yielding the stage to UNCITRAL. In the short term, the Bank hedged its options, in part because some of its consultants were convinced UNCITRAL had no reasonable likelihood of producing a substantive model law, given the vast divergences across national bankruptcy systems.[74]

The belated entry of the Bank into the promulgation of insolvency norms remains a puzzle since the mandate of the Bank itself, and the size of its Legal Department, might well have brought it into the arena much earlier. From its origins in the Bretton Woods agreement, the World Bank was charged with the alleviation of poverty, although how to do so has never failed to be contentious. Its geographical reach extends to all developing nations. In addition to having field offices in many countries, it supports resident staff with regional teams located at the Bank's Washington headquarters near many of the global actors that impinge most heavily on its mission and resources. As well as building physical infrastructure, the Bank now embraces a panoply of issues—education, women's issues, health, government, the environment, and law, to mention but a few. The Bank's long-term programs are punctuated by involvement in emergency financial situations, where it partners with the IMF and regional banks in structural adjustment loans.[75] Commonly the Bank jump-starts reforms with adjustment loans and then follows them through long-term development projects.

As befits an institution committed to long-term change, the Bank's Legal Department has been larger and more reform oriented than any other IFI. During the 1990s, the Bank accepted the theory that sustainable development requires a comprehensive process that must also include legal and judicial reforms, and it invested heavily in both (Dakolias and Said 1999; Dezalay and Garth 2002; Garth 2002; Shihata 1995).[76] This growing awareness of law's impact on markets, inequality, economic development, and governance became intense with the sharp shocks to the international system from the mid-1990s. Yet it took the Asian Crisis to jolt the Bank's Legal Department into the institution building of bankruptcy systems.

As the legal side of the bank moved heavily into institutional reforms, the private financing and investment unit in the Bank was already seasoned by the debt crises of the 1990s and their impact on corporate restructuring.[77] In Ecuador, Mexico, and Venezuela, Bank officials began to develop models for corporate restructuring that could be implemented swiftly and forcefully in the event of a sharp contraction of the economy and widespread corporate insolvency. Originating from the private sector development group at the Bank, the corporate restructuring specialists advocated the creation of special administrative agencies outside the legal system that could quickly effect debt restructuring agreements between debtors and creditors. The Jakarta Initiative (see Chapter 5) is one such instance.

The Asian Crisis brought together the legal and private sector development sides of the Bank in two mutually supporting ways. For the first time, senior members of the Legal Department were included in the country crisis teams. Above the demands of crisis resolution itself, the Bank heeded the call of the G-7 and G-22 for IFIs to pursue comprehensive legal and institutional responses to corporate failure. It began by appointing an American corporate insolvency lawyer to head its response.

World Bank **Principles**   Since it was last to arrive in the field of designing global norms, the Bank began immediately to differentiate itself from previous IFI efforts, while diplomatically acknowledging the shoulders on which it stood. It decided to develop two technologies in tandem—a set of global norms entitled *The World Bank Principles* and two diagnostic instruments, one public and one private.

The Bank sought to legitimize its products by combating the Bank's general reputation for top-down heavy-handedness through a consultative procedure that spread the net widely. The earliest drafts of the *Principles* are fulsome in recognition of the Bank's indebtedness to efforts by the IMF, ADB, and G-22. They acknowledge the value of consultations with leaders in the world's main associations of professionals—INSOL and the IBA. The Bank turns other development banks into "partners" and collaborators.[78] Implicitly, this approach contrasts with those of the other multilaterals, whose products had been crafted by staff and a very small circle of consultants. The Bank similarly cast its net broadly to scholarly and practitioner communities by setting up an elaborate advisory, task force, and working group structure that embraced some of the world's most distinguished practitioners, insolvency law reformers, and academic commentators and no less than eight working groups of judges, practitioners, regulators, bankers, academics, and international civil servants, overwhelmingly from advanced economies.[79]

The Bank Initiative followed an iterative process from 1999 through 2005. Successive drafts were circulated and discussed in forums throughout the world by bankruptcy experts and national officials.[80] Usually a conference began with an overview of the current draft of the *Principles*. National experts from the region followed with descriptions of bankruptcy law and practice in their countries and, sometimes, how closely these conformed to the *Principles*. This consultative process demanded careful scrutiny precisely because it sought to achieve multiple, potentially contradictory, goals. The Bank Initiative clearly endeavored to dispel fears that yet another program would be developed ex cathedra by a deep-pocketed international institution under strong influence from the U.S. to then be imposed heedlessly on weak, poor nations. It showed itself open to expert opinion, both official and private, and exuded responsiveness to comments on its several drafts. The regional forums and their "country delegations" allowed the Initiative to imply something very close to democratic or legislative deliberation. In its search for "international best practice," the extensive consultation gave some verisimilitude to its claim for "the highest level of consensus."[81]

In fact, while the Bank projected a patina of consultation to the extremes, many of those consulted had little confidence that their reactions mattered much at all. The breadth of consultation invoked the image of a legislative process in which each draft Principle was reviewed by a representative body. In fact, the Bank retained complete discretion over the contents of the *Principles*, constrained only by the force of expert opinion outside the Bank and the pressures from the U.S. Treasury, with the ultimate requirement for formal approval by the Executive Boards of the Bank and the IMF. This process cleverly positioned the Bank product vis-à-vis all others in the international field: compared to the EBRD, ADB, and IMF, the Bank appears almost profligate in its range of consultation; yet preemptively the Bank might forestall its only likely competitor for an authentically legislative process in the global community, UNCITRAL.[82] Evidence indicates this was precisely how the Initiative was presented to the U.S. Treasury, which maintained continuing interest in development of a single global standard acceptable to the U.S., and how the Initiative was presented to higher management at the Bank. Extensive consultation was tantamount, it was implied, to global democratic approval.[83]

The Initiative differentiated itself from other global products by the expansiveness of its mandate. Earlier drafts of the *Principles* emphasized the *systemic* nature of its enterprise. While it included the substantive topics common to other enterprises, it went far beyond the IMF's and ADB's black-letter-law focus to include all the institutions necessary for the functioning of a fully defined insolvency regime. These included systems for enforcing security rights, courts, out-of-court procedures, government-restructuring agencies, and professions.[84] Unlike others, it treated systemic crises and bank insolvencies. The Initiative explicitly covered enterprises in the private market and state-owned enterprises. In other words, the World Bank Initiative fully amplified the substantive and institutional aspects of insolvency that the EBRD originally treated in its survey of comprehensive (substantive law) and effectiveness (implementation).[85]

Compared to the ADB and IMF norms, which were published in 1999 without widespread consultation, several drafts of the *Principles* were produced by the Bank between 1999 and 2005. They changed not only in form but content. These changes reflected expert feedback, changes in the competitive environment, and diverse pressures that shifted over time. Initially, numbers of international specialists complained that the *Principles* adhered too closely to U.S. practices, an allegation that also detracted from their legitimacy, let alone potential effectiveness. By early 2002 it became clear that UNCITRAL's Working Group on Insolvency was going to proceed with a global standard on substantive bankruptcy law, and optimism was rising that it might be successful. This forced leaders of the Bank's Initiative either to concede the substantive part of their norm making to UNCITRAL or to compete with it. As other institutions later discovered, it decided to compete with an alternative technology that embraced a more expansive agenda. The substantive leanings of the *Principles* also changed, tilting away from an evenhanded balance of debtors' and creditors' rights in favor of creditors' rights.

The form of the Bank's proposal changed significantly, not least in response to its competition with UNCITRAL (see Chapter 4). Whereas the

ADB offered "standards" and the IMF presented "principal conclusions," the World Bank presented thirty-five "principles and guidelines," which it characterized as "a distillation of international best practice."[86] As norms they were formally similar to the ADB's standards and the IMF's conclusions. The format throughout the *Principles* was consistent: it opened a topical area with the relevant Principle and then provided an explication of its meaning, a discussion of implications, and sometimes indications of variations across legal systems that would provide equally satisfactory conformity with the Principle. The Principles themselves varied significantly in form. Some were general and aspirational;[87] others were precise and prestatutory.[88] Most indicated a preference, but one or two Principles offered alternatives.

The Bank recognized it must eschew any temptation to offer "one-size-fits-all" solutions. It insisted there was a universality to its *Principles*. Yet it hastened to add that insolvency "systems must be rooted in the country's broader cultural, economic, legal and social context."[89] Concessions must be made to underdevelopment, such as "weak or unclear protection mechanisms, weak financial institutions and capital markets, ineffective corporate governance and uncompetitive businesses, and ineffective laws and institutions." And it acknowledged differences in "domestic policy choices."[90] It did not, however, directly engage strong differences among advanced countries on the balance between the rights of creditors and debtors, or differences between support for private commercial interests versus a public interest. It sought to "hive-off" major policy considerations within insolvency law (e.g., those that relate to workers) and to sidestep the practical political and social impact of certain insolvency measures on countries with weak social safety nets. It effectively sidestepped matters of equity and stability in favor of efficiency. Its partiality, however, was clearly with secured creditors.

The commentary that followed each Principle frequently addressed the tension between universality and variation by discussing alternatives and their merits, though opaque presentation often left its own preferences difficult to discern. On the involvement of creditors in the governance of an insolvency process, for example, the commentary noted the English model, where creditors defer mostly to insolvency practitioners, an "alternative approach" (i.e., the U.S. model) where creditors are heavily involved, and an intermediate approach in some civil law systems. The commentary leaned toward the value of a creditors' committee following the U.S. approach. On whether directors and officers should be liable for decisions that harm creditors, the commentary followed the Principle in essentially presenting two contrasting systems—one encouraging entrepreneurial risk versus one focusing on corporate responsibility—and weakly concluded it is necessary to "strike a balance."[91] In both these cases, a sharp division occurred between the English and American versions of common law insolvency systems. In another case, where there was a clear national variation between those countries that have a unitary approach to entering liquidation or rehabilitation (e.g., France, Germany) and those countries that allow a choice of multiple points of entry (e.g., U.S.), the commentary seemed to tolerate both.[92] In one of the most intractable policy choices—on whether secured creditors should be included within bankruptcy proceedings or not—the commentary listed two clear options and noted that many countries fall under each. It slightly favored the U.S. and common law countries and hinted that including secured creditors within bankruptcy might be preferable.[93]

Over time a clear shift occurs in the *Principles*, visibly manifest in the differences between an October 2000 draft and the April 2001 document. The much shorter 2001 version gives primacy to substantive law over institutions and implementation. The systems emphasis is relatively muted, and the heavy institutional and regulatory sections of an earlier version are variously moved to an Annex, reduced in size, and pushed toward the back of the document. The 2001 version champions creditor rights far more heavily than do earlier drafts. The shift is signified by the change in title of the *Principles* from *Effective Insolvency Systems* to *Effective Insolvency and Creditor Rights Systems*. The creditor rights section in the 2000 version is brought from the middle to the front of the document as the point of departure to set the context for the entire insolvency discussion, which is relegated to Section 3.

In addition, the World Bank eventually dropped its thinly disguised preference for making the U.S. model normative for the world and makes many concessions to British and Continental systems. For instance, the 2000 version favored the U.S. practice of leaving management in charge of companies during reorganization. The 2001 version expressly states there are "two preferred approaches," and in both cases it emphasizes the importance of an administrator or supervisor, a move more compatible with Commonwealth and civil law practices. Following resistance by English and Commonwealth countries, Principle 27 backs away from an earlier preference for a specialized bankruptcy court.

The pointed shift toward creditors' rights indicates that the Bank's Initiative had yielded to pressure by secured creditor lobbies and quite possibly the change in U.S. administration. This might be seen as a correction against the overly U.S.-centric earlier versions of the *Principles*. However, the change also supports the view that the extensive consultative process did more than just serve as a legitimation strategy. Whatever the intent, its actual effect was to push the Bank to a more balanced position, indeed, to compel it to live up to the rhetoric of its report—that universality of principles must be combined with variability in implementation.

But, as we shall see in Chapter 4, the competition with UNCITRAL compelled the Bank by 2005 to abandon much of content of the *Principles* and to replace it with a quite different script not of its own making.

The Assessment Techniques   Alongside its prescriptive script, the Bank created two diagnostic instruments. It designed the Assessment Template to enable countries to assess their own compliance with the Bank's *Principles*. The Template, said the Bank, was designed to be "flexible" and neither "restrictive" nor "exhaustive."[94] It tried to be "practical" and to reveal how "rights are generally obtained and enforced." The designers explicitly acknowledged the universality/particularity problem by balancing the Template's recognition of "key features and issues that commonly arise in most insolvency systems" with each system's "own unique blend of legal, institutional and regulatory framework."

Compared to the *Principles*, the Template offered a far more precise set of standards for any country. Under each Principle, the Template raised twenty to forty questions that constitute a practical checklist of Bank-prescribed topics that any policymaker should consider in the reform of bankruptcy law. For example, under the area of judicial remedies for creditor rights in Principle 2, the Template presents fifteen items, such as "Describe the procedure for seizing immovable property to satisfy an unsecured right," "Describe the procedure for disbursement of proceeds from sale of immovable property," or "Describe the procedure for collecting on intangible assets." All these, of course, presupposed that a country *should* have such procedures.

Even more than the *Principles*, the Template underscores the importance of institutions by asking questions that probe into their structures and operations. On registries for securities, for instance, the Template wants to know: "What body is responsible for operating and maintaining the registry? What is the responsibility of the registering body? Where is the registry located? Is the registry electronic or manual?" and so on, through many more questions. The implicit norms are plain: there should be throughout a country a clear, coordinated system of registries whose locations are well known. Preferably, the registry should permit easy electronic access. There should be a hierarchical structure of responsibility and an internal review process. A similar battery of questions on structures and operations applies to courts, regulatory bodies, and professions.

The Template presses countries to take deliberate diagnostic approaches to their own legal systems. It impels countries to discover why problems arise, to undertake hardheaded diagnosis as a precursor to reform. The Template therefore offers a normative model in another guise. An Assessment Template might reinforce or subtly shift the emphasis in the *Principles*. In fact, it does both. The very form of the questions themselves sometimes implies the "correct answer" anticipated by its designers, although sometimes the form of the question reinforces with more clarity how to "operationalize" each of the Principles.

Reports on the Observance of Standards and Codes   The World Bank gives an evaluative edge to its *Principles* in a second way. It complements internal self-evaluations with external Bank-staffed and Bank-funded evaluations of a country's insolvency system. In a four-year program set up by the Bank, with the IMF as a junior partner, the insolvency lawyers stated its intention to undertake some seventy to eighty ROSCs of developing countries. Some of the ROSCs were associated with financial crises, such as in Argentina, but most were intended to help prevent threats to financial stability. All carried at least implicitly the implication that favorable outcomes or favorable adjustments would affect future lending decisions by the Bank.[95]

ROSCs are initiated with agreement among the country team in Washington, the World Bank official on-site in the country, and the country itself. ROSCs proceed in three stages. In preparation, the headquarters team analyzes extant substantive law, using the Template as a checklist. Staff follow this up with a country mission for approximately two weeks during which they interview up to fifty or sixty people, including public and private bankers, government officials (e.g., Central Bank, Ministry of Justice, Ministry of Finance), lawyers (usually those who are in-country counsel to the World Bank, a couple of international law firms, and a couple of local firms), accountants (if possible, a couple of Big Four firms), sometimes officials from debtor organizations (e.g., Chambers of Commerce, representatives of industry associations), judges, and officials in government-restructuring agencies. The World Bank team returns to Washington and prepares and delivers a Report to its government counterparts. Governments have the option to publish nothing, to publish the Executive Summary only, or to publish both the Executive Summary and the full Report.[96] Most elect to publish nothing or the Executive Summary only.[97]

The evaluation itself proceeds Principle by Principle. For every Principle there are three elements: a description of the situation in the country, an analysis of the situation vis-à-vis the Principle, and recommendations. For each Principle the Bank rates the country on a four-point scale of compliance in law and practice.[98] By the conclusion of the analysis nations are ranked on each criterion and given an overall ranking. Unlike the ADB and the EBRD, the Bank publishes no comparisons across countries nor engages in public shaming.[99]

The country evaluations give the Bank several types of leverage. They push countries to take seriously the norms articulated in the *Principles* both by the obvious scrutiny to which they are being subjected and by not so light-handed implications of links between performance in the evaluations and subsequent access to multilateral financing. They also provide systematic information that can be passed along to World Bank programs on infrastructure development and thereby inform Bank priorities among topical areas and across countries.[100]

The Bank's insolvency Initiative articulates a theory of legal development that is heavily weighted toward creditor rights—much more so than when it began its enterprise and certainly more so than the EBRD. What appeared in early drafts to be an ethnocentric Washington Consensus view of the world has attenuated as diversity in implementation of *Principles* has been recognized and honored. A rhetorical analysis of the values in the Principles themselves reveals the governing norms that pervade the Bank's image of an effective legal system. Dominant values, mentioned in approximately a third of the Principles, are independence, integrity, and impartiality of the law and its application. The need for transparency and accountability are expressed almost as often. Such an insolvency system should be efficient, but also fair and equitable. It should allow predictability, particularly by prospective creditors. And it should be practical—affordable and cost-effective, inexpensive, with easy access, and once within the system, prompt and timely.

Legitimation Politics in the Incomplete Road to Consensus

For insolvency experts, international organizations and global norm makers alike, a second phase of constructing an international field of insolvency law—that of creating normative models for insolvency systems in the world's transitional and developing economies—presented a far more daunting challenge than that of creating cross-border protocols among advanced countries. The diversity of national markets, the deep embeddedness of debtor-creditor relations in national legal cultures, radically different levels of capacity in national legal systems, conflicting national policy orientations toward parties in bankruptcies, the dearth of domestic professional and governmental expertise in most nations—all pointed to a lost cause. Yet the quick success of UNCITRAL's Model Law on Cross-Border Insolvency and the urgency injected by the Asian Crisis invigorated insolvency leaders to try again. In close to as many years as it took to develop the Model Law on Cross-Border Insolvency, four international financial institutions produced several versions of normative standards for all countries. These were supplemented by private proposals to forestall the need for formal bankruptcy.

As a result, global norm makers could now add a second layer to the emerging global norms for bankruptcy regimes. The first phase had successfully produced a Model Law to govern corporate bankruptcies that spilled across jurisdictional frontiers of advanced economies. In certain respects this was a less demanding task because it confronted the inertia of already established national bankruptcy systems by seeking grounds for cross-national comity and cooperation. The second phase was more ambitious because it sought to craft norms that could apply across the world to nations with developing and transitional economies. If these norms were legitimately developed and effectively disseminated, there was a good prospect that they could shape emerging bankruptcy systems. Hence international organizations offered several alternatives variously directed to bankers, legislators, economic regulators, courts, and professionals (Table 3.3).

The process in this second phase reveals a logic in which norm-making institutions sought to legitimate their initiatives and maximize their respective forms of leverage. But they did not do so independently, since each organization was aware of the other, and the IMF and World Bank, in particular, drew on the technical authority of professional associations.

TABLE 3.3 Global and Regional Insolvency Standards, 1986–2004

Initiative	Transnational Actor	Economies	Entities Regulated	Formal Instrument: Enabling Institution	Key Audiences: Veto Player(s)
Cross-Border, Advanced Economies (late 1980s–2003)					
MIICA, 1986–1989	Professional association (IBA)	Advanced, adjacent	States	Model law/Legislature	Executive, legislative branches: Governments
Concordat, 1993–1996	Professional association (IBA)	Advanced, adjacent	States	Protocol/Courts	Practitioners, judges: Courts
Maxwell Protocol, 1992	Courts	Advanced	Courts	Protocol/Courts	Professional counsel: Courts
Council of Europe Istanbul Convention, 1990	Regional suprastate body	Advanced, adjacent	States	Convention/Courts, regulatory agencies	
EU Convention, 1990–1996	Regional suprastate body	Advanced, adjacent	States	Convention: National legislatures	National governments: Same
Model Law on Cross-Border Insolvency, 1990–1997	World governance body	All economies	States	Model law—harmonization of procedures: Legislature	Executive, legislative branches: Governments
Principles of Cooperation among NAFTA countries, 2003	Professional association (ALI)	NAFTA: Canada, U.S., Mexico	States	Principles/Courts	

EU Regulation on Insolvency Proceedings, 2001	Regional suprastate body	Advanced, adjacent	States	Convention/ Courts, regulatory agencies	Executive, legislative branches: Governments
National Insolvency Regimes, Emerging Economies (late 1990s–2004)					
Model Bankruptcy Code	Professional association (IBA)	Emerging markets		Model law/Legislature	Executive, legislative branches: Governments
Workout Principles	Professional association (INSOL)	Emerging markets	Banks, creditors	Principles/ Private banks	Banks: Banks/secured creditors
Asian Development Bank Report	IFI	Emerging markets	States, courts	Standards/Legislature	Executive and legislative branches: Governments
International Monetary Fund Insolvency Procedures	IFI	Emerging markets	States, courts, professions	Statute/Legislature	Executive and legislative branches: Governments
World Bank Principles	IFI	Emerging markets	States, courts, professions	Statute/Legislature	Executive and legislative branches: Governments
National Insolvency Regimes: Emerging, Transitional and Advanced Economies (2004)					
UNCITRAL Legislative Guide	World governance body	Emerging, transitional, advanced economies	States, courts, professions	Statute/Legislature	Executive and legislative branches: Governments

The politics of norm production are also a politics of institutional legitimation. A normative standard is developed as a script for persuasion. Like organizations, a template requires legitimation. IFIs designed their normative instruments to appropriate as broad and as salient a set of legitimating warrants as they could manage, including external warrants (ways of giving external support or leverage to the script) and internal warrants (ways of legitimating a template that inhere in the script itself). These warrants sometimes reinforce, sometimes displace, and sometimes substitute for each other. Cross-cutting these are positive legitimation warrants, which strengthen the authority of an institution and its scripts, and legitimation deficits, which subtract from its authority and lessen the probability of adoption.

External warrants fall under representational and effectiveness criteria. Institutions can claim warrants of representativeness based on (1) breadth of consultation, (2) the quality of expertise that they have marshaled, (3) the scope of organizational or institutional cooperation to which they can point, (4) the empirical bases from which norms have been developed, and (5) the kinds of consultative forums in which norms have been presented and debated. If organizations can convince potential adopters that the norms were developed by representatives of nations such as theirs, that their interests were effectively taken into account, then their products are likely to be more readily accepted. If global norm makers similarly display their willingness to benefit from the technical expertise of professionals who will preside over local implementation, they may also pass more readily the most severe test—that of translating norms into practice. In both cases, if a global norm maker has a positive track record of getting acceptable norms implemented, or there is an expectation that the norms of this international organization will likely set the standard, a further warrant of authority is added to the organization and its scripts.

Seemingly, the most potent external warrants are those that connect norms to sanctions, although a reliance on sanctions implicitly acknowledges some insufficiency of legitimacy to induce conformity without sanctions. The connection is implicit when an IFI can plausibly state or imply that a ranking on a scale of compliance will influence the probability of future investment, lending, or grants. Even if they do so informally, EBRD legal officers can induce reform when they indicate that their legal risk assessments are integrated into risk models employed by bank decision makers. And to the extent that such risk ratings find their way into private financial markets, via joint financing with IFIs, incentives for conformity with IFI standards will be all the more influential. The connection between norms and sanctions is explicit when IFIs make loans conditional on particular reforms. This may occur quasi-coercively as in situations where desperate countries must adjust to norms or face financial collapse. It may also occur through mutual understandings where countries make generalized commitments to reform in a good-faith gesture to stimulate IFI financing.

Internal warrants inhere in the procedures by which norms are developed and the rhetorical construction of normative scripts. Since procedure is closely related to fairness, a sense that all parties integrated into the deliberative process are treated in accord with appropriate rules, the salience of variability differed considerably. In the cases of the ABF, EBRD, and IMF, each organization gathered information from experts, but internal deliberations were essentially invisible to outsiders. In the case of the World Bank, an appearance of widespread consultation in its global forums and specialty groups gave a greater verisimilitude of participation, as country specialists reported on their situations, yet final determinations of which norms to develop were also staff driven.

In sum, all the IFIs had positive legitimation warrants from representation of expert opinion, but their legitimation deficits are evident in their failure to obtain authentic representation of interested parties in decision making or to reveal internal procedures that produced norms. In any event, since representation was mostly absent, the significance of procedural legitimation was slight.

Scripts balance differentially the interplay of diagnostic versus prescriptive technologies (Tables 3.2, 3.3). We have observed significant variation across IFIs, from the EBRD, which was predominantly diagnostic, to the World Bank, which has developed both a public and private diagnostic instrument alongside its prescriptive standard. The diagnostic instruments not only carry implicit evaluative standards but are integral to IFI leverage over potential recipients of IFI loans. The regional IFIs ratcheted up persuasive pressures by publicly rating countries on their compliance with standards generated by the banks. In the case of the Asian Development Bank, the tactic was self-consciously adapted to the concept of "face" in Asian culture.[101] Since the Bank is fully aware of the punitive effects of public shaming in many Asian countries, its choice to publish rankings of countries against each other on some thirty-three standards seems quite calculated to motivate "shamed" countries to meet the standards. While less specific and detailed in its public promulgations of norms than its sister IFIs, the EBRD nevertheless offered the broad contours of a system it would find worthy of high ranking. By offering public ratings without detailed specificity for remediation, the EBRD offered two paths of action for low-ranked countries. Either they should consult directly with the EBRD and obtain its tailored prescription for each country, or countries should look to future norms, such as the World Bank's guidelines.

As the EBRD further demonstrates, rankings can be leveraged into ratings. The diagnostic instrument provided criteria for a scorecard on which countries might be given numerical ratings. At once, these carry the verisimilitude of social science (however unwarranted) and enable a bank to monitor and track changes from year to year with an apparently refined instrument. While these scores are partly self-validating, they serve concomitantly to give a bank leverage over a country, by comparing it both to other countries and to levels on an absolute scale, and by providing a weapon in the hands of national reformers who are lobbying for change. This move to legal commensuration simultaneously validates legal initiatives within financial institutions and opens up a new array of technologies that may be deployed by IFIs to precipitate change.

The relationship between external and internal warrants of legitimacy can be complex, for warrants are not simply additive—that is, the more, the better. For instance, the IFI with the strongest coercive mechanism, the IMF, conveys its norms in the softest rhetoric, never naming or shaming countries and never comparing some unfavorably to others. The IFI uses the least direct financial leverage; the ADB, by contrast, employs ranking and naming tactics to shame unreformed nations. It appears that institutions that carry big sticks can speak softly, whereas those with limited financial leverage must script their norm setting and assessments with the strongest rhetorical devices. Ironically, the most forceful lever to obtain compliance with IFI norms may also be delegitimating. We shall discover in the next chapter that the exercise of quasi coercion by IFIs engenders a backlash. National policymakers often resist external constraint, the more so the more detailed the reforms. They resent infringements on their sovereignty. And the reliance on economic pressure carries the self-subverting implication that the intrinsic merits of norms are not sufficient in themselves to induce local action.

The coupling of normative models with assessment tools intensifies the potential influence of international norm-setting institutions. What appears as a diagnostic instrument in one respect readily may be construed as a surveillance mechanism in another. As assessment tools have evolved toward greater specificity, they enable IFIs to dissect laws and practices with considerable precision. With greater and greater forensic accuracy, the assessment tools enable IFIs to achieve multiple ends. Foreign and domestic appraisers of insolvency systems can diagnose national weaknesses by a common metric. The IFI establishes the basis on which negotiations will occur. The tool enables IFIs and nation-states to calibrate the extent and pace of reform. And scores within the tool can be aggregated and recombined in multiple ways to compare and contrast one country with another.

Whatever the particular order or combination of these technologies, however, it is clear that the normative framework created by the international institutions comprises both. While the norms themselves (whether called principles, guidelines, or standards) ostensibly incorporate the standards and the reasoning that justifies them, the assessment tools reinforce the norms and may further define and prioritize them. In fact, for most countries the assessment tools may provide the most immediate and precise versions of norms, for they are substantially better specified than the so-called principles, guides, or standards.

If the paired normative models and assessment tools set up positive and negative incentives to reform, how effectively these models go toward resolving the tension between global uniformity and national diversity remains to be appraised. The imperatives toward uniformity are plain: ideological conformity around the Washington Consensus, geopolitical pressures toward conformity with U.S. preferences, and organizational pressures to provide simplified models as an expression of bounded rationality. The centrifugal pressures toward diversity do not need repetition. How do the norm-setting enterprises manage this tension?

In theory there are at least four possibilities. First, at one extreme, IFIs might continue to confront each nation's problems on an individual basis. This is rather unsatisfactory, indeed impracticable, because resource constraints will not permit invention de novo of a solution for each situation. Second, at the other extreme would be to develop a single, homogenized instrument for a region or the world. The efficiency benefits for IFIs are considerable. However, the legitimation and implementation problems for client nations are insurmountable. Third, an intermediate position closer to the national-variation model would be for international institutions to acknowledge that many types of capitalism exist and the likelihood that many types of insolvency regimes will be functionally equivalent. If this were the path followed, IFIs would specify functions to be satisfied and then offer institutional variations that match types of capitalism. Fourth, an intermediate position closer to a homogeneous model would be for IFIs to adopt a developmental model where it is presumed that emerging markets and transitional societies are on a developmental path that will ultimately lead to a paradigmatic advanced economy, such as that of the United States (it is never assumed to be Sweden). But as a concession to their underdevelopment, they may not be yet ready for reforms that require a more sophisticated infrastructure or a change in commercial mentality.

In practice, the IFIs have moved toward a more sophisticated solution that posits a core model for the world but allows alternatives and variants to satisfy the functional requirements of an insolvency system in particular contexts. Best exemplified by the World Bank, an IFI offers a relatively high-order principle and then shows there may be two to three variations that are currently extant and acceptable to the IFI. However, these systematic variations occur rather infrequently in the Bank's thirty-five Principles. They pertain mainly to areas where there are either sharp divergences among the insolvency systems of advanced nations or where concessions need to be made to the legal incapacity or limited resources of emerging markets.

Norm making by the IFIs has resulted in the selection of core principles without forcing convergence in the areas of most intractable difference among advanced nations. Indeed, as the norm-setting process has advanced, a subtle shift in the depiction of the enterprise has occurred. Whereas earlier aspirations pointed to the harmonization of norms, later expressions indicate that investors will settle for predictability, even if predictable patterns vary considerably across jurisdictions. The World Bank in particular has felt compelled to reflect some of the diversity among common and civil law advanced countries in the variants on themes it will accept. Insofar as consensus has been reached among expert elites, it has not required total convergence.

The proliferation of global norms by international organizations offered both promise and dangers. By experimenting with a variety of technologies, private and public institutions created alternative ways of coping with the varieties of markets and legal systems. A general consensus emerged around the merits of bankruptcy systems that offered companies the alternatives of both reorganization and liquidation. But this progress toward a global standard remained incomplete. A developing country in Central Asia was now confronted with four sets of standards, a transitional country in Eastern Europe with three, a developing country in Latin America with two. Quite apart from confusion, from the point of view of global "legislators," this enabled a country to play one set of global norms against another. The norms stood at varying levels of abstractness, some so vague they provided little guidance, others too specific to permit reasonable cross-national variation. In addition, there was no doubt that the regional and global public institutions had significant leverage, much of it around financing of loans in normal times and emergency packets in crisis situations. The IMF and World Bank in particular, however, were impugned by their use of coercion, considered too close to the U.S. administration. Organizations with significant expert legitimation had little practical leverage. And no IFI or professional association had solved the fundamental problem of representation.

The turn of the millennium therefore left the prospect of a single global standard unrealized. Successive iterations of global norm making within and among international organizations had shown some convergence at the highest levels of abstraction—a theory of law and markets together with principles that might govern insolvency regimes. Scripts began loosely to resemble each other, even if they were labeled distinctively. Both diagnosis and prescription now seemed two sides of the norm-setting enterprise. But none of these organizations had any reasonable prospect of prevailing. It would take a quite different approach, of coordination rather than incipient competition, to push global norm making to a single, consensual standard.

4 Attaining the Global Standard

Terence C. Halliday, Susan Block-Lieb,
and Bruce G. Carruthers

B Y 1999 many of the pieces were in place for a global standard on
national insolvency systems. Professional associations and courts
had undertaken programs on their own account either to stimulate domestic law reform or to engineer mechanisms for complex, cross-border transactions. From IFIs came a variety of scripts and instruments, in the form of
diagnostic tools and codified norms, that pressed developing or transitional
countries toward regional and global standards. Major donor governments
propagated reforms through their aid programs.[1] How did these variegated
efforts culminate in a single global standard?

Several of these solo activities began to coalesce in selective alliances. The
IFIs hired consultants or built networks of professionals to formulate general
guidelines for the reform of insolvency regimes. Sometimes these consultants
served in their individual capacities; at other times they represented or were
taken to represent professional associations where they held leadership positions. IFIs joined with professional associations such as INSOL to stage conferences with organizations like the OECD to broaden their auspices. The U.S.
channeled its national interests through its multilateral agents, such as the
IMF and World Bank. And multilateral governance organizations, such as
the OECD, reached out to sponsor international events focused on insolvency
reforms with IFIs and international professional associations.

Altogether, these activities progressed toward a convergent set of standards, albeit in different forms, sponsored by different institutions, and with

variations in emphasis. At the close of 1999 it was reasonable to ask these questions: Had the loosely articulated field of reform reached its zenith? Were the drivers of global convergence content with their accomplishments? Or could they press on to the goal of a single global standard?

There were good reasons to stop. Practitioners, international institutions, and comparative law professors all knew that insolvency law and practice varied enormously among legal families, a variation magnified across the world and even among countries in the same region with a similar legal heritage. If there were differences among varieties of capitalism within advanced countries, how much more variation might be found among developing and transitional economies? It was implausible to expect that countries with well-entrenched legal and market infrastructures would operate bankruptcy regimes in the same way as countries that historically had little use for law and little investment in legal institutions. Given the plethora of global players, each with its own interests and legal technologies, could any transnational forum enable a consensus to be forged? Not least, potential conflicts could be envisaged between sovereign nations that sought to establish economic spheres of interest in developing markets, just as developing (debtor) countries were not likely to share the same economic interests as developed (creditor) countries.

Nonetheless, the imperative to press forward flowed from several directions. Although the several products of IFIs and professions were somewhat convergent, their form and focus were confusing to potential adopters. For reforms in Asia, for instance, the IMF, World Bank, and ADB each had on offer a different standard, despite the need for all three to work together on national projects, particularly in crisis situations. The United States, a prime mover for reforms that benefited global trade, leaned vigorously on international institutions to produce a single standard on the grounds that convergent laws would facilitate investment.

Forward momentum also continued because each of the global actors confronted its own limitations. While the IFIs could boast much experience and the production of scripts based on research and expertise, they all suffered from legitimation deficits—the states that would be their objects of reform had virtually no voice in the crafting of norms. Some IFIs, such as the IMF, recognized that their coercive leverage in the international financial system worked against the acceptability of any standard promulgated by them. Regional IFIs were just that—local players in the total world system. And all the scripts, while generally convergent around the ideal of corporate reorganization, varied considerably in form, content, and the specificity of norms. The U.S. pressed for some harmony to be brought to this cacophony. So, too, did professional associations, whose members ranged across the world seeking to liquidate or reorganize companies in many jurisdictions.

The pragmatic problems confronted by agents of global reform coincide with the theoretical issues that surround global norm production. Can a practicable and legitimate global script be crafted in the face of such enormous national diversity? Is there any prospect that a legitimate global script could produce convergence among nations, without impinging on national sovereignty? And what kinds of leverage are possible for a global standard to be both legitimate and effective?

Several global reform efforts through 1999 converged on one international organization that might combine a highly legitimate product with an adaptable technology that stood a chance of implementation through leverage of various types. The United Nations Commission on International Trade Law, based in Vienna, offered a forum where global commercial norm making was well institutionalized and had already achieved a singular success in the bankruptcy field—the completion in 1999 of a Model Law on Cross-Border Insolvency. Emboldened by their accomplishment, the principal actors—professionals, IFIs, national delegates, the UNCITRAL Secretariat—now confronted a more daring prospect, the creation of a global standard for national insolvency regimes, embracing both substantive and procedural law.

Success at this enterprise, however, required a solution to a puzzle that bedevils many international organizations. How is it possible to legitimate a global script without subverting the production of meaningful norms? On the one hand, UNCITRAL has developed sophisticated means of integrating widely diverse interests, of obtaining broadly inclusive representation, of establishing expert authority. On the other hand, the very heterogeneity of nations, legal families, and interests could easily consign UNCITRAL to ineffectiveness, to either stalemate or capture or production of vague principles that offer little guidance or little legal convergence. This chapter will show how UNCITRAL managed to craft a legitimate global script that may be leveraged to advance convergence across legal systems. In so doing, UNCITRAL demonstrates how IOs more generally might tackle global norm production in areas of legal regulation hitherto thought intractable. UNCITRAL's success suggests that prospects for some convergence on global norms may be greater than has hitherto been anticipated.[2]

We demonstrate, first, how UNCITRAL overcame legitimation deficits encountered by other international organizations; second, the problems this solution posed for effective norm production; third, the strategies UNCITRAL mobilized to overcome the threats of capture, stalemate, and vacuity; and fourth, the substantive outcomes and their theoretical implications for global norm making. This chapter will show that UNCITRAL's Legislative Guide on Insolvency Law brought to a climax the search for a single global standard that is perceived to be highly legitimate, articulated through an adaptable technology that stands a good chance of implementation, substantially because several types of leverage can be mobilized to aid its diffusion. But this did not occur without contestation among global actors, most notably the World Bank, which resisted its likely displacement as the "gold standard."

Making Global Norm Making Legitimate

An international organization may legitimate itself in three ways (Barnett and Finnemore 2005; Cronin and Hurd 2008; Hurd 2007). First, the organization and its products will be perceived as legitimate by its critical audiences if it is *representative*. The standard of representation may be contestable, changing from organization to organization and sometimes across issues within organizations. A country or INGO may consider an international forum representative if it has a seat at the negotiating table. More broadly, an international organization will likely be perceived as legitimate if it incorporates within its deliberating body all principal sets of interests that surround the organization's mandate and will be affected by its decisions. In the insolvency field, for instance, a representative global body would need to incorporate a cross section of states (including advanced, developing, and transitional economies) from different regions of the world and that reflect the world's principal legal families. It would incorporate representatives of all the main classes of interests that come into play in corporate bankruptcy—creditors and debtors, managers and workers, owners and managers, states and consumers. It would also involve those professions that do insolvency work (lawyers, accountants, insolvency professions, civil servants, judges) and academic specialists. Representation of expertise and interests would also be necessary from international organizations, such as the IFIs active in the field.

Second, an IO is perceived as legitimate when its discussions and decision making are *procedurally fair*. The rules of participation require that any actor has voice (i.e., can express its views) and that rules are clear, transparent, and evenhandedly administered to give equal chance for participation and voting to the powerful and weak alike. Procedural fairness can have the effect of changing the interests and perceptions of all participants as they engage each other and, even further, produce a common discourse and emergent community solidarity. In the insolvency field, procedural fairness would require that the world's most powerful economic actors, for example, not obtain advantages in participation over peripheral countries, that the representatives of creditors are not privileged over debtors, that the common law system does not predominate over the civil law system, that experts do not obtain advantages denied generalists. It must be noted that the fair application of transparent and neutral rules does not preclude the emergence of vocal and dominant actors in discussions. It merely assures all representatives that none will be given special privileges in debate or decision making.

Third, legitimacy depends in a somewhat circular way on the prior *effectiveness* of the institution. If it has been effective on similar projects in the past, it obtains greater legitimacy for its efforts in the present. If nation-states have a history or record of implementing the norms of an international organization, then they will take for granted that the organization has the right to promulgate norms, and it will be natural for nation-states to adopt them.

From the outset of its second initiative in the insolvency field, UNCITRAL staked its claim to be the ultimate producer of global norms on grounds of representation and effectiveness.

Setting the Agenda

In 1998 Australia proposed that in light of the "recent regional and global financial crises," there was a need to strengthen the international financial system, and "strong insolvency and debtor-creditor regimes were an important means for preventing or limiting financial crises and for facilitating rapid and orderly workouts from excessive indebtedness." Given UNCITRAL's previous success and the relationship it had forged with international organizations with expertise in insolvency, Australia asked UNCITRAL to consider a model law in the field.[3]

Heeding this call, in September 1999 UNCITRAL's Secretariat circulated a position paper to the same Working Group on Insolvency Law that had successfully produced a Model Law on Cross-Border Insolvency.[4] The paper invoked the grounds consistent with its founding claims—that a need for coordination existed in order to "avoid inefficient duplication of work" and that UNCITRAL was the appropriate forum given its "universal membership." UNCITRAL could already boast of "its previous successful work on cross-border insolvency" in which it had crafted a Model Law to cover insolvencies involving multiple national jurisdictions.[5] Not only had UNCITRAL established its credentials in this field through the Model Law but it had done so rapidly, from its first Colloquium in April 1994 to adoption by the Commission in May 1997.[6]

UNCITRAL bolstered its claim to leadership by noting that it already had well-established relationships with key expert organizations in the field. INSOL, and later the IBA, both had worked closely with UNCITRAL in the production of the Model Law. INSOL, in particular, had co-hosted international colloquia with the UN agency to solicit input from judges, judicial administrators, government officials, and practitioners.[7]

The more delicate problem lay in UNCITRAL's relationships with the IMF, World Bank, and OECD, which already had completed or had under way the creation of normative codes for bankruptcy regimes. UNCITRAL diplomatically acknowledged this prior work by prominently describing each achievement at the outset of its Proposal and expressing its desire to build on their notable efforts. The Proposal similarly acknowledged the significant work under way in the international professional associations, especially the IBA and INSOL. At the same time UNCITRAL signaled that its voice would embrace more than the Washington-based IFIs, for it championed a less prominent Technical Report of the Asian Development Bank on insolvency.

The Secretariat, with support from the Commission, used the Proposal to convene an "exploratory session" of the Insolvency Working Group in December 1999 at the UN center in Vienna. The Secretariat was charged to explore whether an UNCITRAL project on insolvency law would be practical, since there was much skepticism among experts and states that the huge diversity of laws and interests in bankruptcy could be harmonized at any useful level.

The Secretariat of UNCITRAL consciously cast its net very broadly, not only to get people to the table but to get them early and to get them openly engaged with each other. Said an UNCITRAL official:

> You can't develop law reform on topic "x" without involving all the people who have an interest in topic "x" or have expertise in topic "x" or affected by topic "x" because you'll just never get anywhere. And you'll end up, if you leave one

of the lobby groups or the interest groups outside the process, then the minute you come up with your piece of draft legislation, they'll be jumping up and down and banging on the door and saying, "We don't like this."[8]

Experience showed that the sooner you "get everybody together," the better. "If they're part of the process, you don't have as much problem." In addition to inviting states, therefore, UNCITRAL invited a broad array of INGOs because in these types of proceedings expert organizations are "as much key players as government."[9] All the core global nonstate players participated, including the regional and global banks (IMF, World Bank, EBRD, ADB, European Bank), the principal professional associations (IBA, INSOL), the OECD, and other less prominent organizations. UNCITRAL underlined its inclusive and participatory intentions by co-hosting the Colloquium with INSOL and the IBA and by designating present and former leaders of INGOs as chairs of various sessions.

UNCITRAL officials understood clearly that their late emergence as a prospective global leader in this field required some delicate positioning. Privately, the UNCITRAL leadership saw that their opening stemmed from limitations of other global players. According to an UNCITRAL official,

> the World Bank has a problem, as does the International Monetary Fund—their efforts are seen to be the work of a few experts. And there is always the feeling that Washington might be cramming things down the throats of others. This doesn't go down well with policy-makers in countries when they sit down to reform their laws.[10]

As for the professional associations, "INSOL and the IBA are similarly prejudiced. INSOL is mostly insolvency practitioners. The IBA is mostly lawyers. These are people who charge fees and are seen to have particular interests. They don't carry cachet in key ministries. And they have no effective way of getting things implemented." Furthermore, the ADB and the EBRD "have a regional focus, so that limits their global impact."[11]

Publicly, the UNCITRAL Secretary (the director) opened the 1999 Working Group meeting with a dual claim to UNCITRAL's leadership: UNCITRAL, he said, can contribute expertise in the creation of model laws, and it can set one model law in the context of others already developing or in the process of being developed (e.g., secured transactions). More important, a major advantage of UNCITRAL derives from its "truly universal representation"— the representation of delegates from all countries makes a difference in the "acceptability" of the product. It is one thing to have a group draw up some recommendations, set out ideal goals and purposes; but there should be a sense of realism in the work to see what are acceptable measures and what is possible. The President of INSOL reinforced UNCITRAL's legitimacy by observing that it had already demonstrated that when there was a need, it could act. It could get things done. It is "an incredibly effective machine."[12]

The Working Group meeting demonstrated rather more prospect for a successful project than many participants had expected. After its review of the 1999 meeting, the UNCITRAL Commission in mid-2000 recommended that the Insolvency Working Group hold a Colloquium to get other views, explore what is possible, and draw more constituencies into the process. The Colloquium met in Vienna for one week in December 2000, with some 150 participants drawn from forty countries. Lawyers, accountants, academics, and judges attended alongside insolvency practitioners, civil servants, and representatives of all the major international financial institutions. INGOs dominated the proceedings. But some governments sent delegations, including an active group from the U.S. State Department. The Colloquium itself was sponsored by INSOL,[13] which did most of the organization, and the IBA. The ADB led several of the discussions. All the major players attended and participated.

The Secretariat wrote a preparatory document for the Commission that synthesized two leading reports—those of the World Bank and the ADB—and laid out the pros and cons of the issues. The Working Group recommended that the Commission give it the mandate to prepare a comprehensive statement of objectives and core features of a strong insolvency system, including out-of-court restructuring and a legislative guide that contained flexible approaches to the implementation of the objectives and features, as well as alternative approaches and the pros and cons of each.[14]

The Structure of Representation

UNCITRAL's products are developed through three stages: Working Groups in which "policy decisions" and drafting of an instrument take place; the UNCITRAL Commission itself, which sets the substantive agenda of UNCITRAL and approves products from Working Groups; and the UN General Assembly, which gives pro forma endorsement of Commission decisions. Representation could in principle be incorporated in any of the three stages. In practice, both the Working Group and the Commission are constituted as representative bodies. The General Assembly, fully representative of the world's nations, caps the deliberative process by placing its powerful symbolic imprimatur on UNCITRAL products, although the General Assembly does not debate the merits of UNCITRAL's products.[15]

Representation presupposes criteria against which it can be measured. For insolvency, those criteria might include (1) attributes of nations (e.g., developed, developing, transitional economies, region); (2) attributes of legal systems (e.g., common versus code law, Western versus Islamic law); (3) attributes of bankruptcy-related interests (e.g., creditors vs. debtors, managers vs. owners, workers vs. managers, private creditors vs. state creditors); and (4) configurations of expertise (e.g., lawyers, accountants, insolvency practitioners). Rather than weight these independently, the Working Groups and Commission essentially sought to balance them in terms of the two kinds of authority that help to produce legitimate, competent law—representative authority and expert authority.

Representative Authority   Representative authority was sought by including in the Insolvency Working Group three classes of delegates.

1. *Official State Delegations.* These came from a representative sampling of the world's regions and levels of economic (and legal) development. By constitutional mandate, the delegations had to include representatives from the principal legal systems of the world and from developed and developing countries. At its founding, UNCITRAL selected seven members from African states, five from Asia, four from Eastern Europe, five from Latin America, and eight from Western European and other states. States were chosen by lot, subject to "the adequate representation of the principal economic and legal systems of the world and of developed and developing countries."[16] Until 2004 there were thirty-six state delegations. From 2004 that number was increased to sixty state delegations by the same criteria used at the outset of the Commission. Arguably this selection of almost one-third of the world's nations also spans the diversity of attributes relevant to the drafting of commercial law.

     Lawmaking in technical and complex areas can be impeded when delegates do not have the requisite technical sophistication or when technical experts are too divorced from either practice or politics. To protect against both problems, the Working Group Secretary sought to

populate the Working Group with delegates that were attuned politically to the *enactability* of the product in their own countries. Governments were encouraged not to send generalist diplomats or nonexpert
civil servants, but expert civil servants along with judges or academics with experience and technical expertise in insolvency. Expert civil
servants are acutely attuned to political feasibility of Working Group
recommendations and might also be in a position to influence enactment.[17] Moreover, the Secretariat anticipated that expert civil servants
might lift the general quality of deliberation within the Working Group
while balancing the influence of expert groups.[18]

2. *Observer State Delegations.* In addition to the sixty official delegates,
   the UNCITRAL Secretariat invited all other UN member nations to
   send delegations if they so chose. In the Working Group on Insolvency,
   approximately ten to twenty observer nations also attended regularly.
   The Secretariat insisted that no nation that wished to participate was
   excluded.

3. *International Organizations.* Unlike national legislatures, the UNCITRAL
   Secretariat sought representation from international interest groups. In
   national insolvency politics, those interests are readily identifiable: banks
   (secured creditors), owners and managers of firms, trade creditors,
   workers, state agencies (e.g., departments of commerce and taxation),
   professionals, and consumers. A subset of these—banks, professionals,
   and state agencies—usually dominates national lawmaking (Carruthers and Halliday 1998; Halliday, Block-Lieb, and Carruthers 2008). The
   UNCITRAL Secretariat invited comparable interests at the global level
   to participate at all stages of the proceedings.

   The interest groups that attended the Working Group fell into four
   classes. First, the international financial institutions (most particularly, the IMF, World Bank, and ADB) arguably represented the point
   of view of secured creditors as well as of the largest creditor nations.
   The IMF and World Bank have a special concern with international
   financial architecture. Second, international economic governance organizations (most notably the OECD and the African Common Market—COMESA) attended, although OECD attendance diminished
   over time and the European Union was absent, except to the extent
   that its interests were represented by delegates from member states,
   such as France, Germany, and Spain. Third, international professional

associations of lawyers and insolvency practitioners attended regularly and participated extensively, most notable of which were the IBA, INSOL, the International Insolvency Institute (III), and the international subcommittee of the Business Section, American Bar Association (ABA). Fourth, occasionally other international lawmaking bodies participated, such as the International Institute for the Unification of Private Law (UNIDROIT), the Hague Conference on International Private Law, or other interested expert groups.

As in national lawmaking, certain interests were not directly represented in the UNCITRAL Working Group on Insolvency: although invited, representatives of business (e.g., the International Chamber of Commerce) did not attend; representatives of labor (e.g., International Labor Organization) were invited but attended rarely and scarcely participated; and trade creditors (other businesses) had no direct representation.[19]

The composition of the Commission largely mirrored that of the Working Group. It, too, incorporated official state delegations, any other state that might wish to attend as an observer, and international organizations. Approximately half of the official delegations, including some of its most influential members, were members of both the UNCITRAL Commission and Working Group. International organizations, expert groups, and interest groups appeared less prominently in the Commission than in the Working Group, although the principal organizations ensured they were present and available to participate.

Expert Authority   In the modern state, however, representative authority is not sufficient for competent lawmaking. The complexity of legal regulation requires expertise. Indeed, the legitimacy of the product among its practitioners partly depends on the technical authority manifest in it. Governments incorporate expertise into deliberations and decision making through a variety of methods—forming national commissions, involving experts in developing policy, accepting draft legislation from professional groups, consulting with professional associations, hiring experts for legislative committees, and bringing expert witnesses to testify before legislative committees. Only rarely do experts get explicitly integrated into the decision making, as in the U.K. House of Lords.

UNCITRAL combines representation and expertise by integrating experts directly into the deliberative and decision-making processes. It did so principally by including representatives of international professional associations with extensive experience in insolvency. The Secretariat invited experts to attend the negotiating and drafting sessions and to participate openly in discussions, if not final decision making, on similar terms as official state delegations. The most prominent expert groups were associations of professionals who practice insolvency—lawyers, accountants, and other insolvency practitioners. Their interests did not necessarily coincide (Halliday and Carruthers 2001). On the one side were lawyers' groups, such as the International Bar Association, the International Insolvency Institute, and the American Bar Association. On the other disproportionately were accountants and other insolvency practitioners, most notably represented through the international federation of national insolvency associations, INSOL. A statistical analysis of speech turns in the first two years (or four sessions of Working Group meetings) shows that the four main organizations of practitioners participated extensively in public discussions (Halliday and Carruthers 2003). Of the forty-three states and private groups that participated in debate, the four main professional groups accounted for 25 percent of all interventions. Their participation—while public and open—therefore greatly exceeded their numbers.[20]

The Working Group Secretary also invited small numbers of experts from practice, academia, IFIs, civil service, and the judiciary to meet as an ad hoc expert group between Working Group sessions to advise the Secretary on drafting.[21] The Secretary also used a small circle of responsive professionals for comments on drafts between sessions.

Consequently, several types of expertise were integrated into proceedings by the combination of state and interest-group delegations. These included expertise in the private practice of liquidation and reorganization; public administration of bankruptcy proceedings; adjudication of insolvency proceedings; national, technocratic lawmaking; and institution building of insolvency regimes. Whereas private professionals in particular were active through their international bodies, many national delegations included experts in one or more of the five areas.

Given the inherent difficulties of establishing legitimacy by global institutions, UNCITRAL has succeeded well in integrating the diversity of nation-states on insolvency and by accomplishing what most national legislatures do not manage—including in decision making key interest groups that can both contribute their expertise and express their preferences openly. This accomplishment, however, potentially sows the seeds of its own destruction. The more diverse the constituencies drawn into the lawmaking process, the more difficult it should be, in principle, to reach substantive consensus. While solving through inclusiveness the legitimation problem, UNCITRAL thereby raises the hurdle that must be surmounted for the production of any statutory or lawlike product. The critical question then becomes, Under these circumstances, how is global norm making possible?

Heterogeneity of Practices, Incipient Clashes of Interests

The fundamental challenge faced by UNCITRAL's Working Group on Insolvency can be understood more clearly by identifying principal fault lines that divided national insolvency systems across the world.

Substantive and Institutional Variations in the World's Insolvency Systems

International institutions have long considered insolvency law to be a particularly hard case for any kind of harmonization or global convergence.[22] To begin with, insolvency laws and regimes vary widely across national jurisdictions. For instance, the European Union took several decades to reach agreement on a cross-border insolvency regulation and has never been able to harmonize national bankruptcy laws. As speakers observed in the exploratory Colloquium, insolvency law is deeply embedded in economic and cultural institutions that are not readily susceptible to change. In this section we outline primary differences that separate the world's insolvency laws.

First, nations vary in the range of *options* they offer corporations in financial distress. At one extreme sit insolvency laws that protect creditors' interests and maximize the collection of creditors' claims. These pro-creditor regimes favor creditors' short-term interests in quick repayment of unpaid claims. This type of insolvency law may provide only for the liquidation of an insolvent entity, with the proceeds realized to be dispersed among the debtors' various creditors. At the other end of this spectrum are insolvency laws that protect the interests of a debtor in financial distress, as well as stakeholders whose interests are closely aligned with those of the debtor (e.g., suppliers, employees, and equity owners). Insolvency laws looking to protect the interests of debtors and other stakeholders may focus not just on maximizing collections but also on preserving the added value that inheres in the debtor's continued operations, including employment and other long-term relationships.

Second, capitalist nations vary in the *level of protection* they offer property and contract rights. Insolvency laws permitting the liquidation or winding up of a business entity most strongly promote the property and contract rights of creditors, notwithstanding a debtor's economic demise. At first appearance it might seem that insolvency laws, which provide a stronger emphasis on reorganization and the interests of debtors, thereby derogate strong property rights. However, insolvency laws providing for the reorganization of a business organization might also preserve property and contract rights, albeit by different means. Reorganization laws protective of property interests and contract rights tend to view rehabilitation of a business entity as the prerogative of creditors who, in their own self interest, may decide to waive immediate enforcement of their rights in order to realize long-term benefits and protections.

Third, nations vary in the protections they offer for *cultural, social, and economic interests.* Insolvency laws differ a great deal in how strongly they recognize and protect social and economic welfare of parties affected by corporate failure. The insolvency laws of many nations look to protect stakeholders' interests by, for example, providing enhanced priority in distributions and other protections for environmental claims and to claims held by employees, consumers, and others. Other nations either do not give stakeholders such priorities in insolvency law, or they manage concerns of labor, consumers, and other "weak creditors" in other statutes.

Fourth, nations differ sharply in the degree to which they use insolvency law for *moral or economic regulation.* In some insolvency regimes, an insolvent debtor's failure to commence an insolvency proceeding in a timely fashion constitutes a misuse, indeed, a conversion, of property held at least metaphorically in trust for the benefit of creditors. Under such a regime, the directors and officers of an insolvent debtor are liable to creditors for the harm caused by this dalliance. Insolvency law is thereby used as a form of moral regulation of company directors.[23] Many other insolvency laws do not presume that a debtor's financial distress was the result of actionable misconduct on the part of the debtor's management or board of directors, absent evidence of fraud, gross mismanagement, or other malfeasance. From this perspective, insolvency laws are viewed as economic, rather than moral, regulation. As a result, access to insolvency proceedings is left to the discretion of the debtor's management, who may not be required to establish the debtor's insolvency or other financial distress in order to prove eligibility.

Fifth, comparable cross-national variation is also apparent in the pronounced differences over which institutions have *jurisdiction* to initiate, administer, and resolve disputes arising within insolvency proceedings. For instance, who will administer an insolvent firm? Questions of administration divide principally over the preference of some nations to leave existing management in control of business operations versus the preference of others to replace management with someone who represents the creditors (and possibly other stakeholders). Most countries put an insolvency representative in place to administer a proceeding but differ as to the professional group from which the insolvency representative is drawn. Insolvency administrators can be drawn from five possible pools: business leaders, private lawyers, private accountants, insolvency practitioners, and civil servants.[24]

Sixth, how are *disputes* resolved among the parties? Many nations view the resolution of disputes as the particular province of the judiciary, thus giving interested parties rights of due process pertaining to notice, participation, and appeal. In some instances, judges with jurisdiction to resolve disputes arising in an insolvency proceeding come from the general ranks of the judiciary; in others, dispute resolution is situated in a body with specialized insolvency experience. Other nations do not yield dispute resolution authority to the judiciary. Some resolve the need for technical expertise by vesting an administrative agency or similar entity with authority to resolve insolvency disputes. Others view the need for judicial involvement sparingly. One approach requires judges to defer to the business judgment of the insolvency representative. Another looks more directly to determine the views of groups of creditors (either the general body of creditors or their representatives), requiring the insolvency representative to defer to determinations made by creditors and binding dissenter creditors based only on the lodging of a record of the vote with some central agency or tribunal.[25]

A conceptual overview of the world's insolvency systems therefore reveals deep substantive and institutional fissures that would seem difficult if not prohibitive to bridge in any global lawmaking. What substantive and institutional consensus is possible given such stark differences? In fact, many of these variations are crystallized around the issue of corporate reorganization.

If nations are committed only to *liquidation* of companies that cannot pay their debts, then a set of substantive options follows and the administrative options are also limited. Such nations seek to realize the assets of the corporation for creditors as soon as possible, they will replace management in the interests of realizing those assets, and they will ensure the protection of property interests above all. If nations wish to foster corporate *reorganization*, then they will likely give debtors more discretion in instituting proceedings, restrict unilateral actions by secured creditors to seize assets, seek to bring as many assets as possible into the estate, give more protections and incentives for management to stay in place, offer more time to gather assets and obtain new financing, and frequently if not invariably require an administrative apparatus and court interventions to make collective decisions binding. This contrast overstates the options since variations occur across countries on regimes for liquidation and reorganization.

Nevertheless, reorganization effectively became the touchstone of convergence in the UNCITRAL proceedings. It narrows but certainly does not resolve major fault lines among the world's trading nations (Block-Lieb and Halliday 2006).

Universality's Undersides: Capture and Stalemate

By bringing together a wide diversity of interests, UNCITRAL runs another risk. An open playing field for all the world's most influential actors will likely produce a significant advantage for the bigger, more resourceful players. Most players in the insolvency arena had discernible stakes in the outcomes of UNCITRAL's deliberations. The achievement of universality risks either stalemate or capture.

The Stakes   Developing and transitional nations, whose economies and legal systems were ostensibly the primary beneficiaries of the UNCITRAL initiative, have legal systems usually less developed than those in their markets. Transitional countries, seeking to shift from a command to a market economy, had neither markets nor the commercial legal systems that underwrote them. A decade after the transitions began, all had some insolvency laws, but some were ill conceived at the outset, poorly implemented, or designed at a point when only indigenous national concerns dominated political change. For nations aspiring to membership in the European Union, such as Poland, Turkey, and the Baltic countries, reformers felt compelled to strengthen their case with commercial laws that conformed to EU directives and aligned with the dominant EU economies.

Numbers of poorer countries in negotiations with the IMF, or "under care" by the IMF, or countries anticipating loans from the IMF, looked to the

UNCITRAL product as a means of satisfying IMF pressures for an effective insolvency system.[26] Turkey also illustrates one of the most pervasive reasons for joining the UNCITRAL proceedings—the need to attract foreign capital. One of the clear messages of the rich nations, bearers of the Washington Consensus, and international financial institutions has been that countries will not attract capital if they cannot offer laws that provide investors confidence they can get their investments out in a fair and orderly way if investments go bad.[27]

For *advanced countries*, by contrast, there were few expectations that UNCITRAL would affect their own insolvency laws, although in fact the effects on some were greater than expected.[28] The major powers, which head legal families and who fuel investment in developing economies, participated substantially to influence the creation of a world credit system either in their own image or along lines they could accept. The United States played a dominant role: directly, through its strong continuing presence as a Commission member or observer nation; and indirectly, through mobilization and coordination of expert groups, among others.[29] The stakes were high for Britain, as former head of an empire with lingering loyalties in the Commonwealth, and with London's status as Europe's preeminent financial center. France, similarly, leads the Francophone world and, indeed, French code law, from the Napoleonic Code to the present, arguably provides the strongest alternative to Anglo-American common law in the developed world. With Frankfurt as a European financial center, and Germany's historical influence in Central and Eastern Europe, Germany, too, might strive to shape a set of global norms in a German mold. In Asia, where Japan far exceeds any other country as a financial center, a similar effort might also be anticipated (Gilpin and Gilpin 2000).

Advanced countries vary significantly in their insolvency laws along all dimensions. Crafting a single legislative guide or model law opens up an arena for conflict among them. What is at stake for sovereign countries, therefore, is no less than a system that favors their respective credit institutions, professions, practices, and ways of doing business.

For *international financial institutions* we have seen that UNCITRAL's product might have far-reaching consequences. If the IMF, World Bank, or major regional banks can insert within UNCITRAL's product what might otherwise be questionably legitimate coming from the international financial institutions, then the benefits are obvious. Nations may adopt IFI-acceptable laws without IFI intervention. And IFIs are on much firmer ground if their interventions are accompanied by recommendations to adopt a UN standard.

For *expert bodies*, most notably professional associations, insolvency reforms inevitably affect their jurisdictional rights (Carruthers and Halliday
1998). That is, an insolvency law allocates work and monopolies over work to
particular professions. If, for instance, professional experts could persuade the
UNCITRAL delegates that a British-type system of insolvency practitioners
should prevail in countries that adopt the UNCITRAL model,[30] this system
would offer an enormous competitive advantage over one that uses lawyers.
It would also give the British an added competitive edge over Americans, who
rely principally on lawyers in corporate reorganizations. Most crudely, therefore, UNCITRAL proceedings might be viewed by expert bodies as a site for
occupational development, by defining conditions and institutions that will
shape the global competition for professional services.

Since insolvency law purports to offer an orderly regime in order to protect
property rights, it seems that *financial institutions*, whose lending depends on
the predictability and enforceability of property rights, should also seek to
erect a global normative order that provides them precisely with the protections they covet. Historically, financial institutions have preferred maximum
discretion over their ability to recall loans or realize their security interests,
a system that has worked against rehabilitation of companies. By the same
token, since *company management or corporate debtors* are always the subject
of corporate bankruptcy law, it seems that they would have interests to pursue
through a global model bankruptcy law or legislative guide. And since financial institutions (usually secured creditors) and management (often owners)
find themselves at odds inside bankruptcy proceedings (banks who want their
money and control of the company's assets vs. managers who want to keep
using the bank's money on new terms and maintain control), then the appearance of one should motivate the involvement of the other.

Finally, *UNCITRAL* itself has interests that do not necessarily coincide with
those of the participants in its proceedings. UNCITRAL must justify its own
existence within the UN, even more so with the greater emphasis of the Secre-
tary-General and the UN leadership on the role of the UN in lawmaking, and
lawmaking as a component of peace making.[31] Then, again, UNCITRAL must
forge a fine line between capture by the most powerful global actors, which
would delegitimate it before the great bulk of nations, and unresponsiveness to
the most powerful global actors, which would render the UN marginal.

Given the stakes, UNCITRAL proceedings might therefore be dominated
by (1) a powerful nation, such as the U.S., Britain, France, Germany, or Japan;

(2) countries sharing the same economic stage; (3) the professions of law or accounting; (4) a particular legal family; (5) international financial institutions; or (6) repeat players in bankruptcies—banks or corporations. Complex alliances among groups of actors are also possible: of advanced nations with expert organizations from those countries; of the U.S. with the institutions of the Washington Consensus (i.e., World Bank, IMF) and expert organizations based in the U.S.; of the U.K. with its common law former colonies and expert organizations based in London;[32] of France with other code law countries and other Francophone countries and organizations. Alliances on particular issues might cut across the major divides of legal families and national interests. For example, an alliance between the U.S. and France is possible because American and Continental approaches to insolvency have in common a central role for judges and courts, compared to the British disposition to keep liquidations and restructuring out of the courts. UNCITRAL itself has the potential to dominate proceedings given the significant powers of the Secretariat to set agendas, determine the form of the product, declare where consensus or a preponderance of opinion has been established, and draft the law itself.

Outcomes: Transcending Diversity

At the UNCITRAL Insolvency Working Group discussions in 1999, much skepticism could be heard about the prospect of global convergence on anything so local as national bankruptcy law. Five years later, a four hundred– to five hundred–page document demonstrated that the nay-sayers were wrong. Despite the great diversity among the world's nations, and the ostensible fault lines among actors in the UNCITRAL proceedings, the UN General Assembly approved a consensually forged Legislative Guide in December 2004. In the face of such cross-national heterogeneity, on what terms could such a consensus be crafted?

Substantive Outcomes

The details of the consensus were enabled by an important agreement forged in the Working Group during its first sessions. Delegates adopted a set of high-order principles that would govern the substantive and procedural specifics of the Guide. Most important was the third "key objective."

Striking a Balance between Liquidation and Reorganization   "The first key objective of maximization of value is closely linked to the balance to be achieved in the insolvency law between liquidation and reorganization. An insolvency law needs to balance the advantages of near-term debt collection through liquidation (often the preference of secured creditors) against preserving the value of the debtor's business through reorganization (often the preference of unsecured creditors and the debtor). Insolvency law should include the possibility of reorganization of the debtor as an alternative to liquidation, where creditors would not involuntarily receive less than in liquidation and the value of the debtor to society and to creditors may be maximized by allowing it to continue."[33]

This objective balances the conflict between creditors and debtors, and indeed the conflicts between nations that have prioritized one over the other, and explicitly authorizes reorganization as an acceptable alternative in any insolvency law. The objective forthrightly acknowledges that creditors will need to be satisfied that reorganization will not erode the value of their claims; yet it also states clearly the expectation that a reorganization option will stimulate the economy and thereby benefit all economic actors, including workers.

In part, this consensus was driven by the U.S. and the expert professional groups represented by Americans (IBA, ABA). Decades of success and experience gave them persuasive force. Behind the scenes, the U.S. was strongly supported by the IFIs, especially the IMF, for whom strong reorganization provisions were a sine qua non of its support for a Guide. The IMF and World Bank maintained that reorganization would stimulate entrepreneurship and lead to orderly rehabilitation of companies in ways that would forestall national economic crises. If the private banking industry were present, it might have objected. Yet decades of experience with reorganization seem to have convinced many bankers that unilateral action on their part alienated potential borrowers, destroyed otherwise viable businesses, and was not necessary because they could protect their assets even in reorganizations. Indeed, the third key objective explicitly anticipated this concern by inserting the phrase, "creditors would not involuntarily receive less than in liquidation." Many national delegations also found reorganization appealing, not least because reorganization is a way of softening hard budget constraints that otherwise might cause political difficulties as businesses are closed, employment declines, and the public fisc must pick up the pieces (Carruthers, Babb, and

Halliday 2001). The settlements within the Guide on more specific issues are all constrained by this master compromise.[34]

1. *Eligibility for Bankruptcy.* Bankruptcy laws can reach widely to embrace all economic actors in a society or narrowly to protect only a few. The Guide takes a maximalist position: any debtor engaging in an economic activity, whether state owned or privately owned, whether an industrial or financial firm, whether a legal-person enterprise or natural-person enterprise, whether for profit or not for profit, should be eligible for the protections and opportunities of an insolvency law.[35]

   This highly inclusive provision favors advocates of market rather than administrative solutions to business failure, it elevates the status of bankruptcy law as a regulatory mechanism for market activity, and it expands the potential scope of professional services. Inclusiveness reflects the views of the IFIs, the U.S., and the professionals who can benefit from increased demand for their services.

2. *Initiating an Insolvency Proceeding.* It matters a great deal *who* can initiate a bankruptcy. The ability to push a company into, or to decide if it will be a candidate for, reorganization is an exercise of power by any party that has an economic interest in the firm. If a bank has a categorical right to push a company into bankruptcy, the capacity of managers to rescue a company is weakened. If managers have discretion about if and when to seek bankruptcy protections, they are provided negotiating power with creditors and the prospect of saving the underlying business. The test for bankruptcy can also be critical:[36] a cash flow test is much easier for managers or creditors to demonstrate; a balance sheet test usually takes much time and is contestable, giving courts more discretion. And, finally, if there is no gap in time between application to the court and commencement (the court immediately accepts the application), then creditors have less room for maneuver. By contrast, where courts may take weeks or months to decide on an application, many creditors may scramble to get their money out and thus doom the company to failure.

   The Guide recommends that debtors can voluntarily initiate bankruptcy proceedings. The Guide further permits a gap in time between application and commencement of a bankruptcy so a court can make a careful determination of the debtor's eligibility. This favors a Continental law approach, those who advocate a strong role of judges, and creditors. It is less favored by the U.S. or Australia, where bankruptcy applications do not require court approval to commence certain insolvency proceedings. Further, while the Guide prefers a cash flow test, which favors managers, it accepts a balance sheet test, an option preferred by many code law countries.[37]

3. *Scope of the Insolvency Estate.* Advocates of reorganization in bankruptcy law argue that the more debtors' assets available for turning the company around, the greater the probability of success. In recent decades, the U.S. has shaped its law to keep most assets in a bankruptcy pool or "estate." In many other countries, however, secured creditors (usually banks) have had the right to seize their assets outside bankruptcy, which can effectively destroy a company altogether. If security is held in machinery, buildings, or land, the seizure and sale of those assets can shut the company down.[38]

    The Guide leans in the direction of the U.S. bloc. All assets of all sorts should be included in the estate. Yet protections should be created for both debtors and creditors. Debtors should be given a period of time when there is a "stay" or stoppage of any efforts by creditors to realize their security. Creditors, however, should also be protected. They can apply to courts for relief if they believe the value of their assets is being run down,[39] and they are entitled to protect the economic value of their assets.

4. *Contracts.* Contracts are a particularly valuable, though intangible, form of property rights. Contracts with workers, real property leases, financial contracts, equipment leases—all have economic value. When a company goes into bankruptcy, the continuation or breaking of these contracts can make or break a company. Countries have divided sharply over the inclusion of contracts in an estate. Many laws consider freedom of contract sacrosanct, and bankruptcy should make no difference. Other laws reflect the view that without including contracts in the estate, a reorganization has little hope.

    With the exception of financial contracts, the Guide prefers that all contracts be included in the estate where they can be continued, renegotiated, or rejected.[40] Together, the provisions on the insolvency estate and contracts strongly favor the champions of reorganization—the IFIs, the U.S., and bankruptcy practitioners. Its universality potentially favors advanced economies over developing and transitional countries because the disposition of local assets may be bound by the ruling of a foreign court and assets themselves may be expatriated. The provision to exclude financial contracts is a major victory for the financial centers (e.g., U.S., U.K.) and the IMF, which lobbied strongly against their inclusion on grounds that interfering with financial contracts can create uncertainty and shock in global financial systems that depend on automatic and fast clearing of financial contracts. The inclusiveness of the Guide's provisions on the estate are less welcome for bankers and leasors, especially in countries such as Germany, where the banking sector dominates corporate financing. Their discretion is significantly reduced. Rather than act alone, they are compelled to enter the negotiating arena with other creditors and the debtor. They also must yield more discretion to judges and courts.

5. *Rights of Managers.* If a company goes into bankruptcy, should the managers be replaced or continue to run the company? Most countries replace managers with an insolvency representative.[41] If managers were not skilled enough to keep a company out of bankruptcy, they say, why assume they can turn the company around? Some countries, notably the U.S., conventionally leave management in place. The latter maintain that if managers know they are going to be replaced, then they will delay filing for bankruptcy and thereby doom their enterprises. Moreover, if bankruptcy laws are strong enough, bankruptcy itself can be a creative business strategy (Delaney 1992). Professionals, too, have divided on this issue. Bankruptcy lawyers, especially in the U.S., have leaned in favor of keeping managers on and keeping hope alive, which creates work for them. Accountants, especially in Britain and many Commonwealth countries, have preferred to step in themselves and act categorically, quickly, and decisively (Carruthers and Halliday 1998).

The Guide resolves these differences by giving something to everyone. It states that three options are possible: (a) management can stay in place; (b) management may be displaced in part; and (c) management may be displaced entirely. In so doing it legitimates the less usual practice of the U.S. to enable "debtor-in-possession" of the company, without making it normative for the entire world.[42] But U.K. and Continental delegates were equally adamant that their practices should not be impaired. The outcome, therefore, effectively affirms extant practices in all advanced countries.

6. *Fresh Financing.* Successful reorganizations require new money for operating expenses and turnaround measures, such as new marketing efforts, better equipment, and new managers. But companies in financial
distress have low credit ratings and thus either cannot get new money
or can do so only at prohibitive cost. A solution to this problem, widely
adopted in the U.S. and Canada, is to give either current or new lenders
strong incentives to put in new money. This can be achieved by giving
them a priority in case of future liquidation that ranks higher than
all other existing creditors. This new security, or "super-priority," has
proved successful because new creditors now stand first rather than
last in line if the reorganization fails.

The U.S. bloc successfully pushed for the Guide to include this option in reorganizations. The Guide, however, also satisfies the interests
of other secured creditors, whose economic interests must be protected
by the court.[43]

7. *Confirmation of Reorganization Plans.* If companies are to be rehabilitated, stakeholders must agree on the reorganization plan. On this issue there has been wide national variation. Creditor-friendly countries
prefer creditors or insolvency practitioners to take the initiative, with
or without the approval of the debtor. Debtor-friendly countries prefer
the company's managers to have the first opportunity to present a plan
and to give hold-out creditors—those who simply refuse to go along
with the large majority of other parties—little leverage, sometimes by
"cramming down" a decision by a court against their will.

Given such differences, the Guide takes a minimalist approach:
it prescribes neither who should present a plan nor how much time
they will have to do it. But it does insist there should be a plan and
that the law should be clear on who can take the initiative over what
period of time. It vests courts with powers to alter deadlines in the
light of circumstances. The Guide offers a checklist of matters that
should be required for confirmation of a plan, but it does not prioritize them or distinguish between those that are mandatory and those
that are voluntary. However, it insists that if any party has property
rights that could be altered by a plan (e.g., secured creditors), then that
party should have a vote on the plan or some other way to defend its
rights. On the controversial issue of "cramdown," the Guide permits
but does not prescribe that countries allow courts to confirm a plan

over the objections of an entire class of creditors. Finally, on the much-contested issue of whether courts must be involved in confirmation of plans, UNCITRAL remained open, just so long as specified criteria are met, and not least that minority creditors can protect their rights by raising objections before a court.[44]

In these compromises UNCITRAL gave something to everyone. For those countries where courts are central, they can remain central. For creditors concerned about the loss of their rights in reorganizations, it assures them they will be protected. For strong advocates of reorganization, and proponents of debtor rights, it permits legislation to enable cramdown and otherwise bind hold-out creditors that would prevent confirmation of a plan.

8. *Priorities in Liquidations.* One of the most strongly contested elements of bankruptcy law reaches to fundamental ideological differences over protections for workers, creditors, and the state. When the estate cannot pay all creditors in full, who gets paid first? And for what percentage of their claims? Some countries prioritize workers for back pay, lost vacation time, or unvested pension moneys; others insist that all or most taxes must be paid to the government, or social insurance payments that companies often stop making when they get into financial difficulty, before private creditors get paid. Some countries even permit these privileged creditors to recover assets ahead of secured creditors. Since alternative rankings reflect strongly held policy preferences, for instance, between social democratic and neoliberally inclined regimes, a political compromise would have stalemated UNCITRAL.

Insolvency practitioners from advanced countries generally share two preferences. One is that professionals be paid first, euphemistically entitled "administrative costs" of a bankruptcy. While this clearly serves the pecuniary interests of professionals, the priority of administrative preferences serves an economic and legal function that is difficult to manage otherwise. A second is that the number of priorities be limited, especially of government claims. This gives practitioners more flexibility in the creation of reorganization plans. Since more priorities work against the interests of unsecured creditors, there can be adverse consequences for the cost of credit (many banks are often unsecured as well as secured creditors on a particular loan) and the ability to reorganize. Priorities also seem to work against the governing principle of fairness, pari passu.[45] Moreover, bankruptcy specialists in general prefer that policy goals of governments, such as protecting laid-off workers or protecting state pension funds, be handled by separate statutory or administrative methods.

Given the deep divides over priorities, UNCITRAL takes no position on who should be entitled to priorities. But it does press ahead with its emphasis on reorganization, recommending that the number and size of claims be reduced. The form of the recommendations again allows wide national variation while encouraging legislators to harmonize around UNCITRAL's preference.[46]

Institutional Outcomes

We observed earlier that nations differ widely in the administrative arrangements they make for insolvency and reorganization. On *formal court proceedings*, countries such as Australia seek to proceed so far as possible *without* court involvement, whereas other countries, such as France, require court approval for all important decisions. In general, the Guide has a high view of courts and expects that competent and independent courts will always be available to parties in insolvency, although courts are not always required.

Court proceedings are often slow and costly, and courts can readily be overwhelmed in times of recession. For this reason, many advanced countries have developed *out-of-court workout arrangements*. INSOL, for instance, advocates worldwide a set of principles loosely based on the London Approach for Central Bank–led workouts. The U.S. has developed techniques for expedited proceedings, where most negotiations among creditors take place outside court and outside insolvency proceedings. The Guide decided not to take any position on any informal arrangements or techniques sponsored by organizations such as INSOL.[47] But in response to energetic proposals by the U.S., the Working Group was persuaded to adopt methods very closely aligned with the U.S. practice of *expedited proceedings*. This practice enables a number of major creditors to agree among themselves over the terms of a corporate reorganization. They do not consult with smaller creditors because they ensure that those creditors will be paid in full in any reorganization. However, an agreement that takes place out of court may fail if any of its signatories pull out. As a result, the U.S. method, adopted by the Guide, enables sponsors of an expedited plan to present it to a court for confirmation, in which case it then becomes binding on all creditors.[48]

Finally, countries differ over which *professionals* are given jurisdiction over insolvency work. The Guide permits all manner of professionals under the generic label of "insolvency representatives."[49] Nevertheless, it goes into considerable detail to specify the qualifications, modes of appointment, responsibilities, and regulation of insolvency representatives. Effectively, therefore, the Guide does not favor any of the professions that otherwise compete in domestic and international markets for services in corporate liquidation and reorganization.

While the Guide permits countries to limit the role of courts, as in the U.K. and many Commonwealth countries, the strong emphasis on judicial determinations represents an effective alliance between the U.S. and Continental countries, supported by the IFIs and U.S.-staffed expert delegations. The insolvency practitioners represented by INSOL and supported by the U.K. lost their battle to include their out-of-court INSOL Principles in the Guide, though they are mentioned affirmatively in the commentary. By contrast the U.S., ABA, and III won a major victory by including in the Guide provisions for expedited proceedings that virtually reproduce U.S. bankruptcy law and practice for so-called prepackaged bankruptcies. The Guide clearly supports licensed and regulated insolvency practitioners, primarily delivering professional services in the market. Ostensibly it does not benefit lawyers at the expense of accountants/insolvency practitioners, or vice versa. In that sense it leaves the international division of professional labor intact.

Did the clash of powerful stakeholders in UNCITRAL's proceedings lead to either the extremes of stalemate or capture? The production of the Legislative Guide on Insolvency, with its 450 pages of objectives, purposes, and Commentary, and its 198 Recommendations of statutory provisions, belies the charge of stalemate. Neither can the Guide be characterized as the expression of capture by a dominant actor, if by capture we mean the co-optation of this UN agency to reflect solely the particular interests of some group. We also show later that avoiding these two extremes did not condemn UNCITRAL to vacuous compromises. Indeed, the Legislative Guide represents an outcome led powerfully by a bloc comprising the U.S. official delegation, the U.S. lawyers in the delegations of the IBA and ABA, and the IMF.[50] At the heart of the Guide is the norm of reorganization, the comprehensiveness of a bankruptcy estate, the involvement of debtors and creditors in proposing and confirming a plan, incentives for financing a reorganization, and some specific U.S. practices, most notably expedited proceedings and the handling of financial contracts.

Nevertheless, the U.S. was not able to impose on the world its law of commencement (application and commencement occur simultaneously), its provisions on automatic stays (all actions against the debtor cease at the moment of commencement), its practice of debtor-in-possession (management continues to run enterprises after filing for bankruptcy protection), the ability of its courts to impose plans on hold-out creditors, or its provisions for closing out a bankruptcy case. In each of these cases the U.S. settled for the permissibility of these practices while tolerating alternatives.

A number of the agreements in the Guide paralleled those necessary to obtain legislative passage for the 1978 U.S. Bankruptcy Code, over thirty years ago. For instance, whereas the Guide significantly strengthened the rights of debtors in reorganization, it also enhanced protections for the assets of secured creditors that are kept within the bankruptcy estate during reorganization.

Although the Working Group was often led by the U.S. bloc, agreement depended on numbers of alliances and trade-offs. On the most difficult issues, the U.S. bloc sought agreement with the influential French delegation. Given the significant differences among these competing insolvency systems, and the persuasiveness of both delegations, it was said by a U.S. delegate that "an agreement with France made consensus with the Working Group a 'slam dunk.'" The lawyers' expert organizations developed a tacit agreement early on that the Legislative Guide negotiations would not become a battleground between warring professions over jurisdictions of work. The U.S. bloc accommodated the sensibilities of other vocal delegations, such as deferring to the Australian delegation's preference for liquidations and reorganizations with minimal court involvement, deferring to the civil law jurisdictions and their preferences for substantial court involvement in the public interest, deferring to the U.K. preference for moral regulation within bankruptcy law, and deferring to the flexibility desired by many advanced and developing nations over the types of ordering of priorities. In all these the U.S. bloc conceded to practices different from its own in order to get consensus.

If particular substantive provisions adhered more closely to those in the U.S. than in other countries, it must also be acknowledged that the Legislative Guide was created by advanced countries for developing and transitional countries. While numerically dominant, developing and transitional countries were underrepresented in their formal participation, except Korea and Colombia.[51] Many of their delegates conceded that the Legislative Guide was a rich countries' norm promulgated for all countries. Since developing and transitional countries have very little experience with reorganization, it is not surprising that they could bring less expertise to the table. By contrast, two powerful economic actors contributed relatively less to the proceedings. German and Japanese participation was restrained, as neither country sent large delegations to UNCITRAL and the delegates they did send participated less than economic power would predict. Significantly, the other economic bloc that might have proved a counterpoint to the U.S., the European Union, was conspicuous by its absence and failed to mobilize at all.

Of the world's three major trading blocs, only the U.S. took the UNCITRAL proceedings seriously and sought to create a global script that would reflect U.S. economic and professional interests. The U.S. mobilized with skill and dedication. The U.S. delegation at UNCITRAL concentrated more experience than any other delegation, whether state or private. It usually included four experts: the lead delegate from the U.S. State Department; an eminent judge; one or two leading private practitioners; and sometimes a leading academic. The same delegates attended virtually all sessions and thus had the continuity that is critical to effectiveness in multiyear deliberations. Before each meeting, the State Department official, Hal Burman, hosted nationwide conference calls of experts to hammer out a negotiating position for the next session. During the sessions, the U.S. bloc caucused together and worked with other delegations to find agreements. And between the formal sessions, several U.S. lawyers volunteered to draft language or react to drafts by the Secretariat. If the U.S. bloc dominated, the reason was not only its economic and global power but also its bringing to bear more expertise, expending more energy, and working more diligently than other delegations from any other prospective bloc or alliance.

Strategies for Global Lawmaking

We have shown that UNCITRAL solved the problem of representation but in doing so confronted the dangers of stalemate, capture, or inconsequential norm making. None of these adverse results occurred. How was it possible to stake the broadest claim to legitimation through representation and yet produce a practicable guide for legislative enactment? Global lawmaking in the insolvency field succeeded largely because UNCITRAL adopted three sets of organizational strategies: micropolitical, procedural, and formal strategies.

Micropolitical Strategies

We define *micropolitical strategies* as those employed to exploit and manage power differences within international lawmaking forums. For UNCITRAL, those problems of inequality in power, resources, and expertise influenced the balance between competing legal traditions, the relationship between UNCITRAL's products and the IFIs and their scripts and evaluative technologies, and containment of dominant nation-states, especially the United States.

The Legislative Guide rejects a "one-size-fits-all" approach to global norm making. At the outset the Guide acknowledges "that there is no universal solution to the design of an insolvency law because countries vary significantly in their needs, as do their laws on other issues of key importance to insolvency."[52] Consensus on the nine key objectives of an insolvency system was accompanied by recognition of permissible variations across national insolvency systems that would accommodate alternative policy goals, such as "rescuing businesses in financial difficulty, protecting employment, protecting the interests of creditors, encouraging the development of an entrepreneurial class."[53] Countries might lean in the direction of "creditor-friendly" regimes or "debtor-friendly" regimes, or give more or less prominence to liquidation or reorganization.[54]

The Guide also remains neutral among alternative legal traditions by crafting its script to look quite unlike the law of any one country. Where alternative approaches to an issue are canvassed in the Commentary that precedes each set of Recommendations, there is never any reference to which countries offer what alternatives. Even more important, there is a disengagement between the Guide's expression of preferences for an alternative and who or what legal tradition exemplifies the Guide's preference.[55] In fact, no reference, even illustratively, is made to the law of a particular country. In so doing, the Guide deliberately seeks to forestall crude "counting" of which countries succeeded most in placing their stamp on the final product. Thus, the Guide sacrifices the potential benefits from holding up particular countries as exemplars in favor of appearing above national interests.[56]

The Working Group on Insolvency integrated public and private global organizations into its deliberations and decision-making processes. The IMF sent delegates to the majority of Working Group sessions; the OECD and ADB were represented in earlier sessions; and the World Bank was represented in later sessions. For example, throughout, the Secretariat sought to keep abreast of IMF positions on issues and benefited from implicit IMF support. On at least one issue of particular importance to the IMF, that of financial setoff, the IMF provided funds for an expert group selected by UNCITRAL to meet and draft recommendations.[57]

UNCITRAL also seeks consistency with its own precedents, both those adopted by the UN and those enacted in countries. Apart from the drafting merits inherent in consistency itself, UNCITRAL's reliance on its own precedents offered three benefits (Block-Lieb and Halliday 2007b). One is that earlier Working Groups may have solved problems that eased the task of later groups.[58] Another benefit comes from the legitimation of effectiveness already endowed by an earlier Working Group and the UNCITRAL Commission— both may be considered as earlier political settlements whose terms are best acknowledged.[59] A third benefit also relates to the pragmatism of global reform initiatives: if countries have already enacted laws based on UNCITRAL's earlier products, then it does not behoove UNCITRAL subsequently to introduce inconsistencies since this will compound difficulties of national lawmaking and cast some doubt on the strength of the global consensus that produced each product.

Not least, it was a primary challenge for this global body to "manage the U.S." Part of this "management" occurred procedurally, as we elaborate in the next section. Although UNCITRAL can benefit from U.S. experience and expertise, UNCITRAL clearly understands that its products will be doomed if they look too much like U.S. law. As a result, the Secretariat sought to craft a product that looks unlike U.S. law, however much its contents may reflect positions acceptable to the U.S. For the most part, the Guide excludes all but one term of art in the U.S. Bankruptcy Code.[60] Even on the limited occasions when these concepts find their way into the text, it is usually to illustrate practices of "some legal systems" in contradistinction to others.

Procedural Strategies

Legitimation in international organizations depends also on procedural fairness or the rules of deliberation (Hurd 2005, 2007; Tyler 2001). Fairness requires that all actors have voice, clear rules govern proceedings, and those rules are fairly applied. Indeed, research on procedural justice demonstrates that adherence to certain processes in the administration of justice may be as important, or more important, to parties as the substantive outcome itself (Tyler 2001). Fairness in global metabargaining can be manifest at three points: agenda setting, participation, and decision making.

Agenda Setting   Setting an agenda for an organization or legislature is a prime site for the exercise of power (Kingdon 1995). The actor—nation-state, international organization, norm-making body—who can set the agenda effectively can predetermine what matters will be subject to bargaining and what matters will not. As a result, agenda setting itself is a site for bargaining where all sophisticated actors understand that the shape of the agenda substantially bounds the outcome.

UNCITRAL's Secretariat recognized that this stage requires careful management. When UNCITRAL convened a feasibility meeting in December 1999, it carefully structured the meeting so that leaders of prior initiatives chaired and led sessions and ample recognition was made of their enterprises. This procedural step immediately set UNCITRAL's initiative apart from all previous norm-making enterprises by IFIs.

As a result, the agenda setting influenced both the *substance* and *form* of that law. For both, the Secretariat adopted a pragmatic "modesty concept"— that the Working Group aim for what is possible, not what might be more desirable.[61] On the substance of the law, the initial agenda-setting meetings facilitated a practicable and modest outcome by taking a number of intractable issues off the agenda. The Working Group excluded individual bankruptcies and focused entirely on business bankruptcies.[62] In addition, the Working Group excluded, so far as possible, policy matters related to the use of bankruptcy law as a social safety mechanism; the treatment of corporate groups in bankruptcy; and detailed recommendations on the structure and organization of courts, government agencies, and out-of-court bodies.

The Working Group also decided to craft its product principally for developing and transitional countries, even if it came to have substantial effects on law reforms in several advanced countries, such as France and Spain. This step helped to defuse potential struggles that might have broken out among advanced countries for norms closely related to their own laws, although it did not necessarily mitigate efforts by these countries to press for a guide that was most consistent with their respective regimes. It also influenced the didactic tone of the document since it became imperative to instruct potential legislators in the fundamentals of corporate insolvency regimes and in the reasoning behind choices.

Participation   Since UNCITRAL chose to proceed in its legislative chamber with large, diverse constituencies, it adopted procedures to ensure that all participants were treated fairly. Because the chairmanship of a Working Group, or the position of rapporteur, might allow a delegation to exercise undue influence, UNCITRAL encouraged Working Groups to elect chairs and rapporteurs from developing or smaller advanced countries. For the Working Group on Insolvency, delegates elected as the principal chairman a judge from Thailand, and as interim chairmen a barrister from New Zealand, a lawyer from Switzerland, and a professor from Korea. As rapporteurs, they elected the Colombian director of corporate insolvencies, among others.

The informal rules of participation reinforced norms of procedural neutrality. The three governing rules were that (1) any delegate or observer was free to speak in open session; (2) whoever raised a delegation flag (e.g., a representative of Colombia, China, or the IMF) was called upon to speak in the order in which it raised its flag; (3) all delegates with raised flags were heard before the Chairman called again on a delegate to speak a second or third time.[63]

Since access to information, especially to early drafts, influences the capacities of actors to exercise influence, the breadth of dissemination influences the sense and reality of broad representation. The Working Group Secretary at UNCITRAL e-mailed successive drafts to all delegates. Since forwarding e-mails to nondelegates involved only a click or two on any delegate's computer, fragmentary evidence indicates that this Working Group had its materials disseminated not only to the network of delegates but to each delegate's network, thus ensuring that the successive drafts opened up wide opportunities for response.[64]

Decision Making   Power differences in the international system can be reinforced or mitigated by decision-making rules. They can systematically advantage or disadvantage particular actors, will influence the capacity of an institution to reach optimal solutions, and can reinforce or undermine the legitimacy of products.

Whereas some international lawmaking bodies bring all decisions to a vote that is recorded and publicized,[65] UNCITRAL's Working Groups do not, principally because the Secretariat believes that divided votes on particular provisions weaken the final product and make it easier for nation-states to discard contentious provisions. Rather, UNCITRAL adopts a consensus norm but without formal vote. After debate on a provision, the Chair states what he or she believes to be the agreement reached by delegates. He may either ask for some manifest expression of agreement such as a nodding of heads; or she may pose the question and wait for dissent. If none is forthcoming, this is deemed to express a consensus of the chamber as a whole. If disagreement does arise, further debate may continue. In the quite common cases where disagreement continues, the Chair takes a sense of standing by the most vocal, most influential delegations and will declare a sense of the meeting that supports the "prevailing" view, officially with particular deference to state delegations. Thus, if France and the United States concurred, together with the principal expert organizations (IBA, INSOL, ABA), unless there was vocal dissent led by another respected delegation or observer (e.g., Australia, U.K., Colombia, Korea), the Chair usually declared effective consensus on that decision. Since the Chair was always from a smaller country, and from a country not clearly aligned with any legal family or geopolitical bloc, this method was not challenged.[66]

This method enabled a consensus to be reached that strengthened the overall integrity and authority of the product. Incorporating into the consensus making the voices of observers and international organizations allowed a broader degree of representativeness in the decision making than would be permitted by rules that confined votes only to official delegates.[67]

Yet this method does not dispel all doubts about substantive or procedural fairness. It permits vocal coalitions or blocs to veto provisions that do not satisfy major constituencies even though a straight vote might put the fewer powerful actors in a numerical minority. It gives the Chair a great deal of discretion to pronounce a consensus. By the same token, the mechanism is entirely transparent; and since the signs on which the Chair relies can also be read by any delegation, there is the possibility of diplomatically dissenting, which happened only on rare occasions. The procedural fairness in this decision-making regime, therefore, inheres principally in the option of "voice" for all participants.[68]

Formal Strategies[69]

Finally, consensus was enabled through the interplay of two formal strategies: manipulating technologies of lawmaking; and creating a variety of rule-types that could be deployed and combined as the consensus-building challenge demanded.

Manipulating Technologies UNCITRAL has developed a portfolio of products to match the difficulty of reaching consensus in a particular area of substantive law. These technologies, or alternative forms of scripts, have progressively allowed UNCITRAL to extend its global norm making into areas of law previously thought intractable.

1. *Products.* A *convention* takes the form of a multilateral treaty. Countries accede to a single standard. As a result, the demands for accession are high since countries may not alter any part of the convention to suit domestic political or legal differences.[70] Likewise, conditions of formulation require zero-sum bargaining in order to reach agreement. Both conditions mean that conventions will be applicable only to areas of law that permit agreement across radically different legal families and levels of economic development.[71]

A *model law* relaxes some of the strictures of conventions.[72] It takes the form of a legislative text that the UN General Assembly recommends be enacted in toto by nation-states. However, in order to be responsive to the particular needs of a given state, a model law "permits" states to exclude or modify certain provisions of the model law. As a result, a greater number of countries may be encouraged to adopt some form of it.[73] As an enhancement on a model law, some recent UNCITRAL products have combined a model law with a *guide to enactment* that sets out background information, explanations of decisions, and information on various policy options that might enable legislators to make informed decisions.[74]

It was a short move for UNCITRAL in the last several years to detach the guide to enactment from a model law and to produce a standalone principles-oriented product—the *legislative guide.* At the first Colloquium on the prospects of an UNCITRAL initiative, the Secretariat described the Guide in these terms:

> The purpose of these principles or legislative recommendations would be to assist Governments and legislative bodies in reviewing the adequacy of laws, regulations, decrees and similar legislative texts in a particular field. In order to advance the objective of harmonization, and offer a legislative model, the principles or recommendations . . . would set out a number of issues often addressed in national laws and regulations and address the desirability of dealing with those issues in legislation. The text would provide a set of possible legislative solutions on certain issues, but not necessarily a single set of model solutions for the issues considered.[75]

In the past thirty years UNCITRAL has relaxed the strictures of its legal technologies for harmonization (Block-Lieb and Halliday 2007a). By shifting its emphasis away from strictly binding instruments, such as conventions, and by inventing new technologies, UNCITRAL has been able to embrace more areas of commercial law, widen the circle of countries that will adopt its products, and move more nimbly in response to demands or crises.[76]

2. *The Structure of the Legislative Guide on Insolvency Law.*[77] Three formal elements of the Guide demonstrate how the Secretariat crafted a script that could accommodate the extremes of variation we have observed.

   a. *Glossary.* After the Introduction, the Legislative Guide presents a Glossary. What first appears as a technical aid to an understanding of the text in fact functions as a formal mechanism for defusing national contests over legal concepts and terminology. UNCITRAL both adopts and creates a universal vocabulary to standardize usage within the Guide. In addition to the obvious political advantage of avoiding identification of UNCITRAL's products with any particular legal system, this also has the juridical effect of detaching judges from standard interpretations of terms in their own legal traditions. Said an UNCITRAL official:

      > If you use a particular word in this actual text, the judge in one legal system will give it its own meaning, and we don't want the judge to give it that historical meaning. We want to give the international meaning, which is then spelled out. So we want not to confuse the user of the text by using a text as he learned it in law school.[78]

      The invention of terms in particular spans Working Groups and harmonizing projects, with the effect that UNCITRAL has been elaborating its own specialized language that it proffers for global adoption.

   b. *Commentary.* The Commentary combines several elements. First, it usually identifies an issue and indicates why it is important (e.g., determining which debtors will be subject to the law or which parties can commence proceeding). Second, it may offer a principle in relation to the issue and justify the principle (e.g., "an insolvency law will need to clearly identify the assets" because this will produce "transparency and predictability."[79] Third, where there is considerable cross-national variation of laws on this issue, the Commentary will present principal alternative ways that countries address the issue, without ever identifying the countries.[80] Fourth, it discusses the benefits and deficiencies of the alternatives, focusing both on juridical and practical advantages and disadvantages.[81] And, fifth, it will usually express a preference (e.g., "it is increasingly recognized" that a certain course of action will have more advantages to the economy).[82]

The Commentary thereby serves both internal and external functions. For purposes of reaching agreement, the Commentary provides a space where disagreements can be defused by signaling that dissent has been heard and that points of view have been fairly aired. By including contending views in the Commentary, even if one of those views will be preferred over others, groups may be pacified and country delegates can signal to their ministries that their opinions were expressed and recorded. For purposes of implementation, the Commentary has a significant didactic role, for it expresses a global consensus on what issues must be addressed in legislation, explains to national lawmakers the costs and benefits of alternatives, and offers a guide to judges, providing reasoning to support recommendations.[83]

c. *Recommendations.* At the end of each substantive section of Commentary, the Guide includes Recommendations. These are always prefaced by a set of purposes, which themselves have been negotiated by delegates.[84] The statements of purposes range from a single sentence to four to six specific goals, providing both an introduction to the Recommendations they precede and a statement of their intended reach. The variety of forms in the Recommendations provides the Guide with a repertoire of rule types that alone or in combination enable the Guide to adjust for the degree of diversity and dissent on issues.

Recommendations are grouped along a spectrum of specificity that ranges from broad statements of norms to explicitly detailed language ready for enactment. *Imperative recommendations* propose that national legislatures take specific types of action whose content is expressly stated. Imperative recommendations have in common that they all provide domestic legislatures with proposed statutory language. If a legislative guide were composed of only imperative recommendations, it would closely resemble a model law. *Constraining recommendations* are not explicitly directive as to particular courses of action, but they are conducive to convergence. Often they point in a direction and then give choices. For instance, they may seek to establish that there should be a rule on a topic and it should include certain elements without precluding the addition of others. Or it may permit a country to adopt a certain rule and, if so, what it might include, without requiring it. *Focusing recommendations* look to sharpen the focus of any law adopted by a domestic legislature. They recommend that there should be a rule on a topic without specifying its content. *Policy recommendations* identify and affirm substantive commercial law norms. These are the highest-order principles in the Guide. They are stated at the outset as its nine governing norms or key objectives.[85]

Although these norms might, at first glance, be dismissed as little more than blandishments of "motherhood and apple pie," in fact, they are much more than that. Each addresses either a reorientation of policy in many countries or a ubiquitous problem in the functioning of bankruptcy systems. These four classes of rule types have the virtue that they may be combined and recombined in many ways to adapt to the challenge posed by the degree and type of dissensus.

The combination of choosing a technology (i.e., a Legislative Guide) that permits a great deal of cross-national variation and of creating the flexibility of recommendation types by levels of abstraction have given UNCITRAL great flexibility in dealing with any issue, no matter how divisive. The recommendation type or level of specificity is varied depending both on the difficulty of obtaining consensus in norm making and in the degrees of freedom thought desirable for national legislatures. While this is not so homogenizing as a convention, or even as a model law, it nevertheless presses countries toward a global statutory norm where they will find differing levels of global consensus. The result is a completed Legislative Guide in an area of commercial law thought to be not susceptible to global convergence.

The Politics of Global Legitimation

The rapid progress made by UNCITRAL's Working Group between 2000 and 2003 seemed to confirm agreement among international organizations that it was the appropriate forum in which to formulate a single set of global norms. It therefore came as a great shock to UNCITRAL delegates and the Secretariat to learn in mid-2003 that the World Bank intended to press forward with its *Principles* and effectively propagate a rival standard. World Bank officials took heart from their apparent success at convincing the U.S. Treasury that their enterprise was in the ascendancy, much to the dismay of the U.S. State Department representative to UNCITRAL, who was bent on presenting a single global norm to developing countries.

In the following two years UNCITRAL pressed forward to complete its Legislative Guide while simultaneously engaging in endless meetings, offering one or another complementary solution that was reflected in unstable successive oral and written agreements. The struggle embroiled rivalries not only between U.S. government departments but between the IMF, which supported the UNCITRAL Legislative Guide, and the World Bank, which clung to its own product. Since both the IMF and World Bank are part of the larger United Nations family of organizations, the General Counsel of the UN also became involved as pressures were placed on the World Bank Legal Department to yield or see it become a matter for the Managing Director of the IMF and the President of the Bank.

By mid-2005, a year after the Commission had adopted the Legislative Guide, U.S. Treasury agreed with the State Department that a single standard was preferable—and it was the UNCITRAL standard that should dominate. In late 2005 UNCITRAL and the Bank reached a two-part agreement that was to be ratified by the IMF/World Bank directors.[86] The first part involved the authorization of parallel documents: one would comprise a twenty-five-page severely truncated version of the World Bank *Principles*, listing some thirty-three principles preceded by an executive summary; the other would be the already published 498-page Legislative Guide with its 198 Recommendations and several Annexes, including the Model Law and its Guide to Enactment. In effect, the Guide eclipsed the *Principles*, although the latter retained some significant institutional elements on courts and insolvency professions not treated extensively in the Guide.[87] The second was the design of a ROSC (Report on the Observance of Standards and Codes), jointly deployed by the IMF and World Bank for diagnosis of insolvency systems, which would reflect the options available to nations in the Legislative Guide and had the tacit approval of UNCITRAL.[88]

This agreement codified a bargain in which UNCITRAL provided legitimacy and legislative substantive and procedural specificity and the World Bank fostered diagnosis and economic leverage. At best this would provide UNCITRAL with the leverage for implementation it did not have and the World Bank the legitimacy that it lacked.

The agreement between the World Bank and UNCITRAL brought to conclusion the twenty-five-year-old movement to establish global norms for insolvency law (see Table 3.1). What began with private efforts among professionals and ad hoc experiments by innovative judges transposed into multiple and parallel norm making by global public institutions and came to fruition in the production of a single global institution with a plausible claim to universality. Development of this legal field started with efforts to solve the problems of administering complex cross-border insolvencies for a handful of multinational corporations. The norm-making enterprise lifted its scale and urgency with the market making and market modernization of transitional and developing economies, respectively. But the threat of regional and global financial collapse, and the promise of galloping global trade, induced the UN and its allies to produce the "gold standard" that pioneers of the insolvency field had once imagined to be an impossible dream.

The evolution of this global field resulted from a conjunction of interests among an enormously varied set of actors. The finance ministers and central bankers of the world's largest economies, led by the U.S., pressed their agents of global reconstruction, the IMF and World Bank, to provide comprehensive solutions to protect and invigorate a global economy. International professional associations, based in advanced economies, sought openings for professional services, convergence of national laws and insolvency regimes, and coherence in national laws and practices. Many developing countries recognized the merits in conforming their laws to international standards that might facilitate investment, or at least raise the probability of technical assistance and emergency aid from IFIs. And the UN's primary agency for the production of commercial law norms seized an opportunity to expand its presence as the most legitimate global producer of norms for national lawmakers. The convergence of these interests around a progressive advance in norm-making ambitions and practices culminated in a comprehensive solution for nation-states that purported to embrace all of the core elements in an insolvency law.

The primary actors in the twenty-five-year progression toward the new global standard perceived their struggle as involving a politics of legitimation. What began as technical solutions by private and state legal experts, and moved into a multiplicity of regional and global scripts advanced by more experts, ended finally in a forum where technical authority would be underwritten by representation—of nations and of interests.

Why did so many powerful actors decide ultimately to forgo their solo initiatives and compromise their preferences in a global forum? Each was saddled with limitations in terms of what we have named legitimation warrants and deficits. The United States has ample expertise and massive power, but ultimately its strength is also its weakness: its competitors among advanced nations and its "clients" in developing nations feared its hegemonic capabilities. U.S. negotiators understood this all too well. The leading regional development banks, particularly the Asian Development Bank and European Bank for Reconstruction and Development, had some in-house expertise and access to more consulting expertise, as well as considerable experience investing and advising countries in their regions. But their solutions were bounded by the particularities of their regions. In neither case could the bank claim a democratic authority for its norms. The IMF also had considerable experience and substantial in-house expertise as well as access to outstanding consultants. Most notably it had financial leverage through conditionalities for its loans. Yet again its strengths were its deficits: it well understood that norms produced by an international institution frequently derogated for its coercive intrusions on sovereignty could never be an effective source for global norms.

The World Bank differed from the IMF in two respects: while the Bank was also widely derogated, its leading counsel, an American lawyer, did not comprehend the depth of anti-Bank sentiment in developing and transitional countries; nevertheless, the Bank made valiant efforts over several years to broaden consultations to experts and officials in most regions of the world as it honed its principles of a creditor-debtor system. Of all the actors in the international field, the Bank evidenced until the bitter end a striking gap between its self-perception as a legitimate norm-making institution and the perceptions of its prospective clients. It yielded only after intense pressure by the IMF, the U.S. State Department and Treasury, and the UN General Counsel. The two principal professional associations, INSOL and the IBA, together with the ABA's

International Section, had strong claims to technical authority. Yet they, too, acknowledged that this authority had narrow auspices and could not be perceived as either universal in its warrants or enforceable in its implementation.

With the grudging exception of the World Bank, therefore, legitimation deficits of all the international institutions and leading nations led them to the only institution that seemed to combine the warrants necessary for an effective global standard—the United Nations. Here we find a remarkable correspondence between theoretical analysis of legitimacy in international organizations and the self-understanding of UNCITRAL itself. If legitimacy of international organizations resides in three sets of attributes—representation of affected constituencies; procedural fairness in deliberation and decision making; and perceived effectiveness, past and future—UNCITRAL established its bona fides as the institution of last resort in global norm making precisely in these terms (Barnett and Finnemore 2005; Hurd 2002, 2007). The Secretariat proclaimed the universality of UNCITRAL's representation in the Commission and Working Group in not so veiled contrast to all those other international organizations on whose shoulders it would stand. The Secretariat arguably effected its claim to universality with an excess of inclusiveness: not only were all nations welcomed to the Working Group but so were the principal international interest groups in the insolvency field, even if all did not accept the invitation. Virtually all of the principal fault lines of insolvency policy were drawn inside the chamber. It could boast representative and expert authority to a degree seldom matched by national legislatures.[89] Having brought diverse interests into the chamber, UNCITRAL then ensured that the rules of agenda setting, participation, and decision making were transparent and fair, thereby reinforcing its claims to be neutral and procedurally correct. And from the outset the UNCITRAL Secretariat, and many of its most vocal boosters, pointed to its past effectiveness in norm making and their implementation worldwide. The Working Group adopted a "modesty principle" precisely to assure the enactability of this new standard.

What the theorists of legitimation in international organizations do not adequately address, however, can be observed in the conundrum that this apparent success posed for UNCITRAL's capacity to produce a meaningful product. Expansiveness of representation and participation compounded the difficulty of finding a consensus that would produce the effective norms and legal convergence that most delegates appeared to want. The heterogeneity of interests and asymmetries of power might impede the Working Group's capacity to produce anything but stalemate or vacuous imprecise standards, or possibly capture by the most powerful actors.

None of these eventuated. The Commission produced a Legislative Guide and so avoided stalemate. Neither was it captured by a single bloc. It is true that the U.S. bloc dominated, but it did not impose a U.S. solution. The outcomes were satisfactory to civil law and common law countries; to developed, developing, and transitional countries; to creditor as well as debtor interests (so far as these could be ascertained from their agents); to lawyers and accountants (the IBA/INSOL). Moreover, UNCITRAL managed to sidestep a potential price of such a consensus—vague and imprecise Recommendations. The Legislative Guide deals with all the core elements of a national bankruptcy law. The centrality of corporate reorganization provides a pivot on which the entire Guide balances. Most of its consensually developed Recommendations facilitate convergence in some measure yet allow significant variation in situations when consensus on a single Recommendation would be impossible.

How was this possible? UNCITRAL adopted three strategies that enabled it to harmonize a cacophony of voices. Its micropolitics assimilated to UNCITRAL the major prior players in the field, a representative array of nations, and leading expert organizations. At the same time those politics sought to redress imbalances of power to lend neither the appearance nor reality of U.S. dominance. Its procedural strategies institutionalized practices of participatory fairness in agenda setting and decision making. Its formal strategies combined a choice of technology well suited to the diversity of interests and practices of delegates with the invention of an array of rule types that could ratchet up or down levels of generality, depending on the extent of dissensus among delegations.

The melding of UNCITRAL's substantive proposals with IMF and World Bank instruments subsequently integrated two aspects of global scripts. Viewed diagnostically, the Reports on the Observance of Standards and Codes enabled UNCITRAL's product to be operationalized in the legitimate appraisals of national laws that accompany global lending and technical assistance. Viewed prescriptively, UNCITRAL's Legislative Guide became the norm against which nations could remedy the deficiencies that arise from ROSCs. This potentially sets in motion two changes: nations may conform their laws to the UNCITRAL Guide in order to score highly on ROSCs; or ROSCs may precipitate nations to remedy their faults by adopting Recommendations in the Guide.

This fusion of the evaluative and prescriptive sides of global standards for insolvency laws effectively puts in place a dynamic for national lawmaking that pushes toward isomorphism—or legal convergence—through three of the mechanisms identified by neoinstitutionalists. UNCITRAL's Guide and the IMF/World Bank ROSCs offer a normative standard that can be the basis of modeling by any nation-state. In practice, however, a substantial persuasive apparatus is in place by IFIs, professions, and UNCITRAL itself for countries to align their laws with the script promulgated by the UN. And in the extremes, the IMF and the World Bank will use economic coercion to compel conformity at some level in order for countries to qualify for emergency credit or even technical assistance.

As a result, UNCITRAL not only succeeded in producing a legitimate global script but it managed to leverage its norms by linking them to institutions with the power to persuade and enforce. For nations voluntarily undertaking reforms, the UN imprimatur increases the likelihood that adoption of these norms will be acceptable to domestic political constituencies. For nations involuntarily reforming their insolvency law, it will be some consolation that the standard comes not from the IMF or World Bank but from an entity in which their nation had the right of representation. In either case, the agreement between the World Bank, IMF, and UNCITRAL, together with vigorous proselytization by influential professions, has elevated a single script to the level of a global standard. The degree of actual convergence, however, awaits the verdict that ultimately counts—enactment and implementation by nation-states.

5 Indonesia:
The IMF as a Reformist Ally

THE ASIAN FINANCIAL CRISIS struck Indonesia with double force, plunging its economy into deep recession and shaking its political system to the core. From the 1970s through the early 1990s, Indonesia's rapid economic growth had lowered the nation's poverty rate from 60 percent in 1970 to 11.3 percent in 1996 (Giorgianni et al. 2000). The financial shock wave of 1997 hastened the collapse of Suharto's authoritarian rule and an uneven transition to a more democratic polity. After decades of erosion by authoritarian leaders, Indonesia's legal system had very little capacity to encounter either crisis and, indeed, was undoubtedly complicit in both.

Of our three national case studies, Indonesia represents the most asymmetrical balance of power between a nation-state and IFIs. Compared to China, which scarcely was touched by the Crisis, Indonesia suffered perhaps its severest shock and was most crippled by the destabilizing impact of the Crisis. Compared to Korea, it remained a less industrialized and more agrarian economy and had a correspondingly lower per capita GDP. Indonesia did not have enormous capacities or resiliency of an essentially first-world economy, nor the domestic infrastructures and expertise that Korea had assiduously built over the previous decades. Moreover, unlike politics in China and Korea, Indonesian politics and its market were shaped by a sharp ethnic fault line—the important role played by ethnic Chinese in the economy. Long-standing tensions simmered between the Chinese minority population, which dominated large corporations, and the indigenous Indonesian business class (*pribumi*). As a result, in Indonesia IFIs faced a government shaken by internal and external pressures and without either the assurance or capacity to resist the pressures for reform emanating from the IFIs and their leading sovereign sponsors. In these circumstances it should be expected that IFIs could exert their financial power to maximum effect in order to produce deep and lasting law reforms.

This balance of power in favor of the IFIs encountered a quicksand of institutional shortcomings, social conflicts, incapacities, and outright resistance. The enactment and implementation of law reforms, substantive and institutional, occurred in a context fraught with conflict. IFIs differed fundamentally with each other. Creditor nations took sharply contrasting positions about how to restructure corporate debt. Foreign creditors confronted national resentments and recalcitrant debtors. And entrenched interests in the justice system resisted reformist impulses.

Confronted with financial collapse of its industry, commercial banks, and Central Bank, Indonesia threw itself on the mercy of international banks and international financial institutions to stabilize the free fall of the rupiah. The IFIs and sovereign lending nations offered a massive bailout. Their intervention was coupled with strong macroeconomic and microeconomic medicine—demands that Indonesia reform all its fundamental financial institutions as well as the legal institutions that regulate the economy. Notable among these was Indonesia's institutional incapacity for corporate restructuring, especially when assets involved political and economic elites.

The IFIs sought to revivify law in a nation whose recourse to law had progressively diminished over thirty years of authoritarian rule and whose legal institutions were decrepit, weak, and riddled with corruption (Lev 2004; Lev and McVey 1996). The professions of law and accounting, economics and finance, offered a shallow pool of expertise for activation of legally regulated means of liquidating or rescuing a flood of failing companies. A strong nationalism and the enormous success of Chinese conglomerates at the heights of the Indonesian economy would greet any real or imagined efforts to wrest control away from domestic owners with dogged and creative resistance. Even if political will for reform were real—and doubt would persist on this score—the institutions available to deliver reform had limited capacities.

Yet it is wrong to construe IFI legal interventions as little more than an exogenous imposition of a foreign mandate on a hapless nation-state (Lindsey 1998).

Although IFIs encountered resistance from entrenched elites, they were cautiously welcomed by weak domestic legal elites who saw IFIs as potential agents of institutional reform. Before the Crisis a small core of Indonesian lawyers had kept alive the hope that meaningful law reform remained a desirable prospect. During the mid-1990s first one and then another indigenous proposal for institutional and substantive reforms emerged. It is true that these benefited from the resources of IFIs and donor aid. It is clear, however, that the core features of these plans to reform the courts, bankruptcy law, and administration came principally from within Indonesia, not as a mirror image of a global standard, which in the area of bankruptcy did not then exist. Rather than act as a hegemonic global power using its weight against a unified resistant local actor, the IFIs found local allies who had been waiting for the leverage to accomplish what they had failed to do within the constraints of purely domestic politics. Local reformers had templates but little power. The IFIs had developing norms with fragmentary local knowledge. Hence, a faction of local reformers welcomed IFI conditionality as a means to accomplish ends they could not manage by themselves.

This IFI–domestic alliance entered into repeated cycles of point and counterpoint for law reform, as first one, then another, agreement was reached with the Government, recorded in its Letter of Intent with the IMF, then postponed, frustrated, or weakly implemented, if at all. These cycles of pressure and response encapsulated the substantive law, the courts, the private professions, and out-of-court mechanisms for corporate restructuring. A change in one impeded or facilitated adaptation in another. They began narrowly and broadened successively, sometimes overlapping with complementary initiatives elsewhere in contiguous institutions, in an expanding effort by the IFIs and their domestic allies to wrap their arms around what seemed often to be an elusive quarry. In the process these recursive cycles demonstrate both the expansiveness of IFI ambitions to reconstruct a legal system that can regulate firms and the limits of pressures by IFIs, aid programs, and domestic reformers in the face of unsettled politics, institutional deformities, corruption, and cultural resistance.

We begin with an overview of the antecedents of the Crisis in Indonesia and then turn in detail to the multiple tracks of reform pressed by IFIs. We then circle back to analyze the recursive processes that structured legal change and to appraise how far Indonesia has moved toward the global norms sponsored by international agents of reform.

Up to the Crisis

From the mid-1970s the performance of the Indonesian economy has been substantially affected by oil prices. Winters (1996) has argued that when oil revenues were high, Indonesia reduced its dependency on international investors for capital. But when oil prices declined, the Government worked harder to create a positive investment environment. During the early 1980s, a period of relatively low oil prices, the Indonesian government began to reform the nation's financial system. Banking deregulation was intended to ensure that the financial system would do a better job mobilizing domestic savings and facilitating investment to make the country less beholden to foreign investors (Pangestu and Habir 2002; Schwarz 2000). The number of banks grew rapidly, as did their assets and liabilities. Despite new laws to institute prudential regulations, poor implementation and weak regulatory oversight enabled banks to take on excessive risks (Pangestu and Habir 2002: 6–7).

Foreign investment in Indonesia increased rapidly during the 1990s. Private inflows of bonds, loans, and portfolio investment averaged $5.7 billion between 1990 and 1993, surged to $10.2 billion in 1994, and by 1997 reached $25.6 billion (Bingham et al. 2002: 51).[1] As Indonesian banks and corporations absorbed the inflow of capital, Indonesia's overall level of indebtedness rose to levels even higher than that of other Asian developing economies (Giorgianni et al. 2000: 71). Being so highly leveraged made them extremely vulnerable to even a small downturn. Furthermore, much of the debt was dollar denominated, and Indonesian borrowers rarely hedged against the foreign exchange risks to which they were now exposed. With this additional liquidity, Indonesian banks extended credit into property and real estate investments that produced a real estate bubble (Pangestu and Habir 2002: 12–13). Since many of their loans were secured by real estate, if the bubble burst, banks would quickly suffer financial difficulty.

Politically, Indonesia had long been dominated by President Suharto and his retinue. Indonesia's House of Representatives functioned to endorse policies crafted by a highly centralized executive power (MacIntyre 2003). Strong links joined the business elite to the top levels of government in a quasi-patrimonial system. Suharto and his family played a balancing act between the more numerous *pribumi* business community, which pressed for more access and opportunity, and the ethnic Chinese community, which dominated the largest business groups. Corruption and favoritism were pervasive, but so pervasive that outside investors simply regarded them as unavoidable costs of doing business in Indonesia. A development official observed that corruption "was predictable and reliable, so foreign direct investment came into the country" (Riesenhuber 2001:149–150).[2]

As a former Dutch colony, Indonesia inherited the Netherlands' civil law system.[3] In the decade or more following Japan's defeat after World War II, and the subsequent success of Indonesia's independence movement, a window of opportunity opened for the consolidation and expansion of a postcolonial *Rechtsstaat*, or "state of law," in the new nation (Lev 2000). Some modernization of substantive law was accompanied by the prospect of the judiciary as an emerging center of power. But decades of authoritarian government by Sukarno and Suharto progressively reduced the courts to a cipher (Pompe 2005). By the mid-1990s, judges were poorly trained, poorly paid, and eminently corruptible. The courts moved very slowly if at all. Their independence was assured neither from the regime nor the market. Commercial litigants avoided courts whenever possible, especially foreign businesses, which had no confidence that their claims would be treated on their merits. So, too, did "clean" lawyers, who feared a tainting of their reputation. Although Indonesia had a 1905 bankruptcy law on the books that it had inherited from the Dutch, the law was not widely used, especially against politically connected, and protected, companies.[4]

Unlike Korea, Indonesia had not even an elementary social safety net in place when the Financial Crisis hit, although its relatively large rural sector helped somewhat in cushioning the dramatic rise in unemployment (Lee 1998). Suharto's undemocratic and corrupt regime could do little to protect the populace from the effects of the Crisis, so the political turmoil that accompanied the fall of his regime and the transition to a prospective democratic polity complicated Indonesia's ability to respond to the Crisis.

The Crisis began in Thailand, but it soon spread to Indonesia and there became enmeshed in a full-scale political crisis that eventually toppled Suharto. By October 1997, the value of the Indonesian rupiah had declined more than 30 percent, farther than the currency of any of the other Crisis countries (Lindgren et al. 1999: 54). A three-year $10 billion stand-by arrangement was reached with the IMF on November 5, 1997, with more funding from other international financial institutions for a total package worth $36.1 billion. Despite this intervention, the exchange rate fell again in December as investors pulled their money out of Indonesia. Given a high level of foreign indebtedness, this massive outflow of capital and fall of the rupiah rendered many

Indonesian firms and financial institutions effectively insolvent (World Bank 1998: 61). With nonperforming loans somewhere between 65 and 75 percent of all loans (Kim and Stone 1999), the country was left with a dual massive restructuring task: how to resuscitate salvageable financial institutions from those that were terminally insolvent while also restructuring companies that might be rescued without harming banks.

Foreign Interventions and Local Alignments

Three sets of global actors rushed into the fray. Approximately two hundred foreign private banks met in Frankfurt to hammer out an interim private solution of debt restructured with the Government of Indonesia (GOI), the so-called Frankfurt Accord, in cooperation with IFIs.[5] This later proved controversial since it smacked to some of a special deal to bail out foreign banks that should have been held accountable for their own risks. Not to do so encouraged moral hazard. The World Bank, IMF, and other multilateral banks hurried to put together a comprehensive rescue plan. And behind the IFIs stood the U.S., Japan, Australia, and other sovereign states, which could act bilaterally and through the multilateral institutions.

The first weeks and months of response to the Crisis in Indonesia well exemplify the severe difficulties of coordination and cooperation confronted by international actors—IFIs, nation-states, aid agencies, and others. Not only do rivalries bring agencies into competition with each other but the internal politics of massive institutions such as the World Bank can ramify outside it to complicate domestic and international relations. Foreign states have their own interests, and these are not always internally coherent. Compounding the confusion are the often differing interests of the Crisis government and rivalries among its agencies for determination of the course to be taken out of the Crisis. The initial weeks and even months into a crisis therefore unfold in a complex politics of diagnosis and prescription.

The IFIs entered Indonesia with the belief that they had a very narrow window of opportunity available to prevent massive financial collapse, not only in Indonesia but in the region and possibly for the global financial system. In those few weeks, from February through April 1998, they were compelled both to diagnose the nature of the problem and to craft remedies that the Government of Indonesia would commit to in its Letter of Intent with the IMF—the governing "contract" between Indonesia and world lending institutions. Foreign governments, key ministries of leading creditor nations, and IFIs rushed to Indonesia for intensive discussions with the Indonesian government and, concomitantly, negotiations among themselves over who would lead the Crisis bailout teams and on what terms. But it quickly became clear that some IFIs had higher aspirations, not merely to cauterize the bleeding of capital and stabilize the economy but to reconstruct fundamental market institutions in Indonesia, and for that they also required reform of law and its institutions. Most ambitiously, the IMF was enrolled by Indonesian reformers to lay the foundation for a longer-term solution that would provide orderly mechanisms for dealing with corporate debt and activate the power of law in a nation that had previously marginalized it.[6]

In the insolvency field, the dominant foreign players clustered around a handful of institutions headquartered within a few blocks of each other in Washington, D.C.—various departments and agencies of the U.S. government (e.g., Treasury, State, United States Agency for International Development [USAID]), the IMF, and World Bank. In the background lay other nations—Japan, the Netherlands, Australia—and other multilaterals, such as the Asian Development Bank.

While the economists sorted out the proportions of the Financial Crisis, the lawyers moved swiftly to appraise the extent of failure in the legal system. At this point, two streams of recent experience converged in potential collision. On the one side, within Indonesia initiatives had begun some years before the Crisis to assess and prescribe solutions to problems in the administration of justice, including commercial transactions. On the other side, the IFIs headed into Indonesia with diverse experience of insolvency reforms in Central and Eastern Europe, with debt-restructuring schemes in Latin America, and with the still unfolding crisis of Thailand immediately behind them. In the law reforms, the IFIs initially confronted Indonesia without systematic or consensually developed global norms and neither the IFIs nor norms were necessarily consistent with each other. The IFIs therefore faced a double challenge: how to crystallize and discern what lessons were portable from one national context to another (i.e., the transplant problem) and how to find a balance between implicit global universals and national adaptations. In short, as we shall dissect in greater detail in Chapter 10, the indigenous and global confronted each other in a moment of crisis and considerable confusion.[7]

When the IFI lawyers reached Jakarta in late 1997, they were not confronted with a blank slate. Two global/local partnerships were already on the ground, and each had a different diagnosis and prescription for Indonesia's market regulation difficulties. The IMF and World Bank therefore confronted three options: adopting one or another of the existing approaches or devising yet another. Each also represented an alliance—of the World Bank with Bappenas (a government department) and its reform team; of the USAID-sponsored Economic Law, Institutional and Professional Strengthening Project (ELIPS) in tandem with the Ministry of Finance; and of the IMF with local reformers selected by the Ministry of Justice. These alliances were not so neat, since sometimes they shared the same personnel; nor so bounded, since other vortexes of influence also played into the mix; nor so unified, since even within institutions there were tensions that confounded coordination and co-operation around a coherent program.

World Bank–Funded Diagnosis of the Legal System

The IFIs entered Indonesia with differing levels of exposure to the country, its economics, politics, and law. The World Bank and its investment arm, the International Finance Corporation (IFC), had been active in Indonesia for many years. Indeed, with its rapidly falling poverty rates, Indonesia was one of the Bank's success stories (Mallaby 2004). Between 1995 and 1997 the Bank had funded an extensive domestic research program on law reform in Indonesia, not least, in commercial law (Bappenas 1998).[8] The extensive results generated by this project offered an indigenous diagnosis and set of remedies to many problems that also bedeviled bankruptcy law and practice. Essentially the Bappenas study provided a comprehensive appraisal of law-in-action and thus a social and cultural construction of institutional weakness.

In an adroit blend of bricolage (Campbell 2004) and cultural adaptation, the Bappenas Report urged the development of dispute-resolution mechanisms that were sensitive to Indonesia's cultural context. The Report proposed that alternative dispute resolution (ADR) rather than formal court procedures should be a prominent mechanism for resolving disputes because "the Indonesian people, who are in essence non-litigious, have a socio-cultural basis rooted in society believing that it is a mistake in itself if a dispute is brought out into public" (Bappenas 1998: 109).

Nevertheless, the Report recognized that, in "the era of a global market," alternative dispute resolution would need to be complemented by an "efficient and effective" method of business dispute settlement. Here it found a colonial precedent for its recommendation that policymakers consider specialized courts, including a commercial court, somewhat similar to the Economic Chamber during Dutch colonial times: "[T]he expertise of judges, especially in business law, would be a basic condition for trials in the Economic Chamber so that the justice institutions can retain authority and gain the trust of the business world in settling their cases" (Bappenas 1998: 118). Without expert courts that can "keep the trust of the businesses" bringing cases to them, then "the courts will be permanently left behind the rapid growth of business, and companies will choose to settle disputes outside Indonesia" (Bappenas 1998: 126). In its institutional recommendations, therefore, the Report deftly blended three streams of legal symbols—Indonesia's indigenous practices, the Dutch colonial precedent, and the IFI global norms on the significance of formal courts, and for business, courts that were specialized and competent. It also picked up the frayed threads of the promised *Rechtsstaat* of the 1950s that was crushed by an authoritarian state (Lev 2000). In short, while the Bappenas proposals were enabled by World Bank funding, they demonstrated that an indigenous reform trajectory preceded the Crisis, a trajectory that anticipated two of the IFIs' most notable institutional goals—the formation of a viable commercial court and the creation of an out-of-court dispute resolution body.

The Bappenas project had a broader significance that would be consequential after the Crisis. In its extensive research and consultations the Legal Diagnostic Assessment effectively had also begun to build a civil society and reform constituency around a clear set of reform objectives. At the same time it enlisted support from Indonesia's principal legal institutions. By the time the IFIs arrived in Jakarta, therefore, a partial blueprint for wider institutional change lay waiting for a powerful sponsor to impel reforms.[9]

USAID's Radical Shock Approach

Officially unrelated to the World Bank–funded initiative, before the Crisis the U.S. had been funding the ELIPS program through USAID, one of whose elements included the drafting of economic law. In late 1997, a coordinating Minister of Economics and Finance, anxious about slowing investment, approached ELIPS with the proposition that Indonesia must demonstrate to the international investor community that it could handle the growing burden of debt carried by corporations, since international bankers were "closing their doors" and refusing to invest further. Indonesia fixing its moribund bankruptcy law and providing efficient options for debt restructuring would help open again the flow of fresh money into Indonesia. A new system must maximize efficiency and speed. Even more, it would send powerful symbolic signals to uneasy foreign investors that Indonesia was getting its house in order.[10]

ELIPS formed a team that included expatriate lawyers and accountants from Australia, Singapore, and the U.S., together with Indonesian professionals. The experts moved swiftly to produce an entirely new draft bankruptcy law. Substantively it turned away from a revised Indonesian/Dutch regime and proposed a more drastic turn in the direction of U.S. bankruptcy law. Institutionally, it differed sharply from the U.S., however, in its most radical idea. Convinced that the courts were hopelessly corrupt and incompetent, the ELIPS proposal followed the precedent of an already existing Indonesian Tax Tribunal and proposed to replace completely the courts with a bankruptcy administrative agency inside the executive branch of government. It would be staffed by bankruptcy experts, including, perhaps, foreign professionals, at least in the short term.[11]

IMF versus the World Bank

The relations between the Bank and the Fund in Indonesia during and immediately after the Crisis period were initially strained and conflictual. The Bank had a long presence in Indonesia, and its funds had enabled the Bappenas Report to anticipate many of the institutional reforms that the Crisis precipitated. The IMF Legal Department entered Indonesia only for the second time ever as a member of an IMF Crisis mission team, which previously had included only economists and finance specialists.[12] They had successfully participated in the Thailand emergency intervention and now brought their newfound experience to the next crisis. However, this move into the first wave of the mission, coupled with something of a lawmaking, institution-building orientation, brought them incipiently into conflict with the World Bank's long-standing presumption of IFI leadership in judicial reform, as well as law reform and institution building more generally.[13]

When an IMF/World Bank legal team traveled to Jakarta in April 1998, it confronted a financial *and* legal crisis. On one side, two plans for insolvency and legal reforms were already on the table. On the other side, the legal team needed some basis for making its judgment about whether to follow the Bappenas or USAID plans or to forge yet another. In the absence of the IMF's longtime presence on the ground, the team conducted a rapid appraisal of the situation. Its informants principally were foreign professionals, banks, government officials, local experts, distinguished local lawyers, and academics.

There is no evidence they consulted with debtors—the corporations that the bankruptcy reforms would cause to be liquidated or reorganized.

Their evaluation identified several key problems. Critics of Indonesia's bankruptcy law averred it was "outdated."[14] It relied on a 1905 Dutch law that had never been substantially reformed and had fallen well behind subsequent reforms to the law in the Netherlands. In its translation into Bahasa Indonesia, the Indonesian language, mistranslations and ambiguities appeared. Moreover, since there was virtually no commentary or settled doctrine, the law remained indeterminate. It lacked effective provisions for liquidating companies and had no effective provisions for rescuing companies under court protection. In short, it failed on both sides of the balanced package implicitly at the heart of yet unformalized global norms—a balancing of options for either liquidation or reorganization of failing companies, depending on their prospects for turnaround. Vague deadlines also indicated that turnarounds might be delayed for years and thus be ineffective.[15]

The diagnosis construed the law's indeterminacy from its lack of use. Courts were seldom used for companies in financial difficulty. Since a high point in the 1950s, the stature of courts in society and the market had markedly declined to the extent that public opinion and experts alike agreed that they were protected from neither political interference nor economic corruption. Because being a judge was no longer a prestigious career and had manifestly little power, it failed to attract highly qualified professionals. Those judges the bench did attract had limited experience in bankruptcy law, certainly of major companies. Foreign investors forthrightly stated they could not expect to be treated fairly in Indonesian courts. Courts had no independent authority when major cases involved political and economic elites. As one observer put it, "[L]egal institutions and professions had lost their autonomous function as they turned into extensions of dominant interests."[16] Supports for the courts were also lacking in the private sector. Indonesia had no formalized mechanisms for out-of-court workouts between debtors and creditors. And the market for expert professional services was severely limited.[17]

Yet the course to be taken remained uncertain until another issue was resolved. Would the Indonesian government, in this Crisis situation, move to bail out all corporations by buying their debt? Not only would this create an extra debt burden for Indonesia, possibly reaching $90 billion, but it would create an enormous moral hazard whereby debtors could take on major risks confident that a financial collapse would be covered by taxpayers. Or would the Government of Indonesia compel debtors to face their creditors and ne-gotiate debt restructurings through market and legal mechanisms? Various plans were mooted by domestic and foreign experts. One option pressed by an English banker would persuade the Government of Indonesia to essentially bail out the bankers. The Minister of Finance approached a World Bank of-ficial to bring the authority of the Bank to reject this course of action. Corpo-rations would need to face up to their creditors, and vice versa, to negotiate a way out of an impasse they had created. That decision, on which the IMF and Bank concurred, made all the more imperative that institutions be created in which debtor-creditor negotiations could be resolved, both in court and out of court.[18]

Within these parameters the IMF-led legal team set to work believing it had about three weeks in which to design a legal reform package. The IMF brought together a distinguished trio of Indonesian lawyers.[19] Two of these—Fred Tumbuan and Kartini Muljadi—were nominated by the Government of Indonesia. They had previously worked closely with the principal author of the Bappenas Report. Tumbuan was renowned for his integrity and had extensive experience in some of Indonesia's biggest international corporate financings.[20] Muljadi was arguably Indonesia's most eminent notary and had been legal counsel to Suharto on his personal financial affairs. The appointee of the IMF, Mardjono Reksodiputro, was a name partner in one of Jakarta's leading commercial law firms and Dean of Law at the University of Indonesia. In succeeding months the IMF was also able to draw on several other lawyers: Gregory Churchill, an American corporate lawyer and partner in Mardjono's firm, was fluent in Indonesian; Jerry Hoff was an experienced and outspoken Dutch insolvency lawyer who had been advocating substantive law reforms that would enable Indonesia to do what had been successfully managed in the Netherlands; and Theodoor Bakker, another experienced Dutch lawyer, was a practitioner in the Mardjono firm.[21] Later in 1998 the IMF hired a consultant, Sebaastian Pompe, a Dutch scholar and lawyer with English legal training who had completed a controversial dissertation on the Indonesian Supreme Court and had briefly practiced with the Mardjono firm, to coordinate its programs on the ground in Jakarta.[22]

The alignment of the IMF with leading Indonesian experts was an al-liance of mutual convenience. For the IMF, access to a deep pool of legal talent and experience enabled it to compensate for its weak institutional pres-ence, pre-Crisis, in Indonesia and for it to draw on the pent-up demands and prescriptions for legal change that had been building in the 1990s. For Indonesian reformers, the IMF offered the potential leverage to institutionalize the recommendations of the World Bank–funded Bappenas Report, not least because the IMF effectively had managed to enlist several of its principals. However reluctantly, Indonesian reformers welcomed IMF interventions insofar as they would advance reforms concordant with their reform agenda.

The intensive meetings with informants, officials, and experts in April 2008 sharpened the contrasts between alternative courses of action. The USAID/ELIPS proposals offered a ready-made path forward for substantive and institutional changes. The ELIPS assumption that the Dutch law was "retarded in its own right" and should be replaced by law closer to U.S. bankruptcy law sparked intensive discussions, not least within the IMF/World Bank team and among its Indonesian advisors. The ELIPS proposal to move bankruptcy cases out of the court system also confronted head-on the Bappenas concept of a new commercial court.[23]

Indonesian advisors to the IMF-led team argued forcefully against both directions. A major substantive turn could create far-reaching and unpredictable ramifications for cognate law, such as property law. Said one expert, "[Y]ou cannot parachute a common law solution into a civil law society in the middle of a crisis." Besides, the modern Dutch bankruptcy regime seemed perfectly capable of handling Dutch corporate bankruptcies, for example, the massive Fokker Aircraft restructuring. An abandonment of the courts was even more problematic. In addition to raising constitutional questions, which would be untimely in a time of crisis, many enforcement issues in an out-of-court regime would end up back in court, so courts could scarcely be avoided altogether. Most important, for some Indonesian law reformers, the principal payoff of the IFI interventions was less to do with insolvency and more to do with a renaissance of courts and law in society as a whole.[24]

The IMF and World Bank lawyers in the mission team drew opposing conclusions. The World Bank lawyer preferred the ELIPS approach. The IMF rejected it. The disagreement amplified up to the Washington headquarters of each institution and beyond, as the IMF garnered the support of the U.S. Treasury, and the Bank mobilized the U.S. Ambassador, the State Department, and USAID. According to one well-placed informant, this squabble among Washington-based institutions and U.S. government departments on what should happen in Jakarta was eventually resolved in the White House in favor of the IMF.[25]

Tensions between the Bank and Fund were also manifest over another proposal. A regional legal expert from the Bank presented a plan for corporate bankruptcies that leaned heavily in favor of debtors, seemingly based on a Latin American concept, the *concordato*. According to a lawyer-critic elsewhere in the Bank, this was a "very debtor friendly" approach that "is basically run by lawyers for the debtor, without the interference or supervision of a judge." Debtors are protected from their creditors, and with a very good lawyer, debt repayment can be stretched out for seven to eleven years, which, to bankers, is tantamount to wiping out the debt altogether.[26] To lawyers familiar with U.S. bankruptcy law, this was reminiscent of the state of U.S. law before the 1978 Bankruptcy Code, a kind of 1970s Chapter 11. To Indonesians, schooled in Dutch law, it seemed entirely unfamiliar.

But the aggravating issue, it seemed, was less the plan than the aggressive and public way in which a Bank regional lawyer "grossly undermined the IMF in Indonesia" by speaking out against it in public. In response, "the IMF got ticked off and simply said, '[W]e will not work with her anymore. We will not work with World Bank Legal'" at all. In virtue of conflicts between the Bank and IMF, the Bank pulled its principal lawmaking staff person out of Jakarta and ceded the substantive and court reforms to the Fund, a team headed by the IMF Legal Department's Assistant Counsel.[27]

These differences pointed to the wider question, how should the roles of the IMF and Bank in bankruptcy-related reforms be defined in the immediate and intermediate terms? After the first flurry of reforms, the Managing Director of the Fund, Michel Camdussus, and the President of the Bank, James Wolfensohn, met in mid-1998 to divide up responsibility for their interventions overall in Indonesia. They agreed, broadly, that the IMF would focus on immediate law reforms, particularly of the substantive law and courts. The Bank would take care of medium-term policy, taking over IMF-led reforms at a certain point, as well as focus on the out-of-court mechanisms, most notably, the Jakarta Initiative.[28]

For the next few months, IMF and Bank relationships over insolvency-related issues were mixed. The Corporate Restructuring and Governance Group of the Bank, which had been formed in response to the Asian Crisis, worked closely with the IMF in the development of Indonesia's out-of-court corporate restructuring body, the Jakarta Initiative Task Force, together with Bank lawyers in Jakarta. Yet some months later there were renewed murmurings from some in the Bank's Legal Department that IMF-led reforms were not working and needed revisiting. Said one close observer, "[I]t was important for some in the World Bank to demonstrate that the Fund didn't get it all right." Apart from this perturbation, however, a division of labor and efforts to forge comity settled down to cooperation among the IFIs. At the IMF's invitation, Jakarta-based Bank lawyers joined quarterly IMF meetings with the Indonesian authorities and staffs on both sides and exchanged information on the progress of reforms. Not least, mutual support enabled the IMF to participate in Bank-led coordination of wider donor activities.[29]

The Reform Program

Once the decision was taken to reject the ELIPS approach, the reform team quickly agreed upon master principles of institutional design. In quick order the reform team came up with four sets of proposals: (1) to implement substantive and procedural changes in the law that would enable rapid processing of cases and would give the court powers to hold off creditors while restructuring negotiations took place within the court; (2) to create a specialized Commercial Court with specially selected judges to handle all bankruptcy, intellectual property, and other commercial cases; and (3) to create a receivers' profession, a new profession that would make expert professionals available to handle corporate liquidations and reorganizations in the private professional market (Hoff 1999; Steele 1999; Wessels 1998). Together the IMF and the Bank's Corporate Restructuring & Governance Group added a fourth plank to the reform program, (4) the Jakarta Initiative Task Force, an out-of-court mediation system housed in, but substantially independent of, the Ministry of Finance.

On October 31, 1997, the Government of Indonesia signed the first of many Letters of Intent with the IMF to commit itself to the first of these and subsequent reforms.[30] In principle, future tranches of loans from the IFIs would be dependent on the implementation of these commitments. The compliance of Indonesia was publicly posted on the IMF website in the form of successive Letters of Intent, which included reports of projected dates for action and dates for actual implementation of commitments.

Reforms of Substantive Law

In broad concept, the reform team agreed not to disturb the inherited Dutch colonial law but to modernize it by borrowing some features of subsequent Dutch reforms that had never been incorporated into Indonesian law but were said to work well in the Netherlands. They sought to add other provisions not in Dutch law but that had become common in other advanced economies. In this way the reformers calculated that a balance would be struck between continuity and change, between the disturbance of current law and the dangers of uncertainty, and between the enactment of new law and its prospects for effectiveness and efficiency.

At the recommendation of the reform group, the Government of Indonesia agreed to ninety-eight emergency statutory amendments, most of which facilitated the capacity for reorganization as an alternative to liquidation of companies. Most important, it agreed that the secured creditors (typically large banks) could not act unilaterally outside bankruptcy law to liquidate a company, since this usually would lead to its destruction and forestall any possibility of reorganization no matter what the cost to other creditors. Major creditors would have to participate in court proceedings, although they would obtain various protections for their assets. The reforms also imposed strict deadlines for expediting cases so that procedures would be relatively transparent and the business would not die while in surgery.[31] The reformers supposed that the law would also act as a "hammer"—the increased probability that corporate debtors would be liquidated by a court if they did not restructure their companies would likely impel widespread efforts to reach out-of-court settlements with debtors.

Because statutes take time to wend through legislatures, and often run into complex negotiations and amendments, the Government of Indonesia agreed with the IMF to authorize the reforms by Presidential Decree subsequently to be confirmed by Parliament. All parties agreed that these would be considered as stopgaps on the way to comprehensive reform in an integrated bankruptcy law. However, the lawmaking proceeded without public consultation or hearings. Debtors were excluded from participation. In a last-minute stand, and determined not to be locked out of the process, a group of powerful corporate leaders met with the President on the eve of his decree to urge him not to sign it. Under pressure from the IMF and domestic reformers in favor of the reforms, he rejected their interventions, although parliamentary authorization would come years later.[32]

It became clear very quickly that the 1998 substantive amendments to the 1906 law solved some problems, such as the speedy treatment of cases, but led to others. Early confusion developed in the court over such a basic concept as "debtor" and how the term should be defined.[33] Inconsistencies became apparent in decisions across cases (Suyudi 2004). And the treatment of secured creditors after the 1998 amendments put creditors in an ambiguous position of either participating in the approval of a reorganization plan or giving up some of their security. The "doubtful" decisions of the court also turned an institution designed to compel debtor reorganizations that would satisfy creditors into a haven where high-asset debtors could shelter from creditors.[34]

By 2001, with the immediacy of the Crisis over, the IMF losing its leverage, and Indonesia not cooperating very well in the implementation of the reform program, USAID struck back in tandem with a restive domestic interest group to chart another course. In contrast to the reforms of 1998, which opponents saw as excessively creditor friendly, a rival group in 2001, funded by USAID, brought an opposing debtor-friendly bill into the lawmaking arena.[35] A former banker, turned lawyer and law professor, persuaded the Minister of Justice to permit two drafting teams to proceed toward a revised bankruptcy law. Its team leader believed that after two years the Commercial Court had already shown itself to be corrupt and incompetent in its treatment of bankruptcy cases. Liquidations produced "many victims"—employees, suppliers, even the nation, through tax losses. Much better, he thought, to compel out-of-court private restructurings, where negotiations between creditors and debtors would be facilitated by consultants.[36] The failures of the 1998 reforms demonstrated that a revised Indonesian law did not work for corporate rehabilitation and needed to be supplemented by provisions more like Chapter 11 of the U.S. Bankruptcy Code.

The new team proposed a Restructuring Bill that was intended to be much more facilitative of debtor workouts and indeed to be fairer to debtors than the IMF/Indonesian–led reforms of 1998. The Restructuring Bill had "powerful domestic" support from debtors in Indonesia who saw it to be more "business-like" and realistic and from bankers and debtors who resented creditor-led restructurings that put Indonesian companies under foreign control. The Restructuring Bill would allow debtors to stay in possession of their companies, and voting provisions for confirmation of a plan would strongly favor the debtor. This would apply only to limited-liability companies and would essentially exist alongside the general bankruptcy law. If negotiations failed, then the company would automatically become bankrupt.[37]

To reformers who forged the 1998 reforms this looked like a haven where debtors might shelter indefinitely without being compelled to go to court and face liquidation.[38] The "IMF feared it might solidify and focus debtor support."[39] There was also some concern that USAID and its ELIPS program might be reviving an alternative to the IMF-Indonesian approach by providing a center of gravity around which opposition could build to the 1998 reforms. The opponents of the draft Restructuring Bill therefore mobilized to derail it. They found one opportunity to counterattack when the OECD hosted a Forum on Asian Insolvency Reforms in Bali in 2001. Anticipating this domestic conflict, the OECD in consultation with IFIs and supporters of the IMF's initiative in Indonesia crafted the program to enable international experts to appraise both bills. Speakers presented for both sides and were subject to questioning by the international experts. Overseas specialists argued against the Restructuring Bill while supporting the original reformers' amendments. The OECD convenor summarized proceedings by applauding the concept in the Restructuring Bill but urged that it be held in abeyance for a decade or two.[40] In the meantime members of the original drafting team, together with their technical supporters from the IMF, pressed the Minister to reject the Restructuring Bill and focus on the new Bankruptcy Bill that confirmed and modified the 1998 Emergency Bankruptcy Law, which might achieve restructuring through the courts. Until the Minister made his choice in favor of the Indonesia/IMF law, said a reformer close to the IMF, "we were sweating all the way."[41]

In 2002 a comprehensive restatement of the bankruptcy law was introduced to Parliament. Written in modern Bahasa Indonesia, the consolidated version sought to clarify legal concepts with a chapter on definitions, most notably on the concept of debt. To commence a case and file for suspension of payments, now not just debtors but creditors could take the initiative. The disadvantageous position for secured creditors who participated in voting for a reorganization plan was relieved by provisions that permitted them to keep their security and participate in a vote on a reorganization plan. Related to this new position, creditors could now be broken into classes when they voted on reorganization plans, a practice common in advanced countries, and specifically advocated by Germany's preeminent bankruptcy authority Manfred Balz, who had been integral to the IMF's norm making and its consultant on many national reforms. This was intended to provide secured creditors with an incentive to be involved in reorganizations if they thought there was any chance a debtor could resurrect his or her business.[42] For the most part, however, the amendments were procedural and intended to remove the indeterminacies in the 1998 amendments. The draft law languished in Parliament without a powerful sponsor until 2005, when it was finally passed, thereby bringing to fruition, after seven years, the substantive component of the law reform package urged by the IMF and its domestic partners.[43]

The Commercial Court

Once the disagreement between the Fund and Bank over the ELIPS plan for a new administrative court was resolved in favor of the IMF, discussions turned to the architecture of the new court system. Solutions arrayed along a continuum from gradualist to dramatic.

A veteran observer of Indonesian justice, Dan Lev, maintained that the institution of the courts might be left intact but it required emptying of all current judges on the Supreme Court who were irremediably corrupt or at least tainted with the brush of corruption.[44] Such a cleansing of the Supreme Court, together with an overhaul of court administration (including the employment of new staff), would set the stage for an entirely new era in the administration of justice.[45] The prospect of a radical purge led to "vehement discussions" among the Indonesian reform group, not least because it was difficult to envisage how such a move could be orchestrated and why new judges in old institutions might not succumb to exactly the maladies of their predecessors.[46] While the IMF might have found the outcome desirable, such a step relied on an assumption that lacked systematic evidence—that most senior judges were corrupt. Merely to allege this, even if it were "common knowledge," seemed presumptuous and even unjust. Moreover, an IMF insistence on this measure would have badly compromised the IMF itself: it would be seen at once to be trampling heavily on the sovereignty of a country, even perhaps to be orchestrating "a constitutional-political coup."[47]

Significantly, just as the reform team had decided to build upon Dutch bankruptcy law rather than replace it, so, too, they chose to build upon a model already developed by Indonesian reformers in the Bappenas Report—the creation of a new Commercial Court. Formalized as a commitment by the GOI in June 1998,[48] the Commercial Court would be constituted as a "carve-out" inside the current flawed system. Indonesian reformers had high expectations of a new court. The Court would be "clean, open, accountable, and also modern," a court comparable to those of Singapore, Thailand, and Malaysia. This Court would demonstrate to investors that they could expect fairness and competency. Reformers were led to believe by the Ministry of Justice that the new Court would have its own modern facilities, competent staffing, up-to-date equipment, and handpicked judges.[49] Indonesian institution builders believed that the Crisis provided an opening for a new specialist court that would serve as an exemplar for the entire court system. A leading Indonesian reformer pressed the case that by providing a "wedge" in the court system, even in one model court, reformers might solve two problems—administration of bankruptcy law and generic court reform—by a single stroke, an ambition the IMF was later to endorse.[50]

The Government established the Court in 1998. Almost immediately, limited resources and lack of political will began to compromise the initial concept. The first problem was money: the Government made no new funds available to house a model court with modern equipment. Instead, the Court was housed at the Jakarta Central Court in an old downtown building, where judges were packed, five or six at a time, into a single room with no computers and few staff. The Australian aid program promised technical assistance for computing, but it never made it into the courtroom. Even courtrooms were in short supply. Symbolically, the placement signified business as usual—this would be just another court. The contrast between the first-world corporate headquarters of major corporations and the third-world facilities of the courts emblemized the powerlessness of the latter. Instead of a clean slate, judges were compelled to rely on an "arthritic," compromised bureaucracy. Moreover, the new Court was embedded within the old court system. Rather than being a "carve-out" within the court system, appeals went directly to the Supreme Court, itself an institution with limited experience in sophisticated commercial cases and of doubtful probity.

A great deal, therefore, rested on the selection of judges. Reformers had floated many ideas: finding clean, competent judges in Indonesia; relying on expatriates; or seconding first-rate commercial lawyers to the bench for a limited period. President Wahid even floated the idea of recruiting judges from the Netherlands. However, the Ministry of Justice and Supreme Court prevailed upon the Government to follow established procedures for judicial selection. It was politically unacceptable to employ foreigners and unprecedented to appoint private practitioners. Instead, the Supreme Court set up some selection criteria (for example, at least ten years' experience on the bench) and proceeded to maintain its own (compromised) control by selecting lawyers from the general courts. Even so, most of the judges were ill prepared, with little significant commercial and virtually no bankruptcy experience. The Japanese, Australian, and Dutch governments did provide some funding for a crash training course in bankruptcy law, but that lasted only a few weeks.[51] High salaries might have provided an incentive for a career on the Commercial Court, but that hope, too, was frustrated by the GOI, which decided there were too many bureaucratic hurdles to surmount in order to get pay increases that, in any event, would create problems of equity with the rest of the judiciary.[52]

A reformist minister in the short-lived Wahid government pleaded with the new judges "to regain the trust of the people in the judicial and legal institution" and decide just three "celebratory" cases free of corruption.[53] This was not to be. The Commercial Court's first decision caused a minor sensation: a putatively strong case was carefully prepared by the IFIs, with the World Bank's International Finance Corporation as one of the parties to the case. Other international parties and even international observers participated. The judges were caught between countervailing local pressures, on the one side by reformist officials who wanted a showcase ruling that was competent and clean, and on the other side by allies in the government and private sectors who looked for the courts to protect Indonesia's corporations from foreign interests and rule in favor of local corporations and creditors. The Court ruled in favor of the debtor in a decision widely greeted as "inexplicable" by international organizations and foreign observers.[54] Following several other "inexplicable" decisions, even international agencies began to despair. Within a year of the Court's establishment the World Bank's International Finance Corporation, which had suffered unpredictable treatment at the hands of the Court, no longer considered the courts to be a viable institution for equitable or competent adjudication.[55] It, too, abandoned them. Ironically, subsequent research showed that the great majority of decisions were perfectly consistent with the judgments of expert observers (Schröeder-van Waes and Sidharta 2004; Suyudi 2004). A small number of notable, even notorious, cases had therefore impugned the Court as a whole.

In short, the disturbance that a powerful and independent Commercial Court might have produced for the political elite, accustomed to a subservient court, or for the judicial elite, entrenched in a comfortable patronage system of mild expropriation, never eventuated. The entire infrastructure of the new Court effectively was subverted by a collusion of political and legal interests before the first case was heard.

Chastened by this and subsequent early setbacks, the IMF did not retreat but pushed on with a series of measures to remedy the Court's faults. The IMF believed that these decisions could be a result either of incompetence or corruption. It tried to solve the incompetence problem by a series of measures. The first was the activation of an initiative in the original design of the Commercial Court—appointment of *ad hoc judges*. In November 1998, the GOI announced the creation of ad hoc judges, distinguished specialists from outside the judiciary who would sit on panels of judges, provide their colleagues with the benefits of their expertise, and offer some insulation from external pressures.[56] But this step quickly faltered because, on a panel of three judges, an ad hoc judge could be outvoted by the other two but could not publish a dissent to signal why she disagreed. Without her being able to publish a dissent, her reputation as a competent or "clean" jurist risked sullying.[57] As a result, ad hoc judges refused to serve.[58] To remedy this problem, a further round of reform resulted in a Supreme Court regulation that would allow ad hoc judges to publish dissenting opinions, a decision that broke the deadlock and opened up the bench to such judges. In fact, only one ever served, and only on a handful of cases (IMF 2005).[59]

The IMF tried to solve the corruption problem through a succession of methods in what it called the "governance phase" of reforms, and these, too, have a point/counterpoint character. Initially, the IMF put in place a team of court watchers to monitor all cases closely and provide confidential reports to the IMF. Essentially staffed by foreign lawyers, and therefore politically explosive, the team offered a source of valuable intelligence for the IMF.[60] Subsequently, an IMF grant enabled Bappenas to appoint a team of seven Indonesian lawyers and retired judges to review and publicize all court decisions in order to keep the courts and judges publicly accountable.[61] This "Team of Seven" reviewed every case from the beginning of the Commercial Court (approximately three hundred), created a concordance of the cases with the case law, digested the cases, and for each offered a summary with their evaluation of the case. Essentially they asked of every case: Is the decision good? Does it meet the law? If not, why not? Are there differences between similar cases? What is the reasoning of the judges? And is there consistency between decisions of the Commercial Court and Supreme Court on bankruptcy? For cases whose reasoning was hard to fathom, the team tried to suggest how better it might have been decided. Judges were effectively rated by the "rightness" of their decisions.[62] The analysis was published as a report and forwarded to judges and the Supreme Court, all in an effort to improve consistency and professional engagement.[63] But to the disappointment of some reformers, even professional "publics," such as lawyers and legal academics, failed to take advantage of the breakthrough step that marked publication, for the first time in Indonesian court history, of all cases, and their subsequent evaluation by the Team of Seven. This failure of engagement signified even further the deformities to professionalism wrought by decades of eroding public discourse.[64]

A further initiative, announced in March 1999, proposed legislation to combat corruption in the public sector, including the courts.[65] The Government of Indonesia, with IMF encouragement, set up in 2000 a Joint Anti-Corruption Investigating Team to investigate and prosecute corruption in the court system—but the Supreme Court struck it down.[66] Judges were made subject to review by a new Independent Commission for the Audit of the Wealth of High State Officials.[67] The IMF then pressed the Government of Indonesia to set up an Anti-Corruption Commission to investigate and prosecute cases and an Anti-Corruption Court with strong penalties, including criminal liabilities for judges and inducements for people to cooperate.

Through 2003, the Commercial Court had heard 342 bankruptcy cases and decided 316 (Suyudi 2004). But after a steep rise in cases from 1998 through 2002, the number of petitions for bankruptcy dropped sharply. The number of cases dropped from 52 in 2004 to 44 in 2005 and a similar number in 2006.[68] Since many thousands of companies are going out of business across Indonesia each year, it is clear that formal bankruptcy law through the courts has become almost irrelevant for restructuring or liquidation. Lamented one reformer, "[P]eople have realized it is useless."[69]

An independent evaluation commissioned by the IMF Legal Department concluded that as a "viable judicial institution," the Commercial Court is "widely perceived as disappointing and as having succumbed to the deficiencies of the wider judicial system." In its narrower goal, it has "not contributed as intended to creating an effective bankruptcy system" (IMF 2005). However, even critics, including some of the progenitors of the Commercial Court, are not prepared to write it off completely. The Court might be "unpredictable," its judgments sometimes "irresponsible," its judges of declining quality, its aura of corruption deplorable, but all of these together have not destroyed a Court that remains potentially viable.[70] Put another way:

> [T]he experiences in the sixties and the seventies and the early eighties had been so abysmal that nobody even thought about filing for bankruptcy because of the issues of corruption, malpractice, bad administration. So I think it's fair to say that by 1997 there was no bankruptcy institution in Indonesia. After the

change of the law and the implementation of the law . . . there was a bankruptcy system and there is. It's not functioning well, it's not functioning the way it should function, but there is now a bankruptcy system.[71]

Not to be daunted, the IMF and Dutch government, partners in the Commercial Court reforms, turned last to the more fundamental problem—the deformities of the general court system. By late 2006 foreign donors—AusAid, USAID, the Dutch government, Asia Foundation, World Bank, European Union, Millennium Challenge Corporation (a U.S. government fund), Japan, among others—were pouring millions of dollars into court reforms, focused principally on the Supreme Court. The narrow wedge of the Commercial Court reforms by now had become an expansive opening: IMF-supported domestic initiatives designed Blueprints for all aspects of court reconstruction. The partnership between civil society and Supreme Court reformers benefited from major institutional reforms between 2002 and 2005, including a Judicial Commission and a Constitutional Court. At the request of Indonesian reformers and officials, the IMF has again taken up the cause to provide technical assistance for reforms to the entire court system based in part on Blueprints that can trace elements of their vintage to earlier IMF support.[72]

And in a surprising move, the Economic Growth Office of USAID swept into Indonesia in 2006 with $7 million to revitalize and expand the jurisdiction of the Commercial Court, while aiding capacity to the Anti-Corruption Court.[73] Although the odds are long, this second act of Commercial Court reforms suggests that pronouncement of its death for bankruptcy cases may be premature. The war is not over.

Jakarta Initiative Task Force (JITF)

Even though the IMF and World Bank Legal Departments initially differed, the IMF legal team did agree to work with the Washington-based specialists in the Bank's new corporate restructuring unit. They agreed on two principal goals: corporations that had contracted huge debt burdens should not be bailed out by the government but should bargain with their creditors in a market-driven process; and the government should create an institutional framework in which debtor-creditor negotiations could be located, a site that was "neutral" and competent. In broader systemic terms, the JITF would provide a "safety valve" for resolving large numbers of cases voluntarily so as not to overwhelm a nascent court system.[74] In the background, however, would lie the threat of a bankruptcy court to punish debtors that failed to negotiate out-of-court restructurings. Said one IFI official involved in the design of JITF, "I never believed a voluntary scheme would work unless there was a hammer to make people reasonable."[75]

Leading up to the Crisis and in its immediate aftermath a great deal of private restructuring of the largest conglomerates was already under way.[76] But reliance entirely on private markets provided proved inadequate. Caught between two unsatisfactory options, the IFI officials pressed the Government of Indonesia to set up a semiautonomous restructuring agency. From an IFI vantage point, the concept drew on prior experiences with out-of-court restructuring schemes IFIs had instituted in Thailand and Ecuador, all drawing very loosely on a voluntary program called the "London Approach" (Meyerman 2000). From a domestic perspective, JITF built on customary nonlitigious forms of dispute resolution that authors of the Bappenas Report asserted were part of Indonesia's "living tradition" (Bappenas 1998: 109).

The GOI launched the Jakarta Initiative in September 1998.[77] Companies with more than $10 million in assets could bring their negotiations with creditors to a "neutral" mediation body that was staffed by experts, many of them expatriate accountants and former bankers. Successful workouts would lead to a Memorandum of Understanding (MOU) among the parties, although JITF did not have any powers to enforce the MOUs. Housed in the Ministry of Finance, by March 1999 the JITF was handling some 125 companies with $17.5 billion in foreign currency debt and 7.8 trillion rupiah in domestic currency debt.[78]

Immediately the innovation ran into difficulties. The IFIs had envisaged that if the Court began to liquidate companies, debtors would receive a powerful signal that they would fare better, with less cost and public shaming, by mediating through the JITF. But the market read the establishment of the JITF as "an abandonment of the bankruptcy court," an apparent vote of noconfidence that compounded the problem of the Court's legitimacy and JITF's effectiveness.[79]

It also quickly became apparent that since debtors and corporations were not consulted in the creation of JITF, many corporate owners and managers would use every expedient to resist or distort its adverse impact on their financial affairs or control of their companies. Debtors pursued two strategies. They stayed as long as possible in JITF to prolong negotiations with creditors in the hopes that either creditors would settle for less or circumstances would change and the pressure would be lightened. But, perversely, rather than the Court acting as a stick to drive debtors into serious negotiations with creditors, the Court's first decisions convinced debtors that if ultimately they were pushed into court, it could actually become a haven from restructuring pressures since debtors stood a very good chance of winning cases.[80]

In February 2001 JITF's Chairman, Bacelius Ruru, reported to an OECD-sponsored conference that "it is critical that there be reasonable certainty regarding the results that would be achieved in a legal proceeding." When there is "little confidence" that the insolvency law will be applied, then the pace of restructuring out of court will also be slowed (Ruru 2001). The frustration of the IMF is apparent in its statement of September 2001 that "the Fund recommends a more forceful implementation of the framework for corporate debt restructuring through the JITF. The work of . . . JITF will depend on taking forward, with greater, vigor, legal reforms to tackle continuing debtor recalcitrance and improve the governance of the court system."[81]

Again, the process followed one after another cycle of unsuccessful reforms. Against the advice of IFIs, the Government of Indonesia set up the Jakarta Initiative with too few negative sanctions for noncooperation. This provided few incentives for corporations to negotiate deals with their bankers. They had no realistic fear of being liquidated or losing control of their companies. As a result, a series of measures, mostly in the form of executive orders, followed every few months to provide first positive then negative incentives for debtor corporations to come to agreement with their creditors. Several carrots were offered. For instance, if parties dealt in good faith, they might become eligible for tax incentives, banking incentives, and capital incentives. Debt-to-equity swaps were made tax neutral. And companies would be protected from being delisted on the Jakarta Stock Exchange. When those incentives proved relatively ineffective, the IMF pushed for using sticks, ranging from threats to take away the licenses of companies that refused to cooperate and to allow the Attorney-General to force them into bankruptcy court, to shaming mechanisms such as publicizing the names of companies that dragged their feet. Some measures were implemented but never used. Others were rejected altogether by the Government.[82]

As late as January 2002 the IMF's fourth Indonesia review was still complaining of a continuing need to accelerate corporate debt restructuring under JITF, and it reiterated the problems it perceived with the quality of restructurings and their sustainability, as well as the need for further legal reforms "aimed at tackling continued debtor recalcitrance." Even deals that were done—and there were large numbers—required creditors to take extraordinary "haircuts"

or loan reductions, frequently approaching 90 percent. And to save face, creditors frequently offered long-term bonds with generous terms, never expecting
to see them mature.[83] When JITF wound up in December 2003 with a fanfare
of massive numbers and major restructurings, it took a more skeptical analyst
to question whether the deals were less restructurings than write-offs, whether
Memos of Understanding were meaningful commitments of repayment or
face-saving devices for surrender by the creditors.

It is not surprising, therefore, that many in Indonesia, confronted with
such intractable constraints, wrote off an initiative such as JITF as "an abys-
mal failure." But then again, precisely because JITF faced such long odds, with
"no legal system to enforce rights," with "no leverage" itself, and with no leverage for creditors who have nowhere else to go, a JITF staff person might
have been justified in his conclusion that "given its resources, the JITF has
done bloody well."[84]

At the end of its mandate, in December 2003, the JITF could claim that of
the approximately $60 billion of corporate distressed debt, it had completed
financial restructuring of ninety-six companies with a total debt of $20.5 bil-
lion.[85] But the cards favored the debtors. Without negative incentives, coercion,
or powerful institutional suasion such as that offered by Central Banks in other
contexts, or credible threats of liquidation in the Commercial Court, creditors
were compelled to take massive "haircuts";[86] debtors could drag out the settlement process, and the final outcome, Memorandums of Understanding, did
not imply any settlement in fact. Indeed, there seem to be no reliable statistics
on whether agreements within JITF have led to their execution in practice.

The JITF process, coupled with an uncertain Commercial Court, provided
an arena in which debtors could express their voices and fight again battles
they had lost in the political arena. The IFI diagnosis, as befits creditor-driven
institutions, placed the burden of responsibility for corporate debt overhang
not on the creditors themselves but on the debtor corporations. Its measures
were explicitly intended to give teeth to creditors, to empower them to compel
debtors into repayments and restructurings rather than postponements and
even refusals to deal. Those "teeth" were not very sharp and bit scarcely at all.
Yet again an actor mismatch between implementation and lawmaking was
ultimately fought and probably won in the arena of practice and by the very
actors who had been excluded from the policymaking.

Nevertheless, JITF's dissolution in December 2003 did not remove entirely the function of out-of-court negotiations from the market. While JITF

might not have fulfilled the expectations of creditors, its nonconfrontational, expert-mediated approach served multiple functions: it kept pressure off a nascent and struggling court system; it avoided the confrontational tone of legal proceedings; it lowered the cost of professional services; and it had some continuity with proposals also advanced by the Bappenas Report (Bappenas 1998) before the Crisis. As a result, in yet another example of follow-on effects of initial IFI-supported reforms, the Government closed the doors of JITF and opened up a new institution—the National Mediation Center—with much more expansive reach. It has become mandatory for corporations in civil disputes to enter mediation before a court hearing. Many staff members from JITF moved across to the National Mediation Center, forming the core of a new profession of financial mediators.[87]

A Private Insolvency Profession

The institution builders understood clearly that the construction of an insolvency system depended substantially on the quality of professional services. These were particularly critical in the largest cases where massive conglomerates that had contracted billions in foreign debt required highly sophisticated lawyers and accountants to unravel the intricate financial and legal relationships that bound Indonesian debtors to their domestic, and especially foreign, creditors.

At the outset of their engagement with the Crisis in Indonesia, IFIs and USAID confronted a confusing and inadequate division of labor for corporate restructuring. While Jakarta could boast some excellent corporate law firms, many of which were affiliated with global law firms based in London, the U.S., and the Netherlands, lawyers could not hope to handle the massive volume of bankruptcy work themselves, in part because so much of the restructuring would rely on valuations where accountants were needed. International accounting firms and major local firms also had a notable presence in Jakarta, but they did not have the experience of acting as bankruptcy receivers or administrators, as is common in Britain and many other Commonwealth countries. Government officials who could act as receivers were too few and knew little about modern business or international transactions.

The IFIs considered several options. The Dutch and civil law tradition leaned toward allocating the work to lawyers. Australian and Commonwealth professionals in Jakarta preferred the English-style reliance on accountants. The IMF preferred to let the market choose either accountants or lawyers. The

IFIs and USAID maintained that experienced foreigners could enter the professional services market and train indigenous professionals. Eventually the Indonesian officials agreed with the IFIs to create a new second-order profession, the receivers' profession, that could attract and regulate first-order professionals who developed a bankruptcy specialization, such as accountants and lawyers.[88] It would have responsibility for handling the assets of bankruptcy companies, supervising reorganizations, and acting as the Court's agents in bankruptcy proceedings. Whether lawyers or accountants, they would need to be trained in bankruptcy law and practice, to qualify through examination, and to become members of a self-regulating professional association, the last of these a particularly critical condition given the susceptibility of bankruptcy professionals to economic or political corruption.[89]

Implementation went less smoothly. The Government committed itself in June 1998 to create a new system of receivers and administrators to be drawn from the private profession.[90] Yet, in response to the fierce protectionism of the Indonesian legal and accounting professions, and aware of nationalist sentiment about foreign influence, the Ministry of Justice issued implementing regulations that required receivers to be members of the newly founded Receivers' Association, thus placing it in a gate-keeping and self-regulating role. Regulations prescribed that receivers must pass oral and written examinations in Bahasa Indonesia, thereby at a single stroke excluding virtually all foreign professionals, except the handful of longtime expatriate residents who spoke Bahasa Indonesia.[91]

The merits of this move can readily be debated. Given the significance of Bahasa Indonesia as a defining linguistic characteristic of postcolonial Indonesian society, its abandonment as a necessary condition of membership in a public profession undoubtedly would be politically awkward, especially at a time when foreign influence seemed unusually intrusive.[92] Nonetheless, the understandable retreat by the GOI from facilitating participation by foreign professionals had the effect of subverting an approach that could have overcome the dearth of expert services in an area critical to corporate reorganization.

From the beginning, the new profession ran into difficulties (Survey of Receivers': Final Report n.d.; hereafter Receivers' Report). Little time was available for training the first cohort. The Court's methods of appointing receivers quickly became suspect. Although the regulations envisaged that receivers would be appointed by the Court, it had been mandated and expected in practice that creditors could nominate receivers for Court confirmation. In fact, many sources reported that from the beginning Commercial Court judges frequently rejected creditors' nominees and selected alternative receivers without adequate explanation. Although some qualified receivers were given no cases (for example, one experienced lawyer had been proposed eight times by creditors but was never accepted by the Court), other firms had many.[93] Such arbitrariness and concentration of appointments fueled conjecture that a "bankruptcy ring" of collusion had formed between judges, debtors, and receivers, where judges received a kickback from receivers and/or debtors in order to appoint debtor-friendly receivers.[94]

The reformers had designed an economic incentive system that had worked brilliantly in the 1978 U.S. reforms. Rather than paying court-supervised professionals by the hour, which made them subject to the whims of the bench and much uncertainty about their final fees, the reformers proposed and the Ministry of Justice accepted that receivers be paid a proportion of the estate (the total assets of the debtor) they managed and helped restructure.[95] Like mergers and acquisition legal practice, a proportional compensation system would attract the largest law and accounting firms since their fees would be commensurate with the size and complexity of their clients. In cases where debtors' assets amounted to billions, fees could add up to millions of dollars.

In short order the courts rejected this potential windfall for receivers. They reverted back to court-imposed judgments on fees that were based on hourly rates, starting at three hundred dollars an hour, then dropping to two hundred dollars an hour, irrespective of the magnitude of the case in hand or the normal fee structure of the firm (Receivers' Report n.d.). However, receivers reported that they often had difficulty collecting their fees from debtors, even for hourly compensation. The consequences were immediate: the leading law and accounting firms in Indonesia abandoned receivers' work because it was unprofitable.

Retreat from bankruptcy work by the largest firms resulted also from the conditions under which fees were "negotiated." Since they were not set at the outset of the case, "the imposition of receivers' fees by the judges at the end of the appointment had led to collusive practices [of] 'cow trading' [*dagang sapi*]. The judges often asked for financial 'kick-backs' before making the appointment" (Receivers' Report n.d.). In other words, a "bankruptcy ring" immediately sprang up between supervising judges and professionals in a highly lucrative trade. To maintain their reputations, many firms felt they needed to retreat from the potential taint of corruption.[96]

In principle, unethical practices by the practitioners might have been sanctioned by the new professional association that was given such powers. In fact, the association barely got off the ground. After passing the admission exam, receivers reported that they heard nothing from their so-called association (Receivers' Report n.d.). Ethical enforcement ranged from nonexistent to negligible. When, under significant outside pressure, the Receivers' Association did bring an action against one of the most notorious firms of receivers, the lawyers under investigation promptly broke away and formed a rival association of receivers with a strong debtor orientation. In a move that carried a whiff of corruption, the Ministry of Justice official responsible for government oversight of the receivers eventually endorsed the breakaway group and thus authorized two rival associations of this tiny profession. A potential breakthrough in professional regulation by a single unified body, which had long eluded lawyers in Indonesia, abruptly ground to a halt. Needless to say, no receivers were disciplined.[97]

But the failure of the professional services market cannot be laid entirely at the door of the receivers. In a turn of events startling to the reformers, numbers of debtor corporations with large assets hired lawyers who, it is widely alleged, were both clever and corrupt. These so-called black lawyers simultaneously used the ambiguities of the law, various stratagems for falsifying claims, and bribes, it is alleged, to protect their clients from any actions of the courts adverse to their clients. Well known to other members of the bar, this practice had at least two effects. On the one side, these lawyers captured many of the most important clients. One disgruntled banker said that if your lawyer guarantees he will always win, and does, then he will attract debtors prepared to pay the price that assures that result. On the other side, since the risk of reputational contagion could spread to all lawyers who won in the courts, leading lawyers who sought to preserve their moral capital of being "clean" simply refused to practice in the courts—including some of these engaged in the reforms themselves.[98] In short, judges may have been corruptible, but unscrupulous professionals were prepared to exploit their vulnerability to cash inducements (Schröeder-van Waes and Sidharta 2004).

Making Sense of Failed Implementation

The process of insolvency reforms in Indonesia attracted interpretive communities, some bent on turning their diagnoses into more effective prescriptions, others making attributions that influenced their advice to clients, and yet others in making sense of the matrix of changes more generally since the fall of Suharto and the Financial Crisis.

At one level the reform struggle can be seen as a struggle over legal inheritance. Would Dutch-derived substantive law persist? Could a derogated judicial system recover some of its stature in the 1950s? Could an adversarial system of institutionalized legal conflict, which viewed the courts as a natural arena for dispute settlement, take root in a culture where public displays of business failure were anathema? In contrast to legal theories that consider legal transplants a relatively straightforward matter (Watson 1974), a handful of Indonesian and Dutch lawyers persuaded the IMF to stick more closely to inherited Dutch law and to reforms of similar law that had taken place in the Netherlands but had not yet been adopted in Indonesia. The Fund acceded within a set of parameters defined by the emerging consensus at the global center about norms for bankruptcy systems worldwide. A bankruptcy law must provide a credible threat so that debtors would negotiate with creditors or risk losing everything. It must offer a shelter for debtors in which they could hold creditors at bay while reorganizing their companies. Secured creditors should be inside, not outside, negotiations for reorganizations. For their design and approval, plans for reorganization must mobilize key creditors. These global norms set a threshold for a modernized Dutch-Indonesian law. Thus, the eventual agreement codified in the April 1998 Letter of Intent signed by the Government of Indonesia represents a melding of traditional and modern, indigenous and global approaches to law reform.[99] It was an act of bricolage (Campbell 2004), bringing together legitimate fragments of one set of laws with organically grafted developments in a cognate set of laws. It offered a translation of global master norms into domestic substantive law (Merry 2005, 2006).

Melding contemporary reforms with a moribund tradition, nevertheless, does not go far to recover a flowering of the justice reforms in the first decade after independence (Lev and McVey 1996; Pompe 2005). For some resident officials of IFIs the disappointment and despair with the dramatic failures (in their view) of early test cases mixed with a war-weary resignation to the situation. Hence their recourse to an explanation that turned on lack of a legal tradition: "courts were never used in Indonesia" and until Indonesia learns to "project the rule of law," foreign investors will stay away.[100] Being a judge or lawyer historically in Indonesia, said another, has been a low-status occupation, and the best and brightest have stayed away.[101] Thus, issues of competency should be expected—if judges recruited in traditional civil law systems come to the bench entirely through a bureaucratic career, and have no firsthand experience of business and finance, incompetence alone will account for a great deal of unpredictability in the behavior of courts. A civil law system embedded in a culture averse to law thus strikes a double blow at orientations and capacities for bankruptcy within the court system.

Even the apparent cultural affinity of new institutions with Indonesian customs elicited conflicting interpretations. The Jakarta Initiative appeared to have an affinity with the supposed preference of Indonesians for nonconfrontational methods of dispute resolution (Bappenas 1998). But it is a mistake to conclude that it was designed primarily to reflect cultural sensitivity. The World Bank's approach owed much to practices it had instituted in similar and quite dissimilar cultural contexts. It was serendipity that what the Bank and Fund adapted from Asian and non-Asian contexts alike had an affinity with not only with Indonesian practices of dispute resolution but with explicit recommendations in the pre-Crisis Bappenas Report. The IFIs built upon this serendipity to sell the concept to the Indonesians as consistent with Javanese approaches to dispute resolution. Using a "cultural hook," Bank officials could tell the Indonesians that "this is the way it is going to be—and it is not contrary to your culture . . . [but] a way for people to make their own solutions." But closer examination also revealed that certain aspects of the Jakarta Initiative were quite contrary to cultural constructions of the "Javanese way," said one World Bank official, for it required parties to be specific in their objectives and time bound.[102]

The sense of vexation that characterized many Western reformers found expression in generic attributions of inefficiency, indecisiveness, and a lack of integrity. A longtime expatriate specialist at an IFI alleged that the IMF came into the scene in a "very heavy-handed way." As it attached more and more conditions to its financial bailouts, Indonesians reacted in classic Javanese style: they have "a predisposition to avoid controversy, to save face, to make it work. You do what you need to do in a charming, beguiling way. You smile into someone's face and then stab them in the back." Or less dramatically, you agree to what you must agree, then "do every rearguard action imaginable to protect it." Foot dragging is a classic strategy of noncompliance in any country.[103] And the Jakarta Initiative offered a perfect additional step to delay bankruptcy. Without "a real stick" JITF provided a site for debtors to negotiate in bad faith and to delay getting to court where their strategies would in turn adapt to its weak pressure points.[104]

Yet the discourses of explanation and excuse are not uncontested themselves. While the Javanese elite have long ruled Indonesia, the argument goes, Bataks, Sumatrans, Moluccans, and other non-Javanese cannot be readily subsumed under some myth of universal Indonesian cultural practices or traditions. The tremendous ethnic diversity within modern Indonesia brings together a multiplicity of orientations from face-to-face interaction (numbers of informants spoke of the greater affinity that Sumatrans have for straight-talking, direct interaction with Westerners) to assumptions of deference and sycophancy by a ruling elite.[105]

Then, again, so much of the cultural discourse conveniently sidesteps the Chinese, whose companies controlled the commanding heights of the economy and are, thus, frequently the stereotypical debtors in diatribes against the system (Schwarz 2000).[106] The extensive literature on purportedly Chinese ways of doing business cannot be arbitrated here (Hamilton 1996; Redding 1993, 1996a, 1996b), although it is clear that the overseas Chinese throughout much of Southeast Asia have shunned formal legal settings when they could (contrast Taiwan and Singapore). But the foot dragging that has been everywhere observed in Indonesian corporate reorganizations has a simpler explanation that has much to do with the interaction of ethnicity and economic power and little to do with "culture," except insofar as ethnicity embodies distinctive cultural orientations and practice.[107]

Ethnicity notwithstanding, "culture-talk" in post-Crisis Indonesia attracts strong critics. For an Indonesian "modernizer," who leads a vocal NGO opposed to corruption, it is so much "culture-bullshit." For an IFI manager, it is a cynical effort for "sophisticated, ruthless" businesspeople to suddenly "claim Asian sensibilities when it comes to paying up." This is nothing but a "ruse," and for Westerners to buy into the ruse is not only naïve but smacks of "extreme paternalism." For a battle-tested IFI official who has been on many crisis missions, debts are debts. The so-called Javanese way is "nonsense." He's talked about it and he's read about it and he rejects it: "You can be culturally sensitive" in the way you construct institutions in particular societies, "but you have to pay your debt." And in Indonesia, the only way to assure this is to use a "hammer." Since Indonesians have "a wonderful capacity for pain-avoidance," said another IFI official, you've got to wave a big stick, both in the conditionalities embodied in agreements with the Government and in incentive structures within institutions like the Jakarta Initiative and the bankruptcy law.[108]

This debate over authenticity of cultural difference was at its height at a time of dramatic happenings in the Commercial Court, when several high-profile cases were treated in bizarre or manifestly corrupt ways—which attribution depends on where actors were situated in the drama. It was a time when the GOI found itself under diplomatic pressure from the Canadian government over the strange alleged harassment of a Canadian insurance subsidiary in Indonesia, the infamous *Manulife* case (Schröeder-van Waes and Sidharta 2004; Suyudi 2004). IFIs also closely focused on developments, not least because progress factored into their conditional release of moneys. Several years later, as the cases have disappeared from the courts, and both creditors and debtors have reverted to pre-1997 practices of solving corporate financial distress, tempers are cooler and judgments less charged. In this atmosphere one of Indonesia's most distinguished law reformers reflects that perhaps the cultural argument cannot be dismissed cavalierly. We have "come back in a circle" to the situation before the Crisis.[109] "Bankruptcy cases are settled outside the court because many of the private businesses are family businesses and it will shame the family if you say they are bankrupt . . . The family will help and the creditors will be satisfied when it's not going to court. . . . Settle it amicably."[110] This solution does not help corporations with large foreign investments, precisely a group the Commercial Court was designed to serve.

For cynics or realists a cultural explanation blandly avoids the more obvious minefield astride the route to effective implementation—pervasive corruption. Bankruptcy judges on major cases handle disputes worth tens and hundreds of millions of dollars to the corporations in their courts. It is only reasonable to expect, indeed there may even be a certain justice in the fact, that moneys will flow into their pockets for favorable decisions. Judges are especially susceptible to bribes, particularly in a Commercial Court, said one of the lawyers most often alleged to corrupt the system, because their salaries were so pitifully low given the stakes of the cases they were working on. When judges earn $200 a month on cases where the lawyers are earning $200 an hour, and where it is worth the while of business owners to spend millions to save control of their companies, then of course judges will be vulnerable to the leverage of under-the-counter payments. Is it logical, said a lawyer from the Indonesian Bank Restructuring Agency (IBRA), which lost most of scores of cases it took to the Court as a creditor, that a given lawyer would win 100 percent of his cases? Or is it something other than logic? And if this problem were not pervasive in the Commercial Court, where at least the judges had some rudiments of expertise in bankruptcy law, it could and did rear itself on appeals to the Supreme Court, precisely a fear of Daniel Lev and other longtime observers of the Indonesian courts from the outset of the reforms.[111]

In hindsight the initial instinct of the reformers to raise judicial salaries was especially prescient. Repeatedly, observers of the Court, lawyers, and judges themselves maintained that judicial salaries not only discouraged competent judges but fed temptation. According to one prominent lawyer-reformer, when judges saw the big houses of government ministers, they despaired. Another eminent lawyer proposed that salaries should be set at the level of those of moderately successful corporate lawyers in the private market. Said a Supreme Court Justice, it costs a judge about 10 million rupiah to send her two children to a decent school, but her entire salary is only 6 million rupiah a month. How is it possible to live decently and be a competent clean judge?[112]

To fix the problem of corruption is to alter not only well-entrenched institutional arrangements in the entire public service but to transform an entire moral economy. Daniel Lev (2004) goes much further: to reform a legal system that had been run down and marginalized over the preceding forty years required no less than an alteration of both the orientations and structure of state power.[113] It is for this reason that donors—IFIs, government aid organizations, and private groups—by late 2006 were pouring tens of millions of dollars into the legal system, much of it directly or indirectly targeted at corruption.

The failures of the bankruptcy system were also institutional. Optimistic reformers had high hopes that short of reforming all Indonesian courts and all thirty-three thousand judges, it might be possible to create a "model court." It would be a "wedge" through which reforms might enter the entire court system. If a model court could show how justice could be "more effective, more efficient," then it could offer a powerful demonstration effect. But even creating a model court ran aground on the shoals of judicial careers. An effective court required judges trained in commercial law and with an understanding of business. Recruitment to the judiciary historically followed the course of civil law systems, where judges were recruited from law school and therefore never had any commercial experience as lawyers. Given that a model of the generalist judge also prevailed in Indonesia, the judiciary resisted the notion of specialized bankruptcy or commercial judges. The first wave of recruits to the Commercial Court were given compressed training by Dutch professionals, and they quickly learned on the job. But since the court system offered them no higher career opportunities in commercial law, they were motivated to transfer out of the Commercial Court back to promotion along the generalist career track. Until such times that the court system as a whole could either recruit specialist judges from outside the career judiciary or provide upward mobility for judges specializing in commercial law, the competency of the judges in the Commercial Court and Supreme Court would remain underdeveloped (IMF 2005).[114] Furthermore, the entire reform program in the courts had been premised on the expectation that the judiciary, long chafing under military government, would prove to be an active agent for its own reform, an assumption that proved false.[115]

But however much IFIs and specialist reformers might seek to cabin the bankruptcy law and systems from their political and social contexts, these invariably intruded, sometimes so powerfully that they overwhelmed any prospect for the autonomy of law. The Commercial Court presented an arena of struggle that reproduced in microcosm the contest between, on the one side, the giant conglomerates that led much of the Indonesian state developmental economy and, on the other, the mostly foreign credit institutions that fueled the last years of the Indonesian economic bubble. The foreign lenders sought the repayment of loans, or the transfer to them of property that had collateralized their failed loans, or exchanges of debt for equity (and often control) of major Indonesian firms. In this contest, local "debtors outgunned mostly foreign creditors." The debtor corporations had much more at stake—control of their enterprises and conglomerates—than the foreign creditors, who could write off or write down bad debt or at least postpone it and maintain the fiction in their balance sheets that one day the debt would be repaid. Debtors-in-control of major local corporations, by contrast, stood to lose everything. Because the stakes for them were high, and because their resources were extensive, they could fight their battles on the turf of the local courts by buying the "best" counsel and using extralegal means to get a favorable outcome, even if it meant enabling "money to change hands."[116]

Furthermore, debtors' lawyers could justify some of their extralegal approaches to judges as an ideologically valid means of resisting illicit economic coercion by foreign interests. Judges, too, might find ideological solace in decisions that reflected resistance of many Indonesians to a law and court that seemed to exploit Indonesia's weakness during the economic Crisis. "Someone wants to close this country" was the suspicion. Foreign creditors, it was alleged, sought to force their will on a weakened economic and political system. And even if judges did not act for such grand nationalist ideals, they might exhibit a resistance to following a legally correct solution, when that ruling would throw workers out of their jobs or when it would alienate senior politicians with financial interests in the company. Inexplicable legal decisions, therefore, could reflect a coincidence of personal economic interest, nationalist sentiment, social consciousness, and plain political expediency.[117]

Insofar as the most important reforms also required shifts in the balance of power between the executive and judiciary, or a preparedness to prosecute senior government officials for corruption, or a readiness to put powerful politically connected corporations at the mercy of courts, the salience of political will cannot be underestimated. Much resistance to pushing large corporations into an open Commercial Court was alleged by some foreign observers to come from highly placed officials whose financial interests in businesses had hitherto been invisible. The close intermeshing of affairs between large conglomerates and politicians meant that corporate restructuring frequently had fallout for politicians. The specter of foreign investors taking control of painstakingly constructed Indonesian-owned and -controlled companies threatened incipient nationalism and further pressed politicians to protect their own. Within the court system, it is alleged that an earlier Chief Justice of the Supreme Court resisted the reformist incursions into the court system, even with a small model court. One well-placed IFI official felt that a Minister of Justice in power at a critical period only grudgingly pursued the reforms and, if anything, quietly subverted them.

By late 2006 the climate had changed. A reformist Chief Justice, brought in from an academic institution, energetically supported reforms in the Supreme Court and elsewhere in the court system. The Ministry of Justice and legislature passed major financial and administrative control over to the courts, replacing a "two-roof system," in which responsibilities were divided between the judiciary and executive, into a "one-roof system," where the judiciary took over most control of its own affairs. Not least, several longtime reformers close to the political center believed that President Susilo Bambang Yudhoyono had "positive political will" but "perhaps lacked the courage" or the "political clout" to get it done. Nevertheless, growing pressures from citizens, within civil society and the media, appeared to be strengthening the impetus within Indonesia for systemic change in the justice system. Some guarded optimism was in the air despite the many defeats along the way.[118]

Recursivity, Leverage, and Convergence

Over the nine years from the onset of the Financial Crisis in Indonesia, we have shown that for every two steps forward in formal lawmaking, implementation took at least one and sometimes two steps backward. The IMF-Indonesian team and its donor allies effectively entered into a cat-and-mouse relationship with centers of political resistance and commercial reactionaries in repeated cycles of enactment and frustrated implementation. This fundamentally recursive process has not run its course, although an episode that began with reforms of every part of the insolvency regime shows signs of settling at a level of implementation far below that envisioned by the reformers.

It is clear that while the Financial Crisis precipitated an initial rush of lawmaking and institution building, much of it induced, even coerced, by pressures from IFIs, the slice of reforms involving bankruptcy regimes not only relied substantially on an indigenous vision of legal change that preceded the Crisis but also rested fundamentally on indigenous Indonesian law inherited without amendment from the Dutch colonial period. The enormous leverage of conditionality wielded by the IFIs in part modernized extant law, advanced innovations anticipated by Indonesian reformers, and imported law and institutions at the behest of IFIs and their expert advisors. Yet this combination of indigenous and foreign law, of internal reformist impulses and external economic pressures, of culturally attuned adaptations and imported novelties still ran aground on obstacles on all sides. Why did this occur?

In part the incompleteness of implementation follows from the logic of the theory of recursivity. Ideological and structural contradictions abounded in the reform cycles. On the one side, a universalistic model of bankruptcy law, which would allow pure market forces to determine the fates of Indonesian corporations, ran head-on into nationalist identity, which abhorred the loss of Indonesian control over its flagship corporations and critical economic sectors. Internalized within the bankruptcy reforms was a veiled ethnic and political struggle within Indonesia, between the Chinese, whose businesses dominate many sectors of the economy, and the ethnic Indonesians, who dominate politics. Many ethnic Chinese viewed the corporate restructuring reforms to be a political weapon to undermine Chinese business dominance, just as many powerful ethnic Indonesians resented any prospect of personal loss or of a loss of domestic controls over their Indonesian birthright.[119] On both counts, each reform internalized conflicts that had not been resolved elsewhere and thus sowed the seeds of corrective reform cycles.

Internal structural tensions ramified through the judicial system. While a model court seemed a plausible modest step forward within the judiciary, the subversive implications of its powers, salary levels, career implications, and costs of lost "rents" became immediately apparent to other courts, and the Supreme Court in particular. If this internal resistance by the Judges Association and Supreme Court were not enough, in later cycles the Ministry of Justice resisted a transfer of its powers to the judiciary, just as it was a major political effort to push through the legislature provisions that would increase the financial and administrative autonomy of the court system under one self-determining "roof." For corporate restructuring, even the establishment of what the IFIs had imagined to be a complementary organization to the courts—the Jakarta Initiative Task Force—was read by debtors and creditors alike as a contradictory signal, a vote of no confidence by the Government and its IFI "partners" in the Commercial Court.

The ambiguities and indeterminacies that conventionally accompany law-making compounded the struggles of the Court to revivify bankruptcy law. No one imagined that a legal concept so fundamental to commercial and civil law as "debt" should become the source of so much confusion. In practice, of course, the mere fact of innovation presented openings to creative, and some said, unscrupulous, lawyers to turn the reforms against the reformers. By seizing upon terminological ambiguities, debtors' lawyers in their counter-attack could widen a gap to bring an organization struggling for legitimacy into disrepute. No one anticipated that newly appointed ad hoc judges would refuse to serve if they could not offer dissenting opinions, a refusal that led to another round of reforms where dissents were authorized. It was expected that corruption might undermine court reforms, though the IMF underestimated how difficult it would be to extirpate. IFIs felt compelled to save their initiatives by widening reforms to control corruption not only in the courts but across the entire senior civil service. And even when indeterminacies were recognized from the outset—that a model court embedded in a corrupt and derogated court system might be stifled from within—the lack of time, resources, boldness, or political will precluded the construction of a more determinate solution at the beginning.

The uncertain fates of the Commercial Court and JITF reveal a connection between diagnostic failures and mismatch of players. The diagnosis of the problem was an amalgam of local knowledge by Indonesian academics and practitioners who brokered prescriptions for reform and IFI theories of law and market regulation. Much of the diagnosis was well founded. Indonesian practitioners well understood inherent problems of the law and the weakness of extant institutions. Highly experienced expatriates, thoroughly familiar with Dutch and U.S. law and practice and equally at home in Indonesia, sensed what needed to be corrected and how. Similarly, the diagnosis and prescription for professional development were both on point and well conceived, but reformers misjudged how much overzealous representation by small and unscrupulous lawyers could doom any pretensions of an effective self-regulating profession. The IMF clearly misdiagnosed the pervasiveness of corruption and underestimated the capacity of the Supreme Court and Minister of Justice to frustrate change.

Diagnostic misjudgment bled into biases exacerbated by a mismatch of the actors involved in lawmaking and those on whom it would be dependent for implementation. The short time horizons forced by Crisis events almost completely excluded integral players in practice—the debtor corporations, many private banks, and Chinese commercial leaders.[120] It is not surprising that influential actors, most notably debtor-owners of major corporations, who were excluded from effective participation in the reform process, moved their grounds for resistance to the arena of implementation, where they used great ingenuity, inertia, professional expertise, and raw financial power to frustrate the reforms at every point. The politics of implementation therefore became a site of outright resistance in two respects: when the Government of Indonesia had no capacity to resist external pressures, it shifted the battleground to one where it had more advantage; and when domestic actors were excluded from lawmaking, they fought with whatever weapons they had available—legal and extralegal—in the courts and restructuring agencies.

Together, the ideological contradictions, mismatch of players in implementation and lawmaking, and an exclusion of certain facts and perspectives from the diagnosis intensified the indeterminacies of laws enacted and institutions constructed in crisis circumstances with the unsurprising result that successive iterations of reform continued, as each cycle of lawmaking sought to close the gap between practice and lawmakers' intent.

By late 2006, where did these various cycles of reform—substantive and procedural law, courts, professions, and out-of-court—come to rest?

There is no doubt that the formal legal changes converged toward the global norms at the center of the IFI and UNCITRAL norm-making efforts. At the heart of the Indonesian reforms can be found the core of the UNCITRAL

Legislative Guide—the centrality of corporate reorganization as a viable alternative to liquidation of companies in any bankruptcy regime. The Indonesian initiatives center this emphasis on reorganization in the courts, a choice authorized but not mandated by UNCITRAL, although it is certainly the preferred option for the World Bank and IMF, if not the Asian Development Bank. Moreover, the reforms include out-of-court mechanisms at least with a family resemblance to those derived from the London Approach of the Bank of England and of quite close resemblance to those already tried out by the Bank and Fund in Thailand, Malaysia, and Latin America some years earlier. The reforms of professions go further than UNCITRAL's but are consistent with approaches by Britain and Australia. Yet the reforms were also intended to deliver "the stick," the plausible threat of liquidation that the ADB, IMF, and World Bank considered necessary to compel good-faith bargaining over restructuring debt, whether in or out of court. All this was managed roughly within the Dutch colonial and postcolonial tradition, suitably modernized and sometimes moderately harmonized with the center of the global movement toward reorganization.

Yet this convergence on a substantive principle—reorganization—is not accompanied by institutional isomorphism with court-centered bankruptcy regimes in many advanced economies. In practice, while the substantive law stands and the Commercial Court still exists, the practice of corporate restructuring has almost completely deserted the formal bankruptcy system. With the Jakarta Initiative Task Force gone, the Court and professions are empty shells—on the books but irrelevant in practice. In short, as an eminent Indonesian legal authority takes stock, the reforms have gone full circle: from out-of-court informal restructuring before the Crisis, through a brief moment of potential in-court formal restructuring, and now back to restructurings outside court and bankruptcy law.

This might appear to be a victory for debtors. After all, the reforms were driven by international multilateral banks who listened most attentively to the voices of international and domestic creditors. But the story is more complicated. While the reformers clearly wanted to activate bankruptcy law and make liquidation a credible threat, domestic reformers and their IMF allies crafted a substantive law with judicial powers to protect debtors from unilateral creditor actions. The provisions that gave legal authority to debtors to suspend payment to all creditors, and which halted the capacity of creditors to seize their collateral, while a plan of reorganization was being drawn up, were intended to shelter the business while it could take stock, restructure, and redirect the business. There was a very real danger that in the process owners could lose control of their companies. But the alternative might have been for the companies to be dismembered piecemeal by creditors.

Nonetheless, many in the business community did not see the law as debtor friendly, and business leaders (and their coterie of politician-investors, among others) had no desire for their business incompetence to be shamefully exposed in court. Several of the deformities evident during implementation occurred precisely because debtors and their counsel continued to resist the premise that bankruptcy law and courts should be the means of restructuring firms and the outcome that might wrest control away from owners and Indonesians. The last-minute effort of some debtor interests to withhold the President's signature of the substantive reforms, the corrupting of Commercial Court and Supreme Court judges, the rival bill introduced to the IMF-Indonesian reform team's version, the dragging of feet by debtors during JITF proceedings, the corrupting of lawyers and receivers—all these reveal a two-fold struggle. At one level it is between debtors and creditors over which will retain the upper hand when businesses get into financial difficulty. At another level it is over alternative models of restructuring. The retreat from the Commercial Court indicates that the choice has been to revert to the status quo ante: despite the risks that creditor banks may destroy companies that could be reorganized in a court setting, debtors and their counsel prefer to negotiate privately than in the public spotlight. In practice Indonesian corporations, banks, and professionals have conspired to reject the model affirmed by some domestic reformers in partnership with the IMF and other donors. Pre-Crisis practice has reasserted itself despite post-Crisis reforms.

There are two potentially adverse consequences that might arise from this state of affairs. One is that the prospect of a model court opening up the entire court system is dashed. In an ironic twist, however, precisely the opposite has occurred. Every deficiency in the bankruptcy reforms has led to lateral reforms elsewhere on a grander scale. The fight to get ad hoc judges in the Commercial Court helped it little, but they are now institutionalized elsewhere in the court system. The struggle for written opinions and dissents to become standard administrative practice by the Commercial Court led to their incorporation in the higher courts, including the Supreme Court. The apparent corruption in the Commercial Court merely reinforced widening efforts by the IMF and other donor organizations to set up formal anticorruption machinery. The out-of-court efforts of the Jakarta Initiative have now been mirrored formally in mandatory negotiation proceedings for commercial disputes headed toward the Supreme Court. The Blueprint approach to court reorganization developed for the Commercial Court has now been adopted by the Supreme Court, Human Rights, and Anti-Corruption Courts. The complaints over inadequate self-regulation by a multiplicity of lawyers' associations may be somewhat remedied by a law to unify the professions (IMF 2005). In short, reforms have expanded outward and upward in the judicial system to embrace the Supreme Court and other high-profile courts, such as the Human Rights Court and Anti-Corruption Court.[121]

To effect these many more ambitious reforms of the entire court system, tens of millions of dollars are flooding in from USAID, the Dutch government, AusAid, the Millennium Challenge Corporation, the World Bank, the European Union, and the Asian Development Bank, among others. In another surprising twist, USAID decided that the Commercial Court should again be made a priority and has initiated a heavily funded three-year reform program to upgrade it and expand its jurisdiction. Much of this effort seemingly is fueled by the conjunction of fears that the world's largest Muslim nation will radicalize in the absence of a more stable economic and political situation. However, it must be observed that these reforms are occurring "on the books." It remains to be seen if the expenditure of dollars yields practical consequences commensurate with their cost.

Another potential adverse consequence of the demise of bankruptcy practice goes to the heart of IFI ideology and Indonesian development. IFIs maintain that good law (read an effective Commercial Court) fuels investment that stimulates economic growth and the reduction of poverty. We have seen that international institutions have abandoned bankruptcy law in Indonesia.[122] Does this mean that investment in Indonesia has also dried up? Our data do not directly address this question. While foreign direct investment (FDI) climbed from $5.27 billion in 2003 to more than $10 billion in 2007, this level brought it back to levels in the mid-1990s and far below the $27 billion in 1997.[123] In short, foreign investors have cast their ballots on the risk of investing in Indonesia. This brings to a decisive conclusion all the attempted reforms, actual reforms, and failed reforms—a rising tide but far from its heights at the eve of the Crisis.

An indirect indication comes from experienced corporate lawyers in Jakarta. Summarizing their views, a longtime expatriate lawyer for major infrastructure projects noted that investment will still flow into Indonesia when it can be collateralized outside the country (i.e., companies have assets that can be attached outside Indonesia) or various techniques can be used to protect investors without recourse to Indonesian institutions. But for investment in infrastructure that requires domestic collateral (e.g., roads, ports, minerals, electricity, etc.) or for midsized and smaller companies that do not have foreign assets, then foreign investors are not returning. This was not what Indonesian leaders expected, stated a former director of the IFC in Jakarta. There was a sense that if the storm could be weathered, moneys would flow back into the country as they did before the Crisis. Without access to security outside Indonesia, and in the absence of predictable and certain legal rights within Indonesia, other markets appear more attractive and Indonesia languishes.

A decade has passed since the onset of the Crisis. The IFIs entered Indonesia with an enormous asymmetry of power in their favor, an advantage that predictably might have permitted them to impose macroeconomic and legal regulatory regimes on a defenseless country. In the field of corporate bankruptcy, outcomes were both predictable and not. In contrast to naïve views of unified global centers, IOs and aid agencies fought on the ground in Jakarta as to which would take the lead and in what direction. When the IMF came out ahead, it did not impose an alien framework on Indonesia. While it brought general parameters, principles, and thresholds, together with experience elsewhere, it allied itself with domestic reformers who had explicit and incipient designs for reforms developed before the Crisis, particularly for the courts. From the mix of IMF legal staff, indigenous Indonesian specialists, expatriate practitioners in Jakarta, and Dutch experts with a knowledge of Indonesia, it negotiated reforms that ultimately melded domestic preferences with IO principles and experiences. This fusion produced a multifaceted bankruptcy regime that IMF and World Bank conditionality ensured was adopted into formal law. Implementation was another matter. The bankruptcy court appeared to fail altogether.[124] Professional regulation fared little better. The Jakarta Initiative functioned and yielded to a national mediation service. The most important outcomes, however, may have been the by-products of the Commercial Court initiative. Not only did it bring the courts into the public eye as a new potential center of economic power, but it contributed to a stream of subsequent reforms and more ambitious designs for the entire court system that in mid-2007 seem to have been widely embraced by Indonesians and donors alike. The notion of Commercial Court reforms as a "wedge" for wider reformation of the judiciary may eventually be proved prescient (Lev 2004).

6 Korea:
Legal Restructuring of the Market and State

T HE YEAR 1996 marked the Republic of Korea's economic coming-of-age: a former Japanese colony, subsequently ravaged and
divided by civil war, Korea was admitted to membership of the Organisation
of Economic Co-operation and Development (OECD), a club of the world's
richest nations. By any economic criterion, its rapid transition from a third-
to a first-world country had been notable. After years of phenomenal growth
it could boast the world's eleventh-largest economy, low unemployment, and
balanced budgets. The products of its largest corporate groups were household
names in global markets for shipbuilding, chemicals, construction, and communications. Yet, only months after accession to the OECD, Korea plunged
into an economic crisis so severe that it required the most expensive intervention ever by the IMF.[1]

Integral to the packet of financial bailouts spearheaded by the IMF and
World Bank were massive efforts to restructure the financial and corporate
sectors of the economy, both to stabilize the crisis and to rebuild an economy
that would be less vulnerable to the shocks that had brought Korea to the
brink of sovereign bankruptcy and total economic collapse (Chopra et al.
2001). The international financial institutions led a coalition of international
organizations and private banks to undertake not only financial restructuring but also structural adjustments (Chopra et al. 2001; Kim and Byeon 2002).
By now, the creation of a viable bankruptcy system had become part of the
IFI's reform packet, so it, too, became an object of intervention by global and
regional credit institutions (Mako 2003).

Reforms and institution building of corporate bankruptcy regimes implicated a good deal more than technical commercial law. The bankruptcy reforms must be seen in a matrix of struggles—between the global norms promulgated by international organizations and the contextually situated particularities recognized by domestic reformers; between the continued practices of a developmental state and the new prospect of a rule-governed market; between the epistemologies of economists versus those of lawyers; and between public and policy support for creditors versus debtors. The bankruptcy reforms offer a prism through which to observe conflicts over the restructuring of the state and market—and the lively negotiation of the role of law and its institutions in the governing of market transactions.

The iterations of foreign interventions and the rapid recursive cycles of reform within Korea signify the magnitude and shape of those struggles. Almost every year, and on occasion several times a year, one kind of reform initiative or another followed in one or another lawmaking site (Oh 2003a). Through negotiations between the IFIs and Korean policymakers, and between actors within the state and those in the market, a succession of policy experiments were implemented by contesting actors who sought to craft a system for treating ailing corporations that vindicated contrasting concepts not only of how to manage corporations in distress but of how more fundamentally to restructure the Korean state and market. Out of these struggles emerged a significantly reformed set of laws and institutions—differing from both those that existed before the Crisis and those the IFIs had implanted in other Crisis states, such as Indonesia.

We turn first to sketch the financial context of the post-Crisis reforms. We then review the legal and administrative reforms that predated the Crisis and accelerated dramatically after its onset, culminating in the enactment of the Unified Bankruptcy Act 2005. We then analyze the recursive cycles, their actors, dynamics, and outcomes, with particular attention to the degree of convergence in Korea with the global norms propagated by the IMF and World Bank.

Prelude to the Crisis

At the end of the Korean War, Korea was a country in ruins. But by 1996, when it joined the OECD, South Korea had experienced decades of phenomenal growth (the annual growth of GDP averaged 7.6 percent between 1987 and 1997; per capita GNP climbed from $270 in 1970 to over $10,000 in 1997).

A once undeveloped agrarian economy had been transformed into an industrial economy oriented around the production of goods for export onto world markets (e.g., agricultural production was 23 percent of GDP in 1976, but only 6.3 percent in 1996). Light manufacturing dominated in the 1950s and 1960s, but Korea developed heavy industry in the 1970s. This transformation had been accomplished by interventionist government policy that used the Korean banking system to direct flows of capital into selected industries. So-called policy loans allowed the Government of Korea (GOK) to target investment and build up Korea's industrial capacity (Woo 1991). It was also made possible by the military protection and foreign aid offered by the U.S., which for its own geopolitical reasons wanted to see Korea flourish.

The organization of the Korean economy resembles that of Japan in a number of ways, partly because Korea was a former Japanese colony. As in Japan, corporations in Korea relied heavily on bank loans rather than capital markets to finance their expansion. This allowed the owners of firms to secure additional capital without losing control of the firm. For the Korean government, reliance on banks also gave it a lever with which to influence investment flows over the entire economy. Indeed, before the early 1980s Korean commercial banks had been publicly owned and so directly controlled by the Government. Afterward, Korea's banks were domestically owned yet remained easily swayed by government ministries. Only after the 1997 Financial Crisis did foreign ownership in the bank sector become significant. Korean economic development did not depend on extensive foreign direct investment (Gilpin and Gilpin 2000), nor were Korean securities markets (bonds and shares) well developed.

Also, similar to the Japanese economy, the Korean economy was organized around a small number of large business groups, *chaebols*. A *chaebol* is like the Japanese *keiretsu*, a conglomerate of firms in different industries and sectors (sometimes including a nonbank financial institution) bound together through a network of bilateral ownership ties, exchange relations, loans and cross-loan guarantees, and informal social ties. At the center was the core firm, which was frequently family owned (Chamyeo Yondae 1999; Chodosh 2005; Steers, Shin, and Ungson 1989). In 1994, the top 30 *chaebols* constituted about 15 percent of Korea's GNP.

In the period before 1997 large Korean firms had become very highly leveraged (relying heavily on debt rather than equity for capital) at the same time that Korea's financial markets had been opened up to the outside in preparation for OECD membership (Baliño and Ubide 1999; World Bank 1998). The largest *chaebol*, Hyundai, for example, had a debt-equity ratio of 578.7 percent in 1997 (Nam, Kim, and Oh 1999; Nam and Oh 2000). Compounding the dangers, much credit was extended through short-term loans, which added a degree of potential volatility to financial markets. Thus, Korea was vulnerable to a sudden exit of short-term capital (World Bank 1998).

Korea's financial institutions had not kept pace with its expansion. Foreign banks generally loaned to Korean banks, which in turn loaned money to the *chaebols*.[2] As a consequence of the preponderance of politically directed loans (Woo-Cumings 1999), and an implicit guarantee that *chaebols* were "too big to fail," Korean banks (which had been government owned until 1983) possessed underdeveloped skills in credit analysis and risk management (Baliño and Ubide 1999; Chopra et al. 2001). When not dictated by the state, lending decisions were based on the availability of collateral rather than cash flow projections, on the existence of cross-guarantees among *chaebol* firms, and with less detailed financial information about the borrower than a Western bank typically would require (Borensztein and Lee 2000; Woo-Cumings 1999). Furthermore, loan classification was lax and loan provisioning inadequate, especially given that many Korean banks were undercapitalized.

When the Financial Crisis hit, the won fell sharply in November 1997, banks were unable to roll over their short-term debts, and international reserves dried up (Chopra et al. 2001). The *chaebols* were hit by a sharp fall in sales and the decline in the exchange rate (Nam, Kim, and Oh 1999). The Korean government guaranteed the foreign obligations of Korean financial institutions, but money still flowed out, and Korea was forced to seek help from the IMF in December (Lindgren et al. 1999) and a restructuring of private debt in January 1998 (Kim and Byeon 2002). Meanwhile, many of the *chaebols* were in deep financial trouble, which meant that the banks lending them money also experienced great difficulty. While the highly leveraged *chaebols* were vulnerable to cash flow problems, it turns out that they were not too big to fail. By the end of November 1997, six of the top thirty *chaebols* had filed for court protection, and another filed for bankruptcy in December.[3] As corporations become insolvent, nonperforming loans at the banks grew to a point where they reached about 80 percent of bank capital, a level that seriously threatened the solvency of many banks (Baliño and Ubide 1999) and ultimately the entire financial system.

Korea shared some basic problems with Thailand and Indonesia: how to provide enough liquidity to the financial system to keep illiquid but solvent firms and banks afloat while simultaneously sorting out nonperforming loans to separate salvageable firms and financial institutions from the unsalvageable. However, Korea differed from the other countries in two important respects: first, Korea was central to American diplomatic and security interests in the Far East; second, its economy was organized around the *chaebols* and their close relationship to the Korean state.[4] Even more important, G-8 central bankers informed their private banks that unless they could restructure Korea's private debt, the entire world financial system was at risk (Kim and Byeon 2002). It was not surprising that U.S.-backed international multilateral financial institutions and private multinational banks quickly stitched together a rescue package of unprecedented size.

Corporate Failure and Bankruptcy Law

If sources of finance and commercial banking had not grown apace with Korea's economic expansion, neither had the legal regulation of market relationships, including bankruptcy law. In the preceding decades, Korea had dealt with ailing corporations by two mechanisms, neither of which relied upon conventional bankruptcy practices. On the one hand, since large firms were directly or indirectly supported by the Government, the Government took responsibility when they ran into financial difficulty. This could be done on a case-by-case basis, when government officials would pressure banks to extend rescue loans or renegotiate financing, or through forced mergers or forced liquidations. Industry-wide problems or general economic downturns could also be managed through systemic policy responses by such measures as the Arrangement of Ailing Firms in 1969 or the August 3 Presidential Emergency Economic Decree to freeze outstanding debt (Oh 2003b). This fostering of a moral hazard for lenders cultivated the myth that large firms were "too big to fail." In short, for major firms in those industries at the center of government industrial policy, firm failure was handled at the discretion of powerful government administrators, most notably the Economy Planning Board, established in 1961, and the Ministry of Finance after 1994 (later consolidated into the Ministry of Finance and Economy, or MOFE), which had administrative oversight of Korea's industrial development.

On the other hand, for smaller firms debt enforcement was managed outside bankruptcy law. In contrast to many other countries, when a creditor in Korea filed an application for compulsory enforcement of debt repayment, other creditors were not necessarily disadvantaged.[5] They could be joined to the enforcement procedure to share in the distribution of proceeds without the use of bankruptcy law (Oh 2003b).

The combination of these two practices rendered the use of Korea's three bankruptcy statutes virtually null. Since 1962 Korea had in place three bankruptcy acts, which it had adapted from Japanese procedures.[6] A composition procedure gave corporate management the right to begin initiative proceedings, develop a plan, and remain in control of the company. This legislation, initially intended for small companies with uncomplicated debt structures, limited the power of creditors. More significantly, the management of larger companies began to use this legislation to escape both reorganization and forced liquidation. The Corporate Reorganization Act, designed explicitly to permit court-protected restructuring, had features unattractive to management: the process required them to hand over control of a company to court-appointed receivers, and the court had the power to nullify the shares of dominant shareholders. In the corporate reorganization proceeding, managers and owners also risked losing control (Nam and Oh 2000).

Significantly, neither piece of corporate legislation took stringent measures to liquidate companies that, on any reasonable business projection, had little hope of being turned around. The threat of liquidation, in other words, was sufficiently remote that it did not compel managers and owners to engage in fundamental financial or operational restructurings of their firms or corporate groups (Nam and Oh 2000). As a result, neither liquidation nor reorganization within this particular legal framework was likely to take place, particularly for *chaebols*.

Compounding the entrenched practice of state interventions for major companies and the limitations of substantive law were equivocal attitudes of the Korean state toward the role of law and a skeptical attitude of the Korean public to practices of debtors. While Korea could boast a relatively sophisticated judiciary, whose judges were recruited through a rigorous meritocratic competition, and which arguably had lower levels of corruption than in some other Crisis countries, in fact Korean judges had little experience with corporate bankruptcy and limited competency in complex commercial disputes more generally. Between 1983 and 1996 only 26 cases had been filed under the Composition Act and 678 cases under the Reorganization Act (Nam and Oh 2000).[7] On average, judges might have seen only one or two corporate reorganization cases in their careers and were therefore not in good shape to handle a sudden influx of cases in an economic downturn, let alone a national Financial Crisis. In part this resulted from the practices of a developmental state that ordered the market through administrative rather than law-governed mechanisms. In part it also reflected the minuscule size of the Korean bar, again highly sophisticated but with a very limited capacity to scale up to any broad-based demand for its services in corporate bankruptcy (Ginsburg 2007).

Yet the Korean public also had little tolerance for a bankruptcy system that appeared to coddle incompetent owners and managers. Until 1910 debtors had been treated within the penal code. Although the 1962 laws introduced the concept that debtors might be forgiven (discharged) their debt, this legal provision far outpaced the readiness of a public to tolerate widespread use of a law that would protect debtors from creditors in cases of personal bankruptcy and enable them to turn around their companies and remain in control, one of the principal incentives given management to use bankruptcy laws early in a company's financial slide to arrest its decline before it was too late (Oh 2003b).

The combination of these factors produced a legal system that was competent but institutionally underdeveloped and highly circumscribed by a dominant, imperative state apparatus. In Korea, law had not yet emerged as a serious basis for regulation of market relations or restructuring of failing firms. Legal culture had little public support for court-based protections for debtors that would enable effective reorganization for troubled companies.

Epistemological Conflicts

Underlying the fundamental conflicts between an administratively coordinated market and a law-governed market was an epistemological divide that revealed itself in an incipient struggle between economists and lawyers (Halliday and Carruthers 2004a).[8] The expansion of a market is one of many arenas in which new work opportunities emerge for professionals (Abbott 1988). The opening of opportunities regularly leads to jurisdictional conflicts for control over areas of work. The professions that succeed in establishing their jurisdictional rights benefit from an expansion of their powers in the ordering of institutions, often an enhancement of their prestige, and not infrequently the material rewards that result from a monopoly over a professional services market (Carruthers and Halliday 1998). Korea's economic miracle had been presided over by an elite of domestically and foreign-trained economists who dominated the heights of the government ministries responsible for the economy, most notably the Ministry of Finance and Economy. Because these economists were educated at top universities in the United States and Europe, and supported by prestigious research institutes such as the Korea Development Institute (KDI), Korea's success can be viewed in substantial part as the triumph of a professional project. This technocratic elite had been able to translate its theories of markets and firms into practice through its ascendancy in the administrative state.

The extraordinary success of Korea's economist-driven state planning, globally acknowledged by its admission to the exclusive economic club of the OECD, vindicated the primacy of economic knowledge as an architect of economic change. In the view of the economist–civil servants in the top ranks of public administration, markets needed administrative control, banks could not be given free reign to act as purely commercial lenders, and firms could not be left to their own devices, especially if they were critical to a key industry. If law were to be of use, it was as an instrument for effecting state policy, not as a framework for allowing market actors to chart their own course subject to law's institutional constraints and recourse when things went wrong. The coupling of expert knowledge to power exemplified many professions' widely documented ambitions to translate their technical authority into political action (Halliday 1985).

Ironically, the very success of the economists' project carried within it the seeds of contradiction. And here the lawyers entered a struggle over epistemology and power in relation to the market. Although commercial lawyers themselves were deeply dependent on the state as a client and the patron of their commercial clients, they conceived of a role of law and legal institutions in markets that differed sharply from that of the economists. In their view, markets might be emancipated from arbitrary or systematic state intervention and allowed to function as sets of private transactions, moderated by law and modulated by courts. Firms, managers, and shareholders would function as market actors relying upon the law to regularize their relationships through contract, and courts to arbitrate their disputes. Thus, in the bankruptcy field market actors would use the law to protect their rights and the courts to preside over liquidations and reorganizations, especially in situations where collective action problems produced conflicts among creditors, between creditors and debtors, or between creditors and shareholders. In short, commercial lawyers conceived of a law-regulated market that depended upon a dismantling of the developmental state (Ginsburg 2001). In this, of course, they had their own jurisdictional interests, for a law-governed market would also be a lawyer-governed market. And while the tiny coterie of lawyers in Korea's legal profession had done very well financially, in virtue of its tightly held monopoly, an opening up of the market also opened up opportunity for money and power.

In short, the lawyers and economists had sharply divergent concepts of Korea's economic restructuring. In one, technocrats would continue to guide the economy, administrative interventions would continue to displace nego- tiated relationships among market actors themselves, and restructurings or liquidations of major companies would be handled out of court rather than in court. In another, market actors would be emancipated from the heavy hand of government to manage their own relationships, law would provide the ordering principles for binding market relationships, and courts would provide the arenas in which collective action problems, disputes and conflicts, would be resolved. In the former, economists prevailed; in the latter, lawyers. The jurisdictional conflicts between the professions intimated foundational differences over the future structure of the Korean state—and the role of law in the state and market.

Pre-Crisis Diagnoses and Debates

The conflicts over the future of the developmental state, and its cognate un- derstandings of markets and the law, did not arise with the Crisis. For the previous five years the Korean government had engaged in exhaustive self- diagnosis, resulting in the publication and debate of reports by the Secretarial Office to President Y. S. Kim, the Presidential Commission of the Twenty- First Century, the Ministry of Finance and Economy, the Ministry of Trade Industry and Energy, the Korea Development Institute, the Korea Institute for Industrial Economics and Trade, the Korea Institute for International Eco- nomic Policy, the Bank of Korea, the Korea Development Bank, and the Fed- eration of Korea Industries (Booz-Allen and Hamilton 1997).

Mere months before onset of the Crisis, the Government of Korea had re- ceived a report from the international consulting firm Booz-Allen and Ham- ilton, which drew upon extensive cooperation from government ministries and leading private sector bodies to conclude that the developmental state had now hit a ceiling and must be fundamentally restructured. Stated Booz- Allen, "[T]he curtain is coming down on the Korean economic miracle of the last three decades." The very strategies that Korea used to achieve its success had now turned into barriers to further development. *Revitalizing the Korean Economy* summed up its diagnosis and prognosis in five propositions: (1) the Korean economic miracle is over; (2) a stalemate currently exists over a vision, a strategy, and a way forward, including the question of which institutions should preside over its future; (3) Korea should become "market-led," "knowledge-based," "entrepreneurial," "regionally integrated," and globally connected; (4) the strategy for change will require breaking down systemic problems; and (5) the way forward will require a fundamental restructuring of the government vis-à-vis the market where "the government's direct intervention with the micro-economy will be extremely limited." On the way to this restructured economy (and state), Korea would confront tough transitional issues, most notably, how to control the reorganization of *chaebols*, how to avoid systemic dangers in the financial system that would "trigger a landslide of bankruptcies," and how to cope with dangers of "widespread bankruptcies in the manufacturing sector" (Booz-Allen and Hamilton 1997).

Diagnostic convergence notwithstanding, Korea's fledgling democracy had proved incapable of resolving the clashes among deeply entrenched interests over the shape of reforms (Mo 2001). The National Assembly remained subordinate to government ministries. Extralegislative bargaining among government ministries or between government and interest groups weakened political culture and worked against the creation of public consensus around reforms, especially those as fundamental as a retreat from the development state would require. Domestic politics effectively stymied fundamental or decisive reform—until the Crisis. Hence the Crisis.

By contrast to the analysis and decisive prescriptions of Booz-Allen, international financial institutions approached the Crisis with an attenuated presence in Seoul. Korea had long since matured from needing a close monitoring presence of the Bank or Fund. The IMF had no reason for involvement and saw no clouds on the horizon. On the eve of the Crisis Korea's Deputy Prime Minister and Minister of Finance and Economy blithely told the IMF/World Bank Boards of Governors that "I'd like to point out that Korea's economic fundamentals remain sound and current economic difficulties are manageable."[9] The World Bank's private investment arm, the IFC, had a presence in Seoul, but the Bank's aid program had diminished almost completely. The OECD imprimatur seemed to assure IFIs that Korea had graduated into a new league and did not and would not require undue attention on their part. Seoul was not Jakarta.

Pre-Crisis Reforms

As evidence of corporate distress began to accumulate in the early 1990s, both courts and regulators responded with modest changes. In 1992 the Supreme Court sought to adapt the Corporate Reorganization Act to meet criticisms that court-based reorganizations were subject to political manipulation and the law was used to evade criminal prosecution. The law itself was reputed to be ambiguous, delay limited the prospect of turnarounds for companies, and creditors had little prospect of recovering their assets. The rules changed procedures for initiating cases and confirming reorganization plans. Pro-creditor rule changes enacted in 1996 mandated that shareholdings of owners would be wiped out in a reorganization and that debtor-managers would lose control of companies (Oh 2005).

As the number of bankruptcies mounted on the eve of the Crisis, MOFE stepped in to compel banks to change a lending practice that banned further bank transactions upon *budoo*, namely, the nonpayment of promissory notes. If debtors did not pay up on their promissory notes, banks would stop all further transactions by the debtors, effectively bringing a business to a standstill. This could spell disaster for a company but also set off a chain reaction when the debtor could not pay trade creditors and others. MOFE compelled the commercial banks, for the first time, to act collectively by adopting an Anti-*budoo* Accord in 1997 whereby they agreed they would not automatically prohibit future transactions but work with companies on the edge of default to extend their lives through financial restructuring. This action effectively channeled ailing corporations away from filing bankruptcy cases, thus diverting cases from judicial control in the courts (Nam and Oh 2000).

In the event, neither of these steps went nearly far enough to anticipate the severity of the problems that confronted Korea at the onset of the Crisis.

The Crisis and Its Immediate Aftermath

Alarmed by its severe liquidity crisis, and the imminent threat of such massive corporate failure as might imperil the financial sector, the Government of Korea turned to international financial institutions for an emergency infusion of capital. Acknowledging that they had virtually no time to do "extensive diagnostic work," the legal and private sector restructuring teams from World Bank and IMF consulted quickly with major law firms in Seoul, beginning with the IFC's local counsel, the banking sector, academics and economists, judges and government officials—although not extensively with either the corporate sector or labor. Compared to the other Asian Tigers, Korea did offer major advantages: it had already conducted a succession of previous inquiries into its developmental problems; and IFIs could take advantage of well-developed scholarly and research institutions, such as the Korea Development Institute, ample high-quality data, and government officials with advanced training in (mostly) top U.S. universities. Said a World Bank lawyer who was on the original Korea crisis team:

> Clearly, we recognized that it was not going to be possible to be prescriptive at that early stage about what it is that was needed to be done in an area as complex as insolvency. But what we wanted to do was to, first of all, gain an initial validation of the premise. And then to sketch out some actions that could be taken within a very short period of time to both start to ease the constraints on the insolvency system, and to sketch out further work that could be done over following months. Because we were anticipating, as in fact eventuated, a succession of operations, each of which could build on the preceding one . . . [i]t needed to unleash a reform process. And so really what we were doing was identifying quickly which direction the reform process should go.[10]

In practice, a dual-track reform trajectory emerged for corporate restructuring. This reflected in part the two-pronged involvement of World Bank officials, who were primarily specialists in private sector restructuring (Iskander et al. 1999; Mako 2001, 2003), which specialized in out-of-court mechanisms, and the lawyers from the World Bank and IMF, who specialized in substantive law and legal institutions. The reform packet negotiated with the Government of Korea committed it to actions that would solve, on the one side, problems arising from substantive law and the courts, and on the other side, problems of out-of-court restructuring. The reforms were made the subject of economic conditionalities in general terms at the outset.[11] Thereafter the IFIs would depend principally on persuasion and modeling, together with technical assistance and even shaming (Braithwaite and Drahos 2000).[12]

This twin approach had significant institutional corollaries. The primary affinities of the IFI intervention teams were with the powerful Ministry of Finance and Economy rather than the much weaker Ministry of Justice or the Supreme Court. From the beginning of IFI interventions, this produced an institutional contradiction: the very government ministry most proximate to the IFIs, and able to push through change quickly, was also the butt of critics for its failure to open up the Korean market to rule-governed competition. The IFIs found themselves compelled to rely on a ministry whose failure to allow a mature law-governed market to emerge had arguably helped bring about the very Crisis it was now being called upon to resolve.

The substantive and institutional reforms that flowed out of the Crisis were driven principally by a working relationship between IFI economists and lawyers on the one side, and MOFE economists on the other, with the Ministry of Justice and private and academic legal experts, together with the Supreme Court, reluctantly following along. The cleavage between those solutions situated primarily within the law and those located primarily within the market was widened by the continuing struggle between lawyers, with their weak basis of mobilization from within the state or market, and the economists, whose dominance over the institutions of knowledge and the state, most notably MOFE, endowed upon them significant advantages. The struggle can be observed in the switching back and forth between alternative sites of reform—regulatory interventions in which the economists and MOFE dominated, and statutory and court reforms, in which lawyers and judges had greater capacities for influence (Halliday and Oh 2006). As the economists insisted that the primary difficulties lay in the law and courts, with the obvious implication that problems would be better solved away from the courts, the lawyers insisted that problems lay in the markets, with creditors and arbitrary official interventions, with the corollary that the state should pull back from market interference and allow law and courts to regulate free market exchanges among market actors (Oh 2002a; 2002b).

Yet this apparent imbalance of power between the IFIs, MOFE, and the economists on one side, and the lawyers and courts on the other, decreased as the dangers of the Crisis receded. Lawyers had a twofold advantage for the long run. First, practice ultimately depended upon legal practitioners and judges. Law and the courts were necessary to bind all parties to corporate reorganizations, which could not be achieved outside law, as MOFE came eventually and begrudgingly to recognize. And second, the ideological thrust of the IFIs pressed Korea to strengthen the institutional foundations of its markets while persuading the state to retract its continuing interventions in market transactions or through industrial policy. A strengthened rule of commercial law in the long run offered the best means of accomplishing this end; for this reason, among others, the IMF consistently pressed the Government of Korea to undertake a fundamental unification and revision of all its bankruptcy laws.

From early 1998 until 2005 the protagonists in Korea's bankruptcy reforms offered one solution after another, sometimes through regulatory and out-of-court initiatives, at other times through statutory and institutional reforms to improve in-court solutions. We can observe them by following the sequence from one lawmaking expedient to another.

Administrative Steps:
Bank Workout Accords and "Big Deals," 1998[13]
The IFIs and MOFE both doubted the capacity of courts to handle the volume and complexity of the largest *chaebols*. MOFE and IFIs therefore revived institutionalized practices of administrative control through two variations of administrative innovation.

Workout Accords   The IFIs brought to Korea a series of measures similar in general design to those they had already implemented in Thailand and Indonesia. In their portfolio of structural reform options were recommendations to create out-of-court mechanisms for corporate debt restructuring. As the IMF reported in its Article IV Consultation with Korea in mid-1998, Korea needed to create a framework for debt workouts.[14]

The Workout Accord (or Corporate Restructuring Agreement) proceeded on MOFE's assumption that courts were not ready to handle corporate restructuring or major bankruptcies. Together with the newly created Financial Supervisory Commission (Chopra et al. 2001), a banking regulatory body, and its monitoring arm, the Financial Supervisory Service, MOFE sought to optimize two goals simultaneously: restructure overindebted firms and rationalize banking oversight of corporate borrowers. Without consultation with foreign banks or the legal community, MOFE compelled 210 domestic banks to sign an agreement, on June 28, 1998, that they would adopt a set of out-of-court measures, through tightened bank monitoring and lending practices, against 106 target firms, about half of which were *chaebols* (Mako 2002). A lead bank would bring together the principal banking creditors of a corporation, declare a standstill on any further debt collection that could harm the business, develop a workout plan agreed upon by major creditors, and formalize the plan in a Memorandum of Understanding between the banks and the debtor firm on a set of restructuring measures to be undertaken by its management (Oh 2003a, 2005). Optimally, these procedures would keep corporations away from courts.

The Government legitimated this move to international agencies by labeling it as a variant on the "London Approach," a mechanism by which the Bank of England took the leadership in coordinating banks in financial restructurings for particular firms. The concept of bank interventions may have owed something to the London Approach, but it differed from it markedly and cannot be considered a close transplant (Meyerman 2000; Oh 2005). More properly it was a restructuring scheme for financial institutions (Chopra et al. 2001). Nevertheless, it was administratively organized according to a set of transparent rules and, in that sense, can be seen as a form of rationalization.

Big Deals   A second administrative intervention was arbitrary and directly interventionist in ways entirely familiar from decades of government direction both industry development and particular firms. While the GOK did not openly acknowledge its intervention, the Government apparently orchestrated a series of mergers in the largest *chaebols* that were announced on October 7, 1998.[15] For instance, in the semiconductor industry, Hyundai Electronics and LG Semiconductor were merged into Hyundai Electronics. In the ship engines industry, the Samsung Heavy Industries Co. was merged with Korea Heavy Industries and Construction Co. And in oil refining, Hanwha Energy Co. merged with Hyundai Oil. In railway vehicles, Hyundai Precision and Industry Co., Daewoo Heavy Industries Co., and Hanjin Heavy Industries Co. were merged into a single corporation.

Through the "Big Deals," government regulators compelled conglomerates to restructure through spin-offs and mergers to improve their balance sheets. The mergers served two purposes. In the short term they reduced competition. It is also probable that this step was taken to protect banks whose enormous portfolios of nonperforming loans put them at risk of failure. By removing the worst and most threatening cases to financial stability from the markets and keeping them away from inexperienced or unproven courts, the administrative solution might be viewed as temporary and transitional—even if at the same time it compounded its apparent contradiction by seeding a moral hazard, convincing conglomerates that they were too big to fail and the Government could be relied upon to help restructure them out of trouble.

Striving for Judicial Transparency: Statutory Amendments, 1998

The Government of Korea committed immediately in October 1997 to revise its bankruptcy law in line with "international best practices"; it followed up this general commitment with a more expansive pledge to undertake a "thorough review" of liquidation and reorganization law.[16] Indeed, the GOK went so far as to accept that its three separate bankruptcy laws should be combined into one harmonized, seamless statute, a condition that the economists thought would induce greater efficiency and that IFIs believed would bring Korea into conformity with global norms. This promise, perhaps impetuously given at the time of the emergency, eventually was honored, but not without some reluctance by key actors, most notably many legal experts.

In fact, law reforms were already on the table before the Crisis hit. The Government had earlier decided that the Supreme Court rule changes on corporate reorganization procedure did not go far enough. In 1997 MOFE engaged the prestigious economic think tank the Korea Development Institute to appraise the efficiency of the corporate reorganization law. The KDI Report offered an economist's solution based on theory, a little research and public data, and some consultation with bankers and officials. Without serious consultation with lawyers, judges, or business, KDI concluded in the Report that the problems lay within the courts. The Corporate Reorganization Act did not function efficiently because judges had too much discretion about accepting cases for restructuring or liquidating firms, managers could not predict how courts would act, courts had insufficient expertise with business, and courts acted too slowly. Moreover, the lack of transparency fueled suspicions that courts were subject to political influence—or even that judges might be corrupted by corporate executives eager to obtain a favorable decision.[17]

In fact, judges did have much discretion over whether cases should be accepted for reorganization or whether companies would be simply liquidated. They applied three tests: a public interest test, in which they made a generic appraisal of the impact of liquidation on all stakeholders; a viability test, where they estimated the prospects of a reorganized enterprise; and a financial difficulty test. For the economists the public interest test applied by the court was unduly subjective. The prescription was consistent with an economist's concept of legal instrumentalism: create a bright-line rule that appeared entirely unambiguous and give judges little discretion over the decision to reorganize or liquidate a company. KDI recommended to MOFE that the law be amended to provide for an "economic criterion test" whereby judges would be compelled to liquidate a firm if its liquidation value (what it would be worth if broken up and sold) exceeded its going concern value (what it would be worth if sold as an ongoing enterprise) (Nam and Oh 2000; Oh 2002a).

Supported by the IFIs as a means of improving the transparency of the law, the GOK enacted the Economic Criterion Test in the 1998 Amendments to the Corporate Reorganization Act. In so doing it built into the law two contradictory concepts of how law works: the Economic Criterion Test institutionalized an economist's notion of an objective and mechanical application of law, irrespective of circumstances, itself dependent on the fiction that accounting could be readily reduced to uncontested comparisons among columns of numbers; by contrast, lawyers, law professors, and judges considered it illusory that determinations of enterprise value, now and in the future, would be uncontestable, and believed it imperative that judges have the discretion to respond to variations in circumstances.[18] Nevertheless, it was conceded that public perceptions of judicial vulnerability to political influence might be attenuated by this apparent removal of discretion.[19]

However, the strict economic test served another function. IFI officials consistently stated a belief that any court-based rehabilitation system would only be effective if liquidation were a credible threat to company owners and managers (Mako 2002). With the reduction of judicial discretion that could soften a corporate financial landing, the strict test might increase the likelihood that owners and managers would take seriously the need for cooperation with bankers in fundamental financial and operational restructurings.

Pressing for Judicial Competency: Court Reforms, 1998

Additional reforms were made in the Court Organization Act. If the courts were to have the capacity to handle large numbers of cases previously handled administratively, the IFIs and their MOFE counterparts believed that they needed to be reorganized, mainly to concentrate expertise on corporate bankruptcy. This led to two reforms. A 1998 Amendment enabled courts in cases that involved complex financial and commercial issues to appoint a Bankruptcy Committee of business experts (economists, former bankers, accountants) to advise judges.[20] This worked quite well, by most reports.[21] In the other, the IFIs and the Korean bankruptcy reform committee pressed for the creation of a specialized bankruptcy court whose judges would be selected, trained, and experienced in this technical field of commercial law. The Supreme Court's resistance, ostensibly on monetary grounds, was supported by MOFE and GOK, whose public purse was already under severe strain. More compelling for the Supreme Court was its preference for a generalist model of rotating judges. It also doubted that a specialized court would have enough cases over the longer term to justify its existence. Instead it created a functional equivalent: in Seoul, and in some district courts in major cities, it created a bankruptcy division of the court to which it appointed outstanding judges and around whom it built an infrastructure of published opinions, a practice manual, workshops, and training (Oh 2001).[22]

There is a paradox here. At the very moment when an impetus from the IFIs pressed for improvement of the competence and sophistication of the courts, the 1998 Amendments reduced the discretion of those very judges. Just as the Supreme Court administration office began assigning its most capable judges to the new bankruptcy division, MOFE ensured that a critical element of their jurisdiction—deciding which companies would qualify for reorganization—was heavily constrained by the new mechanical test.

Ensuring Legal Efficiency: Statutory Reform, 1999

In its initial agreement with the IMF and World Bank, the Government of Korea had committed to increase the transparency of court decisions and to expedite court proceedings. An increase in transparency was achieved by the 1998 Amendment. In 1999, the Ministry of Justice, under guidance from MOFE, prepared amendments with the principal purpose of reducing delay, or "fast-tracking" the processing of cases.[23] In the Seoul District Court, several months usually passed between the time a case was filed in the Court and the date at which the Court ruled a case could be commenced.[24] Observers differed sharply over the reasons for this lapse. Those who diagnosed the problem as dilatory behavior could rely on Court statistics that showed long delays between filing and judicial determinations, a lapse that could be attributed either to the inefficiency or lack of diligence by judges. Those who were familiar with actual cases argued that the real causes lay outside the courts: creditors failed to provide critical information, and courts could not trust the accounting in the company's financial records. Here again, charged lawyers, the blame had been shifted improperly from creditors to the courts.

The conflict between the outside observers (MOFE, and some lawyers and businesspeople) and the insiders (judges and lawyers experienced in bankruptcy) was drawn inside the drafting committee, which comprised a representative from MOFE, practicing lawyers, a judge, a public prosecutor, researcher, and law professor. While the first draft was circulated to the Korea Bar Association and Supreme Court, there was little doubt about the outcome. MOFE ensured that the Ministry of Justice delivered an amendment that reduced the time from filing to a decision on commencement to no longer than one month (Oh 2003a). Thereafter court behavior changed from substantial review of facts to a largely nominal overview of formalities. The effect was dramatic: in the two following years the days from filing to commencement dropped from 107 before the reform to 23 and 21 in 2000–2001 and 2001–2002, respectively. It also brought a much larger number of cases into the courts.[25]

Several other substantive amendments were intended to make the reorganization more feasible. A "stick" imposed mandatory liquidation on companies if reorganization failed, a threat that might facilitate greater cooperation by debtors. And to make reorganization more feasible, the courts obtained greater powers to bring more assets into the reorganization pool (the estate) by powers to cancel suspect deals close to the time of filing bankruptcies (akin to "voidable preferences and fraudulent transactions"). Mergers and divestiture of subsidiaries could now be added to the repertoire of options for reorganizing companies. The proportion of creditors necessary to approve a reorganization plan was lowered to get higher acceptance rates of plans. And disincentives were created to lessen the number of appeals, which slowed quick resolution of cases.[26]

Constructing Efficient Market Institutions: Workout Reforms, 2001–2004

After a year or two of experience with the flurry of reforms in 1998 and 1999, it became clear that everything had not been solved and new problems had arisen. The Workout Accords and Big Deals worked up to a point, but the Workout Accords had deficiencies that required repair. Substantive and procedural statutory reforms had quite a mixed effect. While the courts moved more quickly, improved their specialized competencies, and mobilized new expertise, it became obvious that judges could not be treated as ciphers but needed to retain discretion in complex circumstances. In 2001 the contradictions and tensions, indeterminacy or incompleteness, of the previous rounds precipitated further reforms. Having opted primarily for workouts outside the courts, MOFE now saw it could no longer avoid them.

Expediting Market Restructuring: Workout Amendment, 2001

The Workout Accord erected by MOFE in 1998 followed from its definition of the situation: courts were not capable of expeditiously and efficiently handling major bankruptcies, so some other mechanism was necessary. But the 1998 Workout Accord sought to solve the tension between in-court and out-of-court solutions by opting entirely for the latter, a resolution that in practice suffered from two weaknesses. The first was that so-called workouts were entirely private agreements among domestic banks about a debtor-client whose loans they shared. Because the workouts did not include foreign banks, the foreign creditors were able to act as "holdouts" and free-riders, creditors who refused to agree to a restructuring unless they obtained especially favorable terms.[27] There was a little irony here. The Workout Accord had been pushed through without any consultation with foreign banks. Now, in practice, they exacted a price in everyday deals for their exclusion.[28] The second and related difficulty was that a purely private agreement could not be made legally binding, especially on actors that were not parties to the agreement. Further, the process took too long, thought MOFE, and small lenders didn't get involved. In short, it became apparent even to MOFE that the courts were not superfluous.[29]

In response to complaints from the domestic banks, and the obvious limits in practice of the Accord, MOFE proposed a corrective step that would have all the benefits of both the out-of-court workout and court powers of enforcement. Creditors would produce a plan on the terms of the Workout Accord, obtain agreement of creditors holding more than 50 percent of the claims, and file it with a court; a judge would then immediately adopt the privately negotiated plan as a court order. From MOFE's point of view this had the additional merits of appearing quite similar to a "prepackaged" form of corporate reorganization practiced in U.S. Bankruptcy Courts, and it delivered on yet another commitment it had made to the IMF and World Bank for law reforms at the time of the Crisis. In one step the Workout Accord would obtain statutory and court mandates, thus significantly strengthening its legitimacy and effectiveness.

When the Ministry of Justice circulated MOFE's proposed Amendment to key lawyers, judges, and legal academics, they objected strongly. The Amendment was against legal principle, they said, since it would breach due process, would bind third parties to contracts they had not negotiated, required retrospective enforcement, created numerous problems of priority among creditors, and again reduced judicial discretion. Lawyers also claimed it would waste time, not save time.[30] Faced with vigorous opposition from within the legal community, the Ministry of Justice needed to find a way to moderate the objectionable parts of MOFE's proposal, enable MOFE to save face, and signal to the IFIs that Korea was continuing to press forward with the reform program.

In a sense the solution was to make the Amendment indeterminate. A new provision—that the priority of new loans would be honored only by the parties who had signed a Memorandum of Understanding—introduced nothing new into the law, but for neophyte audiences it looked like compliance with international norms and local progress. Similarly, enabling an out-of-court draft plan to be brought into court for the court's consideration saved MOFE's face but added nothing to what already was permitted in current law. The Amendment was enacted, therefore, but was not intended to be implemented—and it never was. Even bankers avoided it. They doubted they could convince the judges—whom they didn't think competent—to follow the prepackaged plan, itself an admission of indeterminacy.[31] In addition to saving MOFE's face, the only value of the 2001 Amendment, it seemed, was as a signal to the IFIs that Korea continued to honor its commitments for reform.[32]

Binding all Creditors:
Corporate Restructuring Promotion Act, 2001

The continuing struggle between the proponents of an administrative track for reform and a judicial track continued with the lawmaking around workouts. MOFE remained steadfast in its analysis that restructuring of major companies continued to be necessary, that it should occur outside courts, and that the deficits of the preceding rounds of reform should be remedied. The 1998 Workout Accord, extended into 2000, lapsed in 2001. The 2001 Amendment for prepackaged bankruptcies had failed. In short, the incompleteness and indeterminacy of previous efforts at reform in administrative sites pushed MOFE toward a comprehensive statutory solution that remedied the faults of previous reform cycles.

The solution came with the Corporate Restructuring Promotion Act (CRPA), which would target 934 of Korea's largest corporations carrying more than 50 billion won in debt.[33] Banks would be motivated to detect at an early stage companies drifting into financial distress. In the restructuring format, a lead bank would bring together the largest creditors. They would undertake a financial analysis of the debtor's situation and develop a plan. If most creditors voted in favor of the plan, it would be binding on all creditors (Nam and Oh 2000).[34]

MOFE, the Financial Regulatory Service, and some legislators joined forces for the statutory reform effort. Their diagnosis remained consistent: a legal basis for workouts that was binding on all parties, including foreign institutions, and that would immunize agreements against subsequent legal attacks. Its appraisal of the situation, however, differed sharply from that of other parties to restructurings. MOFE sought a solution inside the banking sector, driven by bank creditors. It was not coincidental that this sector historically had responded strongly to government institutions and that the legacy of government-led banking persisted not least because government entities (e.g., Korea Deposit Insurance Co., Export-Import Bank/Bank of Korea, KDIC) had become the largest shareholders in the bank restructurings that followed the Crisis.

But three principal sets of players in practice resisted, albeit for different reasons. Business leaders opposed the increased powers that a new law would vest in their creditors. Management might get to submit a plan to the creditors, but management had "no say" over the bankers' decision of life or death for a company.[35] Ironically, domestic banks saw the legislative proposals as another wave of regulatory demands that would require substantial changes to internal banking procedures and much greater monitoring of corporate borrowers. Like the earlier workout accords, it discriminated against trade creditors.[36] Foreign banks doing business in Korea, which by definition were almost always minority creditors, saw themselves as "victims" of an edict that reduced a creditor to an "asterisk," when the creditor was told ex cathedra, "this is what we decided for you."[37] "We see the effects of CRPA as negative," stated another.[38] Even the IMF wondered if the design might be flawed since it did not make court protections available to minority creditors.[39]

Lawyers and judges strongly opposed the statute. The CRPA appeared to be yet another thinly disguised effort to keep corporate exit and restructuring efforts away from the courts, its mandates, and protections. For many lawyers, restructuring could readily have been accomplished through the Corporate Reorganization Act. The CRPA would work against rehabilitation, they alleged, because companies would be kept outside the law and its protections during reorganization. It would also weaken the judiciary because judges would have fewer important cases in which to develop their skills and build a body of law. It might also be unconstitutional.[40]

However, some observers saw this as an explicit effort to *replace*, not complement, the Corporate Reorganization Act, thereby removing corporate restructuring from the hands of lawyers, judges, and courts. In the process, said some legislators in the National Assembly, this would diminish the rights of certain creditors and remove various protections for actors in corporate restructurings that could only be provided by courts. Soogcun Oh (Oh 2003) interprets this as one more instance of industrial policy—a manifestation of the state's inability to allow markets to do their work and for law and the courts to provide the ultimate exit mechanisms.

In short, the CRPA set up a classic mismatch of actors: government administrators who were supposed to maintain a regulator's distance from everyday commercial activity pushed through a piece of legislation that was opposed by the most important players in practice—banks, lawyers and judges, and debtors. More fundamentally it reflected again both the ideological and structural contradictions that run through all the bankruptcy reforms. Two powerful institutions—a historically dominant government agency and an emerging robust legal system—fought over whether administratively constrained out-of-court procedures would prevail over in-court rehabilitation mechanisms. Effectively the draft Bill, and later the Act, assigned the courts to a backstop position—the site for company liquidations if bank-led workouts failed. The law therefore incorporated an inherent tension between concepts of *where* corporate reorganization should occur (market, courts) and *which* institutional processes should have primacy. Most significantly, in its implications for recursivity, the Act set up the conditions of its own subversion by forcing change over the objections of the very economic and legal actors that would implement the Act—and could thereby subvert it. Perhaps the only mitigating factor was the sunset provision built into the new law: it would run for five years only.

Unification of Law as Legal Efficiency: The Unified Bankruptcy Act, 2005

From the first IFI appraisals of the Korean Crisis in late 1997, their legal teams concluded that the partitioning of corporate bankruptcy into three separate laws hindered the efficiency of a court-based insolvency system. Just as the 1978 U.S. Bankruptcy Code had replaced and unified three earlier pieces of legislation, the IFIs concluded that a unified act would modernize the Korean bankruptcy system. Their grounds, which were consistently repeated over several years, turned on overseas experience, misinformation about Korean practice, and MOFE assumptions about law and efficiency.

The global trend, stimulated by the 1978 U.S. Bankruptcy Code, recommended by IFIs in their programmatic documents and country interventions,[41] and brought to a global consensus in UNCITRAL's 2004 Legislative Guide, proceeded on the premise that a single law with multiple entry points that permitted multiple tracks (e.g., liquidation and reorganization) and allowed switching between them (e.g., from reorganization to liquidation) would create a seamless, efficient law that would forestall tactical shopping among laws by debtors or creditors. By reducing delays and jurisdictional confusions among a multiplicity of options, the law would reduce transaction costs of bankruptcy proceedings and minimize loss of value to creditors. A unified law appealed to MOFE because it seemed to remove lawyers' stratagems from the treatment of failing corporations, "efficiency" had its own self-validation, and correctives seemed imperative if corporations were to use bankruptcy law. Further, conformity with IMF and World Bank standards seemed not only expedient but modern and economically sound.

As a result of this pressure from the IFIs and their coincidence with MOFE's own epistemologies about law and markets (Halliday and Carruthers 2004a), the Government of Korea committed privately to the IMF and World Bank in early 1998 that it would review its several bankruptcy laws with a view to unifying them into a comprehensive document. Initial Letters of Intent by the Government in 1998 and 1999 committed only to the amendments to existing laws and to setting up various out-of-court restructuring mechanisms. By mid-2000, however, the public statements of both the IMF and Government begin to signal their agreement for a comprehensive law. Korea's Letter of Intent in June 2000 commits to a harmonization and modernization of laws,[42] in cooperation with the World Bank, and by mid-2002 the IMF was publicly shaming Korea for "outmoded" and "inconsistent" laws and urging it to draft a unitary and comprehensive law that would "bring predictability and certainty to the insolvency regime."[43] Said the IMF, this would reduce delays and help reduce "the significant overhang of insolvent companies for which the insolvency regime has failed to provide an effective exit mechanism." Of course, this lawmaking would also provide the vehicle for numbers of substantive and procedural reforms, which the IMF also recommended.[44]

This diagnosis was not uncontested. Many lawyers and legal academics believed that the real problems lay elsewhere. Extant laws did need amending, where provisions were no longer relevant or where gaps existed in dealing with contemporary circumstances. Various impediments to effective reorganization did need removing. Yet lawyers considered that many of the problems attributed to the legal system in fact lay outside it. Delays occurred in court but often because companies provided unreliable or incomplete financial information. Cases did not come to court because creditors had financial incentives not to put companies into bankruptcy, and thus reveal the true magnitude of their bad loans. Bankers and government administrators alike colluded to keep matters away from courts because the law diluted their power over restructuring and attenuated Government control over industries and firms. The law failed to provide incentives for debtors to bring their companies under the protection of bankruptcy law from debt collection by creditors (Oh 2002a). Lawyers also recognized the dangers of a radical change in the form of law: it would disturb established usage and practice and open up ambiguities and new indeterminacies and inconsistencies. Perhaps there was also an inherent conservatism in the legal community itself—and certainly a much less mechanistic concept of law that was held by MOFE and the IFIs. It also appeared that some of the substantive reforms lawyers thought desirable to effect reorganizations and minimize loss to creditors would not obtain popular or political support (Oh 2002a).

In 1999 the Ministry of Justice initiated a Technical Assistance Loan Project (TALP) with funding from the World Bank to undertake research and propose policy options for a new law. Spearheaded by a leading Korean law firm (Shin and Kim), in association with a New York firm (Orrick, Herrington & Sutcliffe), the consultants submitted a report to the Ministry in December 2000 that contained many policy options. From 2001 through 2003, a Ministry of Justice drafting team worked on various drafts. These were circulated to judges, the Korean Bar Association, and Bankers Association, among others. Labor was little involved, and business, via the Federation of Korean Industry, had a minimal role. The drafting team submitted a unified law that included significant substantive reforms to the Ministry of Justice in 2003. A draft was sent to the IMF for review and comments and forwarded to the National Assembly in 2003. In early 2004 the Government decided to pull out of the unified bill the sections on the rehabilitation proceeding for individuals and enact them in a separate statute: the Individual Debtor Rehabilitation Act. With the change of government in March 2004, and in response to many critical comments from the Judiciary Committee, the draft was further revised and introduced again in 2004. After navigating its way through subcommittees of the National Assembly, amid some considerable controversy over several provisions, the unified law was enacted by the National Assembly in March 2005 to become effective twelve months later.

The massive Act contained significant substantive changes. It abolished the old composition procedure whereby companies could restructure their debts while managers remained in control. But it inserted a new concept in which current debtor-management might remain in control of the company under court supervision. This provision, while lacking popular support, gained the support of lawyers and industry because it provided an incentive for debtors to use bankruptcy law as a haven in which reorganization could occur without necessarily losing control of their companies. It also might appeal to IFIs since it bore some resemblance to the debtor-in-possession provisions of the U.S. Bankruptcy Code. Secured creditors, mostly banks, initially resisted this encroachment on their powers, but later came to accept it as potentially beneficial to creditors as well, if it would save a company (Oh 2003a, 2003b, 2005).[45]

While abolishing the composition track, the new law now has only two tracks for corporations—liquidation or rehabilitation. Parties file for bankruptcy, stating their preference for one or another track. Courts make the determination as to which track will be followed. The Act also includes a straightforward way to convert from the reorganization to liquidation track.

To balance the prospect of debtors continuing to manage their companies, the Act contains benefits for creditors. It continued previous policy to include secured creditors inside bankruptcy proceedings. But against the urging of the World Bank and IMF, the Act did not include an automatic stay on all debt collection at the moment of filing, a policy preferred by creditors. It even includes a provision that the expenses of the creditors' committee can be paid by the debtor, an incentive to increase the involvement of creditors in bankruptcy proceedings, which has been an enduring problem (Oh 2003b).

Not least, for multinational corporations involved in transnational commerce, the Act incorporated significant elements of UNCITRAL's Model Law on Cross-Border Insolvency, which replaces strict territorialism with a principle of universal jurisdiction of a court based in the center of main interests of a multinational company.[46]

Convergence or Divergence on Global Norms?

Engagement between global and local actors continued from the time of the Crisis through the drafting of the Unified Bankruptcy Act. To what extent did this engagement produce formal and substantive convergence with global norms?

It is clear that officials at the IMF and World Bank intended that Korea bring its law into closer conformity with their standards; and it is also clear that MOFE, the Korean government agency most closely linked to the IFIs, had every intention to do so. This bargain was struck quickly and quietly at the time of the Crisis. Lawyers, judges, and law professors—those who would implement changes—were much more ambivalent, for various reasons: they resented outside pressure, they believed that foreign diagnoses and prescriptions were faulty, they thought legal change in Korea had its own indigenous trajectory, and they wanted to preserve a kind of local conservatism and protectionism. Even if they agreed with some of the diagnoses, they did not necessarily agree with the prescriptions.

Eight years later, however, by the enactment of the Unified Act, it was clear that the Korean reforms had moved substantially, if not entirely, toward the IFI models. Formally, Korea's Ministries of Finance and Justice could now display to the IMF and World Bank a comprehensive single statute for all corporate exit mechanisms, including the options to change tracks from liquidation to reorganization. Complementing—and to some extent competing with—this legislation was an elaborate out-of-court set of mechanisms to monitor and reorganize companies through the interventions of major bank lenders. In place, too, was an experienced and sophisticated bankruptcy division of the court system, with reformed procedures, if not the nationwide specialized court advocated by the IFIs.

Substantively, too, the Korean reforms moved toward global norms in several areas. By introducing something close to debtor-in-possession, Korean managers now had an incentive to use bankruptcy protections with some real prospect of maintaining control of their companies, an incentive that would also allow them to begin reorganization before their companies were technically insolvent and had a better chance of surviving. It included ways to "cram down" a reorganization on hold-out creditors who might have blocked confirmation of a plan. We have seen that the Unified Act also adopted core provisions of the Model Law on Cross-Border Insolvency, thus bringing it into conformity with the UN standard.

But Korea did not adopt several provisions strongly recommended by IFIs. It did not include an automatic stay on all debt collection upon application for bankruptcy; the stay came into effect only at commencement, when the court accepted the case. It did not include full debtor-in-possession, following the U.S. model. Nor did it provide a special "super-priority" for new financing while a company was in bankruptcy. Its protection of creditors' assets in bankruptcy was less comprehensive than the World Bank standard. And it did not adopt the UNCITRAL Model Law in toto.

Quite how to interpret this substantial convergence is more difficult. The obvious explanation is that the Government of Korea simply brought its law into compliance with the IFIs under their direct pressure. Yet one of the primary drafters of the law, Professor Oh, was also Korea's delegate to UNCITRAL, so he was well informed about the global consensus emerging during the drafting of the comprehensive law. Influence may have been much more indirect: leading Korean lawyers and academics, in the course of their work, were quite familiar with developments in other jurisdictions. In addition, there was a functional logic within the development of Korean law that pushed indigenous reforms in the direction of exogenous influences. In short, a confluence of factors produced convergence, although the urgency was precipitated by the Crisis and crystallized for negotiation by the interventions and monitoring of the IFIs. In the final analysis, Korea negotiated a compromise with the IFIs that gave them the symbolic recognition they expected without delivering everything. It is too soon to know how much this will produce symbolic decoupling—that is, implementation that looks very different from the formal law-on-the-books.

Recursivity

As in China and Indonesia, the Korean cycles of reforms cannot be extricated from an active global context. International actors, from the IFIs to the UN, regional development banks, international professional associations, the OECD, consulting and professional firms, and other sovereign states directly oriented their interventions in market construction toward Korea. Before the Crisis primarily the OECD and market actors engaged Korea. As a condition of membership, the OECD had analyzed Korea's emerging economy and laid out sets of standards for restructuring the economy and opening it to global markets, which Korea was committed to reach. In its own self-analysis Korea had drawn on leading international consulting firms for advice and policy setting, as the Booz-Allen and Hamilton Report superbly illustrates (Booz-Allen and Hamilton 1997). External influences were intensified and complicated by the international circulation of Korean technocrats, scholars, and professionals. This worked for and against convergence of Korean policies and institutions with exogenous standards. Korean professionals became thoroughly familiar with Western legal and economic trends, but familiarity doesn't necessarily lead to conformity. Indeed, arguably it equipped Korean professionals with more sophisticated bases of adapting, interpreting, or rejecting external influences in support of "Korea-first" dispositions.[47]

With the onset of the Crisis external institutional interventions became immediate and imperative. With its pretense of normalcy stripped away, and the abyss of financial default imminent, the Government of Korea had no option but to throw itself on the mercy of international financial institutions. We have seen that the IMF and World Bank responded with a succession of rapid appraisals and explicit policy recommendations that Korea incorporated into its policy reform matrix and codified in public commitments. The urgent and hurried evaluations of late 1997 and early 1998 set in motion a sequence of more formal diagnoses by international and domestic actors. The two most compelling, arguably because they emanated from international institutions, were the World Bank–funded technical assistance report begun in 1999, which privately laid out steps Korea should take, and the public analysis published by the IMF following its Article IV evaluation of Korea's economy and insolvency issues, which also laid out explicit recommendations.

The diagnoses that international actors offered invariably came with prescriptions for policy reforms. This normative environment progressively consolidated and unified from the time of the Crisis through 2005. In 1997 the Bank and Fund drew on their ad hoc experience in other situations and a loosely formulated concept, not yet codified, of a good corporate restructuring and bankruptcy system. By 2000 the reform context for Korea had systematic norms articulated by the ADB, the IMF, and the World Bank.[48] At international forums, Korea's primary academic drafters of the unified law felt it prudent, perhaps necessary, to measure the proposed reforms against the standard of World Bank *Principles* (Oh 2003b). As the proposed unified bankruptcy legislation reached the National Assembly in 2003 and was debated through 2004, the Minister of Justice now sought advice on how closely the new bill conformed to what had just become a unified global standard—the UNCITRAL Legislative Guide on Insolvency. In these senses the global normative context for insolvency law became increasingly coherent in the course of Korea's adaptations to the Crisis. Now its auspices could rely not only on legitimacy from the expert-driven, and arguably U.S.-constrained, institutions of the World Bank and IMF but also on the UNCITRAL Guide that had been diplomatically negotiated by forty to sixty nations, including Korea itself. The relative flexibility of the Guide also gave Korean drafters international "cover" for their decisions not to follow some of the precise recommendations of the IMF and Bank. In this respect the UN-drafted set of norms could be deployed against their predecessor counterparts from the Fund and Bank, a move that gave Korea some degree of freedom to make its own decisions in view of its own economic, political, and legal circumstances.

The development of legal technologies and normative standards over the years since the Crisis paralleled a shifting basis of external influence on Korea. Before the Crisis the influences followed career paths, institutional relationships between universities and government ministries in Korea and foreign counterparts overseas, the flow of scholars and professionals in and out of Korea, and the transactions of everyday market activities in various industrial sectors. OECD membership had no coercive aspect: it represented a normative model of great prestige toward which Korea oriented its policies in order to mark its economic coming-of-age. These soft forms of influence turned hard very quickly in 1997. Both actual and implied conditionalities accompanied the agreements between the IMF, World Bank, and Government of Korea. The Letters of Intent signed by the Government effectively were contractual agreements with the recognition by all parties that the Fund and Bank had the right to withhold further tranches of capital if Korea failed to deliver on its reform commitments.

In Korea's case the force of economic coercion had a very short life. Korea rebounded rapidly, faster than anyone expected. It was a matter of national honor to repay its loans in short order. In place of the heavy-handed use of conditionality, international institutions now resorted to persuasion and modeling. Rather than threaten economic sanctions, the Bank used technical assistance moneys to fund a consultation that set standards for Korea that conformed to its *Principles*. Without economic sanctions available to it, the IMF used more subtle techniques of "shaming" to induce Korea finally to make good on its promise to unify its three bankruptcy laws into one seamless, comprehensive law. This shift to a modeling and persuasive mode of influence, of course, also gave Korea some measure of autonomy to conform to global standards only so far as Korea itself considered necessary. A strong sense of national honor seems to explain final passage of the Unified Act, for considerable doubt existed within the legal community of its value—and the potential ambiguities, inconsistencies, and indeterminacies that would arise from a massive new piece of legislation that included numbers of innovations. Both IFI officials and Korean reformers took very seriously the commitments made by the Government in 1997 to revise the law comprehensively.

On the domestic side of the reforms the mechanisms of recursivity can be observed repeatedly driving forward cycles of change. The Korean case bears out predictions of both globalization and structural contradictions' theory, namely, that its reforms stem from a fundamental contradiction within Korea's development model. Despite decades of state direction of the economy, and state determination of the life or death of individual corporations, Korea was compelled to open its financial sector as a condition of entering the OECD. But the exposure of sheltered markets to global financial pressures bought OECD membership at a high price, because neither the financial nor legal systems were prepared for global engagement.

Actor mismatch occurred throughout, sometimes in cases where there is a complete absence of certain actors in reform discussions (e.g., debtors, labor); in other cases when these actors are not introduced into discussions at all or too late to make a difference (cf. foreign banks on out-of-court, bank-led restructurings); and in yet others where asymmetric influence placed the force of policy formulation and change in the hands of officials without adequate consultation or agreement with the practitioners who would implement the changes. The failure of lawyers to employ the prepackaged Amendment of 2001, forced upon them against their better advice, perfectly illustrates the ability of practitioners both to forestall change through resistance to reforms and to compel lawmakers to undertake another round of reforms to achieve what they failed to accomplish in the previous round.

The familiar repercussions of law's unpredictability appears as a result of both the unintended impact of the Economic Criterion Test after 1998 and the nonresponse in practice to the prepackaged Workout Amendment of 2001, itself a statutory response to a private scheme initiated by MOFE between 1998 and 2000 that lacked legal authority to bind parties. In these cases, unanticipated or ineffective outcomes drove further rounds of reform in subsequent statutory amendments and enactments.

As we shall shortly elaborate, the reform process turned on repeated conflicts over what needed remedying and how to do it. The cycles were propelled by a series of conflicts, often of diagnosis, first, between MOFE and the Ministry of Justice; second, between the economists and lawyers; and third, between government officials long accustomed to intervening in the market and advocates of market-based solutions. The 1998 reform, for instance, can be attributed to MOFE's distrust of judges and the courts—it sought to restrict judges' discretion and to compel them to apply a simple formula. Domestic diagnoses were interwoven with those pressed from outside Korea. The economists could draw on the formidable resources of the prestigious Korea

Development Institute and on the compelling ideals of market efficiency. Academics and judges countered with research reports on what actually happened in practice: why, for instance, apparent malingering by judges reflected more on corporate financial transparency than on judicial competency.

Judges themselves were caught in a cross fire of competing attributions. To economists and economic technocrats they lacked competency, experience, and often independence. With massive financial stakes on the table, judges were vulnerable, if not to bribes in the moment, to future expectations of employment by law firms that appeared before them. To experienced commercial lawyers and academics, many of whom had been educated and trained with judges in Korea's elite legal institutions, judges' intelligence, meritocratic accomplishments, and capacities to comprehend commercial activities were unquestioned, even if some small changes were necessary in court organization to facilitate their effectiveness.

In this matrix of mechanisms—actor mismatch, diagnostic struggles, contradictions, and indeterminacy of law—it is not surprising that the reform cycles turned quickly, all the more so in a context of unrelenting foreign pressure of various sorts (Halliday and Oh 2007). The stakes were high. Korea's market vulnerabilities had been displayed to the world and seemed to require urgent reconstruction and institution building. As important, however, the future distribution of power among factions of the Korean state was also at stake, as were even more fundamental distributions of power among the state, market, and law, as we shall reflect upon later.

We have also seen that the broad sweep of the recursive episode did not begin domestically in 1997 but years earlier. Throughout the 1990s the Supreme Court and Ministry of Finance took steps to reform the economy, as the Government pressed banks to confront their own bad debts, corporations to confront their heavy debt overhang, and courts to respond effectively. But the Crisis precipitated more rapid reform cycles, not least because it created the opportunity for powerful external pressures to overcame domestic timidity or lack of political will to implement changes that had been mooted for years. The statutory reforms proceeded in a series of small steps, as if the Ministry of Justice and lawyers hoped they might satisfy international demands without the need for wide-ranging reforms. The climax of the episode is the Unified Act. But it may not herald the episode's conclusion. From other major bankruptcy reforms, notably the U.S. Bankruptcy Code, ambiguities in the law and creative compliance by lawyers led to follow-on amendments before the Code substantially settled into routine implementation. Given the scope and new departures in the Unified Bankruptcy Act, we expect that unanticipated consequences, conflicts with other commercial law, and changing economic circumstances will continue the cycles of reform before the episode is rounded out.

Bankruptcy Reforms and Institutional Restructurings

Viewed from organizational and institutional perspectives, the Crisis precipitated three widening circles of restructuring in which bankruptcy reforms were implicated. In its narrowest sense, the interplay between international institutions and the Korean government over insolvency reforms involved ways to restructure corporations, or in Nam and Oh's (2000) terms, design effective "exit mechanisms" for ailing firms. After the Crisis the Government's policy toward restructuring turned on a classification of all firms into a pyramid of relative impact on the economy or industrial sectors. The largest five *chaebols* it treated individually in the Big Deals through complex negotiations that divested and merged corporate groups to save them and their bankers. The next layer in the pyramid, *chaebols* ranging in size from below the top five down to approximately the top eighty, and then to almost one thousand companies above a 50 billion won debt level, it sought to restructure through out-of-court bank accords and later through the Corporate Restructuring Promotion Act, itself essentially an out-of-court procedure. At the lowest level of the pyramid, the GOK was prepared to consign to the courts all mid-sized and small companies if out-of-court corporate restructurings had not done their job.[49] The out-of-court restructurings were designed to be handled primarily by bankers and the largest domestic creditors. They principally involved financial and not operational restructuring (Mako 2002). And they anticipated little cooperation from debtor-managers, shareholders, labor, or trade creditors. As MOFE was to industry, banks were to corporate lenders.

Restructuring might also occur within the courts through the mechanisms of reorganization. The general direction of reforms pushed court reorganizations in a more cooperative direction among the parties to bankruptcy, with incentives for owners and managers to use legal protections, for creditors to negotiate plans with debtors and trustees, and for all parties to expect participation and protection by the court. If none of this worked, then the ultimate exit mechanism was the sale of the firm as a going concern or its breakup into whatever assets still retained value.

The IFIs and Government also recognized that restructuring of the financial sector, not least commercial banking, was critical in its own right and a necessary condition of effective corporate restructuring. In substantial part, the insolvency reforms were effectively banking reforms. The Government had established a powerful and unified financial regulatory body, the Financial Supervisory Commission, and given it extensive powers of bank supervision through its operational arm, the Financial Supervisory Service.[50] The workout accords, and especially, the Corporate Restructuring Promotion Act, required that banks create internal monitoring protocols and workout units that would constantly maintain a vigilant eye over the finances of the companies that borrowed from them. Just as corporate managers now expected bankers to be scrutinizing them more carefully, so bankers anticipated that regulators would be watching them far more closely. Hence the financial and corporate regulatory packages of the IFIs and Government were integrally connected. The health of each depended on the other.

In a wider sense, the story of insolvency reform is an element of a more consequential project—the restructuring of the Korean state. Much of this occurred within the administrative arms of government, as scattered financial regulatory agencies were consolidated into a coherent single agency, or the Central Bank was given new independence and powers, or the Blue House (Korea's "White House") was constrained from arbitrary interventions by bureaucratic regulations. But it was the relationship of the financial ministry to the courts that defined a perceptible struggle over shifting powers. For the previous twenty years, law and the courts had been rising in force and prominence as Korea pursued its democratic transition (Ginsburg 2001, 2003). The power of judges had been evident in a succession of cases where administrative arbitrariness had been held to account, police and security powers were checked, and basic rights defended (Ginsburg 2007). A legal system previously tightly fenced in and kept away from the fundamental exercise of state power now began to insist that executive authority itself had limits. A new Constitutional Court had significant powers ceded to it by all political parties. Koreans elected a parade of lawyer-leaders to the presidency. But relatively little of this advance in judicial power eroded the dominance of MOFE over the economy and market.

The Crisis led to an assault on this redoubt of administrative power. The struggles over judges and courts were more than a clash of professions with competing epistemologies. In fact, those professions championed alternative concepts of the state. For lawyers and judges it was no longer tolerable to accept the long-standing status quo whereby a dominant state apparatus tolerated but scarcely took seriously the constraints of law in market transactions. In this they had an unlikely ally—the IFIs. Whereas the Washington Consensus had advocated the primacy of markets and virtues of privatization, the post–Washington Consensus insisted upon building the institutions that enabled and protected the market. No less than the G-7, speaking through the G-22, had insisted on an international financial architecture that created new debtor-creditor regimes (G-22 1998b). Although IFIs had close relationships to the economic ministries in government, their legal departments insisted that institution building for market economies required muscular courts with competent and decisive judges. In short, law, lawyers, judges, and courts would step in where previously only government regulators had trod. From an institutional perspective, therefore, the bankruptcy reforms expressed in microcosm a much larger project—the shifting of power away from the administrative state to the legal ordering of markets.

This particular step leads to the broadest sense of restructuring in post-Crisis Korea. Bankruptcy reforms were implicated in shifting relations among the state, market, law, and politics. The Booz-Allen and Hamilton Report presented a private sector prescription for Korea that accorded substantially with the ideologies of the IFIs. The developmental state was now over. The administrative state required downsizing and reconfiguration. MOFE needed to trust the market, to override its habitual intervention in market affairs, to allow market actors to proceed on market criteria.[51] Law was integral to this transition. The expansion of legal institutions was a necessary element in limiting the arbitrariness of administrative interventions in society and the market. In relations among institutions law would become constitutive of a new institutional order. Civil society groups increasingly saw law as a means of mobilization in economic affairs, such as corporate governance, as well as for other social causes.[52] Law, said a veteran elite practitioner, "has become much, much more important as a way of regulating society and solving problems."[53] Hundreds of judges have been added to cope with the rapid increase in commercial cases.[54] Moreover, just as the powers of the Constitutional Court rested on a political settlement among competing political parties, so, too, the regulatory power of law in corporate reorganization now rested on a political settlement—the Unified Bankruptcy Act—forged in the National Assembly, not managed away from law and politics by technocrats.

In sum, we can view South Korea's corporate and debt-restructuring debates as a contest of three logics. A political logic rests on national and sectoral interests in the distribution of power, on electoral sensitivity and regional priorities, on national security and strategic industries, on party ideologies and claims to political office. An economic logic rests on the efficiency of markets and the predictability of market players once emancipated from arbitrary political intervention. It envisages a strengthening of market institutions to warrant a mandate for the retraction of state guidance and imagines rational economic actors operating with autonomous institutional frames. A legal logic tempers efficiency with equity just as it tempers political decisions with the rule of law. The corporate and debt-restructuring reforms, therefore, were caught up in a much larger drama—the very restructuring of Korean political, economic, and legal institutions as they struggled to find a new equilibrium for the distribution of power in Korean society. Bankruptcy law was both an object and subject in that drama.

7 China: Global Norms with "Chinese Characteristics"

WHEREAS the buffeting of massive movements of international capital reduced Indonesia and Korea to the status of supplicants to international public and private lenders, China rode out the storm relatively unscathed. Unlike Korea and Indonesia, it suffered no dramatic economic shock and did not have to turn to the IMF or World Bank for assistance. Thus, it did not make itself beholden to IMF loan conditionalities. But the Asian Financial Crisis did not escape the attention of China's leaders. The Crisis and its aftermath offered sharp object lessons about the dangers of losing control over flows of capital into and outside the country, the vulnerabilities that result from depleted foreign reserves, the risks of careless integration in the world economy, and the potential loss of sovereign domestic authority over policy alternatives (World Bank 2007). If the Crisis vividly illustrated how political leaders could be subordinated to international policy preferences, it also flagged weak links in domestic institutions, most notably those regulating the market. Not least, it spurred a renewed interest in law as an economic regulator, or as a safety valve for conflicts and failure, and as a magnet for investment.

The shape of China's bankruptcy reforms, and its degree of convergence with global norms, can be explained in part by China's location in the space of our two-dimensional matrix of countries. On the criterion of the asymmetry of power, China was not particularly vulnerable to external economic pressures, not because it has an advanced economy but because its controls over capital flows sheltered it from the Asian Crisis. China's shield from capital speculators substantially inoculated its economy from external shocks. Powerful weapons of economic coercion could not be brought into play because China did not require any kind of financial bailout. As a result, IFIs and other international actors could rely only upon models and technical assistance leavened with much expert persuasion.

On the criterion of proximity, China in the mid-1990s did not have the close ties between leaders in commercial law reform and global centers that we observe in Korea. Yet this situation changed perceptibly in the later 1990s and rapidly after 2000. In contrast to the paucity of expert intermediaries who were available to broker insolvency reforms from 1980 to 1996, by the time the reformist impetus picked up pace in the mid-1990s, a heavier traffic of scholars, professionals, and government leaders was flowing back and forth between China and overseas. After 2000 China's bankruptcy reformers had as much access and proximity to global leaders and institutions as they could want.

Given China's lack of vulnerability to foreign influences and its late-developing proximity to the global center, we could anticipate modest convergence of its bankruptcy regime with the emergent global standard. Outside China, international organizations, private banks, and sovereign nations had carrots but few sticks. Even the carrots were of doubtful impact since China's growing foreign reserves and the mounting flow of foreign capital seemed to assure the investment conditions for continued rapid economic growth without major concessions from the Chinese. Inside China, its leaders retained great discretion to set their policy course in a direction and at a pace of their own choosing. Yet after 2000, pressures built on Chinese leaders, not least from the European Union, to create market conditions, including a bankruptcy system, that would protect foreign investment. The conjunction of these conditions would predict a bankruptcy system that converged with the global standard only insofar as that was consistent with domestic priorities. Ultimately China's lawmakers would compromise with a legal regime substantially convergent with global norms but nevertheless with "Chinese characteristics."

Bankruptcy reforms in China, however, represent another kind of marker in the globalization of insolvency norms. When the U.S. and Britain began the reform movement in the 1970s and 1980s, the reforms were purely domestic ones directed primarily at weak firms and at most to faltering markets. The law and economy ideology adopted by the G-7, G-22, and later, the IFIs and other international organizations, made domestic bankruptcy law an integral component of international financial architecture. In China, however, more than the economy was at stake in bankruptcy reforms.

Under the terms of China's old social contract (Tang and Parish 2000) workers exchanged long hours, low wages, limited vacations, and few opportunities for consumption in exchange for a rich portfolio of benefits guaranteed by the state-owned enterprise (SOE). The "iron rice bowl" of the SOE offered not only job security but housing, education, child care, health care, and pensions (Lubman 1999; Naughton 1995: 210). The tearing up of the old social contract and its replacement by a new contract in which workers were given more freedom to choose their employer and higher wages, but no job security, no guaranteed housing, education, child care, health care, or pensions for life, entailed a sharp break from the past, a turn from decades of socialist ideology, and a rude thrust into a new economic order with many fewer protections.

This radical dislocation had more than economic consequences. Angered by the repudiation of a once-sacrosanct agreement, shamed by the loss of jobs, fearful of existing with a flimsy safety net, tens of millions of dislocated workers have become a potential source of widespread social unrest (Fewsmith 2007; Minzner 2007). Since the Chinese Communist Party (CCP) takes responsibility for political leadership and economic policy, a restive and displaced workforce potentially poses a political threat, all the more acute in a country whose revolution is still active in the memories of its eldest citizens. A law complicit in firing workers from SOEs thereby reaches to the fundamentals of social and political stability. Ultimately, social and political unrest threatens the grip on power held by the CCP.

In this context, the bankruptcy reforms become far more than a technical piece of economic regulation. They reach to the social order of society and the viability of the one-party state. At the heart of the bankruptcy reforms, therefore, lay a deep tension, even contradiction, between functions a law might perform. On the one side, China's economic development depends on more complete integration into the world trading system and its various markets, a process that requires some adjustment of China's commercial law toward global norms. On the other side, China's leaders and the Party apparatus seek to stay in power (Shirk 2007). Control of 1.4 billion citizens by a 70 million–strong Party requires a social stability that could be ruptured by the adverse effects of bankruptcy law on tens of millions of workers, especially those in SOEs that have benefited least from the economic boom. Caught between these contradictory pressures, with cataclysmic downsides if the law goes wrong, what kind of law can be crafted to produce what kind of market?

The severity of this challenge can be observed by the tortuous route that legal regulation of failing enterprises has followed from 1986 to 2006. China's bankruptcy reforms have gone through three cycles: an Interim Bankruptcy Law for SOEs that was passed in 1986; a series of far-reaching administrative interventions into failing SOEs in the mid- to late 1990s, prospectively culminating in 2008; and, beginning in 1994 and coming into effect in 2007, development of a corporate bankruptcy law that would cover most business enterprises, state owned and private. We begin by briefly setting these reforms in a comparative and historical context and then move to analyze in detail the recursive cycles of reform through 2007.

From a Command to Market Economy

China's trajectory has been quite unlike that of the other two cases, most notably because it is a transitional economy. Whereas Indonesia and Korea had already decades of market building behind them, China's transition from a command economy began in earnest only during the 1980s. By the time its process of comprehensive bankruptcy reform began in 1994, the shift to a growing private sector in the economy was little more than fifteen years old. Since the late 1970s, the Chinese leadership has been reforming the economy, moving away from a traditional socialist planned economy to its self-designated "socialist market economy." The leadership has carefully engineered economic change without losing political power, for it is mindful of the fate of the U.S.S.R.: economic reforms led to a declining economy, the Communist Party lost power, and the country split apart. In pursuing economic reform without democratization, the Chinese strategy has been to avoid dramatic reforms (like mass privatization), to move forward cautiously, to experiment with a number of different policy approaches before selecting one, and to suppress any inklings of political opposition (Wank 1999). In particular, political power has been ostensibly decentralized, and local authorities have gained a significant measure of policy and fiscal autonomy.

Although the development of a legal framework suitable for a market economy has been one priority (Lubman 1999: 174), China has been careful not to adopt features of capitalist economies that would lead to mass un-employment. Since the late 1970s, the leadership has incrementally shifted the governance of economic activity away from centralized plans and toward markets and market prices in direct contradistinction to the "shock therapy" or "big bangs" that launched transitions in Eastern and Central Europe. Rather, China "grew out of the plan" (Naughton 1995): in effect it simply capped the planned portion of the economy and let the market portion grow. Prices were liberalized (shifting from administered to market prices), and enterprises were given greater autonomy. Reform also involved opening up China to foreign investment and trade and creating a commercial-legal framework to help govern market-based economic relationships and trans-actions (Lubman 1999). The production of such law has been the business of the National People's Congress, which previously had been an almost mori-bund institution (Fewsmith 2001: 9). A more gradual approach to economic transition was intended to ensure that initial successes would help create a political constituency in favor of further reform, and thus avoid political controversy and social unrest.

As well, China's sheer size gives all its problems an order of magnitude greater than that of the other two countries. Modest reforms produced mod-est successes that created a political constituency supporting further reform, potentially ensuring a virtuous economic and political cycle. Regional differ-ences increased as redistributive policies that tried to equalize such differences were halted, and the east coast began to pull ahead of the rest of the country (Fewsmith 2001: 171–172).

State firms were permitted to sell their above-plan output at market prices, and they were also allowed to keep their own profits (Naughton 1995: 103, 202). Over time, state firms were granted a measure of autonomy in how they paid and managed their own labor force (at the outset, workers enjoyed lifetime employment, and wages were set according to national scales—the only thing firms controlled was the size of the bonuses they paid to employees). Price liberalization meant that firms became more responsive to market prices, not just to the production targets set by the plan.

State-owned enterprises produce a shrinking proportion of total economic output, but they remain important because they still employ many millions of people. In a country ruled by a Party that nominally represents the inter-ests of peasants and workers, the government cannot be entirely ruthless in how it manages the firms it directly controls. Yet SOEs went from being a major source of public revenues (indeed, more important than tax revenues) to being a substantial burden on the public purse. On narrowly economic grounds, most SOEs should have been closed,[1] but on political and social grounds mass liquidation of insolvent enterprises was out of the question. How then to manage SOEs as market competition extended from domestic to global trade?

China's application for admission to the General Agreement on Tariffs (GATT) and its successor, the World Trade Organization (WTO), involved protracted negotiations. China joined in 2001, after fifteen years of negotiations. China agreed to reduce its tariff and nontariff trade barriers, to open service sector industries to foreign competition (e.g., insurance, banking, telecommunications), and to abide by international intellectual property rules (Lardy 2002: 22, 66). For China, WTO membership would guarantee access to foreign markets; it would help to ensure continued inflows of foreign investment; and the increase in domestic competition would indirectly help to force necessary, but painful, changes in the SOE sector (Fewsmith 2001: 208).

As part of the shift to a socialist market economy, China has reformed its banking sector (the Asian Financial Crisis also underscored to the Chinese leadership the importance of a robust financial sector). Under socialism, a single "monobank" provided all necessary financial services to the entire country. With reform, the monobank was broken up into a Central Bank and a set of state-owned commercial banks (Naughton 1995: 255). Yet the commercial banks continue to loan mostly to SOEs, partly on the grounds that these loans are in effect guaranteed by the government. In addition, local bank branches developed close ties with local government, and the latter often applied political pressure to secure loans for local state firms (Naughton 1995: 265; Wank 1999: 75). Lending to private business has been much slower to develop because the capacities of the banks to assess creditworthiness are too rudimentary, and the transparency of private business too limited (Woo 2002: 391).

The concentration of commercial bank lending to the SOE sector has meant that the economic problems of SOEs became problems for their bankers (Holz 2001: 347). Insolvent SOEs become delinquent in paying back their loans, and nonperforming loans (NPLs) became a very serious problem for the four state-owned commercial banks. In 1998, about 24 percent of all loans had nonperforming status among the commercial banks (Huang 2002: 382). The problem was so great that the government decided to recapitalize the banks, remove the NPLs from bank loan portfolios, and consolidate the NPLs in four asset management companies (Woo 2002: 389). Nevertheless, NPLs have continued to accumulate, and the government may continue to face prospects of other expensive bank bailouts.

Cycles of Reform

The institutionalization of bankruptcy regimes in China has proceeded in three stages. The onset of the recursive episode began in the middle 1980s when a remarkable moral entrepreneur, Cao Siyuan, managed to build a groundswell of political support to implement China's first post-Mao bankruptcy law in 1986. Since the initial law applied only to SOEs, a second stage, initiated in the early 1990s, saw a patchwork of special bankruptcy laws, regulations, and procedures erected for particular categories of companies or regions so that all enterprises of any kind in China were covered. The third stage started in 1994 when the State Council charged the Finance and Economy Committee (FEC) of the National People's Congress (NPC) with the responsibility of creating a single, integrated bankruptcy law for all China.

We shall attend most closely to the first and third stages. The first set the foundation for a market-based approach to corporate liquidation, even if it was limited only to SOEs. The third embraces virtually all categories of enterprises above a certain minimal size, both state-owned and private.

In each of these stages China's leaders struggled with a nested set of issues that ultimately reached to the Party's viability and control of the country. At the narrowest technical level, lawmakers confronted a policy issue relevant to all market economies—how to create mechanisms for orderly treatment of failing firms. Since law was either absent or apparent in a pastiche of differentiated regulations, China's particular challenge to the technical problem was to establish symmetry between a seamless national market and a seamless national bankruptcy system. But most fundamentally, the bankruptcy debates were less about markets and law and more about social stability and political power. For China's leaders and the Communist Party the challenge was acute—how to stimulate market growth without losing political control. In short, how to avoid the fate of the Soviet Union, where the Communist Party fell from power and the country itself fractured into many pieces. Navigating a narrow path between precipices on either side required negotiating contradictions between a liberal ideology of the market and an illiberal polity, between concepts of law that enabled government control and others that might threaten, between actors that were beholden to the Party and those that might undermine it.

Exposing State-Owned Enterprises to Liquidation

No precipitating event launched China's twenty-year undertaking to put in place a comprehensive bankruptcy law and its supporting institutions. The initial step to lay a legal foundation for a socialist market economy grew out of a growing awareness that China's ninety-three thousand state-owned enterprises operated in an economy that dampened productivity, suppressed competition, and impeded economic growth.[2] Estimates of unprofitability in the state-owned sector ranged from 20 to 25 percent to 73 percent, though the true magnitude of their distress was hidden beneath a veil of opaque accounting procedures (Cao 1998a: 17; Zheng 1986). By any measure, vast numbers of SOEs were prime candidates for reorganization at best and liquidation at worst. But no such mechanism existed in the state socialist regime. Not only did Communist ideology make it unthinkable to throw workers out of work but SOEs also served as educational and welfare systems, providing housing, health care, schooling, and pensions or retirement care. As late as 2000 SOEs still "provided 40 percent of jobs in urban areas, 57 percent of pension funds, and about three-quarters of urban housing" (World Bank 2001: 22).

Wider economic distortions and inefficiencies abounded. The state compelled banks to lend irrespective of creditworthiness. No credit market effectively existed. Financial distress either drained state resources to maintain the enterprise as a going concern, or profitable enterprises essentially subsidized weak enterprises. As a member of the Standing Committee later put it: "In the absence of a bankruptcy system, the losses that administrative or governmental intervention and blind commanding create for some enterprises will inevitably have to be made up by the profits of other units; in other words, we extract from the fat ones to compensate the lean ones" (Cao 1998a: 72).

From the "Iron Rice Bowl" to the
Financial Accountability of Enterprises

China's first efforts to implement a bankruptcy law began with the opening up of China's economy in 1979 and culminated in 1986 with an Interim Bankruptcy Law. The movement was driven by an energetic young official, Cao

Siyuan, whose personal account of the reform movement, *The Storm over Bankruptcy*, is a primary source.[3] Cao took it upon himself both to diagnose the ills of China's command economy and to prescribe bankruptcy law as their remedy. Trained as an economist, Cao used the State Council's Technology and Economic Research Center (TERC) as a pulpit for writing and research in favor of a bankruptcy law. Cao's initiative sprang from a growing sense, in a slowly liberalizing economy, that the accretion of maladies in SOEs not only impeded China's economic vitality but exacerbated deformities in the economic and cultural ethos of China that ultimately threatened to rend the social and political fabric itself.

As a child from a poor family, Cao daily heard his tailor father's mantra— "a day without work is a day without food." But the Cultural Revolution demonstrated that this was not true. Workers spent a great deal of time out of their factories, production was partly or completely suspended, yet they still received their wages and other benefits. Cao concluded that the "iron bowl of rice," which guaranteed all workers food and welfare whether or not they earned it, had potentially catastrophic effects on enterprises, the economy, and the political system (Cao 1998a: 15). The "death threat" of bankruptcy might galvanize workers and managers and push China toward economic and political reform that redounded to the benefit of all parties.

Cao began an energetic campaign for enterprises to become responsible for their own profits and losses. External pressures on enterprises would "generate internal motivation," "motivational forces for continuous technological progress and improvement in their operations and management." Cao and the reformers he enrolled understood explicitly that they were engaged in a project of market construction through law. One set of external pressures would build up if competition were unleashed among SOEs. But for competition to produce market discipline, it was necessary to separate enterprises from everyday administrative control by government ministries so that SOEs would become "relatively autonomous commodity producers" (Cao 1998a: 72; Peng 1987: 373–374). Enterprises would be held financially responsible for their own profits and losses (Peng 1987). Workers would be motivated by fear of unemployment. Bankruptcy therefore introduced the threat of survival of the fittest (Cao 1998a: 25).

An effective bankruptcy regime might achieve much more. Since the state in the command economy had been writing off the heavy accumulated losses of nonprofitable state enterprises, a regime that reduced those losses would free up state capital for more productive uses (Zheng 1986). As Cao put it, this would solve "the problem of enterprises eating from the state's communal pot" (1998b: 46). Related to this idea, an orderly exit mechanism for unprofitable companies would stem the practice of effectively taxing stronger enterprises to keep afloat the weak. But to make enterprises autonomous, economic actors would also require that their legal rights and their property rights be clarified by delineating the relative responsibilities of enterprises vis-à-vis the state (Keyser 1998: 7). Thereby bankruptcy law would effectively codify in law the legal rights and responsibilities of debtor enterprises and creditors (p. 7). Cao himself saw farther than most of those he enlisted to his cause. He accurately envisaged that both the enactment and practice of bankruptcy law might promote political reform and produce greater social stability, somewhat ironic because fear of instability was precisely one of the principal objections that critics would raise to passage of the law.[4]

The State Council in late 1984 and early 1985 created a Bankruptcy Law Committee within the NPC Standing Committee and appointed Cao Siyuan group leader of a drafting team (Cao 1998a: 53–55). Cao believed that change would only be possible if officials could be convinced with empirical evidence that a bankruptcy law would change behavior. In 1984–1985 Cao personally persuaded the Mayor of Wuhan to conduct some experiments on the likely impact of a threat to close an SOE on the economic performance of the enterprise. The Mayor identified a chronic money-losing enterprise, the No. 3 Radio Factory, and gave it a "yellow card"—be profitable or be closed down within twelve months. The effect was dramatic. "People came to a rude awakening— suddenly they realized that their personal situations and individual honor were closely related to the status of the enterprise." The factory did some market research, stopped some product lines, opened up others, and absenteeism fell as output rose. By March 1986 the enterprise turned a profit (p. 37).

Emboldened by this success, in 1985 Cao got the Shenyang municipal government to widen the experiment and issue "bankruptcy warning bulletins" to three companies. Two factories turned around; one went bankrupt. But the effects ramified through the city—"its stimulating and encouraging influence was felt throughout all the enterprises, trades and professions, in Shenyang municipality"—as other enterprises realized the iron bowl was no longer so immutable (p. 37).

By attracting the attention of reformist Premier Zhou Ziyang (later forced out during the Tiananmen crisis), Cao obtained high-level sponsorship for a Draft Law that was adopted by the Standing Committee Executive Committee in January 1986 and set down for presentation to the Standing Committee of the National People's Congress (NPC-SC) in June 1986. The Draft Law ran a gauntlet of critics. Cao vigorously, and apparently for the first time, mobilized the media ("the uncrowned kings," as he labeled them) with stories, reports, statistics, and surveys in support of reform. He orchestrated numerous discussion groups held with academics, municipal officials, workers in enterprises, banks, and courts.

Opposition to the draft legislation took two forms. One faction sought to demonstrate from the Wuhan and Shenyang experiments that there was strong resistance among workers that could lead to social instability. Opponents argued that until a safety net was in place, "the time was not right." And until "immature laws" were improved, bankruptcy reforms would be premature (Cao 1998b: 47–48, 70–80). The basis of the opposition is instructive, for it indicates how deeply the bankruptcy law penetrated Chinese ideology, economy, and political system. At the ideological core of the opposition lay a fundamental disquiet that bankruptcy law was tantamount to a retreat from socialism and the introduction of capitalism. To break the iron bowl represented an abdication of socialist ideals. And if there were a bankruptcy law, "what should be the differences between a socialist bankruptcy law and a capitalist bankruptcy law?" (p. 48).

This criticism forced Cao and his supporters to shift ground so they could advocate a law redolent of capitalism within a frame consistent with socialism. Thus, advocates of reform began to speak of a "commodity economy" and to argue that there was nothing inconsistent between socialism and competition, survival of the fittest, and "solving the problem of enterprises eating from the state's communal pot." Cao successfully enlisted a distinguished senior economist, Xu Dixin, a member of the NPC-SC, who wrote an influential open letter in which he redefined the meaning of responsible socialism:

> In the past, under the influence of erroneous "leftist" guiding thought, our country regarded eating from the communal pot and clutching an iron rice bowl as part of the socialist economic system. Now that the responsibility system for production is being implemented, this should mean taking responsibility for losses and bankruptcy at the same time as taking responsibility for profits. (Cao 1998b: 46, 52)

Yet always lurking beneath the surface of opposition was the frequently expressed fear of social instability and political disturbance, a fear made all the more acute by the immense dislocations of the Cultural Revolution. To forestall social instability, it would be necessary, in effect, to separate productive from welfare aspects of the enterprise, and to erect an alternative infrastructure of social welfare and support. In response to criticisms that the state needed to protect unemployed workers with unemployment insurance and protections over employment conditions, contract hiring, and discharging of employees, the State Council drew up a set of temporary regulations on the labor system and unemployment that were implemented on October 1, 1986.

Troubled responses to the proposed reforms signaled not only how far bankruptcy law might destabilize China's core institutions but also mirrored in reverse the expansiveness of some reformers' vision of a modernized China. The law was intended to make firms more efficient and to allocate economic resources to managers who could best deploy them. The market would "generate internal motivation," increase worker productivity, heighten the vigilance of enterprises, and stimulate initiative and constant improvement. The new law would variously "reform the economic system," stabilize the commodity economy, protect the legal rights of creditors and debtors, and permit effective management of the macroeconomy. It would be an integral element in "the steady development of our country's modernization construction" (Cao 1998b: 54, 55–70).

Moreover, Cao believed that if profitable enterprises ended up subsidizing unprofitable factories, which was the case in China, it would create a kind of dependence mentality. If people so depended on their jobs (and all the other benefits that came with them), then they would be passive in seeking any change. A dependence mentality that relied on the "big pot of rice" provided by the state sapped individual incentive, motivation, and responsibility for work. It permeated their lives so that they were prepared to tolerate the chaos of the Cultural Revolution without taking control (Keyser 1998: 5). Thus, ironically, political stability, accountability, transparency, and a growing political maturity through participation by the people, not economic benefits, impassioned Cao to push for reforms.[5]

In the intervening five months between the sixteenth and eighteenth Sessions of the NPC-SC, Cao and his supporters waged a vigorous lobbying campaign on multiple fronts. Cao personally phoned all NPC-SC members and filled their mailboxes with articles and his primer, a book on the enterprise law; he contacted by mail the Premier and Vice-Premiers of the State Council, the Chairman and Vice-Chairmen of the NPC-SC, the General Secretary of the CCP Central Committee, and officials heading agencies. He put together a petition by thirty-two NPC delegates and got letters of endorsement from important people, such as the Venerable Xu, a distinguished economist (Cao 1998b: 52–53). In October 1986, he conducted a forum convened by the NPC Law Commission and the NPC Finance and Economy Committee in the Great Hall of the People for some ninety-two people.[6] From June to December, proponents produced some 161 articles and talks, and the media reported some 167 news stories (Cao 1998b: Appendix C, pp. 102–104).

Debate continued through the NPC-SC's eighteenth Session in November 1986 until the law was put to the vote on December 2, 1986, where it received 101 affirmative votes of the 110 people present. The Enterprise Bankruptcy Law (EBL) as enacted had six principal features (Peng 1987; Zheng 1986):

1. *Scope.* It applied only to SOEs.

2. *Definition of Bankruptcy.* It stated that an enterprise could be declared bankrupt "because of a deficit caused by mismanagement, [it] cannot pay debts which are due." The law provided some exceptions, for example, if an enterprise were of "great significance" to the public interest or national economy.

3. *Reconciliation and Readjustment.* The law gave an enterprise the ability to restructure its finance and operations and in two years to begin repaying its debts.

4. *Liquidation.* If an enterprise was declared bankrupt, it sold all its assets and its employees were dismissed.

5. *Sanctions.* Managers and government officials might be subject to administrative penalties if they were held responsible for an enterprise's failure. Both were subject to criminal penalties in certain circumstances.

6. *Worker Provisions.* After administrative expenses, workers would have first priority for the distribution of assets.

The EBL was enacted in the context of several other labor and social security reforms intended to provide a social safety net for workers to supplement whatever they received from a bankrupt enterprise (Zheng 1986: 712–714).

Recursive Processes

Despite the achievement of enacting China's first bankruptcy law since the 1930s, the process of lawmaking, and the form and substance of the law itself, built in a set of mechanisms that would inevitably drive toward further reforms.

The EBL internalized a set of ideological and structural contradictions. As some of its critics had already pointed out, it held enterprises accountable as market actors while they existed in a command economy where managers had little control over many decisions and where the price system was principally fixed by government (Zheng 1986: 690). The law simultaneously expected that firms be profitable and efficient while continuing to operate as microcosms of social security systems, although the new law would allow bankrupt companies to move some social protections to local communities. Further, the EBL intended to put the "threat of death" over corporations through fear of liquidation, but the reconciliation-and-readjustment provisions in the law potentially softened and even subverted the liquidation provisions.

And while workers were supposed to be motivated through threat of unemployment, they were guaranteed either reemployment or unemployment support—even more so for managers whom it appeared would simply be reassigned. The law also prescribed that while government agencies were removed somewhat from the front end of responsibility for debts (i.e., decision-making responsibility shifted to the enterprise), the government was brought back in during the reconciliation-and-readjustment procedures since the law gave it a decisive role in approving reconciliation schemes. Not least, throughout the EBL was a built-in tension between a putative shift toward market-based decision making on the part of enterprise managers and policy-based decisions on the part of government officials (Peng 1987).

Interestingly, some of these contradictions were advanced as reasons why the EBL should *not* be passed: there was no rational commodity price system in China; enterprises could not compete freely because they were not sheltered from arbitrary administrative interference; and enterprises could not be held legally accountable for failures if they were not independent legal entities (Cao 1998a: 75; Keyser 1998: 7). Technically these criticisms were on point, and their implications rose to the surface as the law came to be imperfectly implemented in subsequent years.

The formal properties of the EBL bred uncertainty and ambiguity. An immediate problem arose from its brevity—many salient topics were not covered, or they were introduced but not elaborated (Zheng 1986: 732). It was ambiguous in numerous places, and terms were not adequately specified.[7] There were also substantive confusions, for example, between liquidity (cash flow problems) and insolvency (liabilities in excess of assets). Many discretionary elements remained, which detracted from the law's certainty. For instance, the state could exempt from the EBL any SOEs that operated public utilities and enterprises of "great significance" to the public interest or the economy (Peng 1987: 387). Perverse incentives in the EBL might actually subvert the law itself.[8] Institutional incapacities presaged the law's effectiveness in two respects: no courts had competency in day-to-day liquidations or restructuring, even though their initial role would be highly constrained; and higher courts had no experience on which to draw for the development of the law in places where the statute was silent, ambiguous, or confusing.

Underlying these outcomes was an enduring diagnostic conflict between reformers and opponents that did not dissipate with passage of the statute. Cao Siyuan and those he enlisted believed the problem was one of motivation—that the socialist system had broken a contingent link between responsible labor and management and the rewards of employment. The perverse incentive of the iron rice bowl undermined work productivity. His opponents viewed the problem quite differently. They maintained that SOEs were deeply embedded in state administrative apparatuses in ways that gave managers little possibility of acting as profit seekers; no effective market existed; and no real alternative could be found for laid-off workers. Moreover, it was inconceivable that workers of liquidated companies could cut loose entirely from the government social safety net, for ideological and pragmatic reasons. The obvious solutions were administrative. The wise course of action would be to edge forward incrementally by fine-tuning the present system. SOE managers and the massive administrative apparatus for the state-enterprise system contributed a deadweight of inertia to the conservative factions within the Party-state leadership.

The actors that pass laws frequently do not include all those actors who implement them. A severe mismatch sows seeds of discontent that will reap the need for further reforms. In part because they were so few in number, lawyers or judges or experts in commercial law or practice were completely missing from the 1986 legislative process. The process was driven by economists and pragmatist politicians. Banks had not become differentiated enough within the government apparatus to act as political interests. And, of course, all enterprises other than state-owned enterprises were excluded. The new bankruptcy law applied only to SOEs, and it came into effect very slowly. In the following decade, the government patched together several regimes to deal with failed market enterprises: (1) for private enterprises that had status as "legal persons," the government included some limited liquidation provisions in its 1991

Civil Procedure Law;[9] (2) for enterprises in special economic zones, such as Shenzhen, Shanghai, Beijing, and Guangdong, it created special bankruptcy provisions; (3) for liquidation of joint ventures with foreign companies, it adopted regulations issued by the Ministry of Finance Trade and Economy Commission (MOFTEC). Other enterprises—the vast number of small business that were not "legal persons," collectively owned enterprises, or the millions of township enterprises and cooperative enterprises, no law or legal regulation existed for companies in distress. Most consequential for the country as a whole, however, was a series of administrative initiatives directed at state-owned enterprises.

Administrative Solutions for State-Owned Enterprises

The enactment of the Enterprise Bankruptcy Law instituted a partial mechanism for the orderly exit of companies from the economy. While notable in its own right as a marker of transition to a market economy, this first step toward the legal constitution of a market was faltering at best. Its limitations became apparent in its implementation. For the first four years of its existence, 1989–1993, the number of bankruptcies averaged only 277 (World Bank 2000: 5). If even the most conservative estimate of insolvent SOEs were correct (i.e., 20 percent), this amounted to about 5 percent of SOEs that needed reorganization or liquidation. Said a Chinese academic bankruptcy specialist, "the Draft Law was just a 'flower pot'—pretty on the outside but meaningless."[10]

The reasons the EBL failed to be implemented were varied. Since initiation of an SOE bankruptcy required government action, it appears no clear policy directives pressed local officials to deviate from business as usual. The impact on labor inhibited action (World Bank 2000). Resistance sprang up from several sides: local municipalities did not want responsibility for laid-off workers; banks were reluctant to write off debt and so make plain the extent of their nonperforming portfolios; and SOE managers and workers faced the unknown world of law and markets with trepidation. The social implications of bankruptcy also loomed large. SOEs accounted for about 70 percent of urban employment. Given that they were estimated to be 10–30 percent overstaffed and that as many as 50 percent were unprofitable, the potential volume of workers dislocated and the strain on services were unsettling for central and local governments.[11]

However, part of the reluctance to implement the law flowed from the EBL itself. As a diagnosis by the ADB made clear, the EBL incorporated within it an acute contradiction that potentially bedevils all bankruptcy laws. Given that the assets of the company cannot satisfy all the creditors, how are the assets to be distributed? If a company is to have any hope of rehabilitation, as many assets as possible need to be deployed to turn the company around and make it profitable again. To do this requires that certain creditors not be paid at all, or be paid partially, or not be paid immediately—these creditors include workers. Although all bankruptcy systems confront this problem, it was acute for China given its ideological commitment to workers, the fear its leaders had of unrest, the absence of institutional supports outside SOEs, and the magnitude of the unprofitable SOE sector. Simultaneously the EBL seemed to maximize two conflicting values—rejuvenating companies and protecting workers.

The legal analysis of the EBL pointed up the uncertainties it created. Law Professor Li Shuguang, who acted as a consultant to the State Economic and Trade Commission (SETC), and other domestic and foreign critics, pointed to numerous unresolved issues. The law did not protect enterprises that went into bankruptcy from continued efforts by creditors to collect debts owed them (i.e., there was no "stay" on creditor actions). The law did not adequately protect property rights of creditors. The law was passive rather than proactive in encouraging rescue of enterprises (e.g., reorganizations could not be initiated by creditors). The process of reorganization was carried out more at the behest of government officials than by creditors. Most fundamentally, it could not meet the needs of labor.[12] Municipalities complained they were being burdened by more unemployed workers than they could support.[13] If it was indeed intended to "clear out garbage enterprises" from an earlier stage of socialism, it failed. On all counts—technical, substantive, and policy—the EBL fell short. Rather than provide confidence, it sowed confusion. A first iteration of reform came from the Supreme People's Court in 1991.[14] But these clarifications did little to increase the trickle of cases.

In 1993 Premier Zhu Rongji pressed the SETC, which had administrative responsibility for SOEs, to coordinate with other agencies to begin coping with the huge number of unprofitable SOEs. Because it was under time pressure, the SETC undertook a hurried three-month study of bankruptcy practices, reviewed the EBL, and coordinated with other agencies, most notably the Central Bank, the Ministry of Finance, the Economic and Planning Commission, the Ministry of Labor, bureaus responsible for state assets, and the

General Tax Bureau.[15] The SETC also for the first time in the bankruptcy field brought in a foreign institution for technical advice—the Asian Development Bank—although its impact was not felt until later.

State Council Document 59, promulgated in November 1994, contained a policy directive to animate the EBL. It signaled two policy preferences. First, the State Council prioritized enterprise reorganization and merger rather than liquidation (ADB 1996: 33). Second, it established a clear priority for workers in the allocation of enterprise assets—and in so doing, tackled directly potential repercussions of worker dislocation.[16] Underlying both was a push to shift enterprise management from the old traditional Chinese factory model, where the Party and union predominated, to a new Western model of corporate structure with Boards of Directors and management accountability.[17]

The Central Bank and the agencies responsible for SOEs and state assets created a controlled program that would be rolled out progressively as its success warranted. On the one side, the government selected certain weak SOEs to be merged with stronger enterprises. On the other, to transfer all the liabilities of a weak SOE to a stronger enterprise might doom the stronger enterprise. It was necessary therefore to find a way to dismiss redundant workers without immiserating them and without fostering social and political unrest. The government employed an ingenious approach to solve the problem. The principal asset of most SOEs was land or the rights to use land ("land use rights"). Since many of these companies had increasingly valuable assets, especially if they were located in urban areas, the land rights presented an asset that could be sold, and the proceeds might be channeled to laid-off workers. Or put another way, "it linked the main off-balance liabilities of enterprises (pensions and severance, as well as other labor 'rehabilitation' entitlements stemming from the SOE employee status) to the main under-valued or off-balance assets (land use rights)" (World Bank 2001: 2).[18]

In order to be certain that workers were adequately taken care of when companies were liquidated, the Capital Structure Optimization Program (CSOP) earmarked the value of land use rights of bankrupt enterprises to be assigned specifically to the rehabilitation or settlement of workers. When the land use rights were sold, workers would be paid a lump sum (approximating three years of salary) that was intended both to cover their living expenses while they searched for new work,[19] and as important, to function as a buyout of a worker's rights as a state employee (World Bank 2001: 7). Other responsibilities for worker support would shift to the local municipality.

The government provided an incentive for enterprises to enter the program by giving creditor banks an ability to write off their debt up to a bureaucratically approved level. This write-off would help clean up the balance sheets of overly indebted enterprises and enable them to reorganize. It would also encourage banks to allow particularly weak enterprises to be liquidated without adversely affecting the bank's balance sheet. Local officials would decide what enterprises should be nominated for liquidation or reorganization under the program within the quota for their city. The experiment began in 1994–1995 with eighteen large cities and some 7 billion yuan in potential write-offs and expanded to fifty-six cities (20 billion yuan) in 1996. The "over-riding consideration" for selection of cities in the experimental programs was a location where the labor force would not cause social unrest.[20] In 1996 support for worker buyouts was sweetened even further with a regulation that gave labor rehabilitation and pension expenses priority over mortgages on land use rights, thereby infringing secured property rights (World Bank 2001: 7).

That the change in policy and program was effective can be seen from the results. The number of cases approved for the program rose from 171 in 1994, to 278 in 1995, and jumped to 2,291 in 1996. Bankruptcy cases approved under the CSOP regulations rose from 44 to 69 to 1,099 from 1994 through 1996, thereafter falling away to 675 and 459 in 1997 and 1998. Since the SETC preferred mergers to outright liquidations, the majority of SOEs were merged with others, after shedding themselves of workers and debt burdens. Approximately 336 firms were absorbed through merger in 1994 and 1995, and 1,192 in 1996, remaining at 1,022 in 1997 and rising to 1,550 in 1998 (World Bank 2001: Table, 4). The mergers involved some 1.25 million workers (World Bank 2001: 4). Liquidations proceeded through the bankruptcy courts and involved 1,212 firms with some 750,000 million workers from 1994 to 1996. During the same period, smaller bankruptcy cases under the bankruptcy law rose from less than 1,000 in 1993 to near 6,000 in 1996. Whether through the bankruptcy law or CSOP, however, the volume of bankruptcies made only a small dent in the vast landscape of enterprises in financial difficulty.

Although the regulatory changes quickened the pace of corporate reorganizations (mergers) and liquidations, it drew many complaints. Designers of the program recognized it had been cobbled together with inadequate research on an unrepresentative number of sites. The loudest complainers were the banks over a practice called "whole takeovers." Local authorities would encourage a stronger enterprise to take over the assets, pension liabilities, and most workers of a weaker enterprise, but the weaker enterprise would walk away from its liabilities to banks and other creditors (World Bank 2000: xiv). In practice, these often amounted to false bankruptcies. A firm would enter reorganization in the Bankruptcy Court, reorganize itself into a new legal entity, then take over all the old firms' assets and most employees—while leaving its debts behind (World Bank 2000: 18, Case Study). Also, the number of workers being transferred to local authorities was overwhelming them.

While the diagnosis of the SETC substantially accorded with that of IFI professionals (i.e., inefficient factories, unproductive workforces), its prescription was distorted since it reflected a mismatch between the actors most involved in everyday business practice and those with most influence in the SETC, which drafted the document. In short, managers and workers were included and banks were excluded. It not only favored workers over banks but it was a simple document based on limited research. Its indeterminacy and incompleteness allowed it to be readily abused by SOEs, which concocted schemes for false bankruptcies and devised techniques that would allow them to escape their indebtedness to banks.

In 1997 the State Council responded with Document 10, which signaled another policy shift—this time more in favor of banks than workers. The role of government in restructuring was strengthened (enterprises had to get permission from a "coordination subgroup" in each city). Acquisition and merger should be the preferred ways to rescue SOEs in trouble. And the government increased the number of trial cities to 111 (and certain industries, such as textiles and defense, elsewhere [World Bank 2000: 4]), and the size of the write-off quota to 30 billion yuan in 1997 and 40 billion yuan in 1998.[21] The new regulations discouraged whole takeovers and opened up some avenues for downsizing besides merger and bankruptcy that would be eligible for the write-off quota.

Results were immediate. The number of cases approved for write-off quotas increased to 2,486 and 2,721 in 1997 and 1998. Bankruptcies plunged while mergers rose. But implementation again produced unexpected and unwelcome results. Foreign specialists and their Chinese counterparts complained about two features of the CSOP program that made China exceptional: the State Council edict that a particular asset (land use rights) had to be used for one particular creditor (workers); and the heavy intrusion of the state, through its insistence on permissions, into the bankruptcy, merger, acquisition, and reorganization processes.[22]

In 1999 the government changed policy course again. It now widened its quota write-off program to any midsized or large loss-making SOEs anywhere in the country. Bankruptcy replaced merger as the government's preferred restructuring mechanism. However, the government realized that many of its initiatives were being foiled by collusion among local enterprises, local authorities, and local branches of banks, essentially to defraud central offices in favor of local interests. Therefore, it reversed its efforts at devolution and moved decisions about which bankruptcies should be implemented from the municipality to the provincial level.

The difficulties confronting bankruptcy in China recur through all these initiatives. On the financial side, according to the World Bank (2000), bankruptcy of SOEs had principally been an administrative process, with little involvement by creditors and little transparency. The difficulty for secured creditors (those with collateral of some sort) to enforce their claims had provided a disincentive for them to lend. Creditors had been treated very differently from one municipality to another and from one SOE to another. It was "socio-political instability from mass unemployment without adequate social protection" that was "a key concern of policy-makers" (World Bank 2000: 14). The state controlled the debtor, the creditor, and the bankruptcy process and thus substituted a principle of hierarchy for one of "market." To forestall unrest, enterprises paid workers up to three to six times their annual salary when SOEs were liquidated. The fear of labor unrest and the "likely militancy" of workers, the priority given to workers' expenses after layoff (including retirement), and the lack of creditor control combined in a process driven by administrative directive (World Bank 2001: 11–22). In bankruptcy itself, there were few options for out-of-court restructurings, or indeed much opportunity for reorganization within court proceedings.

The response of municipalities to the regulatory measures displayed many of the techniques of noncompliance so familiar to sociolegal scholars. Enterprises in collusion with local authorities engaged in creative compliance—creating false bankruptcies within the letter of the regulations, thereby "defrauding" the banks. The rules permitted partial compliance, for enterprises could undertake financial restructuring without restructuring their operations, which was a primary goal of the original EBL reformers. Enterprises used the lack of specificity in the regulations on transparency of asset sales to manipulate the disposal of assets in the enterprise or management's favor.

Moreover, while altering somewhat the shape of the trade-off, the State Council regulations did not resolve the central contradiction in the law—wanting to make SOEs economically viable while expecting them to help solve the labor problem. The regulations enabled ETCs and local authorities to press stronger SOEs to take over weaker SOEs, thus weakening the former and putting them at risk. While it wanted to save enterprises, it took their most valuable asset, land use rights, and earmarked it to pay off workers rather than reinvest in the company.

In part the seesawing between central and local control of CSOPs, and between workers' rights and bank interests, follows the trajectory of classic struggles between debtors and creditors in the bankruptcy reforms of any country (see Carruthers and Halliday 1998). These took the form of interagency rivalries between the SETC, which took the SOE/debtor side,[23] and the Central Bank, which took the side of bank creditors that ultimately it would need to underwrite. Yet shifting lines of conflict at the municipality level sometimes brought banks and local enterprises in collusion against Beijing while at other times pitted local banks and authorities against enterprises. Any significant unanticipated outcome during implementation or deviation from the intent of a regulation provided yet another occasion on which to renegotiate the relative balance of influence of the parties-in-practice over lawmaking.

Toward a Comprehensive Bankruptcy System

From the early 1990s it was apparent that China's patchwork quilt of laws, regulations, opinions, and practices in principle would benefit from integration into a single comprehensive bankruptcy law that treated all enterprises of any sort. From inside the country it was readily apparent that the EBL was scarcely working at all, and when it was used, its deficiencies were manifestly obvious. In November 1993, the 3rd Plenary Session of the 14th Central Committee of the Chinese Communist Party made the decision to take a series of steps toward consolidation of a socialist market economy. As part of a package of commercial laws to realize this vision, the push to create a comprehensive bankruptcy law with responsibility for its drafting was vested in the NPC Finance and Economy Committee.

The drafting of a new law had gone through three phases since 1994: from 1994 to 1996 the NPC drafting team produced a draft bill that failed to obtain approval by the Legal Affairs Committee of the NPC; drafting was suspended from 1996 to 2000; from 2000 the Draft Law went through several revisions before it was introduced for its first review by the Legal Affairs Committee, and once the draft was under review, progress also stalled at several points, both in the second and third reviews. During this same period, various law-making entities reached out for technical assistance from international financial institutions, most notably the Asian Development Bank and the World Bank, and from foreign countries, most importantly the German technical assistance program.

The First Phase: 1994–1996

The Finance and Economy Committee of the National People's Congress established a drafting team in 1994 that was charged with producing a law that saved jobs and turned companies around. The law should establish orderly credit procedures, modernize flexible security transactions, and encourage foreign investment. Bankruptcy should be "marketized," so the state was distanced from direct involvement. The law was to apply to all ownership types, such as privately owned enterprises, state-owned enterprises, joint ventures, and the like.[24] The seven-person team included three scholars, three officials, and a judge. The three academics were drawn from Beijing universities and law schools.[25]

The Asian Development Bank, working principally with the SETC, completed reports in 1995, 1996, and 1997 that offered a wide-ranging critique of the EBL and its implementation, which the new law was expected to remedy.[26] The ADB argued for reform on three principal grounds: the "Byzantine-like quality" of the insolvency system, changes in economic conditions since the mid-1980s (ADB 1996: 25–37), and the formal and substantive limitations we have earlier noted.[27] Arguably, the most important policy problem not solved by EBL was its failure to treat adequately the problems of workers in liquidations or restructurings. The solution in State Council Document 59 did not help much because it kept the possibility of declaring bankruptcy hostage to a prior settlement over the fate of an enterprise's workers. Ironically, it was also peculiar that workers had no role either under the EBL or State Council Document 59 in negotiating settlement or reorganization plans that very much concerned them (ADB 1996: 50). Yet the ADB was entirely mindful of dangers in two directions: the fragility of a banking sector that carried a massive overhang of "old debt"; and the potentially dangerous social and political consequences if SOEs were fully exposed to market forces. The ADB 1996

Report laid out its own formal and substantive criteria for a new Chinese law: "A new bankruptcy law must be detailed and precise; it must contain full interpretative guidelines; and it must emphasize and encourage, as an alternative to liquidation, the possible reorganization and restructuring of insolvent enterprises" (p. 2).

At the outset the drafting team undertook a policy study on ten major problems, which they put before a major conference in Beijing. They produced a first draft code in 1994, but it immediately ran into a wall of resistance over the unemployment of workers.[28] The Finance and Economy Committee, an NPC body of approximately two hundred officials experienced in economic management, broadly reviewed the draft, which was in turn submitted to related government ministries for their reactions. However, when the draft reached higher levels of policymaking in the National People's Congress, the State Council, and the Party, it bogged down because of a fear that the problems with workers remained unresolved.

With the nagging fear that "big trouble" could arise from this enormously sensitive problem, the idea arose to sell the land assets, or more properly, the land use rights, of the company to support the workers. The State Council seized upon this idea and in 1994 produced its regulations through the CSOP program to begin experiments with this putative solution to enduring concerns of workers' concerns and the fundamental fears of the top leadership.[29]

By 1996 the NPC technical drafting committee presented a draft to the FEC that sought to hold in tension, on the one hand, features found in most capitalist countries with, on the other hand, a distinctive Chinese character.[30] The Draft Law proposed the usual provisions for liquidating companies, but it strongly emphasized a capacity for reorganizing companies. It proposed mechanisms, together with specialized trustees and practitioners, that would facilitate the rescuing of businesses. Courts would control either directly or indirectly liquidation and reorganization. The draft recommended setting up committees of creditors to encourage their active participation and monitoring so that their economic interests would be engaged to make proceedings transparent. A theme of "conciliation" ran through the draft with the idea that parties should be encouraged to come to agreement in their collective interest rather than proceed in an adversarial fashion. An element of coercion permitted "cramdown" by a court, whereby it could force a solution on a small number of holdout creditors.[31] The reorganization or restructuring orientation had strong political and grassroots support, for it promised that enterprises would remain in a local municipality and (some) jobs would be saved.

Unlike the 1986 EBL, the Draft Law reflected an increasing awareness of bankruptcy systems in advanced countries, particularly Germany and Australia. It marked a significant shift toward a court-controlled process driven principally by creditors and relying heavily on specialized trustees and practitioners.

The 1996 draft combined political pragmatism with ideological distinctiveness. The Draft Law contained three elements quite unlike the bankruptcy law of any advanced economy. First, what is unique about a *socialist* market economy, stated an academic draftsman, is a heavy emphasis on the "social interest." In the bankruptcy event, workers and the local community and even related enterprises have interests that should be recognized in the formulation of policy. "Sometimes we must force the creditors to accept reorganization if it meets social interests. So we accept the notion of cramdown,"[32] a capacity for courts to overrule creditors who oppose a reorganization plan, subject to numbers of substantive and procedural protections. "So putting workers number one in priorities can be thought of as a Chinese characteristic" and a recognition of "China's national economic and social situation."[33]

Second, the Draft Law ranked second the interests of the state in unpaid taxes. Again, this is a claim unlimited either by amount of claim or length of time.[34] In theory, claims could reach back for several years. Powerful claims by tax authorities, frequently in conflict with other government departments, are familiar in any lawmaking over bankruptcy. China's case added a stronger principled dimension to this general claim, for the "Chinese government believes that it should take the money and use it for the people. There is a kind of philosophical commitment here—the moneys should be channeled to the public good."[35]

Herein reappears the enduring contradiction between the *socialist* and *market* orientations that recur through all the reform cycles. The combined effect of these two priorities almost certainly would nullify any aspirations for restructuring because the worker and state priorities between them invariably would siphon away all the principal assets of the company (such as land use rights, cash, etc.) that might have been used to turn the company around.

Third, the Draft Law was caught in a strong debate over the inclusion of SOEs in this market-driven model of liquidation and reorganization. On the one side, lawyers and the drafters, supported by the World Bank (with some provisos) argued energetically that all business enterprises should be treated equally, including the SOEs. On the other side, the SETC and government officials, afraid of instability and foreign intervention through takeovers, maintained the need for SOEs to be treated differently. A special chapter in the Draft Law sought to "grandfather" in SOEs existing before the law was enacted, requiring SOEs seeking bankruptcy protection to first get the permission of the agency that managed them.[36]

The FEC submitted its draft to the powerful Legal Affairs Committee of the NPC in 1996, which called the reform process to an abrupt halt. Many reasons are given and supposed by actors and observers of the reforms. Some rehearse the arguments from 1985 and 1986—that China's social security system was not developed sufficiently and until China had put in place social insurance, unemployment, and pension schemes to protect workers, it was neither fair nor wise to risk putting them out of work. The most widely held view was that the NPC continued to fear social and political unrest, and until a safety net was well in place, the bankruptcy law would be kept off the legislative agenda. There was also fundamental ideological opposition to the possibility of individual bankruptcies, which natural-person enterprises would produce.[37] Provisions on how to treat SOEs remained a subject of strong difference. Some reformers believed that if they had been prepared to leave that chapter in the Draft Law, it would already have been passed.[38]

The Second Phase: 1996–2000

In the four years that drafting was suspended, activity continued on several fronts. The government watched closely to see how its experiments with the 1988 law were working and whether its regulatory initiatives through the CSOP program would mitigate the potential for social unrest and financial uncertainty. The government also began to lay the foundation for a social security system that was independent of SOEs while concomitantly it developed sets of regulations and new legislation that would support a fully functional bankruptcy regime. Members of the drafting team used this quiet period to inform themselves more fully about developments outside China. They participated in a number of international conferences; learned about new international protocols, such as the UNCITRAL Model Law on Cross-Border Insolvencies; and convened meetings for further academic review within China.[39] These provided a springboard for renewed revisions once the drafters got the go-ahead from NPC leaders.

The Third Phase: 2000–2006

In late 1999 the FEC drafting committee got the green light to proceed with further revisions. If an indicator of political contentiousness is the shifting substantive provisions across successive drafts, then the bankruptcy law thoroughly qualifies. While the drafts became increasingly more sophisticated over time, and as consultants from inside and outside China debated it in one symposium after another, the countervailing forces of conflicting interests can be observed in the instability of its substantive provisions from one draft to the next. At several points, especially in 2004, at the NPC-SC's second review of the Draft Law, and at the third review in 2005, the process stalled for several months as conflicting interests pitted top leaders against each other. In narrow terms, the deadlocks centered on particular provisions, most notably the relative priority of workers or banks in the distribution of corporate assets. In broad terms, the debate reflected the more fundamental divide between those who emphasized market forces and those who feared China was drifting too far from its socialist distinctiveness. Put another way, one side sought some continuity with China's revolutionary past while others sought conformity with perceived global norms. In fact, the difference lay principally at the margins and substantially on the symbolic force of the law, whether for domestic consumption by those who sympathized with workers or international consumption by prospective investors. Moreover, an underlying current of concern related to potential political costs if a law were to quicken the pace of already mounting social unrest in the rust belts and less developed regions of China. When it became apparent that a failure to enact the law in 2006 would effectively require it to go back to the drawing board for an entirely new cycle through the NPC and its committees, a resolution was found that amalgamated pragmatism, symbolic representations, and various protections for a nervous government.

All the drafts from 1996 to 2006 and the final 2006 Enterprise Bankruptcy Law (2006 EB Law) shared a broad consensus that a bankruptcy law should permit three paths of action by failing companies: (1) liquidation, in which companies were either sold as going concerns or broken up and their parts sold off piecemeal to satisfy creditors; (2) conciliation, a simplified process in which smaller companies could negotiate with creditors to restructure their debts and have their settlement made binding by a court; and (3) reorganization, which would allow the financial and operational restructuring of companies, under court protection, in order to make them viable market actors once again (Art. 7).[40] Within these broad contours, however, were many twists and turns as the politics of bankruptcy played out among its stakeholders.[41]

Scope   A great deal of wavering occurred over the scope of the law. What kinds of enterprises would be eligible for bankruptcy proceedings under the new law? This issue was highly consequential. The government would confront risk in a shift from mostly administrative control over failing SOEs and financial institutions, to legal and market processes. The capacity of courts and professions to handle large numbers of enterprises was unproved. There was also an ideological current running through these debates, since it was said that the closer the possibility of bankruptcy came to individuals, the more troublesome this was to the lawmakers of a once Communist society where bankruptcy was unthinkable.

The draft brought back onto the table in June 2000 embraced not only SOEs but all enterprises (both legal person and natural person), partnerships, solely invested enterprises, and other profit-making organizations.[42] The scope of the law approached the scope of the market. Over the next several years, however, nervous top leaders pressed for its scope to be narrowed by excluding natural-person enterprises (i.e., businesses not formally incorporated), and at various times, financial institutions, partnerships, and proprietorships.[43]

In the law finally adopted, all legal-person enterprises are eligible for bankruptcy, including small proprietorships. Under some circumstances partnerships might also be eligible. So, too, would financial institutions, though these would require regulatory permissions in certain circumstances.[44] The law excluded the millions of small businesses undertaken by individuals or families without formal incorporation. This decision intimates an aversion of many leaders to the concept of personal bankruptcy in a socialist country. But there is also an element of pragmatism, since an expansive law might also overwhelm the courts or government agencies.

The treatment of SOEs proved vexing, with various proposals over the years to exclude them altogether and deal with them administratively, to include them in a special chapter that gave them distinctive treatment, or to provide various escape provisions for SOEs only. Leaders feared that an onslaught of SOE liquidations could provoke unrest. Lawmakers adapted in two ways. The government announced that 2,116 SOEs that were particularly troublesome, large numbers of them groups of companies, would be given until 2008 to be restructured by administrative means—so-called policy bankruptcies.[45] This continued the long-standing practice initiated in 1994 by the State Economic and Trade Commission and had resulted in some three thousand mergers, restructurings, or liquidations. The new law incorporated all remaining SOEs.

However, the pipeline into bankruptcy court for SOEs will be regulated by government ministries and agencies, either at the national or local levels, which can turn the faucet on and off, according to political will and circumstances. A number of barriers would keep some central or local government control over reactions to the vagaries of the market and thus ease the political risks of transition to a legally regulated bankruptcy system.[46]

After much hesitancy, financial institutions, including commercial banks, insurance companies, and securities corporations, were also embraced by the bankruptcy law so long as this was consistent with their primary regulatory law, such as the banking law. However, under several circumstances they will need to get permission from their regulatory agencies before using the law.[47] In the new law, partnership enterprises have a more equivocal status: they may proceed to use the new law if it is consistent with the Partnership Law. But in fact, there are so many lacunae in the treatment of partnerships that their coverage in practice by the new law remains equivocal.

In sum, it is anticipated that at its maximum scope the Enterprise Bankruptcy Law will incorporate some 8 million private and state-owned enterprises that previously were subject to a potpourri of laws.

Access to Bankruptcy and Standards for Initiation   The rights given parties (e.g., banks or debtors) to initiate a bankruptcy proceeding confer differential powers on stakeholders. As a result, struggles persisted to the penultimate moment of the lawmaking.

In the 2000 Draft Law, courts were given the power to initiate bankruptcy on their own discretion, a power deplored by the experts, since it abrogated a principle of the market and smacked of a command economy.[48] Later drafts conformed to global norms and restricted this power to debtors or creditors only. The provisions on conciliation for smaller companies were initially vested in debtors, then creditors only, and ultimately debtors only (Art. 95). For reorganization, both debtors and creditors are permitted to file under certain circumstances, a principle that is consistent with global norms (Art. 70). So, too, are significant shareholders, potentially against the wishes of management, which is less common (Art. 70).

Since standards of initiation affect both the size of the pipeline into bankruptcy proceedings and timing, they significantly affect the powers of stakeholders. One international standard is the *cash flow test*—can a company pay its bills on time? But the Standing Committee feared that this test would open the gates to a flood of bankruptcy filings. It therefore added a *balance sheet test* in which companies would be eligible for bankruptcy only if their liabilities exceeded their assets, a calculation that is time consuming, expensive, and often contestable. A balance sheet is also quite susceptible to manipulation, a problem compounded in countries where keeping multiple sets of company books is not uncommon. At one point, they combined the two tests, thereby ensuring that even fewer companies would be eligible.

To counteract this highly restrictive move, experts invented another test, described by one lawmaker as a bankruptcy test "with Chinese characteristics." A court could accept a bankruptcy application if the company both had a cash flow problem and was "obviously insolvent."[49] This solution can be read in two ways. On the one hand, it might be a back door to revive the cash flow test, since judges could simply specify "obviously insolvent" in terms of cash flow.[50] On the other hand, the "obviously insolvent" test also provides a major opening for judicial discretion and, thereby, a means by which political influence can be exercised over judges. Complained one academic draftsman, "[T]his is a way for the government to protect companies that might qualify under the other [two] tests but companies the government doesn't want to fail. This way the government can protect itself from a wave of liquidations." Oddly enough, said an expert economist, this would likely favor debtors over creditors because the judicial test produced a degree of uncertainty that made it difficult for banks to calculate risk.[51]

The Bankruptcy Estate   The size of the pool of assets available for reorganization affects its probability, but frequently secured creditors, usually banks, resist being constrained by bankruptcy proceedings. The 2006 EB Law broadly states that "all the assets" of a debtor will be part of the bankruptcy proceedings, but it does not specify them precisely. The Supreme People's Court interpretation will almost certainly include two of the most important assets—assets for which the enterprise has given some kind of security, such as property, machinery, or possibly receivables; and contracts.[52] If this happens, then secured creditors will need to work within the reorganization process presided over by the Court as it gives both debtors and creditors more assets to work with to effect a successful restructuring.[53]

Priority of Creditors   By far the most heated debates, reflected in the volatility of successive drafts, turned on the *priority* given to different classes of creditors in a liquidation or reorganization. This struggle, familiar from other countries (Carruthers and Halliday 1998; Halliday and Carruthers 2007), conventionally pits secured creditors (usually banks) against workers (usually for unpaid wages, vacation time, or social security contributions) against the state (usually for unpaid taxes including social security withholdings). The fight in China has been particularly acute because the government has been seeking to maximize two contradictory goals—to rehabilitate companies, rather than throw workers onto the street, and to protect workers, for both pragmatic and ideological reasons.

Some early drafts by the FEC drafting team gave secured creditors a right of priority, followed by administrative costs of managing the bankruptcy, but unlimited payments to workers and taxes.[54] Little money would be available for turning around the firm. One draft sought to solve the problem of siphoning off moneys to workers by off-loading worker costs onto the local government, but this was later reversed.[55] The draft submitted in 2004 for the First Reading by the full Standing Committee gave secured creditors (banks) the highest priority, followed by administrative costs, then labor and taxes. This proposal ran into a powerful workers' coalition that asserted that "because we are a socialist country we should be in favor of workers." Led by the Deputy Chairman of the Standing Committee (a former leader of the 200 million–strong All China Trade Union Federation), the Ministry of Labor, and social security officials, the worker bloc insisted that the first position for secured creditors be displaced by the claims of workers. "The top leaders are still worried about social unrest," noted a member of the FEC drafting team, and "because the production of workers' benefits is a key to the whole society, when problems appear to the public they are under pressure to protect worker benefits."[56]

By the Second Reading, the Central Bank had mobilized on behalf of financial institutions. Ironically, the top leadership had been insisting that banks act responsibly according to commercial rather than policy criteria, with the result that banks were compelled to act politically as an interest group. The banks were fully aware that "some SOEs owe workers wages for several years, even five or more, so if the priority of the workers wages comes before secured creditors, they won't get anything."[57] Declared the banks, if workers retained the first priority, then banks would refuse to lend money to enterprises that have heavy debts to workers and that will kill companies. The banking bloc obtained support from economists and academics, but the worker bloc in the NPC stood firm.

The debate brought proceedings to a halt. Insiders reported that China's Premier favored priority for secured creditors, thus taking the side of the banks, while a high-ranking NPC official favored workers, thus taking the side of the workers and their union advocates. In the meantime the NPC Legal Affairs Committee consulted with the Asian Development Bank, which convened a panel of international experts who reported on priority in their countries. The overwhelming response was priority for secured creditors.[58]

After months of stalemate and intensive jockeying the 2006 EB Law produced a Solomonic solution of casuistic drafting. The most salient provision in the EB Law, Article 113, makes it appear that the workers won. On its face it seems to prioritize worker claims, whereas in practice it prioritizes the banks. The government is anticipated to move more quickly to expand social insurance for workers and bolster its still underfunded general social security net, including retirement costs.[59]

Professional Division of Labor   Since bankruptcy reforms open up a politics of conflict over "jurisdictional rights" for professionals (Carruthers and Halliday 1998), it matters which occupations are allocated what domains of work and whether that work is located within the state or in the private market.

At no stage did reformers seriously consider putting insolvency work entirely or predominantly into a state agency, and none, other than the Supreme People's Court, has a primary responsibility for bankruptcy administration. Consistent with government policy to move many previously state-controlled functions to intermediary organizations, successive drafts envisaged that "qualified" and "experienced" institutions (e.g., law and accounting firms) would be primarily responsible to act as administrators of bankruptcies and reorganizations. There is no evidence that lawyers or accountants mobilized to obtain expansive monopolies. Indeed the 2006 EB Law envisages the work will be done by a law or accounting firm or possibly by a specialized bankruptcy firm, although it is open enough to permit officials also to act as bankruptcy administrators (Art. 24). All of these possibilities, as well as individuals, are authorized by a subsequent Supreme People's Court interpretation.[60] However, the language is sufficiently flexible to leave open the prospect of a future specialized insolvency profession with advanced training beyond the generalist qualifications of lawyers and accountants. In its 2007 provisions, the Supreme People's Court went to extraordinary lengths to mitigate corruption in the methods it adopted to allocate administrators to particular cases.[61]

In reorganization, later drafts leaned in an American direction by giving substantial powers to creditors' committees, but they reflected the British and Continental practices of appointing administrators for reorganizing companies because of doubts about management's capacity or interests in reorganization. The 2006 EB Law left much ambiguous. Creditors' committees can exercise substantial powers of supervision (Art. 68), but the Court will appoint the administrator. In a significant gesture to workers, the creditors' committee must include an employee representative of the debtor or union (Art. 67).

Since the formula for setting fees affects the quality of professionals who will be recruited to corporate restructuring, the outcome is critical. The new law remained indeterminate, pending more specific rules and interpretations by government agencies and the court.[62] Fees will be set by the creditors' committee and Court. The subsequent provisions of the Court indicate fees may reflect the financial value of the case, which will be attractive to specialist firms, but the courts will retain ultimate authority over fees if creditors and administrators cannot agree.[63] As the U.S. well remembers, possibilities for corruption, with kickbacks to judges,[64] are considerable if the rules do not specify carefully and the courts do not adhere to the spirit of the law in appointment and remuneration of bankruptcy specialists. Overall, however, it is clear that China has opted for a private market rather than government agency solution for bankruptcy administration.

Courts and Jurisdiction   A running debate took place over institutional arrangements, most notably whether corporate bankruptcies should be handled by specialized courts. International organizations and technical assistance programs emphatically recommended either specialized courts or more powerful higher-level courts with presumptively higher-quality judges. The struggle among advocates for specialized, lower-, and higher-level courts turns on competency, independence, and institutional capacity. Judges in lower courts "are not very familiar with bankruptcy law and the level of their knowledge varies according to the districts. In some districts they may be good; in less developed districts, ignorant." More complex matters would be better dealt with in intermediate courts. On independence, "lower courts are influenced by local protectionism and sometimes they have to do things according to local leaders. Sometimes there is corruption in dealing with bankruptcy cases. If this continues, then they will damage the creditors through the district."[65]

Earlier drafts by the FEC drafting team therefore recommended a specialized court, but top leaders feared that this would be expensive and other areas of law would also want their specialty courts.[66] The FEC team settled for intermediate generalist courts, and when this also encountered opposition, backed down to first-level or intermediate-level courts depending on the value of the company in bankruptcy or on the sophistication of the courts in a given jurisdiction.[67] The 2006 EB Law does not specify the level of the court. This will be up to the Supreme People's Court. The court level may, for instance, depend on the size of a company's balance sheet.

The EB Law states that the jurisdiction will be in the domicile of the debtor (Art. 3), a solution that may create problems because "domicile" might be the locus of a head office, but the real decisions and assets of an enterprise might be elsewhere. No consideration or discussion seems to have occurred over the need for a government agency, akin to the English Insolvency Service, to handle no-asset bankruptcies and to serve as a regulator. This may be a problem yet to surface.

Global Forces

China's insulation from global capital markets enabled its leaders to press forward reform cycles that closely followed domestic issues. Yet, despite China's ability to substantially set its own pace and own course, international influences pressed upon drafters and decision makers. What were the exogenous contexts, the institutions, mechanisms, and structures of power that operated as constraints and opportunities for domestic actors?

At the outset of the bankruptcy reforms in the mid-1980s, China stood at substantial distance from the global center. Since China has never experienced a sustained Western colonial presence,[68] it has no inherited Western legal system to draw upon, although it does lean in the direction of civil law regimes (Lubman 1999; Potter 1999).[69] This deprives it of obvious foreign models to which it could easily turn and thus places it even farther from the global centers than either Indonesia or Korea. And the recency of China's integration into regional and global markets and educational systems means that its penetration or awareness of global paradigms remained quite shallow at least into the 1990s.

By the same token this distance from any particular center offers it a diversity of possibilities—with no sunk costs or predispositions, China can pick or choose the global centers to which it will orient itself in different spheres (e.g., commerce, science, education). Moreover, the vast size of China's economy and its lack of reliance on multilateral financial institutions redress the balance of power that in Korea and Indonesia substantially favored the global center. The diversity and diffuseness of foreign influences therefore gave China's reformers some degree of freedom.

China's engagement with foreign institutions and bearers of norms expanded progressively through the entire recursive episode, beginning with no contact, expanding along parallel administrative and legislative tracks, and converging on the comprehensive bankruptcy law.

China began its twenty-year cycles of reform with the purely indigenous Interim Bankruptcy Law in 1986, which owed nothing to any outside law or legal system since information on foreign systems was not available to drafters or the NPC.[70] China's bankruptcy reformers did have some close models at hand, but they chose not to take them seriously. Taiwan, a thriving "Asian Tiger," might have offered a standard, but it was ideologically impossible for the mainland to acknowledge any influence from its wayward "province"; in fact, drafters suggested that its law was too much like that of Japan and, if anything, was regressive. Hong Kong, too, would have seemed the epitome of a thriving open market economy, yet the FEC drafting team found its reliance on common law and the English system too alien to China's affinity with code law. And if China were to look to common law countries, said one reformer, why go to Hong Kong, when one could go directly to Britain from whom its law is derived? Within China several bankruptcy regimes might have served as experimental sites or models. The Special Economic Zones had the right to enact their own regulations, which varied from zone to zone. Yet the markets in those zones differed so dramatically from that of China as a whole (e.g., they have no SOEs) that the regulations had limited effects on the country as a whole except for the model they offer of a simplified procedure for companies in distress.

The Administrative Track   When the former ministry responsible for state-owned enterprises, the State Economic and Trade Commission,[71] decided to embark on a set of experiments to solve administratively its enormous problem with insolvent SOEs, it turned to the Asian Development Bank for technical advice. In a series of technical reports from 1995 to 2000, the ADB enlisted insolvency experts from Australia, New Zealand, and Hong Kong. The SETC commissioned several reports and recommendations from the Asian Development Bank.[72] In these cases, the mediating personnel were principally ADB staffers and foreign consultants, most notably Australians Ron Harmer (the drafter of Australia's bankruptcy law) and John Lees, a longtime Hong Kong insolvency practitioner and later, President of INSOL.[73] Their positions allowed them to inject into the Chinese bankruptcy debates a vision of a regime that would rely substantially on an insolvency practice profession and less on courts, a model that was more congenial to the Asian Development Bank and different in emphasis from those of the Washington-based IFIs. In the developing market for Chinese professional services, Harmer and Lee sought to legitimate a jurisdiction for insolvency practitioners, but they played the mediating role judiciously, for they advocated that China adhere to various global standards and international norms yet conceded that in certain matters China would need to go its own way.[74] In these studies China allowed the ADB consultants to find Chinese counterparts as informants on Chinese law and practice.[75]

The principal ADB Report, delivered to the SETC in 2000, represented the most systematic formulation or adaptation for China of a global norm for insolvency systems. The Report acknowledged that a shift from a "socialist planned economy" to a "socialist market economy" raised many difficulties, notably that "socialist" and "market" were potentially at odds. The PRC needed bankruptcy law as an element of a market economy, yet on the "socialist" side it sought to promote and maintain public ownership in production. Thus far, said the ADB, the government had maintained a view that insolvency law was an instrument of government policy, a lever to be pulled by officials rather than a mechanism to be used by market players.[76]

Furthermore, any change in the bankruptcy law threatened the basic right to work, guaranteed in Article 42 of the Constitution, and this was the "most difficult and sensitive issue in the insolvency process."[77] During field visits, "several officials and SOE managers put forward the view that SOE employees had sacrificed good wages for the benefit of the SOE and of the PRC generally, and that the insolvency process should reward them for their contributions."[78] Thus, a "difficult environment" existed, said the ADB, in which to introduce new bankruptcy law. There was no legal tradition upon which to draw, and a set of unpropitious economic and political circumstances.

The ADB recommended sweeping reforms, from substantive bankruptcy law with a reorganization emphasis to consideration of a specialized government agency for restructuring, the development of courts and professionalization of judges, and the professionalization of private insolvency practice. In the final analysis the NPC did adopt a comprehensive substantive law that had a strong emphasis on reorganization. But it has yet to put in place the other elements of a functioning bankruptcy system—a government agency, specialized courts, or a specialized insolvency profession. For the moment, the law sits on the books without an institutional infrastructure that can implement it effectively.

While the ADB's Report was relatively muted and delivered privately, the World Bank Report, released in 2001, expressed its criticism publicly and proposed decisive action. Written principally by economists, with some cooperation from the Legal Department of the Bank, including the principal author of the World Bank *Principles* on bankruptcy, its critique echoed and amplified the ADB's approach. It began empirically, by showing the impediments resulting from the old social contract. It explained why the magnitude of the problem was so great:

> In the state planned economy, SOEs were obliged to meet the social needs of their communities, including full employment and comprehensive social services to their employees, retirees, and their families. . . . In the late 1990s, SOEs in China provided 40% of jobs in urban areas, 57% of pension funds, and three quarters of urban housing. Medical institutions that belong to SOEs serve one-fifth of China's population. (World Bank 2000: 10, 22)

Pervading the system were presumptions of the "entitlements of labor"—that workers, when laid off, may expect to get several years of salary, and sometimes even free municipal housing. Fifteen years after the debates in the NPC-SC, "workers largely consider their right" to the iron rice bowl to be intact. This "perception of entitlement" is changing slowly, so much so that many workers appear "traumatized" by the transition. Yet labor, workers, and the public are slowly coming to realize that bankruptcy is a "painful but inevitable ingredient of a market economy" (World Bank 2000: 23–24, 29).

These painful transitions from one to another contract, where old rights were displaced by new mechanisms, where entitlements so thoroughly inculcated over half a century become nullified, threatened to disturb more than workers' consciousnesses. The prevailing fear of the government, acknowledged in every debate over the new bankruptcy law, centered on social stability and its political repercussions. The World Bank echoed the ADB and NPC when it noted that the priority concern of the government was "social stability" and it was the overriding constraint on reforms. The fear was well founded, for the Bank estimated that if only half of the SOEs that were unprofitable in 1998 were to be liquidated, 20 million people would be laid off in urban centers. Nevertheless, the Bank made a direct appeal that reforms proceed even if the government had to make special short-term arrangements for SOEs.

The Legislative Track   While the SETC was obtaining technical assistance from international financial institutions, the Finance and Economy Committee's drafting team relied heavily on technical assistance from the German overseas aid agency Deutsche Gesellschaft für Technische Zusammenarbeit (GTZ). Since the mid-1990s, the GTZ has been providing drafting assistance to the NPC on a cluster of economic laws, including bankruptcy law. The GTZ has a resident office in Beijing with several lawyer-staffers. Its primary technique for exercising suasion has been to host a series of conferences on successive drafts of the bankruptcy law. To these conferences GTZ has invited specialists from across the world's insolvency systems. For example, the 2000 conference included five foreign experts: Salvatore Barbatano, an American lawyer; Sergey Sarbash, a Russian judge; Lusina Ho, an Oxford-trained Chinese law professor from Hong Kong; Lars Lindencrone Petersen, a Danish judge; and Stefan Smid, a German academic and judge. Each foreign expert was allotted chapters of the Draft Law for detailed commentary. GTZ authored a final report that fused expert commentary and subsequent discussion into a set of explicit recommendations for the drafting committee. These were subsumed under a set of principles that GTZ avowed represented "the collective experience [of] those bankruptcy systems which are regarded as highly credible and efficient."[79] The following specialists sat down with two GTZ lawyers and five Chinese experts: Cao Siyuan, author of the 1986 PRC bankruptcy law; Jiang Xinxiong, a member of the NPC Standing Committee; Wang Weiguo, an academic member of the drafting committee; Zhu Shaoping, the Director of the Legislative Office for the Finance and Economy Committee of the National People's Congress; and Zou Hailin, a member of the drafting committee and an academic specialist on bankruptcy law at the Chinese Academy of Social Sciences.[80] In other conferences, experts have been drawn from Australia, Britain, and elsewhere.[81]

Through 2003 the GTZ for internal purposes kept a running scorecard on its impact. Did the drafting committee respond to successive rounds of expert recommendations? It found that of seventy important changes it recommended, thirty improved in the directions it proposed, thirteen were neutral, and fifteen did not follow GTZ expert advice.[82] The German strategy was subtle: rather than pursue a heavy-handed, explicitly German model (which might offend the nationalist sensibilities of the Chinese), the GTZ imported specialists from civil and common law systems alike from across the world's major insolvency systems, which enabled GTZ to forge a global consensus that the Germans merely mediated, a united "global" front at once more coherent and less objectionable than a nationalist global "other."

In the last stages of FEC drafting and during the cycles of review by the Standing Committee, a flurry of technical assistance came from all quarters. The World Bank legal staff appraised the current draft for its conformity with the World Bank *Principles*. In 2004, the Asian Development Bank hosted a conference with the Legislative Affairs Committee. Also in late 2004, a small group of foreign experts and the GTZ participated in an informal workshop held by the FEC. The intense activity reflected a form of expert co-optation because each of the organizations responsible for drafting—the FEC drafting team, the FEC itself, the Legal Affairs Committee, the Standing Committee—sought its own expert advice in order to bolster selectively its authority on contentious provisions.

In no case, therefore, was it possible for international organizations to use financial leverage over China's bankruptcy reforms. Instead, technical assistance came in two contrasting forms. The ADB and GTZ took an insider approach, combining notable foreign expertise with a discreet form of suasion. The World Bank, by contrast, took an outsider approach where expertise was mobilized to persuade publicly and possibly to shame China into action. In all cases the foreign agents of reform offered generalized norms rather than an explicit national model of a bankruptcy system. From the World Bank the normative referent was its own *Principles*. In the last stages the UNCITRAL Legislative Guide was also put on the table for the consideration of the Chinese. From the ADB and GTZ came the core of an expert consensus by specialists from advanced economies. As a result, from the mid-1990s to the final passage of the new law, the Chinese drafters and lawmakers were apprised with increasing frequency and intensity of norms, themselves progressively formalized, which represented a putative global consensus.

International Conformity with Chinese Characteristics

At first glance, China appears to be a limiting case of globalizing law and markets. We have seen that the Asian Financial Crisis had very little direct effect on China, since its leaders had effectively erected barriers to control the inflow and outflow of capital. Moreover, inflows took the less liquid form of foreign direct investment (FDI), which went disproportionately into fixed assets and infrastructure rather than the more liquid form of portfolio capital. Indirect effects, however, were far reaching. China's leaders sought to create institutions that would inoculate the country from future external financial shocks. These included far-reaching institution building within the financial sector, significant reforms of the SOE sector, expansion of massive foreign reserves, and careful monitoring of capital flows in and out of the country (World Bank 2007).

Above all, the leaders of China's Party-state sought to drive forward economic growth at the blistering pace it has sustained for a quarter of a century. The economic logic was straightforward. A controlled release of market forces inside China would consistently and perceptibly improve the material circumstances of China's citizens, lifting hundreds of millions out of poverty within China while positioning China itself as a major player in the world economic system. Yet driving forward economic development is not only an economic but a political imperative. For a 70 million–strong Party to maintain control over 1.3 billion citizens, it has been necessary for China's top leaders to balance their integration into the world economy, which substantially drives growth, with domestic challenges that are far more threatening than the whims of currency speculators.

China seeks simultaneously to advance economic liberalism without permitting political liberalism. In one sense this solves a number of problems that can occur when developing countries seek to transform both their markets and polities simultaneously, an enterprise that has proved difficult in Indonesia and deleterious in Russia. In another sense, the failure to develop a more open political system that is accountable to its citizens and offers them avenues of political expression may threaten the stability that market growth requires (Minzner 2007). This is nowhere more evident than in the legal infrastructure of the state.

Bankruptcy systems are integral to the market. Such is the consensus of the global institutions that have provided China's market makers with global norms and technical advice over the past decade. In any market economy, bankruptcy laws and institutions provide one set of orderly means of dealing with failing commercial enterprises, nonprofits, and even municipalities. In advanced economies the restructuring opportunities provided through bankruptcy law, coupled with the threats of liquidation of uncompetitive firms, provide a kind of self-correcting mechanism in which a legally regulated market handles its weakest enterprises. In China, however, bankruptcy systems provide an alternative mechanism to the bureaucratic decisions that once ruled a command economy. Since enterprises in this economy also served as social security systems, providing workers with housing, education, health care and pensions, the dismantling of the state-owned enterprise sector effectively also significantly increased the risk of unemployment, the loss of benefits, and the increase in personal risk.

Even though China's economic trajectory appears robust (OECD 2007), it has no lack of economic problems: slow rural growth for the majority of the population; sharply increasing inequality; a widening income and wealth gap between urban and rural residents; regional disparity in economic development; unemployment resulting from continuing downsizing and closing of SOEs; increased competition as entry in the WTO lowers China's barriers to foreign firms; a growing trade surplus that is triggering protectionist sentiments, particularly in the U.S.; the possibility of real estate bubbles and stock market busts; energy shortages; environmental hazards; and growing pressures from China's foreign competitors over protection of property rights (Mertha 2005; Naughton 2003, 2006a, 2006b).

It is a short step from an economic problem to a social problem. While China's economy has been booming, social unrest has been increasing, so much so, according to one analyst, that "by the early 21st century social unrest had become a normal feature of Chinese society" (qtd. in Minzner 2007: 5). Between 1993 and 2004 the official count of "mass incidents," which include riots, strikes, demonstrations, and protests, had increased from eighty-seven hundred to seventy-four thousand. While it appears there has been a recent downturn, partly due to a changed metric and to heightened repression, news headlines belie claims of subsiding protests. Expert observers conclude that a new generation of "professionalized protest leaders" and "die-hards," often former military officers, may be refining a "radicalization of tactics" that "fuel an increase in the scale and size of mass petitions" (Minzner 2007).

Social unrest is not remote from either bankruptcy law or its embedding legal system. National surveys show that one of the leading causes of local unrest is unemployment. According to the 2007 Blue Book produced by the Chinese Academy of Social Sciences, 17.5 percent of households have one or more people unemployed, while many more are afraid of layoffs and loss of medical coverage and old age insurance. Indeed, of issues causing most concern to people, unemployment ranked second only to lack of adequate medical care (Fewsmith 2007; Halliday 2008a). The head of a national bureau responsible for handling citizen petitions stated in 2003 that a primary cause of unrest was "restructuring of state-owned enterprises, including the failure to pay wages and benefits" (qtd. in Minzner 2007: 5). At a time when the State Asset Supervision and Administration Commission (SASAC) intends to close 2,167 SOEs and lay off another 3.66 million employees, these retrenchments combined with any downturn in the economy, the bursting of a stock market or real estate bubble, or any foreign policy incident that disturbed China's overseas markets and sources of capital could trigger widespread unrest, especially in the countryside, where China's Communist insurgency began in the 1930s (Naughton 2003, 2005, 2006b).

China's leaders are acutely aware of these dangers and have taken numerous measures both to forestall the problems arising in the first place and to smother them with security forces when they break out. But these measures do not reach to a fundamental problem that is also salient to a bankruptcy regime. The legal system might seem a palliative to these incipient problems. However, it is implicated both in the creation of a bankruptcy regime and the social unrest. For a bankruptcy system to work in China, it must rely on judges, courts, and lawyers who are seen to be competent, fair and, binding (Halliday 2008a). Yet many of the factors causing unrest themselves stem from deficiencies in local justice. A prominent complaint in the 13 million petitions submitted in 2005 focused on "'legally-related' grievances, such as disagreements with court decisions." Local Party committees continue to exercise authority over courts through selection of judges, selection of court presidents and vice-presidents, control of court budgets, and even input on court decisions, although with a frequency that is wrapped in secrecy. The Ministry of Justice and its local affiliates constrain access to lawyers on many types of cases. The result is that administrative law cases have fallen and the civil cases brought in 2005 are back at 1996 levels. Grievances and disputes increasingly are being handled extralegally, even in the streets (Minzner 2007).

Given these domestic pressures on the leaders of China's Party-state, bankruptcy reforms are doubly implicated: directly, insofar as a badly designed law and bankruptcy regime could intensify the pressures already existing in the economy; and indirectly, insofar as the prospect of a bankruptcy regime that works depends on attributes of law, courts, and lawyers, which are proving difficult to institutionalize despite the high aspirations registered by China's judicial leaders (ADB SPC Report). Failure on either or both counts might trigger or reinforce social unrest. And social unrest in a one-party state may ultimately become political disaffection.

How then have China's policymakers navigated among these dangerous shoals? How can they simultaneously meet global expectations and manage domestic threats?

A careful manipulation of the recursive process of reform has been one response. Lawmakers have oriented themselves to international agencies and experts by proceeding through successive iterations of consultation, technical assistance, and participation in international forums in order to familiarize themselves with the range of potential options available from the repertoire of bankruptcy systems in advanced countries. Various bodies in the lawmaking enterprise have sought specialist expertise and authority from different international sources (e.g., FEC with the GTZ; NPC-SC with ADB; SETC with ADB). In the absence of foreign leverage over China, Chinese lawmakers have had ample room to pick and choose among provisions that are considered legitimate by the progenitors of global norms.

Familiarity with both convergence and variety in international norms has led China's leaders to adopt the broad contours of the global consensus, namely, that bankruptcy regimes must provide both credible threats to liquidate failed firms and realistic opportunities for enterprises to be rehabilitated if any prospect of a turnaround seems possible. On one or another of the key features of bankruptcy regimes advocated by the IMF, World Bank, ADB, and UNCITRAL, we have shown that the law enacted in 2006 much more closely adheres to international norms than, for instance, the draft of 1996. As the GTZ evaluation demonstrated to its satisfaction, successive rounds of drafting moved the Draft Law progressively closer to standards acceptable to GTZ experts from many legal systems.

Enactment of the final law depended heavily on cycles of experimentation across China in the preceding decade. Whereas the Interim Bankruptcy Law of 1986 was relatively moribund, and liquidation cases for private firms were handled through the Commercial Law, the most consequential rounds of experimentation occurred through policy bankruptcies, mergers, and reorganizations presided over by the SETC and later SASAC. This administratively driven effort to restructure the state-owned sector ensured the tight control that China's leaders believed necessary to contain the volatility of laid-off workers and related costs to families, local communities, and the flimsy social safety net. It also prepared the state-owned sector for a future moment at which market forces, regulated by law, might take over from administrative directives of the state-owned sector. In principle those moments arrived on June 1, 2007, when the bankruptcy law came into effect, and some time in 2008 by which time all the remaining exempt SOEs would be exposed to market forces.

If the substantive outcomes of law-on-the-books show a convergence on the central tendency of global bankruptcy reforms, there remain many specific variations, even more ambiguous and open provisions, and most of all, much institutional indeterminacy. Large numbers of provisions in the law await specification by an Interpretation of the Supreme People's Court, and until this is completed, the extent of ambiguity remains unknown.[83] But it is the institutional indeterminacy that will affect the magnitude of the implementation gap. No specialized courts have been created, and a specialized chamber for bankruptcy has not been adopted. It is unknown how well local courts will be able to detach themselves from the powerful local economic and political interests that will bias courts against nonlocal creditors. A huge imbalance exists between the status and income of judges and the stakes of many corporations whose economic survival or family control will depend upon their decisions. Opportunities for corruption and political pressure will be legion. Neither have policymakers chosen either to create a government agency for low-asset cases, nor have they formed a specialized insolvency profession, although slow steps toward the latter are anticipated. A combination of the substantive gaps in the law and the suspect autonomy and competence of courts will detract from the certainty that bankruptcy law is supposed to offer market actors.

Over time, potential problems of actor mismatch have been attenuated. Following the recent pattern of broad consultation in policymaking under Premier Wen Jiabao, bureaucratic interests across China's central government had ample opportunity to mobilize. Whether the resolution between banking and worker interests is stable has yet to be tested. An unstable political settlement may drive further rounds of reform. Private firms had little opportunity to participate in the lawmaking. Since their treatment by the courts will send clear signals to foreign investors about the security of their assets, and will thereby influence investment strategies, this absence of key actors in practice from the deliberative process has the potential to induce further rounds of lawmaking.

Most of all, however, certain contradictions remain in the substantive law and its institutions. A backlash has been opening up in China to neoliberalism and its celebration of competition and the lowering of tariff barriers for foreign firms. Some go so far as to charge that foreign bankers are pushing China into conditions that would be conducive to another Asian Financial Crisis, when foreign interventions would be impossible to resist. Critical voices inside China oppose "absolute liberalization, comprehensive privatization, complete marketization, and globalization" (Naughton 2006b). Contradictory analyses of the market situation, and thereby its policy directions, are reflected in the degree to which a market regulated by law should be set free of restraints by government mandarins. Already some aspects of this contradiction can be seen in reliance on courts that are at once supposed to be neutral, fair, competent, and binding, yet are controlled to varying degrees by the Party and cadres. It is very difficult to see how courts can be neutral commercial referees when political controls are quite proximate.

The most important step taken by the bankruptcy lawmakers, however, is to hedge against the risk of an uncertain new law through the retention of administrative controls. Access to the bankruptcy law for SOEs, for financial firms, and possibly for partnerships, is hedged about with administrative approvals that must be obtained from regulators before enterprises can use the law. These administrative channels into the bankruptcy system can be opened or closed, depending on the specific circumstances of an enterprise or the general state of the economy. And, of course, as has been observed with the Interim Bankruptcy Law, in the worst-case scenario access to the courts by private firms can be sharply limited by Party and administrative controls over judges.[84]

At best it can be said, then, that each recursive cycle has pushed the law toward greater formal certainty through a progressive expansiveness of the law's jurisdiction, more detail and specification of legal provisions, the removal of ambiguities, the correction of what seemed to be policy errors, and the response to changed circumstances. At the same time the cycles of reform and putative reform evidence a progressive shift toward the legal rationality articulated in the global norms promulgated by international institutions and professions in order to produce legal and market certainty. In short, the reform cycles have produced increasing "legalization," increasing profession- alization of the lawmaking process, and increasing internationalism in the formal and substantive provisions of the new Draft Law.

Yet China is entering a new phase of development in which its economy will be more open to foreign competition and its economic decision makers will be subject to greater direct pressures from integration into the world trad- ing system. At the same time there is much potential for social conflict that might express itself in challenges to political authority. China's leaders have promulgated a bankruptcy law that broadly conforms to global norms with quite discernible Chinese characteristics. Despite its technical remoteness from ordinary citizens, bankruptcy law has become a potential flashpoint at which law and the economy spark political instability or fuel other unrest that could press for regime change. China's leaders may well have inoculated themselves from the set of conditions that produced the first Asian Financial Crisis. At its best the bankruptcy regime helps serve this purpose. Paradoxi- cally, however, by adopting many of the international norms intended to pre- vent a second crisis, China potentially opens itself to a new set of conditions that may not be unable to forestall instability, but may even provoke it. In the words of a World Bank economic update on China: "Even with all the safeguards in place, though, vigilance remains required, because if there is one lesson that countries can draw from the Asian Crisis it is that it is never enough to prepare for the *last* crisis" (World Bank 2007).

8 Intermediation

RARELY DOES SCHOLARSHIP engage the global/local encounter from both sides. We have already approached the globalization of bankruptcy norms from two orientations. In Part I we viewed the world through the lens of the global center. In Part II we altered the angle of orientation from Vienna or Washington and stood in the shoes of lawmakers in Jakarta, Seoul, and Beijing.

Yet puzzles remain. How does an IO translate its normative pressures into practical reforms? How does it sustain its reform impetus in the face of scarce resources, changing agendas, and multiple demands from across the world? Why does implementation seldom reflect enactment? How is it that the strong appear surprisingly weak, and the weak seem stronger than even they themselves perceive? What can repeated engagements of diverse "locals" with harmonizing global interests tell us about the limits of national law reforms pressed by foreign actors?

Answers to these questions require a third orientation—from the perspective of processes manifest across these global/local encounters. Part III is an exercise in "mapping the middle," as Merry (2006) puts it. We examine tensions between the global and the local that help explain the contingency of globally induced law reforms. The extent of convergence around globalizing norms, we argue, substantially turns on three processes. From the side of the international organizations the problem is one of *intermediation*. How can IOs find effective intermediaries to bridge the gap between the global and the local? From the side of nation-states global/local encounters are shaped by capacities for *foiling*. Can national leaders of putatively weak nations resist IOs? Are they at the mercy of the global powers? And, finally, global/local encounters are subsumed within the dynamics of *recursivity*. Intermediation and foiling set into motion cycles of reform that alternate between a politics of enactment, which is the dominant arena of power for IOs, and a politics of implementation, which is the arena of power in which local actors display greater capacity.

The three chapters in Part III successively demonstrate the salience of these three processes for the degree to which the national cases converge on global norms. We will show that nations in the Global South are not nearly so weak as they may appear—or as they believe. Convergence has its limits precisely because the strong are not so powerful as they usually are alleged to be and the weak have weapons that mitigate their powerlessness. As a result, the globalization of law is always a negotiated process. Globalization is neither imposed imperatively from above nor embraced in its entirety from below. It proceeds through recursive cycles with successive approximations to narrow gaps between aspirations of policy entrepreneurs and realities of practice.

Negotiating Globalization in Asymmetrical Fields of Power

Intermediaries negotiate the global/local relationship. The structure of inter-mediation influences the terms negotiated by both global and local actors. The negotiations in which intermediaries are critical bridges between the global and local occur within asymmetrical fields of power (Figure 8.1).[1] First, nation-states vary in their power relative to global actors. A weak, poor state in finan-cial crisis is much more vulnerable to international financial institutions than a strong, rich state outside a crisis. Second, nation-states also vary in their social and cultural distance from the global. Whereas some states have few leaders or experts who are linked and familiar with global institutions and their scripts, other states are closely integrated with global institutions through revolving personnel, policy influence, and concordance of ideology and practices. States that are weak on both dimensions, or weak on one dimension and strong on another, will experience a sharply different interaction between the local and global than those strong on both dimensions. That interaction has conse-quences for intermediaries, the degrees of freedom for crafting local scripts, and the breadth of the gap between law as enacted and law as implemented.

Indonesia, Korea, and China in the 1990s were differentially vulnerable to global pressures, a variation that affected the role of intermediaries. Indonesia in 1997 had the least power to resist global institutions since its financial vulnerability was so acute. At the same time it was also farthest in cultural and social distance from the global center, with a very small number of potential organizational overlaps or intermediaries who had ties to the global center. Korea, too, was financially vulnerable to global pressure in 1997, but less acutely than Indonesia since it had a much stronger economic base on which to rebuild, as its rapid recovery subsequently demonstrated. In sharp contrast to Indonesia, in Korea the gap between global centers and institutions, officials, and experts was much narrower. Whatever the measure—numbers of economists trained in prestigious U.S. universities, numbers of officials who had worked at the IMF or World Bank, the density of research and researchers in national institutes—Korea was proximate to and familiar with global norms and their propagators. China in 1997 was least vulnerable to global pressures because it had shielded its economy from volatile movements of capital. The IFIs had very little leverage over it. Yet China in the late 1990s was more like

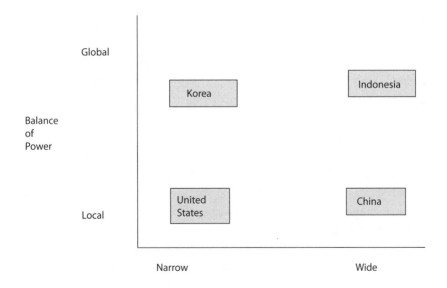

FIGURE 8.1 Situational Vulnerability of Nation-States to Global Pressures
SOURCE: Carruthers and Halliday (2006).

Indonesia than Korea in the distance between the global and local since its integration into the world economy, its depth of expertise, and its affinity to IFIs remained limited.

The location of a country in this two-dimensional space—the balance of power between the global and local and the cultural distance of the local from the global—affects the dynamics and structure of relations between international actors and their local interlocutors. The positioning of countries in relation to these dimensions influences the magnitude of the problem faced by IOs as they seek to bridge the gap between their policy and financial imperatives and the realities of local conditions.

In these locations of nation-states in fields of global power, the global/local interaction depends on who, or what, occupies mediating positions. Mediating bodies, institutions, and organizations add another layer of complexity since their own interests, capabilities, and biases bear on the interaction. For example, the interaction of national legal systems with global legal norms is often mediated by the legal profession, which has its own distinct jurisdictional interests and biases (Carruthers and Halliday 1998). In other arenas, the mediation may be performed by NGOs, academic networks, or particular government agencies. To the extent that such mediating bodies span "structural holes" (Burt 1992), they may be in a position to pursue their own interests by performing a brokerage function.

However they pursue their own interests, intermediaries do so within the locus of the global/local interaction in the two-dimensional space represented by Figure 8.1. We hypothesize that mediation of a lopsided interaction (with a highly uneven balance of power) will work differently than that of a relatively balanced interaction. Balanced interactions offer more opportunities to intermediaries than unbalanced ones, which are primarily dictated by the dominant party. A rough balance creates more openness and prospects for intermediaries to shape the interaction and insert their own concerns. The other dimension matters as well. Distance determines the magnitude of the intermediation necessary to bring local and global into alignment. If intermediation is a kind of work or activity, then distance measures the opportunity to perform such work. Where local and global operate in close proximity, that is, where the distance is small, then less needs to be done to reconcile the two sides. But intermediaries will not necessarily possess the capacity to span large distances. Indeed, the finite capacity of intermediaries sets a limit on the kinds of distances they can cover and creates opportunities for chains of intermediation. Insufficient capacity will undermine their ability to perform or to monopolize the work of mediation. In such cases, mediation is either shared or performed incompletely, so that either the local cannot be fully brought to global standards or the global isn't completely localized (and hence a global/local gap remains).

Yet scholarship on "mapping the middle" remains quite sparse (Merry 2006). We know too little about ways that IOs span the gulf between global centers of power and national capitals. Who are the intermediaries on whom IOs rely to diagnose the problems in developing countries? How do IOs solve problems of agency and control in executing their plans? How do national governments obtain the expertise and authority to obtain or counteract the influence of IO intermediaries? In short, how is the incipient tension mediated between the global and the local? And by whom?

We shall first unpackage the fraught connotations of "global" and "local" before turning to the attributes of global scripts and types of intermediaries, both of which significantly influence the negotiation of the global/local encounter. On this basis we turn to analyze systematically and in detail the mediating agents between the IFIs and Indonesia, Korea, and China. We demonstrate that the structure and dynamics of intermediation vary by the cultural proximity and asymmetries of power that characterize a given state's relationship to the global. Paradoxically, given the potential consequentiality of national conformity with global norms, we show how much reform turns on so few mediating actors—how narrow is the channel through which the global/local reformist encounters flow.

The Global and the Local

Analysis of intermediation is complicated by the conceptual and empirical imprecision of "global" and "local." Intermediation implies an interstitial structural location, but between what? While the shorthand of "global" versus "local" offers a convenient binary classification, the distinction is fraught with difficulty. Insofar as it appears to differentiate sharply two poles of social organization, and to maintain a fiction that the global and local are themselves unitary, the usage can obscure rather than reveal the intricacy of globalization.

To return to our conceptualization of the global in terms of structure and discourse (Halliday and Osinsky 2006), on the one hand, global institutions exhibit structural capacities for global reach. They have organizational mandates that extend to most or all countries, such as those of the UN, and organizational capacities that enable them to reach across the world in pursuit of their mandates. On the other hand, global actors sustain their expansive reach by discursive claims to universality. These claims rest upon ideologies (e.g., rule of law, human rights, free trade) that may be codified in conventions, model laws, UN declarations, global best practices, and evaluation instruments used by international development banks.

In the insolvency field, we have seen that the structure of the global in fact breaks down into several distinct types of organizations: international professional associations; international financial institutions, including both global and regional banks; international governance organizations; and international clubs of nations. Behind these lie some influential nation-states with global scope, such as the United States and Germany, and some other states with important regional influence, such as Australia, in Southeast and East Asia. We have argued that there are wide variations across these international organizations in their legitimacy, ability to develop global scripts, and capacity to obtain compliance by nation-states.

The local, too, is fraught with ambiguity. One danger is to assume that the local is equivalent to the periphery in the world system or to confine its use to developing nations. It is more defensible to begin with the premise that the national or subnational (municipal, village, tribe, professional association, firm, national network) of *any* country is local. "Locals" are found in the North and South. Using this logic, and to escape reification, Santos (2000, 2002) contrasts globalized localisms with localized globalisms. *Globalized localisms* represent the process whereby "a given local condition or entity succeeds in traversing borders and extending its reach over the globe and, in doing so, develops the capacity to designate a rival social condition or entity as local." In the development of global legal scripts, for instance, this process requires that scholars work backward to ask whose localisms are being globally institutionalized. In the case of insolvency law, the central principle of U.S. corporate bankruptcy law, the option that failing companies might be rehabilitated while under the protection of courts has permeated all global standards, and thereby a U.S. localism is globalized. *Localized globalisms* refer to what Merry (2005) calls indigenization, that is, the selective adaptation of a global ideal to a local situation. Hence, while Indonesia, Korea, and China will all admit to the reform of their law in conformity with the global norm of corporate reorganization, each of them has done so rather differently, whether in substantive and procedural law or in bankruptcy institutions in court or out of court.

In the development of global scripts, intermediaries from advanced countries with sophisticated bankruptcy systems—that is, locals from the North—exert more influence than their counterparts from developing countries—that is, locals from the South. Often they accomplish this through international associations of professionals who are called to assist global institutions in norm development. In the institutionalization of global norms locally, however, those intermediaries with loyalty to the nation-state and with influence in practice are likely to exert the greater influence. These intermediaries influence the pace, form, and substance of localizing globalisms.

Just as the global can be disaggregated into groups of not always consonant institutions, so, too, it is useful to unpack the local, especially when a tension between enactment and implementation helps explain the ultimate effects of the global/local encounter. Our attention to enactment in this chapter effectively means that the counterparty to the international financial institutions is not a generalized local but leaders of the nation-state. Government ministers, officials in the government bureaucracy, and sometimes senior judges are the ones who negotiate with their global counterparts. After the outcomes of those negotiations are enacted, however, the field of action shifts to implementation that is truly local—to the corporations, judges, lawyers, workers, and banks who are spread across the mainly urban centers of the country. The interests of state leaders and those of the corporate sector, banks, and workers are not necessarily consonant. In fact, we observe instances where global and nation-state officials join forces against local interests that are reluctant to comply with new regulatory regimes. And there are occasions when local groups, such as the Indonesian NGO, Center for Law and Policy, joins forces with the global to force the hand of nation-state officials. Similarly, academic drafters of the new bankruptcy law in China may invoke global norms and practices in order to push state law-drafting officials more closely to global norms. Thus, intermediaries bridge gaps between the global, nation-state, and truly local, although the last of these may be the most difficult to recruit.

We thus distinguish between the global, which itself may be differentiated into different fractions; the nation-state, which refers to leading officials and politicians from different branches of government; and the truly local, which includes all the actors who actually implement the law. In each of these cases—the global, nation-state, and truly local—we observe internal differences—struggles among global institutions for primacy in establishing the global "gold standard," struggles among government ministries, and struggles among local actors. These struggles get expressed in competing alliances that elide the categories of the global and local and render their relationships highly complex over time and across countries. In this chapter, while we continue to use the labels of "global" and "local" as a useful shorthand, for the most part we focus predominantly on that subset of the global that includes international financial institutions and to that subset of the local that involves officials of the nation-state. Where it is necessary to differentiate within the local between the nation-state and truly local, we do so.

Global Scripts

The negotiation of a settlement between global and local actors depends in part on the coherence of global norms. Does a single global norm exist, or are there multiple competing norms? If there is a dominant or sole set of global norms, has it been codified? And what role do local actors have in crafting these norms? Answers to these questions differentially affect the capacity of intermediaries to exercise more or less discretion and craftsmanship as they translate the global to the local. If a local intermediary has had a hand in crafting a global norm, we expect that there will be closer conformity of a subsequent reform in the intermediary's country to the global standard. If norms are not codified, and they are not manifestly responsive to problems in countries at the periphery, then intermediaries loyal to a nation-state may use the ambiguity to deviate from global standards.

We have shown that in the insolvency field regional and global institutions adopted increasingly convergent formalized scripts from 1999 to 2004 (Chapters 3 and 4). At the height of the Asian Financial Crisis in late 1997 and early 1998, however, no such script existed; not until two years into the reform cycles stimulated by the crisis were the ADB, World Bank, and IMF able to put on the table their respective norms. By 2004 UNCITRAL began to circulate drafts of its substantive Guide, although its emerging norms were already intimately familiar to drafters from countries such as Korea, whose delegate to UNCITRAL was a member of its national drafting team. The Guide was authorized in late 2004.

The variations in these global scripts available to nation-states during the critical reform window from 1997 to 2004 indicate several analytically distinct possibilities, each of which yields varying degrees of discretion to intermediaries.

1. Single-standard, fully explicated formal rules that exemplify the "best" alternative (in this case, what diffuses around the world is a highly formalized and fully articulated optimal version). In the insolvency field, UNCITRAL's Model Law on Cross-Border Insolvency (UNCITRAL 1999) best exemplifies this instance, for it is intended to be adopted in toto by nation-states, although in practice adopting countries have made amendments to it.

This alternative allows for the least discretion. It gives intermediaries little room for movement and requires of translation something closer to transliteration.

2. Minimum-standard, fully explicated formal rules (these set a standardized floor below which countries will not go, however they may exceed minimum standards to varying degrees if they wish). Certain Recommendations in the UNCITRAL Legislative Guide approximate this criterion. They take one of these forms: "if a nation chooses to have a law on 'x,' then it should have the minimal conditions of 'y'"; or "a nation should adopt this provision 'x' with the minimal conditions of 'y'" (Block-Lieb and Halliday 2006).

3. Menus of options, giving alternative viable ways to resolve a problem or meet a standard. The 1999 IMF Guide took this approach, but it has been greatly elaborated by UNCITRAL's Legislative Guide. Although the Guide discusses alternative approaches to each chapter of a bankruptcy law, it often proposes a single Recommendation. In cases where there are substantial differences among legal families that nevertheless conform to the overall objectives of the Guide, it presents alternatives, sometimes expressing a preference as to which is more desirable.

The second and third alternatives allow a moderate degree of discretion by intermediaries. They anticipate local variability and offer interpretive room for maneuver by local intermediaries.

4. General principles, to be specified or interpreted as appropriate (these set overall goals that can be implemented in different ways, depending on the local situation). The World Bank *Principles* take this form in theory,

although operationalization of these *Principles* is allegedly intended to deliver results more closely approximating the U.S. model (this claim has been made by countries under pressure by the World Bank to reform their laws in accordance with the *Principles*) (World Bank 2002).

This fourth form of global script permits the most local variation. It offers intermediaries considerable discretion and creation options in their translation of global principles to local adaptations.

Confronted with these alternative scripts, intermediaries in principle had the capacity to mediate four alternative outcomes to the global/local encounter (Merry 2005).

1. *Acceptance* occurs when there is a one-to-one correspondence between global scripts and national enactments. Common examples are adopting a UN Model Law in toto or ratifying an international Convention without reservations.

2. *Adaptation as replication* takes place when a global frame is translated into local guise without fundamental change in its primary goals or mission.

3. *Adaptation as hybridization* takes the form of a merger of global frames, goal, and mission, with local forms but in ways that are reducible neither to the global nor local.

4. *Rejection* occurs when intermediaries either are unsuccessful in bridging the gap or convince one or other of the parties in the global/local encounter not to pursue a reform. In these situations, intermediaries loyal to the nation-state seek to develop defenses, or to frame issues, in ways that justify a refusal to comply with a global norm.

Intermediaries

If intermediaries are integral to the encounters of the global and local, the primary challenge for globalizing international organizations is to find intermediaries that are competent, influential, and loyal.

First, international institutions and nation-states seek intermediaries with multiple *competencies*. The most important is legal or economic expertise in either the local situation or on global norms that are being applied to that situation. IFIs search for professionals with diagnostic capacities to analyze the current practice in an area of law, whether on its own terms or in relation

to other criteria, such as global standards or scripts. Further, such professionals, usually lawyers, contribute even more value when they have prescriptive
capacities, that is, they can translate the construction of problems in an area
of legal regulation into substantive, procedural, and institutional reforms and
demonstrate how they may be inserted into existing law or fit within current
institutional constraints.

Second, international institutions seek intermediaries with *powers* of several sorts. Perhaps the most important capacity of the intermediary is an
ability to bridge the ideological or cultural divide between the global and
local. This requires a translation of global scripts into frames that are legitimate, recognizable, and appealing to national and local parties (Merry 2006).
To indigenize a global script is no easy discursive task on its own terms, for
it demands a creative leap between that which purports to be universal and
that which in practice is very particular. The task is complicated because not
only is the linguistic equivalent of transliteration impossible but the process
of translation occurs in the midst of power struggles within and between the
global and local. So-called translation in fact becomes a negotiated settlement that will yield either greater conformity to global norms or greater deference to national norms. The power to craft a legitimate frame will be partly
determinative of related powers—to obtain agreement among actors whose
interests are not necessarily consonant, to facilitate enactment of the "translation" into formal law, and ultimately to smooth effective implementation
of the law.

Third, intermediaries differ in their *loyalties.* International institutions
seek loyal experts who are committed to global scripts and the ideologies of
global organizations just as nation-states want assurances that their advisors
will serve single-mindedly the causes advanced by national policymakers. But
a strict dichotomy between loyalty to the source and target greatly simplifies
practice. For an intermediary to be effective in application of global scripts
to a local situation, he or she must be thoroughly familiar with that situation with every likelihood that familiarity may carry with it local sympathies.
Conversely, for a local expert to be an effective advisor likely means that the
expert will be somewhat integrated into international networks of scholars
or practitioners or participate in international organizations with the likely
result that the local expert will be somewhat globalized. For this reason, the
power of intermediaries is ambivalent (Merry 2006). While they exercise the
power that accrues to knowledge brokers, they may also be considered double

agents (Dezalay and Garth 2002), not fully trusted by either side and thereby subject to manipulation and subversion by both sides.

In globally induced bankruptcy reforms we discover two principal classes of interaction that are challenged through intermediaries standing between the global and the local—the direct and mediated.

Direct interaction occurs when the relationship between a global institution and a national government proceeds without an intermediary. When an official from the IMF negotiates with the Minister of Finance in Indonesia or Korea, it may be done face-to-face. When the Government of Indonesia signs a Letter of Intent to codify the agreement between Indonesia and the IMF for financing, the relationship is also direct. Yet practicality makes it impossible for direct relationships to be the primary mode of interaction between the global and national in enactment of law.

Most often, the relationship between the global center and nation-state is aided by *first-order intermediaries*. These simultaneously have a direct relationship with the global center and with the local nation-state. Literally, they stand between the two negotiating parties and translate between them. For instance, in Indonesia the IMF hired an on-site manager who advised the IMF on reforms and monitored implementation.

A *second-order intermediation* occurs when intermediaries have direct contact with one side or the other but not both. They act as advisors or consultants to global or local officials or as negotiators with similar advisors on the opposite side. The drafting team created in Indonesia to draft amendments to the 1905 Bankruptcy Law comprised two nominees from the IMF and two from the Government of Indonesia. Each set of nominees acted as second-order intermediaries, engaging both in direct relations with its respective principal and in indirect relations with the other intermediaries' principal. Thus, the IMF nominees simultaneously acted to advise the Fund and to influence the Government of Indonesia indirectly through negotiations with its intermediaries. On occasion, second-order intermediaries who advise one or the other actor become sufficiently integral and trusted that they move into a first-order position.

Third-order intermediation occurs when intermediaries have direct contact with neither of the principals in the global/local encounter but affect the process of translation, enactment, and implementation indirectly. When international professional associations advocate their own norms or practices to local professional groups, or local professionals influence the thinking of first- and second-order intermediaries, or corporations engaged in restructuring affect the courts or local politics, they all exert an attenuated influence on the negotiation between the global and local, especially in the implementation phase.

Both individuals and organizations act as intermediaries. International financial institutions frequently employ individual consultants to appraise the adequacy or effectiveness of a country's legal system and to advise on remedies. The Asian Development Bank has regularly retained lawyer Ronald Harmer, the principal drafter of Australia's current bankruptcy law, to undertake technical assistance programs. The European Bank on Reconstruction and Development has likewise retained Harmer as a consultant, together with Neil Cooper, an English accountant and insolvency specialist who was a former President of INSOL. Organizations may also be retained or created. We shall later observe how nation-states hire foreign law firms to advise them on negotiations with IFIs. IFIs in turn may either form alliances with local NGOs, who operate as advisors or monitors, or may create organizations if a vacuum exists in civil society or the market.

The role of intermediaries varies in relation to their location in the cycles of lawmaking. We have argued that law reform frequently takes the form of recursive cycles driven from an initial reform of law-on-the-books to law-in-action and then back to corrective reforms of law-on-the-books. The recursive cycles are driven by four sets of dynamics that occur between enactment and implementation until there is some settlement or equilibrium.[2] Some actors in law reform are concentrated on one side or another of the recursive loop. Some straddle both sides. Although our focus here is primarily on enactment, it is helpful to set it in the context of implementation for two reasons. In each of the case studies, the reforms in fact comprise several cycles of law-on-the-books to law-in-action and back to further reforms via law-on-the-books. Just as everyday practice cannot be understood without knowledge of its formal framework, the politics of enactment grow directly out of struggles at the local sites of practice implementation.

The *politics of enactment* consist of ways that national authorities and local agents of implementation negotiate how closely a piece of legislation or regulatory package will adhere to global scripts. The politics of enactment are two-faced. One is shown to global institutions in direct negotiations that occur between a developing country and an IFI over financial support in return for law reform. The other turns to local political constituencies that may resent the terms of externally induced reforms and are responsive to local politics that may have little to do with insolvency as such. The difference between the two has been captured by the notions of symbolic compliance or decoupling.

The *politics of implementation* comprise the variety of ways that nations widen or narrow the gap between formally enacted laws and regulations and their application in everyday practice. Nation-states have adopted a variety of methods for foiling global actors (Halliday and Carruthers 2007a). Frequently resistance is more strategic during implementation because nation-states can fight more effectively on the local terrain where international institutions have less sway. These can take the form of deliberate resistance, or decoupling, where a nation agrees to pass a law that will satisfy its external constituencies (e.g., it is said that Indonesia would adopt any law to get money flowing back into the country in 1998) but then deliberately subverted it through non-enforcement or by failing to erect institutional mechanisms for its effective implementation (such are the weapons of the weak; see Scott 1985).

Some intermediaries, such as foreign law firms or even indigenous academics, will have a much stronger impact on the enactment side of the reform cycles; whereas others, such as industry, trade creditors, or professionals, may have more influence on implementation. The more completely intermediaries can stand astride both sides of the reform process, the greater their influence on the translation of the global to the local.

Globalizing the Local

In the politics of insolvency reforms the movement to globalize the local occurs by socializing individuals, facilitating contacts between international organizations and government agencies, and internationalizing local politics.

Socializing Individuals

In developing and transitional countries, a small number of privileged individuals are socialized into a more cosmopolitan sensibility and habitus through formal education. It is a well-established pattern for the children of indigenous elites in colonial societies to be sent to the metropolitan country for first or second degrees. The children of wealthy families in East Asia commonly are sent to Australia, Canada, the United States, and Europe for first degrees. In professional fields, however, it is more common for the initial professional qualification to be taken in the home country and for an advanced degree to be obtained in the North. Of the handful of Indonesian lawyers who aided the IMF in the drafting of the initial amendments, one key figure, Fred Tumbuan, had fluent English from years of study in Australia. A principal draftsman of all the Korean insolvency reforms has his primary qualifications from the preeminent Seoul National University and a master's in comparative law from the University of Michigan. Of the three scholars in the main drafting committee for China's insolvency reforms, one has had visiting appointments at Uppsala University and the University of British Columbia, another has a doctorate from Moscow State University, and the third has a doctorate in law from Japan.[3]

Qualifications get parlayed into memberships in international NGOs, participation in global networks, and visits and tours. Some of these follow from earlier contacts; others, from language facility. They are frequently reinforced by involvement in initiatives by global and regional institutions. Professor Soogeun Oh, a primary drafter of the Korean insolvency reforms, is thoroughly integrated into global networks through his membership in the prestigious International Insolvency Institute, based in Canada, his regular participation in the regional forums hosted by OECD, as an invitee to regional and global forums hosted by the World Bank, and as one of Korea's official delegates at the UNCITRAL Working Group on Insolvency. Professor Wang Weiguo of the Chinese drafting team has participated in regional research projects led by an Australian team, has traveled with multilaterally funded educational tours of Germany and Australia, and is one of the Chinese scholars most prominently featured in forums on insolvency hosted by the World Bank and OECD.

Conversely, individuals in globalizing societies become integral conveyors of the Northern "local" to the periphery. Their local standing becomes regionally or globally leveraged, often through the sponsorship of multilateral organizations. Three individuals exemplify this pattern in the insolvency field. Manfred Balz, a distinguished German corporate lawyer who served as General Counsel for one of Germany's largest companies, Deutsch Telekom, in the insolvency field is more notable as the principal drafter of Germany's sweeping reforms in the 1990s. Balz's avocation, however, was as a global consultant, roaming the world during his vacations variously drafting and commenting upon current and draft laws. Balz was a favored consultant for the IMF, for instance, as in the drafting of Cambodia's new law in 2003 and as an advisor to the IMF and indirectly to the Korean Ministry of Justice on Korea's new consolidated law in 2003.[4] An Australian, Ronald Harmer, established his credentials by chairing the commission that drafted Australia's strong creditors' rights regime in the 1990s. The Asian Development Bank has employed Harmer extensively from the mid-1990s consultations on China, through the late 1990s eleven-country evaluation, to a multicountry consultation at present. Since the Australian system strongly emphasizes creditor rights and gives courts less prominence in corporate liquidation and restructuring, Harmer's approach has affinity with the ADB's skepticism about relying too heavily on courts in Asia. Harmer has joined forces recently with Neil Cooper, an English accountant and insolvency practitioner, to undertake consultations for the EBRD in its twenty-six countries of operation. Cooper's credentials rest on his longtime leadership of the international federation of insolvency practitioner associations and his integral role in both the two main lawmaking initiatives of UNCITRAL.[5]

The local intermediaries from the North and South intersected. They attended regional and international conferences together. Harmer, Cooper, and Oh have all been delegates at UNCITRAL's Working Group on Insolvency. Balz commented on Korea's comprehensive bankruptcy law drafted by Oh. Harmer and Cooper have sat around conference tables in China with Professor Wang Weiguo on China's Draft Law. The 2002 OECD Asian regional Forum held in Indonesia brought together the Indonesian reformers together with Harmer, Cooper, Balz, Oh, and Weiguo.[6] While some of the insertions of locals in the global are self-generated, particularly at earlier career stages, others are enabled by global actors who constitute and reconstitute networks of locals from the North and South in one forum after another, whether it be in UNCITRAL meetings held in Vienna and New York; OECD forums held in Sydney, Bali, Bangkok, Seoul, New Delhi, and Beijing (OECD 1999, 2003, 2005, 2006); or World Bank forums in each region of the world.

From diverse points of origin, therefore, locals themselves become cosmopolitanized as they enter into an elite network of reformers authoritatively familiar with their national situations (often having "authored" those situations themselves) and broadly familiar with global trends and norms. These potential intermediaries with an authoritative foot in both the local and global are scarce and valuable. There are only two Koreans, Professor Oh and a Supreme Court judge, who are integrated simultaneously into the global networks and have high standing in their own country. There was no such person from Indonesia. And there are only two law professors, Wang Weiguo and Li Shuguang, who at once are integrated into international networks (Wang

Weiguo with the OECD and World Bank; Li Shuguang with the ADB, World Bank, and OECD) and were members of the Chinese drafting team. Because the intermediaries from the South are likely to be more loyal to their country than to international institutions, global institutions are at a disadvantage. However, it puts these individuals in a strategic position between the IFIs and nation-state to broker knowledge in either direction.

Contacts by Government Agencies
Government agencies vary in their proximity to the global. As might be expected from the pervasiveness of economic globalization, ministries of finance tend to have stronger global connections and are more familiar with economic ideologies propagated from global centers, whereas ministries of justice tend to be more local and less connected with international institutions. The IMF, which is a principal agent of economic reform in developing countries, has its primary correspondent relationship with finance ministries. These formal relations are solidified through personal careers as local economists serve in the IMF and former IMF officials return home to senior positions in the finance ministries.

Korea best exemplifies this pattern in the corporate restructuring reforms. The official in the Ministry of Finance and Economy (MOFE) who drove the 2001 Corporate Restructuring Promotion Act through the National Assembly was a former IMF staffer; and when MOFE wanted the IMF to exert some influence on the domestic scene, MOFE channeled its influence through a Korean economist on staff in Washington.[7] Interventions by the Asian Development Bank in China were entirely with the former State Economic and Trade Commission, which was responsible for all of China's state-owned enterprises, rather than the Ministry of Justice.[8]

Even when agreements between the IMF and national governments involve legal institutions and infrastructure, the primary coordinating ministry is the Ministry of Finance, not Justice. Indeed, the IFIs tend to think of justice ministries as regressive, conservative, and resistant to change. When the World Bank entered Korea at the height of the Financial Crisis in 1997 and early 1998, even the lawyers in the World Bank preferred to deal with MOFE since they saw the Ministry of Justice as part of the problem, not the solution. Moreover, since the legal departments of the IFIs are smaller by far than their staffs of economists, the openings for locals to serve within global institutions have been very limited.

In a comparison of the three Asian case studies, the most economically developed country, South Korea, has the closest ties between its finance ministry and the IFIs (Halliday and Carruthers 2004a). South Korea has a pattern of advanced professional education in the U.S. and other advanced countries undertaken by Korea's brightest graduates since the earlier 1990s, a strong status hierarchy in Korean education that links successful careers in Korea to graduation both from top Korean institutions and from elite overseas universities;[9] and a pattern of mobility between Korean think tanks and economic ministries, on the one side, and IFIs, on the other. Indonesia, by contrast, has a much more limited pool of foreign-trained economists, quite apart from lawyers, on which to draw. In the insolvency area we have identified no U.S.-trained economist or Indonesian lawyer in the front ranks of reformers. While China's earlier generation of senior government officials rarely had foreign qualifications, and ministry links to IFIs were few, that is rapidly being remedied. All higher-level officials, such as Directors-General of Legislation, will now bring to consultations with foreign experts their younger staffers with postgraduate qualifications from the U.S. or U.K. and who are fluent in English (or other Western languages).

"Internationalizing Palace Wars"

Dezalay and Garth (2002) argue that the politics of globalization frequently involve a selective engagement by local interests to appropriate the global in order to pursue local politics by transnational means. Rather than the global triumphing over the local, local groups in civil society, counterelites, or marginal segments of the state reach out to enlist the global in order to strengthen their internal political positions. Traces of this phenomenon can be observed in the Asian insolvency reforms.

The reforms in Indonesia well exemplify these contrasting narratives. From one perspective, the reforms stemmed from the projection of raw IFI power. Seemingly without financial alternatives, Indonesia embraced an IMF-led bailout in return for which Indonesia agreed to a long list of macroeconomic and institutional reforms, including substantive reform of its bankruptcy law, the creation of new debt-restructuring institutions, and the establishment of a dedicated Commercial Court that was intended to be modern, well resourced, competent, and clean. In this story Washington imposed a solution on a hapless Jakarta that lacked any capacity to resist.

A fuller version of events, however, recognizes a small law reform movement that had begun to grow among progressive officials during the last years of Suharto's authoritarian rule, and that drew support from a handful of academics at the University of Indonesia and a smattering of indigenous lawyers. In the mid-1990s, the World Bank sponsored locally driven research and an indigenously crafted report that recommended reforms in law, including establishment of a new Commercial Court. Later, on the eve of the Crisis and after Suharto's fall, USAID provided technical support to a bankruptcy initiative launched by a reformist cabinet minister. In this, a reform trajectory was already under way before the Crisis, and in each instance of local initiative its sponsors reached outside the country to draw upon external resources to strengthen a weak reform impulse. The Crisis served to inject urgency and provide external constraints that catapulted a weak reform movement into the driver's seat of political response to a desperate balance of payments situation. This second, amplified, Indonesian account thus views the coercion apparently exercised by the IFIs over the Government of Indonesia as a triumph for an indigenous reform movement that found an irresistible global ally to move otherwise inertial domestic politics. Global institutions were used to pursue a substantially local agenda that garnered support from progressive factions in the Government of Indonesia.[10]

Elements of a similar pattern can be observed in Korea. Before the crisis a macroeconomic report prepared for the MOFE by an American consulting firm, Booz-Allen, pointed to a looming cataclysm if Korea did not take drastic steps to restructure its banking sector, its industry debt overhang, and its state-driven economy (Booz-Allen and Hamilton 1997). Within the legal field modest reforms were already being mooted to make corporate reorganization law more efficient. The Crisis again provided a precipitating event to push each reform further, effectively appropriating politically weak internal reform impulses and giving them powerful external impetus. Again this story interprets the restructuring of relations among the state, market, and law less as a simple foreign incursion against a unified domestic resistance than an alignment of the global with a local progressive faction against the domestic protectors of the status quo. Yet this very alliance of global institutions with local reformers has been construed by its opponents as the "IMF Crisis," thus effectively abdicating domestic responsibility for the Crisis through the classic political maneuver of finding a scapegoat.

Therefore, to construe this globalizing moment in both Indonesia and Korea as a struggle between a monolithic global and local is incorrect. The politics of local and global alliances lead to cross-alignments where a local faction in favor of particular changes obtains an ally in global institutions just as other local factions either seek alternative foreign allies or engage in some kind of resistance. Marriages of convenience enable global actors that require local allies and local reformers that seek global leverage to find each other and wage common cause. An asymmetry often exists in these competing alliances, for in crisis instances one party to internal political struggles will be better able to harness the global to its purposes than another that relies on indigenous claims and legitimation for its preferred course of action.

Mediation of the Global and Local

The gap between the global and local—the area in which they intersect—is an arena of power. Into that arena move actors that mediate the relationship between the global and the local. We find that IFIs seek up to five types of intermediaries, each of which is intended to solve a different problem. For the insolvency reforms, we analyze who were the mediators in each case study, reflect upon the roles they were called upon to play, appraise their capacity to exert influence in either direction (i.e., localizing the global, globalizing the local), and identify the mechanisms they employed. We find that each country's situational context affects which kinds of intermediaries are available to IFIs.

Indonesia

Since in this case a wide gap existed in 1997 between the local and global, it follows that the intervention of the IFIs during the Crisis involved extensive efforts for global institutions to find local counterparts, partners, allies, and sources of information and political support. Yet precisely because the distance between Indonesia and the global center was so great, intermediaries with expertise on Indonesia were difficult to find, and questions of competency and loyalty were acute. And because the asymmetry of power appeared to be pronounced in favor of the IFIs, the mediation over enactment seemed destined to be undertaken on terms dictated from abroad.

In the insolvency field, the Government of Indonesia managed initial and subsequent relations with the IMF—the principal IFI—through negotiations between government finance and justice ministers and the lead IMF legal representative, Sean Hagan. Government ministers diverged over the scope and depth of reforms: the finance ministry was prepared to concede any law reform that would garner international financial support; the justice ministry remained substantially opposed to the broad sweep of reforms and yielded ground on enactment only to the extent necessary for a strategy to shift the battle against the global to the ground of implementation. However, the Government of Indonesia strengthened its negotiating position by hiring a leading American law firm that specialized in insolvency—Hebb and Gitlin of Hartford, Connecticut—to advise it in negotiations with the IMF. Richard Gitlin, the lead lawyer, had impeccable international credentials since he had served as President of INSOL and could engage the IMF with great authority.[11] After enactment of the first wave of measures agreed upon between Indonesia and the IMF, senior civil servants, such as the Director of the Jakarta Initiative (a new corporate debt-restructuring agency), dealt directly with the IMF and World Bank through formal reporting protocols and in periodic conferences about insolvency in Asia where senior Indonesian civil servants and IFI staff would participate.[12]

On the IFI side, the Crisis in Indonesia required rapid action from the IMF and World Bank in particular to get their own personnel on the ground in Jakarta while finding Indonesian counterparts on whom they could rely for local knowledge and connections. The principal World Bank employees were Douglas Webb, a New Zealander from the Legal Department, and Gerry Meyerman, a Canadian businessman at the Private Sector Development Group at the Bank. Meyerman focused on out-of-court mechanisms for corporate debt restructuring that the Bank had used in other crises; Webb attended to the legal and judicial sides of reform. An advantage to the World Bank was that its International Finance Corporation, a private investment arm of the Bank, had an office and long experience in Jakarta; thus, the Bank had immediate access to Bank employees, mostly expatriates, with extensive local knowledge about corporate investment. The Bank had a further advantage because it had funded in the mid-1990s an Indonesian-led research and reform effort that produced a Report (Bappenas 1998) whose recommendations were salient to the interests of the IFIs, such as the creation of a specialized Commercial Court. Thus, the Bank had Washington and Jakarta employees as well as extensive local contacts through the Bappenas project on whom it could call. Further, USAID had also been active immediately before the Crisis in drafting a new bankruptcy law, so the resources and contacts of yet another U.S. agency were available.[13] The IMF by contrast had few local contacts. Yet, after a brief struggle between the IMF and World Bank over who would lead the insolvency reforms, the IMF triumphed as the lead IFI, not least because it effectively brought on board the team of Indonesian reformers who had led the 1996 Legal Assessment Diagnostic and Bappenas Report.[14]

The immediate reforms of Indonesian insolvency law in early 1998 were drafted by a small group whose members were nominated by both Indonesia and the IMF. A Coordinating Minister and Cabinet Secretary nominated two distinguished Indonesian lawyers. Kartini Muljadi had created a very successful commercial law firm that purportedly handled much of President Suharto's personal commercial interests. Fred Tumbuan had a small but distinguished commercial law firm and a strong reputation as "clean." Both the Government of Indonesia nominees previously had worked on the USAID draft bankruptcy law, so they were effectively moved sideways from one Washington-funded reform effort to another. On its side the IMF nominated Mardjono Reksodiputro, the Law School Dean and a name partner of the firm that had produced under contract the Bappenas Report on justice reforms.[15] The IMF was also advised by two lawyers who performed a strong bridging function: Jerry Hoff, a Dutch lawyer with experience in Indonesian and Dutch insolvency law and practice, who could intelligently fuse the best of Dutch insolvency innovations into the 1905 Dutch colonial insolvency law; and Greg Churchill, an American partner of Mardjono's firm who had extensive practice in Indonesia and who could "translate" for the IMF negotiator concepts in American bankruptcy law that might be salient (or not) for Indonesia and consistent with Dutch/Indonesian law and practice. Over three weeks of intensive work, this small group worked together with IMF counsel to hammer out a reform program that could be incorporated into the first Letter of Intent signed by the Government of Indonesia and the IMF.[16]

We have seen that the reform cycles continued for the next several years in a recursive process of enactment, incomplete implementation, and corrective amendments (Chapter 5). To monitor and advise on this process, the IMF hired a Dutch English-trained legal scholar, Sebaastian Pompe, who had written his doctoral dissertation on the Indonesian Supreme Court and had briefly practiced in Mardjono's firm until the Indonesian government in 1996 forced him to leave the country because it disliked the results of his research. Pompe knew the justice system intimately but had the added perspective of an outsider.[17]

For the first two years, the IMF had no ties with domestic NGOs, even though such a partnership might have been productive and legitimating.

Indonesian NGOs were extremely loath to be seen to be associated with the Fund, and some were ideologically opposed to it. After 2000, however, some NGOs accepted IMF funding when it coincided with their own domestic and civil society agendas, although with caution and reluctance. A mutuality of interest enabled a limited low-profile partnership. In addition, civil society initiatives, such as the establishment of a team—the Team of Seven—to scrutinize Commercial Court decisions, indirectly supported IMF interests in a viable court and an engaged civil society and profession to sustain it.[18]

The Indonesian case indicates that the wide distance between the IFIs and the nation-state required the constitution of several types of intermediaries to handle the problems of translation and enactment (Table 8.1).

Bridging Experts. Experts who could perform a bridging function of mutual translation among the key legal systems in play. They included the Indonesian, Dutch, and American systems. The lead IMF lawyer believed that competency in the Dutch system was necessary because the insolvency law was derived from Dutch colonial law,[19] and because the IMF needed to know what current Dutch law and practice would meet IMF standards and yet be readily grafted into the Indonesia law.[20] The IMF lead lawyer therefore brought an unformalized global script, based on the IMF's accumulated experience, to be negotiated with the purveyors of three national scripts—those of Indonesia, the U.S., and the Netherlands. In principle, these translators might equally well have been Indonesian nationals with extensive legal experience in the Netherlands or the U.S.[21]

Indigenous Expert. An indigenous expert who was at once authoritative in his advice to the IMF and legitimate within his own country. That is, the IMF needed to be confident that an expert with views that fell within the parameters of the Fund could advise it on courses of action that his *professional* credentials would guarantee were juridically defensible and practically feasible and that his *political* sensibilities would suggest were enactable. The IMF's bargaining position would be enhanced if its indigenous intermediary had high local cultural capital, and the prospect of reaching an agreement eased if the IMF's indigenous representative had high status in the view of the Government of Indonesia's drafters. Mardjono's credentials appealed to the IMF because he had high local status (as Dean of the Law School), knew commercial law and practice from experience (he was the partner of a prominent local law firm), came recommended by a trusted American, had a track record in legal diagnosis

TABLE 8.1 Cross-National Comparisons of Mediating Agents for International Organizations in the Globalization of Insolvency Reforms

	Indonesia	South Korea	China
Bridging Experts[a]	Dutch and American consultants	Domestic experts Law firm consultants	Domestic consultants
Indigenous Experts[b]	Indonesian legal academics and commercial lawyers, national and expatriate	None	Law professors
IFI On-Site Manager[c]	Present: Dutch specialist on Indonesian courts World Bank/IFC office in Jakarta	Not present	Not present (World Bank office in Beijing)
Domestic Constituencies for International Institutions[d]	Quite limited	Limited	Very limited
IFI Political Sponsor[e]	None	Ministry of Finance and Economy	Limited (Finance and Economy Committee, National People's Congress; State Economic and Trade Commission)

SOURCE: Adapted from Carruthers and Halliday (2006).

NOTES:

a Experts who could perform a bridging function for IFIs of mutual "translation" among the key legal systems in play.

b An indigenous expert whose advice to IFIs is authoritative and legitimate within the expert's own country.

c An on-site manager/monitor/advisor with unquestioned commitment to the IMF or other IFI.

d Domestic constituencies committed to monitoring, intelligence, and lobbying IFI-led or aided reforms.

e A powerful political sponsor.

and prescription (i.e., in the Bappenas Report), and had a positive record of working with multilaterals (in the Bappenas Report).[22]

On-Site Manager. An on-site manager/monitor/advisor loyal to the IMF. Since the IMF had no equivalent of World Bank staffers resident in Jakarta, its Legal Department decided it needed a resident manager both to facilitate and monitor implementation and to feed those experiences into subsequent rounds of corrective law reform. This could be achieved in two ways. By appointing a foreigner, the IMF protected itself from the chance that nationalist identity might compromise the quality of work or that national connections might be used to compromise reports and recommendations. By placing a manager on the IMF payroll, the Fund increased the probability that its agent's primary occupational commitments were to its principal. Both steps also helped ensure integrity, an element of character commonly under assault in Indonesian commerce and politics. A foreigner who was also fluent in Bahasa Indonesia and thoroughly familiar with the evolution of its court system could also provide some authority for the IMF's institutional analyses and recommendations. All these moves, however, needed to be reconciled within the same manager who had strong ties and sympathies with those Indonesian reformers who saw the IMF as the leverage they needed to effect their indigenously generated goals.[23]

Domestic Constituencies. The functions of domestic monitoring and social control, domestic intelligence, and domestic lobbying all add up simultaneously to localize and indigenize the global while allying with local actors whose interests coincided with those of the IFIs. If groups are already in existence, and foster programs consistent with IMF goals, then the IMF may seek ways to work through those that are willing and in parallel with those who resist a direct IMF connection.[24] The IMF, for instance, appeared perfectly happy to engage the Team of Seven's activities alongside its own court-monitoring apparatus. And if there is an institutional vacuum, then it will push for the establishment of such institutions, as we observed in relation to the insolvency practitioners' profession (Chapter 5). Yet the capacities of all these actors were limited. Their mechanisms of analysis, monitoring, publicity, lobbying, and informal regulation were manifestly overwhelmed by stolid political resistance, enormous commercial counterpressures, and a quiescent professional community.

Political Sponsor. A powerful political sponsor. Ideally, an IFI seeks an internal political ally—a minister or government department—that has the willingness and ability to navigate the difficult shoals of local politics and carry the reform program through to enactment and, most important, to implementation. In Indonesia the IMF never did find an enduring partner with the political will and capacity to execute the letter and spirit of the IMF/Government of Indonesia agreements. It appeared that the Minister of Justice showed little interest, even resisted, the reforms; and the finance ministries, where the IMF usually has most sway and affinity, seemed neither willing nor able to push reforms forward.

At the formal enactment stages of the reform cycles, the translation process yielded what Merry (2005) calls replication rather than transliteration, hybridization, or rejection of the global norms. In substantive, procedural, and institutional reforms, the Indonesians either directly imported changes or modified them only enough to be adaptable to local circumstances while satisfying the broad goals of the IMF. However, we shall see later that translation also occurs informally and in the recursive phase of implementation. There a different outcome prevailed. Indonesia also was confronted with changes in the scripts available to it. During the Crisis in early 1998, no formal document existed against which Indonesia's system could be appraised or its reforms calibrated. The IMF relied on an unformalized protocol that it had developed on an ad hoc basis in other crisis situations. Discussions about the IMF's expectations and Indonesia's response began initially in a very small circle of direct and indirect contacts. By the time that the OECD began its annual forums on Asian Insolvency Reform in 1999, the World Bank *Principles* had become available in an early draft. From that time forward both Indonesian and foreign experts were able to compare and debate progress in Indonesia implicitly or explicitly in relation to the World Bank *Principles*, a matter of no small consequence since the IMF was constantly monitoring conformity to its own norms and Indonesia's commitments from 1999 to 2004 as a condition of its continued structural adjustment loans.[25]

Korea

Whereas a large gap existed between Indonesia and the global center, and the balance of power favored global financial actors, the Republic of Korea stood much closer to the global centers, and the balance of power was much more even. In Asia, Korea has a former colonial and strong trading relationship with Japan, the world's second-largest economy. In its relationship with the United States, Korea occupied a key geopolitical position in the Cold War and thus came to have its military, economy, and higher educational systems closely integrated with those of its Cold War protector. And Korea in 1996 was admitted to the OECD, the world's premier club of rich nations.

When the Crisis hit in late 1997, Korea's relationships with IFIs, such as the World Bank and IMF, were handled by the powerful Ministry of Finance and Economy, which had been the technocratic driver of Korea's economic miracle. While it was obvious that this relationship would obtain for macroeconomic and structural adjustments to economic institutions, it also held for legal reforms. The principal World Bank lawyer in the first intervention teams, Douglas Webb, made MOFE his primary counterpart in substantial part because the Ministry of Justice was considered weak and reactionary. Similarly, Gerald Meyerman, who weeks previously had also been part of the Indonesian crisis team of the World Bank, dealt directly with MOFE. Neither the World Bank nor the IMF had offices in Korea since it had graduated from its status as a developing nation in need of foreign aid.[26]

The closeness of Korea to the U.S. changed the structure of mediation between the global and local. Within MOFE, representatives of the IFIs could find economists trained in exactly the same prestigious economics departments in the U.S. as the best and brightest recruited to the IMF and World Bank. Dr. Yangho Byeon, a senior MOFE official who presided over drafting and passage of the 2001 Corporate Restructuring Promotion Act, had himself been an IMF staffer in Washington. The theories and practices of neoliberal economics prevailing at the Bank and Fund were entirely familiar to—if not entirely practiced by—Korean technocrats at the Ministry of Finance. They talked the same language and understood each other. In other words, the global had been internalized within the local in theory if not entirely in practice.[27]

Moreover, Korea had developed a sophisticated cluster of government-funded research institutes that enabled the IFIs to diagnose quickly and efficiently the deficiencies in the Korean bankruptcy system. For example, the efficiency measures introduced into the 1998 insolvency amendments by agreement between the IFIs and Government of Korea came originally from proposals generated before the Crisis by the prestigious Korea Development Institute, which housed some of the nation's leading economists. Later insolvency reforms to speed up the handling of cases relied on research undertaken by Korean scholars and the Korean Economic Research Institute.[28]

On the law side, the IFIs proceeded initially through MOFE to bring on board the Ministry of Justice, which created its own drafting teams. Later the IMF and World Bank dealt directly with the Ministry of Justice, although MOFE always hovered in the background and was always ready to exert pressure on the Ministry of Justice to deliver whatever agreement MOFE had concluded with the IMF.[29] The legal mediators on the Korean side functioned *within* the Ministry of Justice and not in direct relationship with the IFIs, as had been the case in Indonesia. Partly this was possible because the drafting teams themselves included key members whose own biographies assured the IFIs of their familiarity with foreign, and especially American, law and practice (which most closely approximated IFI global norms). In addition to Professor Soogeun Oh's international credentials, Yong Seok Park, the only practicing lawyer also on all the reform committees, has economics and law degrees from Korea, advanced training at Harvard Law School, and six months of practice in a major New York law firm. Although their proposed reforms from 1998 to the present all went back to the IMF in Washington for comments, they were drafted at arm's length from the IFIs.[30]

Where further expertise was needed, the Ministry of Justice retained two leading law firms to advise on the reforms of insolvency law: Kim and Chang, a distinguished Seoul law firm; and Orrick and Harrington, a New York firm. The recommendations of these firms were debated and selectively adopted by the Ministry of Justice in association with a technical assistance project of the World Bank. When the IMF needed further advice on the draft legislation produced in response to those recommendations, it turned not to a Korean specialist but to its longtime consultant, Manfred Balz, whose annotated comments on the draft eventually ended up on the desk of the Minister of Justice.[31]

The structure of mediation in Korea therefore differs markedly from that of Indonesia because greater competence and common professional backgrounds in the former assured the IFIs that Korea could be delegated more discretion to draft its own reforms in response to general goals agreed upon by the IFIs and Government of Korea. Consider again the roles that intermediaries played in this distinctive situation.

> *Bridging Experts.* The IMF or World Bank in Korea had less need to retain experts who could perform the bridging function among the key legal systems in play. Those experts already existed within Korea because they integrated within their own biographies a familiarity with the two most salient legal systems and IFI global norms. Since Korea's bankruptcy law was partially based on earlier U.S. law via Japan, IFIs found it much more familiar to U.S. lawyers.

> *Indigenous Expert and On-Site Manager.* Since the IFIs were persuaded early in the reform cycles that Korea would comply with its agreements for insolvency reforms, and that the capacity of Korea to implement reforms could be relied upon given the sophistication of its professionals, neither the IMF nor World Bank felt any necessity to repeat in Korea what they did in Indonesia, namely, retain the services of an indigenous expert or hire an on-site manager with unquestioned commitment to the IMF.

Domestic Constituencies. In MOFE the IMF had a powerful political sponsor—indeed, the most powerful government ministry that had not only great influence inside the government bureaucracy but long and deep ties with the heights of industry and especially the banking industry. Although the primary responsibility for the insolvency reforms moved over to the Ministry of Justice in the last several years of reforms, the IMF could still continue to rely on MOFE to bring pressure inside the government if progress was slow.

Political Sponsor. The international institutions did not find any need to build domestic constituencies since they believed they could attain their ends entirely through bureaucratic and, later, parliamentary means. Oddly enough, domestic constituencies in the bar and industry opposed parts of each of the reforms, but the IFIs relied rather on the political will of the government and the effective alliance of policy institutions (e.g., Korea Development Institute) and MOFE to overcome residual reluctance for change from the profession, courts, or Ministry of Justice.

Korea therefore exhibits a quite different pattern of intermediation from that of Indonesia. The IFIs retained no Koreans as bridging experts, indigenous experts, or on-site managers. In fact, they relied on direct relationships between the IMF Legal Department and the Ministries of Finance and Justice. While those departments retained their own advisors, essentially as second-order intermediaries, first-order intermediaries were absent. Essentially, the IMF relied both upon its assumption that translation was not a major problem because the Korean bankruptcy law looked close enough to U.S. law and upon the political will of Korea to ensure that a cross between replication and hybridization of the increasingly formalized global script would take place. In fact, Korea did not accept entirely the provisions of that script, most notably in refusing to accept a key procedural step in corporate reorganization.[32] It did yield on the IMF's repeated request that it combine its three bankruptcy laws into a single unified bankruptcy code.

China

Like Indonesia, China stood at some distance from the global center. Since China has never experienced a sustained Western colonial presence,[33] it has no inherited Western legal system to draw upon (although it does have an attenuated civil law heritage via Japan) or even a close relationship with a European country based on a colonial heritage, as does Indonesia or Japan (Lubman

1999; Potter 1999).[34] Thus, China was deprived of obvious foreign models to which it could easily turn so was placed even farther from the global centers than either Indonesia or Korea. And the recency of China's integration into regional and global markets and educational system meant that its penetration or awareness of global paradigms remained shallow. By the same token, distance from any particular center offered China a diversity of possibilities—with no sunk costs or predispositions, China could pick or choose the global centers to which it would orient itself in different spheres (e.g., commerce, science, education), which endowed it with some degrees of freedom. Moreover, the vast size of China's economy and its lack of reliance on multilateral financial institutions redressed the balance of power that in Korea and Indonesia substantially favored the global center. And significantly, China remained relatively immune from the Asian Financial Crisis, although its leaders were alerted to the dangers that could occur in modernizing economies.

With this configuration of a substantial gap between the local and global and a relative symmetry of power between the global and local, the pattern of global/local mediation should differ from the Korean and Indonesian cases. On the one side, China would need to assimilate the part of the global that advanced its local interests without needing to trade off so extensively its national singularities. On the other side, global institutions sought means of engaging and enlisting the nation-state without the ability to exercise the financial muscle available to them in the crisis countries of Korea and Indonesia.

In the 1990s China approached the global for selective incorporation of foreign ideas and practices into China's law and practices, but it has done so experimentally and incrementally. We have seen (Chapter 7) that it occurred on two tracks.

The first, a set of reforms undertaken by the former PRC ministry responsible for state-owned enterprises (the State Economic and Trade Commission),[35] brought China to the IFIs for technical advice. The SETC commissioned several reports and recommendations from the Asian Development Bank.[36] In these cases, the mediating personnel on the ADB side were principally ADB staffers and foreign consultants, most notably Australians Ron Harmer and John Lees, a longtime Hong Kong insolvency practitioner and, later, the President of INSOL. Their position allowed them to inject into the Chinese bankruptcy debates a vision of a regime that would rely more on an insolvency practice profession and less on courts, a model that was congenial to the Asian Development Bank and different in emphasis from that of the Washington-based IFIs. They played the mediating role judiciously, for at once they advocated that China adhere to various global standards and international norms and conceded that in certain matters China would need to go its own way.[37] In these studies the ADB consultants found Chinese counterparts as informants on Chinese law and practice, including legal academics from Beijing.[38]

Later the SETC invited a World Bank team to provide a further analysis that was published in 2001 (World Bank 2001). In this case the Bank relied heavily on its own economists and, to a lesser degree, lawyers, both in Washington and its large office in Beijing. The Bank could further rely on two different types of "locals" to help ensure an indigenous adaptation of the global. American William Mako, a World Bank employee resident in Beijing, came to Chinese reforms from an extensive tour of duty, including negotiating the corporate restructuring conditionality for the $2 billion adjustment loan in Korea, advising the Bank of Thailand on its corporate restructuring program, and advising Turkey and countries in Central Europe and the former Soviet Union on measures to alleviate corporate distress resulting from financial crisis.[39] Mako combined broad global experience with short-term local exposure. The Bank complemented this expertise with the obverse configuration—a PRC-trained staffer with extensive foreign education. Zhang Chunlin had economics training in China, an advanced degree in Soviet and East European Studies from Glasgow University, and advanced training at Oxford University. Before his tenure began with the World Bank in 1999, he had worked in the SETC—that is, the very government ministry most implicated in IFI consultations on the privatization of Chinese state-owned enterprises. The Bank hired two outside consultants—a law professor from the China University of Politics and Law (Beijing), Li Shuguang; and a Chinese finance specialist, Wu Yalin, with Lloyds, the diversified U.K.-based financial services firm.[40]

China's second track of reform, and alternative tactic for obtaining access to the global, began with the decision of the National People's Congress in 1994 to draft a comprehensive bankruptcy law. The small core drafting team included three law professors who performed a boundary-spanning role from the Chinese side.[41]

Professor Wang Weiguo did his legal training in a provincial university and now chairs the Department of Economic Law at China University of Politics and Law in Beijing. Since his formal training, he has had extensive contacts with Western institutions, with some as an arbitrator and with others as a visiting professor, for example, at Uppsala University (Sweden) and the

University of British Columbia.[42] He also has strong contacts with Australian insolvency scholars with whom he has collaborated on comparative research. Li Yong Jun, also a professor at the China University of Politics and Law, has a degree from Shandung University and was slated to do postgraduate study in the U.S. on a Fulbright program. Tiananmen Square and 1989 intervened, Fulbright pulled out of China, and he went instead to the Soviet Union to take a doctorate in debtor-creditor and contract law. Dr. Zou Hailin joined from the Chinese Academy of Social Sciences. After his academic training at prestigious Peking University and the Chinese Academy of Social Sciences, he spent two years in the United States. Later these were joined by Professors Wang Xinxin (Renmin University) and Li Shuguang (China University of Politics and Law). Li Shuguang had been a consultant to both the ADB and World Bank and had served coincidentally as a consultant to the SETC since 1993. While all his formal education has been within China, as a consultant he was sponsored for visits to observe the insolvency systems of Germany, Australia, and the U.S., three legal systems that essentially framed the conceptual universe for China.[43]

The infusion of global scripts into the Chinese reform process was channeled through three global actors. The Asian Development Bank advised government ministries responsible for state-owned enterprises continuously from 1994. In practice, however, its advice strayed beyond that narrow mandate to include all enterprises—private and state owned—and to encompass social security options and implementation and training, among others.[44] The World Bank has become directly involved only since about 2000. Its higher profile can be observed through the Survey published in its 2001 Report. A lower profile of suasion has also occurred through the Insolvency Initiative of the World Bank's Legal Department and its principles of effective and efficient insolvency regimes (1999, 2001, 2003). On at least one occasion the World Bank reviewed the latest Chinese bankruptcy draft against these global norms and met with the Chinese drafting committee in Beijing to review consistencies and discrepancies.[45] In 2006 the OECD hosted its Forum on Asian Insolvency Reforms (FAIR) jointly with the Government of China in Beijing and other IFIs, another opportunity for the latest draft of China's bankruptcy law to be compared with UNCITRAL's global script and the Legislative Guide and for Chinese officials to consider the structure of their emerging bankruptcy experience in relation to other reforms in Asia (Halliday 2006; OECD 2006).

The German aid agency GTZ might lay claim to the most effective technical assistance to the NPC through its long-standing program of technical assistance on economic law. We have seen (Chapter 7) that the GTZ chose a distinctive route to advice. Rather than seek to champion the virtues of German law, it took major successive drafts of the bankruptcy law and invited specialists from many legal systems to sit across the table from Chinese reformers and work their way systematically through the strengths and weaknesses of each section of the Draft Law. GTZ then provided a summary report that encapsulated the principal insights from the international experts and formulated them as recommendations. Together, GTZ averred, these represented principles of "those bankruptcy systems which are regarded as highly credible and efficient."[46] According to the informal scorecard maintained by GTZ, on balance its recommendations found their way into the law more often than not.

Therefore, the global institutions' entry into China was inhibited by a lack of financial leverage and a balance of power generally favorable to China. While China wanted and needed foreign expert advice, it wanted such advice on its own terms, spreading out the sources from which it accepted technical assistance and selectively adopting features in accordance with its own preferences. Again, consider the roles intermediaries have played in the Chinese case in contrast to those of Indonesia and Korea:

> *Bridging Experts.* Regarding experts to play a bridging function of mutual translation among legal systems in play (e.g., Chinese, civil law, Australian, U.S.), the IFIs relied almost entirely on consultants, but their expertise was almost always greater on foreign systems than China's indigenous system. This was partly a function of the limited experience that expatriates had with Chinese bankruptcy practice.

> *Indigenous Expert.* Regarding indigenous experts who might be authoritative with IFIs while legitimate in their own countries, Professor Li Shuguang was retained both by the ADB and World Bank as a consultant. However, his later position on the NPC Drafting Committee (from 2003) and as a consultant to SETC had him straddling both tracks of the Chinese reforms. The World Bank insolvency initiative and the OECD forums on Asian insolvency turned regularly to Wang Weiguo, together with Li Shiguang, both on the NPC Drafting Committee.

These alternative alignments between a particular local expert and an international organization reflect a more general pattern found in other countries—that the IMF, World Bank, or ADB enlist international and local consultants who are identified with a particular international institution and hence are faithful to its distinctive emphases. For international institutions, scarcity in the late twentieth and early twenty-first centuries is not of territory but authoritative expertise—a professional technical facility and bridging knowledge that are also accompanied by linguistic facility. For countries long outside the orbit of British or American influence, the number of professional experts with all the attributes of competency, power, and loyalty, as well as fluency in English, is few indeed. The competition between IFIs and aid programs for indigenous experts is similar in fashion to their competition for loyalty by the leading international experts.

> *On-Site Manager.* Since the IMF and World Bank in China did not have a sustained lawmaking and institution-building program that was linked to a structural adjustment program, as is the case in Indonesia, they had no need of a resident manager. A distant parallel in China might be the lighter touch of the German aid program GTZ, whose resident managers for the economic law program, Immanuel Gebhardt and Hinrich Julius, built up substantial local knowledge and contacts among the lawmakers in government departments and the NPC.
>
> *Domestic Constituencies.* Regarding domestic constituencies, because China discourages independent NGOs, it left IFIs no prospect for finding indigenous nongovernmental allies who might provide domestic intelligence or lobbying. Instead, IFIs must rely on relationships built with contesting government agencies or on factions within the top political leadership that find particular global scripts supportive of their factional preferences.
>
> *Political Sponsor.* In China the IFIs did not find a powerful political sponsor in any internal political allies unequivocally committed to carrying the draft comprehensive law through the NPC into enactment and implementation. By contrast, one or two individuals (or groups) with a veto blocked advancement of the legislation over several years. At most it could be argued that progressive forces within the SETC used foreign legitimation to force reorganization of the state-owned enterprise sector in the face of steadfast resistance by many local and provincial authorities. While membership in the WTO may be used to similar effect in other areas of economic restructuring, the impact of entry into the WTO was attenuated in the insolvency field except for the pressure eventually brought by the European Union for a bankruptcy regime that protected European investments.[47]

The substantive movement in successive drafts of the bankruptcy law and administrative reforms from 1994 to 2004 can be characterized as a shift from translation as hybridization to translation as replication. For instance, earlier versions of the law allowed arbitrary interventions by the State Council in the resolution of bankruptcy cases in a manner that fell outside any version of global scripts. With the removal of this provision and the tightening of others, the World Bank (2001) and the GTZ pronounced that China's local script adhered sufficiently closely to the global script that it should be implemented.

Global Scripts and the Powers of the Intermediaries

We have shown that intermediation differs considerably by the situational vulnerability of nation-states. The gap was widest and the balance of power most asymmetrical in Indonesia, where the availability of experts was also most scarce and the perceived need for action was greatest. The most complex set of intermediating structures were put in place by the IMF. In Korea, by contrast, the ready availability of Korean academics, lawyers, and economists familiar with foreign and domestic situations, and the lesser urgency of reform, enabled the IFIs to take a more relaxed and less directive approach that could rely on domestic availability of expertise. Since protracted institution building was needed only in Indonesia's case, only Indonesia warranted an on-site manager to preside over reform cycles. In Korea the IFIs believed that the elite and sophisticated state apparatus could deliver the reforms agreed upon by the IFIs and the Government of Korea without intrusive foreign presence in Seoul.

Since all externally induced or supported reforms require effective domestic political constituencies, the variation across our cases is more complicated. Paradoxically, while by far the greatest volume of substantive and institutional reforms have actually been enacted or established in Indonesia, the wide gap between law-on-the-books and law-in-action and the need for repeated reform cycles reflect the almost complete absence of diverse domestic constituencies or strong political sponsors. But with much less external leverage, domestic constituencies and political sponsors for IFIs in China remained quite limited, as China's slow and experimental refinement of its administrative system and Draft Law well illustrated. Effectively, China can manage foreign and international influence on its own terms, for the most part keeping enactment at bay until it is ready, whereas Indonesia proceeded substantially on the terms and timing of IFIs, using implementation—with slim domestic sponsors and tepid political will—as its only option for keeping unwanted global incursions at bay. In Korea the IFIs had a ready and powerful partner, but foreign influence was contested internally as the lawyers and economists struggled over the role of law in the reconstruction of Korea's markets. Both China and Korea shared endogenous reasons for reform, although they managed external pressures and resources rather differently. Korea's weakness during the Asian Crisis enabled the IFIs to penetrate more deeply into its endogenous lawmaking process, a vulnerability to which China was much less exposed.

Between 1998 and 2004 the insolvency field moved quickly from a situation where there were no formal global scripts, to a multiplicity of alternatives, to the single prescriptive standard promulgated by UNCITRAL's Legislative Guide on Insolvency. The diversity of global norm makers and the status of scripts available to nation-states and truly local actors set constraints on the role of intermediaries.

First, where there are multiple actors and no formal scripts, intermediaries have more degrees of freedom, other things being equal. Global actors have less discursive power and weaker legitimation because their proposed reforms in the name of the universal can actually be construed as particular to a given global institution.

Second, where there are multiple actors and multiple formal scripts, then the discursive and structural elements of globalization change, other things being equal. Insolvency scripts varied in form. Each gave intermediaries differing degrees of discretion in translation. Intermediaries acting on behalf of nation-states can compare and contrast, play off one against the other, or be empowered by the realization that a global consensus does not exist on all points, and thus undermine claims to universality from the global center. For instance, a leading Korean draftsman refused to include in the Korean bankruptcy law an automatic stay on application by a firm for bankruptcy protection. This is preferred in the World Bank *Principles*, but as a delegate to UNCITRAL Professor Oh knew full well that its draft gave lawmakers options and UNCITRAL could claim a global consensus that the World Bank could not. The capacity to play off one script against another depends on other factors. Korea in 2005 had paid off its debts from the Asian Financial Crisis, IFI leverage was diminished, and a new universal global script had emerged from the UN whose form and substance gave considerable flexibility to lawmakers.

Third, competing scripts from competing global actors might have a quite different effect. The existence of multiple models and paradigms makes it easier to create hybrid forms with creative alternatives, a process akin to bricolage (Campbell 2004). In its insolvency lawmaking, the Chinese took advantage of this multiplicity of alternatives coming from different international agencies and nation-states.

Fourth, where there are multiple global actors who reach consensus on a single global script, such as UNCITRAL's Legislative Guide, then the implications for intermediaries on both sides are quite complex. A single legitimate global standard appears to empower global actors and their agents and diminish the freedom of translation by those intermediaries loyal to nation-states. Yet insofar as intermediaries from developing nations had a hand in creating the global script, the global/local difference was already blurred; thus, the intermediaries themselves can no longer be so clearly identified with one or the other. More important, the form of UNCITRAL's Legislative Guide managed to converge on higher-order objectives and many substantive and procedural recommendations while still leaving considerable discretion for national lawmakers to indigenize the global norms in replicated or hybrid forms, as China manifestly has done.

In the insolvency field, however, together with many other areas of commercial law, recall that there are in fact *two* types of global script (Chapter 4). On the one hand, there are the descriptive/prescriptive codes represented by the IMF, World Bank, ADB, and UNCITRAL documents. On the other hand, the invisible diagnostic tools used by the global and regional financial institutions are devised and applied by a handful of IFI staffers and consultants. There is of course a contingent relationship between these two scripts. The ROSC on insolvency has now been brought into conformity with the Recommendations of UNCITRAL, and any serious lapses in a nation-state's conformity with the norms evaluated by the diagnostic instrument leads back to the relevant Recommendations in the Legislative Guide. Conforming a nation's laws to these Recommendations improves the good standing of a nation-state with IFIs, should it in the future require technical assistance, loans, or investment.

The evolution of the insolvency field therefore substantially blurred the global/local dichotomy. It consolidated the link between a normative consensus and enforcement or tangible incentives, legitimated some freedom of translation by intermediaries, and even tolerated hybrid adaptations that advance the highest-order objectives of the UNCITRAL Guide. In private

negotiations between state officials and IFI representatives, or in public forums such as international conferences, the negotiation of globalization turns
on the capacity of officials directly or through intermediaries to agree on
whether a local translation conforms to a global script or whether a hybrid
solution advances the spirit of global consensus.

Collective Intermediaries

In the international division of labor over global norm making, there are not
only "model-mongers," as Braithwaite and Drahos (2000) picturesquely put
it, but "model missionaries"—those organizations that do not develop norms
themselves but leverage the norms of others. We saw implicitly that the European Bank for Reconstruction and Development (Chapter 3) did not formulate its own codified prescriptive norms but relied on its practical experience
and the norms of others. A rather different role in this international field was
played by a unit of the OECD based in Paris.

A small unit within the Directorate for Financial and Enterprise Affairs
widened the Directorate's long-standing international leadership on development of corporate governance norms by arguing that the incentive framework
for all the stakeholders in business enterprise is affected by the mechanisms
available in a society to exit from the market. Hence, the OECD also should
be interested in insolvency regimes. The OECD had been involved episodically in Central and East European reforms after the collapse of the Soviet
Union. With the Asian Financial Crisis it decided to enter the norm-making
world of insolvency on a different tack to those taken by the international
financial institutions.

The OECD unit had a very limited budget, no deep pockets for technical assistance, and no staff resources that could be dedicated to insolvency
alone. Nor did the OECD have any financial leverage over developing and
transitional countries. How then could it insert itself into the global matrix of
organizations now intent on developing and diffusing norms for bankruptcy
regimes? Rather than compete with the World Bank, IMF, ADB, or EBRD,
it carved out a distinctive niche consistent with the OECD's activities more
generally. OECD experts do publish thorough analyses of national economies,
such as the OECD (1999) report on the Korean economy, and a subsequent
Survey of China (OECD 2005) exemplify. OECD groups do develop norms.
More generally, however, the OECD functions as a cog in the wheel of world

expertise on issues that affect economies. It brings together academic and scientific specialists with professionals, practitioners, and state officials on an array of standard-setting and evaluative activities.

It was in this vein that the OECD unit initiated its Forum on Asian Insolvency Reforms. The OECD proposed, in tandem with funding partners and national governments, to create an arena that did more than bring together experts. Optimally it would permit three kinds of globalization from "across" (Chapter 1). First, it could bring together potentially competitive international financial institutions on neutral ground to hear about each other's programs and to spread comity. Second, it could bring regional neighbors around a conference table to share each other's experience with problems of corporate reorganization. And third, it had the promise of bringing together the national officials who had begun or intended to institute reform programs with experienced lawyer-practitioners and, not least, IFI officials who were embroiled in regional reforms. The OECD relied on the application of a peer review approach to the diffusion of innovation. It argued for a tactical approach to legal change that relied on two kinds of persuasion: it was much more convincing to hear the experts of many jurisdictions experienced in bankruptcy reforms than to be exposed to programmatic imperatives from a single IFI; and it was more immediate and proximate to hear from one's fellow officials in regional Ministries of Finance and Justice, or from judges, or out-of-court bankruptcy administrators than to be lectured by specialists from countries far removed from the region.

The OECD therefore instituted a form of organizational intermediation where it sought to broker funding sources, global norm producers, government officials, and bankruptcy experts in a sequence of FAIRs, each one in a country where bankruptcy reform was an immediate issue. We have seen (Chapter 5) that the FAIR in 2000, held in Bali, became a critical debating ground between contending factions for legal change within Indonesia, a debate held in front of experts from across the world who effectively were drawn into taking sides, which ultimately benefited the IMF-Indonesian reform team. After a FAIR in Bangkok (2002), the third Forum took place in Korea on the threshold of passage of Korea's Unified Bankruptcy Act (Chapter 6). The FAIR in New Delhi (2004) intended to quicken the impetus toward India's own comprehensive reforms. This approach was even more pointed in the Beijing FAIR in April 2006, when the OECD and its organizational partners (World Bank, ADB, INSOL International, UNCITRAL), with funding from the Governments of Japan and Australia, joined with the Development Research Center of China with a hope of breaking China's draft Enterprise Bankruptcy Law out of what appeared to be a political deadlock in the National People's Congress (OECD 2007).

This series of meetings therefore had a capacity for collective intermediation at multiple levels: among IFIs, among regional reformers and officials, between IFIs and nation-states, and even among domestic factions within a reform process. All the leading experts on a country or a region would attend, many giving presentations, together with international experts. Hence another global/local encounter was facilitated in a regional mix where experience and expertise were more focused. The universality of the global became refracted through the immediacy of the regional and local—and, not least, when the aspirations of enactment were confronted with the realities of implementation.

Power and Intermediation in Implementation

In this chapter we have largely restricted ourselves to the politics of enactment and formal translation. However, the politics of enactment are interwoven with the politics of implementation in recursive cycles of legal change. Different actors and different types of intermediaries may be involved on either side of the reform cycles. In fact, it is usually the case in bankruptcy reforms in any country that key actors in implementation, most notably business, trade creditors, and consumers, are not directly involved in enactment, a mismatch that often leads to resistance in practice by those excluded from the formal lawmaking.

But as sociolegal scholarship conventionally asserts, "law" is law as it is experienced, not law as it is encoded in state documents. It follows that translation is not simply a matter of moving from a formal script codified by global agents to a formal script enacted through legislation, regulatory orders, or court cases. While translation can take the forms of formal replication or hybridization, it also takes on an informal character. Formal law may be implemented badly, by design or not. A new kind of truly local intermediary may emerge—the judge, a lawyer or accountant, corporate management, a government tax department—who uses the obscure site of a local court or out-of-court settlement agency to amend in effect or frustrate in result the global norms inscribed in national law. This may be done inadvertently, perhaps out of a simple incapacity to deliver what promises are encoded in formal law (Pistor and Xu 2003), or deliberately, as a political act to resist in practice what could not be defeated in the prior stage.

The opportunities open to these local agents, who are effectively renegotiating the shape of globalization on their home turf, are many. For instance, a country like China or Indonesia may simply not provide the court capacity to handle a substantial volume of complex cases. Or a newly minted structure for implementation, such as Indonesia's Commercial Court, may be staffed with inadequately trained and insufficiently protected judges. In other words, a global script may be adopted formally but indigenized compositionally, with the result that law as it is experienced deviates the further it is removed from global and nationally enacted scripts. This process of symbolic decoupling enables a government to signal to global actors its compliance with global norms, while quietly assuring its local constituencies that it has little interest or ability to comply with them in practice. Put another way, just as global scripts may differ in form and substance from each other, so, too, local scripts may vary between those enacted by the local nation-state and those implemented by the truly local practitioners of law in everyday life. This translation of the global will tend toward rejection or hybridization rather than acceptance or replication.

Informal translation in the implementation phase complicates even further the relationships between asymmetries of power, distance between the global and local, and the structure of intermediation and its outcomes. Once informal translation in implementation enters the analysis, the balance of power between the global and local must be differentiated more carefully. The balance of power will be most favorable to global actors at the point of enactment, but it tilts the other way in implementation. That is, countries that appear relatively powerless over enactment nevertheless have some power to shape implementation. Groups within countries that may be unable to block enactment can undermine or frustrate implementation.

Asymmetries of power influence intermediation depending on where the power lies between global centers, nation-states, and the truly local. If global institutions and nations are dominant, then the local will be pulled in the direction of the global, although how far depends in part on the distance to traverse and the ability of intermediaries to effect that shift. The pull will be stronger for enactment than for implementation. Moreover, a strong global influence will likely empower intermediaries with the global competencies and loyalties that are consistent with the global professional division of labor. In part, those competencies themselves result from spheres of influence in which nation-states have been embedded and, thus, their facility in languages and legal cultures that dominate in the center.

We have argued that a greater distance between the global center and nation-states requires more bridging work. Bridging opens up more structural paths for intermediation and creates more opportunity for multiple intermediaries and multiple intermediation strategies. This process helps explain why the IMF built the most complex of the IFI intermediation structures in Indonesia, for that country lay farthest in distance from global norms and practices. But distance is not "measured" only from a global center, such as IMF Headquarters in Washington and the finance ministry of a nation-state. While this is mostly true at the phase of enactment, even more important may be the distance between the UN in New York and those truly local actors engaged in implementation. While a greater distance of the nation-state from a global center should multiply opportunities for bridging work and the creative compliance of translation, the widening of that gap between the global and truly local also opens up the prospects for hybridization and effective rejection. In short, the degrees of freedom for how the work of liquidating and restructuring companies will be effective are greatest in the phase of implementation.

Our cases also suggest that where the global/local distance is great, and where the former has power relative to the latter, then the bridging work done by intermediaries will consist in a relatively straightforward translation of global institutions and rules into a local idiom for enactment. Global scripts will be given a local name or label and be subject to cosmetic alterations, but otherwise little will change. When the balance of power is a little more even, a more basic reworking of the global may be expected because there is a greater capacity for intermediaries to deliver a hybrid product or even reject parts of the global scripts.

The position of intermediary is a position of power. In all of our cases the most critical actors are professionals and, most important, legal professions. Since these professional mediators stand at the intersection of the local and global, they have a unique opportunity to shape the field of power in directions that benefit professional ideologies and interests. Just as economic actors struggle to obtain control over property rights, professions can use their integral role in lawmaking to obtain jurisdictional rights over work (Carruthers and Halliday 1998). Can this extraction of a "price" for the mediation between the global and local also be observed in Asian insolvency reforms?

In the translation of the global to national lawmaking scripts, the global universal of allocating insolvency work to qualified professionals also finds its way into the laws of Indonesia, Korea, and China. But which professions and which professionals? Advanced economies divide between those in which insolvency work is undertaken principally by accountants qualified as insolvency practitioners (e.g., Britain, Australia) or by lawyers who specialize in bankruptcy (e.g., U.S., Canada, and Continental Europe). At the outset of global norm making it appeared that a struggle between these two professions might break out as each laid claim to new domains of work. In fact, each profession came to realize that a division of occupational territory was unlikely to prevail on its terms and thus they advocated general norms (e.g., credentialing, regulation, competency) at the global level with the expectation that national histories and local contexts would determine outcomes nation by nation. Thus, the Indonesian lawmakers adopted the Dutch model of lawyers and accountants working as insolvency practitioners, the Koreans followed the U.S. model in which lawyers dominate, and China hedged by stressing the general norms without specifying them, despite the dominance of lawyers in the Drafting Committee.

The pervasiveness of lawyers as first- and second-order intermediaries can be observed in the centrality all three laws give to courts as the institutional locus of corporate liquidation and restructuring, an emphasis that echoes the importance of courts to two of the most influential delegations at the UNCITRAL negotiations, the U.S. and France. In this indigenization, intermediaries reflect global norms that also give courts centrality, although this institutional orientation is more emphatic in the earlier IMF and World Bank scripts than it is in the UNCITRAL Legislative Guide. The most striking case of intermediaries using their position as an opportunity for self-interested indigenization was that of Indonesia. We saw that international institutions sought to inject more expert services into Indonesian insolvency practice by opening up practice to Indonesian citizens and foreign professionals. Indonesia agreed with the IMF to do so, but in the implementation phase officials in the Ministry of Justice adopted regulations that required the qualifying examination be taken in Bahasa Indonesia. The result was to nullify almost entirely the goals of the IFIs. This translation as resistance by second- and third-order intermediaries again reinforces the point that implementation is a phase in which the imbalance of power at the point of enactment may be partially redressed.

In sum, even in a relatively confined space—one area of law in one region in one period—the process of negotiating globalization has proceeded in systematically different ways. Standing at the nexus of those negotiations are a quite small number of collective and individual actors. Their relative capacity to shape the encounter of the global with the local varied in some measure by the relative balance of power and distance between their nation-states and the global actors that drove legal change. Each locus in this space produced a different structure of intermediation that gave local actors differing degrees of freedom vis-à-vis the global centers.

9   Foiling

I F IFIs confront the challenge of intermediaries in global norm making, national lawmakers confront the threat that IFIs pose to their degrees of freedom in policymaking. Repeatedly political leaders and interest groups state a preference for discretion, some freedom of action, or adaptation in order to shape their relationships with global actors on their own terms. Whether this is seen as an issue of sovereignty, national integrity, self-determination, or pride, national actors characteristically resist the imposition of global norms that are not sensitive to national situations or responsive to national particularities or political sensibilities. Rarely can be found the local actor who subscribes entirely to the prescriptions of international organizations.

Local developing states that confront global institutions usually do so from a position of relative weakness. Tremendous power differences can exist between global and local actors, particularly at the height of a financial crisis. In these circumstances, reform of bankruptcy law in Asia since the Asian Financial Crisis presents a prime site for analysis precisely because the circumstances should have been optimal for effective transplantation and rapid convergence of local with global norms.

On the one side, nations such as Indonesia and Korea confronted financial meltdown and desperately required massive infusions of credit that they could obtain from no source other than international financial institutions. The IFIs were truly the lenders of last resort, not only for their own funds but for the guarantees they effectively provided to private lenders. On the other side, the world's financial powers could exercise maximal leverage as they controlled the conditions under which credit would flow. We have seen that the IFIs sought to sustain their direct leverage over country bankruptcy reforms after the Crisis through a variety of expedients, ranging from persuasion to assistance. Opportunities for economic coercion could not have been more intensive. IFIs can sustain leverage through sequences of conditionalities for subsequent loan disbursements, monthly or quarterly monitoring of progress, the setting of strict deadlines for reforms, and public shaming. In addition, the IMF has increasingly been using its mandated annual Article IV consultations on the economy of each country to put pressure on recalcitrant governments (Stiglitz 2002).[1]

Herein lies a puzzle. The enormous asymmetry in financial power presented conditions that were optimal for the adoption of transplanted law and institutions. The combination of external pressure and internal need should have ensured ready conformity with global models of bankruptcy law and institutions. Yet we have shown that the enactment and implementation of global norms in Indonesia, Korea, and China were neither smooth nor certain. Given the enormous coercive powers of global financial actors, why did the implantation of new bankruptcy regimes prove so difficult? Put another way, what capacities do national actors have to maintain some degrees of freedom, to compel IFIs to negotiate rather than to impose, to chart the course of their own future? Can developing nations foil the intentions of their powerful global counterparts?

It is a mistake, however, to assume that all local actors are bent on resistance to foreign interlopers. As Dezalay and Garth (2002) demonstrate for Latin America, frequently local political conflicts become internationalized because local reformist groups, political outsiders, or minority factions welcome overseas allies to strengthen their position in domestic political struggles. Indeed, government leaders themselves may quietly welcome foreign interventions that local politicians blame for domestic reforms they want to carry out and that otherwise would be politically risky. Foreign intervention can break political logjams and force deadlocked local interest groups to reach agreement. The capacity to foil, therefore, not only sets conditions for exchanges between the global and local but often expresses local political conflicts, as potential losers from foreign interventions mobilize their force to blunt overseas influence and potential winners seize the new opportunities that foreign intervention may offer them.

For reasons of international and domestic politics, therefore, we shall show that even in cases of extreme asymmetry of power, supposedly weak countries can foil financial hegemons. As we juxtapose the strengths of the weak and the weaknesses of the strong, it will become clear that the imbalance of power between the global and local is not nearly as unbalanced as may first appear. While the arena of enactment favors the global actors, the arena of implementation favors locals. Through adroit maneuvering and deployment of weapons of the weak, developing nations can retain substantial autonomy.

Transplants

Under circumstances of concerted global financial power, it should follow that mandated law reform, especially during national financial crisis, will be more readily adopted and implemented. Watson (1974) and his followers maintain that legal transplants can readily be lifted from one legal system and embedded in another. Since law has some autonomy from social and cultural institutions, it is portable, and commercial law more so than areas of domestic legislation such as family law (Harding 2002; Heydebrand 2002). If this is so in general, it should be even more the case under the extreme circumstances witnessed following the onset of the Asian Financial Crisis.

In addition to direct incentives, such as IFIs' withholding access to requisite capital if change is not implemented, there are also indirect inducements for foreign capital inflow. Some research indicates that countries adopting the property rights and corporate governance standards considered normative by creditor nations, and that are effectively enforced, attract significantly more foreign direct investment (FDI) or weather financial crises more successfully (Pistor et al. 2002; Pistor, Raiser, and Gelfer 2000). This creates domestic demand for laws that will speed the flow of foreign credit and is reinforced when IFIs press for changes that are consistent with the models or practices of the "suppliers" of a country's capital (Pistor 2000). Whether better law does increase FDI and subsequent economic development remains contested. Clearly, China, or the Asian Tigers before 1997, offer striking counterexamples. Countries manifestly lacking in the very rule of law championed by leading creditor

nations and IFIs nonetheless managed to attracted massive overseas investment. The statistical evidence also is far from definitive.

A substantially larger body of scholarship, supported by the indifferent
experiences of some of those global practitioners who must deal with transplants, remains wary—if not skeptical—of any assumptions that importation
and implementation of laws and institutions will be easy. While the debate
over legal transplants has been declared "tired and often confused" (Nelken
2002), new empirical scholarship in law and finance, heavily influenced by
the experiences of legal transplants in the 1990s, has reinvigorated work on
the concept. Initial work purported to show a strong empirical association
between property rights and economic development (Shleifer and Vishny
1997). It seemed a short step to conclude that the enactment of rights would
produce immediate, effective implementation; and in response, flows of capital, successful privatization, and emergence of effective corporate governance
regimes would follow.

More sophisticated research casts significant doubt on whether transplants can be taken for granted. Indeed, Pistor and her colleagues, who have
undertaken extensive historical and cross-sectional empirical work on law
and development, have coined the term *transplant effect* to label ineffective
transplants. This scholarship uncovers two aspects of the transplant effect—
demand and context.

On the *demand* side, the evidence suggests that laws will not be effective
unless there is demand from within a country. That demand comes from
strong interest groups or key policymakers or opinion leaders who want
change and have the capacity to select what they want. Legal professionals are
critical: lawyers, judges, and related professionals must understand the new
rules, the concepts behind the rules, and the compatibilities between those
rules and concepts and others extant in current law. There must also be a sufficient supply of professionals to satisfy the demand (Berkowitz, Pistor, and
Richard 2003). Yet the status and qualifications, as well as reputation, of most
lawyers in countries into which transplantation is being considered means
that the professional constituency able to demand reform will be quite limited
in size and likely also quite limited in its capacity to satisfy demand (Lev and
McVey 1996).

On the *context* side, evidence suggests that transplanted laws will not
work if they are (1) not adapted to local circumstances, (2) unfamiliar to
the population, and (3) bear little resemblance to the recipient country's

own laws or practices. Familiarity might arise from geographic proximity, a shared history, or immigration (Pistor, Raiser, and Gelfer 2000). Context also relates to culture and institutions. It is probable that an imported law must in some manner be related to the myths and narratives of the recipient country's identity, both national and legal (Campbell 2004; Nelken 2002). Unless an imported law can be conformed to a country's "invented traditions" or "imagined communities," and given its own local cultural warrants, it may be viewed as culturally alien (Heydebrand 2002). Effective transplants require not only that the new law fit that immediate moment but that there be sufficiently creative and authoritative institutions to undertake the adaptations that will necessarily result from the law's incompleteness (Pistor and Xu 2003).

Moreover, choice requires alternatives. The implication is that alternatives exist and a country's political leaders have had the chance to review and select what laws seem best suited to the country's exigencies (Pistor 2002). Context also implies institutional affinities, since transplants will not work if the institutions that are to implement them are weak or absent (Berkowitz, Pistor, and Richard 2003).

The local story is invariably more complex because domestic demand for reform is frequently contested, just as a variety of strategies may be deployed to "manage" foreign imports. Local contestants—elites excluded from power versus entrenched elites, entrenched professionals versus insurgent professionals, locals versus cosmopolitans—may play out their own struggles for influence on the international stage (Lev and McVey 1996), just as international organizations and countries reenact their global competition on the national scene (Dezalay and Garth 2001, 2002). Struggles ramify at the center, at the periphery, and between center and periphery. Thus, the indeterminacy of successful legal transplants stems from the outcomes of contests in multiple arenas, themselves unpredictable.

Transplant scholarship therefore offers extremes with many points along the continuum. Optimists would predict that IFI initiatives in commercial law will be readily transplanted (Watson 1974). Pessimists hold that wholesale transplantation is simply impossible because law is always so deeply embedded within a social and cultural situation and in interpretative communities. Other views are arrayed between these extremes. Harding (2002), for instance, proposes that it may be more constructive to view legal transplants and imports into Southeast Asia as "an accretion of layers of law." Support for the possibility of successful transplants may also vary by the degree of coercion and length of time given transplants to take root.

Our country studies demonstrate that transplants are not mysterious graftings of alien species on indigenous institutions. Even putatively weak nation-states are active agents who can substantially shape their own fates. They do so by deploying a range of weapons whose combined impact can retard or destroy the prospect of a successful transplant from a global norm to a national law.

Weapons of the Weak

How does the asymmetry between enormous financial power and manifest vulnerability permit partial freedom for the subordinate party? Or in Scott's (1985) memorable title, the "weapons of the weak"? Under what circumstances are particular strategies of resistance likely to be most effective? The insolvency reforms display varieties of techniques wielded alone or in combination by Indonesia, Korea, and China. These techniques are not confined to East Asian countries alone. The IMF Legal Department acknowledges that they bedevil its efforts across the world.[2]

Avoid or Reject Conditional Foreign Capital and Aid

Two notable instances have occurred in recent years where nations have refused the terms of the IMF or have avoided relying on IFI interventions—in Malaysia and Argentina. In contrast to its neighbors in Thailand and Indonesia, Malaysia in 1997 refused to accept the IMF bailout package. Its judgment was courageous, for the economic risk and exceptionalism, but in hindsight it is arguable that its decision was defensible and the results acceptable because Malaysia did not suffer such drastic domestic reversals in its economy as its neighbors did (Stiglitz 2002).[3] Of our case studies, China was most inoculated against the Asian Financial Crisis and therefore had no need to expose itself to pressures from IFIs, although the repercussions of the Crisis elsewhere led to numerous domestic reforms on China's own terms.

The ability to reject pressure from the IFIs appears more likely in three circumstances: when there is no crisis and thus no desperate demand for short-term capital and thereby less external leverage for investors; when there is a crisis, but capital can be found elsewhere or a country is prepared to ride out the crisis while sustaining domestic economic damage (e.g., Argentina since

2003); and when there is a powerful, entrenched national leadership that can speak to outside institutions cohesively and remains in control domestically.

Accept Recommendations Selectively

On occasions a country may accept IFI-led bailouts but will refuse explicitly to implement major recommendations of international agencies. It simply says no. More common is the practice of accepting some recommendations but obtaining relief from others. Korea bargained hard and did reject some important recommendations of the IFIs, such as creation of a specialized bankruptcy court.[4] Indonesia was prepared to enact positive sanctions to get debtors to restructure through the Jakarta Initiative, but potentially vulnerable politicians successfully resisted enacting negative sanctions just as sympathetic officials refused to implement negative sanctions already available.[5]

Refusal to adopt important recommendations may be possible under three conditions. First, if levels of external leverage are low, as subsequently became the case in Korea, then the country obtains degrees of freedom to go its own way. Second, if a country can show general compliance with IFI demands, and demonstrate a readiness to undertake major initiatives at least on the books, as did Indonesia, then the IFIs tolerated resistance to some other proposals, even if in the end the proposals would prove troublesome for the general reform program. Third, if a country can persuade IFIs that local circumstances will create more problems than the solution, rejection can be justified, but this is a reasoned justification rather than a straightforward refusal and thus looks more like the invocation of "cultural incompatibility" (see discussion later).

Fragment International Influence

Since the dominant financial powers have a large advantage, the force and focus of pressure can be relieved by either forestalling concerted action or segmenting and dispersing it. In its selective acceptance of assistance from IFIs and sovereign creditor nations, China essentially controlled the inputs from outside the country.[6] And by spreading those inputs over time and among different reform bodies within China, bodies that might not have agreed with each other or competed as centers of power, the Chinese government gave itself maximal degrees of freedom to make its own choices in its own time. Indeed, China so successfully pursued its two-track program of reform (of bankruptcy law through the NPC, and of state-owned enterprise reform through SETC and now SASAC) that leading officials on one track were sometimes unaware of developments on the other. Moreover, each of the major aid agencies—the German GTZ, the World Bank, and the Asian Development Bank—were given a particular fragment of the overall reforms with limited opportunity to combine forces or develop a concerted approach. Significantly, the World Bank itself operated on two tracks—the report prepared for the SETC on SOEs was primarily driven by economists; the contributions of the Bank to the Draft Law prepared by the NPC committee came from the World Bank's Legal Department, though they were quite limited by comparison.

Of course, attempts to fragment the powerful may not be necessary if the IFIs are already divided. In cases such as Indonesia, where certain national constituencies knew that IFIs themselves were divided, as indeed were different agencies of the U.S. government, keeping those differences alive when problems arise on the path actually taken may be enough to perpetuate fragmentation. An alternative path not taken that had been advocated by a powerful external agency provides some legitimacy for resistance.

The divisions that give power to recipient countries therefore arise from both outside (i.e., global institutions) and inside (i.e., domestic institutions). International institutions not only disagree with each other but often compete with each other for primacy in program leadership and recognition. If the distance between the local and global is narrow (Halliday and Carruthers 2004a), then a nation-state will be aware of these differences and can exploit them. To do so will be more possible when diminished pressures for reform, or an absence of crisis, do not require concerted action by IFIs. But if fragmentation of external agents of change can occur without domestic pressure, and if nation-states may also on occasion have the capacity to exploit a lack of external policy coherence, fragmentation might occur as a by-product of intrastate rivalries. Fragmentation of the powerful can occur less as a result of calculated state tactics and more as a result of state disorganization. In this sense, the existence of many competing and powerful state agencies provides its own protection from IFI intervention.

Invoke Cultural Incompatibilities

Countries sometimes fend off IFI recommendations by claiming that implementation would conflict with cultural mores. This can be a rather powerful shield because the IMF and World Bank, among other international agencies, are often caught in a cleft stick. On the one hand, they usually propagate convergent norms or global scripts, in the form of best practices, model laws, global principles, among others. On the other hand, they are very sensitive to accusations that they force "one-size-fits-all" solutions on countries regardless of their culture and institutions. Finding a resolution of this tension often proves elusive. For instance, Indonesia successfully sidestepped negative sanctions on debtors that might have been administered by the Jakarta Initiative by maintaining that the sanctions were culturally inappropriate, an approach that echoed an earlier report on commercial law reform drafted before the Crisis (Bappenas 1998). China in turn frequently invokes its own exceptionalism by championing models of its development that combine a global label (e.g., market) with a local qualifier (e.g., *socialist* market economy, or democracy *with Chinese characteristics*).

The effective use of this weapon increases when global institutions are already under attack by critics for cultural insensitivity. Since this is a rallying cry of antiglobalization movements, it strikes IFIs in a weak place and may compel them to ease their pressure for adoptions of global norms. On the domestic front, effective playing of the "culture hand" requires some plausible basis. Domestic authorities must be able to point to well-known cultural practices or rely upon cultural stereotypes (e.g., "Indonesians avoid conflict") or even construct a cultural practice that seems authentic to outside observers. It is likely, however, that this strategy will be more effective in minor rather than major elements of structural adjustment and externally induced reform programs.

Comply Symbolically

Countries, like organizations, can offer signals of compliance to external constituencies but proceed divergently with internal practices (DiMaggio and Powell 1983; Hirsch and Rao 2003; Meyer and Rowan 1977). This strategy is relatively easy since promulgation of regulations or enactment of legislation appears to be compliant but does not cost much. Nor does it create the political and administrative problems that might be entailed if implementation were to be taken seriously. There are several variants of symbolic compliance.

1. The country enacts the principle but implements it partially. Indonesia set up the Commercial Courts but starved them of resources. Instead of a new modern courthouse that symbolized the primacy given to commercial disputes by the Government, the Court remained sequestered in a rundown building with several judges to a room and minimal infrastructural support—a radical contrast to the elegant, air-conditioned, and marble-lined buildings in which many of the

bankrupt corporations were housed. The Government of Korea committed to create a specialized Bankruptcy Court with the not altogether enthusiastic support of the judiciary itself. But when that proposal came to the Budget Office, it, too, was ruled too costly and instead the Bankruptcy Court was constituted as a division of the Commercial Court in Seoul and other major centers elsewhere in Korea.

2. The country implements principles perversely. The IMF's advisors were experts on the Indonesian court system. Daniel Lev, a political scientist, was the veteran social science observer of Indonesian courts from the 1950s. Because he was pessimistic that any reforms would be effective without wide-ranging restructuring of the judiciary, he advocated replacing all Supreme Court judges to ensure that a new Commercial Court would exist in a competent and uncorrupted judicial system. The Ministry of Justice and Chief Justice strenuously objected to wholesale reforms of the judiciary and urged the IMF not to take such a radical step. Instead, the IMF reached agreement that the Indonesians would establish a Commercial Court from which appeals could be made to an unreconstituted Supreme Court. But, if possible, recruitment to the Commercial Court would involve both competent and "clean" judges already in the judiciary, and possibly private lawyers or foreign lawyers seconded to the court for the short term.

   In fact, senior judges and allies in the Ministry of Justice dismissed the possibility of either importing foreigners or breaking their usual pattern of recruitment and seconding leading Indonesian commercial lawyers. Instead, they recruited judges from within the system who were subject to all the bureaucratic constraints of the judiciary in general. Even once recruited and trained, judges would be required to rotate off the Commercial Court to maintain their career trajectories. And because the Supreme Court maintained its jurisdictional status as an appellate court, appeals to the Supreme Court led to several ignominious and inexplicable rulings that counteracted any expertise or independence of the Commercial Court. Lev, in short, was proved right as the embedding of a new structure within a flawed existing institution led to the subversion of the former by the latter.[7]

3. The country enacts a law but qualifies or subverts it through enabling regulations. The IMF and World Bank doubted that Indonesian domestic legal and accounting professions had the capacity to handle the

mountain of major corporate reorganizations and bankruptcies. Not only was the volume of cases likely to overwhelm the relatively small number of professionals experienced in complex, international cases but professional self-regulation in Indonesia had not worked well. Private lawyers were regulated, for instance, by several competing associations. Their regulation involved very little continuing education and no effective disciplinary action (Kendall 2001).

To adapt to this potential weak link in the chain of reforms, the Government of Indonesia agreed on two initiatives. First, it would permit foreign insolvency specialists to practice in Indonesia. However, when the Ministry of Justice subsequently released its detailed regulations, it demanded that all prospective bankruptcy administrators or receivers would need to pass an examination in Bahasa Indonesia, a provision that effectively kept foreign specialists out of the domestic market. Second, as agreed, Indonesia did create a new hybrid receivers' profession in which lawyers, accountants, and others could qualify as receivers in bankruptcy cases. But as a self-regulating body it failed. While it took responsibility for admissions to the profession, it did not discipline members suspected of corruption. A rump group closely associated with reputedly "corrupt" lawyers broke away to form a rival group that was subsequently authorized as an alternative self-regulatory body by the Minister of Justice.[8]

4. The country enacts a law but fails to enforce it. IFI officials insisted that a bankruptcy system would not work unless there were sanctions against company directors that would compel them to use the system and negotiate in good faith. Even more, when debtors used illegal methods to evade payment to creditors, the IFIs pressed the government to enact criminal sanctions. The Government of Indonesia complied. New laws gave prosecutors authority to bring criminal charges against debtors. These were never used.

5. The country enacts statutes, but courts subvert them. In practice, countries exploit the classic sociolegal gap between law-on-the-books and law-in-action. They send a signal to international organizations with their law-on-the-books but resist in the phase of implementation. In this respect, the process of recursivity presents an opportunity for nation-states to resist IOs. New statutes encounter the exigencies of practice and lead to court cases. In developing countries rarely is

a court system immune from political influence. The IFIs' insistence on "strengthening" courts potentially plays into the hands of local officials. Courts can be "strengthened" but still remain under the sway of national leaders.

In the Indonesian reforms, the failure of IMF-led institutional changes in the legal system to embrace far-reaching restructuring of the judiciary put the new Court in a compromised system. Reactionaries within the court system could readily accept the new Commercial Court so long as it was nested within a system that could be managed politically—and where corruption would be tolerated. That the courts became a new battleground can be seen from the subsequent rounds of foreign aid efforts by the IMF, World Bank, Dutch government, European Union, and USAID to reform the court system from the top down, beginning with the Supreme Court. But long before this succession of foreign aid initiatives gained significant momentum, bankruptcy cases had slowed to a trickle in the courts as dissatisfied parties sought alternative forums and mechanisms for restructuring or liquidating their firms.

Symbolic compliance will not work on all circumstances. It requires that external regulators have limited surveillance or enforcement capacities and that internal practices be relatively invisible. It depends upon the attention span and will of the IFIs. If a new crisis, such as 9/11, distracts the IFIs, then pressure for compliance relaxes. An IFI's term of action may come to an end, as did the IMF's in Indonesia, and then it may be impelled to hand off its reform efforts to another IFI (e.g., World Bank, USAID) or donor (e.g., Netherlands), if the other IFI is willing and able. But if their priorities differ, countries have further room for maneuver. Symbolic compliance also works when nation-states can plausibly plead incapacities of resources, bureaucratic limits, corruption, and asymmetries of power between government authorities and those they attempt to regulate.

Defer Compliance

Perhaps the least risky and most common tactic is for a country to delay and stall. The government will advise the IFIs that it accepts conditions and recommendations but then "drags its feet"—doing as little as possible for as long as possible. Governments, of course, use this strategy with domestic constituencies, by creating commissions and blue-ribbon committees, hoping all the while that the public interest will wane, the responsibility will fall to a new government, or other events will overtake the problem. Some IFI officials believed this was how Korea reacted to the IMF's most challenging expectation—the unification of bankruptcy law. The constant extension of completion dates for commitments in the Indonesian Letters of Intent to the IMF reveal a similar pattern. And China suspended the drafting of its bankruptcy reforms for the four years from 1996 to 2000 because domestic concerns were of much greater moment to its leaders than external pressures.

Stalling or slowing implementation is an effective tactic because it avoids direct confrontation and has a surface plausibility as an excuse. It blurs unwillingness and inability to comply. Slow execution of government programs is also ubiquitous in developed and developing countries. Its effectiveness may increase in two circumstances: when IFIs appear reluctant or unable to penalize nation-states for noncompliance; and when weak countries have less administrative and expert capacity to implement programs.

Segment Reforms

A complementary or alternative strategy for stalling can be to break down a larger commitment into innumerable smaller steps. The experience of any one step may then influence the course and pace of later steps. Arguably, China adopted this strategy when it undertook (with SOEs through SETC) a series of progressive experiments in successively wider circles of cities. This strategy now has the implicit endorsement of the former Chief Economist of the World Bank and Nobel Prize winner, Joseph Stiglitz (2002), because a gradualist, experimental advance might offer more learning from trial and error, and with less risk. While prudent from a government's point of view, and thereby defensible, this approach gives the government greater opportunities to stall compliance. Korea countered the IFI proposals for reforms to its bankruptcy system by undertaking a series of modest statutory amendments in annual reform cycles. This could be interpreted as a strategy for complying minimally in the hope that the maximal demand—integration of all its bankruptcy laws in a single, unified, comprehensive statute—might vanish.

This strategy can work when IFI pressures are not sufficient to obtain a comprehensive solution at the outset. The salience of a crisis for segmentation of reforms is more complicated. On the one hand, a crisis gives IFIs maximal short-term leverage and thus offers a critical moment in which to obtain a major commitment from a government for comprehensive reform. On the other hand, comprehensive reforms cannot readily be designed in a few short weeks. In these circumstances, IFIs might settle for segmented reforms in the short term and a longer-term commitment for comprehensive reform.

Substitute a Solution

A country may offer a home-grown solution to solve an IFI-designated problem. The IFIs wanted Korea to make liquidation a credible threat to firms and to speed up court procedures. Korea responded by adopting the strict economic criterion test, which was close enough to IFI intent that the Government could maintain it was compliant in its reduction of judicial discretion. Similarly, Korea passed the Corporate Restructuring Promotion Act (2001), which seemed responsive to IFI pressures for out-of-court work-outs, but it did so in ways that subverted various rights, including those of foreign creditors.

Substituting an alternative will be possible when a country has some degree of freedom from IFIs, when for instance the imbalance of power diminishes. However, national officials must be sophisticated enough to craft an alternative and persuasive enough to convince IFIs of its functional equivalence to their proposals. That, in turn, depends upon the presence of experts within a nation-state who can communicate as peers with experts from IFIs. An alternative to a global model may also be more acceptable if the IFIs believe a nation-state is generally executing the broad contours of an agreement between the nation-state and IFIs, if not all its particulars.

Construct Exclusions and Escape Routes

Governments recognize that compliance with IFIs may bring risks or threats to domestic power relations or forms of market regulation. To preserve these, governments sometimes build in "back doors," exclusions, and escape routes.

1. Governments carve out exceptions to the new law so that politically troublesome or economically risky prospective subjects are removed from the law's purview. Thus, China showed considerable reluctance to include all state-owned enterprises in earlier versions of its Draft Law and later carved out a time-bound exception for some two thousand SOEs when the law came into force.

2. Governments create escape routes so that unanticipated consequences of law reform may be mitigated on an ad hoc basis. In earlier versions

of the Chinese Draft Law, the State Council was given the right to intervene arbitrarily in particular cases. The Enterprise Bankruptcy Law, for instance, requires permissions from state agencies for certain financial enterprises and SOEs to gain protection under the law.

3. Governments maintain channels of influence that attenuate the force of reforms. When the Government of Korea enacted the Corporate Restructuring Promotion Act, its officials knew that the Government would still have back-door channels, through its equity interest in banks, to be able to interfere in the very market processes the Act was intended to promote. Likewise, the Chinese government was and continues to be anxious about the consequences of handing over corporate reorganizations or liquidations entirely to courts, especially if a particular case might be politically sensitive or cause widespread economic dislocation. Since the Party-state controls the judiciary, it retains the discretion to turn on and off the pipeline of cases into the courts as circumstances dictate.

Weakness of the Strong

We have seen that IFIs exercise initial and continuing powers from conditionalities for loans to close monitoring and surveillance through periodic reviews (Art. IV), technical assistance, and aid programs. Yet successes appear incommensurate with leverage. In Indonesia, laws were amended, institutions constructed, processes initiated; and the new Commercial Court, the Jakarta Initiative, the new receivers' profession, and the substantive and procedural law reforms have produced flattering statistics (for example, number of cases coming to court, speed of disposition, extent of assets restructured in JITF Memoranda of Understanding, numbers of qualified receivers) but also widespread disappointment. In Korea, the Government undertook formal reforms consistent with IFI preferences, albeit on its own schedule, but those reforms still confronted inertia and resistance from some parties. In China, experiments widened and deepened reform of SOEs, but it took thirteen years for the creation of a comprehensive bankruptcy law and a comprehensive bankruptcy system.

Given the asymmetries of power, how is it possible for the weak to get away with these tactics? The IFIs are not naïve. They have been in many comparable situations. Their officials may have knowledge of the region or the country. They will have ample access to the best and brightest experts inside the country. They get immediate access to any government officials. And they have their formidable negative sanctions. In practice, however, it looks rather different.

Time Pressures

IFIs, and the IMF in particular, operate under severe time constraints in emergency situations. They move from crisis to crisis, their attention span is limited, and their resources are stretched thin. For instance, each lawyer in the IMF Legal Department has responsibilities for many countries on several continents. And during the Crisis, the World Bank Legal Department had no lawyer-specialist completely dedicated to insolvency.

Diagnostic Limitations

The quality and potential efficacy of "prescriptions" for ailing economies rely on the accuracy of "diagnoses." And those diagnoses depend largely on the abilities of the practitioner-diagnosticians. Thus, diagnoses may suffer from lack of experienced in-country staff or access to experts in institutions. Indeed, adequate institutional analysis requires skills that IFI experts conventionally do not have (Halliday and Carruthers 2004a). All IFIs are dominated by economists who often are unfamiliar with the political economy of a country and whose training reflects little sophistication in institutional analysis, including institutional economics. IFI lawyers are trained in substantive law and a mode of reasoning that seldom treats the behavioral and institutional conditions of legal practice. The lawyers do obtain on-the-job training, but the scope of their responsibilities is so broad and their targets are constantly moving so that an earnest intent to understand institutional and cultural complexities in a given situation simply cannot be sustained.

Inappropriate Borrowings

IFIs draw on precedents from other crises. This seems positive on its face, for it cross-fertilizes global learning. But the relevance of the precedent depends on contextual, institutional, and cultural conditions in which previous actions initiated by IOs either succeeded or not. Discerning the conditions under which success or failure occurred is a challenge for expert institutional analysts in the social sciences. It is very rare that IFI professionals have such training or, indeed, know how to compensate for lack of it.

Exclusion of Significant Local Constituencies
Time pressures also influence the failures of IFIs to build support and consensus within countries and political commitment from key constituencies. In bankruptcy law, for instance, the IFIs effectively represent the foreign creditor community. Laws based on the preferences of creditor institutions inside and outside a country may run into vigorous opposition from other parties in the market, including debtors and workers, who then act to subvert the agreement, especially when they have not been consulted in the policymaking. Such exclusions of interested parties—a mismatch between actors involved in implementation and lawmaking—drives subsequent cycles of reform.[9]

Formulaic Solutions
Additional problems in transplantation stem from the tension-ridden relations between global exporters of norms and national importers. The strongest critics of IFIs charge that some IFIs compel countries to accept "one-size-fits-all" solutions. Countries are not given enough time to make them work or to craft adaptations that fit with the culture (Stiglitz 2002). While this criticism is not always fair, it does draw on the widespread view in adopting nations that IFIs do not comprehend adequately the complexity of the situations in which they are seeking to implant global norms. And in this the critics are substantially correct. Given the limited depth on the bench of country experts, whether in the head office or in the field, having a global template of sorts has an organizational logic that makes sense on its face. By labeling norms as "best practices," the template forestalls or short-circuits all the complexities that political scientists, sociologists, anthropologists, and comparative lawyers might introduce about what will work where. "One-size-fits-all," or its close cousin, "best practices," offers a perverse efficiency. In this sense, an ideological grab bag of formulas for solving the problems of enormously diverse markets and legal systems not only reflects the dominant politics of global power centers but presents a handy simplified packet that offers institutional reforms on the cheap. Putatively efficient, yes. Practically effective, no.

Shame and Face
In the heat of emergency negotiations, IFIs can appear careless of national sensibilities, of the loss of face of rulers in sovereign nations, and of the limitations

in their powers. The exercise of economic muscle from Washington fuels the presumption that the laws represent the imposition of foreign interests. These, in turn, engender nationalist resentment that can be appropriated by local constituencies for political gain. In Korea, for instance, the Crisis of 1997 has entered popular usage as the "IMF Crisis." Such alienation fosters passive opposition and the resort to stratagems of evasion and noncompliance, not necessarily based on the merits or otherwise of reforms. Resentments are intensified when "rescue" leads to heavier indebtedness and a sense of perpetual dependency, thus vindicating premises of dependency theory (Tamanaha 1995). Nevertheless, it must also be remembered that what alienates one section of a debtor nation may be viewed as an opportunity by other national constituencies, especially those oriented toward Western and global norms and actors.

Time-Bound Leverage

In the face of this mounting potential resistance, the real powers of enforcement by the IFIs are diminishing. As one veteran of debt crises observed, the real window for opportunity of successful interventions by IFIs lasts for three, or maybe, six months from the onset of a crisis. Beyond that, governments know that the IMF and World Bank are extremely reluctant to, and in fact, virtually never do, withhold additional tranches of loans because of noncompliance.[10]

Asymmetry of Expertise

Alongside the asymmetry of financial power in crisis situations is an asymmetry of expertise. IFIs have access not only to their own expertise but to experts and expert organizations worldwide, who can be mobilized very quickly. Developing nations usually have limited expertise and limited resources to mobilize it from elsewhere. The more extreme that asymmetry, the less local resistance can rely on technical expertise. But in countries such as Korea, when the asymmetry is much less pronounced, a national technocratic elite can buy itself significant degrees of freedom by countering external experts with national experts, especially when the latter have credentials similar to those of the former. And if a country does not have its own world-class experts, it may follow Indonesia's example of retaining one of the best specialist law firms in the U.S. to trade punches with IOs on a more equal footing. But outside counsel can only go so far.

Foiling and the Transplant Effect

If foiling is effective, it facilitates the "transplant effect," or ineffective transplants. To what extent does the activist orientation of national leaders coincide with the conditions of demand and context that produce the transplant effect?

If effective transplants require domestic constituencies, especially legal professionals, we should expect to find a critical mass of professionals who understand the new rules, their animating concepts, and the affinity of the imported concepts with current law. Their absence would bolster foiling at the points of enactment and implementation. A small fraction of professionals in Indonesia foresaw the implications of the bankruptcy reforms. Anticipating improvements in the justice system that they had previously advocated, they welcomed the IMF intervention so long as it was consonant with their aspirations. Later they were joined by other lawyers who came quickly to understand how the new system could be perversely exploited for their economic benefit—and some nationalist effect. One or two hundred other professionals sought qualifications as receivers. But IFI officials remained long puzzled why lawyers or accountants as a whole, or even leading spokespeople for either profession, did not mobilize to support the Commercial Court and new bankruptcy regime in the court of public opinion. This quiescence combined with official resistance to impede the transplant.

In Korea, too, support by lawyers and judges for bankruptcy reforms initially was grudging. Eventually the bar acceded to the reform agenda but only because it became clear that the Ministry of Finance and Economy was determined to push through changes to fulfill commitments to the IFIs. Yet, once convinced that some sorts of law reforms were inevitable, the courts and lawyers swung in behind the reforms to ensure that the bankruptcy system, at least, functioned effectively. However, it is too early to know how effectively reforms in the 2005 Unified Bankruptcy Act will be implemented.

Imported laws are more likely to be adopted if they are adapted to local circumstances. The IMF in Indonesia sought precisely to do this by accepting advice from its Indonesian advisors to graft amendments onto existing Indonesian law, which itself was derived from Dutch commercial law. While the idea of handling corporate liquidations in courts was new, as was the prospect of corporate rehabilitation, reformers presented these changes as consistent with Indonesian cultural preferences for nonadversarial negotiation. Arguably, by pulling cases into courts, the new regime was also intended to push debtors and creditors to negotiate outside court, initially through the Jakarta Initiative

Task Force, and later through negotiation services. Unfamiliarity with court-based liquidations and reorganizations also stalked the Chinese reforms, since the principal channel of SOE liquidations and reorganizations had occurred through administrative actions by the SETC and one of its successors, SASAC. China's history of corporate bankruptcy in courts has existed only in the margins of practice for the last twenty years. The reforms therefore inaugurate a marked break with the past, a break compounded by the institutional incapacities of courts, even if they have been slowly upgrading. In Korea the situation was different insofar as judges were prestigious, courts had a high reputation, and legal practice was an elite profession. It is true that political interventions and administrative direction of the economy before 1997 were characteristic ways of handling large corporations in distress. In this sense giving courts after 1997 power to handle massive financial restructurings or liquidations as an outcome of judicially adjudicated disputes between debtors and creditors also represented a new departure. It is an initiative that has gained some momentum after initial stumbles, although its true test awaits an economic downturn where bankruptcy proceedings are governed by the new law.

Pistor and others (Pistor et al. 2002; Pistor and Xu 2003) have argued that transplants are more likely to take root when nation-states can choose the best fit of several alternatives. Giving national policymakers real choices also adds legitimacy to the legal change. China has had the most discretion over its choices because its legal experts had broad access to IFIs and expertise across the world's leading legal systems, including those of Japan, Germany, Britain, Australia, and the U.S. Neither was it subject to economic coercion by an IFI that advocates a single model. Korea might have had a narrower rate of choice since it began reforms with a fairly complete trio of bankruptcy laws. Furthermore, the high level of professional expertise and cosmopolitanism among practicing and academic professions of law gave Korean lawmakers access to options in Japan, the U.S., and Europe, as well as the developing global norms being drafted by UNCITRAL's Working Group on Insolvency.

This expertise and Korea's quick economic rebound gave Korean reformers more degrees of freedom to follow their own course, which enabled them to choose among the options of advanced countries and global norms, and if necessary, to create new options. Two "metachoices" and a midcourse "mesochoice" confronted Indonesian reformers. The first metachoice confronted Indonesian negotiators with the IFIs, as the IFI-led package of conditionalities was finalized in the 1998 agreements between the Government of

Indonesia and the IMF. Leading commercial lawyers in Indonesia who were advising the IFIs swiftly rejected any suggestions that the Dutch-based Indonesian bankruptcy law should be replaced in toto by provisions more like those of the U.S. bankruptcy system. Once the IMF and Indonesians agreed on this determinative choice, then any subsequent options occurred within the constraints set by the original decision to maintain continuity with Dutch-derived law and to fit seamlessly with cognate commercial and civil law. Another metachoice occurred in the struggle among foreign agencies, especially USAID and the IMF, over the location of an adjudicatory body. Should it be located in an executive agency, and thus follow the precedent of a tax body, as USAID argued, or should it be grafted onto the court system, as the IMF preferred? Here a coincidence of interest between the IMF and Indonesian reformers decided in favor of the courts, a key decision that shaped the series of court-related measures we have seen continue to the present. In midcourse another decision point arose when a legal academic and practicing lawyer in Jakarta led a group of lawyers to propose to the Government an alternative to what now looked to be the failed experiment. The Ministry of Justice authorized two parallel tracks of proposed reforms to proceed before deciding ultimately to back the alternative favored by the IMF, OECD, and other international bodies.

The rejection of transplants is more likely when institutions are underdeveloped or ill suited to the changes. Although we consider a related question of institutional capacity later, it is clear that substantial variation existed across the three countries. We have seen that bankruptcy systems require interrelated institutions—courts, out-of-court options, and expert professions. China and Indonesia both suffer from severe institutional capacities on all three institutional foundations, but for somewhat different reasons. China's courts have evolved rapidly since 1978. Judges are better qualified, courts are increasingly used as forums for dispute settlement, and a hierarchical national court system is developing with some overall coherence injected by the Supreme People's Court (Peerenboom 2002). Yet a substantial number of judges have limited or no legal qualifications and little more than a rudimentary capacity to handle complex corporate cases. Courts are not autonomous, either from markets (corruption) or from the Party-state. Creditors, especially those from out of town, from another province or country, can have no confidence that they will be treated equitably. Similarly, a legal profession has been built from the ground up in the last twenty-five years and at its apex, in major commercial cities, is highly sophisticated, both in domestic and foreign law firms. But this layer of expertise is very thin indeed.

Indonesia, by contrast, in the 1950s had a court system that heralded a *Rechtsstaat*, but its successive dismantling, loss of status and power, lack of autonomy, and corruption created an enormous problem of reconstruction, as the faltering steps since 1997 have shown in the Commercial Court and Supreme Court. The Jakarta Initiative did set a precedent for out-of-court settlements because it contributed to the creation of a broadly expansive national arbitration center. But professional competence and effective self-regulation have proved elusive, with such widespread allegations of corruption that elite commercial lawyers who guard their reputations avoid bankruptcy work. By contrast, Korea already had in place reputable and competent institutions on which could be grafted new functions and structures. Although corruption, too, had been an issue in some courts, it has been controlled. The court system has shown the capacity both to engraft new commercial functions and to move first-rate judges onto the bankruptcy bench. An out-of-court mechanism does not exist after the Government refused to reenact the Corporate Restructuring Promotion Act. The legal profession has the inherent competence and probity to handle bankruptcy cases, but its severe protectionism has led to a shortage of practitioners. It is under strong pressure to expand, as commercial work as well is expected to shift from administrative direction into the market for financial and legal services.

Finally, the failure of imports to transplant follows from either the lack of coherence from the center, political struggles in the adopting nation, or both. We can explain Indonesia's relative failure to implement a bankruptcy regime in part from differences between international agencies, such as the conflicts among the IMF, World Bank, and USAID. Much more significant, however, were internal struggles. So long as senior officials, the Chief Justice, and a faction of lawyers resisted the foreign intrusion, it would prove exceedingly difficult to get beyond the enactment of reforms favored by those reformers who saw the Crisis as an opening for long overdue reforms in the justice system. The domestic constituency for reform proved shallow. In effect, the IFIs aligned themselves with consonant domestic allies who were politically weak.

In China conflicts ran along fault lines defined by ministries and factions of the NPC and Party that favored priority for workers versus those of bankers, commercial academics, and market modernizers who favored creditors. A division sprang up over whether and how to include SOEs under the law.

Many other differences occurred on one or another provision. But the Party leadership, via the NPC, ultimately decided at least on enactment of a law that purportedly draws in most SOEs and gives priority to banking creditors. Yet the degree of political will remains to be tested in the implementation phase as does the capacity of losing factions to frustrate effective practice. Differences in Korea turned primarily on the primacy of continued administrative guidance via the Ministry of Finance and Economy versus a new power for the courts as a locus of restructuring. Although differences were fairly evenly balanced in the first years, with an advantage to the administrative solution, the refusal of the Government to reenact the MOFE-friendly Corporate Restructuring and Promotion Act, and the successful passage of the Draft Law, indicates that the political weight is on the side of the law, courts, and profession. Should a competency in treatment of major bankruptcies continue to build in the courts, we expect that a market/legal alternative to administrative interventions will dominate the restructuring scene.

Korea is the strongest case for adoption of global principles that will be implemented in practice.[11] Strong pressure from the Government for conformity with IMF and international norms overcame most domestic resistance and converted initial reservations in the professions to acceptance and even support, especially as the promise of expanded legal services gets realized. The changes were conformed to Korean law and commercial practice in part because the IFIs gave Korean drafters discretion to reach IFI goals in ways acceptable to Korea and in awareness of international alternatives. Institutional capacity was high and needed relatively limited adjustments rather than wholesale reconstruction. An absence of conflicts among IFIs, and an eventual political settlement in Korea in favor of law-based bankruptcies rather than interventions by government ministries, further suggests that the reforms will be implemented effectively in practice.

The Chinese case is much more equivocal. Domestic demand came principally from political leaders and the financial sector. Other than progressive law professors, several of whom spearheaded the drafting, support from professionals was not highly visible. Although the Chinese clearly had ample choice of alternatives, and the law has been adapted to Chinese exigencies, institutional capacities remain severely compromised. This is partly a matter of political will—do the Party, top leaders, and even leading judges seek a powerful, competent, independent court? If political will is directed to implementation as well as enactment, it then becomes a matter of how rapidly it is possible to build a mode of settling disputes that will find wide acceptance among debtors and creditors in China and overseas alike. China is investing substantially in upgrading its courts and professions. But the path is long, and there are many pitfalls along the way. Not least, the political will exercised in Beijing may not be sufficiently effective in the provinces and municipalities.

In Indonesia the probability is that the battle for the Commercial Court per se is already lost. Few domestic groups mobilized energetically for the bankruptcy reforms, including lawyers at large. Resistance to a process that brings commercial disputes—and financial failure—into a public forum suggests that Indonesian aversions to confrontation on a public stage will keep bankrupt debtors away from courts, even if they were to offer debtors protections from creditors. The failure of the Commercial Court in bankruptcy cases reduced them to a trickle. Institutional capacities and bureaucratic impediments compound pessimism. Yet, just as monitors of this apparently failed transplant were about to declare defeat, more propitious developments indicate that all may not be lost. While USAID now mounts a well-funded rear-guard action to revive the Bankruptcy and Commercial Court, aid funds are pouring into a multiplicity of efforts to reform the Supreme Court, not least with a reengagement of the IMF in partnership with the Dutch aid agency. A new Minister of Justice supportive of reforms, a President who at least does not discourage them, and progressive leaders among Supreme Court judges have injected some optimism that public demand coupled with foreign resources might now move the entire court system forward in ways that ultimately might benefit bankruptcy proceedings.

Intentionality and Incapacity

The argument that the weak may be stronger than either they or IOs suppose turns in part on the premise that they are rational actors, intentionally holding global powers at bay. But is this premise correct? To what extent is the frustration of IFI goals a function of deliberate efforts or a result of constraints or inertia that accompanies change anywhere? And how is it possible to tell the difference?

The distinction is more than academic. It is theoretically and pragmatically meaningful to differentiate between resistance, which implies a deliberate effort by nationals to forestall external pressure, and ineffectiveness, which implies cooperation but an inability to execute. The issue is even more complex because the most sophisticated strategies by governments will be to disguise intentional noncompliance as unanticipated and uncontrollable institutional inertia.

The excuse, of course, has a surface plausibility. No matter how great the pressure, states may be too overburdened, politics too contentious, institutions too fragile, costs too high, resistance too entrenched for reforms to be implemented effectively. The issue becomes one of inability rather than unwillingness. And where countries are undergoing many transformations simultaneously (e.g., economic, political, and legal), which now seems the norm in financial crises, the inability exception seems plausible.

Nevertheless, Scott (1985) would suggest that precisely because the developing countries are weak, they must adopt strategies that limit their culpability and therefore their vulnerability. The "inability" move offers a strong defense. The most artful of governments will tailor its compliance to an "inability" defense, predicting that through its design, intervention, or neglect compliance will be subverted in practice. This suggests that scholars and practitioners alike might proceed on the premise that all circumstances that forestall IFI compliance are within the control of the government. While this premise is manifestly wrong, it serves as a useful heuristic in order to avoid the mistake too often made about the weak—that they are powerless.

It may also be the case that law reform lends itself to being foiled rather more than economic reforms. The latter are relatively easy to measure, and the immediacy of their impact can readily be evaluated. Economic levers, such as interest rates, seem far simpler to manipulate than legal compliance. Moreover, long lags occur before the effectiveness of law reforms becomes apparent.

Transplants of law entail far more than law itself. On the surface, it appears rather simple to enact statutes, issue regulations, or even erect new institutions. But the advocates of law reform, especially in an area such as bankruptcy law, with its enormous distributive implications, often fail to understand how extensively law reform reaches to the fundamental institutional order of a society. It potentially threatens deeply entrenched power elites. It demands extensive changes in market relations (e.g., in the prevailing concept of the firm). It may demand changing the balance among a society's central institutions (e.g., substitution of market for hierarchy).

Thus, the imposition of a "Western" bankruptcy system penetrates far into economic, social, and political life. By so doing, it confronts the heavy weight of path dependence, institutional inertia, and historical momentum. Successful reform in this technical area of commercial law, therefore, entails not simply debt restructuring but institutional restructuring (Halliday and Carruthers 2004b).

As Malaysia demonstrated, countries are not compelled to accept IFI capital or prescriptions. But even for those countries that do, "old hands" at the IFI reconstruction game strive for bold changes but will settle, reluctantly, for less. For the most hardened realist, *any* movement whatsoever can be considered a small victory, for without IFI intervention, no movement at all might have occurred. For champions of more comprehensive reform, such as those pursued in Indonesia, a window of opportunity has opened, complete with new indigenous champions, and shells of institutions and laws now exist that might be completed and made effective over time. For these IFI officials, therefore, the Crisis provided an opening. Subsequent IFI leverage kept up a momentum. Over the longer term, lessons will be learned on all sides about the limits of IFI power and extent of indigenous resistance. For the IFIs, the bridgehead has been established. For the developing nations, or, more precisely, clusters of interest groups within them, the choice remains whether to repel, resist, co-opt or appropriate the options through IFI interventions. The evidence from corporate bankruptcy law makes plain that developing nations do have choices and, if they or powerful groups within them so choose, they may significantly foil the financial hegemons, even in the most extreme circumstances.

10 Recursivity

T O INDUCE global legal change, international actors must find intermediaries to institutionalize global norms in domestic law. This occurs principally through the *politics of enactment* whereby nation-states and local authorities respond to international influences, under particular circumstances, by institutionalizing formal law-on-the-books. The problem of global legal change from the vantage point of developing nations turns on their ability to determine their own fates in the shadow of powerful exogenous constraints on their resources and policy-making. Maintaining a space for self-determination involves a dynamic of foiling in which putatively weak nations can hold at bay powerful international organizations. Foiling occurs principally through the *politics of implementation*. Local actors who are weak on the international stage find their best last defense in frustrating unwanted global agents and pressures at the point where law is translated (or not) into action. A potent strategy for weak developing nations is to engage in guerrilla warfare on the ground of their choosing—everyday practice.

The dynamics of intermediation and foiling are brought together in a process of legal change we call the *recursivity of law*. These cycles of enactment and implementation express the incipient contests and cooperation, alliances, and struggles between the global and local (Figure 10.1). Within each developing country in a global context, law reforms follow a recursive process: an event such as the Asian Financial Crisis triggers cycles of reform; the reforms

oscillate between formal law and law-in-practice; reforms eventually will settle at a new equilibrium if they have taken root at all. The dynamics of recursivity help explain the variance in the scope of legal change in practice and the
degree of convergence between global and local legal norms.

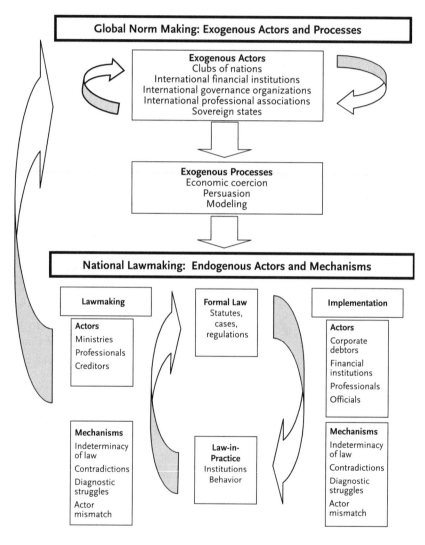

FIGURE 10.1 Recursive Cycles of Bankruptcy Lawmaking in Global Contexts
SOURCE: Adapted from Halliday and Carruthers (2007b).

Through a reanalysis of our empirical cases, we elaborate the logic of recursivity as a general framework for legal change. We then extend the framework by showing the impact of intermediation and foiling on reform cycles, all of which reflect power strategies exercised by actors who are intent on stamping their interests and ideologies onto legal change.

The Logic of Recursivity[1]

The analysis of legal change in a global context benefits from a framework for comparisons over time and place. The recursive framework holds in dynamic tension processes that conventionally are segregated in scholarly analysis, with the result that partial and incomplete explanations distort and fragment understanding. Legal change invariably is a cyclical process. The recursivity approach to legal change is premised on a fundamental distinction in sociolegal scholarship between law-on-the-books and law-in-action. Legal enactment of law-on-the-books leads to variable levels of law-in-practice. The successes or failures of implementation eventually lead to subsequent reforms of law-on-the-books. In contrast to the conventional orientation of sociolegal scholars to the first process (from enactment to implementation) and political scientists to the second process (from practice to enactment), the entire cycle from enactment to implementation and back to enactment becomes the unit of analysis for theoretical explanation. The elements of this process can be specified conceptually by explicating the empirical findings in terms of recursivity (see Figure 10.1). Concomitantly a comparison of the three cases through the conceptual lens of recursivity amplifies the variety of ways that legal change manifests itself even in a single area of law.

Poles

A recursive cycle has two poles (see Figure 10.1). For our purposes, we define *law-on-the-books* positivistically as law binding in form or in effect, most often by a sovereign authority, and increasingly, by a transnational authority, such as the European Union or global regulatory bodies.[2] It is codified in statutes, regulations, and cases. Hence the 1998 amendments to the Indonesian Bankruptcy Law, the 2005 Korean Unified Bankruptcy Act, and the 2006 Chinese Enterprise Bankruptcy Law constitute one type of formalization. But so, too, do the regulations implemented by the Indonesian Ministry of Justice to administer the Commercial Court or to regulate the receivers' profession.

Court cases handed down by the Seoul District Court or the Jakarta Commercial Court likewise are binding law. In all cases, of course, the law is binding de jure, and not necessarily de facto. It is for precisely this reason that socio-legal scholarship and the sociology of law emphasize that formal law means little if implementation does not follow. Hence the unit of analysis for legal change must hold in tension enactment and implementation as they engage each other in both directions.

Law-in-practice refers to behavior and institutions that constitute and enact law as it actually is experienced. For the latter, law-in-practice effectively is law, but it cannot be understood without the frame of law-on-the-books. By the same token, it makes little sense to develop a theory of legal enactment without considering the problems or situations in everyday life that stimulated political action in the first place.

Global Contexts

In many areas of national lawmaking, cycles of reform and implementation derive from or respond to the global norms articulated by international organizations and sovereign states. The field of global actors in the insolvency domain comprises international financial institutions (IMF, World Bank, ADB, EBRD), international organizations (UNCITRAL, OECD), international professional associations (IBA, INSOL, International Section of the ABA), clubs of nations (G-7, G-22), and powerful states (e.g., U.S., France).

Global actors formulate norms that they seek to propagate across the world. From the orientation of the global center, the probability of adoption turns not only on the legitimacy of the global actors but also on the mechanisms they can deploy to exercise leverage over adopting states in order to persuade local lawmakers that legal change is in their interests. While the mechanisms by which these global institutions influence national regulation are many (Braithwaite and Drahos 2000; Halliday and Osinsky 2006), in the field of insolvency law three predominate. The most potent is *economic coercion* exercised in the form of conditionalities by the IMF and World Bank. The case of Indonesia in particular reveals the scope of financial and law reforms to which the Government of Indonesia was required to commit over successive contractual Letters of Intent in order to receive multilateral financing from IFIs and the consortium of state lenders they led. Economic incentives also feature in grants for technical assistance by the ADB (Indonesia, China), the World Bank (Korea, China), IMF (Indonesia), and sovereign nations (U.S. via

USAID, Indonesia; Germany via GTZ, China; Australia via AusAid, Indonesia). More subtle forms of economic incentives can occur in the reciprocity understandings between nations (Braithwaite and Drahos 2000), as in the European Union's pressure on China to enact a comprehensive corporate bankruptcy law in order to stimulate continued foreign investment.

Persuasion accompanies or may substitute for economic pressure. Alongside its economic levers, the IMF sought to convince Korean lawmakers that their bankruptcy regime needed to be upgraded to a world-class standard, especially as Korea was now a member of the OECD, the exclusive club of thirty mostly-rich nations. The appeal to international reputation may have been more effective once the Crisis was over and economic pressures disappeared. Even more so, without any coercive levers to influence China, the ADB and World Bank, as well as GTZ, episodically reinforced the message both that China's economy required a rationalized bankruptcy system and that foreign investors and commercial interests expected the rule of law in commercial relations when companies were in distress. The OECD deliberately held its Asian Forum on Insolvency Reforms in Beijing at a critical moment (April 2006) before adoption of the new law in order to provide some impetus to Chinese policymakers.

Global actors influenced China and Korea in particular through *modeling* of global norms. We have seen that the World Bank drafted *Principles* that were featured in World Bank and OECD forums in Korea and Indonesia while their laws were being reformed. The IMF and the ADB generated standards. Most important, UNCITRAL's Legislative Guide on Insolvency convened an international deliberative process to formulate a set of principles and rules, indeed a shadow law, that would be considered legitimate by potentially adopting states and would guide their reforms. Since both China and Korea, respectively, were drafting de novo and comprehensively revising their laws, drafters compared and contrasted their provisions with the UNCITRAL model. Indeed, the Korean Ministry of Justice requested a systematic comparison of the draft Korean comprehensive law with the UNCITRAL Legislative Guide to assure Korean lawmakers that their reforms satisfied the new global standard.

Cycles

It is a rare law that does not proceed through enactment-implementation and implementation-enactment cycles. Laws originate from social movements, interest groups, elites, parties to litigation, and officials precisely because they perceive some deficiency in the regulation or organization of current institutions. Laws are "solutions" to "problems." They usually proceed from formalization to have an impact on practices, although seldom of precisely the kind that their designers imagined.[3] We have shown that cycles between formal law and practice are stimulated by the engagement of global and national actors in the processes of enactment and implementation, as the imperfections of intermediation and the stratagems of foiling push for yet another round of adoption or resistance.

The cyclical character of the insolvency reforms can be observed from the case studies. In Korea for several years after 1997 it seemed as if a new law each year was pushed through the National Assembly as first one approach and then another did not work or did not have sufficient scope to satisfy IFIs or solve domestic problems. In Indonesia the reform of the substantive bankruptcy law went through two major cycles in 1998 and 2005, and the flurry of laws, cases, and regulations kept the Commercial Court in constant flux. While the Chinese were continually experimenting with new administrative regulations on SOEs, the NPC-based drafters of a new comprehensive law lost count of how many versions they produced between 1994 and 2006.

In Korea and Indonesia cycles were also driven by the diagnostic-prescriptive interventions of international organizations. While both countries were operating within the constraints of their agreements with the IMF and World Bank, quarterly and sometimes monthly progress reports fed information back to Washington, which in turn led to calls for new or quicker cycles of enactment and implementation. After Indonesia and Korea were released from the intensive care of IFI monitoring, periodic evaluations from ROSC surveys and Article IV reviews of the IMF kept up pressures for rounds of reform. The World Bank and German aid program in Beijing served a similar function in China.

Episodes

An explanation of legal change must account for three aspects of cycles: why they begin, why they continue, and why they stop. It is useful to encapsulate the first and third of these questions within the concept of "episode."

A new set of reform cycles often has discrete beginnings: although underlying problems in social practice or contradictions and tensions may build up pressure for change of state law, some kind of triggering event is frequently required—a tragedy or scandal or crisis—to precipitate lawmaking at a given moment. In global bankruptcy reforms two triggers energized the entire field. The fall of command economies in 1989 required that all former Communist countries create a new legal apparatus to support their new market economies, and thus the first wave of comprehensive corporate bankruptcy reforms was born. This did not, however, stimulate the crafting of global scripts. It took a second and more alarming event, the Asian Financial Crisis, both to accelerate the forging of a consensus on global norms and to change the law and practice of Indonesia, Korea, and China. We have shown that in all three countries a low level of reformist activity occurred before 1997. But the dangers and dramatic impact of the Crisis kicked off the effective beginnings of reform cycles in Korea and Indonesia and injected new urgency into the Chinese.

Cycles also come to an end. In Asian insolvency reforms China has moved to a midpoint in an episode that has yet long to run. While massive reconstructions of SOEs have taken place through administrative channels, and a new comprehensive bankruptcy law has been enacted, there still remain to be promulgated extensive regulations that specify the law, especially those on substantive law and procedures. Implementation has scarcely begun. It seems likely that multiple cycles of regulations and cases and possibly amendments to the statute in response to practice will be required before any settling occurs.

The situation in Indonesia by the end of 2006 indicated that settling had occurred but at a level far below that anticipated by the IMF and its Indonesian supporters. Negligible numbers of bankruptcy cases in the courts signified that the grand experiment had mostly failed. The retreat of the IMF, World Bank, AusAid, and the Dutch aid program, all supporters of the Commercial Court experiment, indicated that they, too, had given up hope. Only a few signs remained that something might bring bankruptcy cases back to life. USAID's funding of new Commercial Court initiatives, a major push to reform the Supreme Court and much of the court system, a new President and Minister of Justice, the establishment of a national mediation center—all gave optimists a lingering hope that the episode had not ground to a fruitless halt.

Korea's effective establishment of a bankruptcy chamber in major courts, the lapse of the Corporate Restructuring Promotion Act, and the new prominence of law and courts in corporate restructuring, indicate that its active mobilization on bankruptcy reforms will lead to settling of legal changes at noticeably higher levels than those that preceded the Crisis. Yet the Unified Bankruptcy Act of 2005 inevitably will lead to a series of regulations and cases before the new law settles as a predictable and effective legal change. It is likely that this level will be higher than before 1997, but how much higher, and with high broad a scope, cannot easily be predicted.

Moreover, a legal change that appears settled, whether in Indonesia at a low level or Korea at a higher level, may be jolted into new cycles of reforms if there is a powerful domestic or international shock to the economy. A downturn in the business cycle or another credit crisis would suddenly put pressure on each of these bankruptcy regimes that would both test the robustness of institutional construction since the Crisis and show cracks and fissures that require rapid attention.

Actors

Both the lawmaking and law practice sides of the recursive loop are populated by international and domestic actors. A recursive analysis of reforms emphasizes that legal change takes place in both arenas, and the tension between them reflects the respective actors in play. These actors differ by the issue at hand.

Lawmaking   The lawmaking side involves parties capable of legal and political mobilization. Common to each of the bankruptcy reforms were government ministries. They are natural institutional counterparts to international organizations and also executors and often crafters of policy decisions. In each country the finance ministries had the closest affinity to IFIs, especially in Indonesia and Korea, although China's State Economic and Trade Commission (SETC), which supervised SOEs, was the prime interlocutor with IFIs on SOE reforms until it was dismantled and reorganized. While the finance ministries exerted immediate and predominant influence on the fact of enactment in all countries, the justice ministries and courts characteristically injected cautionary responses to calls for change and presided over the regulations and cases that specified, qualified, and on occasion nullified legislative intent. In each country, but especially China and Indonesia, the justice ministries rank much lower in prestige and power than those that regulate the economy, and an incipient tension exists between them. Where law has far higher prestige, as in Korea, the Ministry of Finance and Economy (MOFE) and the Ministry of Justice skirmished repeatedly across the years after the Crisis, a balance of power that altered as the Government took steps to diminish administrative intervention into the economy and to stimulate rule-governed commercial activities in the market. Nevertheless, our analysis of foiling has shown that Ministries of Justice can exercise their powers to issue regulations or pursue prosecutions and lawsuits quite effectively to nullify or qualify lawmaking in the legislature.

Each ministry had its own domestic constituencies and allies. In principle, finance ministries might expect support from creditor institutions, but insofar as reforms after the Crisis involved tighter and closer regulation of the banking sector, in all three countries the Ministries of Finance and their supervisory agencies, as well as the Central Banks, could not assume unqualified support from the financial sector. Lawyers are the natural allies of the Ministry of Justice and courts. Apart from a handful of elite commercial lawyers and law professors, however, lawyers in Indonesia exerted no coherent influence on lawmaking; lawyers in China have had limited involvement in the statutory lawmaking; and lawyers in Korea, while well organized, reacted cautiously to legislative reforms. Yet the indirect influence of renegade lawyers in Indonesia arguably subverted the legitimacy of the Bankruptcy Court. By using a brilliant array of legal and extralegal means to advance the cause of their debtor-clients, a small coterie of lawyers got favorable case rulings that undermined the intent of the reform movement.

Judges are capable of making their own law through cases that govern parties to litigation and criminal prosecution. While research indicates that the majority of cases in Indonesia were decided correctly by the Commercial Court judges (Suyudi 2004), a small number of widely publicized early cases were decided inexplicably by the Commercial Court judges and on appeal by the Supreme Court. This disillusioned key potential constituencies of the courts, particularly on the creditors' side. In Korea, MOFE initially exerted statutory pressures to restrict judges' discretion precisely to fetter their lawmaking powers. Even judges initially expressed reservations about powers conferred upon them to decide cases with huge economic repercussions. Yet the courts did respond by appointing some of Korea's most outstanding judges to special bankruptcy chambers and built up a body of case law that affirmed its authority as a source of law. Korean judges consistently were canvassed about statutory reforms and had an impact through notable cases. The Supreme People's Court has filled a legal vacuum in China through its powers to issue occasional Interpretations, statutory-like provisions to fill in gaps in the otherwise vague and incomplete statutory law. It did so in 1991 and 2002. However, no judge sat on the NPC drafting committee; and although the Supreme People's Court was party to discussions of various drafts, along with many other groups, there is little evidence that it exerted a strong influence on the comprehensive law. But its lawmaking through Interpretations and rulings on cases under the new law will be influential as cycles of implementation and formal lawmaking operationalize the new statute in the next several years.

In developing countries legal academics can have an impact that significantly exceeds that observed in advanced countries. In Indonesia, Korea, and China, a tiny number of law professors with specialties in commercial or bankruptcy law became the drafters of the principal statutes, the prime intermediaries or interlocutors between governments and international actors, and the carriers of global norms into the domestic situation. By the same token they also have empowered the political leaders of these countries to resist pressures from IFIs, in part because the leaders could mobilize expertise and authority from international organizations. Indirectly, we have seen several instances in Indonesia and Korea where governments hired foreign law firms to strengthen their negotiating hand with IFIs. Since lawmaking usually involves interagency struggles, or even contests among different levels of the same organization (e.g., Finance and Economy Committee of the NPC versus the Standing Committee), agencies have drawn in IFI allies, as did the Standing Committee of the NPC seek technical assistance from the Asian Development Bank, to strengthen its negotiating position within China's complicated political system.

In advanced economies, the creditors' lobbies, and particularly the banking sector, have powerfully shaped statutory reforms. In Indonesia and Korea, by contrast, weakness and imminent collapse discredited the banking sector in the immediate years after the Crisis with the effect that its political influence was attenuated. Rather than act as independent actors in the political economy, the banking sector was effectively put into administrative receivership as executive agencies sought first to stabilize, then reform, then normalize new banking practices and structures of monitoring and control. The major banks in China have also been undergoing a wrenching restructuring in order to reduce their overhang of nonperforming loans and to transition toward commercially viable lending, monitoring of clients, and early and active interventions in the financial affairs of distressed borrowers.

Nonetheless, their hand in lawmaking can be seen in two arenas. During the 1990s banks actively fought for regulatory provisions that favored them during SETC's major SOE-restructuring campaign. They did not always win, but their voice demanded a hearing. And in the last several years, as NPC drafts of the bankruptcy law have been circulated, through the Central Bank and other representations they have become a vocal lobby, as was manifest in the penultimate struggle between the lobbies of banks and workers over priority for creditors in bankruptcies. But banking influence less visibly can be observed through the cases that banks choose to take to court and how far they will go in obtaining expert counsel to shape court judgments. In many notable cases that shaped opinion in Indonesia, for instance, banks lost, even if overall judgments were in their favor. These cases indicate that the relative impact of the banking sector in developing countries, in comparison to that of advanced countries, is diminished, first, in relation to advanced economies, and second, in times of fiscal crisis.

Other creditors had limited impact on enactment. Trade creditors—those companies that extend credit to another company by conveying goods and services before they are paid—had no obvious channels for mobilization and, like advanced economies, were ignored as the stepchildren of reforms. Labor, which is always a creditor for unpaid wages and vacations or unfunded pensions in corporate insolvency cases, had no discernible influence in Indonesia, quite limited influence in Korea, and most influence in China. Since China's leaders are particularly nervous about worker unrest, the liquidations and restructurings of SOEs carried out by the SETC since the mid-1990s were usually accompanied by lump-sum payments to workers in compensation for their unemployment in those circumstances where mergers (which shifted workers from an unprofitable firm to a viable acquirer) would not work. In the NPC and Standing Committee debates, the All China Trade Union Federation and sympathetic factions in the NPC, State Council, and Party actively pressed the case that workers' interests must be recognized in the new law. The fight between factions sympathetic to workers and those favoring secured creditors can be observed in the constant flux of the priority to be given workers in successive drafts of the law. In the final event, however, the victory has gone to bankers. The interests of workers are given a high ranking in the case of company liquidations, but the lawmakers have essentially externalized worker costs and grievances to China's developing but still underresourced social security system.

As in advanced economies, debtor corporations in Indonesia or Korea failed to mobilize either individually or collectively to influence specific provisions in the statutory law. Their impact came most strongly in the courts. When Indonesia debtors were confronted with the potential loss of (family) control over their corporations to creditors, and especially foreign creditors, or where a threat loomed of dismemberment of their conglomerates, they fought with every legal, and sometimes extralegal, weapon available. The combination of deep-pocketed debtor corporations fighting for survival, brilliant and sometimes unscrupulous lawyers, vulnerable judges in a fragile newly institutionalized court, a disorganized self-regulating bar, together with hostility or skepticism in higher courts and the Ministry of Justice, in an atmosphere of nationalist backlash against foreign takeovers of Indonesian industry, enabled debtors, who had little to say at the point of statutory enactment, effectively to subvert the reforms through court decisions.

In Korea, by contrast, the growing powers and manifest competence of the Bankruptcy Court in a much less corrupt atmosphere led to debtor use of courts, thereby affirming their legitimacy and power as formal law-producing sites. Debtor SOEs in China had their collective interests represented by SETC, many of whose senior officials had previously been senior managers in the kinds of enterprises they now regulated. We have noted that the relative influence of the SETC fluctuated in relation to the banking sector in successive sets of corporate restructuring rules. After its breakup the interests of state-owned debtors were dispersed among government agencies. Yet, because the fate of SOEs ties in so closely with potential social unrest, top leaders have ensured they will retain administrative controls over the pipelines of cases into bankruptcy courts, a move that signifies the continuing capacity of large SOEs to use political leverage rather than legal mechanisms to handle creditors. Through the entire drafting process, private firms, while the most dynamic and expansive segment of the economy, had no effective voice.

Law Implementation   In the case of bankruptcy law, national or domestic actors on the implementation side involve all the parties to the practice of corporate bankruptcy—debtor corporations, secured creditors such as banks, unsecured creditors, trade creditors such as suppliers, workers, the state (for taxes and social security withholdings), the courts, government agencies (e.g., the English Insolvency Service), and insolvency-related professions (e.g., lawyers, accountants, insolvency practitioners). These groups have the capacity to widen or narrow the gap between the letter of the law and law-in-practice through the long-attested mechanisms of avoidance, creative compliance, resistance, and the like. The ultimate test of legal change takes place on the ground of practice. In the final analysis the actors involved in the everyday work of corporate reorganization and liquidation embody the failure or success of attempted change.

We observe some commonalities across the cases. Since implementation is the arena of resistance that has most affinity with debtors, they become pivotal actors in practice. The more that bankruptcy procedures harm the control of debtors over their companies, the greater the probability that they will resist. Where debtor-managers are also debtor-owners, the resistance will be intense, particularly if the business is family owned. This certainly characterizes the orientations of owner-managers of Indonesia's larger companies, and especially its family-controlled conglomerates, toward the new laws introduced after 1997. Initial resistance quickly turned to distortion and ultimately co-optation of the law, aided and abetted by the courts. Reluctance to use courts, and a preference for out-of-court workouts, can be observed in Korea, although that may be changing with the sunset of the Corporate Restructuring Promotion Act, the competent performance of the courts, and the enactment of the Unified Bankruptcy Act 2005. SOE debtor response to China's State Council Document 59 and Document 10, among others, compelled state regulators to move first one way, then another to respond to use and misuse of new rules. But until the new comprehensive law is implemented in 2007, it will not be known for some time how debtor behavior will affect the formal legal change.

Secured creditors are the mirror image of debtors. Following the Crisis the banking systems and practices of all three countries underwent close scrutiny and far-reaching reforms. In all three countries new regulatory agencies with stronger powers and closer supervision sprang up to forestall casual, personalistic, or politically animated lending. Each country took steps to reduce the proportion of nonperforming loans and recapitalize the banks (OECD 2004). Regulatory agencies in Korea and Indonesia demanded that banks put in place workout regimes to identify early and intervene quickly in cases where borrowers became distressed. There are indicators of substantial changes in banking practices. However, the efficacy of lenders to troubled companies depends heavily on the predictability that courts will liquidate companies that don't effectively reorganize. In Indonesia that predictability never came; indeed, courts became a haven for debtors, an unanticipated outcome that reduced the inclination of bankers to go to court and lessened their leverage over debtors in practice. In China the use of bankruptcy law and institutions by courts is too little, too variable, too uncertain, and too understudied to know how much banking action in practice is being conditioned by the changing legal environment.

Trade creditors are not well studied in any country. Some estimates put the credit they extend at levels close to those of secured creditors (Santella 2003). In each of our cases there is no research to indicate what role their practices play in implementation or how their practices are affected by the reforms.

Professionals provide the bridge between formal law and its practical use. Their disposition toward formal legal change will make or break it. At one extreme, professionals may ignore the law altogether, in which case it becomes irrelevant. When Korean commercial lawyers refused to use a MOFE-initiated statutory innovation to allow prepackaged reorganizations, the lawyers effectively killed the innovation and forced the Government to find another path forward. At another extreme, professionals may embrace the law and use it for the mutual benefit of themselves and their clients. This is what creditor-lawyers did initially and debtor-lawyers did subsequently in Indonesia. In between are many shades of gray as lawyers, accountants, and insolvency practitioners gauge the potential value of the law for their practice and their clients. After initial optimism, in Indonesia elite professionals have turned their back on the bankruptcy system, which effectively reduces it to a cipher. In Korea, elite commercial lawyers slowly have come to terms with the reforms and now use bankruptcy law as part of their repertoire of client representation. It expands their market for legal services, especially in the next dip of the business cycle. By appropriating the reforms, they institutionalize them in practice. In China, the bankruptcy bar is quite underdeveloped, as is commercial law more generally. Undoubtedly the new law will be seen as an opportunity to expand the market for legal services, but how much market opportunity exists will depend on a set of imponderables, such as the regulations and interpretations yet to be issued by state agencies and the Supreme People's Court, the degree of administration interventions in those cases where it is possible, the competence and neutrality of judges, and the extent of local political intervention in cases.

Since bankruptcy systems are always backstopped by courts, the orientations of judges similarly affect the impact of change, even more so when judges are potential lawmakers themselves. Most IFIs premise their reform packages on the belief that without an assurance that judges will liquidate a company, or eject its managers, then debtors in particular will have little economic incentive to renegotiate their indebtedness to creditors. The economic criterion test amendment to Korean bankruptcy law was intended explicitly to reduce the discretion of judges and so compel them to liquidate companies whose liabilities exceeded their assets. The liquidation by a court of Dong-Ah Corporation, the huge multinational construction company, sent a powerful signal to financial markets that restructuring was a much more desirable alternative. Professionals and their clients shifted perceptibly to a culture of reorganization once it became clear that neither government regulators nor judges would save failing companies. The behavior of judges similarly changed the market behavior of Indonesian firms. When it became clear that by incompetence or misconduct, judges in the Commercial Court or Supreme Court might side with large family-owned conglomerates against their creditors, then the threat of liquidation became hollow. Ironically, the courts became a shelter for precisely the opposite end for which they had been designed. And in China, since judges have been essentially irrelevant for years under the 1986 SOE law, and their actions under the new law will not be tested for private firms or SOEs until it comes into effect in 2007, it cannot be predicted how behavior will change in practice.

Officials, too, will be salient for legal change in practice if they have substantial regulatory powers. Indeed, in Korea and China the reform process intended that officials progressively withdraw from direct interference in particular firms in order to allow the market to operate according to the new rule-making regime of the bankruptcy reforms. From the mid-1990s, when regulators at the SETC controlled all mergers, reorganizations, and liquidations of SOEs, to the later 2000s, when SOEs supposedly are to manage their own affairs in a creditor economy whose limits are defined by bankruptcy law, the secular change involves a shifting of the boundary between state and market control. Similarly, under pressure from the IMF, the leading role of the Ministry of Finance and Economy in Korea's state development economy was to be attenuated so that officials would forgo interventionism and allow debtors and creditors to negotiate their way out of financial distress within parameters and using mechanisms established by the bankruptcy law. It is clear that withdrawal from guidance of firms was not easy; officials exercised their diminished powers indirectly through government-controlled and regulated banks until the Corporate Restructuring Promotion Act expired. The practice of corporate reorganization in a law-regulated market therefore turns both directly and indirectly on the adjudicatory and regulatory behaviors of judges and officials.

Mechanisms

Cycles of national lawmaking are driven by four primary mechanisms that hold each side of the recursive loop in dynamic tension.

The Indeterminacy of Law   All statutes, court opinions, and regulations contain ambiguities and gaps that create uncertainty and lead to unanticipated consequences. As an entire school of jurisprudence—Critical Legal Studies— has argued, law inherently is ambiguous and subject to interpretive confusion or maneuver. This view has been reinforced by scholarship on law and finance that champions the precision of property rights as a prerequisite for economic development (Pistor and Xu 2003). The more diverse and less integrated its implementing agencies and courts, the greater variation will occur in its application. And the more sophisticated its professionals, the greater the probability for creative misapplication or redirection of statutes and regulations in unexpected directions and to unimagined purposes. Moreover, indeterminacy may be compounded by institutional pathologies such as judicial corruption or incompetence. The occurrence of indeterminacy and unintended consequences regularly drives a turn of the reform cycle, as original crafters of law seek to remedy its deficiencies in order to achieve their original purposes, or subjects of the law react to unwanted outcomes, or courts seek to settle meanings. And more contentious lawmaking is likely to result in vague, ambiguous law that will produce inconsistency in application and provide ample opportunity for creative compliance.

The case studies reveal several types of indeterminacy. Indeterminacy can stem from *ambiguity* of concepts. The fight in the Indonesian courts over the seemingly established meaning of *debts* well illustrates how even a fundamental legal term in peculiar circumstances can become an unexpected site of professional quarrels. Indeterminacy stem from *gaps* in the law. Rather than being a seamless web, statutory law frequently fails to treat certain issues that spring up in practice. Indeed, countries like China purposefully design their commercial law very openly with the expectation that gaps will be filled by regulations and interpretations of agencies and the court. While the gaps may allow freedom for flexible adjustments by courts, they also permit another manifestation of indeterminacy, namely, *inconsistency* between statutes or the regulations and interpretations that are meant to clarify them. Inconsistency can come not only through direct contradictions between lawmaking sources but through the *multiplication* of sources of law. The perception of confusion, delay, and cost resulting from Korea's three bankruptcy laws fed the drive of the IMF to persuade Korea to unify them in a single law. Similar issues explain one impetus for China's comprehensive law to replace a muddle of statutory, judicial, and regulatory laws that applied in different circumstances. While any of those options alone creates indeterminacy, the problem is compounded where more than one option comes into play. Together they are conducive to an unpredictability of how law will be used and therefore uncertainty in the market about the calculus of following a legal rather than some other path.

Contradictions   Cycles of lawmaking and implementation frequently are driven by contradictions internalized within the law. When lawmakers cannot definitively resolve underlying economic, political, or ideological contradictions, they settle for partial or temporary solutions. If these are not based on a political settlement that reflects a compromise among actors powerful enough to derail the law, then tensions or contradictions get internalized into law. Such unstable resolutions within lawmaking make the law vulnerable to subsequent disturbances or triggering events that precipitate another round of attempted solutions. Contradictions are of two kinds.

Contradictions often express clashes of underlying *ideologies*. For instance, the Washington Consensus stressed openness to global trade, lowering of national barriers, and exposure of local markets to international competition and investment (Falk 1999; Salacuse 2000). This ideology is supposed to lead to more investment and economic growth. Yet many developing and transitional countries confront that ideology with one of national sovereignty, that is, they resist losing the flagships of industrial sectors to footloose foreign owners with much less interest in the country for its own sake. Bankruptcy lawmaking catches lawmakers between these countervailing ideologies, and they will likely make their policy decisions partly to satisfy both—thus building contradictions into what may be an inherently unstable settlement.

One form of ideological contradiction reflects a clash between global and local perspectives. The Indonesian reforms pitted a universalistic model of bankruptcy law, which would allow pure market forces to determine the fates of Indonesian corporations, against nationalist identity, which abhorred the loss of Indonesian control over its flagship corporations in critical economic sectors. Similarly, successive drafts of the Chinese bankruptcy law reflected a struggle between some Chinese lawmakers, who wanted to maintain discretionary powers by the state over interventions in bankruptcy cases, and international experts and institutions, who insisted that global norms required administrative restraint. Not infrequently this and other instances of a domestic-international tension were acknowledged in China's insistence that it adopt a bankruptcy law "with Chinese characteristics," that is, a law that in important respects might not conform to global norms.

Other forms of ideological contradictions stem from domestic conflicts. A subtext of resistance in Indonesia occurred because internalized within the bankruptcy reforms was a veiled ethnic and political struggle within Indonesia between the Chinese, whose conglomerates dominated many sectors of the economy, and the ethnic Indonesians, who dominated politics. This division of labor itself was a political settlement that had dampened ethnic strife. If ethnic Chinese viewed the corporate restructuring reforms as a political weapon to undermine Chinese business dominance, then the wider interethnic settlement might dissolve. In China, too, divisions periodically reappear between leaders who emphasize a *socialist* market economy and those who advocate a socialist *market* economy. This difference in relative emphasis has consequences for bankruptcy systems, not least in the relative priorities it gives to workers and bankers. It reflects emphases on administratively directed interventions into market activity versus those that allow a rule-governed market to operate without arbitrary interventions.

Contradictions may also be *structural*. Ideological contradictions, for instance, can be institutionalized in competing social structures. In bankruptcy lawmaking such contradictions can be observed among branches of government and within branches. In both Korea and Indonesia we saw that economic and justice ministries confronted each other not only over their relative status in the government, an unequal competition since finance ministries usually prevailed, but also over the ideologies they reflected. In Korea the intimate ties between MOFE and the IMF endowed upon the finance ministry a set of beliefs about what motivates firms and how the justice system should reflect an economic logic. But the tension between the finance and justice ministries was magnified in Korea, and to a lesser extent in Indonesia, between the finance ministry and the courts. On the one hand, MOFE found it difficult to relinquish the tight controls over the economy that had propelled Korea from a third- to a first-world economy. On the other hand, the judiciary was imbued with rule-of-law values that championed the independence of courts, the discretion of judges, and the neutrality of the courtroom. In cases such as these, contradictions can be effectively institutionalized when implementation is parceled out among rival agencies. In China this impediment to settled reforms is overlaid with yet other conflicts among levels of government, most notably among Beijing, the provinces, and local municipalities, each of which may have strong local reasons for building into their regulatory apparatus interpretations or ideological emphases that are at odds with each other.

Diagnostic Struggles   Since legal (and other) professionals are so heavily invested in lawmaking, there is value in adapting the conceptual apparatus of diagnosis and treatment that has been applied to professional work more generally (Abbott 1988). Diagnosis involves the identification of a problem, the application to that problem various rules of relevance for a given reform (e.g., how broadly construed will be the depiction of the problem), and relating the problem so construed to a way of classifying problems for purposes of law reform (e.g., in relation to a profession's diagnostic classification system or the body of laws that govern a country and to which this reform must be fitted).[4]

Diagnosis in law reforms takes the form of a social construction of how a problem is to be understood and classified. It usually contains an implicit theory of relations between parts of a society, market, and government. More important, diagnosis is a field of contestation among actors for whom the definition of the problem and its subsequent classification will influence prescriptions that yield differential benefits. Diagnosis therefore plays a role analogous to agenda setting in legislative politics. It sets constraints, filters information, and orients perceptions that point toward one set of putative treatments rather than another.[5] The contest among actors in diagnosis will often carry over into conflicts over treatment. However, if the politics that surround diagnosis lead to clear victory of one diagnosis, the advocates of the rejected diagnosis may be excluded from the formulation of legal prescriptions and thus fight against their exclusion in later stages (e.g., law reform in the legislature, or more likely during implementation). Those actors who were successful in gaining acceptance for their diagnosis will usually also get to prescribe the legal solution.

Some of the contest over treatment turns on how measurable will be the results, since commensurability allows closer monitoring, and so favors some actors (e.g., international financial institutions) over others (e.g., national governments not meeting their commitments). Power differences between national actors (e.g., professions) and the global institutions lead to considerable cross-national variation in the ability of external actors to impose their diagnoses and treatments. Lawmaking in a global context often occurs through the mediation of professionals so that struggles break out among the professionals (e.g., lawyers and economists) within the IFIs as well as among professions in the nation-state. Lawmaking in crisis circumstances may pit diagnosticians from international institutions against diagnosticians in the nation-state. In lawmaking, diagnosis and prescription are undertaken both by professionals and all other collective actors for whom lawmaking has relevance. Contests over diagnosis and prescription can ramify equally widely. Yet it is a common strategy of professionals to seek technical diagnoses and specialized treatments in order to encapsulate a sphere of regulation within their own professional jurisdiction.

Diagnostic failures are of different types. *Misdiagnoses* occur when later events prove the diagnosis was wrong at the outset. The IMF, when it decided that Indonesia's legal system could be revived, did not adequately perceive how corrosive was the degree of corruption in the courts and how difficult it would be to extirpate. By not flagging corruption as a problem to be solved at the outset, the IMF and its Indonesian allies were forced to undergo one after another round of subsequent reforms to try to remedy the initial diagnostic failure. Arguably that failure was the single most damaging lapse in its law reform package. Diagnosis by IFIs often can be flawed because diagnosis requires quick action. When IFIs intervene in economic emergencies, *hasty diagnoses* can lead to lapses and faulty prescriptions that again require further corrective rounds of lawmaking. The intense time pressures that the IMF and World Bank confronted in Indonesia and Korea required snap decisions based on access to biased samples of informants about the functioning of the current system and recommendations about how it should be changed. Hastiness in part turns on *incomplete diagnosis*—the reformers do not have sufficient access to the cross section of participants in practice, particularly those farthest removed from the political center, such as workers on the shop floor and managers in the provinces. It is precisely this failure in the chain of intelligence gathering about the state of affairs that a senior Chinese official described as the reasons for difficulties confronted by SETC in its experiments with SOE liquidations and reorganizations.

> There is a massive gap between what happens on the ground and the drafting of the law—in fact, there is almost no relationship between the two. The law-drafters don't really know what's going on on the ground. And the people on the

ground, actually dealing with SOEs, which are in terrible shape, don't know and don't care about the bankruptcy law. They have 50 years of terrible management to recover from. A huge gap exists between the two, and law lags well behind it and it will take a huge amount of time before and practice are in synch.[6]

Diagnostic struggles frequently center around disciplinary differences among professions. In the bankruptcy field these are most pronounced between economists and lawyers, as the Korean debates well exemplified (Halliday and Carruthers 2004a). Economists had an incentive-driven mechanistic notion of how the levers of law could be manipulated as if they were interest rates. Judges could be disciplined by accounting formulae as if judges were miscreant agents seeking to escape the control of their principals. Lawyers had a rights-driven organic notion of how law worked, as well as a tested sense of its limits for compelling sharp turns in behavior. Judges required discretion because facts were always more complicated and contingent than bright-line rules could contain. Consistently, therefore, each profession construed the problems to be solved in different terms. Since each profession also had the particular ear of competing government ministries—economists with the Ministry of Finance and Economy and lawyers with the Ministry of Justice and the courts—they also had the capacity to try to weld their technical authority to different centers of power.

As a result, contention occurs on either side of the recursive loop. The effect is to produce a strong recursive momentum between diagnosis and prescription. These are sometimes driven by changes in diagnosis. Often they are driven by experimentation with prescriptions precisely because actors confront problems that are highly complex and defy ready diagnosis. Sometimes this diagnostic challenge is "solved" by the application of a priori models to which supporting evidence is adduced.[7]

Actor Mismatch   Almost always a mismatch occurs between parties in practice and lawmaking actors. In bankruptcy politics, for instance, corporations or debtors are always actors in practice but scarcely ever actors in lawmaking. In bankruptcy lawmaking, international institutions or state officials may be primary actors in setting up a regime but play only episodic roles in its administration. The merit of the concept of actor mismatch inheres in its challenge to examine systematically all those actors integral to practice, since that is ultimately where legal change succeeds or fails, and all those actors proximate to lawmaking. The difference between the two, an asymmetry, sets up a dynamic integral to repeated cycles or eventual settlement at a kind of equilibrium. In other words, there is a form of power that is mobilized for lawmaking and another form of power that is activated in law implementation. Neither can be ignored.

The mechanisms that produce or mitigate "mismatch" are critically important in the recursivity of law, for they set in play numbers of subsidiary adjustments. Actors in lawmaking who rely on a diagnosis that excluded key practice groups are likely to find their remedies faultily designed. Actors in practice who are excluded from lawmaking can use their control of implementation to undermine and subvert legal changes prescribed by reforms. Indonesian debtors make the point forcefully. The diagnosis of what had contributed to Indonesia's financial collapse relied heavily on a sampling of proximate players—law firms that had represented the World Bank's International Finance Corporation, international lawyers and accounting firms, a few judges, government officials—that mostly excluded the very actors toward whom the law reforms were primarily directed—the debtors, leaders of Indonesia's corporate sector. These players did not have the power to forestall reforms on which they had not been consulted but did have the power to frustrate reforms in practice. The politics of implementation became a site of outright resistance. Domestic actors excluded from lawmaking fought with whatever weapons they had available—legal and extralegal—and these proved decisive in the flawed implantation of a new regime.

Actors in practice who fail to participate in lawmaking through ignorance, failure to recognize their own interests, or an inability to mobilize often find that legal reforms crystallize their interests, help mobilize their members, and motivate intervention. A new and unwelcome law, regulation, or court ruling jolts them into action for the next round of lawmaking.

Mismatch issues are particularly acute for professionals, since they sit astride the implementation process, but are not always integral to statutory lawmaking. On the one hand, a failure to incorporate professionals into lawmaking provokes them to fight anew the lawmaking battle on the terrain of practice they dominate. To alienate the occupation that sits astride the process of implementation sows seeds of subversion in practice. These are all the more corrosive since, unlike formal law, legal practices are substantially invisible much of the time.

On the other hand, by "professionalizing" lawmaking, where technical authority trumps the balancing of interests by all parties, the mismatch is likely to engender a backlash from excluded parties either in implementation or in a further round of reforms. Since lawyers are the profession most proximate to change in law, they have a special status in which their technical authority can be turned to substantive effect.

．　．　．

In sum, each side of the recursive loop has a contingent relationship with the other. There is a politics of enactment that influences compliance and implementation. If the lawmaking process is considered procedurally unjust or illegitimate, if power at the point of enactment grossly distorts the distribution of interests in everyday life, then parties in practice may react by mobilizing their own capacities to avoid or resist change. Parties defeated in lawmaking may make the site of practice another battleground to fight again the battle they lost during enactment (see Pierson 2004: 135). What is notable in these scenarios is that implementation cannot be adequately understood without awareness of its lawmaking antecedents.

By the same token, there is a politics of implementation whereby actors in the very process of variably implementing law will influence the next round of lawmaking. Noncompliance or creative compliance with the law implicitly, and often explicitly, points to the prospect of corrective formal adjustments that will narrow the gap between legislative or regulatory intent and its working out in practice. Lawmaking involves the mobilization of actors, usually a biased subset of those who are engaged in practice.

Both the politics of enactment and the politics of implementation, the two sides of recursive loops, are arenas of power. On the implementation side, power is manifest in differing capacities of actors—lawyers, judges, debtors, creditors—to mobilize. In everyday practice mobilization more often takes the form of an aggregate of individual actions by debtors, trade creditors, or others, who respond similarly to perceived inadequacies of legal enactments. But it is possible in principle for collective action to occur on the implementation— for a bar association to take an adverse position on a new law that its members then carry into practice, or for a trade association to respond likewise.

Power is more visible in the politics of enactment. Here actors vary in their capacities to make diagnoses, to ensure those diagnoses stick, and to set agendas for responsive lawmaking. In crisis situations where banks are discredited, their usual prominence in bankruptcy reforms is muted, and the initiative lies in the hands of government agencies that are negotiating with international institutions. In more temperate times, bankers and lawyers frequently play a more dominant role than other parties to everyday bankruptcies, except perhaps unions in countries where they are strong and accurately perceive the interests at stake. The exercise of power at the enactment phase is reflected in provisions inserted into statutes and regulations that are beneficial to the strongest parties. The ability to mobilize through courts can even the balance of power between creditors and debtors, as both retain skilled professionals to advocate their causes.

Just as configurations of actors vary on either side of the recursive loop, so, too, do certain resources benefit some actors in their proximity to law-makers and others in their proximity to practice. Those actors who are repeat players in bankruptcy proceedings, who readily perceive their interests, can mobilize easily, and can commit major resources to influence lawmakers will exert their power effectively through lawmaking. Those actors who are repeat players in practice, as well as those whose reputations, fortune, and power are immediately at stake in specific bankruptcies, mobilize in a different way, outside and inside courts, in ways that can nullify law-on-the-books. Argu-ably the brake of inertial influence, of slowing or resisting reform, gives the advantage to practitioners. Again it is the battleground of last resort, the final retreat for parties whose prominence in practice was not matched by their centrality to lawmaking.

Trajectories of Recursivity

The rapidity or speed of cycles from the onset of an episode to its settling also varies. Speed matters, often perversely. A very quick lawmaking move from the onset of a problem, such as a crisis or moral panic, can rapidly lead to a poten-tial remedy, but at a price. Hair-trigger enactments leave little time for research, whether to identify all the players whose opinions are necessary to canvass in order to understand the full dimensions of a problem, or to accumulate suffi-cient evidence to decide if the frequency and distribution of a problem warrants the strictures of legal sanctions and remedies. The pressure of time amplifies the probability of contradictions that are not resolved, of faulty diagnosis or misdiagnosis, of a failure to draw the interests of all stakeholders in practice into the politics of enactment, and of badly drafted law. Truncated time gives little opportunity to forge alliances and compromises that will be binding in practice. Moreover, a hastily authorized initial law, case, or regulation increases the likelihood that a chain reaction of subsequent rapid cycles will occur in order to compensate for the faults of the initial rush to enactment.

Here each site of lawmaking is not equal. In emergencies, legislatures, courts, regulatory agencies, and sometimes presidential offices can move very quickly. In the ordinary course of lawmaking, however, it takes a long time for clarifying or corrective cases to wend their ways from first-level to supreme courts. Legal change can be in limbo until that meandering path is negotiated. Part of the uncertainty for creditors and debtors alike in Indonesia during the first flush of reforms stemmed from surprising decisions that signaled the law was far from settled. More important, they also signaled that many structural and organizational problems were not adequately treated in the initial wave of reforms. It took several quick cycles to put in place structures, such as ad hoc judges, to try to stabilize the situation to the satisfaction of the IMF and its domestic allies.

Yet delay, too, has its costs. If IFIs want major rapid changes while an emergency is fresh, national policymakers may increase their negotiating power by dragging out reforms. When the need for emergency credit has diminished, IFIs have been distracted by crises elsewhere, and initial panic has subsided, then reforms become harder to engineer. From the vantage point of nation-states greater deliberation offers the benefit of more research, a better chance of forging lasting compromises, and a law better suited to their circumstances. Time, in principle, mitigates the pathologies of legal change that are reflected in each of the recursive mechanisms.

Rapid cycles can reflect the overwhelming pressure of IFIs demanding governments to commit to particular reforms on a given calendar. But they also may reflect imbalances in domestic politics. Contrast Korea and China. In Korea, the long-standing dominance of MOFE in economic lawmaking manifested itself in several MOFE-initiated statutes in quick succession. With IFI support, these were pushed through the National Assembly with little chance for dissidents to raise exceptions. By the time of the Unified Bankruptcy Act in 2005, however, that influence had attenuated through an extended process of consultation with stakeholders and lessened IFI pressure, although the IMF and World Bank maintained some involvement through the last drafts of the law. In China, by contrast, the government faced no emergency but a steady increase in economic and social pressures within the country in the context of cohering global norms. While workers and an interventionist State Council might have had primacy of influence in the mid-1990s, by the mid-2000s changes in the banking sector, the growth of private professions, and extended interchanges between Chinese and foreign experts led to some balancing of otherwise opposing interests.

Rapid lawmaking favors the metric of enactment. It presents symbolic and potentially dramatic signals of change to alert constituencies, domestic and international.

Slower lawmaking favors the metric of implementation. It can increase the probability of political settlements that obviate the pathologies of recursive mechanisms. Its principal constituency is local.

Time, therefore, is a resource to be manipulated by actors with varying capacities to do so (Table 10.1). Rapid formal change favors global actors with economic weapons in emergencies. Slow operational change favors local actors when emergencies dissipate. Rapid change is a prerogative of leaders and those who control lawmaking institutions. Slow change is the prerogative of practitioners and their clients. Rapid change can therefore be ephemeral, whereas slow change is more durable. By the same token, rapid formal change, while highly visible, can be illusory; slow operational change, while largely invisible, can be substantial.

The issue of the magnitude of change is connected to the control of time and speed. For simplicity we can imagine a continuum from one extreme,

TABLE 10.1 Metrics of Change for Formal Law and Operational Law

	Formal Law Statutory, Case, Regulatory	Operational Law
Metric of Change	Formal enactment	Behavioral change
Pace of Change	Regulatory (fast) Statutory (slow) Case (slowest)	Very slow
Primary Agents	Officials, International institutions	Practitioners
Primary Locus	State agencies	Everyday life
Primacy Functions	Symbolic, Expressive, Institutional	Effectiveness
Ease of Change	Easy	Difficult
Visibility of Change	High	Low
Principal Constituencies for Change	International observers Domestic policy audiences Mobilized interests	Mobilized interests Nonmobilized stakeholders

a small procedural amendment to one provision in a statute, to another extreme, a massive comprehensive act that covers the entire substantive and procedural terrain of the law.[8] The case studies show how governments can use the packaging or incrementality of formal enactments to produce differing patterns of change. In any recursive episode, a variety of distinctive trajectories are possible, depending on various manipulations of time, speed, and increments. One measure of power in legal change is precisely this ability to expand or contract the temporal window of change, to increase or decrease the speed of reform cycles within that window, and to divide or consolidate the package of reforms.

Observe Table 10.2, which summarizes each recursive episode. In the Korean case, a series of modest amendments kept comprehensive reforms at bay until external pressure built up sufficiently to induce a unification of its three bankruptcy laws. This was no happenstance. The quick repeated amendments of 1998 and 1999, followed by the Corporate Restructuring Promotion Act of 2000, reflected the power of MOFE, fortified by pressures from the IFIs, and the Korean government's own determination to escape from the shame of financial failure. The instrumental use of law as a lever of quick behavioral change at the same time reflected the weakness of the legal complex whose skepticism about instant behavioral change derived from their wariness of what legal experts thought to be naïve economistic solutions. But the foot dragging by the legal establishment was also induced by doubts that consolidation of Korea's three bankruptcy laws was necessary or desirable. Not a few elite experts hoped that repeated minor reforms, coupled with Korea's quick economic rebound, would relieve the pressure to produce a comprehensive law. Thus, the Korean trajectory follows a distinctive pattern—a series of minor and incremental amendments to statutes and institutions (e.g., the bankruptcy division of the courts) that climax in one massive reform almost a decade later.

The Indonesian case presents a sharp contrast. Here a comprehensive packet of reforms was agreed upon by the Government, inscribed in Letters of Intent, and put on the books within months of the IFI's assertive presence in Jakarta. The reform package involved presidential decrees, statutes, regulations, cases, institutional changes. It was truly systemic. But all the pathologies we have previously identified in this process led to years of corrective statutory, regulatory, and administrative actions, all aimed at institutionalizing the initial concept of an effective insolvency system purportedly agreed to by the IMF and Government of Indonesia. The interim comprehensive

TABLE 10.2 Recursive Episodes of Insolvency Lawmaking in East Asia

Attributes of Recursive Episodes	Indonesia	Korea	China
Onset	Financial crisis: Transition from national to global capital markets	Financial crisis: Transition from national to global capital markets	Progressive transition from command to market economy
Period	1998–2005	1998–2005	1994–2006
Frequency	Rapid/Annual	Rapid/Annual	Periodic
Pressure	Foreign	Foreign/Domestic	Domestic
Indeterminacy	Vagueness of concepts Faulty grafting onto outmoded substantive law Institutional failure	Inflexibility of bright-line rule Nonuse of prepackage innovation	Drafting vagueness Ambiguous discretionary powers Creative noncompliance
Contradictions	Global creditor vs. national debtor interests Market neutrality vs. ethnic expropriation	State-directed vs. law- or market-driven economy Global opening vs. local protectionism Economic vs. legal models of change	Socialist market economy vs. socialist market economy Firms as rational economic actors vs. firms as social safety nets
Diagnosis	Local legal elites, major law firms, bankers, officials Indigenous research	Local legal elites, major law firms, bankers, officials, government ministries (MOFE) Indigenous research	State agencies (judges, academics) IFI research (World Bank, ADB)
Mismatch: Practice actors missing from lawmaking	Debtors (corporations) Labor Trade creditors/suppliers	Debtors (corporations) Labor Trade creditors/suppliers	Insolvency and legal practitioners Private firms
Cycles: Problem based or institution based	Substantive law Courts: Competence or corruption Out-of-court	Substantive law Courts Out-of-court	SOEs (SETC agency track) All corporations (NPC legislative track)
Episode trajectory	Significant reforms followed by corrective steps	Successive limited reforms leading to comprehensive reform	Progressive steps culminating in comprehensive reforms

SOURCE: Halliday and Carruthers (2007b).

statutory reforms to which the Government of Indonesia committed itself in 1998 did not wend their way through the legislature until 2005. Now the legal changes have largely settled, with major formal changes but minor operational effects. The "big bang" of the Indonesian trajectory therefore reflects a quite different structure, beginning with a comprehensive package at the beginning of an emergency-induced episode and followed by rapid cycles of corrective measures to fill holes, clarify ambiguities, and correct prescriptions based on faulty diagnoses.

China displays a more complicated pattern because its state agencies undertook many incremental experimental measures to compensate for the failings of the 1986 Interim Bankruptcy Law.[9] So, too, did the Supreme People's Court endeavor to fill gaps in the 1986 law with interstitial interpretations. While the legislature stood still, regulatory agencies and the courts over two decades spearheaded massive changes in the state-owned sector. Indeed it is certain that top leaders held back on passage of a comprehensive bankruptcy law until the potential harms it could do to the economy, society, and political system were mitigated by administrative interventions in the state-owned sector. At first this looks more like the Korean model. But on closer examination it is apparent that the Chinese were in greater control of their calendar. Government leaders showed their own substantial freedom from external pressures by widening the window of change to suit their domestic situation. Within this expandable window they moved at a speed of administrative reform, on one track, and of statutory drafting revisions, on another, that always were headed toward some formal coherence for the entire market and legal system. Although time, speed, and steps marched to the beat of their own drum, the Chinese could also hear the drumbeats from international organizations and major markets, such as the European Union. While more autonomous than Korea, the Chinese nevertheless were not deaf to calls for formal change from significant global actors.

These are certainly not the only patterns of recursive change. In countries where formal law is promulgated by multiple agencies, for example, where legislatures, courts, regulatory agencies, and presidential offices each are sources of significant legal pronouncements, many complex patterns are possible. Contrast situations in which a single statute, such as the U.S. Civil Rights Act of 1964 or the U.S. Bankruptcy Code of 1978, gives rise to many cycles of regulations and case law that qualify and extend legislation, with other situations where a presidential decree or dramatic opinion from a constitutional court sparks legislative and regulatory responses. Furthermore, countries with multiple levels of lawmaking, such as federal regimes, similarly multiply the centers from which formal law can emerge. When these two sources of variation are added together, the opportunities for inconsistencies and contradictions are multiplied, but so, too, are potential remedies for actor mismatch and diagnostic struggles. Multiple centers of lawmaking power enable actors with very different resources to search for the lawmaking forum most proximate and favorable to them.

Recursivity and Intermediation

In a world of interpenetrating legal and market regimes, cycles of domestic legal change are embedded within global/local exchanges, trade-offs, negotiations, and contests. Although endogenous recursivity driven by identifiable mechanisms is logically possible, it is empirically difficult to partition these dynamics from global/local encounters. It follows that intermediation, the problem IFIs confront in extending their normative influence, and foiling, the stratagems that nation-states use to assure themselves some degrees of freedom, will also be drivers of recursive legal change.

Patterns of intermediation affect cycles of change. The case studies offer useful evidence about the interplay of recursivity and intermediation. The difficulties in intermediation for international actors derive, we argued, from the situation of countries in the Global South in a two-dimensional space: the imbalance of power between global and local actors; and the proximity of actors in the Global South to the dominant actors and mores in the Global North. It should follow that (1) the greater the imbalance of power, especially in an emergency, the stronger the capacity of IFIs to initiate an episode of reform. The cases of Korea and Indonesia support this proposition for bankruptcy reforms with the qualification that each country already had begun to consider reforms. The Crisis moved them from deliberation to action. China is also consistent with this proposition because the power differences between China and the IFIs were smaller, the 1997 Asian Crisis had a much less direct impact, and the onset of the episode antedated it by several years: the NPC started its drafting in 1994; the SETC administrative reforms of SOEs began in the mid-1990s. When the imbalance of power is great, international organizations can obtain enactment of law reforms in exchange for access to multilateral capital. Financial coercion got law-on-the-books in Korea and Indonesia in a matter of months. Without that asymmetry between IFIs and the nation-state, China could afford to take its time to enactment, which it did, some nine years after the Crisis struck elsewhere on the continent. The trajectories of reforms are also influenced by differences among the East Asian nations in their power relative to international organizations.

The cases in East Asia are also consistent with the proposition that (2) the greater that asymmetry of power, the more capacity IFIs had to drive forward successive rounds of enactments as corrections to incomplete implementation. The IMF drove Indonesia hard through rapid cycles of statutory, regulatory, and institutional change, frequently in quick reaction to failures in practice. Korea's cycles of formal reforms were also rapid. Yet only in part did these stem from Korea's desperate situation in 1998. Korea rebounded quickly. Several of the iterations of formal changes owed more to domestic will to remedy perceived flaws in the legal architecture of the economy than raw pressure from the IMF or World Bank. Even more so China's nimble changes in SOE-restructuring schemes reflected its domestic situation, although it was not unmindful of dangers that could arise domestically as its economy opened up to foreign competition. However, the evidence does not support the proposition that (3) the greater the imbalance of power, the higher the probability that implementation will take effect, in other words, that IFIs will have the power to bring formal reforms to completion in practice. The widest imbalance, between Indonesia and the IFIs, did not produce much perceptible change in practice. Nor did the narrowest gap, between IFIs and China, permit the most change in practice.

Does proximity of a country in the Global South to the change agents of the Global North make a difference to cycles of enactment and implementation? We find that (4) the greater the distance from global institutions, the more limited the choice of intermediaries to guide reforms. It follows that (5) greater cultural distance will likely produce more ideological contradictions between global and local norms, in part based (6) on more difficulty in making empirically justifiable diagnoses because practices are more obscure and resources to study them are scarce. The contrasts between Indonesia, the most culturally remote of the three cases, and Korea, the most culturally consonant with global norms, lend support to these propositions. China is a somewhat anomalous, or at least unknown, case because its rapid administrative reforms of SOEs in the 1990s stemmed less from "cultural" remoteness from global centers than the magnitude of the domestic task to prepare state-owned enterprises for competition in the emerging socialist market economy. Because the comprehensive bankruptcy law is so new that its implementing regulations are only slowly taking shape, it is too early to tell if the changing proximity of its elite academic drafters, officials, and policymakers to the crystallizing global norms for bankruptcy law will have reduced ambiguity, contradictions, and inadequate diagnosis. But the brevity of the law and some of its inherent strains, for example, over autonomy of courts and competence of judges, suggest that its normative conception of law-regulated markets has not assimilated closely to the dominant global norms articulated by UNCITRAL and the World Bank. In that case there will be repeated cycles of statutory amendments, court interpretations, and regulations, as is not uncommon in other Chinese lawmaking.

The attributes of available intermediaries will also affect the configurations of recursivity. For instance, other things being equal, (7) the greater the supply of expert intermediaries to IFIs and governments, the less ambiguity might be anticipated in formal enactments.[10] Shorter chains of communication and more direct relations between culturally consonant negotiators presumably increase clarity of communication. Yet the argument might go the opposite way. If a nation-state has many sophisticated experts on which it can draw, these experts may be mobilized to resist IOs on the IOs' own terms. Former IMF officials from Korea, now responsible for negotiating with the IMF on behalf of Korea via MOFE, know full well how to position Korea's preferences to deviate from IMF expectations. In addition, one of Korea's leading negotiators with the IMF indicated that he needed only pick up the phone, which he had done, to talk to Korean nationals currently at the IMF to get advice about how best to respond to pressure from Washington. This could result in two alternative outcomes: a successful negotiation that brought the Korean law into substantial concordance with IFI norms; or an effort by Korea to go its own way, particularly as the urgency of the Crisis waned, with successive rounds of reforms as Korea and the IFIs struggled to imprint their preferences on the law. In fact, Korea followed more closely the first alternative, responding in broad outline to not only IMF expectations but also to the norms developed by UNCITRAL in which Korea itself had been a delegate nation. As the numbers of Chinese academic experts in bankruptcy increased, as China consulted more widely with overseas organizations, and as Chinese drafters traveled more extensively in advanced economies, China's substantive bankruptcy drafts conformed progressively more closely to global norms, at least on the books.

Do the qualities of intermediaries, their competence, loyalty, and power also affect the shape of legal change? On purely technical grounds it might be expected that (8) the greater the competency of intermediaries, the less ambiguity and possibly the fewer contradictions internalized in the law. But ambiguity and contradictions result not only from technical expertise but from unresolved struggles between competing stakeholders. The intermediaries retained by the IMF and Government of Indonesia were superb technical lawyers with wide experience in Indonesia and in international commercial practice. But the technical quality of their statutory drafting could not withstand or anticipate the hostile reception to the law by legal representatives of stakeholders who felt they had been excluded from the politics of enactment. In this sense technically sophisticated intermediaries built their proposals on a foundation of inadequate diagnosis, actor mismatch, and contradictions. Technical competence could not compensate for these deficiencies. For the same reason, higher-quality intermediaries do not necessarily lead to fewer reform cycles. Since intermediaries are only one of many parties to reform, and often those with technical resources but not political power, their competence alone cannot guarantee a more rapid progression to settling, although, other conditions being equal, they can be influential. That influence is not only seen in drafting. Part of the function of China's academic drafters of the bankruptcy law was to brief top leaders about role of bankruptcy law in a market economy. By helping top leaders find potential affinities between the law and their policy concerns, the academic drafters paved the way for a policy choice. In one of the periodic seminars held by top leaders with policy experts, Professor Wang Weiguo advised President Zhang Zemin and his colleagues that bankruptcy law should include rehabilitation of ailing companies. Because the prospect of corporation reorganization held out hope that workers might not lose jobs, this alternative to liquidation alleviated fears about unrest from unemployed workers and thus made a law that converged with global norms more attractive domestically. The mediation here essentially took the form of arbitrage between the global and local.

In principle the availability and concordance of global scripts should also influence trajectories of reform. We have too few cases to explore variations, but our cases lead us to some conjectures. There are five properties of global scripts that likely influence the configurations of recursivity: whether there are multiple or single scripts; whether the scripts are substantively convergent or divergent; whether they are more or less legitimate; whether they are in the form of principles or rules; or whether they offer a single standard versus options. Let us contrast two extremes. If a single global script lacks legitimacy but is promulgated as a sole standard in the form of precise rules, then it increases the probability of a misfit with national norms and preferences. In a situation of marked asymmetry the nation-state may respond to the global purveyor of norms in ways that increase ambiguity in the law, set up the likelihood of inconsistency between the law to be reformed and other national laws, and build in contradictions between the global and local. This might well lead to round after round of legal enactments in the search for a mutually agreeable formal law. At another extreme, imagine a situation where single or multiple global scripts that are considered to be legitimate converge on substantive norms but give nation-states options for conformity, perhaps at the level of principles rather than rules. In this case, it is probable that national lawmakers can find solutions that resolve potential contradictions, that fill gaps and forestall inconsistencies, and that can respond to the diverse interests of stakeholders in their distinctive situation. This kind of matching, of choice within fairly broad normative parameters, would seem to reduce the need for many corrective cycles of formal lawmaking. This latter alternative comes closer to the state of affairs since 2004 when UNCITRAL and the World Bank essentially converged on common norms at a high level but gave countries significant degrees of freedom to enact and implement their laws in ways that were culturally appropriate and politically feasible. UNCITRAL's script combined not only a legitimacy born of representativeness and procedural fairness but also provided options at various levels of abstractness and particularity. This approach is implicitly respectful of national sovereignty and allows creative adaptation to local circumstances. Again, net of other considerations, it will be more likely that the trajectory of reforms will require fewer corrective cycles.

Foiling and Recursivity

If intermediation influences recursive change principally from the vantage point of international actors, foiling represents the counterpoint of nation-states. From Chapter 9 we have already anticipated the impact that foiling has on many aspects of change, from the properties of the recursive episode itself, to the magnitude and durability of legal change.

Foiling is inherent in the tension between the politics of enactment and the politics of implementation. It explains *why* foreign actors and their domestic allies keep pressing for new rounds of enactment; and it explains *how* domestic actors compel IOs to negotiate, compromise, cooperate, retreat. Foiling is therefore an integral dynamic of globalization and an omnipresent force in the shaping of recursivity.

Consider the implications of techniques used by nation-states to foil globalizing actors. When a nation rejects the assistance of IFIs, as Malaysia and Argentina did in the last ten years, it simultaneously removes IOs from direct intervention in reforms and substantially insulates domestic reforms from explicitly coercive external influence, though the threat of private capital flight might still be realized. By indigenizing reforms, it significantly reduces the array of possibilities for legal change that can produce contradictions and indeterminacy. It also reduces foiling to a single decisive act at the outset of global/local engagement and thus forestalls the mobilization of all the other foiling techniques as reforms proceed. Of course, the rejection of IFI intervention also proceeds on a domestic diagnosis that is sharply at odds with that of the IFIs, but it will not necessarily stop all internal struggles over how to respond to a debt crisis. The decision to cordon off local legal change, so far as possible, from forceful foreign interventions will likely reduce the number of cycles, although it may also lengthen the entire episode of reforms as national policymakers set their own pace for change. Of our cases China most approximates this situation. It accepted technical assistance and advice from the Asian Development Bank, the World Bank, the German aid agency, among others, on its own terms at its own pace. Because it was partially engaged with international experts and felt the pressure of international investors, it did not fully immunize itself from foreign influence. But its slower pace of drafting and regulatory reforms reflected its freedom from economic coercion.

When national law reformers accept some reform recommendations pressed upon them by IFIs but refuse others, they simultaneously acknowledge the value of compliance with some global norms and signal that their domestic situation requires some measure of deviation. This signal by national policymakers warns IOs that law reform will be negotiated, not imposed, and it can have salutary effects on the trajectory of reforms. Korea refused to institute an automatic stay on all debt collection because such a stay would require many changes in law and practice in the Korean banking sector. Legal experts warned that a stay would produce too much change, too much uncertainty, too much resistance, all of which would have led to further supplementary forms of lawmaking. At once this capacity to refuse reduced indeterminacy and removed a potential contradiction in the law that would have made implementation problematic. Korea's example might be generalized. If a nation-state has the capacity to challenge international actors on recommendations that will lead to a transplant effect, then reforms are likely to be better adapted to the domestic situation, and recursive cycles will be less contested, less frequent, and less enduring.

Nation-states often have the capacity to fragment international influences. If there are multiple global scripts and they lack normative consensus, if varieties of international actors bring assortments of alternatives, then national policymakers can pick and choose. In this situation domestic law reformers recognize the value of international norms but retain discretion to manage them selectively. They can also manage reforms at their own pace and with technical assistance and foreign resources of their own choice. Degrees of discretion in the choices made by domestic lawmakers can reduce the contradictions between global and domestic ideologies and concomitantly permit local leaders to test the salience of external diagnoses with local data and analysis. Selection from a menu of alternatives will likely reduce a transplant effect and reduce the number and complexity of recursive cycles. Yet the Chinese reforms also suggest that fragmentation sometimes reinforces alternative tracks of domestic reforms by aligning one government agency with one outside agency (e.g., the NPC with the GTZ, the SETC with the ADB), each global/local relationship reinforcing particular local orientations to change. If international organizations were not in accordance (in China they largely were), political settlements would be more difficult, and contradictions and ambiguities might occur in the law and its enabling institutions.

The stratagem of invoking cultural incompatibilities as a reason for noncompliance with global norms or those of global actors has mixed effects. When used in Indonesia to resist efforts to bring debtors to the bargaining table, it expressed actor mismatch (i.e., the exclusion of debtors from the initial reform negotiations) and also marked another step by which the excluded debtors eventually brought the cycles of reform to a halt. By contrast such a cultural defense might be used to better adapt reform measures to local orientations toward law, capacities of local professions, and attitudes of citizens to debt and debt-restructuring alternatives. Freedom for cultural adaptability would remove from the recursive process much of the tension between evangelizing global "norm mongers" and their local antagonists.

The strategy of symbolic compliance can also cut in opposite directions.

When national lawmakers put a law on the books without any intent to en-force it, or perhaps with the intent but not the capacity to implement, it may simply sit in place. Cycles of reform don't occur because stakeholders know it will not impinge on their everyday activities or tread on their interests. But sometimes, as in Indonesia's disabling professional regulations, a further cycle of reform is required to ensure that the symbolic gesture in a statute does not get implemented in practice. A court can similarly act to constrict or even block enactment. But symbolism is not without efficacy. Even if a government initially intends passage of a new law to be a symbolic gesture to global actors, laws on books can be activated later by domestic interest groups, frequently in ways neither anticipated nor desired by the lawmakers. In such cases, a largely symbolic law may sit on the books for a period with few cycles of reform to clarify and settle it. Effectively, settlement has occurred without implemen-tation. New circumstances, however, can stimulate entrepreneurial actors to seize upon moribund law and activate it. Symbolic compliance, therefore, sometimes creates latent opportunities for reform that can be actuated in practice under new circumstances without any further statutory reform.

Protracting compliance and segmenting or partitioning reforms allow local leaders to use the properties of recursivity to resist international pres-sures. Protracting compliance pits implementing actors who want to slow down change against proponents of enactment who seek to speed it up. Seg-mentation and partition slice up a larger reform package into many smaller pieces, thereby ensuring that cycles will continue perhaps more frequently but certainly longer than impatient international organizations expect. Indeed, because attention to recursivity highlights the multiple points of lawmaking and the many more combinations of relations among them, it thereby also points to the range of opportunities given national lawmakers to deploy strat-egies of segmentation and partition.

Nevertheless, time complicates these propositions. In the short term, if a country is not extensively integrated into foreign markets, its capacity to foil may lead to a more domestically attuned set of legal changes. In the longer term, however, these very changes may institutionalize a national distinctive-ness that is ill suited to closer integration into prevailing global norms and practices. The likely effect may be to precipitate new rounds of reforms to bring a national legal system into greater conformity with global norms, a conformity that might have occurred earlier but with more resistance and disjunction.

11   The Implementation Gap

THREE DOMINANT FINDINGS emerge from our study of globalizing law and markets. First, there has been significant convergence in the formulation of global norms for corporate bankruptcy law. Second, despite this convergence, strict conformity among nation-states is found nowhere. Considerable variation occurs across nations, time, and jurisdictions. Third, variation from global norms arises most noticeably at the point where it matters most—perceptible changes in practice. It is in implementation, the ultimate test of legal change, where the correspondence between global norms and local practices is most doubtful.

In this conclusion we return to the issues raised at the outset of the book, to the empirical evidence we have brought to bear, to the theoretical interpretations of our evidence, and to implications for the world of institution building, where law and markets intersect. By focusing on the implementation gap, we begin to identify contingencies and limits of globalization of law and markets. This is an issue of far greater consequence than academic score settling, for the policy world contains a two-sided puzzle: on one side, ostensibly powerful global agents seem relatively powerless in the face of the implementation gap; on the other, seemingly weak nation-states find themselves to be surprisingly powerful, even when most vulnerable. To solve this puzzle is to understand something of the fate of globalization, and the solution leads to the recursivity of law. It is in dynamics that drive cycles of change within nations, among global organizations, and between global and local actors that can be found many of the impediments to seamless globalization of law.

Emergence of Global Norms

Where do global norms come from? In the past thirty years, the norms for corporate bankruptcy regimes passed through three phases. In the first phase, two leading capitalist economies, the United States and Great Britain, each enacted major revisions of bankruptcy laws that had stood unchanged for decades. The U.S. Bankruptcy Code of 1978 consolidated several laws into one. The English Insolvency Act 1986 set new directions for law that had not been substantially revised since the 1890s. These reforms were shaped by domestic circumstances, and even though the reforms would echo around the world, the lawmakers themselves proceeded as if the rest of the world were not relevant (Carruthers and Halliday 1998). Many other advanced countries followed suit in revising their laws over the next two decades (Halliday and Carruthers 2007b).

In neither the U.S. nor British reforms was much attention given to bankruptcies of multinational corporations spanning multiple national jurisdictions. Yet notable corporate bankruptcies in North America, such as *Olympia and York* and *Bramalea*, and *Maxwell Communications* in Britain, sparked a second phase of reforms that would provide cross-border solutions to corporate bankruptcies. In the absence of an encompassing framework, multinationals would be dismembered piecemeal as creditors raced to seize assets in their home jurisdictions. More often than not this reduced the overall value to creditors, and it undercut the possibility that a company could be saved through reorganization. These multinational collapses stimulated a variety of private and public efforts to develop legal technologies that would constitute an orderly regime: the Model International Insolvency Code of the International Bar Association, court-based protocols for cooperation among judges on particular cases, the International Bar Association's Concordat, an American Law Institute initiative for North American cross-border cases, and several efforts by the European Community/EU to produce a convention. The climax to this search came with UNCITRAL's 1995 agreement on a Model Law for Cross-Border Insolvency, a product so successful that it has been adopted by most advanced economies and many developing economies.

The fall of the Berlin Wall and the Asian Financial Crisis precipitated a third wave of global norm making, this time for developing and transitional economies. The second phase of reforms effectively showed that the wholesale convergence of bankruptcy systems in advanced countries was not possible. Faced with this inertia, lawmakers decided that the prudent strategy was to develop procedural rules for those occasions when diverse legal systems needed to cooperate. For transition economies, however, bankruptcy law was completely absent (or if still on the books, entirely moribund). And for most developing economies it was either absent, unused, or outmoded. In neither case were lawmakers confronted with extant substantive law or established interests to protect the status quo. Thus, new opportunities opened for the construction of entire bankruptcy regimes from the ground up.

IFIs and cooperating international organizations, such as the OECD, initially responded to the fall of the Berlin Wall with ad hoc efforts to erect bankruptcy systems for the transition economies. While the international organizations themselves worked from implicit models, these models were not codified until after the Asian Financial Crisis. The collapse of the Asian Tigers, nations celebrated for decades-long economic growth, threatened to plunge not only Asia but the entire world into economic crisis. Alarmed, the G-7 and G-22 group of "economically significant nations" joined the call of the Clinton administration for a new international financial architecture. Domestic bankruptcy systems were to function as key building blocks by ensuring that mounting corporate distress could be handled in an orderly way long before it threatened domestic banks or shook world financial markets.

Charged with a mandate to build models of domestic bankruptcy systems, the IMF, World Bank, Asian Development Bank, and European Bank for Reconstruction and Development developed their own versions of global norms, each choosing a somewhat different legal technology. So, too, did private associations of lawyers (the International Bar Association) and insolvency practitioners (the International Federation of Insolvency Practitioners). This period of experimentation in the late 1990s can best be understood as a race to produce a set of global norms that satisfied three criteria: the legal technology had to work; the norms had to be considered legitimate by prospective adopting nation-states; there had to be incentives, levers, or mechanisms that would encourage countries to adopt the norms.

As of 2001 no international organization had produced a satisfactory solution. Although the IMF, for instance, could impose its principles through economic coercion, its legitimacy was suspect, as was that of the World Bank. Although the ADB produced strong standards and could offer technical assistance to have them implemented, it had only regional impact. The EBRD was regional, and its technology, a survey, did not include substantive prescriptive standards. Reacting to these failures, the section of the U.S. State Department that dealt with commercial law worried about the adverse impact of competing alternatives from multiple global organizations.

This iterative process came to a climax in 2004. The intervention of the UNCITRAL, with the active support of most international organizations and professional groups, led to agreement on a single set of global norms. UNCITRAL's Legislative Guide had the merit that it embraced all substantive topics of bankruptcy law, but the specificity of its particular Recommendations depended on the degree of consensus its Working Group had been able to attain. On many issues the Guide gave countries reasonable alternatives, thereby signaling that varying practices among advanced countries could be followed and adapted to the specific circumstances of developing countries. The legitimacy of the product relied on UNCITRAL's skillful melding of representation of interests and expertise with the full diversity of the world's countries, procedural fairness, and a prior record of effectiveness, as the Model Law of Cross-Border Insolvency well demonstrated. UNCITRAL brought together experts with national delegates to forge a compromise that was broadly agreeable to the sixty nations of the Commission and most expert groups. Its leverage, however, remained in question since UNCITRAL lacked financial clout.

This final problem was supposedly resolved after difficult negotiations between UNCITRAL and the World Bank, whose Legal Department insisted on pressing a rival technology even after the UN General Assembly adopted the Legislative Guide. After intensive rounds of discussion with the IMF, U.S. Treasury, U.S. State Department, and several delegations to UNCITRAL, the World Bank agreed that it would combine its *Principles* with the UNCITRAL Guide as a set of substantive standards. The World Bank's emphasis on bankruptcy institutions, including courts and professions, usefully complemented UNCITRAL's focus on procedural and substantive law. Most important, however, the UNCITRAL/World Bank/IMF agreement meant that the diagnostic instruments used by the Bank and Fund to evaluate national bankruptcy systems could be aligned with the prescriptive measures recommended in the Guide. Since the Fund and Bank also have technical assistance capacities, and sometimes use coercive measures to secure national compliance, the combined

UNCITRAL/World Bank instruments appear to satisfy the criteria of (1) an effective technology produced by (2) legitimate international organizations with (3) accompanying levers to facilitate compliance by national policymakers. Nevertheless, there is a risk for UNCITRAL, whose legitimation warrants are strong, being associated with the IMF and World Bank, whose legitimation warrants are weak. Some of the odium of the IFIs may detract from the authority of the UN Commission. Nor is it yet clear how enthusiastically the World Bank Legal Department, whose insolvency group is under new leadership, will champion UNCITRAL's Guide. Nonetheless, a fifteen-year-long phase has produced a single set of norms backed by close to a universal consensus. Filled with conflicts, disagreements, missteps, and unintended consequences, the process of consensus building bore almost no resemblance to that proposed in world polity theory, in which institutions mirroring a unified global culture unproblematically proliferate around the world.[1]

By 2007, global bankruptcy institutions had been constructed to help manage the disarticulation between the legal particularity of nations and the economic generality of global markets. Globalization per se did not spur them on; rather, they were motivated by specific events and crises with global implications, as interpreted by a particular community of experts. For market transactions that cross national jurisdictions there now exists a legal framework that can regulate insolvent multinational corporations. And in the face of legal pluralism, there is now a set of global norms that reduces the bewildering heterogeneity of laws to a small number of authorized options. This does not at all preclude private economic actors from continuing to engage in institutional arbitrage.[2] Economic actors will still exploit elements of bankruptcy regimes that favor their business interests. But to the extent that global norms put limits on national variations and encourage comity between jurisdictions, there now exists a normative framework that brings "symmetry" between insolvency law and markets, in the words of a one of the world's leading insolvency jurists (Westbrook 2000).

Global norm making always involves the exercise of power. It poses the question, whose norms? World systems theory predicts the dominance of a world center (Wallerstein 2002). Postcolonial globalist theorists anticipate the instantiation of a particular nation's laws (Jenson and Santos 2000; Santos 2000). Neoinstitutionalists posit a universal set of values that emerge from the world polity (Boyle and Meyer 1998). Had the global standard settled with the World Bank *Principles*, then it would have closely approximated the U.S.

bankruptcy system. Had it adopted the Asian Development Bank's standards, it would have followed Australian bankruptcy practice. By moving to the UN, powerful nations and IFIs essentially traded an imprint of their particular concept of a bankruptcy system for a more generic set of norms that might be enactable in diverse countries. Too much "world culture" would risk a nationalist political backlash.

One underlying assumption is widely held by global actors: that good law produces the certainty that investors require for investment in developing countries, which in turn stimulates economic growth and global trade (Halliday and Carruthers 2007b). This premise animates the reformist impulses of the IFIs, U.S. Treasury, UNCITRAL, the international professional associations of lawyers and insolvency practitioners, international governance organizations such as the OECD, and the UN. It makes assumptions about the relations between property rights and economic activity and, more fundamentally, about the necessity of law for the regulation of advanced economies. Academic critics have argued that other institutions and relationships may substitute for law in many market situations (Gessner 1998; Gessner, Appelbaum, and Felstiner 2001; Ginsburg 2000; Karpik 2007), and even Max Weber himself recognized that predictability might be achieved without formal rationality of laws and institutions (Swedberg 1998). But so far, these criticisms have not yet really had an effect on official policy.

Two key principles in the global consensus reflect core principles in U.S. insolvency law and practice. Debtors must have a chance to reorganize their companies if there is a prospect that the business can be saved. Creditors must be protected in liquidation and reorganization, but not by destroying potentially viable firms. For both debtors and creditors the goal of a bankruptcy system is to maximize the value of the distressed firm and to equitably treat all parties involved in liquidation or reorganization (UNCITRAL 2004). Yet the U.S. did not get all the particularities of U.S. practice it initially wanted in the Guide.[3] While every aspect of the Guide at least authorized U.S. practice, many parts of the Guide permitted practices consistent with French or British law. Differences across major legal jurisdictions in advanced economies compelled participants in UNCITRAL's negotiations to accept the legitimacy of alternatives. These options, which also reflected much international variation in former colonies and client-states, allowed developing and transitional nations to vary on the principal themes. While the voices of developing nations were relatively muted, therefore, so long as they framed their laws within the general parameters set by the advanced countries, they enjoyed some degree of freedom. Legal variation among advanced countries created the possibility for variation among developing countries.

The final consensus, therefore, rests on an ideology of law and markets that is espoused in the Global North and is expressed through a range of authorized options that are found in the Global North. It assumes that economic development in the Global South will follow a similar course to that of the North, and that law enables and regulates markets, empowers debtors and protects creditors, and rescues firms. The consensus also presumes that the casualties of firm liquidation and reorganization, most especially workers, will be handled outside bankruptcy law.

Politics of Enactment and Implementation

Beginning in the late 1990s, the global scripts progressively codified by international organizations (IOs) were exported across the world. Our cases in Northeast and Southeast Asia vary in both the balance of power between them and global agents of change as well as in their cultural proximity to global centers. We anticipated that the impact of the IOs would be greatest when the imbalance of power was most pronounced, particularly during an economic crisis, and that the greater the "cultural distance" from global centers, the more difficult it would be to bring a nation-state into conformity with those norms. There was no "global culture" to make the design and diffusion of such scripts uncontested or unproblematic (Bartley 2007; Beckfield 2003; Dobbin, Simmons, and Garrett 2007).

Yet it is consistent with a key sociolegal premise that the power of global agents of change will differ sharply depending on whether the outcome is enactment or implementation. The full influence of global norms occurs through the interplay of a politics of enactment, which relate to law-on-the-books, and a politics of implementation, which concern law-in-practice. The correlation between these two varies considerably from nation to nation, as we observe in Indonesia, Korea, and China. It is out of these dynamics of recursivity that the magnitude of legal change can be ascertained.

Politics of Enactment

At the point of enactment the balance of power often favors global organizations. Getting statutes passed through legislatures, decrees promulgated by presidents, regulations issued by government ministries, new regulatory bodies set up by executive agencies—all these can be usually managed by government leaders when there is strong external constraint and domestic political will. Nevertheless, not all forms of enactment are equal. IFIs frequently prefer that changes in formal law be made by executive agencies since IFI officials can negotiate directly with senior politicians and bureaucrats. Legislatures inevitably involve more complex bargaining, as politicking on the narrow issues of a particular bill entails trade-offs that relate to other political bargains (e.g., logrolling). Comprehensive statutes take longer to prepare, and their fates can be caught up in changing circumstances, especially when the pressure of a crisis begins to dissipate.

Indonesia, Korea, and China each created new bankruptcy laws and built new bankruptcy institutions. Enactment converged on the core principles of global norms. But there was much variation on substance, in considerable part because the politics of enactment also varied. Most vulnerable to global leverage, Indonesia at the depths of the Crisis swiftly adopted scores of amendments to its law via Presidential Decree. Given its cultural distance from the global center, it was closely monitored to ensure its conformity with the global standards expressed by the IMF. Less vulnerable economically and closer to the global center, Korea, too, mostly conformed to global norms with its new Unified Bankruptcy Act, but in its own way and at its own pace. Because its reformers were already familiar with global standards, and the government made a commitment to the IFIs that it would undertake comprehensive bankruptcy reforms, it was less intensively monitored by IFIs, whose leverage decreased with the rapid recovery of the Korean economy. China was least vulnerable to direct leverage by IFIs. With limited capacity to exercise more than modeling and moral suasion, IFIs had to be satisfied with the passage of a comprehensive bankruptcy law in 2006 that deviated from global norms in its insistence on preserving many "Chinese characteristics."

Variation in adoption of new bankruptcy institutions exceeded that of formal bankruptcy law. The most vulnerable country, Indonesia, effectively erected an entire bankruptcy system, including a specialized court, an out-of-court restructuring agency, and a specialized private profession. The IMF and other IOs and foreign donors closely monitored and guided this institution building. Korea made quite modest adjustments to its institutions, creating a bankruptcy division within its court system, putting in place some interim out-of-court restructuring mechanisms, but doing little to the private professional sector. Despite much urging by IFIs and consultants, China has done the least institution building. This may be a function of slower development, but when its bankruptcy law came into effect (June 1, 2007), it had no specialized courts or chambers of courts, no out-of-court mechanisms, no government agency, nor any indications of how its professional services sector would respond to demands for its specialized services. China has retained most power in administrative agencies, a response to fears that law may not have the capacity to cope with market demands or political imperatives.

Altogether, vigorous interchanges between IOs and national leaders since the late 1990s produced widespread formal lawmaking and institution building in our three cases. Initially through Presidential Decrees and executive regulations, later through legislative actions, each country has moved its formal bankruptcy system much closer to the global norms that began to be formalized after the Asian Financial Crisis. Moreover, Indonesia, the country most vulnerable to international influence, conformed most closely on substantive and institutional criteria. China, the country least susceptible to external influence, remained focused on its domestic concerns while symbolically expressing adherence to the broad contours of global standards.

The Politics of Implementation

To measure globally constrained legal change solely in terms of formal enactment, a common practice by IFIs, legal scholars, and some social scientists, vastly overestimates the extent of change.[4] It is more important—and far more difficult—to discover whether enactments produce behavioral changes in practice. For the study of globalization and law, implementation becomes a particularly acute issue because it is the ground of political struggle that most favors "locals." Not only is everyday legal practice largely invisible to official eyes but local businesses, creditors and debtors, lawyers, and judges are adept at exploiting their local knowledge to frustrate powerful international agents of change.

A large literature on regulation and in the field of sociology elaborates the well-honed techniques that frustrate efforts to obtain compliance with law. Sometimes behavioral changes follow the spirit of the law. Very often, however, the targets of regulation engage in symbolic compliance, decoupling, and creative compliance—all techniques to give the appearance of conformity with legal norms without the actuality. Transitional and developing nations, long accustomed to dealing with international aid and financial institutions (and very often hosts to large informal economies), also develop sophisticated means of delivering enactment without implementation.

Indonesia, the country that enacted the most wide-ranging substantive and institutional reforms, is also the country that implemented them most imperfectly. Despite close to a hundred amendments to its bankruptcy law in 2005, a new Commercial Court, years of out-of-court workouts, and a formal insolvency profession, bankruptcy practice in 2007 had advanced little beyond the situation in 1996.[5] It is true that side effects and unexpected reformist outcomes, such as Supreme Court reforms, might redeem the Commercial Court experiment and elevate the prospect of law as an ordering mechanism for markets. But the high hopes of enactment fell far short in practice. At best, there is now an infrastructure in place, ready to be activated during the next economic downturn. In Korea, by contrast, reforms already under way before the Crisis gained momentum and scope through the interventions of the IOs. With far greater capacity in its courts and private professions, and with political will to conform to supposed global best practices, Korea narrowed the gap between enactment and implementation, although the impact of the 2005 bankruptcy law is yet to be accurately gauged. China's reforms of SOEs through administrative interventions pushed the state-owned sector far toward a market-oriented prospect of corporate restructuring. Although the novelty of China's bankruptcy law does not permit any analysis of implementation, the severe limitations of implementing institutions, together with the government's continued administrative controls over entry of cases to the courts and even their dispositions in the courts, suggest that national and local politics will open up a substantial implementation gap that varies significantly across China.

Enactment and implementation are the two sides of legal change in a global context. By the former, each of the case studies reveals greater conformity to global norms than existed either before those norms were formalized or before the Asian Crisis intensified pressures on countries to reform their legal systems. By the latter, the case studies show that convergence in practice frequently belies easy assertions of homogenization that are based on checklists of accessions to treaties or adoption of model laws. In other words, much of the ground won by international organizations at the point of enactment is subsequently lost in rear-guard battles over implementation.

As a result, the globalization of law involves two types of deviation. In the first, nation-states diverge in their formal law from the standards pressed upon them by foreign advocates. In the second, practitioners within countries deviate from the letter or intent of laws promulgated by their own legislators and officials. Since this latter deviation can be almost invisible, it deprives outside parties—foreign banks, international corporations—of the predictability that IOs insist is a necessary feature of effective bankruptcy regimes.

An implementation gap emerges out of the interplay between enactment and implementation. The extent of that gap, and the dynamics that widen it, limits the globalization of law and markets. It also complicates arguments about institutional change, which often stipulate that institutions are generally stable except for short periods of dramatic change (e.g., theories of "punctuated equilibrium"). Here, it is clear that both continuity and change can occur at the very same time, but at different levels. Big shocks at the level of enactment may be dampened down to the modest perturbations at the level of implementation (Streeck and Thelen 2005).

Recursivity and the Implementation Gap

The politics of enactment and implementation can be analyzed through the framework of the recursivity of law. In this approach to legal change, three cycles of activity combine: (1) iterations of norm making by international organizations; (2) domestic rounds of lawmaking by legislatures, executives, and courts; and (3) the interplay of the international and domestic as the global and local maneuver around each other (see Figure 1.1).

Iterations of Global Norm Making
By 2005 global norm making had produced a single script—a Legislative Guide that offered norms for substantive and procedural law. The Guide, in turn, was paired with World Bank *Principles* and IMF practices that embraced institutions. The latter rendered diagnoses of local conformity with global norms; the former presented prescriptive standards to bring nation-states into compliance with global expectations.

The scripts channel the heterogeneity of national law into a finite set of alternatives, but they still permit much variation. Consider UNCITRAL's Legislative Guide. The very process that enabled consensus about the Guide also internalized much variety. Its Recommendations, the most rulelike of its prescriptions, contain significant numbers of flexible rules. The most open propose that there should be a rule on a topic without specifying its content;

or that a rule on a topic might contain certain baseline provisions, but that others could be added. More constraining Recommendations offer choices among two or three courses of action. And if these modest constraints prove unduly restrictive, then the Guide offers nine high-level principles that tolerate considerable national variation. As a result, even if the most frequent Recommendations in the Guide are imperative rules that approximate precise statutory language, large numbers of other rules permit considerable latitude (Block-Lieb and Halliday 2006).

The most forgiving rules are often on the most controversial topics. Indeed, rules that offer multiple options or minimal thresholds or even no substantive content at all are crafted that way precisely to span deep fissures among legal systems within the Global North, quite apart from heterogeneity in the Global South. Thus, an implicit presumption has emerged in the Legislative Guide. If it is possible for advanced economies to engage in high volumes of trade and investment despite considerable variation in their commercial laws, then it is also possible for global trade to flourish so long as (1) there is some convergence on master principles, (2) certain minimum standards of laws are shared among nations, and (3) the laws (or their functional equivalent) of any given nation are transparent and predictable.

Interplay of the Global and Local

Between the global and local unfold processes of intermediation, foiling, and negotiation, each of which contributes to the implementation gap. The transmission of global norms to local actors, or the injection of local preferences into global norm making, occurs through intermediaries. In the flows between nation-states and international organizations, the number and expertise of intermediaries from advanced economies greatly exceeded those from transitional and developing economies. In fact, UNCITRAL delegates were disproportionately weighted in favor of U.S. experts. The four-person U.S. delegation, always the best prepared and staffed, invariably included a representative from the State Department, one or two leading private lawyers, a veteran judge who had long been involved in international norm making, and sometimes a law professor. The two usual delegates of the International Bar Association were from the U.S. The two delegates from the international business law section of the American Bar Association were U.S. specialists. These were sometimes supported by more U.S. delegates from the International Insolvency Institute, delegates from the IMF Legal Department, and the U.S. lawyer who headed the

World Bank insolvency initiative. Insofar as substantive reforms were directed to corporate rehabilitation, a practice in which the U.S. has the most extensive experience, the size and prolixity of U.S. participants disproportionately shaped the norms under development. While it is an overstatement that the Guide is a "globalized localism" of the U.S., the flow of expertise, experience, and influence from the U.S. exceeded that of any other country and roughly equaled that of all other advanced countries put together.

The strength of intermediation from advanced countries also benefited from the authority of professionals either with extensive experience in their own bankruptcy systems or with global reach. The British delegate was an official in the U.K. government's Insolvency Service and so very familiar with Britain's alternative model of an insolvency system. INSOL representatives brought not only their extensive experience of insolvency reforms in their respective countries, Britain and Australia, but their wide-ranging practice and consulting in Asia, Central Europe, and Central Asia. The Canadian leader of the International Insolvency Institute was a veteran of transnational lawmaking as well as Canadian and cross-border restructurings. France's principal delegate drew on many years' practice as an insolvency judge.

By comparison delegates from the Global South had much less experience and expertise. Neither were their countries very thoroughly integrated into international networks of practitioners—the IBA, INSOL, or the International Insolvency Institute. Exceptions included the Korean delegate (but then Korea might reasonably be classified as an advanced economy); the Working Group Chair, who was a Thai bankruptcy judge; and the Colombian delegate.

Consequently, intermediation between nation-states and UNCITRAL's forum heavily favored delegates from the U.S. and advanced nations. In no small way this imbalance simply reflected the financial resources of nations, organizations, and professionals. Whereas advanced nations could afford to send one or more delegates to every meeting, poorer nations often could not, or they compromised and sent a diplomatic representative from their missions in Vienna or New York, persons who rarely had the necessary expertise. National and international professional organizations from Europe and the U.S. funded their delegates, and others relied on their law firms or even personal resources. Delegations from developing countries also made tactical errors. The most common, exemplified by China, was to send constantly changing delegations, a practice that effectively denied delegations the cumulative experience and relationship building so critical to effective participation.

Intermediation is also a problem for international organizations as they try to induce national reforms. International organizations may require up to five kinds of intermediaries to effect change:[6] (1) experts who perform a bridging function by translating among the key legal systems; (2) an indigenous expert who can offer authoritative advice to an IO and remain legitimate to local audiences; (3) on-site managers and advisors with unquestioned loyalty to the IFI; (4) domestic constituencies that can lobby for change and provide ongoing intelligence to the IOs, as well as exercise local leadership and social control; and (5) a powerful political sponsor. The combination of all five localizes and indigenizes global interventions.

Rarely were all these intermediaries in place. In Indonesia, the first three were available, but reformist domestic groups were limited in number, and a powerful political sponsor committed to reform never emerged. In Korea, not all five kinds of intermediaries were needed since Korea was already headed in a direction consistent with IFI preferences. Moreover, in Korea the very strength of its intermediaries in the Ministries of Finance and Economy and the Ministry of Justice bolstered Korea's hand when it deviated from some global norms in its bankruptcy law and institutions. In China, international organizations had very few foreign experts on whom they could rely, and Chinese experts had primary loyalties to domestic rather than international policymakers.

We find that the nexus between the global and local in a particular issue area can turn on a handful of people. As in an hourglass, although there are many people involved in global norm making and many others in national lawmaking, the flow of information and influence between the two sides occurs through a narrow conduit. In each of the cases, less than a dozen experts, and sometimes less than a handful, control the critical flow of information and influence in the cycles of norms and response between global norm makers and national lawmakers. Who those intermediaries are, where their loyalties lie, and how they align indigenous interests and global norms become determinative of how wide the implementation gap opens up between the global and the local.

The engagement between global and local is not only about flows of information; it is also about power. Yet the ostensible imbalance of power in favor of the agents of globalization, particularly in times of crisis, turns out to be not so one-sided. Local actors possess sophisticated repertoires for foiling the hegemons of the Global North.[7] Often local lawmakers manipulate time, using delay as a form of resistance. Delay can be combined with the decomposition of international expectations into smaller and smaller pieces, each of which can then be dragged out little by little. Policymakers in developing nations also exploit their local knowledge. In local political arenas they can engage in structural filibusters, finding one after another hurdle over which formal law reforms must jump. They may divide to conquer, allocating some international interventions to one set of domestic institutions and other interventions elsewhere in the state, while segmenting the domestic institutions from each other. And they can manipulate local institutions, whether through market corruption or the arbitrary interventions of Party officials. In response to complaints about noncompliance from international organizations, they sometimes respond, disingenuously, that incapacity to comply should not be mistaken for unwillingness. And of course, incapacity frequently is a form of structural inhibition of legal change.

Domestic Lawmaking and Practice

The success of foiling in Indonesia, Korea, and China buttresses arguments that foreign legal transplants will not succeed unless certain conditions pertain (Nelken 2002; Pistor et al. 2002). Local demand is critical (Djelic and Quack 2003: 10). Unless vocal national leaders perceive that domestic reform is imperative, and that the reforms must converge with global norms, the prospects of enactment are dimmed. Political will, therefore, is a necessary condition for narrowing an "enactment gap." Equally important for narrowing the "implementation gap" are demands for reforms from skilled professionals who are committed to the intent of enactments. Since they mediate locally between designers of formal law and the practitioners who follow the new rules, their understanding of the necessity for reform, and their constructive engagement in change make the difference between success and failure (Pistor 2002).

Integral to the alignment of practice with formal law is the practice of bricolage—the skill of local practitioners in blending global norms with local customs, practices, and beliefs (Campbell 2004). This involves much more than technical adjustment. Very often it demands cultural realignment. For instance, after the Crisis it was repeatedly stated in East Asian countries that use of formal bankruptcy procedures required not only institutional capacities (which were often lacking) but also a sea change in cultural orientations. Taking a bankruptcy case to court is tantamount to a public admission of failure. It requires the disclosure of many private details of business practice, and it puts the fate of family businesses in the hands of unknown third parties. Above all, it brings public shame and loss of face (ADB 2000; Meyerman 2000).

Cultural realignment is particularly difficult when it involves elevating law to a status and power previously unknown in a society. In China, law is being asked to take on functions unprecedented in China's postrevolutionary history. In Indonesia, law was regenerated after almost half a century of derogation and neglect. Even in Korea, where courts and private professional practice were well developed, IFIs pressed courts into the center of commercial decision making, a role that previously had been undertaken with great success by Korea's finance ministry. This adoption of Western-style practices to bring business failures into powerful courts involved a structural transformation in which states shifted responsibilities onto institutions hitherto unaccustomed and unequipped for them, and a cultural transformation in which people had to reshape customary practices and beliefs about the proper way to handle troubled enterprises.

Even if both transformations occurred, intense reeducation is required merely to comprehend the possibilities, risks, and opportunities of a new way to handle corporate distress. The process of translation therefore requires two steps in this context. In the first, national lawmakers must translate new and often alien concepts into national laws, somehow conforming them to other extant legal concepts in the web of commercial law and creating hybrids that are locally meaningful (Merry 2005). In the second, lawyers, accountants, and judges must make abstract legal concepts meaningful for practical outcomes. They themselves must understand and then package their understandings for comprehension by business leaders, creditors, and others whose financial decisions will now be made under a different set of incentives and constraints.

The case studies show that these transformations, structural and cultural, follow a recursive logic. The implementation gap will not be closed until cycles of enactment and implementation settle at a new level of law-in-action. Of course, there are ad hoc bases for settling. Lawmakers run out of energy. Crises pass and political agendas change. Before even these ad hoc outcomes, however, in every case we observe that cycles of change continue so long as lawmakers and law implementers seek to reduce the implementation gap. The forward momentum of those cycles is fueled by failures to resolve four problems—actor mismatch, diagnostic struggles, contradictions, and indeterminacy.

Actor mismatch occurred in all three cases where those interests drawn into lawmaking did not reflect all the interests of actors in practice. The failure of IFIs and Indonesian lawmakers to include fully the business community in its formal lawmaking provides a striking example. Kept away from the reforms at the height of the Crisis, business leaders led a last-minute effort to persuade the President not to implement his decree. When that failed, business leaders were faced with a regime they had not designed and with provisions with which they did not agree. Their response was to subvert the new regime by every possible method: by not using out-of-court options until induced or compelled to do so; by using the Commercial Court perversely, effectively destroying the legitimacy of the Court as they defended their interests; by corrupting private practitioners and practice. Many of the subsequent rounds of corrective formal lawmaking stemmed from this initial mismatch, one that was never adequately corrected. In failing to resolve it, the lawmakers allowed the implementation gap to become so wide that corporate bankruptcy as a formal process virtually disappeared.

The failure to align actors in lawmaking with actors in practice can be attributed to several causes. In a financial crisis, creditor-oriented IFIs drive reforms and generally respond to banking, not corporate or labor, interests. In bankruptcy law reforms in many countries, creditors are better organized than debtors for collective action, not least because corporate failure is a recurrent problem for creditors, whereas it is an exceptional situation for debtors, who, in any event, find it a distasteful topic to consider. Creditors are also less numerous than debtors and so easier to organize. Trade creditors, those firms providing everyday credit in the selling of goods and services, are even more difficult to organize collectively.

Moreover, a country's history of political deliberation and public administration may work against inclusion of all parties in practice within lawmaking. If private corporations are remote from public decision making and government agencies, as has been the case for private businesses in China's National People's Congress, the Party, and State Council ministries, then failure to include them in bankruptcy reforms merely perpetuates their exclusion elsewhere. In countries that have followed a state-led model of development, government ministries have been accustomed to directing the corporate sector, not listening to it. Finally, some interests are excluded because they simply didn't exist before reform. Thoroughgoing institutional transformation can sometimes create new interest groups who are charged with implementing new institutions. They could not participate in lawmaking, although they subsequently play a role in practice. Exclusion from bankruptcy lawmaking, therefore, sometimes results from conditions unique to bankruptcy, but at other times reflects domestic politics more generally.

The implementation gap also follows *diagnostic contests*. If interest groups differ sharply over what is wrong with practice, they are also likely to quarrel over remedies. Diagnosis precedes prescription. Hence it is a significant political advantage for an actor in practice to get adopted its analysis of what needs changing. Such a diagnostic struggle came sharply into focus in Korea (Halliday and Carruthers 2004a). Economists believed that failures in the corporate reorganization system substantially lay in deficiencies of formal law. For that reason the Ministry of Finance and Economy was quick to agree with the World Bank and IMF that Korea's three bankruptcy laws be combined to make them more "efficient." Lawyers disagreed. The problem arose, they said, not because these laws were so deficient but because economists did not demand that banks act as responsible commercial lenders. Government ministries, too, distrusted the law's capacities to handle what they had been managing for decades. The result was predictable. One after another reform followed as the economists pushed through reforms consistent with their diagnosis and lawyers refused to cooperate—or waited for reforms to falter. Skeptical about the value of a unified law, legal drafters dragged their feet, hoping that less drastic amendments would satisfy the IMF and World Bank.

Diagnosis in a globalizing world is a two-level political game: foreign and domestic. Regional development banks and IFIs regularly undertake external diagnoses of national performance. The IMF's Article IV reviews, the World Bank and IMF's ROSCs, the EBRD's annual surveys, periodic reviews by the ADB—all inform nation-states how well their countries perform by metrics designed in reference to regional and global norms. Some of these reviews are publicized (e.g., Article IV reviews on the IMF website, EBRD surveys published in *Law in Transition*). Others are conveyed privately to senior government officials, such as precise ratings on World Bank/IMF ROSCs. Too little is known about the degree to which public disclosure is subject to negotiation or how much in public reports has been excised to satisfy national sensitivities. The quality of data also varies sharply by the intensity, representativeness, and systematicity of the review.

Alongside the external reviews, and sometimes in engagement with them, domestic politics proceeds through diagnostic struggles as interest groups seek to define the situation. The two-level game can benefit local constituencies if they can enlist international support for their point of view (Djelic and Quack 2003: 10). Yet this can also backfire since alignment of local banking interests (e.g., commercial banks) with international capital (e.g., IMF) might simply confirm suspicions that they had capitulated to international pressures. Some local "diagnosticians" have especially strong global connections, which can bias international understanding of what reforms are desirable. The IMF and World Bank, for instance, habitually make their first calls to international law and accounting firms with which they have prior relationships. It is much more difficult to find and be informed by local practitioners in regional cities or remote provinces. Selective perceptions of facts on the ground can therefore set up situations where diagnoses of leading national interests inform international diagnosticians, but the full scope of that misdiagnosis does not become apparent until law reforms are put into practice.

Cycles of reform continue when *contradictions* get integrated into formal law and then play out in legal institutions. We have seen contradictions of several sorts in Indonesia, Korea, and China. When enterprises are expected simultaneously to pursue profits and yet act as social security systems for workers, to pay off creditors yet underwrite unemployment protection, as was the case for Chinese SOEs, then the conflicting demands can fail to serve either goal. A law that does not resolve these tensions but internalizes them can subvert itself. The instability contained within the law then breaks out in successive attempts to solve the contradiction, which is one way to interpret China's repeated administrative efforts to restructure the state-owned sector. The issue is not so much that contradictions occur, for this is frequent in many kinds of lawmaking (Calavita 1993; Chambliss and Zatz 1993; Grattet 1993), but that contradictions are not resolved through political settlements.

In a globalized context, recursivity can be driven by contradictions between global ideologies and the ideas of domestic policymakers. To varying degrees this contradiction recurs in each of our cases, as the IFIs, with the U.S. Treasury behind them, endorsed variants of the Washington Consensus that insisted on privatization, deregulation, free trade, and capital market liberalization—all this on nations whose success had depended on state-led economic development models. Overlaid onto the Washington Consensus is a development ideology that pairs rule of law with economic development (Easterly 2007). The current debates over Chinese bankruptcy and property laws, among others, can be understood as a clash between alternative development ideologies that reflect deeply conflicting economic interests (Naughton 2006b). The external/internal clash, in fact, may matter less than domestic conflicts that draw on alternative international authorities for legitimation.

Contradictions also break out through conflicts among different branches of the state. One of the principal hurdles to institutionalization of a court system in a state where courts have been marginal is the immediate tension between the increased power of courts and the decline of the executive branch (Halliday 2008b). Much of the tension in restructuring Korea's bankruptcy system derived from the reluctance of the Ministry of Finance and Economy to shift its role directing the economy to courts that had never enjoyed such powers. Cycles of reform moved the center of action back and forth between executive initiatives and reliance on courts. Similar tensions can be observed among government agencies, as in China, where the Central Bank took the side of commercial banks and creditors, the former SETC championed the cause of SOE managers, and the All China Trade Union Federation carried the flag for labor.

Both ideological and structural contradictions contribute to *indeterminacy* in formal law and the institutions that implement it. New concepts or vague formulations in statutes are classic adaptations to political struggles that are not resolved by authentic bargains. By leaving concepts ambiguous, leaving holes in statutes, or internalizing contrary interests in seemingly inconsistent provisions, the formal law begs for clarification. The demand for specificity and clarity or the removal of inconsistencies leads to further rounds of lawmaking and amendment by the courts and regulatory agencies. Since this process can take years, law settles slowly, if it settles at all.

Where the ambiguities are reduced has political implications. If lawmakers, such as China's National People's Congress, deliberately write vague or incomplete laws with the expectation the Supreme People's Court and regulatory agencies will fill in the gaps, then they deliberately shift responsibility elsewhere. But access by practitioners or interested parties to decision making in the Supreme People's Congress is much less than in the National People's Congress, so the change in locus simultaneously changes the politics. Moreover, regulatory agencies may compete over who has authority to interpret statutory intent, an institutional conflict that exacerbates rather than resolves the problem (Ruru 2001). Expertise also shifts from one lawmaking site to another. The strongest argument for *not* embedding the Commercial Court in Indonesia's hierarchy of courts was the expectation that an expert decision in the Commercial Court would be subject to appeal to a much less competent and apparently corrupt Supreme Court. Different loci are also differentially vulnerable to interference. Critics of the IMF's decision to allow appeals to the Supreme Court anticipated that such appeals would shift the final decision to judges more susceptible to political interference.

The four mechanisms of recursivity help explain where implementation gaps remain. Because Indonesian debtors were excluded from participation in lawmaking, it was predictable they would respond by undermining the law-in-practice. The fact that China's private businesses have had little opportunity to influence the new law may also force it to be amended quickly in an economic downturn. By accepting overseas advice that labor issues should be largely resolved outside bankruptcy law, and in the absence of an adequate social security system, China's lawmakers may be setting themselves up for unsettled practice and law. By not yet clarifying which branches of government will fill in the gaps of China's bankruptcy law, the law will not settle in ways that produce certainty and predictability of legal action.

The recursive framework provides a means to appraise the probability of implementation gaps at two levels. On the side of the global, it points to mechanisms that will widen or narrow the gap between international norm makers and national lawmakers. On the side of the local, it predicts where failures are likely to occur in implementation and thus when cycles of reform and practice will continue until law-on-the-books and law-in-action settle at a new equilibrium.

Limits to Globalization of Law

Globalization of law has its successes and failures, and the case of corporate bankruptcy law provides a look into both possibilities. In addition to its integral role in a market economy, corporate bankruptcy law is a particularly useful case for two reasons. On the one hand, its circumstances were such that global norms should be strongest—a global consensus backed with multifaceted leverage that is maximized at a time of economic crisis. On the other hand, the three national cases we have followed—Indonesia, Korea, China— have all brought to closure their cycles of formal enactment.[8] Thus, we are able to appraise not only the impact of global norms on *formal enactment* but also to observe in some cases and anticipate in others their impact on *practice*. And it is at the point of practice that the limits of globalization are to be appraised. If enactment is the "idealist" measure of global influence, implementation is the "realist" measure. Implementation gaps reveal the limits to global convergence of law and markets.

Our principal findings can serve as hypotheses for other areas of law and other world regions. First, even for types of law that are widely divergent across the world, it is possible to reach substantial consensus on global norms. Through multiple iterations among international organizations, this consensus, legitimated by the UN, centered on core principles that were nevertheless quite permissive. In the heated debate over the relative merits of principles versus bright-line rules in commercial lawmaking, UNCITRAL in effect followed John Braithwaite's argument for law in rapidly changing fields with high economic stakes: to create binding principles complemented by nonbinding rules (Braithwaite 2002).[9] Nation-states are urged to adopt the jurisprudential core of bankruptcy norms—balancing corporate liquidation with corporate reorganization, creditor and debtor rights—but they are given considerable latitude to adapt those principles to suit local circumstances.

Second, the substance of global norms reflects the disproportionate influence of dominant global actors—most notably the United States—international financial institutions, international governance organizations, and international professional groups. Yet that impact on global scripts is not simple. Because there are varieties of law and varieties of capitalism among advanced economies, the global norms could find consensus only if they acknowledged variation around the principles and thus permitted latitude in adoption by nation-states. Similarly, for norms to be promulgated by a UN body, where nations of the Global North and Global South sat in deliberation, the power of the global center had to be veiled and restrained. Veiling is reflected in the linguistic distance between U.S. law and global norms; restraint is apparent where dominant powers concede to alternatives that minimally conformed to their own particular systems.

Third, the combined effect of UNCITRAL's Model Law on Cross-Border Insolvency and its Legislative Guide on Insolvency is to help bring global law into some balance with global markets. This creation of symmetry between law and markets (Westbrook 2000) operates at two levels. It seeks to bring a measure of mutual translatability among national bankruptcy systems by pressing transitional and developing nations to bring their legal systems into closer conformity with those of advanced nations. It complements this push for convergence with procedural rules for managing corporate bankruptcies that cross national frontiers. The ultimate consequence of this two-pronged enterprise is to create a web of law that equals the scope of the global market: all market activity would be regulated by national and transnational bankruptcy law. If fully implemented, law would catch up with the market.

Fourth, even though globalization of law involves power, the imbalance of power between the global center and periphery is more complex than it appears. We observed two cases where financial crisis rendered nations as vulnerable to global financial actors as was possible. But even then, supposedly weak nations have their own capacities to foil global hegemons. Local power manifests itself through the distinction between enactment and implementation. While the politics of the former favor powerful international actors, the latter favor nation-states. And since implementation in a global context involves two steps—from global norms to national enactments, and from national enactment to local implementation—there are two points where national actors can open a gap between global and local. This power of the weak manifests in a global context what others have observed as weapons of the weak in national contexts (Parker et al. 2004; Scott 1985, 1990). We observe that weak nations are stronger than they may appear and stronger than they may suppose.

Fifth, globalization must be negotiated, not imposed. The economic leverage employed by the IMF and World Bank to compel national compliance is substantially illusory. Not only does economic coercion not work as intended but it frequently engenders a backlash. If the politics of implementation help level the playing field for international and national actors, then global actors seeking more than symbolic compliance must negotiate with national leaders (Carruthers and Halliday 2006). Similarly, national leaders must negotiate with their domestic interest groups.

The term *negotiation* has several meanings relevant to the global/local encounter. Negotiation between the global and local manifests itself cognitively as "translation" (Merry 2005). Negotiation between national lawmakers and domestic players unfolds as "bricolage" (Campbell 2004). Negotiation among international and domestic interest groups produces "recursivity" since a stable political settlement emerges through cycles of enactment and implementation. Moreover, negotiation requires that the so-called weak are treated by global actors with the respect that their local power demands. Local knowledge and power mean that nation-states can (implicitly) veto global actions, so global actors can truly "globalize" only on terms approved by their local counterparts. Furthermore, since some nation-states (e.g., China) have greater negotiating power, the negotiations themselves will introduce additional variability in responses to global norms.

Sixth, when national actors are strong enough to require "bilateral" negotiations between global and local, convergence stops far short of complete harmonization. Indeed, UNCITRAL itself has progressively given up on either unification or harmonization of laws (Block-Lieb and Halliday 2007a). Our evidence shows substantial convergence between global norms and the local national laws, and many of the specifics in global norms are adopted for local enactment. But there remains quite substantial variance between global norms and local statutes, and even more difference among the three national statutes informed by the same global norms. In China, where global actors had the least leverage, the national law least conforms to global norms. The law most aligned with global norms is that of Korea, a country already part of the OECD club of rich nations. Therefore, a side-by-side comparison of enacted legislation and institutions reveals some convergence on common principles, but with substantial variation. Divergence widens far more in the arena of implementation, where predictability matters more for market players.

Seventh, local institutions persist—even in the face of competitive markets. The interconnectedness of the world is a central premise of globalization theories. Flows of investment represent the leading edge of global connectedness, yet global flows of capital are very uneven. Most foreign investment capital moves among advanced countries. Foreign direct investment to transitional or developing countries goes overwhelmingly to China, a country that has been without basic commercial laws until quite recently and that still lacks effective legal implementation. International organizations challenge political leaders to reform their laws in order to attract capital, but these admonitions ring hollow until it can be shown that better-*enacted* law attracts capital. If foreign investment seldom flows to transitional and developing countries, then local interests in lawmaking are going to dominate global pressures for conformity. Neither positive nor negative incentives, therefore, will ensure mass convergence on global norms.

Eighth, if local enactment and implementation attenuate the convergence of laws and markets, then the possibility of varieties of capitalism and varieties of law should come as no surprise. It is obvious that distinct varieties of capitalism exist among advanced economies in North America and Western Europe (Hall and Soskice 2000, 2001), and it seems likely that further varieties may be found elsewhere (Crouch 2005). Variations in the organization of markets correspond to variations in law. It cannot be entirely accidental that Continental coordinated market economies overwhelmingly are code law countries and Anglo-Saxon liberal market economies have common law. But even in common law countries with liberal economies we see two major variations of bankruptcy law, one historically more oriented to debtors (U.S.) and others to creditors (U.K., Australia), although these differences are narrowing.

This varieties-of-capitalism analysis could be extended to transitional and developing economies so that clusters of market economies align with clusters of legal systems. These clusters could be regional (Gilpin and Gilpin 2000) or based on close trading relationships. In any case, if markets are to be legally regulated, there is ample reason to suppose that trade can thrive despite significant differences between legal systems. Trade between Britain and the Continent, or the U.S. and European Union, are paramount cases in point. Do legal differences prevent the certainty and predictability that supposedly underpin enduring commercial relationships? Clearly not.

Two legal/market configurations can support the global economy short of full convergence. In the global bankruptcy field, for example, a set of core principles for all legal regimes, with room for local variation, provides sufficient continuity to encourage economic integration. The "transaction costs" that result from local discrepancies benefit professionals whose expertise will be required to manage these differences. Here market integration would proceed on a foundation of law and involve professional consultation. In another configuration, markets cluster into discernible "families" accompanied by corresponding clusters of laws—varieties of capitalism associated with varieties of law. These, too, can be tracked by market players and their professional advisors.

Ninth, it remains an open question how necessary "good law" is either for investment or economic development. The central assumption of contemporary development policy turns on a causal relation between rule of law and economic growth. In part those ideas extrapolate from a simple correlation: current advanced economies usually also have sophisticated legal systems. But we turn to legal and economic history to discover if advanced countries achieved economic success *because* they had good law. What recent East Asian history does demonstrate is the possibility of rapid and sustained economic growth, often fueled by foreign investment, without viable law or legal institutions (Pistor and Wellons 1999). And even within advanced economies, market transactions occur outside the formal legal framework (Bernstein 1990;

Macaulay 1963). Of course, there is much variation within Asia. Singapore, Malaysia, and India have had comparatively better legal systems; and China, Indonesia, and Thailand thrived without them. China has built its legal system over the past fifteen years, but it is highly questionable that high levels of foreign direct investment or high growth rates are attributable to those legal changes that have occurred.

That Asian economies have thrived without law requires the champions of law and economic development to shift toward a "threshold" theory. Economic development may go so far without law, but at a certain point it stalls unless a legal infrastructure is put in place. That legal infrastructure is especially important in a world where other forms of market control—state oversight, family or ethnic social control, political connectedness, or networks of trust-based relationships—cannot cope with the scope and impersonality of a worldwide market.

Our Asian case studies do not yet provide much support for the threshold argument. In part the reason is that the implementation phase in China and Korea has just begun, and Indonesia's mixed reform accomplishments have not yet restored the large sums of capital that flowed into the country in the pre-Crisis period. China's magnetism for investment and its economic growth show no signs of abatement, even though law's development substantially lags market development. Korea's rapid post-Crisis rebound surely owed much to state interventions, imperative bureaucratic actions, and the founding of new agencies, and it is difficult to argue that its shift toward legal rather than administrative regulation of markets deserves primary credit. In other words, even if the threshold argument were correct, it is not at all clear *when* law needs to be in place to push through the threshold nor exactly *where* the threshold lies.

These doubts point to an alternative conceptualization of the relationship of law to markets. Rather than global actors prescribing similar medicine for all developing nations, whatever their level of growth, state capacity, robustness of law, or integration into world markets, it behooves global norm makers to offer models of relationships between law and economies that allow developing nations to make appropriate adaptations.[10] The timing of those adjustments and the degree of convergence with global norms then occur principally at the discretion of nation-states. National policymakers respond less to the supply of global norms than to the demands from their domestic constituencies, which, even in a globalizing world, are far more immediate.

The reality of the politics of implementation thereby limits the idealism of global norm makers.

In some measure, the shift of global standards from the IFIs to the UN in the bankruptcy field recognizes the necessity of such accommodations. This move is not merely from less to more legitimate global norm makers. It follows from the form of the norms themselves—a legislative *guide* that is far more respectful of local sovereignty and circumstance than conventions or model laws. This Guide combines high-level principles that allow much national variation, with rule recommendations that likewise offer choice and creative adaptation. Yet the common presumption of all the global norm makers remains—that good law fuels investment and growth. It is this premise on which developing nations may decide to remain agnostic until obviously successful runs of growth slow or stall.

Understanding the recursivity of law underscores that without global respect for the local, and local awareness of the vagaries of domestic legal change, the contribution of law to markets will be uncertain and compromised. Legal predictability will not be achieved by having countries don institutional straitjackets, and the real limits on global power can be observed in each of the three linked cycles of legal change.

Although global norm making settled on UNCITRAL's Guide and the World Bank's *Principles*, five aspects limit their impact. First, to obtain a high-level consensus, UNCITRAL had to embrace a combination of broad principles, many options for choices, and much local specification. Second, UNCITRAL has no coercive powers, and its reliance on World Bank and IMF diagnostic instruments may erode its moral authority. Third, IFIs are less able to press conformity in the absence of a financial crisis, in the backlash against economic coercion, and as a result of their own institutional difficulties. Fourth, it is not yet clear how energetic private professionals and their associations will be in acting as "model missionaries,"[11] carrying the ideals of global norms to national capitals. Finally, the underlying premises of the law and development movement, itself a tributary of a post–Washington Consensus, has come under increasing criticism by experts in the Global North (Easterly 2007; Stiglitz 2002) as well as by its primary audiences—local policymakers. Ironically, the climactic moment of normative convergence in the global center may have created more degrees of freedom for local lawmakers than those previously offered by the IFIs.

Recursive legal change within countries further illustrates the unpredictability of how law will settle. We have seen four conditions in which change remains unstable and the benefits of legal regulation are questionable. First, legal change in countries that either have not had bankruptcy law or where it has been moribund tends to be confounded by unresolved policy contradictions that are reflected in struggles between institutions that once dominated the economy and those that purportedly will now referee it. Second, these contradictions compound the uncertainties that result from any new law. Such indeterminacies drive further rounds of reform and may even lead stakeholders to abandon the new law. Third, actors in practice can veto formal legal change if they are not parties to its enactment or are otherwise unhappy with the outcome. Yet a mismatch between those who implement and those who formulate law occurs frequently in countries with underdeveloped mechanisms of political representation. Fourth, diagnosing the problem is no easy matter, especially when diagnostic capacities are limited, local actors are ignored, and ideologies too readily substitute theories of what works for empirical evidence of what does not.

The interplay of international agents of global norms and national lawmakers can generate several impediments to closing the implementation gap. If global norms seem illegitimate, they are unlikely to be persuasive in the long run. Nakedly coercive pressures from IFIs may achieve short-term success via national enactment but trigger long-term failure through local implementation. Furthermore, foiling techniques mobilized through national politics of enactment enable putatively weak nations to maintain far more autonomy than naïve views of globalization suppose. And because local responses to global pressures involve *both* enactment and implementation, the latter serves as a formidable line of last defense in global/local encounters.

In view of the limits revealed by a recursive approach to globalization of law and markets, we take issue with strong theories of globalization. Seemingly, evidence for these theories abounds: powerful states, institutions of global capital, and market professionals clearly dominate the heights of global norm making in the bankruptcy field; access to capital for troubled economies is controlled by IFIs during financial crises; the sanctity of property rights, rule of law, and open markets is institutionalized in global norms of commercial law. Developing and transitional nations enter playing fields that are tilted against them. In these contexts, imposing global standards onto local soil would seem unproblematic.

Yet close investigation of these seemingly unstoppable forces shows that they are blunted and even fought to a standstill. The dynamics of recursivity ensure that the penetration of global laws, global capital, and global ideals is ultimately decided at the local level, in national capitals remote from Washington, and in cities and provinces remote from national capitals. It is not that global norms are irrelevant, nor that their impact is negligible. Many do get institutionalized in national laws and new and reformed local institutions. But by the time they reach practice, they are translated and redefined, adapted and domesticated. Local rules are changed by their encounter with the global, but they do not mirror or reproduce it slavishly. "Globalized localisms" are held in tension with "localized globalisms."

Recursive processes of legal change do not guarantee that a global norm will deliver anything like its promise when implemented. Implementation gaps are the rule, not the exception. To close that gap requires a nuanced awareness of the contingencies of legal change and careful adjustments to anticipate their dysfunctions. It requires that power between the global and local be reconceived and, in so doing, that the relations between global centers and global peripheries be reconstituted.

Notes

Preface

1. We combine multiple sources of data. From 1999 we participated in public meetings and conferences hosted by the International Monetary Fund (IMF), World Bank, Asian Development Bank (ADB), Organisation for Economic Co-operation and Development (OECD), International Bar Association (IBA), and International Association of Restructuring, Insolvency & Bankruptcy Professionals, previously International Federation of Insolvency Practitioners (INSOL International). We attended all sessions but two of the Working Group on Insolvency, United Nations Commission on International Trade Law (UNCITRAL) in Vienna and New York from 1999 to 2005. Between 1999 and 2007 we conducted hundreds of formal and informal interviews with officials and delegates to these organizations as well as with officials at the European Bank on Reconstruction and Development (EBRD). We had access to public primary sources and often private documents from these organizations as well as the G-22. We also undertook a statistical analysis of all bankruptcy reforms worldwide that we could discover from 1973 to 1998. Many officials in these organizations contributed to our conclusions by commenting on earlier presentations, publications, and versions of chapters in this book.

2. For the country studies, we again relied on extensive interviews and documentary analysis. In Indonesia we conducted fifty to sixty interviews in 2002 and 2006; many additional formal and informal interviews with Indonesian reformers, international specialists, and IFI officials from 2000 to 2008; and analysis of principally public and some private documentary sources. In Korea we conducted approximately forty interviews between 2002 and 2008 with Korean reformers, domestic and foreign bankers, and IFI officials. In China we have interviewed more than thirty key informants repeatedly on successive field trips from 2001 to 2007 as well as officials from

international organizations, overseas consultants to China, and aid organizations. In all three countries we have taken advantage of the considerable scholarly literature produced within and outside the country on the legal impact of the Asian Financial Crisis in general and on bankruptcy reforms in particular.

3. INSOL later changed its name to International Association of Restructuring, Insolvency & Bankruptcy Professionals.

Chapter 1

1. The so-called Asian Tigers—Thailand, Indonesia, Korea, Malaysia, and Taiwan—were a group of countries that had sustained extraordinary economic growth over the two decades before the Asian Financial Crisis.

2. In the case of bankruptcy law, primary legislation and institutions are national rather than international. Nevertheless, the architects of the new international financial architecture presumed that national institutions designed to be in accordance with global norms would also be connected internationally not only in their normative convergence but in legal provisions that would facilitate cross-border, cross-jurisdictional proceedings.

3. A promising opening in the work of Chambliss and others has been underdeveloped (Chambliss 1979: 149–171; Chambliss and Zata 1993; Grattet and Jenness 2001: 11–50).

4. It should be noted that we adopt a highly restrictive and positivistic concept of law that is far more circumscribed than its conventional definitions in sociolegal scholarship and the anthropology of law. We do so deliberately in order to contain the variation we seek to explain through the recursivity framework. In practice, recursivity also occurs through nonpositivistic dynamics of legal change, although this is a step further than we elaborate in this book.

5. In fact, the sociology of law has not done well in predicting or explaining when cycles of reform will slow or stabilize. One promising line of inquiry can be found in work on "settling," which focuses on stabilization of interpretations by courts (Grattet and Jenness 2001: 11–50) and enforcement agencies (Grattet 2005: 893–941).

6. For a more detailed treatment of intermediation in situations of asymmetrical power, see Carruthers and Halliday (2007b).

7. They can be counterposed as relatively bounded structures—of an organization (e.g., the IMF) on one side and a nation (e.g., Indonesia) on another; or as distinguishable but intersecting sets; or as neighborhoods in vast networks of relationships.

Chapter 2

1. All monetary amounts are expressed in U.S. dollars unless otherwise noted.

2. The *Bramalea* case was handled by the Ontario courts and involved a reorganization of more than thirty American and Canadian subsidiaries with liabilities in ex-

cess of $4 billion. See also *In re Olympia and York Realty Corp.*, Case Nos. 92-B-42698, 92-42702, U.S. Bankruptcy Court for the Southern District of New York.

3. For further on the theoretical debates in this field, see Clift (2002); Westbrook (1991, 1994, 2000, 2001a, 2001b, 2002a, 2002b), and analyses from the perspectives of private international law.

4. Interview 2021.

5. While original country committees included Australia, Canada, England, the Federal Republic of Germany, Israel, Italy, Japan, Nigeria, Scotland, Switzerland, and the U.S., the teams expanded to include Argentina, Brazil, France, Mexico, Portugal, South Africa, and Spain (Panuska 1993: 398n201; Powers, Mears, and Barrett 1994).

6. Interview 2035. Most European countries prefer to replace managers with the appointment of administrators to liquidate or reorganize a company (Lechner 2002: 1006).

7. Argentina, Australia, Brazil, Canada, Denmark, England, France, Germany, Israel, Italy, Japan, Mexico, Nigeria, Norway, Portugal, Scotland, South Africa, Spain, Switzerland, Uruguay, and the U.S., i.e., overwhelmingly countries whose private practitioners had participated in the drafting (Powers, Mears, and Barrett 1994: note 43).

8. Interview 3001; Clift (2002).

9. Interview 2052.

10. The U.S. Examiner, Richard Gitlin, was a distinguished insolvency lawyer who subsequently was President of INSOL.

11. Comity refers to a practice whereby one court chooses to defer to another, even though both have grounds for claiming jurisdiction. It thus is a legal courtesy that forestalls conflict.

12. *In re Brierly*, 145 BR 151 (Bankr. SDNY 1992). Quoted in Flaschen and Silverman (1994: 46).

13. Although we cannot yet establish a direct connection, it seems probable that the leading bankruptcy practitioners and judges in Manhattan, New York, were aware of each other's initiatives.

14. Sigal and Wagner were fully away of failures of the EU Convention and the Istanbul Convention. Yet they use the ongoing EU efforts as point and counterpoint, showing similarities and deviations. They explicitly build on the example of Maxwell Communication Corp. and Olympia and York.

15. These included Argentina, Australia, Bermuda, Canada, France, Germany, Italy, Japan, the Netherlands, New Zealand, Scandinavian nations, South Africa, Switzerland, the U.K., and the U.S.

16. Interview 2055.

17. Interview 2052.

18. Ibid.

19. Ibid.

20. RevDraft 1.

21. Interview 2055.

22. The Principles indicate coordination mechanisms in areas such as how to sell

assets of a company, how to recover assets for the company's estate, and how to file claims. They discuss the corporate governance of a debtor during a reorganization, including how to appoint directors, how boards should conduct their affairs, and how courts provide review of efforts to remove directors. The Concordat indicates the recommended rights of insolvency practitioners, including an ability to appear in foreign courts and a capacity to obtain information (Clift 2002).

23. These include "one insolvency proceeding that governs assets and claims on a worldwide basis; one major insolvency proceeding with one or more supporting insolvency proceedings in other countries; multiple insolvency proceedings that proceed on the basis of territoriality; and multiple insolvency proceedings whose jurisdiction over assets and claims overlap" (Nielsen, Sigal, and Wagner 1996: 538).

24. Letter from Mike Sigal to Country Chairs on Cross-Border Insolvency Concordat, January 3, 1996, in RevDraft, Tab 2. See also Nielsen, Sigal, and Wagner (1996: 557–562).

25. Since 2005, UNCITRAL Working Group V (Insolvency Law) has returned to the problem of coordination and cooperation among courts by using, among other things, cross-border insolvency protocols. See A/CN.9/WG.V/WP.83, Draft UNCITRAL Notes on cooperation, communication, and coordination in cross-border insolvency proceedings for draft text and many examples. See

http://daccessdds.un.org/doc/UNDOC/LTD/V08/563/53/PDF/V0856353. pdf?OpenElement (last accessed December 12, 2008).

26. The EU was established on November 1, 1993, out of the twenty-five nations that had previously joined in a less tightly integrated EC.

27. The Convention has five chapters. Chapter 1 sets out the scope of the instrument and indicates what laws will apply in jurisdictions. Chapter 2 deals with recognition of proceedings and the powers of liquidators in EC countries once a main proceeding has begun. Chapter 3 deals with issues of how secondary proceedings will work alongside main proceedings. Chapter 4 covers the rights of creditors. Chapter 5 lays out how this Convention will relate to other Conventions and how it will come into force (Woodland 1994: Annex 1).

28. Final Report on Trans-National Insolvency, quoted in Law Commission: 42–43.

29. It is curious that this event was hosted by INSOL and not the IBA, given the extensive work the IBA had previously undertaken in this area.

30. UNCITRAL (1999: Model Law, pp. 20–22).

31. Ibid.

32. UN General Assembly resolution 52/158, December 15, 1997.

33. UNCITRAL (1999: Model Law, paras. 1–202).

34. Ibid., pp. 20–22.

35. Ibid.: Guide, pp. 23–24.

36. Ibid., para. 54, p. 35.

37. Some delegations, led by Spain, argued strongly for UNCITRAL to develop a treaty or convention approach, principally on grounds that reciprocity is neces-

sary among jurisdictions. But the weight of opinion elected a more feasible approach (Interview 2026).

38. UNCITRAL (1999: Model Law, Art. 2; Guide, para. 20, p. 26; para. 71, p. 41).

39. Ibid.: Guide, para. 24, p. 27.

40. Ibid., para. 25, p. 27.

41. Ibid., para. 125.

42. The Guide then encourages nations to view these public policy exceptions quite narrowly.

43. UNCITRAL (1999: Guide, para. 27).

44. Ibid., paras. 125, 135, 122.

45. Ibid.: Model Law, Arts. 25–27; Guide, paras. 38–39, p. 31.

Chapter 3

1. Self-executing laws are those that automatically require compliance once they have been formalized. Domestically this occurs through passage of a statute or the ruling of a court case. Internationally it occurs through accession to a convention. Of course, to the extent that lawyers are able to enlist the powers of courts or to ally with international organizations, they can leverage their technical expertise.

2. Interviews 2042, 2030, 2035, 2023.

3. Interview 2024.

4. Interview 2020.

5. See INSOL Lenders' Group, Statement of Principles for a Global Approach to Multi-Creditor Workouts, PowerPoint Presentation, 1997.

6. Interview 2024.

7. Interviews 1963, 5114.

8. See note 5.

9. Finance ministers and central bankers participated from England, Hong Kong, Argentina, Australia, Brazil, Canada, France, Germany, Japan, Malaysia, Thailand, and the U.S. (G-22 1998, 1998b).

10. The Working Group focused on limiting government guarantees to the private sector (Chap. 2.1); insurance facilities (Chap. 2.2); liquid domestic bond markets (Chap. 2.3); exchange rate regimes (Chap. 2.4); and insolvency and debtor-creditor regimes (Chap. 2.5) (G-22 1998a, 1998b).

11. Report of the Working Group on International Financial Crises, Executive Summary, p. 3 (G-22 1998c).

12. In fact, the meaning of *tacit* is more complicated than this. Variants occurred according to whether diagnoses and prescriptions were tacit to all nation-states, to all nation-states except the target state, or to no nation-states. Put obversely, sometimes diagnoses of a nation-state were made known to that country either privately or in public evaluations.

13. Interview 2022.

14. EBRD, *Annual Report 2002: Annual Review*, London: EBRD, p. 85; EBRD, *EBRD Information: Legal Transition Programme*, 1999.

15. Between 1996 and 1998, for instance, of the fifty-six projects undertaken by the EBRD Legal Transition Programme, only four concerned bankruptcy law, and only two of these were substantial.

16. Originally the Survey covered pledge, bankruptcy, and company law. In 1998 it added banking, financial institutions, and the regulation of capital markets. And in 1999 it added general questions on the effectiveness of the legal system and courts (EBRD 1999: Annex 2.2, p. 43).

17. Ibid., p. 1.

18. Ibid.: Annex 8.1.

19. Countries could also be ranked by the sum of their indicator scores for several areas of commercial law. See Ramasastry (2002: 16).

20. EBRD (1999: Annex 8.1).

21. Interview 5913.

22. EBRD (1999: Annex 8.1).

23. The EBRD Annex (Annex 8.1) does point to the international guidelines being drafted by the World Bank.

24. EBRD (1999: Annex 8.1, pp. 160–162).

25. For an extensive analysis of the rhetorical character of IFI documents, and their internal logic of self-legitimation, see Halliday, Carruthers, and Block-Lieb (2008a).

26. The two leaders were Ron Harmer (an Australian lawyer, chief draftsman of the Australian insolvency reforms, consultant to the Asian Development Bank and World Bank) and Neil Cooper (English insolvency practitioner and former president, INSOL).

27. "These include the International Monetary Fund ('Orderly and Effective Insolvency Procedures,' May 1999), the World Bank ('Principles and Guidelines for Effective Insolvency and Creditor Rights Systems,' April 2001), the Asian Development Bank ('Good Practice Standards for an Insolvency Regime' in Law and Policy Development at the Asian Development Bank, April 2000) and the UNCITRAL Working Group on 'Legislative Guidelines for Insolvency Law' (ongoing work)."

28. The first Assessment was undertaken by the principal consultants. It was verified by experts from each of the countries.

29. Interview 5913.

30. The Legal Indicator Survey uses a case-based methodology whereby the EBRD creates a scenario of a failing company and then asks local practitioners what would happen in those circumstances. See http://www.ebrd.com/country/sector/law/insolve/insolass/index.htm.

31. Interview 5911.

32. See ADB at http://www.adb.org/About/membership.asp
(last accessed November 21, 2008).

33. Its subscribed capital in 2000, at the time of release of the ADB Insolvency Report, amounted to $47.6 billion with paid-in shares of $3.3 billion and callable shares

of $44.3 billion. (All monetary units are expressed in U.S. dollars unless otherwise noted.) While the Bank's sphere of operation focuses on Asia and the Pacific, more than a third of its capital comes from nonregional countries, overwhelmingly from Europe and North America (ADB 1999: Annual Report, pp. 180–181).

34. Ibid., pp. 236–238.

35. In 1999 the cofinancing roughly equaled direct financing (ibid., p. 245).

36. A total of $7.4 million in 1999 (ibid., p. iii).

37. The 239 grants totaled $135 million in 1999 (ibid., p. 272).

38. Interview 2054.

39. The six countries are Japan, Korea, People's Republic of China (PRC), Indonesia, Thailand, and India.

40. ADB, unpublished private document.

41. Regional Technical Assistance (RETA) (TA No. 5795-REG).

42. Lees was subsequently president of INSOL.

43. Those of Hong Kong, Singapore, Malaysia, India, and Pakistan are modeled after English common law, with some influence more recently of Australian reforms. Those of Korea, Japan, and Taiwan bear traces of a German civil law heritage and later American law. Indonesia reflects its Dutch colonial origins. The Philippines and Thailand have a mixed heritage (ADB 2000: fn9).

44. Ibid.: 7.

45. ADB (1999: 11).

46. Ibid.: 9.

47. Ibid.: 16.

48. Ibid.

49. Ibid.: 10n10, 29–30.

50. These include variations in legal tradition, effects of cultural practices, differences in public policies, and variations in institutional capacities (ADB 2000: 25).

51. Ibid.: 25–26.

52. Ibid.

53. These include what entities are covered by the law, whether the liquidation/ reorganization processes are separate or dual, access to the process, commencement of proceedings, administration of proceedings, processing of liquidation, rescue processes, the role of creditors, the formulation of a plan, the supervision of the process, implementation of the plan, creditor priorities, avoidance of transactions, civil sanctions, and cross-border issues (ibid.: 27–53).

54. Interview 2044.

55. Since the IMF must cover all developing nations, it could be anticipated that its norms will be articulated at a high level of abstraction, high enough to encompass all variants.

56. Cf. the Korea Article IV review in Chapter 6 in this volume.

57. For a more detailed discussion of ROSCs, see the section following on the World Bank.

58. Interviews 2256, 2305, 4203.

59. Ibid.

60. *Insolvency Procedures*, p. vii.

61. Ibid., p. 1.

62. The reasons given include that such allocation of risk will increase confidence in credit systems, produce growth, increase predictability, and ensure equitable treatment for creditors, etc. Moreover, "interested participants must be given sufficient information for them to exercise their rights under the law." That is, "risk allocation rules" should be integrated into law (ibid., p. 6).

63. Ibid., pp. 5–8.

64. Interview 4203.

65. *Insolvency Procedures*, p. 12. Countries that give a lot of discretion also tend to create an appropriate infrastructure, including specialized courts.

66. Ibid., p. 76.

67. Ibid., p. 50.

68. Ibid., p. vii.

69. Interview 4203.

70. *Insolvency Procedures*, p. 2.

71. Interview 4203.

72. *Insolvency Procedures*, p. 2.

73. Ibid., p. 8. *Insolvency Procedures* is explicitly aware of varieties of law and implicitly alludes to varieties of capitalism. *Insolvency Procedures* also has deficits. From the inside it was intended as a handbook for officials at the IMF, not as a diagnostic tool or as a formal normative standard, even if some countries began using it that way. Others saw it as "the work of a few experts." There is "always the feeling," said a centrally placed official of another IO, "that Washington might be cramming things down the throats of others. This doesn't go down well with policy-makers in countries when they sit down to reform their law" (Interview 2065).

74. Interview 2044.

75. We will observe its role in both Indonesia and Korea during the Asian Financial Crisis. See Chapters 5 and 6.

76. "Legal and judicial reform," states a recent publication of the World Bank (2000: 1), "is one of the main pillars of the Comprehensive Development Framework that James D. Wolfensohn, president of the World Bank, proposed."

77. The International Financial Corporation.

78. For instance, in an October 2000 Consultation Draft on the *Principles*, the Bank includes as "partner organizations" the African Development Bank, ABD, EBRD, Inter-American Development Bank, INSOL, the IBA, International Finance Corporation, IMF, OECD, and UNCITRAL (*Effective Insolvency Systems: Principles and Guidelines*). See also *Principles and Guidelines for Effective Insolvency and Creditor Rights Systems*, April 2001, World Bank.

79. Working Groups included those on Institutional Capacity, Regulatory Framework, Business and Financial Sector, Debtor-Creditor Rights, Rehabilitation and Insolvency Alternatives, Economic Dimensions and Systemic Crises, State-Owned

Enterprise Insolvency, and Bank Insolvencies. Of the eighty-six people (with some duplication) listed in the Advisory Panel, Task Force, and Working Group, approximately eight were from developing countries. None were from transitional countries.

80. Forums have been held in South and Southeast Asia, Central and Eastern Europe and the Baltics, Latin America and the Caribbean, Africa and the Middle East. Often these are cosponsored by regional multilateral institutions, such as the EBRD in Central Europe and the OECD in Sydney, with support from national governments.

81. Foreword, October 2000 draft.

82. See Chapter 4 for the Legislative Guide developed by UNCITRAL.

83. Interviews 4001–4007, 5501–5506.

84. The October 2000 draft of the *Principles* illustrates the extent of this shift toward institutions, and perhaps is its high point (although the 2001 version pulls back somewhat from the institutional emphasis): of the nine chapters in the *Principles*, only one, "The Legal Framework," approaches pure black-letter law; other chapters include "The Institutional Framework," "The Regulatory Framework," "Creating a Corporate Rescue Culture," "Systemic Crises," and "Bank Insolvencies."

85. We shall show in Chapter 4 that pressure from other international organizations compelled the World Bank Initiative to reformat radically its earlier versions so that the *Principles* contain only principles and none of the commentary. This was a concession to the Legislative Guide on Insolvency created by UNCITRAL in 2004, which contained extensive Commentary (see World Bank/UNCITRAL 2005).

86. *Principles*, 2001, para 6.

87. See Principle 1 ("A modern credit-based economy requires predictable, transparent and affordable enforcement of both unsecured and secured credit claims . . . ") and Principle 18 ("The law should provide for a commercially sound form of priority funding . . . "). *Principles*. Ibid.

88. See, for instance, Principle 12 (" . . . The law should provide for such things as general creditors assembly for major decisions, to appoint the creditors committee and to determine the committee's membership, quorum and voting rights, powers and the conduct of meetings"). Ibid.

89. Ibid., para 4.

90. Ibid., para 6.

91. Ibid., para 81.

92. Ibid., para 84.

93. Ibid., paras. 132–135.

94. World Bank, "Principles and Guidelines for Effective Insolvency and Creditor Rights Systems: Template," Draft 2, January 8, 2003.

95. The Bank's public description of this process reads: "Working together in the Financial Sector Assessment Program (FSAP), the World Bank and the IMF jointly developed a system of benchmarks as an early warning mechanism, based on such international best practices as the World Bank's *Principles and Guidelines for Effective Insolvency and Creditor Rights Systems*. At the global level, these FSAP benchmarks set minimum international standards for transparency, market efficiency,

and financial discipline. At the national level, they guide policy reform by identifying economic and financial vulnerability. Countries are then evaluated against
the benchmarks in *Reports on the Observance of Standards and Codes (ROSCs)*. In
the insolvency context, ROSCs provide an opportunity for countries to evaluate the
strength of their insolvency and creditor rights systems in the context of their legal
and institutional frameworks, the relative rights, and the opportunities for alternatives to liquidation."

http://web.worldbank.org/WBSITE/EXTERNAL/TOPICS/LAWANDJUSTICE/
GILD/0,,contentMDK:20139835menuPK:146210pagePK:263900piPK:263909theSite
PK:215006,00.html (accessed September 17, 2006).

96. As of September 17, 2006, postings of ROSCs were found at http://web.world-
bank.org/WBSITE/EXTERNAL/TOPICS/LAWANDJUSTICE/GILD/0,,menuPK:1462
10pagePK:264057piPK:263913theSitePK:215006,00.html. Only six national reports were
posted.

97. Interview 1952.

98. Where "4" indicates that law and practice are satisfactory, "3" indicates that
law but not practice is satisfactory, "2" indicates that there is no material conformity
in law but there is some conformity in practice, and "1" indicates there is neither law
nor practice.

99. Interview 1952.

100. Interview 2044.

101. Interview 2032.

Chapter 4

1. See Chapters 5 and 7 on the United States Agency for International Development (USAID) program for economic law reform in Indonesia and the German commercial law reform program in China.

2. A scholarship on private legislatures in the U.S., as well as its extension to international forums, argues that convergence is only likely to occur either at the level
of vague generalities, when there are strong contending norm makers, or at the level
of bright-line rules, when one norm maker manages to dominate the others (Schwartz
2002: 1147–1152; Schwartz and Scott 1995: 595–653; Schwarz 1995: 909–989; Scott 1994:
1783–1851; Stephan 1996: 681–735).

3. UNCITRAL A/CN.9/WG.V/WP.50. For this and other documents cited from
UNCITRAL Working Group V, see http://www.uncitral.org/uncitral/en/commis-
sion/working_groups/5Insolvency.html.

4. We will variously call Working Group V (Insolvency Law) the Working Group,
the Working Group on Insolvency, the Insolvency Working Group, or the Working
Group on Insolvency Law.

5. UNCITRAL, Possible Work on Insolvency Law, Working Group on Insolvency
Law, Doc. A/CN.9/WG.V/WP.50, para 1.

6. UNCITRAL Model Law on Cross-Border Insolvency with Guide to Enactment,

United Nations, 1997. Available online at http://www.uncitral.org/uncitral/en/uncitral _texts/insolvency/1997Model.html.

7. Ibid., pp. 20–22.

8. Interview 2066.

9. Interviews 2066, 2065A, 4008, 4009.

10. Interview 4008.

11. Interview 2065.

12. Working Group on Insolvency Law, UNCITRAL, Twenty-second Session, Vienna, December 6–17, 1999.

13. INSOL already had a relationship with UNCITRAL that dated from the cross-border initiative (see Chapter 3).

14. Interview 2066A.

15. To say it is symbolic is not to detract from the authority of the most prominent global forum in which all nations exercise their vote.

16. Official Records of the General Assembly, Twenty-first Session, Agenda Item 88, Documents A/6396 and Add.2, September 23, 1966 (hereafter UN 1966), Art. 5, pp. 49–50.

17. For example, the U.K. delegate was a senior policy official of the Insolvency Service and therefore intimately familiar with the day-to-day operations of bankruptcy law in England and with English law and procedure. The influential French delegate was an experienced bankruptcy judge. The Indian delegates were senior civil servants in Ministries of Commerce and Justice.

18. How successful this was cannot be easily established. Delegations often have perverse incentives to send unqualified people: a fully paid trip to Vienna or New York for a week can be a reward for bureaucratic service whether or not the delegate has any knowledge of insolvency; or countries cannot afford to send a delegate and therefore rely on local diplomats. On balance it appears that most delegations included civil servants from government agencies with broad policy interests in corporate liquidation or rehabilitation, such as Ministries of Commerce, Justice, or Trade, or from the Central Bank. They were not usually specialists.

19. In fact, secured creditors themselves were not directly represented by private banks. Arguably, however, indirect representation of secured creditors occurred both through international financial institutions and lawyers, and especially insolvency practitioners who act on behalf of secured creditors. Arguably, some indirect representation of debtors (owners, managers), trade creditors, and other businesses occurred through the handful of private lawyers who serve as trustees or counsel to management, individual creditors, or creditors' committees.

20. A "speech turn" is a linguistic term for the change in conversation from one speaker to another. Research by Halliday and Carruthers (2003) recorded and analyzed all speech turns during the biennial meetings of the Working Group from 2001 to 2004. Speech turns provide a convenient empirical indicator of participation by actors in a political process. For analysis of influence, however, they cannot be the only indicator because some speakers have more force than others and much influence is exercised outside the formal deliberations in the Working Group.

21. The Secretariat used these meetings to resolve issues brought up in the Working Group (WG) sessions, to draft language to specify decisions taken in the WG, and to advise the WG Secretary on technical matters. Drafting decisions taken in the expert group were taken back to the WG for approval. They were inserted in the draft text inside square brackets to indicate they were new materials or materials that could require discussion.

22. This section reproduces and extends sections from Block-Lieb and Halliday (2006). A detailed technical analysis of cross-national variation in substantive corporate bankruptcy law and institutions can be found in Block-Lieb and Halliday (2006).

23. For more on the moral regulation of markets by insolvency practitioners, see Halliday and Carruthers (1996: 371–413).

24. Typically, insolvency proceedings are administered by a combination of these professions.

25. In such a system, reversal of creditor determinations could occur in the event of fraudulent voting practices.

26. Turkey, for instance, which currently seeks entry in the EU and endeavors to meet IMF demands, attended UNCITRAL precisely to inform itself of alternatives acceptable to the global insolvency community and IMF. This might enable Turkey simultaneously to satisfy the IMF without being seen to buckle to pressure from the Fund, which would be politically difficult.

27. It should be noted that the presumption of a relationship between good law and investment remains open to empirical confirmation. However, it is a widely held belief among many global and national actors that such a relationship does pertain.

28. For instance, Spain and France were revising their bankruptcy laws during the Working Group's proceedings, and in both cases the national delegates to UNCITRAL were influential in domestic law reforms and brought back innovations from the Working Group to their new laws.

29. For instance, for a period of time, before each meeting of the Working Group on Insolvency, the State Department delegate would coordinate a conference call of U.S. bankruptcy specialists to consider the appropriate U.S. position at the forthcoming meeting. This had the effect, at best, of coordinating U.S. expert groups, or at least, enabling the U.S. official delegation to anticipate where there might be dissent among U.S. professionals who were representing various expert groups.

30. Insolvency practitioners conventionally are specialized accountants who have taken credentialing courses and exams in the field of insolvency in order to be awarded exclusive rights to undertake statutorily defined tasks in the liquidation and reorganization of companies. They operate principally in the private market, representing banks and other creditors. Some qualified insolvency practitioners staff government insolvency services.

31. Interview 2065.

32. The U.K., Australia, Singapore, and perhaps Canada could forge an expert alliance with INSOL, the federation of insolvency practitioners that is based in London and is significantly influenced by English concepts and practices.

33. UNCITRAL (2004: 14–15; hereafter Legislative Guide on Insolvency Law, Legislative Guide, or simply Guide).

34. See further Block-Lieb and Halliday (2006).

35. UNCITRAL Legislative Guide on Insolvency Law (2004), available online at http://www.uncitral.org/pdf/english/texts/insolven/05-80722_Ebook.pdf. Compare Guide at Part Two, I(A)(3) and Part Two, I(A)(4).

36. Bankruptcy laws differ over whether a cash flow test (e.g., failure to pay bills on time) or a balance sheet test (e.g., more liabilities than assets) is the proper basis for putting a company into insolvency. The Guide, at Recs. 15 and 16, allows both, though it prefers the cash flow test. Rec. 15 indicates that "[t]he intention of this recommendation and the recommendation on creditor applications is to allow legislators flexibility in developing commencement standards, based on a single or dual test approach."

37. Guide at Recs. 18, 18(b), 19.

38. More precisely, if banks have taken security over part or all of the debtor's property, when a default is triggered, the bank can seize the assets over which security has been taken. When these assets include machinery, factories, inventory, and cash that are critical to running the company, or turning off the power and water, then the company's operations may be stopped entirely and all other value that comes from a going concern are lost to the business and other creditors.

39. Guide at Rec. 35.

40. Ibid., 69–83.

41. *Insolvency representative* is a catch-all term and can include a lawyer, accountant, insolvency practitioner, or state official—whoever is given responsibility for corporation liquidation and reorganization by the law.

42. Guide at Rec. 112.

43. Ibid., 63–67.

44. Although very few countries include provisions for adoption of a plan despite the opposition of an entire class of creditors, this is a vexing issue because on occasions a single class may derail a reorganization plan that is acceptable to the overwhelming majority of creditors. The Guide follows U.S. practice by indicating that if the rights of a creditor are not affected by a plan, then that creditor is not entitled to vote. The Guide leaves open—does not proscribe—the U.S. practice of "cramdown," which enables a court to confirm a plan over the objections of a class if the plan seems on balance to be better for all other actors. Whether a court is involved at all in confirmation differs widely across the world. The Guide accepts that in some cases it might, and in other cases it might not, be involved. In all instances, however, certain criteria need to be met (ibid., 139–151).

45. Described in the Guide as "the principle according to which similarly situated creditors are treated and satisfied proportionately to their claim out of the assets of the estate available for distribution to creditors of their rank" (p. 9).

46. Guide at Recs. 187–188.

47. It does, however, specifically mention both the London Approach and INSOL's Principles for Multicreditor Workouts (p. 34).

48. Guide at Recs. 160–168.

49. Guide, Part Two, III(B).

50. At the midpoint of the Working Group's deliberations, for instance, fully 27 percent of all interventions in the chamber were made by these four delegations (Halliday and Carruthers 2003).

51. Korea is a member of the OECD; Colombia was represented by the national commissioner for corporate affairs, who had vast experience in corporate bankruptcy and was a persuasive speaker. At midpoint in the deliberations of the Working Group, delegates from these two countries were participating in a higher proportion of interventions than any other countries except France, the U.S., the U.K., and Spain (ibid.).

52. Guide, Part I, A/CN.9/WG.V/WP.70, para. 25.

53. Ibid., para. 23.

54. Ibid., para. 25.

55. Of course, here and elsewhere in the Guide knowledgeable comparativists will often recognize similarities between Recommendations and the laws of particular countries, especially those most prominent in international legal fields, such as the U.S., France, Germany, and England.

56. This approach might also be seen as a way of disguising for the unwary how extensive is the influence of particular countries on parts or the whole of the Guide.

57. Interview 4008. Curiously, the EU was little involved in UNCITRAL's proceedings.

58. Such is the case, for instance, in the inclusion of the concept of "centre of main interests" by the Model Law of Cross-Border Insolvency. This concept and others like it are simply brought forward into the Legislative Guide (indeed the entire Model Law constitutes a chapter of the Guide).

59. This precedent in successful prior action is another legitimation mandate (cf. Hurd 2005).

60. Only one key term of U.S. bankruptcy practice (*debtor-in-possession*) earns an entry into the Glossary. See Guide, pp. 6–11.

61. "What we have seen in other projects is that you have to be very careful in choosing, in carving out, the area you are in. You should not go too far. Because perhaps by not being as ambitious as you might want to be, you enhance the acceptability of the text."

62. Commercial actors were defined expansively, however, to include state-owned enterprises and individuals whose debt was commercial in its origin. Rec. 8 of the Guide prescribed that "[t]he insolvency law should govern insolvency proceedings against all debtors that engage in economic activities, whether natural or legal persons, including state-owned enterprises, and whether or not those economic activities are conducted for profit."

63. Compare the U.S. to France. The Working Group met during a time of tension between the U.S. and France over the Iraq war. Although the U.S. and France were among the most prominent national delegations in the Working Group on Insolvency,

and their agreement often prefigured a broader agreement of the Working Group, the wider diplomatic quarrels seemed not to affect Working Group deliberations at all.

64. In the final stages of the project, the Secretariat circulated very widely a draft version of the Legislative Guide and solicited comments.

65. Cf. the Hague Conference on Private International Law (http://www.hcch. net/index_en.php) and UNIDROIT, the International Institute for the Unification of Private Law (http://www.unidroit.org/).

66. Note that this "sense of meeting" basis for consensus might lead the Chair to be influenced disproportionately by the strongest voices, those most articulate in the languages of the UN (Chinese, Russian, English, French, Arabic), or the voices of those countries and expert organizations thought to be most important geopolitically or technically.

67. This method could be read as a way of diluting the influence of official delegations or of ensuring that the major powers—U.S., France, etc.—will always have voice and a "vote" even when they are not official delegations.

68. This method may give advantage to the most vocal delegations and observers. By using consensus as the norm, however, the product may be more authoritative for most nation-states. Exceptions may occur in those cases where dissenters within the WG proceedings decide that their voices will not be persuasive and thus reserve their opposition to particular provisions for the politics of implementation in their own country.

69. This section presents an abbreviated version of Block-Lieb and Halliday (2006).

70. It can be argued that conventions are easier to "enact," because there is no legislative process (Interview 2071).

71. Said one senior official of UNCITRAL, "[T]he realities of many subjects are that you couldn't do a convention on it" (Interview 4003).

72. UNCITRAL, Possible Work on Insolvency Law, Working Group on Insolvency Law, Doc. A/CN.9/WG.V/WP.50, paras. 162–168.

73. In practice, UNCITRAL observes that "deviations from the Model Law text have, as a rule, very rarely been made by countries adopting enacting legislation, suggesting that it has been widely accepted as a coherent model text" (ibid., para. 165). In fact, there is a need for systematic research on how widely countries' variants of the Model Law on Cross-Border Insolvency has deviated from that text.

74. UNCITRAL, Doc. A/CN.9/WG.V/WP.50, para. 164.

75. Guide, para. 168.

76. Interviews 2071, 2065, 2066, 4001, 4009.

77. For a more extensive treatment of the Guide's structure and contents, see Block-Lieb and Halliday (2006, 2007a).

78. Interview 2065A.

79. Guide, para. 155.

80. For example, on standards for commencing a bankruptcy action, the Guide

distinguishes between the liquidity test and the balance sheet test. The former is associated with the U.S., the latter with Continental countries (ibid., 103–105).

81. Ibid., 104, 105, 106.

82. Ibid., 161.

83. Interview 2071.

84. An example of a purpose is "[T]he purpose of provisions relating to the reorganization plan is to: (a) facilitate the rescue of businesses subject to the law, thereby preserving employment and, in appropriate cases, protecting investment . . . " (Guide, p. 203).

85. These include the following: provision of certainty in the market to promote economic stability and growth; maximization of value of assets; striking a balance between liquidation and reorganization; establishment of a framework for cross-border insolvency (ibid., 12–19).

86. Agreement was aided by the fact that the Senior Counsel of the World Bank resigned to take up a position in the private sector and two new officials were appointed with responsibility, among other things, for obtaining the approval of the *Principles* and ROSCs by the IMF and World Bank boards, an approval that would require the agreement of the U.S. Treasury and State Departments.

87. World Bank/UNCITRAL (2005); Interview 4013.

88. The UNCITRAL Secretariat and some members of its expert consultative group reviewed and revised the diagnostic instrument.

89. However, it must also be recognized that delegates from nations were not directly elected by citizens but selected by governments.

Chapter 5

1. All monetary units are expressed in U.S. dollars unless otherwise noted.

2. Interview 2263.

3. It is not possible here to discuss in detail the nature of that "inheritance," but more than one lawyer fluent in Dutch and Bahasa Indonesia observes that translation, updating, and a very limited academic and legal commentary on its meaning and application made it a porous foundation for much specialty law that built upon it (Interview 2356).

4. There is disagreement among specialists over the use of the law before 1998. Several commentators allege that it was almost never used (Lindsey 1998) and was effectively moribund before the Crisis (Interviews 2256, 2305, 2040). Others claim there were at least 250 bankruptcy decisions reported by the courts in the five years before 1998 (Interview 5709).

5. Interview 3002.

6. On the concept of "enrollment," whereby weak actors harness the powers of more powerful actors, see Braithwaite and Drahos (2000). Interviews 2256, 2305.

7. We shall see that this dichotomy was quite blurred in practice, for the indig-

enous in part was constructed through global auspices, and the global relied upon local knowledge and local agents (Carruthers and Halliday 2007).

8. The Bank awarded the contract for the research to a Jakarta law firm, Ali Budiardjo, Nugroho, Reksodiputro, one of whose principals, Mardjono Reksodiputro, was also Dean of Law at the University of Indonesia. Mardjono, the Project team leader, included in the team Gregory Churchill, an American, a longtime resident of Indonesia, and a consultant to IFIs in Indonesia. The Project formed teams of consultants and advisors. Its extensive research included in-depth interviews with experts and other resource people; a survey of 1,425 people from seven cities in the business community, legal community, and the general public; and an analysis of archival data (laws, statistics, reports, etc.)

9. Interview 5706.

10. Interview 2273.

11. Interviews 2258, 2256, 2273, 5706.

12. Interviews 2256, 2305.

13. Interviews 3002, 5910.

14. We are indebted to Sebaastian Pompe for the observation that all parties to the reforms required this diagnostic labeling, however true it was in reality. If it was not outdated, why was there any reason to change it? Yet, as one experienced Dutch practitioner pointed out, much the same law worked very well in the Netherlands. Why could it not work equally well in Indonesia?

15. Interviews 2276, 2268, 5117, 2356.

16. Interview 5708.

17. Interviews 5111, 2318, 2269, 2263, 2261, 2262, 5706.

18. Interview 5910.

19. Interviews 2276, 2268.

20. Interview 5111.

21. Interviews 5101, 2356, 2271, 2318, 2250, 2268, 5111, 5115.

22. Interviews 5706, 5705.

23. Interview 5706.

24. Interviews 5706, 5910.

25. Interviews 3002, 2256, 2350, 5706, 5711.

26. Interview 3002.

27. Interview 5910.

28. Interview 3002.

29. Interviews 5910, 5712.

30. The Letter of Intent can be found online at http://www.imf.org/external/np/loi/103197.htm (last accessed June 8, 2007).

31. Interviews 2252, 2306.

32. Interview 2306.

33. Whether this confusion reflected genuine misunderstanding or deliberate efforts at obfuscation, possibly fueled by extraneous interventions, remains an open question (Interview 5708).

34. Interview 5113.

35. Interview 5704.

36. Interviews 5113, 5111, 5117.

37. Interviews 5114, 5100.

38. Interviews 5111, 5118.

39. Interview 5100.

40. Interviews 2306, 5110, 5111, 5708.

41. Interviews 2306, 5100.

42. Interviews 2306, 5111.

43. Interview 2306.

44. In the small world of Indonesian bankruptcy reforms, Dan Lev was a mentor and supervisor of Sebaastian Pompe's doctoral dissertation on Indonesian courts. Lev later was asked by the IMF Legal Department to be an outside reviewer of its entire reform engagement, a courageous move by the IMF since it did not follow his original advice.

45. Interviews 2273, 2276, 2249.

46. Interview 5708.

47. Interviews 5708, 5712. In retrospect, at least one IFI official indicated that more radical surgery might have been wise when IFI leverage was greatest (Interview 4203).

48. Government of Indonesia, Memorandum to IMF, June 24, 1998. http://www .imf.org/external/np/loi/062498.htm (last accessed June 8, 2007).

49. Interview 2265.

50. Interviews 5114, 2265. An experienced expatriate in Jakarta argued effectively that you cannot change the traditional legal structure in the middle of the Crisis (Interview 2278).

51. Interviews 2279, 2277, 2265; GOI, Letter of Intent, July 29, 1998. http://www.imf .org/external/np/loi/072998.htm (last accessed June 8, 2007).

52. Interview 2265.

53. Interview 2257.

54. Interviews 2273, 2256, 2269.

55. Interview 2263.

56. GOI, Letter of Intent, November 13, 1998. http://www.imf.org/external/np/ loi/1113a98.htm (last accessed June 8, 2007).

57. The language of "clean" and "dirty" forms part of a professional moral discourse in Indonesia, where the professional community attributes to its prominent members a label of corruptibility or incorruptibility quite independently of competence, training, or other status markers. This labeling is reminiscent of Abbott's (1981) analysis of professional status strain, but with an important twist, since in these cases the label of "dirty" applies not to low-status clients but to unethical and illegal behavior on behalf of often very high-status clients.

58. Other reasons kept away some appointees: one because he would only take an oath before the Supreme Court, another because of statutory restrictions on his activities as an arbitrator (Interview 5708).

59. Even in this case at considerable cost to herself, as the Ministry of Justice did not pay her extensive travel costs or honoraria (Interview 5708).

60. Interview 2250.

61. Interview 2278.

62. Interviews 2254, 2268.

63. Interviews 2318, 4110.

64. Interview 5708.

65. GOI, Letter of Intent, March 16, 1999. http://www.imf.org/external/np/loi/1999/031699.htm (last accessed June 8, 2007).

66. Government Regulation No. 19 of 2000 (PP-19/2000).

67. Government of Indonesia, Letter of Intent, August 27, 2001. For these and other Letters of Intent, see the IMF website, Indonesia, at www.imf.org.

68. Interviews 5102, 5107.

69. Interview 5116.

70. Ibid.

71. Interview 5115.

72. Interviews 5708, 4203, 5107, 5109, 5112, 5104, 4204.

73. Interview 5103.

74. Interview 5712.

75. Interviews 2251, 5910.

76. Interview 5116.

77. GOI, Letter of Intent, October 19, 1998. http://www.imf.org/external/np/loi/101998.htm (last accessed June 8, 2007).

78. GOI, Letter of Intent, March 16, 1999. http://www.imf.org/external/np/loi/1999/031699.htm (last accessed June 8, 2007).

79. Interviews 5001, 5111.

80. Interviews 5001, 5113, 5114.

81. News Brief No. 01/87. www.imf.org.

82. Interviews 2277, 2251.

83. Interviews 2260, 2277, 2251.

84. Interviews 2260, 2251.

85. Companies reduced their debt by approximately 50 percent. Jakarta Initiative Task Force, "Successful Completion of the Jakarta Initiative Task Force," Press Release, December 18, 2003. *www.indonesia-oslo-no/pr-10.htm* (last accessed October 19, 2004).

86. A term of art in debtor-creditor negotiations where a creditor, such as a bank, agrees to write down or reduce its claims by a large percentage in return for some other favorable terms agreed to by the debtor, such as a commitment to long-term payment at a lower interest rate on the remaining debt.

87. Interviews 5101, 5115.

88. Compare a conceptually similar move in Britain (Halliday and Carruthers 1996).

89. Interviews 2273, 2256, 2266.

90. GOI, Memorandum to IMF, June 24, 1998. http://www.imf.org/external/np/sec/nb/1998/nb9817.htm (last accessed November 24, 2008).

91. Interviews 2273, 2266, 2258.

92. We are indebted to Christoph Antons for pointing out the political sensitivity of implementing what on its face seemed a plausible instrumental solution to a vexing problem of limited supply of expert services.

93. The Receivers' Report (n.d.) stated, "We have found that the distribution of appointments among receivers were imbalanced. Very few receivers (less than 30% or 32 out of 116 certified receivers at commencement of the Program) had been appointed."

94. Interviews 2265, 2268, 2266, 2305. This close financial tie between lawyers and judges is reminiscent of the "bankruptcy ring" in the U.S. that the 1978 Bankruptcy Code sought to remedy (Carruthers and Halliday 1998).

95. Minister of Justice Decree No. M.09.HT. 05.0, dated September 22, 1998, regarding Guidelines for Receivers and Administrators Fees (*Pedoman Besarnya Imbalan Jasa Bagi Kurator dan Pengurus*, or "MoJ Decree").

96. Ironically, given the corruption and uncertainty, most receivers reported that they would prefer a hard-and-fast hourly rate (although it is likely that there is a strong selection bias toward smaller firms in this reporting) (Receivers' Survey n.d.)

97. Interviews 5114, 5116, 5708.

98. Interviews 2268, 5102, 5116, 5114. Interestingly, the problem of capture by "black lawyers" applied only to high-stakes bankruptcy cases. In the intellectual property cases handled by the Commercial Court, a responsible bar of high reputation is said to have maintained its activity in the courts (Interviews 5101, 5116).

99. See at http://www.imf.org/external/np/loi/041098.htm (last accessed November 25, 2008).

100. Interview 2263. The degree of potential and actual litigiousness in Indonesia past and present cannot be debated here, but at least one expert notes that voluntary civil litigation in the 1930s was three times higher in absolute terms than civil litigation in 2000 (Interview 5714).

101. Interview 2276.

102. Interview 2278.

103. For a detailed analysis of techniques used by weak countries to foil pressures from powerful international institutions, see Chapter 9.

104. Interviews 2261, 2263.

105. Interviews 2261, 2250.

106. One study estimated that the ethnic Chinese controlled as much as 70 percent of economic activity in Indonesia. In mid-1993 an economist estimated that 80 percent of the companies listed on the Jakarta Stock Exchange were owned by ethnic Chinese (Schwarz 1994).

107. The Chinese in Indonesia have had a varied recent history when their vulnerabilities to civil disorder and expropriation have been heavily underscored. During Suharto's years in power, the Chinese, who controlled the economy, and the Indonesia

pribumis, who controlled government, negotiated a relatively stable equilibrium to their mutual advantage. Both the Chinese and the ruling elite profited enormously. Since the fall of Suharto, political instability has perpetuated uncertainty on the part of the Chinese over whether the politics of postreform Indonesia will choose "blood or money." Their hedging mechanisms, according to a leading consulting firm, are to keep as much of their cash as possible outside Indonesia and to drag out as long as possible the dismemberment or restructuring of their conglomerates until such time that they get a clear political signal that their future is secure (Interview 2267).

108. Interviews 2250, 2261, 2258, 2278.

109. Interviews 5116, 5114, 5101, 2262, 2263.

110. Interview 5116.

111. Interviews 2259, 2249, 2270, 2277, 2257.

112. Interviews 5117, 5109, 5111.

113. Lev (2004) argues further that the real impact of the Commercial Court experiment may have less to do with the Commercial Court itself than the general reform program for the entire judiciary that grew in part from the manifest difficulties of reforms of the Commercial Court.

114. Interviews 2256, 5116, 5117, 5102.

115. Interview 5714.

116. Interview 2259.

117. Interviews 2278, 2265.

118. Interviews 5117, 5111, 5116.

119. Interviews 2032, 2267.

120. Here and elsewhere it might seem puzzling that without direct representation by debtors, reforms would press for reorganization (which favors debtors) over liquidation (which tends to favor bankers). In fact, the IFIs and governments had a coincidence of interest over reorganization provisions, the former because it reflects U.S. law and practice to enable companies to adapt to changing economic circumstances, and the latter because it enables governments an alternative to politically risky hard-budget constraints that drive businesses out of the market and make workers redundant (Carruthers, Babb, and Halliday 2001). A reorganization can be a relatively cheap way to try to maintain employment, support industry, or encourage continued growth. It doesn't require public ownership, subsidies, bailouts, or other forms of direct intervention (except when the state has to bail out the banks whose loans are being renegotiated), so politically it appears consistent with neoliberal imperatives.

121. Interviews 5117, 5115, 5111, 5101, 5100.

122. This is not the case in the area of intellectual property rights, where talk about town indicates the Commercial Court is working quite well.

123. www.locomonitor.com (last accessed December 5, 2007).

124. Even if its baleful reputation was not entirely deserved (cf. Suyudi 2004). It should also be noted that some observers argue the Commercial Court has been quite effective on intellectual property cases.

Chapter 6

1. The IMF, World Bank, Asian Development Bank, and several countries authorized a three-year standby arrangement of $58 billion (Coe and Kim 2002).

2. International interbank lending to Korea grew from $15 billion in 1994 to $108.5 billion at the end of 1996, with most of the latter debt having a maturity of less than a year (Lindgren et al. 1999: 69). This differs from Indonesia, for example, where foreign banks generally loaned directly to Indonesian firms and circumvented local banks (Iskander et al. 1999).

3. Mako (2002: 209) reports that thirteen *chaebols* entered court-supervised insolvency in 1997, and eleven of them went into receivership. Investment bankers estimated that another eighteen of the largest *chaebols* in Korea were at substantial risk of insolvency.

4. In the wake of U.S. military intervention in Afghanistan and Iraq, and as the world's most populous Muslim nation, Indonesia has recently assumed greater importance in U.S. foreign policy.

5. Bankruptcy law can be seen as a mechanism to solve a collective action problem—that one creditor will benefit unfairly from debt collection at the expense of others.

6. Japan had two insolvency-related procedures in the commercial code and three separate acts: the Bankruptcy Act (modeled after Prussian-German law), the Composition Act (modeled after Austrian law), and the Corporate Reorganization Act (modeled after U.S. Chapter 11).

7. These fluctuated between 15 and 52 cases from 1983 to 1990 and then climbed to fluctuate between 45 and 89 until the eve of the Crisis in 1996.

8. An extended treatment of the epistemologies of economists and lawyers, not least over their theories of law and markets, can be found in Halliday and Carruthers (2004a).

9. IMF/World Bank 1997 Annual Meetings Boards of Governors, Hong Kong, China, IMF Press Release No. 42, September 23–25, 1997. Statement by Kyong Shik Kang, Deputy Prime Minister, Minister of Finance and Economy[o].

10. Interview 2040.

11. See Government of Korea, Letters of Intent, December 3, 1997; December 24, 1997; February 7, 1998; May 2, 1998; July 24, 1998; March 10, 1999; November 24, 1999; at www.imf.org. See also an overview of structural conditionality and those other "nonconditional" commitments by the Korean government in Chopra et al. (2002: Box 3, pp. 50–51).

12. Note Coe and Kim's (2002: 1) observation that "many Koreans considered the 1997 Crisis to be the most critical national crisis since the Korean War in the early 1950s, and the worst national disgrace since the 1910 Japanese Annexation." See also the use of shaming language in the Article IV review of Korea by the IMF in IMF Country Report No. 02/20, February 2002, particularly Section VII, "Reform of Korean Insolvency Laws: A Review of Critical Issues."

13. The sections on legal and out-of-court reforms are drawn substantially from Halliday and Oh (2006).

14. "IMF Concludes Article IV Consultation with Korea," News Brief No. 98/39, June 19, 1998; Government of Korea: Letter of Intent, July 24, 1998, at www.imf.org.

15. For more details on the "Big Deals," see Nam and Oh (2000: 106–109).

16. GOK, Letter of Intent, October 31, 1997; Memorandum to IMF from GOK, January 15, 1998, at www.imf.org.

17. Interview 2298.

18. A case shortly after the new amendments were implemented vindicated this concern. The Dong Ah Construction Company, one of Korea's leading construction firms, was pushed into liquidation despite the fact that its creditors and the Government felt that the appraisal was flawed and that the company could readily be reorganized and save thousands of jobs (Interview 2294).

In addition to the economic criterion test, procedural rules sought to speed up the disposition of cases so that reorganizations not completed in a year consigned firms to liquidation. Amendments made it easier to move a corporation from one track—reorganization—to liquidation, and they took measures to forestall delays caused by appeals (Interviews 2280, 2281, 2285; Letter of Intent, May 2, 1998, http://www.imf.org/external/np/loi/050298.htm (last accessed November 24, 2008); Nam and Oh (2000); Oh 2002, 2003).

19. Interview 2284.

20. Interview 2298.

21. Interview 2280.

22. Oh reports that in three years, from 1998 to 2001, the bankruptcy division judges handled as many cases as all the cases from 1962 to 1997 (p. 3).

23. Interview 2285; Oh (2002a).

24. Between August 1, 1998, and July 31, 1999, for instance, the average number of days from filing to commencement was 135. See Oh (2003a, 2003b).

25. Interview 2285.

26. Government of Korea, Letter of Intent, July 12, 2000, http://www.imf.org/external/np/loi/2000/kor/01/index.htm (last accessed November 24, 2008); Interview 2285.

27. Interview 2290.

28. In our interviews foreign bankers complained that "in Korea we have a difficult environment, not a level playing field" (Interview 2297).

29. Interview 2329.

30. Interview 2294.

31. Interview 2290.

32. This intent was signaled again by the Government of Korea (Letter of Intent, July 12, 2000) and encouraged by the IMF ("IMF Concludes Article IV Consultation with Korea," Public Information Notice No. 01/8, February 1, 2001).

33. Two major corporate failures underlined the need for the Act, according to one of its primary drafters: the Jindo case, over two years and more than one hundred

meetings the creditor banks simply did not want to take responsibility for a decision; and the Hyundai Construction case, where the bank restructuring plan took an interminable amount of time to get agreement among banks and nonfinancial banking institutions (Interview 2290).

34. MOFE, Slide Presentation on CRPA, 2002; Interviews 2290, 2284, 2292, 2301, 2280, 2292.

35. Interview 2297.

36. Interview 2294.

37. Interviews 2299, 2303.

38. Interview 2297. According to a MOFE drafter of the Act, the foreign bankers didn't like it for self-interested reasons: "They enjoyed free-riding in the past," demanding full payment on their nonperforming loans, and this they would no longer enjoy (Interview 2290).

39. Interviews 2299, 2305. Some dissensus existed within MOFE among senior officials on the impact of the Act.

40. Interview 2294.

41. See IMF (1999); World Bank (1999).

42. Government of Korea, Letter of Intent, July 12, 2000.

43. IMF, Country Report 02/20, Chapter VII, "Reform of Korean Insolvency Laws: A Review of Critical Issues." http://www.imf.org/external/pubs/cat/longres. cfm?sk=15644.0 (last accessed November 24, 2008).

44. Ibid.

45. For subsequent developments, see Oh and Halliday (forthcoming).

46. "Territorialism" is a label for bankruptcy practice in which judicial orders inside a sovereign jurisdiction are binding only on property located in the country adjudicating the bankruptcy. Courts and other parties to bankruptcy do not recognize orders that cover other parts of the bankruptcy estate from outside the jurisdiction.

47. Interview 2299.

48. See Part I, Chapters 3 and 4.

49. In fact, this pyramid overstylizes what happened in practice. The Government did permit some very large firms to enter the courts, but there seems little doubt that its preference was for their treatment outside the courts.

50. Interviews 2300, 2303, 2297, 2292, 2301.

51. This retraction of Government guidance proved exceptionally difficult. Foreign bankers, lawyers, and legal academics stated repeatedly that the Government continued to intervene on any significant matter, "no matter what the law." The structure of banking, with the Government as a major shareholder, provided one such ready point of entry for the exercise of indirect influence (Interviews 2297, 2301).

52. Interview 2304.

53. Interview 2324.

54. Interview 2298.

Chapter 7

1. In 2001 a senior official responsible for medium and small SOEs speculated that they were *all* technically insolvent (Interview 2001: 101).

2. In the mid-1980s China had some 93,000 state-owned industrial enterprises, 360,000 collectively owned enterprises, and 12 million township enterprises or cooperative enterprises. Collectively owned enterprises typically received their capital from local authorities (county or town governments), but they held substantial responsibility for their debts. Township or cooperative enterprises were formed by individuals pooling their funds, although they might receive some community assistance. But essentially they operated as independent enterprises (Peng 1987: 375–376, citing Peng Zhen, "Bankruptcy Law Is Also a Promotive Law," *People's Daily*, November 30, 1986, a speech delivered to the NPC Standing Committee on November 29, 1986).

3. There is a danger of relying primarily on a single source, particularly an author who is skilled at self-promotion. While it is likely that Cao amplifies his singular contribution to passage of the Interim Bankruptcy Law, there are two controls that provide some support for his point of view. On the one hand, his autobiographical account was widely published in Chinese and English and thus has enabled any other participants or observers to provide their own perspectives. On the other hand, we have interviewed later reformers of bankruptcy law who do not dissent from the broad contours of Cao's account.

4. In the passage of the Enterprise Bankruptcy Law through the NPC, he opened a media debate as well as, for the first time, a visitors' gallery to observe the NPC-SC (NPC Standing Committee) debates (Cao 1998a: 17).

5. Cao writes that "in my view, the people's congress system ought to become the focal point of our construction of socialist democracy. . . . In order for our country to become truly democratic, we need to educate and train our people in democratic ways gradually and slowly" (1998b: 86).

6. Forty-two were from the NPC-SC, nine from the two convening committees, thirteen from central government departments, and twenty-six from local authorities (Cao 1998b: Appendix C, pp. 102–104).

7. For example, the test for bankruptcy includes this ambiguous clause: if "a deficit has been caused by mismanagement" (Art. 3). How is "mismanagement" to be determined?

8. For example, reconciliation agreements allow the state to make decisions based on policy interests to the disadvantage of creditors; they may prefer bankruptcy, in which case the rate of bankruptcy might be higher than it might otherwise have been (Peng 1987: 384).

9. See the bankruptcy provisions in Chapter XIX of the Code of Civil Procedure. http://www.lehmanlaw.com/resource-centre/laws-and-regulations/civil-proceedings/law-of-civil-procedure-of-the-peoples-republic-of-china-1991.html (last accessed November 24, 2008).

10. Interview 2001: 107.

11. ADB R-38-95, para. 4.

12. Interview 2001: 101.

13. ADB 2748:4.E14–15.

14. Fa (jing) (1991), No. 35, "Opinions of the Supreme People's Court on Several Problems Re the Implementation of Enterprises Bankruptcy Law." It dealt with two problems. The EBL's vague standard for deciding whether or not a company was insolvent contributed to confusion over whether an SOE was eligible for bankruptcy. The Court opinion set out three criteria, including the standard cash flow and balance sheet tests used widely in advanced bankruptcy systems. Although the EBL called for reorganization plans to turn a company around, it did not provide details. The Court stipulated five substantive areas the plan must cover (ADB TA 2748-PRC, Li Shuguang Lecture 4, "Restructuring of Insolvent State-Owned Enterprises: The Legal Framework of Restructuring in China," cited as ADB 2748:4.E8; ADB 2748:4. E9–10).

15. Consultations went well beyond these to some twenty-two departments of the State Council, together with unions, municipal authorities, and the Supreme People's Court, among others (Interview 2320).

16. The ADB's Report noted that workers got top priority under State Council Document 59, "in order to maintain order and stability in the society" (1996: 32).

17. Interview 2001: 101.

18. State Council Circular No. 59.

19. Interview 2001: 104.

20. Interview 2333.

21. ADB 2748:4.E14–15; World Bank (2000: 4).

22. For problems with implementation, see World Bank (2000: 3ff.). Part of the problem lay in the regulation itself: Did Document 10 apply to nontrial cities? To enterprises other than SOEs? Creditor rights remained weak for mergers or acquisitions. The sale of assets lacked transparency since State Council Document 10 did not require sale in an open market and auctions were neither open nor transparent. The government itself was not satisfied with the quality of restructuring in mergers and confronted large numbers of unprofitable SOEs being transferred to local economic bureaus (World Bank 2000: 3, 18; ADB 2748:4; ADB 1996: 51).

23. Many SETC officials were former senior managers of SOEs.

24. Interview 2001: 108, 109.

25. Professors Wang Weiguo and Li Yongjun, Chinese University of Politics and Law; Dr. Zou Hailin, Chinese Academy of Social Sciences.

26. R38-95 (1995), "Report to ADB Directors"; TA 2271-PRC (1996), "Final Report on State Enterprise Insolvency Reform"; TA 2748-PRC (1997), "Draft Final Report on Restructuring of Insolvent State Enterprises."

27. Terms were unclear and undefined; gaps were apparent where topics were untreated or procedures were unspecified; the rights of creditors were very limited; and sanctions for malfeasance were lacking. Oddly enough, the law emphasized liquidation of enterprises rather than reorganization; where it did treat reorganization, it did so too briefly and without measures that would make reorganization attrac-

tive or possible. On institutional grounds, EBL made the judiciary "subservient to the government administrative involvement." Government intervention and control intruded, not always predictably, at several points in a bankruptcy process. In practice, at the macroeconomic level government controls limited competition; at the microeconomic level government controls compelled enterprises to take decisions inconsistent with effective restructuring (e.g., compelling strong SOEs to take over weak SOEs). Moreover, China lacked any effective bankruptcy infrastructure—a competent and independent court system; a government agency that specialized in certain types of bankruptcies; and professionals, such as lawyers, accountants, and insolvency practitioners, to provide expert support for practitioners (ADB 1996: 25–37, 39).

28. Interviews 2001: 104; 2311, 3010.

29. Interviews 2328, 2311, 3101.

30. We refer here to the Bankruptcy Law of the People's Republic of China (draft), hereafter cited as Draft Law, dated April 26, 2001.

31. This is a key feature of American bankruptcy law and an integral component of the Legislative Guide on Insolvency prepared by UNCITRAL (2004).

32. Interview 2001: 104. In advanced economies, cramdown is not usually employed against the body of major creditors in favor of a generalized public interest but against a handful of powerful creditors who stand in the way of an agreement that has been approved by most other powerful creditors.

33. Interview 2001: 101, 106. In fact, the Draft does more than place workers at the top of the priority list—it provides no limit to their claims, and as we have seen from the SOE examples, those may extend for several years at enormously high levels by the standards of any advanced economy. Art. 156, Draft Law: "Insolvency property shall liquidate according to the following sequence after paying off in prior the insolvency costs and common debts: (1) salaries owed to laborers, owed costs for social security that shall be paid and other costs which shall be paid to laborers according to laws and administrative regulations."

34. Art. 156, Draft Law: "Insolvency property shall liquidate according to the following sequence after paying off in prior the insolvency costs and common debts: (1) salaries owed to laborers . . . ; (2) taxes owed by the insolvent person."

35. Interview 2001: 108.

36. Chapter VIII, Draft Law.

37. Interview 2001: 100.

38. Ibid.: 104.

39. Ibid.: 106, 104; Interview 2320.

40. Interviews 4102, 4108, 4106. Some disagreement occurred over conciliation, a process very similar to the concept of composition in Britain and many Commonwealth countries, such as Australia, and Japan, among others. One member of the drafting committee argued that it would be too complicated—too difficult for a court to decide (and perhaps too discretionary) whether a company should proceed through either reorganization or conciliation. It would be expensive as well. The rest of the

drafting committee and NPC did not share this opinion, since it promised to offer an easy and cheap method for small companies to solve their problems.

41. For a more detailed treatment of the principal elements of the law, see Halliday (2007).

42. Law of Enterprise Bankruptcy and Restructuring of the People's Republic of China (Draft as of June 2000), source Deutsche Gesellschaft für Technische Zusammenarbeit (GTZ); Arts. 2, 155.

43. Interviews 4105, 4101.

44. If creditor initiated, they would not require permission. Regulatory agencies could also put a financial institution into bankruptcy despite creditor or debtor preferences (Art. 134).

45. These SOEs were principally administered by the State Asset Supervision and Administration Commission (SASAC), the agency created to regulate SOEs that top leaders designated as especially sensitive to national security, defense, and the like. Some skepticism remains from key designers of the new system that any more than a fraction of 2,116 restructurings or liquidations could be handled in such a short time. If not, many of these firms may end up under the bankruptcy law (Interview 5703).

46. These were the barriers: to use the law, SOEs would first need the approval of their regulatory agency; they would be required to prepare a detailed report on how workers' employment benefits will be treated in bankruptcy; and if the SOE has huge credits from banks, it must resolve those first (Interview 4108).

47. More precisely, when financial institutions themselves (i.e., debtors) apply for bankruptcy protections, they will require regulatory permission.

48. GTZ (2004), "Brief on Recent Developments in Chinese Bankruptcy Law," Internal Report, p. 8.

49. Art. 2 reads, "Where an enterprise legal person fails to clear off its debt as due, and if its assets are not enough to pay off all the debts, or if it is *obviously incapable of clearing off its debts*, its liabilities shall be liquidated" (emphasis added).

50. Interviews 4101, 4105, 4102, 4100, 4106.

51. Ibid.

52. Interview 5403.

53. June 2000 Draft Law, Arts. 86, 90; 2004 Draft Law, Arts. 71, 74.

54. 2000 Draft Law, Arts. 136, 142.

55. GTZ (2003), Beijing Office, "Report," p. 31.

56. Interviews 4108, 4100, 4106, 4105.

57. Interview 4108.

58. Interview 5401.

59. In Art. 113, administrative expenses had first priority; workers claims, second; and extensive tax and social security claims, third. But Art. 132 in the final Chapter XII on Supplementary Provisions qualifies this by stating effectively that the Art. 113 priorities will only apply until June 1, 2007. After the implementation date the prior-

ity will be administrative expenses, secured creditors, worker expenses incurred *only since June 1, 2007,* and tax claims.

60. Supreme People's Court, Provisions of the Supreme People's Court on the Designation of Administrators during the Trial of Enterprise Bankruptcy Cases, April 12, 2007.

61. Ibid. See Art. 20 on "random means such as taking turns, casting lots and using lucky numbers[0]" to appoint administrators.

62. Cf. GTZ (2003), "Report," pp. 15–16.

63. 2004 Draft Law, Art 26.

64. Problems of financial collusion between judges and lawyers (labeled a "bankruptcy ring") were a significant factor in the drive for reforms that resulted in the 1978 U.S. Bankruptcy Code.

65. Interview 4108.

66. Interview 4102.

67. For example, lower courts in Guangzhou, in a heavily commercialized region, might easily manage bankruptcy cases, but in Tibet they would be moved to an intermediate court (Interviews 4101, 4102, 4106, 4108).

68. Hong Kong and Macau are exceptions.

69. Oddly enough, it seems to draw little in law from its two most proximate Sino-capitalist systems—Hong Kong and Taiwan. In the insolvency field, it dismisses the former as too common law oriented; and the latter cannot be an exemplar on ideological grounds.

70. Interview 2001: 100.

71. In April 2003, the SETC was abolished and its functions absorbed into other agencies, such as the Ministry of Commerce and SASAC. For more on SASAC's strengthening role, see Naughton (2005).

72. TA 2271-PRC, "State Enterprise Insolvency: Final Report," March 1996; TA 2748-PRC, "Restructuring of Insolvent State Enterprises," December 7, 1997.

73. On some of these consultations they worked through a corporate reorganization firm, Ferrier Hodgson, that is active in several South and East Asian countries. On another, Harmer's Australian law firm won the contract, though principally as an organizational vehicle for Harmer's activity.

74. For example, they conceded that the enduring problems of state-owned enterprises, especially those most strategic to the Chinese economy, required a special, perhaps administrative, solution that stood outside the structure of a conventional insolvency regime.

75. See ADB, TA 2186-PRC, October 18, 1994; TA 2271-PRC, "State Enterprise Insolvency: Final Report," March 1996; TA 2748-PRC, "Restructuring of Insolvent State Enterprises," December 7, 1997.

76. Confidential Document on file with authors, pp. 41, 72.

77. Ibid., p. 110.

78. Ibid., p. 111.

79. GTZ Expert Conference on the Draft Bankruptcy Law, Beijing, 2001, "Conclusions to Symposium, 2000." For instance, three recommendations read:

1. [I]t is strongly suggested, that in the event that it becomes necessary for the State Council to act pursuant to Art. 174, such actions should be governed by the fundamental principles articulated above. (p. 9)

2. Chapter 2 Section 5 of the Bankruptcy Law dealing with bankruptcy costs and common debts should be amended to include, in Art. 46, the following:—The first priority of distribution should apply to secured loans made to fund business operations during the bankruptcy case; the second priority of bankruptcy costs should be the claims of secured creditors arising from the use of such creditors' collateral to fund operation during the bankruptcy case; the third priority should include items 1 through 5 in the present Art. 46 of the Bankruptcy Law. (p. 10)

3. [I]t is strongly recommended that Art. 114 and the last paragraph of Art. 115 of the Bankruptcy Law be deleted. (p. 4)

80. GTZ Expert Conference on the Draft Bankruptcy Law, Beijing, 2001, "Biographies."

81. Interview 2001: 103; 2317, 3009; Gebhardt and Olbrich (2000).

82. Private internal memorandum, GTZ, Beijing.

83. Estimates range from two to five years (Interview 5701).

84. Interview 2328.

Chapter 8

1. For an expanded version of this chapter, see Carruthers and Halliday (2007).

2. Cycles of national lawmaking are driven by (1) the indeterminacy of law-on-the-books, (2) diagnostic struggles to determine which actors will get to define the situation that is to be reformed, (3) contradictions built into the formal law that were necessary to satisfy conflicting constituencies, and (4) actor mismatch, as actors involved in practice are excluded from policymaking.

3. Interviews 2268, 2281, 2001: 106, 104.

4. Interview 4202.

5. Interviews 2063, 2032.

6. Forum for Asian Insolvency Reform, OECD with ADB and APEC, hosted by the Ministry of Finance of Indonesia and the Ministry of Justice and Human Rights, supported by Government of Japan and AusAid, "Insolvency Reform in Asia," Bali, Indonesia, February 7–8, 2001.

7. Interview 2290; UNCITRAL field notes, 2004.

8. ADB, R38-95, "Report to ADB Directors," 1995 ; TA 2271-PRC, "Final Report on State Enterprise Insolvency Reform," 1996; TA 2748-PRC, "Draft Final Report on Restructuring of Insolvent State Enterprises," 1997.

9. For example, in November 2003, on a panel on debt restructuring held at the elite Korea Development Institute, all four Korean presenters and two Korean commentators quite coincidentally held doctorates from the Economics Department at

the University of Chicago, something pointed out with amusement (and pride) by the KDI Chairman.

10. Interviews 2306, 4011.

11. This relationship ended on a sour note over a dispute about fees between the Government of Indonesia and Hebb and Gitlin.

12. Interviews 2252, 2305, 2306, 2025, 2253.

13. Interviews 2251, 2261, 2263, 2273, 2040, 3002.

14. Interviews 2305, 2271, 2250, 2256, 2305.

15. The IMF discovered Mardjono through an indirect route. One of the IMF lawyers had worked with a Harvard program where he had come across the Bappenas diagnostic report on law in Indonesia (Bappenas 1998). He contacted a principal author, Greg Churchill, who in turn pointed the IMF to his senior partner, Mardjono (Interview 2305).

16. Interviews 2306, 4010, 2268, 2318.

17. Interviews 5705, 5706, 5708.

18. Interviews 2528, 2254, 2318, 5706.

19. Unless otherwise indicated, the IMF hereafter refers to the IMF Legal Department.

20. Nationality mattered in a quite tangible way. The appointment of Dutch citizen Sebaastian Pompe as the IMF manager in Jakarta later facilitated technical assistance aid from the Dutch government after 2000 (Interview 5705).

21. Interviews 2250, 2305, 4010, 2306.

22. Interviews 2301, 2271, 5705.

23. Interviews 2250, 2305, 5705, 5706.

24. One close observer notes that the IMF appeared unwilling to engage with NGOs until its program got into difficulty and its interventions wound down. Thereafter, it tolerated and accommodated to NGO activities consistent with its broader agenda (Interview 5706).

25. See Government of Indonesia, Letters of Intent, June 24, 1998; November 12, 1998; March 16, 1999; April 9, 2002; Government of Indonesia, Memorandum to IMF, June 24, 1998. http://www.imf.org/external/country/IDN/index.htm.

26. Interviews 2040, 3002.

27. Interviews 2040, 4010, 2290.

28. On Korean insolvency reforms in general, see Nam, Kim, and Oh (1999); Nam and Oh (2000); and Oh (2002a, 2002b, 2003a, 2003b).

29. An incipient conflict between the economists and lawyers in the respective ministries continued as a backdrop through the reforms, since each profession had a different notion of law's capacity to regulate markets (Halliday and Carruthers 2004a).

30. Interviews 2283, 3004, 2313, 2314, 2315.

31. Interview 2316.

32. The automatic stay is a provision pioneered in the 1978 U.S. Bankruptcy Code that upon filing and commencing a bankruptcy case "stays" or stops all efforts by creditors to collect on their debts from the company until a court permits. Korea

successfully persuaded the IMF that including such a provision would interfere with banking law and practice in Korea.

33. Hong Kong and Macau are exceptions.

34. It bears repetition (see Chapter 7) that China drew little on law from its two most proximate Sino-capitalist systems—Hong Kong and Taiwan. In the insolvency field, it dismisses the former as too common law oriented; and the latter cannot be an exemplar on ideological grounds.

35. In 2003, the SETC was abolished and its functions absorbed into other agencies, such as the Ministry of Commerce and the State Asset Supervision and Administration Commission (SASAC).

36. ADB, TA 2186-PRC, October 18, 1994; TA 2271-PRC, "State Enterprise Insolvency: Final Report," March 1996; TA 2748-PRC, "Restructuring of Insolvent State Enterprises," December 7, 1997.

37. For example, they conceded that the enduring problems of state-owned enterprises, especially those most strategic to the Chinese economy, required a special, perhaps administrative, solution that stood outside the structure of a conventional insolvency regime.

38. See ADB, TA 2186-PRC, October 18, 1994; TA 2271-PRC, "State Enterprise Insolvency: Final Report," March 1996; TA 2748-PRC, "Restructuring of Insolvent State Enterprises," December 7, 1997.

39. Biography, Proceedings of Third FAIR Conference, hosted by the OECD and Government of Korea, Seoul, November 2003.

40. Interviews 2001: 107, 106; 2309, 2310.

41. The other drafters are civil servants.

42. He has served as a co-arbitrator at the Arbitration Court of the International Chamber of Commerce and the Arbitration Institute of the Stockholm Chamber of Commerce. Biography, GTZ Expert Conference on the Draft Bankruptcy Law, GTZ, Beijing, 2001.

43. Biography, GTZ Expert Conference on the Draft Bankruptcy Law, Beijing, 2001; Interviews 2001: 106, 107; 2311, 3010, 2320.

44. See ADB, TA 2186-PRC, October 18, 1994; TA 2271-PRC, "State Enterprise Insolvency: Final Report," March 1996; TA 2748-PRC, "Restructuring of Insolvent State Enterprises," December 7, 1997.

45. Interview 2307.

46. See Chapter 7, note 79.

47. Interviews 2328, 2001: 100, 3006.

Chapter 9

1. Interviews 2278, 2305.

2. Proceedings of a seminar, "Incomplete Implementation: Responses by Developing Nations to Law Reform Initiatives Advocated by International Financial Institutions," Legal Department, International Monetary Fund, January 27, 2005, Washington, D.C.

3. Debate continues over whether Malaysia paid a subsequent price in a reduction of foreign investment.

4. For detailed discussion of examples in this chapter from Korea, see Chapter 6.

5. For detailed discussion of examples in this chapter from Indonesia, see Chapter 5.

6. For detailed discussion of examples in this chapter from China, see Chapter 7.

7. See Chapter 5, however, for the discussion of medium-term outcomes that potentially turned the relative failure of the Commercial Court experiment into a springboard for wider court reforms.

8. Chapter 5; Interview 5111.

9. This is also true in the U.S. and Britain (Carruthers and Halliday 1998).

10. Interview 2277.

11. Compare, however, Oh and Halliday (forthcoming), who show that key Korean reforms had domestic origins that coincided with international norms.

Chapter 10

1. This section presents a sometimes abbreviated and sometimes extended treatment of recursivity in Halliday and Carruthers (2007b).

2. By focusing on positive law primarily, we make what may appear as a regressive move to sociolegal scholars. We are not unaware that much sociolegal theory rejects a positivistic concept of formal law. We do not disagree with more expansive definitions of law, lawlike rules, and norms that constrain behavior and shape legal consciousness. For purposes of theory development, however, we accept initially some of the costs of artificially restricting our concept of law with the expectation that this heuristic limitation can be relaxed and become more embracing of expansive definitions of law as theory and data advance.

3. Of course, all laws contain symbolic elements. Lawmakers may purposefully put a law on the books that symbolizes their response to a vocal constituency, often in quick reaction to a scandal or public outcry, with no expectation that the law will be enforced. Even ostensibly symbolic laws, however, can lie dormant for years and then be activated by interest groups.

4. Abbott (1988: 40–48) offers a more sophisticated analysis of diagnosis (and its constituent elements of colligation and classification) and treatment (e.g., measurability of results, acceptability to clients) than can be developed here.

5. Although Abbott (1988: 44) appears to distinguish between *prescription* and *treatment*, we use the terms interchangeably.

6. Interview 2001: 101.

7. For a compelling analysis of diagnostic weaknesses in Russian law reforms, see Hendley (2004), who finds that one-shot empirical indicators usually are weak; intense time pressures for reforms can lead to superficial or mistaken diagnoses; outside observers place undue reliance on formal documents, i.e., written law; little attention is given to outside organizations on either the ways laws evolved in a

society or the ways laws actually work; and little consideration is given to variations in legal culture.

8. This distinction truly does simplify a quite complex issue. Because a law purports to be comprehensive does not thereby necessarily mean that it is substantively important. For instance, it can reasonably be claimed that the new Chinese law is both comprehensive and substantial. The new Korean law, however, has a formalistic quality to comply with the Government of Korea's commitment to the IMF. Its comprehensiveness is much more formal than substantial (Oh 2003a, 2003b).

9. The Supreme People's Court also issued an "opinion" in 2002 that sought to clarify ambiguities and fill gaps in the 1986 Interim Bankruptcy Law.

10. In advanced economies the relationship is more complex. As McBarnet and Whelan (1997) have shown, skilled lawyers and accountants may be hired to exploit ambiguity and sidestep the intent of the law.

Chapter 11

1. Schofer and Hironaka (2005) represent an important step forward for the world polity approach by dealing with final outcomes, such as actual environmental effects of institutional change. See also Boyle (2002).

2. See discussion on arbitrage in the Preface of this volume.

3. The most emphatic particular insistence of the U.S. delegation, backed by the Reserve Bank, was the chapter on financial contracts, which was in effect written by U.S. delegates.

4. Cf. the world polity school of sociologists whose research overwhelming focuses on formal legal provisions. But see exceptions (Boyle 2002).

5. In virtually identical form these amendments had been previously formalized by Presidential Decree in 1998.

6. See Chapter 8.

7. See Chapter 9.

8. This is not entirely true for China, which is yet to issue all its Interpretations from the Supreme People's Court, various administrative regulations, and professional regulatory standards. It may not even be true for Korea, whose Unified Bankruptcy Act will certainly require judicial clarification and possibly future statutory amendment.

9. In fact, UNCITRAL's principles would only become binding when adopted by national legislatures, which, of course, is the intent of the Legislative Guide.

10. The notion of "national ownership" of policy, in the context of recent discussions of conditionality, reflects an appreciation of just such complications.

11. See this usage in Braithwaite and Drahos (2000).

References

Abbott, Andrew. 1981. "Status and Status Strain in the Professions." *American Journal of Sociology* 86:819–835.

———. 1988. *The System of Professions: An Essay on the Division of Expert Labor.* Chicago: University of Chicago Press.

Abbott, Ken, and D. Snidal. 2000. "Hard and Soft Law in International Governance." *International Organization* 54:421–456.

Allen, Franklin, and Douglas Gale. 2000. *Comparing Financial Systems.* Cambridge, MA: MIT Press.

Armour, John, and Simon Deakin. 2001. "Norms in Private Insolvency: The 'London Approach' to the Resolution of Financial Distress." *Journal of Corporate Law Studies* 1.

Arrighi, Giovanni. 2003. "The Social and Political Economy of Global Turbulence." *New Left Review* 20:5–71.

Asian Development Bank (ADB). 1996. *Final Report, State Enterprise Insolvency Reform.* People's Republic of China: Asian Development Bank.

———. 1999. *Law and Development at the Asian Development Bank.* Manila: Asian Development Bank.

———. 2000. "Insolvency Law Reforms in the Asian and Pacific Region." Pp. 10–90 in *Law and Policy Reform at the Asian Development Bank.* Manila: Asian Development Bank.

Averch, Craig, Hsiamin Chen, Frederique Dahan, Paul Moffatt, and Alexei Zverev. 2002. "The EBRD's Legal Reform Work: Contributing to Transition." *Law in Transition*: 37–47.

Babb, Sarah. 2001. *Managing Mexico: Economists from Nationalism to Neoliberalism.* Princeton: Princeton University Press.

———. 2003. "The IMF in Sociological Perspective: A Tale of Organizational Slippage." *Studies in Comparative International Development* 38:3–27.

Baliño, Tomás J. T., and Angel Ubide. 1999. "The Korean Financial Crisis of 1997—a Strategy of Financial Sector Reform, Working Paper." Washington, DC: International Monetary Fund.

Bappenas. 1998. *Law Reform in Indonesia: Diagnostic Assessment of Legal Development in Indonesia.* Edited by Ali Budiardjo, Nugroho, and Reksodiputro. Jakarta: Cyberconsult.

Barnett, Michael, and Martha Finnemore. 2005. *Rules for the World: International Organizations in Global Politics.* Ithaca, NY: Cornell University Press.

Bartley, T. 2007. "Institutional Emergence in an Era of Globalization: The Rise of Transnational Private Regulation of Labor and Environmental Conditions." *American Journal of Sociology* 113:54.

Beckfield, J. 2003. "Inequality in the World Polity: The Structure of International Organization." *American Sociological Review* 68:24.

Berends, Andre J. 1998. "The UNCITRAL Model Law on Cross-Border Insolvency: A Comprehensive Overview." *Tulane Journal of International and Comparative Law* 6:309–399.

Berkovitch, Nitza. 1999. *From Motherhood to Citizenship: Women's Rights and International Organizations.* Baltimore: Johns Hopkins University Press.

Berkowitz, Daniel, Katharina Pistor, and Jean-Francois Richard. 2003. "Economic Development, Legality, and the Transplant Effect." *European Economic Review* 47:165–195.

Berle, Adolph A., and Gardner Means. 1968. *The Modern Corporation and Private Property.* New Brunswick, NJ: Transaction Books.

Bernstein, David S. 2002. "Process Drives Success: Key Lessons from a Decade of Legal Reform." *Law in Transition*: 2–13.

Bernstein, Lisa. 1992. "Opting Out of the Legal System: Extralegal Contractual Relations in the Diamond Industry." *Journal of Legal Studies* 21:115–157.

Bingham, Ben, Paul Heytens, Jung Yeon Kim, Andrea Richter-Hume, Alexander Wolfson, Max Aolier, and Sanjaya Panth. 2002. *Indonesia: Selected Issues.* IMF Country Report No. 02/154. Washington, DC: International Monetary Fund.

Block-Lieb, Susan, and Terence C. Halliday. 2006. "Legitimacy and Global Lawmaking." In *Fordham Law Legal Studies Research Paper No 952492.* Social Science Research Network (SSRN).

———. 2007a. "Harmonization and Modernization in UNCITRAL's Legislative Guide on Insolvency Law." *Texas International Law Journal* 42 (3): 481–514.

———. 2007b. "Incrementalisms in Global Lawmaking." *Brooklyn Journal of International Law* 32:851–903.

Boli, John, and George M. Thomas. 1997. "World Culture in the World Polity: A Century of International Non-Governmental Organization." *American Sociological Review* 162:171–190.

Booz-Allen and Hamilton. 1997. "Revitalizing the Korean Economy towards the 21st Century." Seoul, Korea.

Borensztein, Eduardo, and Jong-Wha Lee. 2000. *Financial Crisis and Credit Crunch in Korea: Evidence from Firm-Level Data, Working Paper.* Washington, DC: International Monetary Fund.

Boswell, Terry, and Christopher Chase-Dunn. 2000. *The Spiral of Capitalism and Socialism: Toward Global Democracy.* Boulder, CO: Lynne Rienner Publishers.

Boyer, Robert. 1996. "The Convergence Hypothesis Revisited: Globalization but Still the Century of Nations?" In *National Diversity and Global Capitalism*, edited by Suzanne Boyer and Ronald Dore. Ithaca, NY: Cornell University Press.

Boyle, Elizabeth Heger. 2002. *Female Genital Cutting: Cultural Conflict in the Global Community.* Baltimore: Johns Hopkins University Press.

Boyle, Elizabeth Heger, and John W. Meyer. 1998. "Modern Law as a Secularized and Global Model." *Soziale Welt* 49:213–232.

Braithwaite, John. 2002. "Rules and Principles: A Theory of Legal Certainty." *Australian Journal of Legal Philosophy* 27:47–82.

Braithwaite, John, and Peter Drahos. 2000. *Global Business Regulation.* Cambridge: Cambridge University Press.

Calavita, Kitty. 1993. "The Contradictions of Immigration Law-Making: The Immigration Reform and Control Act of 1986." *Law and Policy* 11:17–47.

Campbell, John L. 2004. *Institutional Change and Globalization.* Princeton: Princeton University Press.

Canan, Penelope, and Nancy Reichman. 2001. *Ozone Connections: Expert Networks in Global Environmental Governance.* New York: Greenleaf Publications.

Cao Siyuan. 1998a. "The Storm over Bankruptcy (I)." *Chinese Law and Government*: 3–93.

———. 1998b. "The Storm over Bankruptcy (II)." *Chinese Law and Government*: 3–103.

Carruthers, Bruce G., Sarah L. Babb, and Terence C. Halliday. 2001. "Institutionalizing Markets, or the Market for Institutions? Central Banks, Bankruptcy Law and the Globalization of Financial Markets." Pp. 94–126 in *The Rise of Neoliberalism and Institutional Analysis*, edited by John Campbell and Ove Pedersen. Princeton: Princeton University Press.

Carruthers, Bruce G., and Terence C. Halliday. 1998. *Rescuing Business: The Making of Corporate Bankruptcy Law in England and the United States.* Oxford: Oxford University Press.

———. 2000. "Professionalization from Abroad: International Financial Institutions in the Globalization of Business Rescue." Paper presented at the American Sociological Association annual meeting, Washington, DC, August.

———. 2006. "Negotiating Globalization: Global Templates and the Construction of Insolvency Regimes in East Asia." *Law & Social Inquiry* 31:521–584.

———. 2007. "Law, Economy and Globalization: Max Weber and How International Financial Institutions Understand Law." Pp. 128–151 in *The Spirit of Global Capitalism*, edited by Victor Nee and Richard Swedberg. Stanford, CA: Stanford University Press.

Chambliss, William J. 1979. "On Law Making." *British Journal of Law and Society* 6:149–171.

Chambliss, William J., and Marjorie S. Zatz (Eds.). 1993. *Making Law: The State, the Law, and Structural Contradictions*. Bloomington and Indianapolis: Indiana University Press.

Chamyeo Yondae (People's Solidarity in Participatory Democracy). 1999. "White Paper on Chaebol (Chaebol Baekso)." Seoul, Korea.

Chodosh, Hiram 2005. *Global Justice Reform: A Comparative Methodology*. New York: New York University Press.

Chopra, Ajai, Kenneth Kang, Meral Karasulu, Hong Liang, Henry Ma, and Anthony Richards. 2001. *From Crisis to Recovery in Korea: Strategy, Achievements, and Lessons, Working Paper WP/01/154*. Washington, DC: International Monetary Fund.

Clemens, Elisabeth, and J. M. Cook. 1999. "Politics and Institutionalism: Explaining Durability and Change." *Annual Review of Sociology* 25:441–466.

Clift, Jenny. 2002. "The UNCITRAL Model Law on Cross-Border Insolvency—an Answer to Insolvency Issues in the Framework of International Trade and of International Projects." In *UCL/Siena Symposium on International Insolvency*. Louvain-la-Neuve, Belgium.

Cotterrell, Roger. 1995. *Law's Community: Legal Theory in Sociological Perspective*. Oxford: Oxford University Press.

Cronin, Bruce, and Ian Hurd. 2008. "Chapter 1. Introduction." In *The United Nations Security Council and the Politics of International Authority*, edited by Bruce Cronin and Ian Hurd. New York: Routledge.

Crouch, Colin. 2005. *Capitalist Diversity and Change: Recombinant Governance and Institutional Entrepreneurs*. Oxford: Oxford University Press.

Dakolias, Maria, and Javier Said. 1999. "Judicial Reform: A Process of Change through Pilot Courts." Washington, DC: World Bank.

Darian-Smith, Eve. 2004. "Ethnographies of Law." Pp. 545–568 in *The Blackwell Companion to Law and Society*, edited by Austin Sarat. Oxford: Blackwell.

Delaney, Kevin J. 1992. *Strategic Bankruptcy: How Corporations and Creditors Use Chapter 11 to Their Advantage*. Berkeley: University of California Press.

Dezalay, Yves, and Bryant G. Garth. 2001. "The Import and Export of Law and Legal Institutions: International Strategies in National Palace Wars." Pp. 241–255 in *Adapting Legal Cultures*, edited by David Nelken and Johannes Feest. Oxford: Hart Publishing.

———. 2002. *The Internationalization of Palace Wars: Lawyers, Economists, and the Contest to Transform Latin American States*. Chicago: University of Chicago Press.

DiMaggio, Paul J., and Walter W. Powell. 1983. "The Iron Cage Revisited: Institutional Isomorphism and Collective Rationality in Organizational Fields." *American Sociological Review* 48:147–160.

Djelic, Marie-Laure, and Sigrid Quack (Eds.). 2003. *Globalization and Institutions: Redefining the Rules of the Economic Game*. Cheltenham, UK: Edward Elgar.

Dobbin, Frank, B. Simmons, and Geoffrey Garrett. 2007. "The Global Diffusion of

Public Policies: Social Construction, Coercion, Competition, or Learning?" *Annual Review of Sociology* 33:449–472.

Easterly, William. 2007. *The White Man's Burden: Why the West's Efforts to Aid the Rest Have Done So Much Ill and So Little Good.* New York: Penguin.

European Bank for Reconstruction and Development (EBRD). 1999. *Transition Report 1999: Ten Years of Transition.* London: EBRD.

Falk, Richard A. 1999. *Predatory Globalization: A Critique.* Cambridge: Polity Press.

Fewsmith, Joseph. 2001. *China since Tiananmen: The Politics of Transition.* Cambridge: Cambridge University Press.

———. 2007. "Assessing Social Stability on the Eve of the 17th Party Congress." *China Leadership Monitor* 20.

Fiss, Peer C., and Paul M. Hirsch. 2005. "The Discourse of Globalization: Framing and Sensemaking of an Emerging Concept." *American Sociological Review* 70:29–52.

Flaschen, Evan D., and Ronald J. Silverman. 1994. "Maxwell Communication Corporation plc: The Importance of Comity and Co-operation in Resolving International Insolvencies." Pp. 41–57 in *Current Issues in Cross-Border Insolvency and Reorganisations*, edited by E. Bruce Leonard and Christopher W. Besant. London: Graham and Trotman.

Fletcher, Ian F. (Ed.). 1990. *Cross-Border Insolvency: Comparative Dimensions.* London: United Kingdom National Committee of Comparative Law.

———. 1996. *The Law of Insolvency.* London: Sweet and Maxwell.

———. 1997. "The European Union Convention on Insolvency Proceedings: An Overview and Comment, with U.S. Interest in Mind." *Brooklyn Journal of International Law* 23:25–55.

———. 1999. *Insolvency in Private International Law: National and International Approaches.* Oxford: Clarendon Press.

Fligstein, Neil. 2001. *The Architecture of Markets: An Economic Sociology of Twenty-First-Century Capitalist Societies.* Princeton: Princeton University Press.

Flood, John, et al. 1995. "The Professional Restructuring of Corporate Rescue: Company Voluntary Arrangements and the London Approach." In *ACCA Research Report No. 45.*

Freeland, James R. 2003. *The IMF and Economic Development.* New York: Cambridge University Press.

G-22. 1998a. *Key Principles and Features of Effective Insolvency Regimes.* Washington, DC: G-22 Working Group on International Financial Crises.

———. 1998b. *Report of the Working Group on International Financial Crises.* Washington, DC: World Bank.

———. 1998c. *Summary of Reports on the International Financial Architecture.* Washington, DC: G-22.

Garrett, Geoffrey. 1998. *Partisan Politics in the Global Economy.* Cambridge: Cambridge University Press.

Garth, Bryant G. 2002. "Building Strong and Independent Judiciaries through the New Law and Development: Behind the Paradox of Consensus Programs and Perpetually Disappointing Results." *DePaul Law Review* 52:383–400.

Gebhardt, Immanuel, and Kerstin Olbrich. 2001. *New Developments in the Reform of Chinese Bankruptcy Law.* Beijing: GTZ.

Gessner, Volkmar. 1998. "Globalization and Legal Certainty." In *Emerging Legal Certainty: Empirical Studies on the Globalization of Law,* edited by Volkmar Gessner and Ali Cem Budak. Aldershot, UK: Ashgate.

Gessner, Volkmar, Richard P. Appelbaum, and William L. F. Felstiner. 2001. "Introduction: The Legal Culture of Global Business Transactions." Pp. 1–135 in *Rules and Networks: The Legal Culture of Global Business Transactions,* edited by Volkmar Gessner, Richard P. Appelbaum, and William L. F. Felstiner. Oxford: Hart Publishing.

Gilpin, Robert, and Jean M. Gilpin. 2000. *The Challenge of Global Capitalism: The World Economy in the 21st Century.* Princeton: Princeton University Press.

Ginsburg, Tom. 2000. "Does Law Matter for Economic Development Evidence from East Asia?" *Law & Society Review* 34:829–856.

———. 2001. "Dismantling the 'Developmental State'? Administrative Procedure Reform in Japan and Korea." *American Journal of Comparative Law* 49:585–626.

———. 2003. *Judicial Review in New Democracies: Constitutional Courts in Asian Cases.* Cambridge: Cambridge University Press.

———. 2007. "The Northeast Asian Legal Complex and Democratization in Korea and Taiwan." Pp. 43–64 in *Fighting for Political Freedom,* edited by Terence C. Halliday, Lucien Karpik, and Malcolm M. Feeley. Oxford: Hart Publishing.

Giorgianni, Lorenzo, Uma Ramakrishnan, Peter Dattels Rhoda Weeks, and Perry Perone. 2000. *Indonesia: Selected Issues.* IMF Staff Country Report No. 00/132. Washington, DC: International Monetary Fund.

Goldman, Michael. 2005. *Imperial Justice: The World Bank and Struggles for Social Justice in the Age of Globalization.* New Haven, CT: Yale University Press.

Grattet, Ryken. 1993. "Structural Contradictions and the Production of New Legal Institutions: The Transformation of Industrial Accident Law Revisited." Pp. 404–420 in *Making Law: The State, the Law, and Structural Contradictions,* edited by William J. Chambliss and Marjorie S. Zatz. Bloomington and Indianapolis: Indiana University Press.

———. 2005. "The Reconstitution of Law in Local Settings: Agency Discretion, Ambiguity, and a Surplus of Law in the Policing of Hate Crime." *Law & Society Review* 39:893–941.

Grattet, Ryken, and Valerie Jenness. 2001. "Examining the Boundaries of Hate Crime Law: Disabilities and the Dilemma of Difference." *The Journal of Criminal Law and Criminology* 91:11–50.

Hall, Peter A., and David Soskice. 2000. "An Introduction to Varieties of Capitalism." Pp. 1–68 in *Varieties of Capitalism: The Institutional Foundations of Comparative Advantage,* edited by Peter A. Hall and David Soskice. New York: Oxford University Press.

———. (Eds.). 2001. *Varieties of Capitalism: The Institutional Foundations of Comparative Advantage.* New York: Oxford University Press.

Halliday, Terence C. 1985. "Knowledge Mandates: Collective Influence by Scientific, Normative and Syncretic Professions." *British Journal of Sociology* 36:421–447.

———. 1987. *Beyond Monopoly: Lawyers, State Crises and Professional Empowerment.* Chicago: University of Chicago Press.

———. 2006. "Lawmaking and Institution-Building in Asian Insolvency Reforms: Between Global Norms and National Circumstances." Presentation at Fifth Forum on Asian Insolvency Reform (hosted by the OECD, World Bank, and Asian Development Bank in cooperation with the Governments of China, Australia, and Japan), Beijing, China.

———. 2007. *Policy Brief: The Making of China's Corporate Bankruptcy Law.* Edited by Randall Peerenboom. Oxford Series in Law, Justice and Society.

———. 2008a. "Lawmaking and Institution Building in Asian Insolvency Reforms: Between Global Norms and National Circumstances." Pp. 17–50 in *Asian Insolvency Systems: Closing the Implementation Gap,* edited by OECD. Paris: OECD.

———. 2008b. "Architects of the State: International Organizations and the Reconstruction of States in the Global South." American Bar Foundation Research Paper No. 08-01, Center on Law and Globalization Research Paper No. 08-01. Accessible at Social Science Research Network (SSRN).

Halliday, Terence C., Susan Block-Lieb, and Bruce G. Carruthers. 2008. "Missing Debtors: National Lawmaking and Global Normmaking of Corporate Bankruptcy Regimes." Presentation at Interdisciplinary Conference on Debt, University of Illinois College of Law and the American Bankruptcy Institute, May 2–3.

Halliday, Terence C., and Bruce Carruthers. 1996. "The Moral Regulation of Markets: Professions, Privatization and the English Insolvency Act 1986." *Accounting, Organizations and Society* 21:371–413.

———. 2003. Conformity, Contestation and Culture in the Globalization of Insolvency Regimes: International Institutions and Law-Making in Indonesia and China, Working Paper 2214. Chicago: American Bar Foundation.

———. 2004a. "Epistemological Conflicts and Institutional Impediments: The Rocky Road to Corporate Bankruptcy Reforms in Korea." Pp. 114–33 in *Korean Law Reform,* edited by Tom Ginsburg. London: Routledge Press.

———. 2004b. "Legal Certainty, Market Uncertainty, and Social Instability: The Confounding Case of Stalled Bankruptcy Law in China." Presentation at annual meeting of the Law and Society Association, Chicago.

———. 2007a. "Foiling the Hegemons: Limits to the Globalization of Corporate Insolvency Regimes in Indonesia, Korea and China." Pp. 255–30 in *Law and Globalization in Asia: From the Asian Financial Crisis to September 11,* edited by Christoph Anton and Volkmar Gessner. Oxford: Hart Publishing.

———. 2007b. "The Recursivity of Law: Global Norm-Making and National Law-Making in the Globalization of Corporate Insolvency Regimes." *American Journal of Sociology* 112:1135–1202.

Halliday, Terence C., Bruce G. Carruthers, and Susan Block-Lieb. 2008. "Rhetorical Legitimation: Global Norms as Self-Validating Formal Scripts." In *Conference on*

Law and Legitimacy in the Governance of Transnational Economic Relations, Villa Vigoni, Lake Como, June 21–24.

Halliday, Terence C., and Soogeun Oh. 2007. "A Recursive Theory of National Lawmaking: Site-Switching in Korean Corporate Insolvency Reforms, 1992-2007." Paper presented at Max Planck Institute for the Study of Society, Cologne, Germany, July 16.

Halliday, Terence C., and Pavel Osinsky. 2006. "Globalization of Law." *Annual Review of Sociology* 32:447–470.

Hamilton, Gary. 1996. "The Organizational Foundations of Western and Chinese Commerce: A Historical and Comparative Analysis." In *Asian Business Networks*, edited by Gary Hamilton. Berlin: Walter de Gruyter.

Harding, Andrew. 2002. "Comparative Law and Legal Transplantation in South East Asia: Making Sense of the 'Nomic Din.'" Pp. 199–222 in *Adapting Legal Cultures*, edited by David Nelken and Johannes Feest. Oxford: Hart Publishing.

Held, David, Anthony McGraw, David Goldblatt, and Jonathan Perraton. 1999. *Global Transformations: Politics, Economics and Culture*. Stanford, CA: Stanford University Press.

Hendley, Kathryn. 2004. "Business Litigation in the Transition: A Portrait of Debt Collection in Russia." *Law & Society Review* 31 (1): 305–347.

Heydebrand, Wolf. 2002. "From Globalization of Law to Law under Globalization." Pp. 117–137 in *Adapting Legal Cultures*, edited by David Nelken and Johannes Feest. Oxford: Hart Publishing.

Hirsch, Paul, and Hayagreeva Rao. 2003. "The Schweik Syndrome: The Narrative Power of Resistance by Agreement." Pp. 137–148 in *Narratives We Organize By*, edited by Barbara Czarniawska and Pasquale Gagliardi. Amsterdam and Philadelphia: John Benjamins Publishing.

Hoff, Jerry. 1999. "Indonesian Bankruptcy Law." P. 1v. (loose-leaf) in *Indonesian Law and Practice Series 2*, edited by Gregory Churchill. Jakarta: Tatanusa.

Holz, Carsten A. 2001. "Economic Reforms and State Sector Bankruptcy in China." *The China Quarterly* 166:342–367.

Huang, Yiping. 2002. "Is Meltdown of the Chinese Banks Inevitable?" *China Economic Review* 13:382–387.

Hurd, Ian. 2002. "Legitimacy, Power, and the Symbolic Life of the UN Security Council." *Global Governance* 8:35–51.

———. 2005. "Deliberation, Procedures, and Effectiveness: A Model of Legitimation in International Organizations." Working Paper, Department of Political Science, Northwestern University.

———. 2007. *After Anarchy: Legitimacy and Power in the United Nations Security Council*. Princeton: Princeton University Press.

———. 2008a. "Legitimacy." In *The Princeton Encyclopedia of Self-Determination*. Available online at http:www.princeton.edu/~/lisd/projects/encyclopedia/ep_description.html.

————. 2008b. "Myths of Membership: The Politics of Legitimation in UN Security Council Reform." *Global Governance* 14:199–217.

International Monetary Fund (IMF). 1999. *Orderly and Effective Insolvency Procedures: Key Issues*. Washington, DC: IMF.

————. 2005. *IMF/Netherlands Program: Legal and Judicial Reform in Indonesia, 2000–2004; External Evaluation, Final Report*. Washington, DC: IMF.

Iskander, Magdi, Gerald Meyerman, Dale F. Gray, and Sean Hagan. 1999. "Corporate Restructuring and Governance in East Asia." *Finance and Development* 36:42–45.

Jenson, Jane, and Boaventura De Sousa Santos (Eds.). 2000. *Globalizing Institutions: Case Studies in Renovation and Innovation*. Aldershot, UK, and Burlington, VT: Ashgate.

Karpik, Lucien. 2007. *L'Economie des singularities*. Paris: Gallimard.

Kendall, Patricia J. 2001. *Inventory and Assessment of Indonesia Bar Associations*. USAID/ELIPS Bridge Project.

Keyser, Catherine H. 1998. "Introduction: The Storm over Bankruptcy (II)." *Chinese Law and Government*: 7.

Kim, Se-Jik, and Mark R. Stone. 1999. *Corporate Leverage, Bankruptcy, and Output Adjustment in Post-crisis East Asia, Working Paper WP/99/143*. Washington, DC: International Monetary Fund.

Kim, Woochan, and Yangho Byeon. 2002. "Restructuring Korean Banks' Short Term Debts." Pp. 405–448 in *Korean Crisis and Recovery*, edited by David T. Coe and Se-Jik Kim. Washington, DC: International Monetary Fund / Korea Institute for International Economy Policy.

Kingdon, John W. 1995. *Agendas, Alternatives and Public Policies*. 2nd ed. New York: Addison-Wesley.

Kornai, Jâanos. 1992. *The Socialist System: The Political Economy of Communism*. Princeton: Princeton University Press.

Lardy, Nicolas R. 2002. *Integrating China into the Global Economy*. Washington, DC: Brookings Institution Press.

Lechner, Roland. 2002. "Waking from the Jurisdictional Nightmare of Multinational Default: The European Council Regulation on Insolvency Proceedings." *Arizona Journal of International and Comparative Law*: 975–1024.

Lee, Eddy. 1998. *The Asian Financial Crisis: The Challenge for Social Policy*. Geneva: International Labour Office.

Lempert, Richard, and Joseph Sanders. 1986. *An Invitation to Law and Social Science: Desert, Disputes, and Distribution*. New York: Longman.

Leonard, E. Bruce. 2001. "The International Scene: The International Year in Review." *ABI Journal* (December/January): 34–35.

Leonard, E. Bruce, and Christopher W. Besant (Eds.). 1994. *Current Issues in Cross-Border Insolvency and Reorganisations*. London: Graham and Trotman.

Lev, Daniel S. 2000. "Judicial Authority and the Quest for an Indonesian *Rechtsstaat*." Pp. 215–244 in *Legal Evolution and Political Authority in Indonesia: Selected Essays*, edited by Daniel S. Lev. The Hague and Boston: Kluwer Law International.

———. 2004. "Comments on the Judicial Reform Program in Indonesia." Unpublished paper, International Monetary Fund. Washington, DC.

Lev, Daniel S., and Ruth McVey. 1996. *Making Indonesia.* Ithaca, NY: Cornell SEAP.

Levi-Faur, David. 2005. "The Global Diffusion of Regulatory Capitalism." *Annals of the American Academy of Political and Social Science* 598:12–32.

Lindgren, Carl-Johan, Tomás J. T. Baliño, Charles Enoch, Anne-Marie Gulde, Marc Quintyn, and Leslie Teo. 1999. *Financial Sector Crisis and Restructuring: Lessons from Asia.* Washington, DC: International Monetary Fund.

Lindsey, Timothy. 1998. "The IMF and Insolvency Law Reform in Indonesia." *Bulletin of Indonesian Economic Studies* 34:119–134.

Lubman, Stanley B. 1999. *Bird in a Cage: Legal Reform in China after Mao.* Stanford, CA: Stanford University Press.

Macaulay, Stuart. 1963. "Non-contractual Relations in Business." *American Sociological Review* 28:55–69.

MacIntyre, Andrew. 2003. *The Power of Institutions: Political Architecture and Governance.* Ithaca, NY: Cornell University Press.

Mako, William P. 2001. "Corporate Restructuring in East Asia: Promoting Best Practices." *Finance & Development* 38:2–5.

———. 2002. "Corporate and Financial Sector Restructuring: Links and Necessary Conditions." In *Second Annual International Seminar on Policy Challenges for the Financial Sector in the Context of Globalization.* Washington, DC.

———. 2003. "Uses and Limitations of Out-of-Court Workouts: Lessons from East Asia." Presentation at Global Forum on Insolvency Risk Management, Washington, DC.

Mallaby, Sebastian. 2004. *The World's Banker: A Story of Failed States, Financial Crises, and the Wealth and Poverty of Nations.* New York: Penguin.

McBarnet, Doreen, and Christopher Whelan. 1997. "Creative Compliance and the Defeat of Legal Control: The Magic of the Orphan Subsidiary." In *The Human Face of Law,* edited by Keith Hawkins. Oxford: Oxford University Press.

Merry, Sally Engle. 2003. "From Law and Colonialism to Law and Globalization." *Law and Social Inquiry* 28:569–590.

———. 2004. "Colonial and Post-colonial Law." Pp. 569–588 in *The Blackwell Companion to Law and Society,* edited by Austin Sarat. Malden, UK: Blackwell.

———. 2005. *Human Rights and Gender Violence: Translating International Law into Local Justice.* Chicago: University of Chicago Press.

———. 2006. "Transnational Human Rights and Local Activism: Mapping the Middle." *American Anthropologist* 108:38–51.

Mertha, Andrew C. 2005. *The Politics of Piracy: Intellectual Property in Contemporary China.* Ithaca, NY, and London: Cornell University Press.

Metzger, Barry. 1996. "Opening Remarks: Seminar on Legal Aspects of Cooperation." Twenty-ninth annual meeting of the Board of Governors, ADB.

Meyer, John W., and Brian Rowan. 1977. "Institutionalized Organizations: Formal Structure as Myth and Ceremony." *American Journal of Sociology* 83:340–363.

Meyer, John, John Boli, George Thomas, and Frank Ramirez. 1997. "World Society and the Nation-State." *American Journal of Sociology* 103:144–181.

Meyerman, Gerald E. 2000. "The London Approach and Corporate Debt Restructuring in East Asia." Presentation at Conference on Emerging Markets in the New Financial System: Managing Financial and Corporate Stress, New Jersey.

Minzner, Carl. 2007. *Social Instability in China: Causes, Consequences, and Implications*. New York: Council on Foreign Relations.

Mo, Jongryn. 2001. "Political Culture and Legislative Deadlock: Politics of Economic Reform in Precrisis Korea." *Comparative Political Studies* 34:467–492.

Montgomery, John. 1997. *The Indonesian Financial System: Its Contribution to Economic Performance, and Key Policy Issues, Working Paper*. Washington, DC: International Monetary Fund.

Moss, David A. 2002. *When All Else Fails: Government as the Ultimate Risk Manager*. Cambridge, MA: Harvard University Press.

Nam, Il Chong, Joon-Kyung Kim, and Soogeun Oh. 1999. "Insolvency Mechanisms: Korea." Presentation at Conference on Insolvency Systems in Asia: An Efficiency Perspective Conference, hosted by OECD and World Bank, Sydney, Australia, December.

Nam, Il Chong, and Soogeun Oh. 2000. *Bankruptcy of Large Firms and Exit Mechanisms in Korea*. Seoul: Korean Development Institute.

Naughton, Barry. 1995. *Growing Out of the Plan: Chinese Economic Reform 1978–1993*. Cambridge: Cambridge University Press.

———. 2003. "An Economic Bubble? Chinese Policy Adapts to Rapidly Changing Conditions." *China Leadership Monitor* 9.

———. 2005. "Incremental Decision Making and Corporate Restructuring." *China Leadership Monitor* 15.

———. 2006a. "The New Common Economic Program: China's Eleventh Five Year Plan and What It Means." *China Leadership Monitor* 16.

———. 2006b. "Waves of Criticism: Debates over Bank Sales to Foreigners and Neoliberal Economic Policy." *China Leadership Monitor* 17.

Nelken, David. 2002. "Towards a Sociology of Legal Adaption." In *Adapting Legal Cultures*, edited by David Nelken and Johannes Feest. Oxford: Hart Publishing.

Nielsen, Anne, Mike Sigal, and Karen Wagner. 1996. "The Cross-Border Insolvency Concordat: Principles to Facilitate the Resolution of International Insolvencies." *American Bankruptcy Law Journal* 70:533–562.

North, Douglass Cecil. 1981. *Structure and Change in Economic History*. New York: Norton.

Obstfeld, Maurice. 1998. "The Global Capital Market: Benefactor or Menace?" *Journal of Economic Perspectives* 12:9–30.

Oh, Soogeun. 1999. *An Institutional Perspective on Financial Reform in Korea*. Seoul: Korea Development Bank Report.

———. 2001. "Bankruptcy Division and Commissioner." Presentation at conference on Insolvency Reform in Asia: An Assessment of the Recent Developments and the Role of the Judiciary, hosted by OECD and Government of Indonesia, Bali, Indonesia.

———. 2002a. "Drafting of New Insolvency Law of Korea." Presentation at Forum on Asian Insolvency Reforms, OECD and Government of Thailand, Bangkok, Thailand.

———. 2002b. "Government Intervention in Corporate Exit Mechanisms: The Corporate Restructuring Promotion Act of Korea." In *Hong Kong University Faculty of Law.* Hong Kong.

———. 2003a. "Drafting of New Insolvency Law of Korea." Presentation at World Bank Forum on Insolvency Risk Management, Washington, DC.

———. 2003b. "Insolvency Law Reform of Korea: A Continuing Learning Process." In *Forum on Insolvency Risk Management.* Washington, DC.

———. 2003c. "Setting Insolvency Rules: A Course of Understanding and Persuasion." Presentation at Forum on Asian Insolvency Reforms, OECD and Government of Korea, Seoul, Korea.

———. 2005. "Changes in Insolvency Practice, Restructuring of Ailing Firms and Risk Management after the Economic Crisis: The Korea Case." In *International Workshop on Reform of Corporate Governance: Corporate Rehabilitations in East Asia and Its Lesson for China.* Forum on Asian Insolvency Reforms, OECD and Government of China, Beijing, China.

Oh, Soogeun, and Terence C. Halliday. Forthcoming. "Rehabilitating Korea's Corporate Insolvency Regime, 1992–2007." In *Pushing Back against Globalisation,* edited by John Gillespie and Randall Peerenboom. London: Routledge Curzon.

Oh, Y. S., and Keun Byung Lee. 1998. "Korean Insolvency Laws Protect Foreign Investors." *International Financial Law Review* 17:30–33.

Organisation for Economic Co-operation and Development. 1999. "Insolvency Systems in Asia: An Efficiency Perspective." Proceedings of a Conference in Sydney, Australia.

———. 2003. *Informal Workouts, Restructuring and the Future of Asian Insolvency Reform: Proceedings from the Second Forum for Asian Insolvency Reform—December 2002.* Paris: OECD Publishing.

———. 2004. *Maximising Value Of Non-performing Assets.* Paris: OECD Publishing.

———. 2005. *Insolvency Systems and Risk Management in Asia.* Proceedings of a conference held in New Delhi, India.

———. 2006a. *Credit Risk and Credit Access in Asia.* Paris: OECD Publishing.

———. 2006b. "Legal and Institutional Reforms of Asian Insolvency Systems." Proceedings of a conference jointly sponsored by the OECD, World Bank, Asian Development Bank, Government of Japan, Government of Australia, and Government of China in cooperation with the Development Research Institute. Beijing, China.

———. 2007. *OECD Economic Outlook.* Paris: OECD Publishing.

———. 2008. *Asian Insolvency Systems: Closing the Implementation Gap.* Paris: OECD Publishing.

Pangestu, Mari, and Manggi Habir. 2002. "The Boom, Bust, and Restructuring of Indonesian Banks." In *IMF Working Paper WP/02/66*. Washington, DC: International Monetary Fund.

Panuska, Tandi Armstrong. 1993. "The Chaos of International Insolvency: Achieving Reciprocal Universality under Section 304 or MIICA." *The Transnational Lawyer* 6:374–411.

Parker, Christine, Colin Scott, Nicola Lacey, and John Braithwaite. 2004. "Conclusion." In *Regulating Law*, edited by Christine Parker, Colin Scott, Nicola Lacey, and John Braithwaite. New York: Oxford.

Patchel, Kathleen. 1993. "Interest Group Politics, Federalism, and the Uniform Laws Process: Some Lessons from the Uniform Commercial Code." *Minnesota Law Review* 78:83–165.

Peerenboom, Randall. 2002. *China's Long March toward Rule of Law*. New York: Cambridge University Press.

Peng, Xiaohua. 1987. "Characteristics of China's First Bankruptcy Law." *Harvard International Law Journal* 28:373–384.

Pierson, Paul. 2004. *Politics in Time: History, Institutions, and Social Analysis*. Princeton: Princeton University Press.

Pistor, Katharina. 2000. "Patterns of Legal Change: Shareholder and Creditor Rights in Transition Economies." *European Business Organization Law Review* 1:59–108.

———. 2002. "The Standardization of Law and Its Effect on Developing Economies." *American Journal of Comparative Law* 50:97–130.

Pistor, Katharina, Yoram Keinan, Jan Kleinhesiterkamp, and Mark West. 2003. Evolution of Corporate Law and the Transplant Effect: Lessons from Six Countries." World Bank Research Observer 18 (1): 89–112.

Pistor, Katharina, Martin Raiser, and Stanislaw Gelfer. 2000. "Law and Finance in Transition Economies." *Economics of Transition* 8:325–368.

Pistor, Katharina, and Philip A. Wellons. 1999. *The Role of Law and Legal Institutions in Asian Economic Development: 1960–1995*. New York: Oxford University Press.

Pistor, Katharina, and Chenggang Xu. 2003. "Incomplete Law—a Conceptual and Analytical Framework and Its Application to the Evolution of Financial Market Regulation." *Journal of International Law and Politics* 35:931–1013.

Polanyi, Karl. 1944. *The Great Transformation*. Boston: Beacon Press.

Pompe, Sebaastian. 2005. *The Indonesian Supreme Court: A Study of Institutional Collapse*. Ithaca, NY: Cornell University Press.

Potter, Pitman (Ed.). 1999. *Domestic Law Reforms in Post-Mao China*. Armonk, NY: M. E. Sharpe.

Pound, Roscoe. 1913. "Legislation as a Social Function." *American Journal of Sociology* 18:755–768.

Powell, Michael J. 1988. *From Patrician to Professional Elite: The Transformation of the New York City Bar Association*. New York: Russell Sage.

———. 1993. "Professional Innovation: Corporate Lawyers and Private Lawmaking." *Law & Social Inquiry* 18:423–452.

Powers, Timothy E., Rona R. Mears, and John A. Barrett. 1994. "The Model International Insolvency Act." Pp. 233–244 in *Current Issues in Cross-Border Insolvency and Reorganisations*, edited by E. Bruce Leonard and Christopher W. Besant. London: Graham and Trotman.

Prasad, Monica. 2006. *The Politics of Free Markets: The Rise of NeoLiberal Economic Policies in Britain, France, Germany, and the United States*. Chicago: University of Chicago Press.

Redding, S. Gordon. 1993. *The Spirit of Chinese Capitalism*. New York: Walter de Gruyter.

———. 1996a. "Societal Transformation and the Contribution of Authority Relations and Cooperation Norms in Overseas Chinese Business." In *Confucian Traditions in East Asian Modernity: Moral Education and Economic Culture in Japan and the Four Mini-Dragons*, edited by Wei-ming Tu. Cambridge, MA: Harvard University Press.

———. 1996b. "Weak Organizations and Strong Linkages: Managerial Ideology and Chinese Family Business Networks." In *Asian Business Networks*, edited by Gary Hamilton. Berlin: Walter de Gruyter.

Riesenhuber, Eva. 2001. *The International Monetary Fund under Constraint: Legitimacy of Its Crisis Management*. The Hague: Kluwer Law International.

Ruru, Bacelius. 2001. "Role of Indonesian Insolvency System: Case for Optimism and Case for Caution." *OECD Forum for Asian Insolvency Reforms: An Assessment of the Recent Developments and the Role of the Judiciary*. Bali, Indonesia.

Salacuse, Jeswald W. 2000. "From Developing Countries to Emerging Markets: The Legal Challenges of Economic Change." *International and Comparative Law Journal* 2:277–295.

Santella, Paolo. 2004. "Advantages of Inter-firm Credit in Dealing with Non-performing Assets." In *Maximising Value of Non-performing Assets*. Paris: OECD Publishing.

Santos, Boaventura De Sousa. 2000. "Law and Democracy: (Mis)trusting the Global Reform of Courts." Pp. 252–281 in *Globalizing Institutions: Case Studies in Regulation and Innovation*, edited by Jane Jenson and Boaventura De Sousa Santos. Aldershot, UK, and Burlington, VT: Ashgate.

———. 2002. *Toward a New Legal Common Sense*. London: Butterworths.

Santos, Boaventura De Sousa, and César A. Rodríguez-Garavito (Eds.). 2005. *Law and Globalization from Below: Towards a Cosmopolitan Legality*. Cambridge Studies in Law and Society. Cambridge: Cambridge University Press.

Sassen, Saskia. 2006. *Territory, Authority, Rights: From Medieval to Global Assemblages*. Princeton: Princeton University Press.

Schofer, Evan, and Ann Hironaka. 2005. "The Effects of World Society on Environmental Protection Outcomes." *Social Forces* 84:23.

Schofer, Evan, and John W. Meyer. 2005. "The Worldwide Expansion of Higher Education in the Twentieth Century." *American Sociological Review* 70.

Schollmeyer, Eberhard. 1997. "The New European Convention on International Insolvency." *Bankruptcy Developments Journal* 13:421–442.

Schröeder-van Waes, Marie-Christine, and Kevin Omar Sidharta. 2004. "Upholding Indonesian Bankruptcy Legislation." Pp. 191–203 in *Business in Indonesia, New Challenges, Old Problems*, edited by M. Chatib Basri and Pierre van der Eng. Institute of Southeast Asian Studies.

Schwartz, Alan. 2002. "The Still Questionable Role of Private Legislatures." *Louisiana Law Review* 62:1147–1152.

Schwartz, Alan, and Robert E. Scott. 1995. "The Political Economy of Private Legislatures." *University of Pennsylvania Law Review* 143:595–653.

Schwarz, Adam. 2000. *A Nation in Waiting: Indonesia's Search for Stability*. Boulder, CO: Westview Press.

Schwarz, Steven L. 1995. "A Fundamental Inquiry into the Statutory Rulemaking Process of Private Legislatures." *Georgia Law Review* 29:909–989.

Scott, James C. 1985. *Weapons of the Weak*. New Haven, CT: Yale University Press.

———. 1990. *Domination and the Arts of Resistance: Hidden Transcripts*. New Haven, CT: Yale University Press.

Scott, Robert E. 1994. "The Politics of Article 9." *Virginia Law Review* 80:1783–1851.

Shihata, Ibrahim F. I. 1995. "Legal Framework for Development: Role of the World Bank in Legal Technical Assistance." *International Business Lawyer*: 360–368.

Shirk, Susan L. 2007. *China: Fragile Superpower*. New York: Oxford University Press.

Shleifer, Andrei, and Robert W. Vishny. 1997. "A Survey of Corporate Governance." *Journal of Finance* 52:737–783.

Silbey, S. 1997. "'Let Them Eat Cake': Globalization, Postmodern Colonialism, and the Possibilities of Justice." *Law & Society Review* 31:207–235.

Slaughter, Anne-Maria. 2004. *A New World Order*. Princeton: Princeton University Press.

Smismans, Stijn. 2004. *Law, Legitimacy, and European Governance: Functional Participation in Social Regulation*. Oxford Studies in European Law. Oxford: Oxford University Press.

Steele, Stacey. 1999. "The New Law on Bankruptcy in Indonesia: Towards a Modern Corporate Bankruptcy Regime." *Melbourne University Law Review* 12:144–160.

Steers, Richard M., Yoo Keun Shin, and Gerardo R. Ungson. 1989. *The Chaebol: Korea's Industrial Might*. New York: Harper and Row.

Stephan, Paul B. 1996. "Accountability and International Lawmaking: Rules, Rents and Legitimacy." *Northwestern Journal of International Law and Business* 17:681–735.

Stiglitz, Joseph E. 2001. "Bankruptcy Laws: Basic Economic Principles." Pp. 1–24 in *Resolution of Financial Distress: An International Perspective on the Design of Bankruptcy Laws*, edited by Stijn Claessens, Simeon Djankov, and Ashoka Mody. Washington, DC: World Bank.

———. 2002. *Globalization and Its Discontents*. New York: Norton.

Streeck, Wolfgang, and Kathleen Thelen. 2005. "Introduction: Institutional Change in Advanced Political Economies." In *Beyond Continuity: Institutional Change in Advanced Political Economies*, edited by Wolfgang Streeck and Kathleen Thelen. New York: Cambridge University Press.

Suchman, Marc C. 1995. "Managing Legitimacy: Strategic and Institutional Approaches." *Academy of Management Review* 20:571–610.

Supit, Frank Taira. 1998. "Indonesia's Phoenix?" *Far Eastern Economic Review* 161:26.

Sutton, John R. 2001. *Law/Society: Origins, Interactions, and Change*. Thousand Oaks, CA: Pine Forge Press.

Suyudi, Aria. 2004. *Does the Court Impose Different Treatment for Different Kinds of Creditors in Bankruptcy Petitions? A Jurimetric Analysis of Indonesian Commercial Court Decisions on Bankruptcy*. Rotterdam: Erasmus University.

Swedberg, Richard. 1998. *Max Weber and the Idea of Economic Sociology*. Princeton: Princeton University Press.

Tamanaha, Brian Z. 1995. "The Lessons of Law-and-Development Studies." *The American Journal of International Law* 89:470–486.

Tang, Wenfang, and William L. Parish. 2000. *Chinese Urban Life under Reform: The Changing Social Contract*. New York: Cambridge University Press.

Thelen, Kathleen. 1999. "Historical Institutionalism in Comparative Politics." *Annual Review of Political Science* 2:369–404.

Trubek, David M. 1996. "Law and Development: Then and Now." *Proceedings of the 90th Meeting of the American Society of International Law*.

Tyler, Tom. 2001. "A Psychological Perspective on the Legitimacy of Institutions and Authorities." In *The Psychology of Legitimacy: Emerging Perspectives on Ideology, Justice, and Intergroup Relations*, edited by John T. Jost and Brenda Major. Cambridge: Cambridge University Press.

United Nations Commission on International Trade Law (UNCITRAL). 1999. *UNCITRAL Model Law on Cross-Border Insolvency with Guide to Enactment*. New York: United Nations.

———. 2004. *UNCITRAL Legislative Guide on Insolvency Law*. New York: United Nations.

Wade, Robert. 1990. *Governing the Market: Economic Theory and the Role of Government in East Asian Industrialization*. Princeton: Princeton University Press.

Wallerstein, I. 2002. "Opening Remarks: Legal Constraints in the Capitalist World-Economy." *Transnational Legal Processes: Globalization and Power Disparities*: 61–64.

Wank, David L. 1999. "Producing Property Rights: Strategies, Networks, and Efficiency in Urban China's Nonstate Firms." In *Property Rights and Economic Reform in China*, edited by Jean C. Oi and Andrew G. Walder. Stanford, CA: Stanford University Press.

Watson, Alan. 1974. *Legal Transplants: An Approach to Comparative Law*. Edinburgh: Scottish Academic Press.

Weber, Max. 1978. *Economy and Society*. Berkeley: University of California Press.

Weber, Steven. 1994. "Origins of the European Bank for Reconstruction and Development." *International Organization* 48:1–38.

Wee, Clare. 2000. "Insolvency Initiatives at the Asian Development Bank." Presentation, IBA Committee J Conference, Milan, Italy, June.

Wessels, Bob. 1998. "Towards a New Indonesian Bankruptcy Law." *International Insolvency Review* 7:171–192.

Westbrook, Jay Lawrence. 1991. "Theory and Pragmatism in Global Insolvencies: Choice of Law and Choice of Forum." *American Bankruptcy Law Journal* 65:457–491.

———. 1994. "Comment: A More Optimistic View of Cross-Border Insolvency." *Washington University Law Quarterly* 72:947–953.

———. 1996. "Creating International Insolvency Law." *American Bankruptcy Law Journal* 70:563–574.

———. 2000. "A Global Solution to Multinational Default." *Michigan Law Review* 98:2276–2328.

———. 2001a. "Global Development: The Transnational Insolvency Project of the American Law Institute." *Connecticut Journal of International Law* 17:99–106.

———. 2001b. "Systemic Corporate Distress: A Legal Perspective." Pp. 47–64 in *Resolution of Financial Distress: An International Perspective on the Design of Bankruptcy Laws*, edited by Stijn Claessens, Simeon Djankov, and Ashoka Mody. Washington, DC: World Bank.

———. 2002a. "Multinational Enterprises in General Default: Chapter 15, the ALI Principles, and the EU Insolvency Regulation." *American Bankruptcy Law Journal* 76:1–40.

———. 2002b. "Setting Global Standards for Cross-Border Insolvency." *International Financial Law Review* 21:9–11.

Winters, Jeffrey A. 1996. *Power in Motion: Capital Mobility and the Indonesian State.* Ithaca, NY: Cornell University Press.

Woo, Jung-En [Meredith Woo-Cumings]. 1991. *Race to the Swift: State and Finance in Korean Industrialization.* New York: Columbia University Press.

Woo, Wing Thye. 2002. "Some Unorthodox Thoughts on China's Unorthodox Financial Sector." *China Economic Review* 13: 388–393.

Woo-Cumings, Meredith. 1999. "The State, Democracy, and the Reform of the Corporate Sector in Korea." In *The Politics of the Asian Economic Crisis*, edited by T. J. Pempel. Ithaca, NY: Cornell University Press.

Woodland, Philippe. 1994. "The Proposed European Community Insolvency Convention." Pp. 1–32 in *Current Issues in Cross-Border Insolvency and Reorganisations*, edited by E. Bruce Leonard and Christopher W. Besant. London: Graham and Trotman.

World Bank. 1998. *East Asia: The Road to Recovery.* Washington, DC: World Bank.

———. 1999. "Building Effective Insolvency Systems." Presentation at Conference on Insolvency Systems in Asia: An Efficiency Perspective, Sydney, Australia.

———. 2000. *Bankruptcy of State Enterprises in China: A Case and Agenda for Reforming the Insolvency System.* Washington, DC: Private Sector Development Unit, East Asia and Pacific Region, World Bank.

———. 2001. *Principles and Guidelines for Effective Insolvency and Creditor Rights Systems.* Washington, DC: World Bank.

————. 2003. *Principles and Guidelines for Effective Insolvency and Creditor Rights Systems.* Washington, DC: World Bank.

————. 2007. *Quarterly Update—China.* Washington, DC: World Bank.

World Bank/UNCITRAL. 2005. *Creditors Rights and Insolvency Standard.* Washington, DC: World Bank.

Zheng, Henry R. 1986. "Bankruptcy Law of the People's Republic of China: Principle, Procedure and Practice." *Vanderbilt Journal of Transnational Law*: 683–732.

Zysman, John. 1983. *Governments, Markets, and Growth.* Ithaca, NY: Cornell University Press.

Index

Abbott, Andrew, 381, 446n57, 461nn4,5
Abbott, Ken, 13, 18, 217
accountants, xxii, 34–35, 375, 415, 440n30;
in Indonesia, 193–94, 347, 355; vs.
lawyers, 58, 66, 72, 82, 133, 136, 144,
148, 278–79, 335, 376. *See also* International Federation of Insolvency
Practitioners (INSOL)
actor mismatch, 192, 205–6, 261–62,
290–91, 332; definition, 19; in China,
261, 266, 290; in Korea, 233, 241–42;
in Indonesia, 192, 205–06; and intermediation, 332; and foiling, 353; and
implementation gap, 416–417; relationship to recursive cycles in law, 17,
19, 241, 242, 353, 364, 383–85, 390, 395,
415, 416–17, 427, 458n2
African Common Market (COMESA),
131
African Development Bank, 436n78
Allen, Franklin, xv
American Bar Association (ABA):
Business Section/international
subcommittee, 132, 133, 366, 411; and
UNCITRAL Legislative Guide, 141,
148, 155, 162–63, 411
American Law Institute (ALI): and
NAFTA, 59, 114; Principles of Coop-

eration among NAFTA countries,
114, 401; Transnational Insolvency
Project, 40, 42, 99
Antons, Christopher, 448n92
Appelbaum, Richard P., 405
arbitrage situations, xix
Argentina: financial crisis in, 111; relations with IMF, 28, 342–43, 397
Armour, John, 83
Arrighi, Giovanni, 5
Asia Foundation, 189
Asian Development Bank (ADB), 21,
39, 73, 74, 76, 87, 105, 172, 305, 331,
417, 429n1, 434n33, 436n78; good
governance standards of, 31, 93, 95,
434n27; vs. IMF, 101, 103, 118, 123, 300,
322–23; and Japan, 92; Legal Department, 92–93, 95; loan policies, 92;
and public shaming, 74, 95, 97, 112,
117–18; relations with China, 263,
264, 269–70, 278, 281–83, 285, 289, 308,
309, 310, 322–23, 324, 325–26, 327–28,
343–44, 370, 372, 390; relations with
Indonesia, 207, 366; relations with
Korea, 239, 450n1; relations with
UNCITRAL, 127, 128, 129, 131, 151;
Report of, 40, 93–96, 101, 103, 115,
117–18, 127, 300, 367, 403, 405, 435n53;

481